The Wl Earth On-Line Almanac: Info from A to Z

Don Rittner

The Whole Earth On-Line Almanac: Info from A to Z

Don Rittner

New York　London　Toronto　Sydney　Tokyo　Singapore

Brady Publishing

A Division of Prentice Hall Computer Publishing
15 Columbus Circle
New York, NY 10023

ISBN: 1-56686-090-3

Library of Congress Catalog No.: 93-1950

Printing Code: The rightmost double-digit number is the year of the book's printing; the rightmost single-digit number is the number of the book's printing. For example, 93-1 shows that the first printing of the book occurred in 1993.

96 95 94 93   4 3 2 1

Manufactured in the United States of America

Limits of Liability and Disclaimer of Warranty: The author and publisher of this book have used their best efforts in preparing this book and the programs contained in it. These efforts include the development, research, and testing of the theories and programs to determine their effectiveness. The author and publisher make no warranty of any kind, expressed or implied, with regard to these programs or the documentation contained in this book. The author and publisher shall not be liable in any event for incidental or consequential damages in connection with, or arising out of, the furnishing, performance, or use of these programs.

Trademarks: Most computer and software brand names have trademarks or registered trademarks. The individual trademarks have not been listed here.

Dedication

Dedicated to

Nancy & Christopher

Credits

Publisher
Michael Violano

Acquisitions Director
Jono Hardjowirogo

Managing Editor
Kelly D. Dobbs

Production Editor
Bettina A. Versaci

Developmental Editor
Perry King

Copy Editors
John Burek
Tyrone Prescod

Marketing Director
Lonny Stein

Marketing Coordinator
Laura Cadorette

Editorial Assistant
Lisa Rose

Artist
Mary Engels

Book Designer
Kevin Spear

Cover Designer
Tim Amrhein

Cover Illustrator
Kathy Hanley

Production Team
Diana Bigham, Katy Bodenmiller,
Scott Cook, Tim Cox, Mark Enochs,
Linda Koopman, Tom Loveman,
Beth Rago, Carrie Roth, Greg Simsic

Acknowledgments

A book of this size and magnitude is the collective efforts of many people. I want to thank the following people for their permission to reproduce their work and acknowledge their efforts:

Ellen S. Keech, Newsnet; Mike Light, BRS Afterdark; Edward Vielmetti (ftp sites list); Dr. Art St. George, library list; Arthur R. McGee, africanlists; David Avery, Dartmouth Internet list; Jack Crawford, K12 net; Gene Spafford (Usenet); Kathy Ryan, AOL; Kent Filmore, GEnie; David J. Kishler, CompuServe; Phil Eschallier, Nixpub; Mike Fuchs, Fidonet; and to my editor Perry King from Brady and Tracy Smith for getting the ball rolling.

stioll need

ORBIT

KI

WELL

Contents

Part 1

How to Use This Book

By purchasing this book, you enter a universe full of millions of people and information resources that are available directly to you by using your personal computer, a modem, and your phone line.

Each day millions of computer users sign on to networks such as the Internet, commercial services like America Online, or private computer bulletin boards to do the following:

- seek advice or answers to questions;
- send electronic mail to colleagues across the continent;
- look for information for research projects;
- search databases or online library catalogs;
- download software programs and publications;
- check stocks and analyze financial resources;
- meet people who share similar interests;
- create work groups separated by thousands of miles;
- read the latest off-the-wire news; or
- just to chat on various topics that interest them with people from around the world.

As personal computers become more affordable, and information providers broaden their reach and increase services, more and more people are joining this online community. More than 25 million Americans have access to the online world and it's quickly becoming possible to satisfy almost any kind of information need without leaving your office or home. As the online world expands, however, it becomes more difficult to know which provider holds the information you are seeking.

The Whole Earth On-Line Almanac will serve as your guide to the thousands of available research materials and millions of people who comprise the electronic online community. Whatever your interests—astronomy, business, social issues, environment, geography or any of the other major disciplines— the *On-Line Almanac* will have something for you.

This book is a compilation of hundreds of online forums, databases, discussion lists, searchable libraries, bulletin boards, and CD-ROM titles covering a wide range of subject areas from Astronomy to Zoology. If you have a computer and a modem, you don't need to guess whether a commercial online service, global network, or bulletin board has the information you need. You can easily look up your subject alphabetically in *The Whole Earth On-Line Almanac* and get pointed in the right direction.

This book is not a tutorial on telecommunications. It assumes you already know how to use your computer, modem, and phone line. But, for a good introduction on telecommunications, see the author's book, *EcoLinking— Everyone's Guide to Online Environmental Information* (Peachpit Press, 1992). In a nutshell, all you need is a personal computer, modem, phone line, communications software, and this book to become part of the global electronic frontier. This book is an easy-to-use reference tool that will save you money and prevent wasted hours combing the networks and commercial online providers.

The Information Providers

The next section of this book provides descriptions of all the featured information providers and explains how they are organized, how to navigate their services, and how to subscribe to them. These services include global computer networks such as the Internet, Bitnet, Usenet, UUCPnet, and

Fidonet; commercial online providers such as America Online, CompuServe, GEnie, and The WELL; searchable online libraries from BRS, Dialog, ORBIT, NewsNet; and finally hundreds of private, government, and business computer bulletin boards. CD-ROM databases are also listed, rounding out the information reservoir.

Many of these providers offer their services for free or at low cost. Some information sources like CD-ROM can be expensive and are best used at your local library.

The Online Resources

Section Three of the *On-Line Almanac* is the compendium of information resources, arranged by category and in alphabetical order. The book heavily favors those resources that promote human communications such as online discussion forums, or lists, echos, and newsgroups (all explained later).

General subject areas covered in this book are:

Academia, Aeronautics, Agriculture, Anthropology, Archaeology, Architecture, Art, Astronomy, Aviation, Biology, Botany, Business, Chemistry, Communications, Computers, Culture, Current Events, Dance, Design, Ecology, Economics, Education, Electronics, Engineering, Environment, Games, Geography, Geology, Government, History, Hobbies, Humanities, Journalism, Justice, Labor, Language, Law, Library Science, Literature, Mathematics, Meteorology, Military, Music, News, Philosophy, Photography, Physics, Politics, Planning, Political Science, Potpourri, Preservation, Psychiatry, Psychology, Publications, Public Health, Recreation, Radio, Religion, Science Fiction, Science, Security, Social Issues, Sociology, Space Science, Sports, TV, Technology, Theater, Transportation, Travel, Writing, Zoology.

Each of the subject areas are further organized by Forums, Databases, Network Discussion Lists, Online Libraries, Bulletin Boards, and finally CD-ROM.

Part 2

The Information Providers

Guide to the Services

The hundreds of information resources presented in Section Three are compiled from the following sources:

- Four commercial online services: America Online, CompuServe, GEnie and The Well
- Five Global Networks: The Internet, Bitnet, Fidonet, Usenet, and UUCPNet.
- Individual Bulletin boards: A selection from the thousands of bulletin boards that exist in the United States.
- Online Libraries and Databases: Knowledge Index, Orbit, BRS After Dark, and NewsNet, and the Internet accessible libraries.
- CD-ROM: A selection from the hundreds of available CD-ROM titles.

To better understand how to access this wealth of information, this section provides a description of each of these services, how you can connect to them, cost, basic structure and how they operate, and how to navigate through them to reach the information.

Commercial Online Providers

The four commercial online providers that offer inexpensive access to a wealth of information are: America Online, CompuServe, GEnie, and The Well. All of these services charge an hourly fee, and all but America Online can be accessed by using any standard communications program.

The commercial information providers offer a host of services from computer or special interest clubs called forums, roundtables, or conferences; searchable databases; online news feeds; financial analysis services; home shopping; educational services; private mail and fax services; and files for downloading. They charge an hourly fee and/or monthly minimum for membership. Rates are as low as $2 per hour to as high as $18.50 or more an hour, depending on the level of service.

The forums, conferences, or roundtables are bulletin board type services that usually offer public discussions on specific topics, news, weekly conferences, and file libraries for downloading. These are subject oriented—Mac Roundtable, Environmental Forum, The Writer's Club—and are good sources for your specific interests.

Searchable databases are large compendiums of information, such as an encyclopedia, technical support, or other collection of specific data that can be accessed by using keywords. Most databases carry an additional fee for use.

This book concentrates on the forums, roundtables, conferences, and databases. It assumes the reader knows how to use e-mail services.

America Online (AOL)

America Online caters to users of Apple II, Macintosh, and IBM PC-compatible computers. You connect to America Online by using your own proprietary graphic-based software program, provided free, and customized to your Apple II, Mac or PC. By using windows, pull-down menus, and the point and click of a mouse, users of all experience levels from novice to expert can navigate AOL with ease.

Getting Online

You cannot use any communications software to get on AOL. You must obtain an America Online software kit for your Apple II, Macintosh, or IBM PC-compatible personal computer, which is available at no charge by calling (800) 827-6364. The software kit includes easy, step-by-step instructions for getting online. Most bookstores also carry the official AOL book written by Tom Lichty and published by Ventana Press, that also provides the software and ten hours of free online time.

Cost

Online fees are $5 per hour for nonpeak time (evenings and weekends) and $10 per hour for peak time (business hours), for either 1200 or 2400 bps. 9600 bps will be offered shortly. A monthly membership fee of $5.95 includes one nonpeak hour free per month. Local telephone access is provided through the SprintNet and Tymnet networks. Other pricing structures are available.

Organization

America Online services are divided into the following eight departments accessible by clicking their Icon:

- News & Finance
- Entertainment
- Travel & Shopping
- People Connection
- Computing & Software
- Lifestyles & Interests
- Learning & Reference
- What's New & Online Support

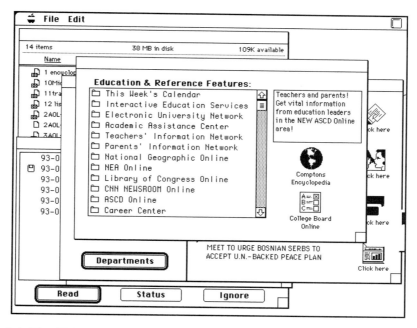

Figure 2.1. The Education & Reference Features menu of America Online provides access to a wide variety of educational networks and databases.

Forums

AOL forums are mini-bulletin boards. They are run by forum leaders (called AFLs), who are responsible for maintaining the message boards and libraries, and running forum events like weekly real time chats. Each Forum is comprised of file libraries, public message boards, public and private conference areas, and a member directory.

File Libraries

Each file library in an AOL forum contains software and articles related to the special interest of that forum. Downloading the file to your own computer is as simple as clicking a few buttons. AOL uses a proprietary download protocol so that you don't have to worry about setting the right protocol.

AOL has a special area that contains the entire collection of the files on AOL called QuickSearch. It enables you to search, by using keywords, the entire AOL database of files enabling you to bypass going into each forum.

Public Message Boards

On the message boards, you can participate in discussions with other forum members, or post information of interest to all members.

You can look through messages that interest you by chronological order or since the last time you logged on. After you have selected a message that interests you, you can reply to it or start a new dialogue by posting your own.

Public & Private Conference Areas

In AOL's live conference areas, you can participate in formal and informal real-time discussions with other forum members. All of the AOL forums have weekly or monthly meetings. You can also create private conference rooms.

Member Directory

Finding other people who share your interests is a snap. The first time you join AOL you are asked to enter information about yourself—a small bio—in the forum Member Directory. This database can be searched by any member by user ID, name, and interest.

Getting Around

Navigating through AOL can be accomplished a couple of ways. You can use the mouse to point and click through a hierarchical path of services symbolized by icons and menus (Mac and Windows users will feel at home); or you can use keyword commands that take you directly to the information you seek. To use a keyword command, you hit the COMMAND and keyword letter keys at the same time—for example, "COMMAND - News" takes you to the News and Finance section.

Databases

AOL has a number of databases covering a wide range of topics and are searchable by using keywords. These databases do not carry a surcharge for use.

Keeping Up-to-date

To stay abreast of new forums and developments on AOL, use the Keyword "New."

CompuServe (CIS)

CompuServe Information Service is the largest and oldest commercial online service with over one million members worldwide and over 1700 online offerings.

Unlike America Online, CompuServe is command-driven but does have a graphical user interface for Mac, PC, and Windows users.

How to Get Online

You need a CompuServe Membership Kit to gain access for the first time. The kit includes a user ID number and a temporary password to use the first time you sign on (you can change the password later). CompuServe Membership Kits are available nationwide at computer software retailers and many bookstores. Call CompuServe customer service at (800) 848-8199 for more information.

Cost

The CompuServe Membership Kit retails for $39.95 but includes $25 of connect time. Online charges vary based on your modem speed: 1200 to 2400 bps is $8 per hour, to 9600 baud at $16 per hour. You pay a $2 online support fee every month to maintain your subscription to CompuServe. They have several pricing structures. A basic charge of $8.95 per month gets you an assortment of e-mail, news, and other features, 36 in all. The more services you use, the more expensive it is.

In addition, members are charged network communications surcharges for use of SprintNet and Tymnet telephone numbers for each session on CompuServe. Some features, particularly reference and financial databases, carry a premium surcharge.

Organization

CompuServe services are divided into ten major subject areas in a menu hierarchy:

- Communications/Bulletin Boards
- News/Weather/Sports
- Travel
- The Electronic Mall/Shopping

- Money Matters/Markets
- Entertainment/Games
- Home/Health/Education
- Reference
- Computers/Technology
- Business/Other Interests

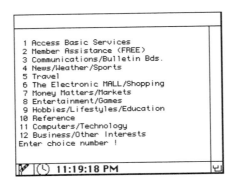

```
 1 Access Basic Services
 2 Member Assistance (FREE)
 3 Communications/Bulletin Bds.
 4 News/Weather/Sports
 5 Travel
 6 The Electronic MALL/Shopping
 7 Money Matters/Markets
 8 Entertainment/Games
 9 Hobbies/Lifestyles/Education
10 Reference
11 Computers/Technology
12 Business/Other Interests
Enter choice number !
```
⌨ | 🕐 11:19:18 PM

Figure 2.2. CompuServe's main menu leads to a wide variety of services.

Getting Around

Finding your way around CompuServe is by possible using one of three methods—a system of menus, GO commands, or CompuServe Information Manager.

CompuServe offers a system of menus; by selecting an item off each one you come to, you branch down from top-level menus into submenus.

By using GO commands and quick reference words (Go Mac) you can jump immediately to the service you are looking for, without branching through menus and submenus. Each of the CIS services outlined in the next chapter have the GO Keyword command listed.

CompuServe offers a software program called CompuServe Information Manager that acts as a graphic front end and is available for IBM PC compatibles, Windows, and the Macintosh. It uses the windows, pull-down menus, and icons that are familiar to Mac users and becoming increasingly familiar to PC users. Information Manager makes it easy to navigate through

CompuServe, because you don't have to memorize commands. You can find Information Manager at many software retailers, and you can order it online.

Forums

CompuServe forums are similar in structure to America Online's. They are mini-bulletin boards run by forum administrators, who are responsible for maintaining the message boards and libraries, and for running forum events. Each Forum has a welcome message that lists the names and ID numbers of the forum administrators and other new member information.

File Libraries

Each file library in a CompuServe forum contains software and articles related to the special interest of that forum. To enter the file library, you type its number—3. You are then presented with a list of the library subtopics. After you have chosen a subtopic, you are offered options that let you browse through descriptions of available files or examine a directory of files without descriptions.

When you have selected a file you want to download, CompuServe asks you to select a file-transfer protocol. Make sure you select a protocol supported by the communications program you use to access CompuServe.

Message Boards

On message boards, you can participate in discussions with other forum members or post information you feel is of interest to the entire membership.

CompuServe enables you to look through messages that interest you by subject matter or in chronological order. After you have selected a message that interests you, you can follow the thread of replies to it or add a message of your own. Compuserve alerts you when you have messages addressed to you in the Forum message area.

Conference Areas

You can participate in formal and informal real-time discussions with other forum members in CompuServe's live conference areas. Many forums have weekly or monthly meetings. You can find conference schedules by selecting the Announcements menu item of each forum.

Member Directory

The first time you enter a CompuServe forum, the system prompts you to join the forum by entering your name. This database can be searched by user ID, name, and interest. It's a great way to find other folks who share your interests.

Databases

CompuServe has a number of databases covering a wide range of topics and are searchable using keywords. These databases often carry a surcharge for use.

All of the CompuServe Forums and databases are featured in the next chapter along with their navigational keyword for fast location and entry.

Keeping Up-to-date

Each time you log on to CompuServe, you are greeted with a menu of new items. Also, all CompuServe members receive a free monthly magazine.

General Electric Network for Information Exchange (GEnie)

GEnie is owned and operated by General Electric Company. GEnie has over 350,000 subscribers and offers similar services as AOL or CIS.

How to Get Online

You are not required to purchase any type of membership kit to sign on for the first time. Any communications program that works on your computer is all that you need. To sign on for the first time using your modem, you need to follow these steps:

- Set your communications software to half duplex.
- Dial (800) 638-8369
- When you are connected, type `HHH`.
- When you see the U#= prompt, type `XTX99515,GENIE` and then press ENTER or RETURN.

ᔕ Follow the online instructions.

ᔕ Call (800) 638-9636 if you want information about GEnie services and pricing before you sign on for the first time. You can order a GEnie user manual online.

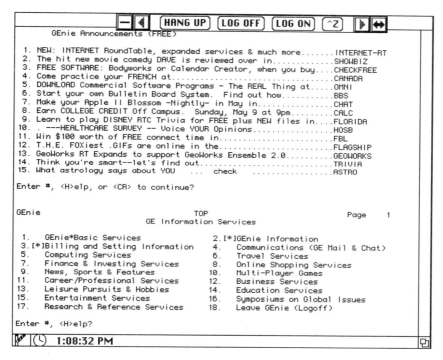

```
 ─ ◄  [ HANG UP ]  [ LOG OFF ]  [ LOG ON ]  [ ^Z ]  ► ↔
         GEnie Announcements (FREE)

  1. NEW: INTERNET RoundTable, expanded services & much more.......INTERNET-RT
  2. The hit new movie comedy DAVE is reviewed over in............SHOWBIZ
  3. FREE SOFTWARE: Bodyworks or Calendar Creator, when you buy....CHECKFREE
  4. Come practice your FRENCH at................................CANADA
  5. DOWNLOAD Commercial Software Programs - The REAL Thing at.....OMNI
  6. Start your own Bulletin Board System.  Find out how..........BBS
  7. Make your Apple II Blossom -Nightly- in May in...............CHAT
  8. Earn COLLEGE CREDIT Off Campus.  Sunday, May 9 at 9pm........CALC
  9. Learn to play DISNEY RTC Trivia for FREE plus NEW files in...FLORIDA
 10. . ---HEALTHCARE SURVEY -- Voice YOUR Opinions................HOSB
 11. Win $100 worth of FREE connect time in......................FBL
 12. T.H.E. FOXiest .GIFs are online in the......................FLAGSHIP
 13. GeoWorks RT Expands to support GeoWorks Ensemble 2.0.........GEOWORKS
 14. Think you're smart--let's find out..........................TRIVIA
 15. What astrology says about YOU   ...  check   ...............ASTRO

 Enter #, <H>elp, or <CR> to continue?


 GEnie                        TOP                        Page    1
                       GE Information Services

  1.   GEnie*Basic Services        2. [*]GEnie Information
  3. [*]Billing and Setting Information   4.   Communications (GE Mail & Chat)
  5.   Computing Services          6.   Travel Services
  7.   Finance & Investing Services    8.   Online Shopping Services
  9.   News, Sports & Features     10.   Multi-Player Games
 11.   Career/Professional Services   12.   Business Services
 13.   Leisure Pursuits & Hobbies   14.   Education Services
 15.   Entertainment Services      16.   Symposiums on Global Issues
 17.   Research & Reference Services   18.   Leave GEnie (Logoff)

 Enter #, <H>elp?

 [  ] [ ] 1:08:32 PM
```

Figure 2.3 GEnie has 350,000 members and provides services similar to those of CompuServe and America Online.

Cost

GEnie charges a $4.95 monthly membership fee that enables unlimited use of certain services, including mail (with an Internet gateway service for an additional charge) and some entertainment, reference and news services. For other services, you pay $6 per hour (Monday through Friday 6 p.m. to 8 a.m. local time, all day on weekends and holidays) or $18 per hour (8 a.m. to 6 p.m. weekdays). Certain services and databases, like CIS, are subject to additional charges.

Organization

GEnie is arranged by using menus that group services into 18 sections from Computing Services, Finance & Investing Services, News, Sports, & Features; Career/Professional Services; Leisure Pursuits & Hobbies; Entertainment Services; Research & Reference Services; Communications; Travel Services; Online Shopping Services; Multi-Player Games; Business Services; Education Services; to Symposiums on Global Issues. To go to any of the services listed there, simply type the menu item number at the prompt, or you can type MOVE and the page number.

Getting Around

GEnie is menu driven but allows keywords for quick access. At the top of each menu are keywords and page numbers. To move to an area, you select either a keyword at the prompt, for example, "mail" to get to the mail menu, or you type a page number with the word move, for example "Move 200."

Roundtables

GEnie's forums are called Roundtables and are similar to the forums of AOL and CIS. They are mini-bulletin boards run by forum administrators, who are responsible for maintaining the message boards and libraries and running forum events. When you first enter a roundtable and join, the administrator usually follows up with a welcome message with an explanation of how the forum is run.

File Libraries

Each file library in a GEnie forum contains software and articles related to the special interest of that forum. To enter the file library, you type its number (usually 3). To find sublibraries, type 8. After you have chosen a library, you are offered options that let you browse through descriptions of available files or examine a directory of files without descriptions.

When you have selected a file you want to download, GEnie will prompt you to select a file-transfer protocol. Make sure you select a protocol supported by the communications program you use to access GEnie.

Message Boards

On message boards, you can participate in discussions with other forum members or post information you deem important for all to read.

GEnie enables you to look through messages that interest you by subject matter (categories), topics, or by all, new or last entries, by author, date, and other options.

Conference Areas

You can participate in formal and informal real-time discussions with other forum members. Many GEnie forums have weekly or monthly meetings.

Databases

GEnie has a number of databases covering a wide range of topics and are searchable by using keywords. These databases often carry a surcharge for use.

Keeping Up-to-date

Each time you log onto GEnie, you are presented with a menu of new items. Also, each member receives a periodic magazine called GEnie LiveWire. New information or updates about the forums you participate in are presented when you enter the forums.

The WELL

The WELL (Whole Earth 'Lectronic Link) is a conferencing network that is housed at the California offices of the Whole Earth Catalog and the Whole Earth Review. Although it is not as large as the other services, The WELL is certainly comparable in terms of dialogue; it is mostly composed of a series of discussions, or conferences, on a wide range of issues. The WELL's sole specialty is online conversation and members do have the ability to chat live with other users online, and to download and upload files.

How to Get Online

You do not need special software, any communications program can access The Well. To register, use your communications software to dial (415) 332-6106. For more information before you try to connect, call (415) 332-4335.

Cost

The WELL charges a monthly membership fee of $10 plus an online fee of $2 per hour (for any calls made anytime). If you dial the Sausalito, California number listed previously, you will also pay all applicable long-distance fees. You are allocated 500K of disk space free but charged $20 a month per megabyte for additional storage space.

As an alternative to dialing into The WELL long-distance, you can use a local phone number from the CompuServe Packet Network at an additional cost of $5 per hour inside the continental United States or $9 per hour in Alaska and Hawaii.

Organization

The WELL is divided into fourteen major conference sections. You need to know how to use navigational commands to get there:

- Social Responsibility and Politics
- Media and Communications
- Business and Livelihood
- Body/Mind/Health
- Cultures
- Place
- Interactions
- Arts and Letters
- Recreation
- Entertainment
- Education and Planning
- Grateful Dead
- Computers
- The WELL

Each major conference is divided into more specific conferences, that are subdivided into topics and responses to that topic.

Getting Around

Because The WELL operates on the UNIX operating system and is command-driven, you need to be specific about typing the right commands for navigation. Instead of seeing menu items, you see an OK: prompt. Entering commands at the prompt takes you to the various areas of interest. For example, by typing ?conf, you can get a list of conferences. By typing ?, you can get online help. Typing exit at the OK: prompt takes you off the system. Basically to get to the conferences, you type "g" and the conference name—for example, "g environment."

An extensive user manual is available to download from The WELL. When you sign onto the service for the first time, you are sent a WELL basic command card and a tutorial that helps you find your way around.

Conferencing on The WELL
Discussions on a wide variety of topics is the focus of The WELL.

Entering a conference is as simple as typing g and the conference keyword. When in a conference, you can get a list of the topics, read any or all of them, and respond to a topic, or create a new one. In the next section you will find a list of the conferences, their navigational keyword, and a summary of the purpose.

Global Networks

Five global computer networks: the Internet, Bitnet, Usenet, UUCPnet, and Fidonet reach millions of users in more than 45 countries. Although each network operates for different reasons, all of them have the ability to exchange mail and information between them. This gives the computer user a broad reach to scientists, professionals, business leaders, students, and other users.

On all of these networks, human to human discussion areas called lists, newsgroups, or echoes have evolved. No matter what they are called, people from around the world can discuss their area of interests with similar minded people 24 hours a day, seven days a week, no matter where they are located. Not surprisingly, hundreds of discussion lists exist covering almost every subject imaginable.

Although these networks offer other services such as the ability to log on to a computer and grab files, software, or documents, or the ability to remotely log on to a computer, only human to human discussion lists are emphasized in the Online Navigator. The other services are briefly mentioned.

The Internet

The federally funded Internet is the largest computer network in the world linking individuals and organizations in more than 45 countries. The Internet is not a single large network—the Internet is a conglomeration of more than 5000 smaller networks, connecting more than a million and one-half hosts, and an estimated 10 million users.

The three primary uses of the Internet are electronic mail, file transfers (ftp), and remote log on (Telnet).

We will examine each of those uses as well as Internet resources that you can take advantage of: mailing lists, online libraries, and scientific databases.

How to Get Online

The Internet, while originally intended to support government and academic research, is now opening up to the general computer user. Getting on the Interent can be accomplished a number of ways—by establishing an account with a research or educational institution that is already on the Internet or by subscribing to one of a number of network gateway services described below.

Because the Internet is not one network, but rather a group of interconnected networks, if you gain access, you still may not be able to connect with the whole Internet since many areas are used for private or government research. Other parts allow public access only if you can get the proper clearance. All of the Internet resources described in this book are available to all users.

The primary way to get involved on the Internet is by using Internet mail. Internet mail links you to many leading individuals and research and academic institutions worldwide. Internet mail is also the way to get access to the discussion lists described later.

Because the Internet is command-driven and every host requires different commands, this chapter does not attempt to teach you how to use various text editors. It assumes you already know how to use the text editor of your connecting network. However, there are several good books that explain how to use all of the Internet resources.

Cost

Because the Internet is not a commercial network, the only costs associated with it are with your access method. If you are affiliated with an institution or business that is an Internet site or can get an external account with such an institution, your only costs will likely be only those of your telephone calls. If you subscribe to a service that acts as an Internet gateway, you may pay a subscription cost to that service.

For More Information and Connections

As a loose affiliation of academic, private, and government networks, the Internet has no central administration. You can get more information from:

The NSF Network Service Center (617-873-3400) offers the Internet Resource Guide, an excellent reference that explains what is available on the Internet.

The DDN Network (Defense Data Network) Information Center (415-859-3695) also offers information about the Internet.

Worldlink

Worldlink is a special service for PC and Macintosh computer users that gives you a front end to the Internet using your own PC. You call one of thousands of access lines (in over five countries) to log on. InterCon offers two flavors—Worldlink-Email and WorldLink-Basic.

The e-mail version gives you off-line and batch reading and creation of e-mail. This enables you to compose your text and the software then sends it, picks up any mail waiting, and then logs off, saving money. There is a flat rate of $19.00 per month (2400 bps) with no limited usage charges. For 9600 bps access, its $29 per month.

The Basic service gives you the e-mail features but also gives you FTP—file transferring capabilities, and Usenet news— thousands of conferences on a variety of subjects from Art to Zoology. As of this writing, only the PC version has Usenet access. January 1993 is the target date for the Mac version.

The Basic service is also done in real time, so you stay connected to the network to send and receive mail, transfer files and view the Usenet news. There is a monthly fee of $29 for 2400 bps access, $39 for 9600 bps. You are allowed 50 megabytes per month and an additional charge of $1 per meg if you exceed the fifty. InterCon may have Telnet capabilities in the future.

For those who do not have a local access point, InterCon will shortly have an 800 number for a small fee.

DASnet

DASnet is a service that provides a mail and file transfer gateway to the Internet and more than 60 commercial e-mail services and networks that otherwise do not have a direct link. Each of these subscribing networks enables their users to send mail (and distribution lists) to any other network or service through DASnet's gateway.

The initial start-up fee is $33.50 (includes a $20 deposit and a DASnet user directory). After that, you will pay $4.75 a month, plus usage (message) time. Message charges depend on the network, but the average is about 45 cents for the first 1000 characters (about one single-spaced page) and 20 cents for each additional 1000. Overseas costs are a bit higher. File transfers cost $15.75.

Contact DA Systems, Inc., 1503 East Campbell Avenue, Campbell, CA 95008, or call (408) 559-7434.

UUNET

UUNET Technologies is a non-profit organization that provides access for a fee to the Internet, UUCP mail, Usenet, and affiliated network services to organizations and individuals that do not have other means of connection.

You can connect to UUNET from thousands of American cities using the CompuServe telecommunications network as a local call, or you can connect directly to them through your modem. An 800 number is available for $10 per hour for nighttime use. Otherwise, you are billed a $35 monthly fee plus $2 per hour connect time if you call them directly. UUNET has several pricing schemes, including $20 a month for low volume users that includes 2 hours of connection per month.

Contact UUNET Communications Services, Suite 570, 3110 Fairview Park Drive, Falls Church, VA 22042, or call (703) 876-5050 for subscription information.

DIAL n' CERF

CERFnet, (California Education and Research Federation) a mid-level network of NSFNET that links up more than 70 research and education centers, has DIAL n' CERF. This is a dial-up service and enables Internet access to organizations and individuals who have legitimate needs, want short-term access, or who already have access but need access when traveling. Users have access to terminal services (Telnet, remote login), SLIP—Serial Line Internet Protocol, a process that enables you to use a modem to connect to the

Internet host—Usenet news, and Internet mailboxes.

When you use this service, you connect to one of the five CERFnet locations in California. Cost for this connection is a one-time installation fee per organization of $250 (regardless of how many users are on your system), and a monthly fee of $20 per user plus connect charges of $5/hour.

Contact CERFnet, c/o San Diego Supercomputer Center, PO Box 85608, San Diego, CA 92186, or call (619) 534-5087—or their hotline (800) 876-CERF. They can be reached through electronic mail as help@cerf.net.

DELPHI

fill in

Electronic Mail

Internet uses the simple mail transfer protocol (SMTP) to send e-mail around the network. Sending mail electronically is very much like sending regular mail. You need to address it to a person and his/her address. In the case of the Internet, it is a mail-addressing scheme called domain addressing. The generic format for this type of address is userid@site.domain. Internet domains include edu (educational institutions), com (commercial sites), gov(government sites), mil(military sites), net (network centers), and org (nonprofits and other organizations that don't belong in the other categories). Domains are often broken down into subdomains. This domain scheme makes it easier to route mail and helps users get a handle on where their mail is coming from (a university, business, and so on).

My Internet address, afldonr@aol.com is a typical Internet ID. The @ sign separates the user ID in this case afldonr from the domain address. The user ID plus the destination address describes for each person on the Internet (or for that matter on any of the networks) his or her own personal mailbox.

The second part of my address aol.com stands for America Online. The site, in this case, ia an online service with an Internet mail gateway. The "com" domain means it is a commercial company. No one else has the id afldonr@aol.com. But other people, members of America Online, do have the same destination ID—aol.com. This helps users know where their mail is coming from or going to. If I get e-mail with the domain address as compuserve.com, I know it is from CompuServe. If it is uacs1.albany.edu, I know it is from the University at Albany, New York. A great book from O'Reilly Associates, called *A Directory of Electronic Mail: Addressing and Networks*, by Donnalyn Frey, lists all of the domain and subdomain addresses.

To use the services in this book, you need to have access to the e-mail facilities of the Internet.

File Transfer (FTP)

The Internet's file transfer protocol (FTP) enables users to log on to remote computers, grab files, and bring them back to their own computers. Many sites have set aside part of their system, called a server, and allow general public access. This is called anonymous FTP. A special user ID called anonymous along with a password (usually guest), enables you to log on to those public areas and download files, documents, and any other information the server wants you to have. There are hundreds of anonymous FTP sites scattered around the world. Fortunately, there is a new way to find out what is on these servers quickly by using the Archie Server.

Archie was created by students and staff from McGill University (Montreal). Archie is a searchable database that lists more than 1000 anonymous FTP sites that collectively hold over two million files. Each month Archie calls each site and updates the directory.

You can access Archie by using Internet mail. You send e-mail to archie@archie.mcgill.ca with a request in the subject line or in the body of the message (with a blank subject, either way works). Archie then processes the request and sends you back the results.

To get a complete explanation on how to use Archie, send e-mail to archie@archie.mcgill.ca with the command HELP as the subject or body of the message. If you use the word LIST, it will return to you a complete list of all 1000+ FTP sites. The amount of files and documents covered by the Archie server is beyond the scope of this book.

You can also log onto the Archie server in the following regions:

Northeast US—archie.rutgers.edu

Southeast US—archie.sura.net

Western US—archie.unl.edu

Telnet

Telnet, also known as remote virtual terminal, enables you to log on to a computer on the Internet as though you were directly connected to it, in real time, no matter where it is located. You can access a database at another site, or you might want to peruse a library card catalog in Germany.

Logging on to a site with Telnet is as simple as typing the Telnet site name, and then following instructions.

Human to Human Discussion Lists

The Internet enables people from around the world to carry on discussions on a variety of topics with each other by using discussion or mailing lists. Internet discussion lists are similar to Usenet's newsgroups, FidoNet's echoes, and BITNET's mailing lists described later. In fact, some of the mailing lists are shared among the networks; if you post a message in one of those lists, it is automatically placed in the other networks' lists.

Because it is possible to subscribe to these discussions lists using e-mail and to the other networks, Dartmouth College has put together and maintains a complete list of all mailings lists. According to David Avery, Dartmouth maintains a merged list of the Listserv and manually maintained lists on Bitnet and the Interest Group lists on the Internet, and UUCPnet lists. It is a single file with one line for each mailing list. The list has been updated monthly for the last year and has a stable format. Each line consists of seven fields, delimited by tabs. The list contains information about approximately 2,500 lists. The fields are:

Field	Size
Category (Computing, Science, Humanities, etc.)	1
List group	3-11
"Mail to" E-mail address for submitting mail to the list for distribution	8-80
"Command to" E-mail address for subscribing, signing off and other administrations	8-80
One line description of the list subject	8-60
Name and E-mail address for the owner of the list	0-80
Long description of the list	0-450

This list-of-lists differs from some similar lists and the list returned by sending the LIST GLOBAL command to a backbone LISTSERV in that:

a) Duplicate entries are deleted

b) Lists obviously intended only for local use are omitted

c) Information about the lists is field delimited, allowing simple parsing

d) Internet and Bitnet lists are included

e) A text description of the purpose of the list is provided

The flat data file containing the list-of-lists information can be obtained by mail, by sending the command SEND LISTTEXT PACKAGE to LISTSERV@DARTCMS1. This will return five files which can be concatenated to form the full list. An editor can then be used to crudely search this text file.

The file LISTSERV LISTS contains the full list-of-lists known on Bitnet and the Internet with the long descriptions. When a list exists on Bitnet and the Internet, it presents the Bitnet address. The file INTERNET LISTS contains the same lists as the LISTSERV LISTS file, but the Internet address is presented for dual network lists.

A short form of the text form of the list can be obtained with the command SEND LISTSHRT PACKAGE to LISTSERV@DARTCMS1. This will return five lists (by category) containing only three fields: Mail to Address, subscription to Address, and a one line description of the list.

A Macintosh Hypercard application is available to format, display and search the list-of-lists. To get the Binhexed Hypercard application as well as the data files it uses, use the command SEND MACSIG PACKAGE to LISTSERV@DARTCMS1.

A VM/CMS Xedit/Rexx application is available to format, display and search the list-of-lists. To get the VM/CMS application as well as the data files it uses, use the command SEND CMSSIG PACKAGE to LISTSERV@DARTCMS1.

A VAX/VMS application written in Pascal is available to format, display and search the list-of-lists. It requires the VMS Pascal compiler. To get the VMS application source code as well as the data files it uses, use the command SEND VAXSIG PACKAGE to LISTSERV@DARTCMS1.

A generic UNIX application written in C is available to format, display, and search the list-of-lists. It requires a C compiler and the curses library. To get the UNIX application source code as well as the data files it uses, use the command SEND UnixSIG PACKAGE to LISTSERV@DARTCMS1.

These are big files; the text data file alone is around a half mbyte. If you are on the Internet, you may want to recover the files via FTP rather than mail. The files are available by anonymous FTP to DARTCMS1.DARTMOUTH.EDU <129.170.16.19> in directory SIGLISTS.

To obtain the text file by anonymous FTP, enter the following commands:

FTP DARTCMS1.DARTMOUTH.EDU

ANONYMOUS

CD SIGLISTS

GET READ.ME

GET LISTSERV.LISTS

QUIT

The list-of-lists is updated monthly. You can use the LISTSERV AFD command to automatically get fresh copies by mail whenever the files are updated, or use the LISTSERV FUI command to get an automatic notification of the update by mail so you can get a new copy by FTP. To use either command you will probably want to assign yourself a password on the DARTCMS1 listserv. Send the following commands to LISTSERV@DARTCMS1:

PW ADD <new_password>

AFD ADD <package_name> PACKAGE SIGLISTS

Or

PW ADD <new_password>

FUI ADD <package_name> PACKAGE SIGLISTS

David Avery (DAVID@DARTCMS1) is the person to contact for the Dartmouth project.

The format of the discussion lists in the On-Line Almanac follow the Dartmouth style except that the category has been omitted because the lists are arranged by category and the descriptions of the lists have been edited.

It is important to remember that when you subscribe to a discussion list there is one address to subscribe to and another address to send mail to for distribution to all subscribers. Do not get them confused. It is considered bad protocol to send subscription requests to the id that is used to post actual information.

The following sample list template is used throughout this book:

⑤   *Alcohol & Drug Studies* **<—List Subject**

Offers the BITNET Community a chance to voice their opinions about the abuse of alcohol, illegal and other commonly abused drugs. **<—Annotated description**

`ALCOHOL@LMUACAD.BITNET` **<—E-mail address for submitting mail to the list for distribution**

`LISTSERV@LMUACAD.BITNET` **<— E-mail address for subscribing**

Contact: Phillip Charles Oliff
`<FXX1@LMUACAD.BITNET>` **<—List Owner**

Online Libraries

More than 100 online library catalogs are available through the Internet, from some of the finest libraries in the country. By using the Telnet and FTP protocols, you can access millions of published reference sources for your research; thumb through their card catalogs as though you were standing in the lobby—no matter where they are located on the globe.

Online Databases

You can retrieve a great deal of research information using e-mail, Telnet, or FTP from several specialized scientific database archives on the Internet. To learn how to access these databases get a copy of the Internet Network Resource Guide. The Guide is available via anonymous FTP, from nnsc.nsf.net, in the directory "resource-guide".

There are three mailing lists available for updates to the Guide.

1) sends updates via e-mail in PostScript format

2) sends updates via e-mail in plain-text (ASCII) format

3) sends an announcement via e-mail when new entries are available via FTP

To get added to one of these lists, send an e-mail message to: resource-guide, `request@nnsc.nsf.net`, and make sure you specify which list you prefer.

If you do not have FTP access, the Internet Resource Guide is on an Info-Server which is an automatic retrieval system that uses ordinary e-mail.

To receive the "help" file with instructions for using the Info-Server, and the "index-resource-guide" file with a list of the sections and chapters in the Guide, send an e-mail message to: info-server@nnsc.nsf.net.

In the body of the message, type:

Request: resource-guide

Topic: help

Topic: index-resource-guide

For people who are unable to use either FTP or e-mail, the NNSC also publishes printed copies of the Guide at a price of $25.00 per guide. Send a check or money order made payable to: Bolt Beranek and Newman Inc., in the amount of $25.00 (U.S. dollars), to:

NSF Network Service Center (NNSC)
Bolt Beranek and Newman Inc.
10 Moulton Street
Mail Stop: 6/3B
Cambridge, MA 02138
ATTENTION: Alanna MacDonald

Include the following account number on your check: 4001-49-06480.

A sample of the databases available is: INFO-SOUTH Latin American Information System. This database provides information relating to the social, political, and economic climate of Latin America. Sources include newspapers and journals published in Latin America, the United States, and throughout the world.

Latin America Data Base

This database is a full-text database of four weekly publications on Latin America: Chronicle of Latin American Economic Affairs, Central America Update, SourceMex—Economic News & Analysis on Mexico, and NotiSur—SouthAmerican & Caribbean Political Affairs. The database is updated four days a week and contains more than twenty thousand articles—from 1987 to present.

The International Centre for Distance Learning (ICDL)

This database specializes in collecting and disseminating information on distance education worldwide.

NASA/IPAC Extra-galactic Database

This database is a continuing project to organize, in one place, a broad range of published extra-galactic data into a computer-based central archive that can access and search using electronic networks. It contains the positions, names, and basic data for more than 200,000 extra-galactic objects, related bibliographic references, and notes from catalogs and other publications.

The Medieval and Early Modern Data Bank

This database provides researchers with a constantly expanding reference library of information concerning the medieval and early modern periods, circa A.D. 800-1800.

Dartmouth Dante database

This database contains approximately 600 years of line-by-line commentary to Dante's Divine Comedy, as well as the Petrocchi version of the poem. Texts are in their original languages (Italian, Latin, and English) with no translations. Ancient commentaries have been parsed for the users' convenience. The search program utilized is BRS/Search.

GenBank Server

This server, sponsored by the Institute for Molecular Biology, provides protein information resource (PIR), protein sequence database entries, and software for molecular biologists. Other files are available, and you can search by e-mail for a protein sequence. The server is accessed through Internet, BITNET, and UUCP. This server also includes the Matrix of Biological Knowledge database.

COSMIC

Hundreds of programs are distributed here including many for physics and engineering programs. This database is funded by NASA.

IuBio Archive for Molecular and General Biology

This database contains software programs and data for biologists, chemists, and other scientists.

PENpages

This service provides thousands of publications on research-based agriculture and consumer issues. It is supported by Penn State's College of Agriculture.

LiMB Database

The Listing of Molecular Biology database contains information on molecular biology databases. Accessible through e-mail only.

Southwest Research Data Display and Analyses System

For people doing research on space physics, magnetospheric physics, and the upper atmosphere. Contains data from the Dynamic Explorer Satellites 1 and 2.

Keeping Up-to-date.

Online resources are not stagnant. New lists and services are being added daily but there are ways to keep up-to-date. There are a couple of mailing lists that will help keep you updated:

- ⟲   NETSCOUT (NETSCOUT@VMTECMEX)
  The BITnet/Internet scouts.

  Send e-mail to LISTSERV@VMTECMEX.BITNET with the text:
  SUB NETSCOUT yourfirstname yourlastname

- ⟲   HELP-NET (HELP-NET@TEMPLEVM)
  BITNET/CREN/INTERNET Help Resource.

  Send e-mail to LISTSERV@TEMPLEVM.BITNET with the text:
  SUB HELP-NET yourfirstname yourlastname

  Be warned, this list is very busy and you can expect 10 to 20 messages per day.

- ⟲   NEW-LIST (NEW-LIST@VM1.NoDak.EDU) or (NEW-LIST@NDSUVM1.Bitnet)

  This list publishes announcements of new lists (about two to three per week). To subscribe to NEW-LIST send mail to:
  LISTSERV@vm1.nodak.edu (or LISTSERV@NDSUVM1.BITNET) with the BODY of the mail containing the command:
  SUB NEW-LIST yourfirstname yourlastname

☽ SRI NIC Maintained Interest-Groups List of Lists

You can obtain the Internet Interest Groups List of lists by anonymous FTP from ftp.nisc.sri.com (192.33.33.22).

FTP to ftp.nisc.sri.com as user "anonymous" (password is Guest) and CD to "netinfo" then GET interest-groups. The file is available as one large file at this time (really large).

The SRI NIC list-of-lists is available via electronic mail.

Send a message to `mail-server@nisc.sri.com` with the following line in the message body:
    Send netinfo/interest-groups

You will receive the file in several pieces. Further information on the server itself is available with the command:
    Send help

☽ Network Accessible Database Server

The Internet Interest-Groups list is in a format that can be searched (called the INTGROUP database). This is only available on the LISTSERV at `NDSUVM1` (or `VM1.NoDak.EDU`).

For example, to search these databases for lists on "astronomy" you would send the following statements in the text/body of the mail to `LISTSERV@VM1.NoDak.EDU` or on BITNET just `LISTSERV@NDSUVM1`:

//DBlook JOB Echo=No

Database Search DD=Rules

//Rules DD *

Select astronomy in lists

index

Select astronomy in intgroup

index

Select astronomy in new-list

index

These statements would search the global LISTSERV list of lists ("in lists"), and the local copy of the SRI-NIC Interest Groups ("in intgroup"), and the archives of the "new-list" list ("in new-list"). For more information, send LISTSERV the command INFO DATABASE .

⑤   The Dartmouth Merged List

Dartmouth, as explained previously, maintains a merged list of the LISTSERV lists on Bitnet and the Interest Group lists on the Internet. It is a single file with one line for each mailing list. The files can be obtained by anonymous FTP from:

DARTCMS1.DARTMOUTH.EDU <129.170.16.19> in directory SIGLISTS. They can also be obtained (except the large data stack) via Bitnet from mail using the command SEND fn ft. To obtain a list of the files via LISTSERV send mail to LISTSERV@DARTCMS1 (LISTSERV@DARTCMS1.DARTMOUTH.EDU) with the command in the body of the mail:
    INDEX SIGLISTS

For more information contact David Avery, DAVID@DARTCMS1.BITNET or david@dartcms1.dartmouth.edu.

Bitnet

BITNET is three interconnected networks that span 40 countries and link up approximately 4000 academic and research organizations. The North American link is also called BITNET, the European link is called EARN (European Academic Research Network), and the Canadian link is called NetNorth.

BITNET's primary use is correspondence among researchers around the world and has gateways for the exchange of electronic mail with the Internet, FidoNet, and many other networks worldwide.

The network was originally restricted to universities with IBM mainframes, but software was developed to allow the network to run on UNIX or Digital Vax computers running the VMS operating system, as well as on other systems that use IBM's RSCS/NJE mail and file transfer protocols. Bitnet seems to be getting absorbed into the Internet.

Getting Online

To access BITNET from your own computer, you must set up an account at a facility that is a member of the network. Getting a BITNET account is easy if you are a student or faculty member at, or otherwise affiliated with, a university that is a BITNET node. Also, many universities will provide external accounts to members of nonprofit organizations or the general public.

After you find a local node, obtain a user ID from that institution. Then, because nodes use different operating systems, you need to become familiar with the text editor of your local node and learn how to send mail to BITNET.

To find a local node or for further information about BITNET, contact the BITNET Network Information Center, EDCUCOM, 112 16th Street NW, Suite 600, Washington DC, 20036; (202) 872-4200. You can download a Bitnet Node list but it is extremely large.

Cost

In most cases, the service is free or available at a minimal cost. A small hourly fee is usually charged for external accounts.

Electronic Mail

All computers on BITNET use Internet-style domain addresses. If you know that someone is on the network at the same time you are, you can send that person interactive real-time mail. It takes only a few simple commands, although those vary depending on the host computer's software and operating system.

BITNET can exchange mail with FidoNet, Internet, and other networks through gateways that direct your mail to the proper destination. This is important because you will use the e-mail to subscribe to discussion lists.

List Servers

BITNET uses servers to store and forward information and files. Each server resides on a host computer and has its own address. The server responds to the commands that you send to retrieve documents, help files, software, mailing lists, and other data.

BITNET has many servers, each with its own contents and purpose: Listservers control mailing lists, Fileservers control file lists. Some servers do both.

In the Online Navigator, we are only interested in the Servers that deal with human to human discussions lists.

Human to Human Discussion Lists

As on the Internet, a wide variety of interesting discussions go on among users of BITNET and some of them are gatewayed to the Internet, FidoNet and Usenet. BITNET discussion groups are called mailing lists and include forums, digests, and electronic magazines. About 1000 discussion groups can be found on BITNET. The Online Navigator lists BITNET, Internet, and UUCPnet lists together by category making it easier to locate the ones that interest you.

To join a mailing list, you subscribe using e-mail like you do the Internet lists. Each list in the Online Navigator tells you how to subscribe to it.

Keeping Up-to-date

You can obtain a current list of the discussions lists.

⊙   BITNET LISTSERV Servers

Global List of Public LISTSERV Lists

On BITNET, the LISTSERV servers keep a composite of their lists online. To get a basic "one line per list" of all lists (about 2000 lines at present) send LISTSERV@VM1.NoDak.EDU mail with the following command in the TEXT or BODY of the mail:

LIST GLOBAL

IMPORTANT: LISTSERV wants the commands in the text of the mail and you can supply more than one per line.

The Subject: field is NOT used for commands (you can put anything there or leave it blank).

The global list can also be searched online. For details send LISTSERV the command INFO DATABASE. The global lists is called the "LISTS" database and is available at some of the major backbone LISTSERVs.

FidoNet

FidoNet is an amateur network of more than 16,000 individual bulletin boards (BBSs) electronically connected to 48 countries and growing.

FidoNet bulletin boards have typical bulletin board services such as private and public mail and file libraries, but expands on those services by offering three additional ones: Netmail enables you to send private messages to any participant on the FidoNet; Echomail consists of public conferences on a variety of topics; and file transfers allow you to send reports, software programs, spreadsheets, or other files, to anyone on the FidoNet.

Echos are the equivalent to the Internet & Bitnet discussion lists and some of them are gatewayed. Similarly, you will find discussions on a wide range of topics on Fidonet.

With thousands of locations across the United States, chances are you can find a Fido BBS in your own city.

How to Get Online

To participate in FidoNet, you must dial into a BBS that is a part of the FidoNet. You can find local Fido boards by looking in computer magazines like BoardWatch, Computer Shopper, Computer Monthly, or almost any BBS list that can be found on the commercial online services like America Online, CompuServe, or GEnie, or other bulletin boards. The Fido NodeList which is the complete phone directory of all Fido boards can be downloaded from many bulletin boards. However this file is large and takes more than one hour to download.

Cost

If you find a local BBS that belongs to FidoNet, access will cost you only the price of a local call in most cases. The entire cost of maintaining the network is distributed among the participating BBS operators. Many boards allow you to send private mail for a small fee, or charge you to enter the Echo conference area. However, most boards are free.

Gateways to Other Networks

Special software called UF-Gate allows the FidoNet to share mail and discussions with the Internet, BITNET, and Usenet. Several Fido boards now gateway certain echoes to BITNET and the Internet.

FidoNet mail to the Internet is routed through the various FidoNet BBS gateways. FidoNet administrator David Dodell explains how to do this:

Internet via FidoNet

FidoNet is fully coupled into the Internet. You do not need to know any specific gateways to send mail from FidoNet to Internet; all you have to do is address the message correctly into the Fidonet.org domain, and the message will be routed automatically. Here's how to address messages through FidoNet to the Internet: The basic FidoNet address format is:

`FirstName.LastName@pww.fzz.nxx.zyy.fidonet.org ww`, =, Point number (this is usually not needed unless specific to a subsystem)

zz, =, FidoNet node

xx, =, FidoNet network or region

yy, =, FidoNet zone

As an example, my name David Dodell, resides at FidoNet address 1:114/15. My FidoNet Internet address is:

<code>David.Dodell@f15.n114.z1.fidonet.org</code>

Now, how do you go from a FidoNet node to an Internet-style address? It's just as easy; however, you need to find a gateway on FidoNet first, since no automatic routing to Internet gateways is available at this time. For example, you could use my gateway at `1:114/15`. You would send a message to the user uucp at `1:114/15`.

In the first line of text, you put the Internet-style address, followed by two returns:

<code>To: user@site.domain</code>

For example, to send to my BITNET account of `ATW1H@ASUACAD`, the FidoNet message would go to uucp at FidoNet address `1:114/15`. The first line of text in the body of the message would be:

<code>To: atw1h@asuacad.bitnet</code>

Or, to my uucp address:

<code>To: postmaster@stjhmc.uucp</code>

Echos

Special public topics or conferences on the FidoNet are called Echos, short for Echomail. About 500 echos now dot the Fidonet landscape. New echos are constantly created, and unpopular ones come and go. Each echo has a moderator, usually the person who originally proposed the echo.

Members of an echo do not communicate with each other in real time. Instead, like the Internet or Bitnet, each comment and response from a member is distributed to the echo where members can read it and in turn respond at their leisure.

Each echo has a set of rules describing the conduct that participants agree to follow. Most rules are developed to ensure the enjoyment and productivity of all participants. The use of profanity and name-calling is discouraged. Infractions of the rules can result in a sound scolding, called flaming, from the entire membership of that echo, or barred from the net. If you are unsure about the rules and etiquette for an echo, you can request them from the moderator or your local system operator.

Not all Fido boards carry every echo. You can make a request to the operator of your local Fido board asking to carry those you have an interest in. Usually the system operator will accommodate you. All of the current echoes carried on Fidonet are listed in the Online Navigator.

The list of Fido echoes contains the general name of each echo, the official echo name (all CAPS—use this to request an echo), a description of the list's purpose. Some echoes are gatewayed to other networks; some are by invitation only, are for system operators only, or require moderator approval.

Keeping Up-to-date

Mike Fuchs is the keeper of the Fidonet echo list. Ask the system operator of the Fido board you are using to send you a copy of the latest EchoList. I believe it is updated monthly.

Usenet

Usenet is a public series of conferences called newsgroups carried primarily over UNIX-based computers. There are 3000 newsgroups currently.

Usenet reaches over 280,000 readers on about 55,000 hosts spanning five continents. Usenet users access the network on all kinds of equipment, from small PCs at home to supercomputers at large universities, commercial online services, research organizations, and even corporations. Although Usenet newsgroups are primarily distributed over computers that use the UNIX operating system, Usenet has gateways to Internet, BITNET, Fidonet, and other networks.

Like the Internet, Bitnet, and Usenet participants subscribe to newsgroups that interest them. Subscribers post messages called articles and replies all of which are circulated to all other members of that particular newsgroup. Unlike FidoNet and BITNET, Usenet itself does not support e-mail. Another network, UUCPnet, carries the e-mail generated for Usenet and, in fact, transports the Usenet transmissions themselves from host to host. Much of the traffic though is now being picked up by the Internet.

How to Get Online

Usenet is similar to FidoNet in that there is no central administration and anyone can join. To participate, you must first get an account with a network or institution that carries Usenet newsgroups. Places to find Usenet newsgroups include:

Wordlink

This service, described in the Internet section, enables you to subscribe, read, and send Usenet from your own PC using their software.

Your local college or university

If you are a student and your school is a Usenet site, you can probably get an account and participate for no cost. Many local academic institutions grant external accounts to qualified organizations and individuals.

The WELL

The WELL online service, described in the Commercial Online Service chapter, carries many of the Usenet newsgroups. The WELL is a subscription service that carries a monthly membership fee and hourly connect charges.

FidoNet

A number of the FidoNet boards carry Usenet newsgroups.

UUNET

If you have trouble finding a local Usenet feed, contact UUNET Communications Services (see Internet section) and subscribe to UUCP, the network that carries the Usenet newsgroups from host to host. UUNET will set up your personal computer as a UNIX site so that you can subscribe to the Usenet newsgroups that interest you.

Other personal bulletin board services

Many bulletin boards across the country carry Usenet newsgroups. Phil Eschallier, maintains an updated list of these bulletin boards called Nixpub (for UNIX Publication). The most current listing of these sites is included in Appendix B with his permission, along with a description on how you can obtain updated lists.

After you find a host site or a BBS that carries Usenet newsgroups, check whether it carries any in your area of interest. (Because Usenet carries some 4 megabytes of information per day, it is not possible for each host site to carry all newsgroups.) If the site does not carry the newsgroups that interest you, ask the system operator or the host of the site to consider carrying them.

Software programs called "readers" enable you to read and reply to Usenet articles. Three common readers are vnews and rn (which have screen-oriented interfaces) and readnews (which is line oriented). These programs are found on most Usenet sites, along with instructions on how to use them. A commercial program called mAccess from ICE Engineering (8840 Main Street, Whitmore Lake, MI 48189), gives Macintosh users access to Usenet newsgroups using the familiar Mac interface. The Mac and PC software from WorldLink has its own built in Usenet reader.

You can also subscribe to a monthly CD-ROM of the complete year's worth of netnews from Sterling Software, 1404 Fort Crook Road South, Bellevue, NE 68005 (1-800-643-6397). It has reading software for various personal computers.

Cost

The costs of the network are shared by participating hosts, and each host pays for its own transmission costs. Usenet is a noncommercial network, but some private bulletin boards and online services charge for access to their Usenet areas.

Usenet Newsgroups

There are hundreds of newsgroups and they cover a variety of subjects. The major Usenet newsgroups are distributed worldwide, and fall into seven main categories:

- comp (computer)
- misc (miscellaneous)
- rec (recreation)
- sci (science)
- soc (social issues)
- news (about Usenet news groups)
- talk (chatter).

There are other groups outside of the main categories that may or may not be carried worldwide, or by every host.

- alt (alternative, not carried by everyone)
- Biz (for computer products)
- Bionet (for biologists)
- Clarinet (newsgroups gatewayed from commercial news services and other "official" sources. The host has to pay a fee to carry these)
- inet/ddn (This consists of many newsgroups bearing names similar to traditional Usenet groups and corresponding to Internet discussion lists)
- Pubnet (or public-access systems)
- unix-PC (groups devoted to users of the AT&T UNIX-PC), and others .

Newsgroup names consist of an abbreviation of the category name followed by a period, and an abbreviation of the group name. For example, the name "sci.astro" signifies that this group astronomy falls in the science category. Subgroups are designated by an additional period and abbreviation; for example, sci.astro.hubble stands for the science/astronomy/Hubble newsgroup, referring to a discussion of the Hubble Telescope.

Most newsgroups distribute everything sent in by subscribers. Others are moderated, meaning a moderator screens submissions to determine which get posted into the newsgroup.

Newsgroups are created and deleted democratically by votes in a newsgroup called news.groups. Anyone can subscribe to this newsgroup.

A number of Usenet newsgroups have Internet, Fidonet, or bitnet equivalents that are shared by the two networks, expanding participation on the topic.

Alternative Newsgroups

A number of newsgroups outside the seven main categories are distributed as alternative newgroups

Alternative Groups

The alternative groups (alt) are a small collection of newsgroups distributed by sites that choose to carry them. You can join the "alt subnet" by finding a site in your area that carries the groups. Either send mail to the administrators of the sites you connect to, or post something to a local general or wanted newsgroup in your area. If no sites nearby distribute the alternative groups, you can get them from UUNET.

Bionet

Bionet is a collection of newsgroups of interest to biologists and is carried by a growing number of hosts including Rutgers, phri, mit-eddie, ukma, and all of the machines at UCSD. Contact Eliot Lear (Usenet@NET.BIO.NET) for more details. Most of these groups have an equivalent on BITNET.

ClariNet

ClariNet consists of newsgroups gatewayed from commercial news services and other official sources. More information may be obtained by sending mail to info@clarinet.com.

Inet/ddn

The inet/ddn distribution consists of newsgroups bearing names similar to traditional Usenet groups but corresponding to Internet discussion lists. The groups are circulated by means of the NNTP transport mechanism among sites on the Internet in an attempt to reduce the number of copies of these groups flowing through the mail. Further details may be obtained by writing to Erik Fair at fair@ucbarpa.berkeley.edu.

Regional

Regional newsgroups are those created by the university or site on topics of local interest. These are usually not sent out over the net and are not included in the Usenet listings in this book.

All of the main newsgroups except the regional ones are listed in this book.

Keeping Up-to-date

The Usenet News list of groups and mailing lists are available in newsgroups "news.announce.newusers" and "news.lists."

The following files are also available via anonymous FTP from VM1.NoDak.EDU in the "BITINFO" directory. After they are connected enter CD BITINFO. These may or may not be the most current versions of these files.

Name on	
vm1.nodak.edu	Source
INTEREST.GROUPS	Recent Interest-Groups from ftp.nisc.sri.com
NETNEWS.MAILLIST	Usenet News Mailing Lists from news.lists
NETNEWS.GRPLIST	Usenet Groups from news.lists
NETNEWS.ALTERNAT	Usenet Alternate Groups from news.lists

UUCPNet

Usenet does not have its own system for transporting newsgroups and e-mail among host sites. Most e-mail is sent via UUCP (UNIX to UNIX Copy Program) software. UUCP runs on computers that use the UNIX operating system and is estimated to be operating on over 10,000 hosts with a million users.

UUCP enables you to send mail and files and execute commands on a remote system. You need the UUCP programs, a modem and a phone line, direct dial, and a public data network. As with Usenet and Fidonet, each host on UUCP pays for its own calls, and there is no central authority.

As with BITNET and the Internet, you can subscribe to UUCP-based discussion lists. These lists have been incorporated into the Dartmouth list and are included in the discussion lists found in the Online Resources section of this book.

Keeping Up-to-date
Subscribe to the Dartmouth lists.

Online Libraries

Imagine being able to electronically look through a card catalog in Belgium, Germany, or across the U.S. without leaving your home computer? Or perhaps you remember the time consuming task of preparing a complete bibliography on a particular subject for a classroom project or professional meeting.

Computerizing the world's published and unpublished literature has been going on for more than a decade. Today, you can search through millions of records finding almost anything that has been published or not published on virtually any topic.

There are several specialized bibliographical retrieval companies that offer the computer user access to this immense bibliographical warehouse. Additionally, many university libraries are becoming part of the Internet where you can log onto their main catalog and peruse at your leisure. Companies like Dialog and Maxwell Communications offer the user an inexpensive access to a selection of their many databases. In the Online Navigator four such bibliographical retrieval companies are featured: Knowledge Index, BRS AfterDark, Orbit, and NewsNet.

Knowledge Index

In 1981, Dialog Information Services launched Knowledge Index (KI) to appeal to the individual computer user who needed information in science and education. Dialog is the largest online bibliographic company with over 200 million items available for searching in 370 databases. Of those databases, 120 have been carefully selected and priced for the home user covering a wide variety of topics from agriculture to travel. These databases include the complete text of 33 major newspapers, scientific abstracts, business and corporate news, government publications, legal and reference information. Knowledge Index is easily searched using menus.

Dialog also has many more databases, available for a higher fee, than those included in KI. Dialog provides a *Dialog Medical Connection* (a menu driven search service of 27 medical and technical databases), and *Dialog OnDisc*, (a series of CD-ROM disks on some of their databases).

In April, 1993, KI became an exclusive service on CompuServe. CompuServe members pay $24 per hour to access KI up to 9600 bps. This is the same pricing charged to members when it was offered by Dialog.

Source

Dialog Information Services, Inc., 3460 Hillview Avenue, Palo Alto, CA 94304, 1(800) 334-2564, or CompuServe (800) 848-8199

Operating Cost

$24/hour off-peak time using CompuServe (extra for all connecting network phone charges—Telenet, Tymnet). No monthly minimum. Users pay only for their actual usage.

Online Availability

Monday-Thursday, 6PM-5AM; Weekends, 6 PM Friday to 5AM Monday.

Databases

All of the current databases offered are included in the next section.

BRS AFTERDARK

BRS/After Dark is similar to Knowledge Index because it is a low cost service from BRS Information Technologies, a division of Maxwell Online Inc., that offers more than 130 databases covering a variety of disciplines including science, biomedicine, education, business, life science, arts and humanities, and current events.

BRS/After Dark is geared more to science, medical, and environmental-related databases than Knowledge Index. Unlike KI, each database has a different cost for access.

BRS provides a users manual that is well thought out and extensive online help is available if you need it. You can quickly locate a summary of any database and its cost before use and can display documents in short form giving you enough information (title, author, publication, and date) to find the document easily in your library, or you can read the entire text of some of the databases.

For additional fees, you can have the complete search or text mailed to you within 24 hours.

BRS Colleague and Search Service

BRS also offers BRS Colleague and Search Service geared more to medical or health care researchers. Most of the information is produced by medical publishers, health agencies and associations. Most of the databases comprise the world's biomedical literature for the last 20 years. Besides database searching, Colleague offers daily updates of medical news stories, electronic mail, and interactive bulletin board and access to over 100 other databases in business, science, education and social sciences.

Rates are more expensive than BRS/After Dark, ranging from $8 to over $100/hr. Daytime searching is available for higher costs. BRS/After Dark is menu driven.

Source
BRS Information Technologies, Division of Maxwell Online Inc., 8000 Westpark Drive, McLean, VA 22102, (800) 955-0906

Startup Cost
One time subscription fee of $75. Includes 44 page manual (punched for three ring binder), complete set of database sheets, and support services. (Customer support is available Monday-Friday, 8 AM to 1 AM eastern time; Saturday 8AM to 5 PM; and 9 AM to 5 PM Sunday, 1(800) 345-4277.)

Operating Cost
Monthly minimum of $12 (applied toward monthly use). Online charges depending on database used from low of $8/hour to high of $48/hour. Connect time and communication fees included. Additional charges per citation display from 0 to 45 cents with the average around 10 cents per citation.

Online Availability
Monday-Friday, 6 PM (local) to 4AM (eastern time), Saturday, 6 AM to 2 AM(ET), Sunday, 9 AM to 4 AM (ET). Available worldwide.

Getting Online
Use Telenet, Tymnet, and Datapac (Canada) national communication networks for access.

Databases

All of the BRS AfterDark databases are described in this book.

Orbit

Orbit, from Orbit Search Service, is also a division of Maxwell Online Inc. Orbit is an ideal bibliographic retrieval service for science researchers. Orbit has more than 100 databases in chemistry, earth sciences, energy, engineering, environmental, material science and many databases not available on other services.

Orbit is command not menu driven and full boolean searching (using connectors like AND, OR, BUT) is available, making searching easy and less time consuming. They have specialized search functions to determine information like the most prolific authors of a given subject, or allowing you to use the same search terms on complementary database. Also users have the option to retrieve only data needed from each record, or just browse a set of records to select those that are of real interest.

Source

Orbit Search Service, Division of Maxwell Online Inc., 8000 Westpark Drive, McLean, VA 22102, (703) 442-0900.

Startup Cost

Annual subscription fee based on number of users: 1-5 users, $40 per user ID.

Operating Cost

Monthly minimum of $15 (no charge if you don't use it during the month). Online charges, depending on database used, from low of $10/hour to high of almost $200/hour. Connect time and communication fees using Telenet or Tymnet extra. Additional charges per citation display from 10 cents and up.

Online Availability

Monday-Friday, all day except 9:45 -10:15 PM Saturday, all day until 9:45; Sunday, 10 AM-Midnight. Available worldwide.

Getting Online
Call 1(800) 45-Orbit.

Databases
All of Orbit's current databases are described in the next section.

NewsNet

Since 1982, NewsNet has provided online the *full text* (no graphics, charts, or ads) of more than 600 specialty newsletters and other news sources.

NewsNet covers a variety of topics from Advertising to news like the Chinese Xinhau English language News Service. NewsNet has a strong focus on the business information world. NewsNet provides many informative publications in science and technology as well.

Users can access their database by using boolean searching (AND, OR, BUT). NewsNet gives you the option to create your own clipping service (called NewsFlash) that will automatically send you when you sign on any new reference material you selected.

NewsNet is organized into Newsletters, directories, wire services, and gateway services. Newsletters are grouped in more than 30 fields. NewsNet is command-driven not menu driven.

Source
NewsNet, Inc., 945 Haverford Road, Bryn Mawr, PA 19010. (800) 345-1301.

Startup Cost
Various payment options exist. There is an annual, half-year, or monthly subscription fee of $120, $75, or $15 respectively. Excellent user manuals make searching easy.

Operating Cost
Online charges are $60/hr for 300 to 1200 baud and $90/hr. for 2400 baud. On top of these charges are hourly charges by the publisher of a title—a

validated charge (for those who subscribe to the printed version and is cheaper) and a non validated charge (those who do not subscribe).

The NewsFlash clipping service has a fifty cents charge per "hit." By preparing your search carefully before signing on to NewsNet, your final search cost can be held at a minimum.

Online Availability
NewsNet can be reached through the national communication carriers Telenet, Tymnet, and Datapac in Canada. Available worldwide.

Getting Online
Call (800) 345-1301.

Databases
All of NewsNet's current databases are described in the next section.

Bulletin Boards

One of the more interesting avenues for obtaining information is from computer bulletin boards (singularly known as a BBS). Bulletin boards are operated by individuals, businesses, nonprofit organizations and government agencies, all for the purpose of providing information to their users and often at no cost or low cost. There are thousands of bulletin boards around the world.

Bulletin boards were born during the late seventies as people began to use their own personal computers to share electronic mail and programs among friends. In the early eighties, bulletin boards became popular with computer user groups because it was an easy way to share public-domain programs with their members. Bulletin boards boomed during the mid-eighties as businesses and government agencies found them an ideal method of storing and retrieving large amounts of information for their customers or public.

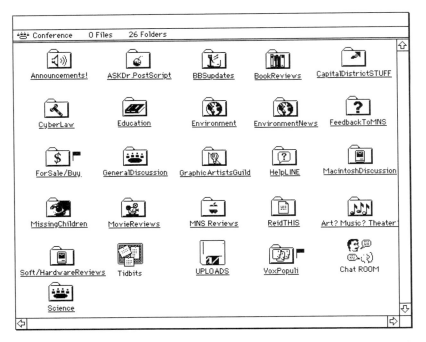

Figure 2.4. This graphics-based bulletin board provides many discussions forums for its members.

Bulletin boards generally cater to people with a particular type of computer (for example, Atari, IBM PC, Amiga or Macintosh) or a particular interest (for example astronomy, public health, economics or record collecting). You can participate in most bulletin boards around the clock, seven days a week at no cost other than the cost of your telephone calls. Some bulletin board operators request donations from regular users; some charge a yearly fee for complete access.

Bulletin boards operate at the whim of their owners and at tremendous personal cost (unless government or business sponsored). As a result, they have very short life spans, often as brief as a few months. Those boards that have lasted more than a year or two usually have an active membership base, a great deal of online expertise, and provide timely information.

Each bulletin board takes on the identity of its sponsor and its membership. One may be popular for its volume of files for down-loading, while another may be popular for the special conferences it carries or because of a special interest of the membership. Although bulletin boards employ different user interfaces, determined by the type of bulletin board software used by the system operator, all follow similar methods of operation, and offer similar services: private e-mail, public conferences, and file libraries. Some have additional features like searchable databases.

Finding a Bulletin Board

The bulletin boards listed in this book are just a sample of what you can find in each of the categories. You can find other boards from this list. Most boards carry BBS lists that are compiled from various sources or the system operator of that board. Many of the boards listed here provide specialized BBS lists.

Several publications also list bulletin boards. Vulcan's Computer Monthly, Computer Shopper, and Boardwatch Magazine can all be found in your favorite bookstore or magazine store. Many local computing newspapers also publish lists of bulletin boards, and local computer user groups and computer stores can often make recommendations.

CD-ROM

Although not technically "online" by using a modem, Compact Disk Read-Only Memory (CD-ROM) technology is a great benefit for those needing access to large amounts of data. One CD-ROM disk can contain the equivalent of 250,000 pages of information, or more than 1500 floppy disks, and the same disk can include data, graphics, and sound.

CD-ROM is commonly used for lengthy reference materials such as bibliographies, scientific collections, databases, and specialized dictionaries. Although some commercial CD-ROMs disks cost more than the drive that reads them, they are nonetheless a convenient way to access and store large amounts of information. One CD-ROM disk saves the equivalent of a ton and a half of paper, which would cost over $4000 to mail (a CD-ROM disk costs 70 cents to mail). If you needed to transmit that amount of data over a phone by way of modem, it would take about 3 weeks at 2400 baud.

To read a disk, a CD-ROM drive spins the disk while a laser beam scans the disk's underside, reflecting off a series of pits, or lack of them. A detector measures the strength of the reflective beam (a pit scatters the laser light, making the reflection weaker) and translates the results into data that is sent to the computer.

You can find CD-ROM readers in most libraries and the price for individual ownership now runs less than $500 for a good one. Some of the specialized CD-ROM databases however are expensive, costing several thousands of dollars. If you buy a CD-ROM Drive, all of them come with straightforward instructions and the necessary software. Macintosh CD-ROM drives attach with a cable to the SCSI port in the back of the Mac. A few files are dropped into the Macintosh system folder and enable the Mac to read the CD-ROM's format. For IBM PC-compatibles, you must insert an interface card and MS-DOS CD-ROM extensions (software drivers).

The most important factor in determining a CD-ROM purchase is speed of access to the data. Read reviews of the latest models in your favorite computer magazines and realize that current models access data at 280 milliseconds or less for a good drive. Toshiba and NEC currently offer models at those speeds.

There are several hundred CD-ROM titles available covering a wide variety of disciplines. A sample of titles falling within each category featured in the Online Navigator are listed. Search your local library for the ones that interest you first or write to the companies for pricing and description.

Keeping Up-to-date

There are several CD-ROM publications produced monthly or quarterly. Check them out at your local library or subscribe to them. The CD-ROM Handbook is published by EBSCO Subscription Services (PO Box 1943, Birmingham, AL 35201, (205) 991-6600) and contains the descriptions of hundreds of CD-ROM titles and prices.

Resources

Part 3 is where the fun begins. Here is where you will find resource listings for the major networks, online services, bulletin boards, library databases, and CD-ROM titles. The topics begin with listings for academia and continue their march through 54 more areas of interest, ending with zoology. On the way, you will encounter the addresses of thousands of fascinating forums and conferences in which you can discover the newest developments in anthropology, business, public health, science fiction, and technology. The listings are presented in alphabetical order by address and usually include short descriptions of the forum or bulletin board.

A complete discussion of the on-line information listed for America Online, CompuServe, and the other networks and services is included in the first two parts of this book. The listings provide the addresses and names you will need to connect with your targeted conference area. The moderator or sysops of the resources listed here will be able to provide you with further information about the service. Happy voyaging!

Academia Resources

Forums & Databases

America Online (AOL)

No services available.

CompuServe (CIS)

🅢 *Peterson's College Database*
Keyword: GO PETERSON+
Describes more than 4,000 accredited or approved U.S. and Canadian colleges that grant associate or bachelor degrees.

🅢 *Students' Forum*
Keyword: GO STUFO
A forum for students to share their ideas and interests with other students around the world; also for teachers.

GEnie

🅢 *College Aid Sources for Higher Education*
Keyword: CASHE or Page 408
A searchable scholarship database for undergraduate and graduate assistance. Includes leads on scholarships, fellowships, loans, internships, and work cooperative programs.

🅢 *Rensselaer Polytechnic RT*
Keyword: RPI or Page 265
A forum to help students and parents explore opportunities available to them at Rensselaer Polytechnic Institute.

The Well

No services available.

Network Discussions Lists
Internet (Includes Bitnet & UUCPNet)

Academic

🅢 *Association of Discussion Groups & Electronic Journals for Scholars list.*
Discusses more than 600 discussion groups, newsletters, digests, and electronic journals on topics of scholarly interest.
    ARACHNET@UOTTAWA.BITNET
    LISTSERV@UOTTAWA.BITNET
Contact: Diane Kovacs
    <dkovacs@kentvm.BITNET>

🅢 *Computers and Academic Freedom Mailing lists.*
    caf-talk@eff.org
    LISTSERV@eff.org

🅢 *Computers and Academic Freedom Mailing lists.*
A daily digest of comp-academic-freedom-talk.
    comp-academic-freedom-batch@eff.org
    LISTSERV@eff.org
Contact: Carl Kadie
    <kadie@eff.org>

🅢 *Chinese Students and Scholars Discussion list.*
    CSS-L@UBVM.BITNET
    LISTSERV@UBVM.BITNET

🅢 *Academic Freedom*
Discusses general principles of academic freedom as applied to university computers and networks.

```
SUBSCRIBE COMP-ACADEMIC-FREEDOM-TALK
```
Contact: Carl Kadie
```
<kadie@eff.org>
```

Accounting

🔊 *Big 10 EDP Auditors list.*
```
B10EDP-L@PSUVM.BITNET
LISTSERV@PSUVM.BITNET
```

🔊 *Contract and Grant Representatives list.*
```
CANDG-L@UCSFVM.BITNET
LISTSERV@UCSFVM.BITNET
```

🔊 *ESIA Budgeted Faculty Discussion list.*
```
ESIABUDG@GWUVM.BITNET
LISTSERV@GWUVM.BITNET
```

🔊 *FPS-L Discussion list—created 19 Oct 88.*
```
FINPROG@VTVM1.BITNET   (Ray Stell)
```

🔊 *Interactive Financial Planning System.*
```
IFPS-L@VTVM2.BITNET
LISTSERV@VTVM2.BITNET
```

Activist

🔊 *College Activism Information list.*
Data on college activism and issues relating to students, faculty, and administration.
```
ACTNOW-L@BROWNVM.BROWN.EDU
LISTSERV@BROWNVM.BROWN.EDU
```
Contact: <ST710852@brownvm.brown.edu>

🔊 *SU Women Faculty, Staff, and Student list.*
```
FEMNET@SUVM.BITNET
LISTSERV@SUVM.BITNET
```

Administration

🔊 *American Association of State Colleges and Universities list.*
```
AASCU-L@UBVM.BITNET
LISTSERV@UBVM.BITNET
```

🔊 *American Association of University Administrators*
```
AAUA-L@UBVM.BITNET
LISTSERV@UBVM.BITNET
```
Contact: Larry Deni
```
<DENI@CANISIUS.BITNET>
```

🔊 *Faculty Development Committee list.*
```
AAUFD-L@UNBVM1.BITNET
LISTSERV@UNBVM1.BITNET
```

🔊 *Association of American University Presses*
```
AAUP-L@PSUVM.BITNET
LISTSERV@PSUVM.BITNET
```

🔊 *Academic Computing Center Directors Forum*
```
ACADDR-L@MCGILL1.BITNET
LISTSERV@MCGILL1.BITNET
```
Contact: <ALAN@MCGILL1.BITNET>

🔊 *Academic Advising Forum*
For professional academic advisors and faculty members with academic advising responsibilities.
```
ACADV@NDSUVM1.BITNET
LISTSERV@NDSUVM1.BITNET
```
Contact: Harold Caldwell
```
<00HLCALDWELL@BSUVAX1.BITNET>
```

🔊 *Association of Collegiate Licensing Administrators list.*
```
ACLA-L@WSUVM1.BITNET
LISTSERV@WSUVM¦.BITNET
```

🔊 *UCLA Administrative Leadership list.*
```
ADMLEAD@UCLACN1.BITNET
LISTSERV@UCLACN1.BITNET
```

🔊 *AJCU Arts and Sciences Deans list.*
```
AJCUASD@GUVM.BITNET
LISTSERV@GUVM.BITNET
```

🔊 *Administrative Management Council list.*
```
AMC@UCLACN1.BITNET
LISTSERV@UCLACN1.BITNET
```

🔊 *Administrative Resource Center Participants list.*
```
ARCLIST@UCLACN1.BITNET
LISTSERV@UCLACN1.BITNET
```

🔊 *Middle States Accreditation Budget Task Force list.*
```
BUDGETTF@UBVM.BITNET
LISTSERV@UBVM.BITNET
```

🔊 *Bogazici University Graduates Communication list.*
```
BURC@TREARN.BITNET
DJAVI@TRBOUN.BITNET
```
Contact: Ferhat Djavidan
```
<DJAVI@TRBOUN.BITNET>
```

🔊 *Canadian Association of College & University list.*
```
CACUSS-L@UOGUELPH.BITNET
LISTSERV@UOGUELPH.BITNET
```

🔊 *Academic Chairpersons Discussion list.*
Deals with daily issues and problems facing an academic chairperson. Unmoderated.
```
CHAIRS-L@FAUVAX.BITNET
MAILSERV@FAUVAX.BITNET
```

🕲 *Higher Education Chief Information Officers list.*
CIO-L@WVNVM.BITNET
LISTSERV@WVNVM.BITNET

🕲 *Big Ten Degree Audit Reporting System Discussion list.*
11DARS-L@UIUCVMD.BITNET
LISTSERV@UIUCVMD.BITNET

🕲 *Executive Information Systems Special Interest Group*
EISSIG@ASUACAD.BITNET
LISTSERV@ASUACAD.BITNET
Contact: Nancy Dickson
IACNLD@ASUACAD.BITNET

🕲 *Association of Physical Plant Administrators list.*
ERAPPA-L@PSUVM.BITNET
LISTSERV@PSUVM.BITNET

🕲 *ESIA Faculty Discussion list.*
ESIAFAC@GWUVM.BITNET
LISTSERV@GWUVM.BITNET

🕲 *AAU Faculty Development Committee list.*
FACDEV@UNBVM1.BITNET
LISTSERV@UNBVM1.BITNET

🕲 *Facilities and Services Discussion list.*
Discusses facilities and services, including physical plant operations, security and public safety, and more.
FACSER-L@WVNVM.BITNET
LISTSERV@WVNVM.BITNET
Contact: Roman Olynyk
<VM0BA9@WVNVM.BITNET>

🕲 *UCSF Faculty Scholarship and Related Academic list.*
FACULTY@UCSFVM.BITNET
LISTSERV@UCSFVM.BITNET

🕲 *Financial Aid Systems—Technical Discussion list.*
FAMSTECH@AUSACAD.BITNET
LISTSERV@AUSACAD.BITNET
Contact: DEVBWED@TCSTSO.BITNET

🕲 *Administration of Student Financial Aid list.*
For university financial aid administrators and related personnel to discuss administrative concerns.
FINAID-L@PSUVM.BITNET
LISTSERV@PSUVM.BITNET
Contact: Robert E. Quinn
<REQ1@PSUADMIN.BITNET>

🕲 *FISC-L Fee-Based Info Services in Academia list.*
FISC-L@NDSUVM1.BITNET
LISTSERV@NDSUVM1.BITNET

🕲 *List for the discussion of university fundraising.*
Discusses computer support of fundraising programs at various universities.
FUNDLIST@JHUVM.BITNET
LISTSERV@JHUVM.BITNET
Contact: Joe Meister
ECF_GJWM@JHUVMS.BITNET

🕲 *Human Resources Information (Canada) list.*
HRIS-L@UALTAVM.BITNET
LISTSERV@UALTAVM.BITNET

🕲 *IAUP-UN: International Association of University Presidents list.*
IAUP-UN@BITNIC.BITNET
LISTSERV@BITNIC.BITNET

🕲 *Instructional Technology Advisory Committee list.*
INSTEC-L@UTKVM1.BITNET
LISTSERV@UTKVM1.BITNET

🕲 *Collaborative Study on Academic Information list.*
ITCOLLAB@HARVARDA.BITNET
LISTSERV@HARVARDA.BITNET

🕲 *Ivy+ Administrative Computing Group list.*
IVY+@MITVMA.BITNET
LISTSERV@MITVMA.BITNET
Contact: Donald E. Heller
heller@mitvma.BITNET

🕲 *Topics Related to the Cleaning of Buildings list.*
For those engaged in the cleaning of public buildings.
JANITORS@UKANVM.BITNET
LISTSERV@UKANVM.BITNET
Contact: Phil Endacott
<ENDACOTT@UKANVAX.BITNET>

🕲 *Local Government Administration list.*
LGA-L@UREGINA1.BITNET
LISTSERV@UREGINA1.BITNET

🕲 *Long-Term Planning list.*
LONG@MIAMIU.BITNET
LISTSERV@MIAMIU.BITNET

🕲 *AAU MBA Student Curriculum*
MBA Student curriculum discussion list for administrators, faculty, and MBA students.
MBA-L@MARIST.BITNET
LISTSERV@MARIST.BITNET

↻ *Conference on Minority Recruitment and Retention list.*
```
MINCON@UKCC.BITNET
LISTSERV@UKCC.BITNET
```
Contact: M. Yasar Iscan
```
<Iscan@acc.fau.edu>
```

↻ *College Business Office list.*
For discussion by college business, finance, and administrative professionals.
```
NACUBO@CTSTATEU.BITNET
NACUBO@CTSTATEU.BITNET
```
Contact: Janet Chayes
```
<CHAYES@CTSTATEU.BITNET>
```

↻ *Forum to discuss faculty development issues list.*
```
NP-FCLTY@UMUC.BITNET
LISTSERV@UMUC.BITNET
```

↻ *NUSVM General Discussion Group list.*
```
NUSLIST@NUSVM.BITNET
LISTSERV@NUSVM.BITNET
```

↻ *Public Administration Network list.*
```
PA_NET@SUVM.BITNET
LISTSERV@SUVM.BITNET
```

↻ *Discussion List for International Volunteers.*
```
PCORPS-L@CMUVM.BITNET
LISTSERV@CMUVM.BITNET
```

↻ *Personnel Directors, Associates, Managers list.*
```
PERDIR-L@UBVM.BITNET
LISTSERV@UBVM.BITNET
```

↻ *Professional Organizational Development Discussion list.*
```
POD-L@TAMVM1.BITNET
LISTSERV@TAMVM1.BITNET
```

↻ *Professional Office Staff Advisory Board list.*
```
POSAB-L@VTVM1.BITNET
LISTSERV@VTVM1.BITNET
```

↻ *UB Professional Staff Senate Discussion list.*
```
PROSEN-L@UBVM.BITNET
LISTSERV@UBVM.BITNET
```

↻ *Registrar Discussion list.*
```
REGIST-L@GSUVM1.BITNET
LISTSERV@GSUVM1.BITNET
```

↻ *Registrars and Other Records & Registration Professionals.*
Shares information, experiences, concerns, and advice about issues affecting records and registration professionals.
```
REGISTRAR-L@CORNELL.EDU
REGISTRAR-L-REQUEST@CORNELL.EDU
```
Contact: Paul Aucoin
```
<Paul_Aucoin@Cornell.edu>
```

↻ *Extramural Funding*
For those people interested in applying for outside funding support from government agencies, corporations, and foundations. Forwards information from potential sponsors.
```
RESEARCH@TEMPLEVM.BITNET
LISTSERV@TEMPLEVM.BITNET
```
Contact: Eleanor Cicinsky
```
<V2153A@TEMPLEVM.BITNET>
```

↻ *Society for College & University Planners Digest list.*
```
SCUPNEWS@UCBCMSA.BITNET
LISTSERV@UCBCMSA.BITNET
```

↻ *The Senate of Warsaw University discussion list.*
```
SENAT@PLEARN.BITNET
LISTSERV@PLEARN.BITNET
```

↻ *SGANet—Student Association of Virginia list.*
```
SGAN-SAV@VTVM1.BITNET
LISTSERV@VTVM1.BITNET
```

↻ *Student Government Global Mail Network list.*
An international mailing network for student government associations. Developed and implemented at Virginia Polytechnic Institute and State University.
```
SGANET@VTVM1.BITNET
LISTSERV@VTVM1.BITNET
```

↻ *Student Government Asian/Australian Mail Network list.*
```
SGANET-A@VTVM1.BITNET
LISTSERV@VTVM1.BITNET
```

↻ *Student Government European Mail Network list.*
```
SGANET-E@VTVM1.BITNET
LISTSERV@VTVM1.BITNET
```

↻ *Student Government North American Mail Network list.*
```
SGANET-N@VTVM1.BITNET
LISTSERV@VTVM1.BITNET
```

↻ *Student Government Latin American Mail Network list.*
```
SGANET-S@VTVM1.BITNET
LISTSERV@VTVM1.BITNET
```

↻ *SGANet Technical Discussion Group list.*
```
SGANET-T@VTVM1.BITNET
LISTSERV@VTVM1.BITNET
```

↻ *Staff Governance in Higher Education list.*
```
STAFFGOV@NDSUVM1.BITNET
LISTSERV@NDSUVM1.BITNET
```

🌐 *Dialogue on Educational Reform list.*
UKERA-L@UKCC.BITNET
LISTSERV@UKCC.BITNET

🌐 *University of Maine System Facilities Management list.*
UMSFAC-L@MAINE.BITNET
LISTSERV@UMSFAC.BITNET

Alumni

🌐 *ALUMNET (Trinity University Alumni) discussion list.*
ALUMNETZ@TRINITY.BITNET
LISTSERV@TRINITY.BITNET

🌐 *Alumni and Friends of Croatian Universities list.*
AMCA-L@MCGILL1.BITNET
LISTSERV@MCGILL1.BITNET

🌐 *AOU Legislative Alert System list.*
AOUNET-L@UMDD.BITNET
LISTSERV@UMDD.BITNET

🌐 *Alumni of Brown University*
Brown University alumni and friends discuss issues affecting the university's students, faculty, staff, and alumni.
BRUNONIA@BROWNVM.BITNET
LISTSERV@BROWNVM.BITNET
Contact: Anne Diffily
<ADBAM@BROWNVM.BITNET>

🌐 *Catalyst*
A refereed quarterly journal serving community college educators, published by the National Council on Community Services and Continuing Education.
CATALYST@VTVM1.BITNET
LISTSERV@VTVM1.BITNET
Contact: Lon Savage
<SAVAGE@VTVM1.BITNET>

🌐 *Canadian Association for University Continuing Education list.*
CAUCE-L@UREGINA1.BITNET
LISTSERV@UREGINA1.BITNET

🌐 *UCSB GSE Alumni Discussion list.*
GSEAA-L@UCSBVM.BITNET
LISTSERV@UCSBVM.BITNET

🌐 *Banner Alumni System Implementation list.*
LLU-ALUM@LLUVM.BITNET
LISTSERV@LLUVM.BITNET

🌐 *MIT Class of 1962 E-mail Network list.*
MIT1962@MITVMA.BITNET
LISTSERV@MITVMA.BITNET

🌐 *MIT Class of 1966 E-mail Network list.*
MIT1966@MITVMA.BITNET
LISTSERV@MITVMA.BITNET

🌐 *Muslim Student Association list.*
MSA-L@PSUVM.BITNET
LISTSERV@PSUVM.BITNET

Club

🌐 *Lista de Informacion de la U.T.F.S.M y su que.*
Provides general information about Universidad Tecnica Federico Santa Maria. For use by anyone related to the university. Chilean subscriptions are screened but international ones are accepted as is. Preferred language is Spanish, although English is accepted.
CLUB-USM@UTFSM.BITNET
LISTSERV@UTFSM.BITNET
Contact: Douglas Sargent
<POSTMAST@UTFSM.BITNET>

🌐 *Academic Interactive Conferencing Discussion list.*
Devoted to discussing how academic conferencing via interactive messaging can be implemented and utilized.
CONFER-L@NCSUVM.BITNET
LISTSERV@NCSUVM.BITNET

🌐 *DEOSNEWS—The Distance Education Online Symp list.*
A weekly publication for professionals and students in the field of distance education. Published by The American Center for the Study of Distance Education (ACSDE) at Pennsylvania State University.
DEOS-L@PSUVM.BITNET
LISTSERV@PSUVM.BITNET
Contact: Morten Flate Paulsen
<MFP101@PSUVM.BITNET>

🌐 *Sigma Nu Fraternity list.*
For discussion by members of the Sigma Nu fraternity. Fraternity archives can be listed by sending the command INDEX Sigma-Nu to LISTSERV@HEARN.BITNET.
SIGMA-NU@HEARN.BITNET
LISTSERV@HEARN.BITNET
Contact: Brett Barnhart
<BARNHART@KNOX.BITNET>

Communication

🌐 *Departmental Network Administrators list.*
DNA-L@UCSFVM.BITNET
LISTSERV@UCSFVM.BITNET

- *DOCDIS Discussion list.*
  DOCDIS@UA1VM.BITNET
  LISTSERV@UA1VM.BITNET

- *A list to discuss residence halls.*
  DORMS-L@TECMTYVM.BITNET
  LISTSERV@TECMTYVM.BITNET

- *The European Association of Work and Organization list.*
  EAWOP-L@HEARN.BITNET
  LISTSERV@HEARN.BITNET

Consult

- *Business School Computing Support list.*
  BSCS-L@EMUVM1.BITNET
  LISTSERV@EMUVM1.BITNET

- *Canadian Association of Campus Computer Stores list.*
  CACCS-L@UOGUELPH.BITNET
  LISTSERV@UOGUELPH.BITNET

Education

- *University Council for Educational Administrators list.*
  UCEA-L@PSUVM.BITNET
  LISTSERV@PSUVM.BITNET

- *USC Office of International Student Services list.*
  USCINT-L@USCVM.BITNET
  LISTSERV@USCVM.BITNET

- *Student Government Net list.*
  USGA-L@SIUCVMB.BITNET
  LISTSERV@SIUCVMB.BITNET

- *Conference Announcements list.*
  KONFER-L@TREARN.BITNET
  LISTSERV@TREARN.BITNET

Fraternity

- *Delta Chi Fraternity Discussion list.*
  DELTACHI@UBVM.BITNET
  LISTSERV@UBVM.BITNET

- *Phi Kappa Theta National Fraternity.*
  PHIKAP-L@SRU.BITNET
  PHIKAP-R@SRU.BITNET

Contact: Michael Hillwig
<MLH4125@SRU.BITNET>

- *Sigma Alpha Mu Discussion list.*
  SAM-L@TEMPLEVM.BITNET
  LISTSERV@TEMPLEVM.BITNET

- *Discussion list for Theta Xi Fraternity*
  THETAXI@GITVM1.BITNET
  LISTSERV@GITVM1.BITNET

Contact: David Lester
CC100DL@GITVM1.BITNET(f)Law

- *Law School Financial Aid Discussion list.*
  LAWAID@RUTVM1.BITNET
  LISTSERV@RUTVM1.BITNET

Media

- *Campus Editors Discussion Group list.*
  CAMPED-L@UAFSYSB.BITNET
  LISTSERV@UAFSYSB.BITNET

- *American Schools of Oriental Research in Canada list.*
  CASTOR@YORKVM1.BITNET
  LISTSERV@YORKVM1.BITNET

- *Conference On College Composition And Communication list.*
  CCCCC-L@TTUVM1.BITNET
  LISTSERV@TTUVM1.BITNET

- *Campus Computing Newsletter Editors*

An electronic forum for Campus Computing Newsletter Editors to exchange ideas, problems, and experiences.
CCNEWS@BITNIC.BITNET
LISTSERV@BITNIC.BITNET

Contact: Wendy Rickard
<RICKARD@BITNIC.BITNET>

- *Chinese Students list.*
  CSSWU-L@WUVMD.BITNET
  LISTSERV@WUVMD.BITNET

- *Communication Committee list.*
  CUMCC-L@ULKYVM.BITNET
  LISTSERV@ULKYVM.BITNET CUMREC

- *Graduate College News list.*
  GRADCOLL@UVMVM.BITNET
  LISTSERV@UVMVM.BITNET

- *Graduate Employment Issues Discussion list.*
  GRDEMP-L@UBVM.BITNET
  LISTSERV@UBVM.BITNET

- *Huntington High School Discussion list.*
  HHS-L@UB.VMBITNET
  LISTSERV@UBVM.BITNET

Regional

- *Chinese Graduate Student Association list.*
  CGSA-L@UBVM.BITNET
  LISTSERV@UBVM.BITNET

Florida Atlantic University Interest Group Discussion list.
For alumni, students, faculty, visitors, and friends of FAU.
```
FAU-L@FAUVAX.BITNET
FAU-REQUEST@FAUVAX.BITNET
```
Contact: M. Yasar Iscan
```
(ISCAN@FAUVAX.BITNET>
```

FULBRIGHT Educational Advising Newsletter list.
```
FULBNEWS@BRLNCC.BITNET
LISTSERV@BRLNCC.BITNET
```

Hungarian Academic & Research Networking Discussion list.
```
H-NET@HUEARN.BITNET
LISTSERV@HUEARN.BITNET
```

METU-Middle East Technical University Graduate list.
```
METU-L@TRMETU.BITNET
LISTSERV@TRMETU.BITNET
```

Management Department Listserv list.
```
MGT-L@NMSUVM1.BITNET
LISTSERV@NMSUVM1.BITNET
```

Chinese Scholars and Students Discussion list.
```
NCUS002@TWNMOE10.BITNET
```

North Dakota Issues list.
```
NODAK-L@NDSUVM1.BITNET
LISTSERV@NDSUVM1.BITNET
```

Tohoku University Students Forum
```
STUDENTS@JPNTOHOK.BITNET
LISTSERV@JPNTOHOK.BITNET
```

Texas Information Services Faculty Research Forum
```
TEXIS-L@UTDALLAS.BITNET
LISTSERV@UTDALLAS.BITNET
```

Turkish Students Assistance Association list.
```
TSAA-L@PURCCVM.BITNET
LISTSERV@PURCCVM.BITNET
```

Members in Taiwan and Abroad list.
Seeks to provide a better understanding among Chinese scholars.
```
TWUNIV-L@TWNMOE10.BITNET
LISTSERV@TWNMOE10.BITNET
```

SUNY/Buffalo Undergraduate College Discussion list.
```
UGCOLL-L@UBVM.BITNET
LISTSERV@UBVM.BITNET
```

Student

Alpha Phi Omega
```
APO-L@PURCCVM.BITNET
LISTSERV@PURCCVM.BITNET
```

Linkages for Students from Asian Nations list.
```
ASPIRE-L@IUBVM.BITNET
LISTSERV@IUBVM.BITNET
```

Community Service Project Discussion list.
```
CSNPROJ@IUBVM.BITNET
LISTSERV@IUBVM.BITNET
```

Eta Kappa Nu Discussion list.
```
HKN-L@ASUACAD.BITNET
LISTSERV@ASUACAD.BITNET
```

Honors Education
For the discussion of honors education, learning communities, and scholarships for under-graduates. Contributors are honors students, faculty, and administrators.
```
<HNREDIT@GWUVM.BITNET>
```

The National Collegiate Honors Council Honors Newsletter Editor
```
HONORS@GWUVM.BITNET
LISTSERV@GWUVM.BITNET
```

International Studies Association FPAS list.
```
ISAFPAS@ASUACAD.BITNET
LISTSERV@ASUACAD.BITNET
```
Contact: Holly Lee Stowe
```
<IHLS400@INDYCMS.BITNET>
```

Latin American Scholarship Program For American Universities
```
LASPAU-L@HARVARDA.BITNET
LISTSERV@HARVARDA.BITNET
```
Contact: Cesar Galindo-Legoria
```
cesar@harvard.harvard.edu
```

Bulletin Board for Student Exchange Mexico list.
```
MEX-ENP6@UNAMVM1.BITNET
LISTSERV@UNAMVM1.BITNET
```

Polish Student Governments list.
```
SAMORZ-L@PLTUMK11.BITNET
LISTSERV@PLTUMK11.BITNET
```

Student Discussion list.
```
YCIAS-L@YALEVM.BITNET
LISTSERV@YALEVM.BITNET
```

Fidonet

🌀 *College Echo*
COLLEGE
A general discussion echo for students, faculty, and staff.
Moderator: Jim Vargas
1:117/120.666
Distribution: BACKBONE, ZONE 3

🌀 *Non-Traditional Student*
NON_TRAD_STU
Discusses the difficulties and accomplishments of the adult returning to college.
Moderator: Butch Walker
1:157/2
Distribution: BACKBONE

Usenet

🌀 *Penn State gets its own.*
alt.flame.psu

🌀 *Collegiate humor.*
alt.folklore.college

🌀 *College, college activities, campus life, etc.*
soc.college

🌀 *General issues related to graduate schools.*
soc.college.grad

🌀 *Information about graduate schools.*
soc.college.gradinfo

Online Libraries
After Dark

🌀 *Academic Index*
This database indexes more than 400 publications of primary importance in undergraduate research.
Academic Index
Coverage: 1985 to present
Updated: Monthly

Knowledge Index

No services available.

Orbit

🌀 *Food Science and Technology Abstracts*
Covers the literature on food science and technology. Includes articles on the basic food sciences and related topics from more than 2,000 journals and other sources in 40 languages. Contains approximately 380,000 records.
Coverage: 1969 to present
Updated: Monthly

NewsNet

No services available.

Bulletin Boards
Federal Information Exchange
(FEDIX) BBS
For colleges, universities, and other research organizations. Contains news releases, speeches, legal issues, and other information useful to higher education.
Baud Rate: 300, 1200, 2400, 9600
BBS Number: (800) 783-3349 or (301) 258-0953
Help Line: (301) 975-0103
Comment: logon as FEDIX
Internet E-Mail: comments@fedix.fie.com

Minority On-Line Information Service

Provides current information about historically Black and Hispanic colleges and universities.
Baud Rate: 300, 1200, 2400, 9600
BBS Number: (800) 783-3349 or (301) 258-0953
Help Line: (301) 975-0103
Comment: logon as FEDIX
Internet E-Mail: comments @fedix.fie.com

COMER BBS NetWork

Dedicated to the exchange of ideas and information between the U of I, WSU and their surrounding communities.
Baud Rate: 300, 1200, 2400, 9600
BBS Number: (208) 885-7812 or (208) 885-6920 (9600)
BBS Software: WILDCAT
Sysop: Ken Gordon

Wisconsin Education Network Bulletin Board System (WISENET).

Operated by the Wisconsin Department of Public Instruction; for schools and teachers.
Baud Rate: 300, 1200, 2400, 9600
BBS Number: (608) 267-0360
Sysop: Sam Bush
Help Line: Susan Bleimehl (608) 266-2529

CD-ROM

⑤ *Career Opportunities*
Quanta Press.

⑤ *Educational Counseling & Credit Transfer Info Service*
Educational Counseling & Credit Transfer Info Service

⑤ *Peterson's College Database*
SilverPlatter Information Inc.

⑤ *Peterson's Gradline*
SilverPlatter Information Inc.

Agriculture Resources

Forums & Databases

America Online (AOL)

No services available.

CompuServe (CIS)

No services available.

GEnie

No services available.

The Well

🌀 *Agriculture*
  (g agri)
Discussions among producers and consumers of food.

Network Discussions Lists

Internet (Includes Bitnet & UUCPNet)

🌀 *Ag Communicators in Education list.*
  ACEWEST@WSUVM1.BITNET
  LISTSERV@WSUVM1.BITNET

🌀 *Airfield 4H Center list.*
  AF4H-L@VTVM1.BITNET
  LISTSERV@VTVM1.BITNET

🌀 *Expert Systems*
Discusses expert systems in agricultural production and management with an emphasis on practitioners, extension personnel, and experiment station researchers in the land grant system.

  AG-EXP-L@NDSUVM1.BITNET
  LISTSERV@NDSUVM1.BITNET
Contact: Sandy Sprafka
  <NU020746@NDSUVM1.BITNET>

🌀 *Agricultural Engineering list.*
  AGENG-L@DGOGWDG1.BITNET
  LISTSERV@DGOGWDG1.BITNET

🌀 *Agriculture Discussion list.*
Discusses grassland husbandry, crop science, simulation of ecological processes, and crop production, (tropical) forestry, plant physiology, land development, water resource management, irrigation science, soil science, plant propagation, cattle breeding, pig farming, and more.
  AGRIC-L@UGA.BITNET
  LISTSERV@UGA.BITNET
Contact: Harold Pritchett
  <HAROLD@UGA.BITNET>

🌀 *The Food and Agriculture Organization Library list.*
  AGRIS-L@IRMFAO01.BITNET
  LISTSERV@IRMFAO01.BITNET

🌀 *Automated Milking Systems list.*
  AUTOMILK@UMDD.BITNET
  LISTSERV@UMDD.BITNET

🌀 *Beef Specialists list.*
  BEEF-L@WSUVM1.BITNET
  LISTSERV@WSUVM1.BITNET

🌀 *Dairy Discussion list.*
For professional educators and extension workers advising the dairy industry. Problems faced by dairy producers are discussed, as well as requests for educational tools.

```
DAIRY-L@UMDD.BITNET
LISTSERV@UMDD.BITNET
```
Contact: Mark Varner
```
ANSC6@UMDC.BITNET
```

🕑 *Food and Agriculture Organization list.*
```
FAO-BULL@IRMFAO01.BITNET
LISTSERV@IRMFAO01.BITNET
```

🕑 *Food and Agriculture Organization—*
Computer list.
```
FAO-DOC@IRMFAO01.BITNET
LISTSERV@IRMFAO01.BITNET
```

🕑 *The Food and Agriculture Organization INFO*
list.
```
FAO-INFO@IRMFAO01.BITNET
LISTSERV@IRMFAO01.BITNET
```

🕑 *Food and Agriculture Organization Open*
Discussion list.
```
FAOLIST@IRMFAO01.BITNET
LISTSERV@IRMFAO01.BITNET
```

🕑 *Jamestown 4H Center list.*
```
JT4H-L@VTVM1.BITNET
LISTSERV@VTVM1.BITNET
```

🕑 *Northern 4H Center list.*
```
N4H-L@VTVM1.BITNET
LISTSERV@VTVM1.BITNET
```

🕑 *Discussion list for New Crops list.*
```
NEWCROPS@PURCCVM.BITNET
LISTSERV@PURCCVM.BITNET
```

🕑 *Southwest 4H Center list.*
```
SW4H-L@VTVM1.BITNET
LISTSERV@VTVM1.BITNET
```

Gardening

🕑 *Automated Milking Systems list.*
```
AUTOMILK@UMDD.BITNET
LISTSERV@UMDD.BITNET
```

🕑 *Beef Specialists list.*
```
BEEF-L@WSUVM1.BITNET
LISTSERV@WSUVM1.BITNET
```

🕑 *Gardens and gardening list.*
Promotes exchange of information about home
gardening. Discussions at all levels of experience
on topics such as vegetable gardens, herbs,
flowers, ornamental gardening, container
gardening, and more.
```
GARDENS@UKCC.BITNET
LISTSERV@UKCC.BITNET
```
Contact: Bob Crovo
```
<Crovo@UKCC>
```

🕑 *Holiday Lake 4H Center list.*
```
HL4H-L@VTVM1.BITNET
LISTSERV@VTVM1.BITNET
```

🕑 *Virginia Tech Horticulture Dept.—Monthly*
Releases list.
```
HORT-L@VTVM1.BITNET
LISTSERV@VTVM1.BITNET
```

🕑 *Virginia Tech Horticulture Dept. list.*
```
HORTPGM@VTVM1.BITNET
LISTSERV@VTVM1.BITNET
```

🕑 *Smith Mountain Lake 4H Center list.*
```
SMT4H-L@VTVM1.BITNET
LISTSERV@VTVM1.BITNET
```

Fidonet

🕑 *Sustainable Agriculture*
```
SUST_AG
```
A forum for information exchange on natural,
biologically-oriented, low-input regenerative
agriculture. Farmers, market gardeners,
homeowners, homesteaders, landscapers,
nurserymen, seedsmen, orchardists, per-
maculturists, greenhouse growers, and others
are welcome.
Moderator: Lawrence London
```
1:151/502
```
Distribution: BACKBONE

Usenet

No services available.

Online Libraries
After Dark

🕑 *AGRICOLA and Backfile*
Worldwide coverage of agricultural economics,
rural sociology, agricultural products, animal
industry, agricultural engineering, entomology,
nutrition, forestry, pesticides, plant science,
soils, and fertilizers.
Coverage: 1970 to present
Updated: Monthly

🕑 *CAB Absracts*
Worldwide agricultural information covering
crop science and production, animal science
and production, forestry, crop protection (pest
control), machinery and buildings,
biotechnology, economics, and sociology.
Coverage: 1980 to present
Updated: Monthly

🌀 *Current Contents: Agriculture, Biology &*
  Environmental Sciences
A subset of Current Contents Search™
corresponding to the Current Contents:
Agriculture, Biology & Environmental Sciences
print edition.
Coverage: Most current 12 months
Updated: Weekly

🌀 *Wilson Biologial and Agricultural Index*
Provides cover-to-cover indexing of over 225
key English-language periodicals in the
biological and agricultural sciences.
Coverage: 1983 to present
Updated: Monthly

Knowledge Index

🌀 *Agricola*
Provides worldwide coverage of journals and
monographs on agriculture and related subjects,
such as animal studies, botany, chemistry,
entomology, fertilizers, forestry, hydroponics,
and soils.
Coverage: 1970 to present
Updated: Monthly

🌀 *CAB Abstracts*
A comprehensive file of agricultural and
biological information containing records from
the 26 main abstract journals published by the
Commonwealth Agricultural Bureau. Abstracts
over 8,500 journals in 37 languages.
Coverage: 1972 to present
Updated: Monthly

🌀 *Food Science and Technology Abstracts*
Accesses developments in food science and
technology and allied disciplines. Other
disciplines are included when relevant to food
science. Also includes Vitis, a subfile on
viticulture and enology. Indexes over 1,200
journals from over 50 countries, patents from
20 countries, and books in many languages.
Coverage: 1969 to present
Updated: Monthly

Orbit

🌀 *Tropical Agriculture*
Covers worldwide literature on tropical and
subtropical agriculture. Sources include journal
articles, monographs, theses, conference papers
and proceedings. More than 75,000 records.
Coverage: 1975 to present
Updated: Quarterly

NewsNet

FOOD AND BEVERAGE (FB)

🌀 *The Food Channel*
Reports on topics of interest to food-related
businesses.
Frequency: Monthly
Earliest NewsNet Issue: 5/1/91

🌀 *Food Chemical News*
Provides information on government
regulation of food and food additives, early
warnings of changes in government food
regulation policy, FDA and USDA proposals,
major enforcement actions, precedent-setting
cases, and more.
Frequency: Weekly
Earliest NewsNet Issue: 12/23/91

🌀 *Food & Drink Daily*
Features key worldwide developments in the
markets for food and drink products.
Frequency: Daily
Earliest NewsNet Issue: 2/2/89

🌀 *Ice Cream Reporter*
Provides news and analysis of events and
decisions that affect the ice cream industry.
Frequency: Monthly
Earliest NewsNet Issue: 11/1/89

🌀 *Kane's Beverage Week*
Devoted to the business of marketing beer,
wine, and spirits. Covers legislation, mergers
and acquisitions, products, research, and the
activities of the anti-alcohol lobby.
Frequency: Biweekly
Earliest NewsNet Issue: 12/9/91

🌀 *Washington Beverage Insight*
Discusses government actions affecting the
soft drink and alcoholic beverage industries.
Coverage includes Congress, federal agencies,
state legislatures, associations, and courts.
Frequency: Weekly
Earliest NewsNet Issue: 4/27/84

🌀 *Wine Business Insider*
Covers the wine industry, providing timely
news and information for everyone from
winegrape growers and suppliers to investors
and exporters.
Frequency: Biweekly
Earliest NewsNet Issue: 10/29/91

Bulletin Boards

Agricultural Electronic Bulletin Board (AgEBB)

Operated by the University of Missouri Agriculture Extension Project. Facilitates agricultural information exchange among Missouri farmers, faculty, extension staff, government agencies, and agribusiness. A Crop Performance Testing database lets a farmer explore possible options and variations for crop performance retrieval. Offers a hardcopy edition of their user's manual.

Availability: 24 hours/ 7 days
Baud Rate: 300,1200,2400
BBS Number: (314) 882-8289
BBS Software: UMC AgEBB
Parameters: 8-O-1
Sysop: John Travlos
Help line: (314) 882-4827

Agriculture Library Forum (ALF)

The National Agricultural Library's BBS; provides an agricultural datebook listing upcoming symposia, conferences, and events. Libraries can request interlibrary loans directly from ALF from various online services. Maintains an excellent list of related bulletin boards.

Availability: 24 hours/ 7 days
Baud Rate: 300, 1200, 2400
BBS Number: (301) 344-8510
BBS Software: RBBS-PC
Parameters: N-8-1
Sysop: Karl Schneider
Help Line: (301) 344-2113

Compu-Farm BBS

Operates from the Farm Business Management Branch of Olds, Alberta, Canada. An online version of their agricultural software directory lists more than 500 different agricultural software products sorted by category. Most computers are supported and the database is constantly updated. You can order hardcopy as well. Features include weekly grain news, crop and livestock market reports, and Farm Business management branch publications.

Availability: 24 hours/ 7 days
Baud Rate: 300, 1200, 2400, 9600
BBS Number: (403) 556-4104

BBS Software: RBBS-PC
Parameters: 8-N-1
Sysop: Bruce Waldie
Help line: (403) 556-4243

Computer Applications Group BBS

Operated by the College of Agriculture at the University of Arizona; there are 12 files covering newsletters and programs in agriculture, human nutrition, communications, and biotech.
Baud Rate: 300, 1200, 2400
BBS Number: (602) 621-2097
BBS Software: FIDO Comments
Parameters: 8-N-1
Help line: (602) 621-2134

Integrated Pest Management BBS

Operated by the University of Wisconsin Extension at Madison. Dedicated to integrated pest management using methods— chemical and non-chemical—to control pest populations while having the least impact on the environment. Bulletins contain local BBS information on droughts. File sections for IPM and communications.

Availability: 24 hours/ 7 days
Baud Rate: 300, 1200, 2400, 4800, 9600
BBS Number: (608) 262-3656
BBS Software: RBBS-PC
Parameters: 8-N-1
Sysop: Roger Schmidt
Help line: (608) 262-0170

Nutrient Data Bank (NDB) Bulletin Board

Operated by the Department of Agriculture's Human Nutrition Information Service in Hyattsville, Maryland. Provides current information on food composition and nutrient databank conferences. You can order disks of the USDA nutrient databases corresponding with Agricultural Handbook #8 and containing 5,000 food items.

Availability: 24 hours/ 7 days
Baud Rate: 1200/2400
BBS Number: (301) 436-5078
BBS Software: RBBS-PC
Parameters: 8-N-1
Help Line: (301) 436-8491, 8:00 am to 4:30 pm

Rutgers' Cooperative Extension BBS

Operated by Rutgers University Cooperative Extension. Holds extensive file library sections containing hundreds of publications and programs. A "door" area contains the Alternative Farming Systems Literature database. Some keyword searching for files is possible.
Availability: 24 hours/ 7 days
Baud Rate: 2400, 9600
BBS Number: (800) 722-0335; (New Jersey only) (201) 383-8041
BBS Software: PCBoard
Parameters: 8-N-1
Sysop: Bruce Barbour
Comments: Costs $15 per year

Southern Production And Resource Analysis Team (SPRAT) BBS

Operated by the Southern Production and Resource Analysis Team, University of Tennessee. Provides a forum for problems of natural resources, the environment, and agriculture. The board has instant access and no validation procedures.
Baud Rate: 300, 1200, 2400
BBS Number: (615) 974-7484
BBS Software: PCBoard Comments
Parameters: 8-N-1,
Sysop: Rob Alexander
Help line: (615) 974-7485

CD-ROM

🌎 *About Cows*
Quanta Press

🌎 *AgMil*
OCLC
6565 Franz Road
Dublin, OH 43017

🌎 *Agribusiness U.S.A.*
Dialog Information Service
3460 Hillview Avenue
Palo Alto, CA 94304

🌎 *Agricola (1970-now)*
SilverPlatter Information Inc.,
100 Ridge Road
Norwood, MA 02062

🌎 Agricola, CRIS, AgMIL
OCLC
6565 Franz Road
Dublin, OH 43017

🌎 *Agricola/CRIS (1983-now)*
OCLC
6565 Franz Road
Dublin, OH 43017

🌎 *Agriculture Library*
OCLC
6565 Franz Road
Dublin, OH 43017

🌎 *Agriculture & Human Resource Series: Agriculture*
ALDE Publishing.

🌎 *AGRIS*
SilverPlatter Information Inc.
100 Ridge Road
Norwood, MA 02062

🌎 *Agrisearch*
SilverPlatter Information Inc.
100 Ridge Road
Norwood, MA 02062

🌎 *AgriStats I*
Hopkins Technology
421 Hazel Lane
Hopkins, MN 55343

🌎 *BEASTCD*
SilverPlatter Information Inc.
100 Ridge Road
Norwood, MA 02062

🌎 *CAB Abstracts (current)*
SilverPlatter Information Inc.
100 Ridge Road
Norwood, MA 02062

🌎 *CABPESTCD*
SilverPlatter Information Inc.
100 Ridge Road
Norwood, MA 02062

🌎 *Census of Agriculture*
Slater Hall Info Products
1522 K Street NW, Suite 1112
Washington, DC 20005

🌎 *Food, Agriculture & Science*
Knowledge Access International
2685 Marine Way, Suite 1305
Mountain View, CA 94043

🕉 *Food & Human Nutrition*
SilverPlatter Information Inc.
100 Ridge Road
Norwood, MA 02062

🕉 *Food Intelligence on CD*
SilverPlatter Information Inc.
100 Ridge Road
Norwood, MA 02062

🕉 *Food Science and Technology Abstracts*
SilverPlatter Information Inc.
100 Ridge Road
Norwood, MA 02062

🕉 *HORTCD*
SilverPlatter Information Inc.
100 Ridge Road
Norwood, MA 02062

🕉 *The Plant Doctor*
Quanta Press

🕉 *SOILCD*
SilverPlatter Information Inc.
100 Ridge Road
Norwood, MA 02062

🕉 *TOPAG & RURAL*
SilverPlatter Information Inc.
100 Ridge Road
Norwood, MA 02062

🕉 *TREECD*
SilverPlatter Information Inc.
100 Ridge Road
Norwood, MA 02062

🕉 *VETBEAST*
SilverPlatter Information Inc.
100 Ridge Road
Norwood, MA 02062

🕉 *VETCD*
SilverPlatter Information Inc.
100 Ridge Road
Norwood, MA 02062

🕉 *WLAS*
SilverPlatter Information Inc.
100 Ridge Road
Norwood, MA 02062

Anthropology/ Archaeology Resources

Forums & Databases

America Online (AOL)
No services available.

CompuServe (CIS)
No services available.

GEnie
No services available.

The Well
No services available.

Network Discussions Lists
Internet (Includes Bitnet & UUCPNet)

Aborigines

🕉 *This list is for issues pertaining to Aboriginal peoples.*
```
NAT-1492@TAMVM1.BITNET
LISTSERV@TAMVM1.BITNET
NATCHAT@TAMVM1.BITNET
LISTSERV@TAMVM1.BITNET
```

Anthropology

🕉 *General Anthropology Bulletin Board list.*
Deals with discussions of various techniques and fields of research in anthropology.
```
ANTHRO-L@UBVM.BITNET
LISTSERV@UBVM.BITNET
```
Contact: Ezra Zubrow
```
<APYEZRA@UBVMS.BITNET>
```

Archaeology

🕉 *Archaeology list.*
For discussions of archaeological matters, especially dealing with research, excavations, conferences, job announcements, calls for papers, publications, and bibliographies.
```
ARCH-L@DGOGWDG1.BITNET
LISTSERV@DGOGWDG1.BITNET
```
Contact: Sebastian Rahtz
```
<s.p.q.rahtz@ecs.southampton.ac.uk>
```

Aztec

🕉 *Aztec Studies and Nahuatl list.*
Focuses on Aztec studies in general and the Aztec language, Nahuatl, in particular.
```
NAHUAT-L@FAUVAX.BITNET
NAHUAT-REQUEST@FAUVAX.BITNET
```
Contact: J. F. Schwaller
```
(schwallr@acc.fau.edu /
schwallr@fauvax.bitnet)
```

NATIVE-L

🕉 *NATIVE-L list.*
```
NATIVE-L@TAMVM1.BITNET
LISTSERV@TAMVM1.BITNET
```

PACARC-L

🕉 *Pacific Rim Archaeology Interest list.*
For discussions on Pacific Rim archaeology, including meetings, articles, software, theories, materials, methods, tools, and related topics.
```
PACARC-L@WSUVM1.BITNET
LISTSERV@WSUVM1.BITNET
```
Contact: STAFF-L
```
CROES@WSUVM1.BITNET
```

Fidonet

🌀 *Indian Affairs*
    INDIAN_AFFAIRS
Devoted to topics of Native American interest, including anthropology, archaeology, current affairs, and history.
Moderator: Dolores Jensen
    1:327/999
Distribution: NATIONAL BACKBONE ZONE 1

Usenet

🌀 *All aspects of studying humankind.*
    sci.anthropology

🌀 *Studying antiquities of the world.*
    sci.archaeology

🌀 *Natural languages, communication, and related areas.*
    sci.lang

Online Libraries

After Dark

No services available.

Knowledge Index

No services available.

Orbit

No services available.

NewsNet

No services available.

Bulletin Boards

The Dakota BBS Bulletin Board

Promotes self-sufficiency and economic well-being of American Indian and rural peoples through modern technology, while valuing frontier and cultural traditions.
Baud Rate: 2400,14.4
BBS Number: (605) 341-4552
BBS Software: RemoteAccess
Help Line: (605) 341-7293
E-Mail: anne.fallis@oldcolo.com

Black Data Processing Associates(BDPA)—Bay Area Chapter BBS

Supports the Black community and maintains a list of minority bulletin boards across the country.
Availability: 24 hours/ 7 days
Baud Rate: 2400,19.2
BBS Number: (707) 552-3314
BBS Software: WILDCAT!
Sysop: Jerry Kirkpatrick
Help Line: (707) 552-1982

The SF NET

A network of computers with conferences found throughout coffee houses in San Francisco. Also has interactive games, matchmaking, chess, and FIDONET & USENET conferences.
Availability: 24 hours/ 7 days
Baud Rate: 2400
BBS Number: (415) 824-7603

CD-ROM

🌀 *Cross Cultural CD*
SilverPlatter Information Inc.
100 Ridge Road
Norwood, MA 02062

🌀 *Languages of the World*
NTC Publishing Corp.

🌀 *North American Indians*
Quanta Press

Architecture/ Design Resources

Forums & Databases
America Online (AOL)
No services available.

CompuServe (CIS)
No services available.

GEnie
No services available.

The Well

🌎 *Design*
(g design)
The Design Conference is the place to discuss anything that involves building, drawing, planning, designing, or physically making it.

Network Discussions Lists
Internet (Includes Bitnet & UUCPNet)

Architecture

🌎 *Architronic: The Electronic Journal in Architecture list.*
ARCITRON@KENTVM.BITNET
LISTSERV@KENTVM.BITNET

🌎 *Basic Design (Art and Architecture) list.*
DESIGN-L@PSUVM.BITNET
LISTSERV@PSUVM.BITNET

🌎 *Landscape Architecture Electronic Forum list.*
LARCH-L@SUVM.BITNET
LISTSERV@SUVM.BITNET

🌎 *Landscape Architecture list.*
LARCHNET@UOGUELPH.BITNET
LISTSERV@UOGUELPH.BITNET

Industrial

🌎 *Industrial Design Forum list.*
For all involved in industrial design, including designers, design educators, and students. Subscribers receive Voice of Industrial Design (VOID) newsletter.
IDFORUM@YORKVM1.BITNET
LISTSERV@YORKVM1.BITNET
Contact: Maurice Barnwell
<GL250267@Venus.Yorku.CA>

🌎 *Graphic and Industrial Design Educators list.*
NDDESIGN@IRISHVMA.BITNET
LISTSERV@IRISHVMA.BITNET

Visual Design

🌎 *Art, Architecture, Design list.*
For faculty in art, architecture, and visual and basic design.
FACXCH-L@PSUVM.BITNET
LISTSERV@PSUVM.BITNET
Contact: Howard Ray Lawrence
<HRL@PSUARCH.BITNET>

🌎 *Art, Architecture, Design list.*
For students in art, architecture, and visual and basic design.
STUXCH-L@PSUVM.BITNET
LISTSERV@PSUVM.BITNET
Contact: Harold Ray Lawrence
<HRL@PSUARCH.BITNET>

Fidonet
No services available.

Usenet
No services available.

Online Libraries
After Dark
No services available.

Knowledge Index
No services available.

Orbit
No services available.

NewsNet
No services available.

Bulletin Boards
HOUSENET
HouseNet shares information about do-it-yourself home repairs, improvements, and home-owning.
Availability: 24 hours/ 7 days
Baud Rate: 2400
BBS Number: (410) 745-2037
BBS Software: WILDCAT!
Sysop: Gene and Katie Hamilton

CD-ROM

ICONDA
SilverPlatter Information Inc.
100 Ridge Road
Norwood, MA 02062

Art Resources

Forums & Databases
America Online (AOL)

🌀 *Desktop Publishing Forum*
Path: Computing & Software Department; Macintosh Forums; Desktop Publishing
Keyword: Mac DTP
Contains rich message boards, and the libraries are especially useful, treating such topics as DTP Utilities, Fonts, Postscript, Printer and Font Utilities, and Sample Documents. Supporting their products in this forum are DeltaPoint and Manhattan Graphics.

🌀 *Graphic Arts & CAD Forum*
Path: Computing & Software Department
Keywords: Mac graphics, PC graphics
Maintains separate graphics forums for PC and Mac users. Each contains message boards and conference rooms. Library categories include Japanimation, QuickTime Movies, Animations, APS, and EPSF/Postscript. Companies supporting their products in these forums include Digital F/X, Thunderware, The Weigand Report, Animated Software Company, Diamond Computer Systems, Tseng, POV Ray-Trace, Dynaware USA, and ZSoft.

CompuServe (CIS)
No services available.

GEnie
No services available.

The Well

🌀 *Art Com Electronic Net*
(g acen)
Dedicated to cultural applications of new communications technologies. Information on contemporary art, special events, global networking, and an electronic art gallery and shopping mall, as well as a growing number of art periodicals. *Art Com Magazine* is posted in ACEN's newstand and in `alt.artcom` on USENET. E-mail your address or proposal to `artcomtv@well.sf.ca.us`.

Network Discussions Lists
Internet (Includes Bitnet & UUCPNet)

🌀 *Ability*
Journal for the study and advancement of academically, artistically, and athletically able people.
```
ABILITY@ASUACAD.BITNET
LISTSERV@ASUACAD.BITNET
```
Contact: A. DiGangi
```
<SAMUEL@ASUACAD.BITNET>
```

🌀 *Arts Libraries Discussion list.*
```
ARLIS-L@UKCC.BITNET
LISTSERV@UKCC.BITNET
```
Contact: Mary Molinaro
```
<MOLINARO@UKCC.BITNET>
```

Art

🌀 *Art-Related Topics Forum*
ART-SUPPORT@NEWCASTLE.AC.UK
MAILBASE@NEWCASTLE.AC.UK

🌀 *Art Criticism Discussion Forum*
Topics reflect the diversity of critical discourse—postmodernism, marxism, feminism, curatorial practices, funding, and any issue affecting the art world.
ARTCRIT@YORKVM1.BITNET
LISTSERV@YORKVM1.BITNET
Contact: Michele Macaluso
<GL253001@YUORION.BITNET>

🌀 *L-ARTECH: Les Arts et les nouvelles technologies list.*
L-ARTECH s'adresse aux organisations (centre, studio, association, etc.) et aux individus s'interessant a l'art et aux nouvelles technogiles. L-ARTECH est en premier lieu une liste de discussions et d'echanges. De plus, L-ARTECH donne acces a deux annuaires: le premier regroupe les organisations, et le deuxieme, les individus.
ARTECH@UQAM.BITNET
LISTSERV@UQAM.BITNET

🌀 *Student Artist Discussions list.*
ARTIST-L@UAFSYSB.BITNET
LISTSERV@UAFSYSB.BITNET

🌀 *List for ad-hoc, transient, mobile, time-based, formless, and decentered art.*
ARTNET@UK.AC.NEWCASTLE
MAILBASE@NEWCASTLE.AC.UK

🌀 *Art History Forum list.*
CAAH@PUCC.BITNET
LISTSERV@PUCC

🌀 *Ceramic Arts Discussion list.*
Discussion of issues in the fields of ceramic arts/pottery.
CLAYART@UKCC.BITNET
LISTSERV@UKCC.BITNET
Contact: Joe Molinaro
<ARTMOLIN@EKU.BITNET>

🌀 *October Downtown Art Show Interest list.*
DOWHATDO@SJSUVM1.BITNET
LISTSERV@SJSUVM1.BITNET

🌀 *ASCII Art Appreciation list.*
For ANSI or ASCII art lovers.
DZZA1005F%SA.BIRMP.AC.UK@NSF.AC.UK
DZZA1005F%SA.BIRMP.AC.UK@NSF.AC.UK
Contact: Chris Davis
<DZZA1005F%SA.BIRMP.AC.UK@NSF.AC.UK>

Fine Arts

🌀 *Fine Arts Forum list.*
For discussions regarding the use of computers in the fine arts.
FINE-ART@EB0UB011.BITNET
LISTSERV@EB0UB011.BITNET
Contact: Ray Lauzzana
FINEART@UMAECS

🌀 *International Fine Arts Forum list.*
Seeks international collaboration among artists and scientists regarding the use of computers in the fine arts.
FINEART@ecs.umass.edu
FINEART@ecs.umass.csnet
Contact: Ray Lauzzana.BITNET
<lauzzana@ecs.umass.edu>

Performance Studies

🌀 *Performance*
Exchange of ideas, texts, hypertexts, syllabi, and book lists regarding performance in various contexts.
PERFORM-L@ACFCLUSTER.NYU.EDU
LISTSERV@ACFCLUSTER.NYU.EDU
Contact: Sharon Mazer
<mazers@ACFcluster.NYU.EDU>

🌀 *Medieval Performing Arts*
PERFORM@IUBVM.BITNET
LISTSERV@IUBVM.BITNET

Visual Design

🌀 *Art, Architecture, Design list.*
For faculty in art, architecture, and visual and basic design.
FACXCH-L@PSUVM.BITNET
LISTSERV@PSUVM.BITNET
Contact: Howard Ray Lawrence
<HRL@PSUARCH.BITNET>

Fidonet

🌀 *Japanese/General Animation*
ANIME
Mainly about Japanese animation, but open to discussions of general animation (including American cartoons and animation) and topics related to Japanese animation such as *manga*.
Moderator: Randall Stukey
1:387/255.150
Distribution: BACKBONE, 1:387/255

🜨 *Fine Arts Conference*
    FINEARTS
For anyone who enjoys the fine arts.
Moderator: Tomas Hood
    1:352/777
Distribution: 1:352/777, ICDMNET, REGION17
Gateways: ICDM_NET

Usenet

🜨 *Artistic community, arts, and communication.*
    alt.artcom

🜨 *Art or litter—you decide.*
    alt.cascade

🜨 *Electronic fan club for animator Mike Jittlov.*
    alt.fan.mike-jittlov

🜨 *Fractals in math, graphics, and art.*
    alt.fractals

🜨 *Discussion of various kinds of animation.*
    rec.arts.animation

🜨 *Japanese animation fen discussion.*
    rec.arts.anime

🜨 *Fine arts & artists.*
    rec.arts.fine

🜨 *The Japanese storytelling art form.*
    rec.arts.manga

🜨 *Discussions about arts not in other groups.*
    rec.arts.miscrec

🜨 *Handiwork arts not covered elsewhere.*
    rec.crafts.misc

🜨 *Sewing, weaving, knitting, and other fiber arts.*
    rec.crafts.textiles

Online Libraries
After Dark

🜨 *Arts & Humanities Search®*
A citation index to the arts and humanities, including archaeology, architecture, television, folklore, history, language, linguistics, and literature.
Coverage: 1980 to date
Updated: Weekly

🜨 *Wilson Art Index*
Provides information indexed from 2231 domestic and foreign periodicals, yearbooks, and museum bulletins.
Coverage: 1984 to present
Updated: Monthly

Knowledge Index

🜨 *Artbibliographies Modern*
Provides comprehensive bibliographic coverage of the current literature, articles, books, dissertations, and exhibition catalogs on art and design.
Coverage: 1974 to present
Updated: Biannually

Orbit

No services available.

NewsNet

No services available.

Bulletin Boards
Occupational Safety and Health BBS

For organizations and individuals with occupational health and safety concerns to exchange information and ideas, and get technical assistance. Emphasis is on the arts.
Availability: 24 hours/ 7 days
Baud Rate: 2400
BBS Number: (212) 385-2034
BBS Software: PCBoard
Sysop: Michael McCann
Help Line: (212) 227-6220

The Arts Place BBS (TAP BBS)

Provides a meeting place for those creatively or artistically inclined and their supporters, as well as a venue for video or film industry aficionados.
Availability: 24 hours/ 7 days
Baud Rate: 300, 1200, 2400, 9600, 14.4
BBS Number: (703) 892-1921
BBS Software: PCBoard
Sysop: Ron Fitzherbert

The Spiral Sea BBS

Services the art community.
Baud Rate: 300, 1200, 2400, 9600
BBS Number: (703) 684-9124

CD-ROM

⑨ *Art Index*
H.W. Wilson Co.

⑨ *Croate's Art Review—Impressionism*
Quanta Press

⑨ *Notable Americans—The National Portrait*
   Gallery
Abt Books

⑨ *Pubique Arte*
Quanta Press

Astronomy/
Aviation/
Aeronautics/
Space Science
Resources

Forums & Databases

America Online (AOL)

○ *Astronomy Club*
Keyword: Astronomy
Path: Lifestyles & Interests Department > Astronomy Club
For beginning astronomists. Offers basic information about locating galaxies, tracking comets, following planetary movements, and more. Library includes calculation/plotting programs and good quality photographs.

○ *Aviation Forum*
Keyword: Aviation
Path: Lifestyles & Interests Department > Aviation Forum
Discussions for users who fly for recreation, for a living, or have military flight experience. Message boards for all levels of pilot. Library includes flight simulation programs and GIF images of aircraft.

○ *The National Space Society*
Keyword: Space
Path: Lifestyles & Interests Department > The National Space Society
Seeks to rally support for NASA and the national space program. Offers electronic mail version of NASA Update, society magazine, and message board discussions. Library includes NASA information and charts.

CompuServe (CIS)

○ *Astronomy Forum*
GO ASTROFORUM

For stargazers at all levels. Announces national and international events; archives contain public domain astronomy software and reference articles.

○ *Aviation Forum*
GO AVSIG
For users interested in computers and airplanes. Covers general flying issues (safety, weather, air traffic control, balloons and soaring).

○ *EMI Aviation Services*
GO EMI
For pilots of any aircraft. Makes available flight-planning programs. Other services offered include abbreviated summaries of local conditions, radar weather maps, and time and distance checks.

○ *Space/Astronomy*
GO SPACE
For all interested in astronomy. Offers current sunspot and solar flare information, NASA news, and access to Sky and Telescope Online.

○ *Space Forum*
GO SPACEFORUM
For all users interested in space exploration. NASA news releases are posted regularly.

GEnie

○ *Aviation RoundTable*
Keyword: AVIATION or Page 410
For users interested in flying and aircraft.

○ *Space and Science Information Center*
Keyword: SCIENCE CENTER or Page 461
Supports space exploration, astronomy, and all avenues of science.

The Well

⑤ *Flying*
    (g flying)
Deals with objects that generate lift (not only aircraft—balloons, kites, birds, and so on) and the people, places, and things associated with them.

Network Discussions Lists
Internet (Includes Bitnet & UUCPNet)

⑤ *Aviation list.*
Moderated. Deals with technical aspects of aviation.
    aeronautics@rascal.ics.utexas.edu
    aeronautics-REQUEST@rascal.ics.utexas.edu

⑤ *Aircraft Discussion Forum*
Devoted to aircraft and helicopters, modern and old.
    AIRCRAFT@GREARN.BITNET
    LISTSERV@GREARN.BITNET
Contact: Giorgos Kavallieratos
    <GIORGOS@GREARN.BITNET>

⑤ *Airline and Airliner Discussion list.*
For users interested in airlines and civil aircraft.
    AIRLINE@CUNYVM.BITNET
    LISTSERV@CUNYVM.BITNET
Contact: Geert K. Marien
    <GKMQC@CUNYVM.CUNY.EDU>

⑤ *Preprint server for Astrophysics list.*
    ASTRO-PL@JPNYITP.BITNET
    LISTSERV@JPNYITP.BITNET

⑤ *General Aviation list.*
    AVIATION@BRUFPB.BITNET
    LISTSERV@BRUFPB.BITNET

⑤ *Aviation list.*
Information of interest to pilots.
    AVIATION@MC.LCS.MIT.EDU
    AVIATION-REQUEST@MC.LCS.MIT.EDU
Contact: Christopher Maeda
    <cmaeda@CS.CMU.EDU>

⑤ *Aerospace Engineering list.*
Deals with theoretical aspects of aerospace engineering.
    AVIATION-THEORY@MC.LCS.MIT.EDU
    aviation-theory-request@MC.LCS.MIT.EDU
Contact: Rob A. Vingerhoeds
    <ROB@BGERUG51.BITNET>

⑤ *Canadian Space Geodesy Forum list.*
    CANSPACE@UNBVM1.BITNET
    LISTSERV@UNBVM1.BITNET

⑤ *Flight Simulation Software list.*
Discussions of flight simulation topics, including hardware and software questions, product reviews, rumors, and more.
    flight-sim@grove.iup.edu
    flight-sim-request@grove.iup.edu
Contact: Mark J Strawcutter
    <mjstraw@grove.iup.edu>

⑤ *Gravity Topics for Spacetime Course list.*
    GRAVITY GRAVITY@UWF.BITNET
    LISTSERV@UWF.BITNET

⑤ *Investing in Space-Related Companies list.*
Information on space-related investment opportunities and events affecting these investments.
    Invest space-investors@cs.cmu.edu
    space-investors-request@cs.cmu.edu
Contact: Vince Cate
    <vac@cs.cmu.edu>

⑤ *James Clerk Maxwell Telescope list.*
    JCMT-L@UALTAVM.BITNET
    LISTSERV@UALTAVM.BITNET

⑤ *Astronomy Events list.*
Information on astronomical events and meetings, mostly in the Boston area.
    koolish@BBN.COM
Contact: Dick Koolish
    <koolish@BBN.COM>

⑤ *Students for Exploration and Development of Space list.*
Distributes information from several national labs involved in space research. Enhances the SEDS-L open discussion list.
    SEDSNEWS@TAMVM1.BITNET
    LISTSERV@TAMVM1.BITNET
Contact: H. Alan Montgomery
    FHD@TAMCBA

⑤ *Israeli Space & Remote Sensing list.*
An interactive forum for the announcement of events and publications.
    SPACE-IL@TAUNIVM.BITNET
    LISTSERV@TAUNIVM.BITNET
Contact: Beth Eres or Abraham Tal
    C40@TAUNOS

⑤ *Space Discussions Forum list.*
Discussions on space-related topics.
    SPACE@UGA .BITNET
    LISTSERV@UGA .BITNET

⑤ *Spacetime Topics for BITNET (Audit List).*
ST-AUDIT@UWF.BITNET
LISTSERV@UWF.BITNET

⑤ *Sun Spots Discussion list.*
SUNSPOTS@RICEVM1.BITNET
LISTSERV@RICEVM1.BITNET
Contact: Bob Greene
RGREENE@RICECSVM.BITNET

Fidonet

⑤ *Observational Astronomy Echo Conference*
ASTRONOMY
Devoted to observational astronomy and related topics. Reports from the Hubble Space Telescope, plus comments and interpretation.
Moderator: Bill McCauley
1:161/42
Distribution: BACKBONE

⑤ *Skylights.*
For astrology and astronomy conversations.
Moderator: Jeanne Garner
1:267/128.1201
Distribution: Privately distributed

⑤ *Space Base's Electronic Space Related Newsletters*
SB-E/N/L
Carries electronic space-related newsletters. Read-only; Q&A and remarks to the SPACEBASE-QUESTIONS echo.
Moderator: Hugh Gregory
1:153/719
Distribution: BACKBONE, ZONE-1, ZONE-2, ZONE-3

⑤ *Space Base NASA News And Press Releases*
SB-NASA_NEWS
Carries the latest daily NASA news. Read-only; Q&A and remarks to the SPACEBASE-QUESTIONS echo.
Moderator: Hugh Gregory
1:153/719
Distribution: BACKBONE, ZONE-1, ZONE-2, ZONE-3

⑤ *Space Base Technical News and Deep Space Probe Reports*
SB-NASA_TECH
Carries the latest daily Shuttle Status Reports, as well as reports on Galileo, Magellan, Ulysses, and more. Read-only; Q&A and remarks to the SPACEBASE-QUESTIONS echo.
Moderator: Hugh Gregory
1:153/719
Distribution: BACKBONE, ZONE-1, ZONE-2, ZONE-3

⑤ *Space Base Discussion and Q&A Echo*
SB-QUESTIONS
For the discussions related to the read-only Space Base echoes.
Moderator: Hugh Gregory
:153/1
Distribution: BACKBONE, ZONE-1, ZONE-2

⑤ *Amateur Satellite Tracking Discussion and Information Forum*
SB-SAT_TRACK
Carries the latest NORAD Satellite Elements weekly and satellite activity bulletins. Answers questions about Satellite Tracking Software. Questions and discussion encouraged.
Moderator: Hugh Gregory
1:153/719
Distribution: BACKBONE, ZONE-1, ZONE-2, ZONE-3

⑤ *Space Base's Solar Flare Activity Alerts and Reports*
SB-SOLAR_RPT
Carries the latest information on solar activity. Q&A, discussion and outside imput encouraged.
Moderator: Hugh Gregory
1:153/719
Distribution: BACKBONE, ZONE-1, ZONE-2, ZONE-3

⑤ *Space Base Sysops Only Conference*
SB-SYSOPS
For Space Base Sysops only to swap ideas and discuss administration and improvements to these echoes.
Moderator: Hugh Gregory
1:153/719
Distribution: BACKBONE, ZONE-1, ZONE-2, ZONE-3

⑤ *Space Base's Rest of The World in Space*
SB-WORLD_NWS
Carries reports from the CIS, ESA, NASDA Japan, China, Australia, Canada, and more. Read only; Q&A and remarks to the SPACEBASE-QUESTIONS echo.
Moderator: Hugh Gregory
1:153/719
Distribution: BACKBONE, ZONE-1, ZONE-2, ZONE-3

⑤ *Space Development Conference*
SPACE
Covers space and related sciences and technologies, plus political and industrial issues. News and issues of current space development activity.

Moderator: Bev Freed
   1:129/104
Distribution: BACKBONE

◈ *Advanced Astronomy Echo*
   STARNET
For advanced observers. Tips and techniques for finding hard-to-spot objects, reports of observations, and reviews of equipment. Distribution is private.
Moderator: Bill McCauley
   1:161/42
Restr: MOD-APVL
Distribution: Private

Usenet

◈ *Discussions on the Astronomical Image Processing System.*
   alt.sci.astro.aips

◈ *Aviation industry and mishaps. (Moderated)*
   clari.news.aviation

◈ *Aerospace industry and companies. (Moderated)*
   clari.tw.aerospace

◈ *Defense industry issues. (Moderated)*
   clari.tw.defense

◈ *NASA, astronomy & spaceflight. (Moderated)*
   clari.tw.space

◈ *Aviation rules, means, and methods.*
   rec.aviation

◈ *Traveling all over the world.*
   rec.travel

◈ *Airline travel around the world.*
   rec.travel.air

◈ *The science of aeronautics and related technology.*
   sci.aeronautics

◈ *Astronomy discussions and information.*
   sci.astro

◈ *Issues related to the Flexible Image Transport System.*
   sci.astro.fits

◈ *Processing Hubble Space Telescope data. (Moderated).*
   sci.astro.hubble

◈ *Space, space programs, space-related research, and so on.*
   sci.space

◈ *Announcements of space-related news items. (Moderated)*
   sci.space.news

◈ *The space shuttle and the STS program.*
   sci.space.shuttle

◈ *Modelling the universe. (Moderated)*
   sci.virtual-worlds

◈ *Non-technical issues affecting space exploration.*
   talk.politics.space

Online Libraries
After Dark
No services available.

Knowledge Index
No services available.

Orbit
No services available.

NewsNet

◈ *Aerospace Daily*
Frequency: Daily
Earliest NewsNet Issue: 9/23/91
For the defense and space industries and the government agencies they serve. Monitors aerospace programs from concept through development and procurement.

◈ *Aerospace Electronics Business*
Earliest NewsNet Issue: 11/4/88 through 6/14/91
Archive file only; not currently updated. Reports on business and technology developments in aircraft electronics.

◈ *Aerospace Financial News*
Frequency: Biweekly
Earliest NewsNet Issue: 7/9/91
Analysis of the latest financial news and business developments in the defense and aerospace marketplace.

◈ *Airline Financial News*
Frequency: Weekly
Earliest NewsNet Issue: 9/24/90
Provides detailed information on financial news and developments in the airline industry, including an airline financial index.

᛫ *Airports*
Frequency: Weekly
Earliest NewsNet Issue: 1/2/90
Focuses on key airport issues such as operations, landing rights, legal decisions, and more.. Includes information on FAA airport grants and opportunities for business in airports.

᛫ *Air Safety Week Accident/Incident Log*
Frequency: Weekly
Earliest NewsNet Issue: 7/10/89
Covers aviation accidents and incidents under investigation by the National Transportation Safety Board.

᛫ *Air Safety Week Newsletter*
Frequency: Weekly
Earliest NewsNet Issue: 7/10/89
Covers developments at the FAA, and investigations and enforcement actions by the National Transportation Safety Board.

᛫ *Air Safety Week Regulatory Log*
Frequency: Weekly
Earliest NewsNet Issue: 7/10/89
Provides comprehensive reports on U.S. air safety regulations mandated by the FAA and other relevant agencies.

᛫ *AsiaPacific Space Report*
Frequency: Monthly
Earliest NewsNet Issue: 3/1/92
Devoted to covering space news from an Asian-Pacific perspective.

᛫ *Aviation Daily*
Frequency: Daily
Earliest NewsNet Issue: 9/16/91
Covers the commercial aviation industry and commercial air transportation issues worldwide.

᛫ *Aviation Week and Space Technology*
Frequency: Weekly
Earliest NewsNet Issue: 9/30/91
A weekly magazine for the aerospace industry; covers military, commercial, and corporate aircraft, rockets, missiles, space vehicles, power plants, and related topics.

᛫ *Commuter/Regional Airline News*
Frequency: Weekly
Earliest NewsNet Issue: 10/1/90
Covers the U.S. and Canadian commuter/ regional marketplaces. Provides market information from manufacturers, quarterly financial reports, updates from the FAA and other government agencies, new technologies, and key personnel changes.

᛫ *Commuter/Regional Airline News International*
Frequency: Weekly
Earliest NewsNet Issue: 2/18/91
Deals with the international commuter/ regional airline marketplace, concentrating on Europe, Asia, the Middle East, and Australia.

᛫ *Helicopter News*
Frequency: Biweekly
Earliest NewsNet Issue: 4/17/87
Current information on the helicopter industry, concentrating on operations, manufacturers, users, and support.

᛫ *Japanese Aviation News: Wing*
Frequency: Weekly
Earliest NewsNet Issue: 4/25/84
Japan's leading aviation weekly. Covers air transport, industry, space, defense, and more. Particular attention to Japan's defense industry and other aviation news in Asia.

᛫ *Official Airline Guides Electronic Edition*
A special gateway service, providing night schedules for more than 650 airlines worldwide, as well as complete fare information and on-time performance ratings for major North American airlines. Provides extensive travel and lodging information in many databases; consult the Special Gateway Services section in the NewsNet Reference Guide. Updated daily.

᛫ *Regional Aviation Weekly*
Frequency: Weekly
Earliest NewsNet Issue: 1/5/90
Of interest to users in the regional aviation industry. Covers business news, equipment, and market changes.

᛫ *Satellite Week*
Frequency: Weekly
Earliest NewsNet Issue: 5/11/81
Covers satellites and satellite communications.

᛫ *Space Business News*
Frequency: Biweekly
Earliest NewsNet Issue: 9/8/86
Covers space commercialization developments worldwide.

᛫ *Space Calendar*
Frequency: Weekly
Earliest NewsNet Issue: 5/16/88

International information on space development and exploration: upcoming launches, business deals, conferences, space technology/transportation, and lunar enterprise.

ⓢ *Space Commerce Week*
Frequency: Weekly
Earliest NewsNet Issue: 6/8/84
Focuses on space commercialization, including space transportation, remote sensing, materials processing, and space defense.

ⓢ *Space Daily*
Frequency: Daily
Earliest NewsNet Issue: 11/2/84
Daily coverage and analysis of space technologies, with related developments in industry and government.

ⓢ *Space Exploration Technology*
Frequency: Biweekly
Earliest NewsNet Issue: 9/1/90
Covers space exploration technologies developed worldwide.

ⓢ *Space Station News*
Frequency: Biweekly
Earliest NewsNet Issue: 12/21/87
Latest news regarding the building of the first U.S. space station. Also covers the Soviet space station Mir and related advances in robotics, computers, and more.

ⓢ *Speednews*
Frequency: Weekly
Earliest NewsNet Issue: 1/1/88
A weekly newsletter covering technical and business developments in the aviation industry.

ⓢ *The Weekly of Business Aviation*
Frequency: Weekly
Earliest NewsNet Issue: 1/8/90
Supplies information on corporate flight departments, fixed-base operators, aircraft and component manufacturers, and relevant vendors.

ⓢ *World Airline News*
Frequency: Weekly
Earliest NewsNet Issue: 9/30/91
Covers the latest trends in global commercial aviation: market changes, mergers and consolidations, significant labor costs, financial trends, and so on.

Bulletin Boards
Aerospace Technology BBS
Covers aerospace and science; home to the International Emergency Network. Extensive BBS listings covering astronomy, aviation, military, and more. Bulletins in space and aviation studies.
Availability: 24 hours/ 7 days
Baud Rate: HST 14.4K
BBS Number: (707) 437-5389
BBS Software: Opus 1.03b
Parameters: 8-0-1
Sysop: Guy Hokanson

Aviation Total Information Systems (ATIS)
Dedicated to all areas of aviation interest
Baud Rate: 300, 1200, 2400
BBS Number: (703) 242-3520 or (703) 242-3534
BBS Software: PCBoard
Sysop: Bill Downing
Help Line: (703) 242-0161

Centreville BBS
Deals with all aspects of flying.
Availability: 24 hours/ 7 days
Baud Rate: 300, 1200, 2400, 9600
BBS Number: (703) 830-4298
BBS Software: RBBS-PC
Sysop: Sigurd P. Crossland

ENVIRONET: The Space Environment Information Service
Contains the EnviroNET Database—Natural and Induced Environment Information and the Spacecraft Environmental Anomalies Handbook.
Baud Rate: 300, 1200, 2400
BBS Number: (301) 286-9000 or (301) 286-9500
Help Line: (301) 286-5690
Comment: Type NSSDCA after connect (ENVNET if asked for number), environet for user ID, and henniker for password.

FAA Safety Data Exchange
Baud Rate: 300, 1200, 2400, 9600
BBS Number: (800) 426-3814

NASA SpaceLink

Geared towards teachers and educators. Large amount of educational resources, including teacher and student files which cover educational topics and classroom materials. Educators can receive NASA publications.
Availability: 24 hours/ 7 days
Baud Rate: 300, 1200, 2400
BBS Number: (205) 895-0028
Parameters: 8-0-1
Sysop: Bill Anderson
Help Line: (205) 544-0994
Comments: Enter NEWUSER as your user name and as your password.

National Space Society BBS

Covers space science and technology issues. Carries several USENET conferences. File libraries and bulletins include NASA press releases and articles, NSS Space Hotline news and more than 20 downloading libraries.
Availability: 24 hours/ 7 days
Baud Rate: 1200, 2400, 9600
BBS Number: (412) 366-5208
BBS Software: Opus
Sysop: Bev Freed

NOAA/SEL BBS

Provided by the Space Environment Laboratory (SEL) of NOAA; makes available text message products produced by the Space Environment Service Center (SESC). Monitors solar activity in collaboration with USAF, providing advisories and forecasts.
Baud Rate: 300, 1200, 2400
BBS Number: (303) 497-5000

NODIS BBS

NSSDC's on-line data and information service; supplies data concerning astronomy and earth sciences, satellites and more.
Baud Rate: 300, 1200, 2400
BBS Number: (301) 286-9000 or (301) 286-9500
Sysop: Angelia Bland
Help Line: (301) 513-1687
Comment: Type NSSDC after connect (or when asked for a number), then for user enter NSSDC or NODIS.

StarBase III

Discussion conferences on astronomy, space science, physics, and UFOs. Supplies on-line NGC and Messier catalogues, a calendar of events, space and astronomy programs, and much more.
Availability: 24 hours/ 7 days
Baud Rate: 2400
BBS Number: (209) 432-2487
BBS Software: MAXIMUS
Sysop: John Pickens

CD-ROM

⑤ *Aerospace*
Dialog Information Services

⑤ *The Aircraft Encylopedia*
Quanta Press

Audio/ Acoustics/ Sound Resources

Forums & Databases

America Online (AOL)

⟡ *Dolby Audio/Video Forum*
Keyword: Dolby
Path: Lifestyles & Interests Department > Dolby Audio/Video Forum
On-line access to Dolby publications and direct communication with Dolby staff.

CompuServe (CIS)

No services available.

GEnie

No services available.

The Well

⟡ *Audio*
  (g aud)
A conference for neophytes and techies, music and video lovers, and equipment mavens.

⟡ *Audio-Image (CD's)*
  (g cd)
Conference/interactive newsletter for discussions of compact disc techology and compact disc sound recordings.

⟡ *Digital Domain*
  (g dig)
For discussion of digital technical matters, equipment reviews, purveyors of information, and tape recordings.

Network Discussions Lists

Internet (Includes Bitnet & UUCPNet)

⟡ *Canadian Electro-Acoustics Community (CEC) list.*
  CEC@QUCDN.BITNET
  LISTSERV@QUCDN .BITNET

⟡ *Digital Acoustic Signal Processing list.*
Discussions of digital acoustic signal processing and related subjects.
  DASP-L@CSEARN.BITNET
  LISTSERV@CSEARN.BITNET
Contact: Frantisek Kadlec
  <FKADLEC@CSEARN.BITNET>

⟡ *Audio Equipment list.*
Discussions of high-end audio equipment and modification of high-end pieces.
  INFO-HIGH-AUDIO@CSD4.csd.uwm.EDU
  INFO-HIGH-AUDIO-REQUEST@CSD4.csd.uwm.EDU
Contact: Thomas Krueger
  <tjk@CSD4.csd.uwm.EDU>

⟡ *Compact Discs list.*
Discussions about the compact audio disc medium and related hardware.
  INFOCD@CISCO.NOSC.MIL
  CDREQUEST@CISCO.NOSC.MIL
Contact: Michael Pawka
  <MIKE@CISCO.NOSC.MIL>

Fidonet

🜨 *Adlib and Compatible Sound Cards Discussion Forum*
    ADLIB
For discussions about all types of sound cards.
Moderator: Todd Toles
    1:396/1.4
Distribution: BACKBONE

Usenet

🜨 *High fidelity audio.*
    rec.audio

🜨 *Discussions of automobile audio systems.*
    rec.audio.car

🜨 *High-end audio systems. (Moderated)*
    rec.audio.high-end

🜨 *Professional audio recording and studio engineering.*
    rec.audio.pro

Online Libraries

After Dark
No services available.

Knowledge Index
No services available.

Orbit
No services available.

NewsNet

🜨 *Audio Week*
Covers the consumer audio industry. Offers reports on corporate financial performance, new products and ventures, and legal developments affecting the industry.
Frequency: Weekly
Earliest NewsNet Issue: 6/19/89

Bulletin Boards

The Audiophile Network
A BBS for high-end audio lovers. Includes music and video reviews.
Availability: 24 hours/ 7 days
Baud Rate: 3-9600
BBS Number: (818) 988-0452
Help Line: (818) 782-1676

CD-ROM
No services available.

Biological Science Resources

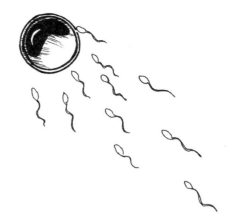

Forums & Databases

America Online (AOL)
No services available.

CompuServe (CIS)
No services available.

GEnie
No services available.

The Well

🖐 *Bioinfo*
(g bioinfo)
Discusses the emerging coevolutionary links between the biological/natural sciences and the information sciences.

🖐 *Wildlife*
(g wild)
Discussions of the flora and fauna of our planet.

Network Discussions Lists

Internet (Includes Bitnet & UUCPNet)

🖐 *Discussion of Bee Biology*
Discusses research and information concerning the biology of bees, and including flower nectar and pollen production.
```
BEE-L@ALBNYVM1.BITNET
LISTSERV@ALBNYVM1.BITNET
```

Contact: Mary Jo Orzech
`<MJO@BROCK1P.BITNET>`

🖐 *BIOCIS-L Biology Curriculum Innovation Study list.*
```
BIOCIS-L@SIVM.BITNET
LISTSERV@SIVM.BITNET
```

🖐 *Biological Applications of Electron Spin Resolution list.*
```
BIOESR-L@UMCVMB.BITNET
LISTSERV@UMCVMB.BITNET
```

🖐 *Biomechanics and Movement Science list.*
For members of biomechanic societies and for anyone interested in biomechanics and human or animal movement.
```
BIOMCH-L@HEARN.BITNET
LISTSERV@HEARN.BITNET
```
Contact: H. J. Woltring
`<ELERCAMA@HEITUE5.BITNET>`

🖐 *Association of Biomedical Communications Directors list.*
For directors of biomedical communications centers in medical schools, veterinary schools, and schools of allied health sciences.
```
BIOMED-L@MCGILL1.BITNET
AD38@@MCGILLA.BITNET
```
Contact: Bill Hillgartner
`<AD38@MCGILLA.BITNET>`

🖐 *Bureau Of Biometrics At Albnydh2 list.*
```
BIOMET-L@ALBNYDH2.BITNET
LISTSERV@ALBNYDH2.BITNET
```

🖐 *Biotechnology discussion list.*
```
BIOTECH@UMDD.BITNET
LISTSERV@UMDD.BITNET
```

🖐 *Brine Shrimp Discussion list.*
```
BRINE-L@UGA.BITNET
LISTSERV@UGA.BITNET
```

🌑 *Classification, clustering, and phylogeny estimation list.*
For researchers in classification, clustering, phylogeny estimation, and related methods of data analysis.
```
CLASS-L@SBCCVM.BITNET
LISTSERV@SBCCVM.BITNET
```
Contact: Jim Rohlf
```
<ROHLF@SBBIOVM.BITNET>
```

🌑 *Confocal Microscopy list.*
Deals with all aspects of confocal microscopy and confocal microscope design.
```
CONFOCAL@UBVM.BITNET
LISTSERV@UBVM.BITNET
```
Contact: Robert Summers
```
<ANARGS@UBVMS.BITNET>
```

🌑 *Biosym Technologies Software Users*
For users of Biosym Technologies, Inc., software, including InsightII, Discover, Dmol, Homology, and Delphi.
```
DIBUG@AVOGADRO.BARNARD.COLUMBIA.EDU
dibug-request@avogadro.barnard.columbia.edu
```
Contact: Peter S. Shenkin
```
<shenkin@avogadro.barnard.columbia.edu>
```

🌑 *Drosophila list.*
Deals with topics of interest to drosophila workers.
```
DIS-L@IUBVM.BITNET
LISTSERV@IUBVM.BITNET
```

🌑 *Computers in Biotechnology, Research, and Education list.*
Seeks to facilitate the use of computers in biotechnological training and research in Europe.
```
EBCBBUL@HDETUD1.BITNET
LISTSERV@HDETUD1.BITNET
```
Contact: Arie Braat
```
RCSTBRA@HDETUD1.BITNET
```

🌑 *Catalogue of Biotechnological Software*
Information about public-domain and commercially available software for biotechnological research and teaching.
```
EBCBCAT@HDETUD1.BITNET
LISTSERV@HDETUD1.BITNET
```
Contact: Arie Braat
```
RCSTBRA@HDETUD1.TUDELFT.NL
```

🌑 *EMBNet(European Molecular Biology Network) list.*
```
EMBINFO@IBACSATA.BITNET
LISTSERV@IBACSATA.BITNET
```

🌑 *Nitrogen Fixation*
Discusses biological nitrogen fixation.

```
<Eng-
Leong_Foo_%KOM.KOMunity.SE@VM1.NODAK.EDU>
<Eng-
Leong_Foo_%KOM.KOMunity.SE@VM1.NODAK.EDU
Eng-leong Foo <Eng-
Leong_Foo_@KOM.KOMunity.SE>
```

🌑 *ENTOMO-L Discussion list.*
```
ENTOMO-L@UOGUELPH.BITNET
LISTSERV@UOGUELPH.BITNET
```

🌑 *Forum on Molecular Biology*
Operated by Unite d'Informatique Scientifique at the Institut Pasteur Foundation, Paris.
```
FORUMBIO@BNANDP11.BITNET
LISTSERV@BNANDP11.BITNET
```
Contact: Bruno Durasse
```
DURASSE@BNANDP11
```

🌑 *BIOSCI GENBANK-BB Bulletin Board list.*
```
GENBANKB@IRLEARN.BITNET
LISTSERV@IRLEARN.BITNET
```

🌑 *Human Biology Interest Group Discussion list.*
Deals with biological anthropology, adaptation, environmental stress, biological race, growth, genetics, paleoanthropology, skeletal biology, forensic anthropology, paleodemography, paleopathology, primate biology and behavior.
```
HUMBIO-L@FAUVAX.BITNET
MAILSERV@FAUVAX.BITNET
```
Contact: M.Y. Iscan
```
<ISCAN@FAUVAX.BITNET>
```

🌑 *Human Evolutionary Research*
Examines human biological evolution, adaptation, variation, and evolutionary medicine.
```
HUMEVO@GWUVM.BITNET
LISTSERV@GWUVM.BITNET
```
Contact: Noel T. Boaz
```
<BOAZ@GWUVM.BITNET>
```

🌑 *International Arctic Project Wildlife list.*
```
IAPWILD@NDSUVM1.BITNET
LISTSERV@NDSUVM1.BITNET
```

🌑 *Color and Vision Discussion Forum list.*
For discussions on any topic relevant to color science or vision research.
```
LIVE-EYE@YORKVM1.BITNET
LISTSERV@YORKVM1.BITNET
```

🌑 *Laboratory Primate Newsletter list.*
```
LPN-L@BROWNVM.BROWN.EDU
LISTSERV@BROWNVM.BROWN.EDU
```

🌑 *Biological Morphometric list.*
```
MORPHMET@CUNYVM.BITNET
LISTSERV@CUNYVM.BITNET
```

⑤ *Neuroscience Information Forum list.*
```
NEURO1-L@UICVM.BITNET
LISTSERV@UICVM.BITNET
```

⑤ *Methods in Modern Neuroscience list.*
```
NEUS582@UICVM.BITNET
LISTSERV@UICVM.BITNET
```

⑤ *Oxygen Free Radical Biology and Medicine list.*
```
OXYGEN-L@UMCVMB.BITNET
LISTSERV@UMCVMB.BITNET
```

⑤ *Photosynthesis Researchers' list.*
For news and information exchange concerning photosynthesis research.
```
PHOTOSYN@TAUNIVM.BITNET
LISTSERV@TAUNIVM.BITNET
```
Contact: Robert S, Knox
```
RSKN@UORVM.BITNET
```

⑤ *Population Biology list.*
Pursues a unified theory to explain the structure, functioning and evolution of populations of living beings.
```
POPULATION-
BIOLOGY<BIOSCI%NET.BIO.NET@VM1.NODAK.EDU>
LISTSERV@IRLEARN
```
Contact: Vincent Bauchau
```
<VINCENT@BUCLLN11.BITNET>
```

⑤ *Potato Research list.*
```
SPUD@WSUVM1.BITNET
LISTSERV@WSUVM1.BITNET
```

⑤ *Biological Systematics Discussion list.*
```
TAXACOM@HARVARDA.BITNET
LISTSERV@HARVARDA.BITNET
```

Fidonet

⑤ *Evolutionary Mechanism Theory Discussion list.*
```
EVOLUTION
```
Discusses evolutionary theory topics, field biology, relevant observations in ecology, geology, astronomy, genetics, and population biology.
Moderator: Wesley Elsberry
```
1:347/303
```

Usenet

⑤ *Discussion of agroforestry.*
```
bionet.agroforestry
```

⑤ *Announcements of interest to biologists. (Moderated)*
```
bionet.announce
```

⑤ *Computer and mathematical applications. (Moderated)*
```
bionet.biology.computational
```

⑤ *Discussions about tropical biology.*
```
bionet.biology.tropical
```

⑤ *General BIOSCI discussion.*
```
bionet.general
```

⑤ *Information about the Arabidopsis project.*
```
bionet.genome.arabidopsis
```

⑤ *Discussion of Chromosome 22.*
```
bionet.genome.chrom22
```

⑤ *Discussions about research in immunology.*
```
bionet.immunology
```

⑤ *Discussions about biological information theory.*
```
bionet.info-theory
```

⑤ *Scientific job opportunities.*
```
bionet.jobs
```

⑤ *Contents of biology journal publications.*
```
bionet.journals.contents
```

⑤ *Discussions of cell and organism aging.*
```
bionet.molbio.ageing
```

⑤ *Computer applications to biological databases.*
```
bionet.molbio.bio-matrix
```

⑤ *Information about the EMBL Nucleic acid database.*
```
bionet.molbio.embldatabank
```

⑤ *How genes and proteins have evolved.*
```
bionet.molbio.evolution
```

⑤ *Messages to and from the GDB database staff.*
```
bionet.molbio.gdb
```

⑤ *Information about the GenBank Nucleic acid database.*
```
bionet.molbio.genbank
```

⑤ *Hot off the presses! (Moderated)*
```
bionet.molbio.genbank.updates
```

⑤ *Discussions about genetic linkage analysis.*
```
bionet.molbio.gene-linkage
```

⑤ *How genes are organized on chromosomes.*
```
bionet.molbio.gene-org
```

⑤ *Discussion of Human Genome Project issues.*
```
bionet.molbio.genome-program
```

🌐 *Requests for information and lab reagents.*
bionet.molbio.methds-reagnts

🌐 *Discussions about the molecular biology of HIV.*
bionet.molbio.hiv

🌐 *Research on proteins and protein databases.*
bionet.molbio.proteins

🌐 *Research issues in the neurosciences.*
bionet.neuroscience

🌐 *Discussions of all aspects of plant biology.*
bionet.plants

🌐 *Technical discussions about population biology.*
bionet.population-bio

🌐 *Information about funding agencies, and so on.*
bionet.sci-resources

🌐 *Information about software for biology.*
bionet.software

🌐 *Software sources relating to biology. (Moderated)*
bionet.software.sources

🌐 *Who's Who in biology.*
bionet.users.addresses

🌐 *Discussions about protein crystallography.*
bionet.xtallography

🌐 *Biology and related sciences.*
sci.bio

🌐 *Discussions in the field of biomedical engineering.*
sci.engr.biomed

🌐 *Medicine and its related products and regulations.*
sci.med

🌐 *AIDS: treatment, pathology/biology of HIV, prevention.* (Moderated)
sci.med.aids

Online Libraries

After Dark

🌐 *BIOSIS Previews,® Backfile, and Merged File*
International coverage of journal articles, research reports, reviews, conference papers, symposia, books, and other sources in biology, medicine, and other life sciences.
Coverage: 1970 to date
Updated: Monthly

🌐 *Cambridge Scientific Abstracts Life Science*
A superfile providing access to the following abstracting services: The Sciences Collection, Aquatic Sciences and Fisheries Abstracts, Oceanic Abstracts, and Pollution Abstracts.
Coverage: 1981 to present
Updated: Monthly

🌐 *Current Contents: Agriculture, Biology & Environmental Sciences*
A subset of Current Contents Search™ corresponding to the *Current Contents: Agriculture, Biology & Environmental Sciences* print edition.

🌐 *Current Contents: Life Sciences*
A subset of Current Contents Search™ corresponding to the *Current Contents: Life Sciences* print edition.

🌐 *TOXLINE*
Bibliographic files from the National Library of Medicine, with over 850,000 citations from 1965-present, covering the pharmacological, biomedical, physiological, and toxicological effects of drugs and other chemicals.
Coverage: Pre-1965 to present
Updated: Monthly with about 5000 documents per update

🌐 *TOXLINE Subset*
A subset of TOXLINE containing documents from all TOXLINE subfiles except the MEDLINE-derived subfile, TOXBIB. Subset contains approximately 30 percent of the documents from TOXLINE.

🌐 *Wilson Biological and Agricultural Index*
Indexes over 225 of the key English-language periodicals in the biological and agricultural sciences.
Coverage: 1983 to present
Updated: Monthly

🌐 *Zoological Record Online®*
Indexes every aspect of zoology, including information on waterborne diseases, animal husbandry and fossils.
Coverage: 1978 to present
Updated: Monthly

Knowledge Index

Current Biotechnology Abstracts

Online version of the print publication produced by the Royal Society of Chemistry. Subjects include genetic manipulation, monoclonal antibodies, immobilized cells and enzymes, single-cell proteins, and fermentation technology. Includes industrial applications.
Coverage: 1983 to present
Updated: Monthly

Life Sciences Collection

Abstracts information on animal behavior, biochemistry, ecology, endocrinology, entomology, genetics, immunology, microbiology, oncology, neuroscience, toxicology, virology, and related fields.
Coverage: 1978 to present
Updated: Monthly

Orbit

Biotechnology Abstracts

Covers all technical aspects of biotechnology from genetic manipulation and biochemical engineering to fermentation and downstream processing.
Coverage: July 1982 to present
Updated: Monthly

NewsNet

Applied Genetics News
Frequency: Monthly
Earliest NewsNet Issue: 10/1/89
Monitors the business and technology of biotechnology.

Biotech Business
Frequency: Monthly
Earliest NewsNet Issue: 7/1/88
Provides news and information on biotechnology products, developments, and companies.

Biotechnology Newswatch
Frequency: Biweekly
Earliest NewsNet Issue: 1/15/90
Examines business, legal, and industrial ramifications of biotechnology, including developments in genetic engineering.

Comline Japan Daily: Biotechnology
Frequency: Daily
Earliest NewsNet Issue: 1/5/90
Concentrates on new pharmaceuticals, medical devices, and research. Includes articles on basic research equipment, industrial applications, developments in agricultural science, and results of current research.

Genetic Technology News
Frequency: Monthly
Earliest NewsNet Issue: 1/1/89
Focuses on genetic engineering and its uses in the chemical, pharmaceutical, food-processing, energy, and other industries.

High-Tech Separations News
Frequency: Monthly
Earliest NewsNet Issue: 9/1/89
Covers the fast-growing fields of organic and biomolecular separations, including the technologies, economies, markets, and business.

Industrial Bioprocessing
Frequency: Monthly
Earliest NewsNet Issue: 1/1/89
Focuses on industrial production of chemicals and energy, including the conversion of biomaterials via fermentation, enzymatic conversion, and biodegradation.

Membrane & Separation Technology News
Frequency: Monthly
Earliest NewsNet Issue: 9/1/89
Explores the scientific, technological, and business aspects of separation, focusing on short- and long-term benefits of new membrane technology and the growth of U.S. membrane markets.

Bulletin Boards

The BioTron
Sponsored by the American Foundation for Biological Sciences, Biotron contains employment opportunities in the biological sciences before they appear in BioScience Magazine. Users can post job opportunities a well as read listings.
Availability: 24 hours/ 7 days
Baud Rate: 300, 1200, 2400
BBS Number: (202) 628-2427
BBS Software: TBBS
Parameters: 8 N 1
Help Line: (202) 628-1500

The National Biological Impact Assessment Program BBS

Operates from Virginia Polytechnic Institute and State University. Facilitates safe performance evaluation of genetically modified organisms in the environment. Includes lists of biotechnology companies, job opportunities, and an international plant biotechnologist directory.
Baud Rate: 300, 1200, 2400
BBS Number: (800) 624-2723 or (703) 231-3858
BBS Software: PCBoard
Cost: 1/2 hour toll free per 24 hours
Parameters: 8-N-1

National Science Foundation BBS

Contains bulletins and information on NSF-funded studies in science and engineering.
Availability: 24 hours/ 7 days
Baud Rate: 300, 1200, 2400
BBS Number: (202) 634-1764
BBS Software: RBBS-PC
Parameters: N,8,1
Help Line: (202) 634-4250

Taxonomic Reference File BBS

Operated by BIOSIS, a non-profit organization that produces biological abstracts and zoological records for the biological and life sciences.
Availability: 12 noon-8 am M-F; 24 hours Sat/Sun
Baud Rate: 300, 1200, 2400
BBS Number: (215) 972-6759
BBS Software: RBBS-PC
Parameters: N,8,1
Sysop: Bob Howey, Carol Lock, Keith Pittman, Yolanda Bryant
Help Line: (215) 587-4917

HerpNet

Operational since 1984. Assists those with an interest in reptiles or amphibians. Offers annual herpetological conference calendars.
Availability: 24 hours/ 7 days
Baud Rate: 300, 1200, 2400, 9600
BBS Name/Sponsor: HerpNet
BBS Number: (215) 464-3562 (9600 HST, call (215) 698-1905)
BBS Software: TBBS

Parameters: 8-N-1
Sysop: Mark Miller
Help Line: (215) 464-3561

Osprey's Nest

For birders, naturalists, and conservationists; part of the National Birding Hotline Cooperative.
Availability: 24 hours/ 7 days
Baud Rate: 300, 1200, 2400
BBS Number: (301) 989-9036
BBS Software: ROBBS
Parameters: 8-0-1
Sysop: Fran & Norm Saunders

CD-ROM

⑤ *ADONIS*
Adonis B.V.

⑤ *AGRICOLA*
SilverPlatter Information Inc.
100 Ridge Road
Norwood, MA 02062

⑤ *AGRIS*
SilverPlatter Information Inc.
100 Ridge Road
Norwood, MA 02062

⑤ *Aquatic Science & Fisheries*
Compact Cambridge
7200 Wisconsin Avenue
Bethesda, MD 20814

⑤ *Arctic & Antarctic Regions*
National Information Service Corp.

⑤ *Biological Abstracts*
SilverPlatter Information Inc.
One Newton Executive Park
Newton Lower Falls, MA 02162

⑤ *Biological & Agricultural Abstracts*
H.H. Wilson Co.

⑤ *Biotechnology Abstracts*
SilverPlatter Information Inc.
100 Ridge Road
Norwood, MA 02062

⑤ *Lasergene*
DNASTAR, Inc.
1801 University Avenue
Madison, WI 53705

⑤ *Life Sciences*
Compact Cambridge
7200 Wisconsin Avenue
Bethesda, MD 20814

Botanical Resources

Forums & Databases

America Online (AOL)
No services available.

CompuServe (CIS)
No services available.

GEnie
No services available.

The Well
No services available.

Network Discussions Lists

Internet (Includes Bitnet & UUCPNet)

Biology

🔄 *Fungus and Root Interaction Discussion list.*
MICRONET@UOGUELPH.BITNET
LISTSERV@UOGUELPH.BITNET

🔄 *Potato Research list.*
SPUD@WSUVM1.BITNET
LISTSERV@WSUVM1.BITNET

🔄 *Biological Systematics Discussion list.*
TAXACOM@HARVARDA.BITNET
LISTSERV@HARVARDA.BITNET

Botany

🔄 *Carnivorous Plants list.*
Discusses all aspects of carnivorous plants. Information on archived files can be listed by sending the command: "INDEX CP" to listserv@opus.hpl.hp.com.
CP@opus.hpl.hp.com
LISTSERV@opus.hpl.hp.com
Contact: Rick Walker
<walker@hpl-cutt.hpl.hp.com>

🔄 *Medicinal and Aromatic Plants Discussion list.*
HERB@TREARN.BITNET
LISTSERV@TREARN.BITNET

Orchids

🔄 *Orchid Growers list.*
Discusses types of orchids grown, cultivation techniques of certain orchids, tips to assist growers, scientific and biological issues relating to growth, and seeding and propagating techniques. Also lists The Orchid Society's events.
ORCHIDS@SCU.BITNET
MAILSERV@SCU.BITNET
Contact: Willis Dair
<DAIR@SCU.BITNET>

Fidonet

🔄 *Herbal Delights for Anyone*
HERBS-N-SUCH
For anyone who enjoys growing, buying, and using legal herbs. Discussions center on

medicinal, culinary, aromatic, and aesthetic usage.

Moderator: Tomas Hood
  1:352/777
Distribution: BACKBONE

Usenet

No services available.

Online Libraries

After Dark

No services available.

Knowledge Index

No services available.

Orbit

No services available.

NewsNet

No services available.

Bulletin Boards

Taxacom

A service of the Buffalo Museum of Science. For those working in the botanical and natural sciences. Offers an online electronic journal, a bimonthly magazine, and an electronic newsletter for legume specialists. TaxacomNet is a bitnet listserver with discussion topics in systematic biology. Subscribe by sending a mail request to `listserv@msu`. The first line of the message should read "`signup taxacoma John Doe` (your name)."

Availability: 24 hours/ 7 days
Baud Rate: 300, 1200, 2400
BBS Number: (716) 896-7581
BBS Software: FYI-MCD
Parameters: 8-N-1
Sysop: Richard Zander
Help Line: (716) 896-5200

The Orchid Database

A non-profit corporation that perpetuates rare and endangered orchid species. Growers send in listings of their collections of orchid species.

Contact: The Orchid Database, Inc.
626 Humboldt St.
Richmond, CA 94805
(510) 235-8815

CD-ROM

⑤ *Cab Abstracts*
SilverPlatter Information Inc.
100 Ridge Road
Norwood, MA 02062

⑤ *Natural Resources Megabase*
National Information Services Corp.

⑤ *The Plant Doctor*
Quanta Press

⑤ *TREE-CD*
SilverPlatter Information Inc.
100 Ridge Road
Norwood, MA 02062

Business/ Economics/ Labor Resources

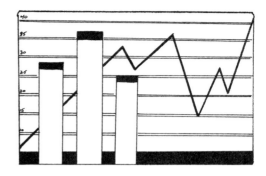

Forums & Databases

America Online (AOL)

○ *Ernst & Young Business Series*
Keyword: Ernst & Young
Path: News & Finance Department > Ernst & Young Business Series
Offers online advice about starting and managing your own business.

○ *Investor's Network*
Keyword: investors network
Path: News & Finance Department > Investor's Network
An interactive forum run by Art Bechhoefer dedicated to helping people make educated investment decisions.

○ *Stock Marketing Timing and Charts*
Path: News & Finance Department > Stock Market Timing and Charts
The forum is run by Carl Swenline, publisher of Decision Point Alert, a market timing service, to enhance your chances of stock market survival and profit through the techniques of market timing and technical analysis.

○ *StockLink*
Keyword: stocks
Path: News & Finance Department > Search for Quote
Users can search for 15-minute delayed single quotes. If a person doesn't know his stock's symbol, he can search the database of companies online. Serious users can buy and sell stocks online through a gateway to TradePlus.

○ *Your Money*
Keyword: Your Money
Path: News & Finance Department > Your Money
Forum leader Richard A. Allridge teaches money management and basic financial principles in easy to understand terms. Features a "Profile of the Month" showing how various America Online members should approach their unique financial goals.

○ *Real Estate Online*
Keyword: Real Estate
Path: Lifestyles & Interests Department > Real Estate Online
Run by real estate expert Peter Miller to help people buy, sell, rent, finance, and invest in real estate. Offers stat-by-state listings.

○ *Microsft Small Business Center*
Keyword: MSBC
Path: News & Finance Department > Microsoft Small Business Center
Offers information about financing, marketing, advertising, and taxes for small businesses. The Service Corp of Retired Executives holds weekly live online conferences to answer questions about running your business.

○ *Strategies for Business*
Path: Lifestyles & Interests Department > Strategies for Business
Hosted by the staff of Attard Communications, a small business consulting firm, it is a resource for business owners and managers to network with other business owners, executives, and managers across the country.

⑤ *Career Center*
Keyword: Career
Path: Learning & Reference Department > The Career Center
Includes background articles on the job market, the interview process, the perfect resume, self-exployment, and job listings. Members can get individualized attention by posting their questions on message boards, or by scheduling private online appointments with a career counselor.

⑤ *Business Forum*
Path: Computing & Software > Mac Forums > Business Forum
Keyword: Macbusiness
Focuses on Macintosh computer tools for business and productivity.

CompuServe (CIS)

⑤ *AdNet Online*
GO ADNET
Enables users to easily search large numbers of employment opportunities. It is updated twice weekly to provide current information on employment opportunities in a variety of careers.

⑤ *Company Information*
GO EUR-25
Provides users with resources for finding financial information about European and American companies.

⑤ *The Electronic Mall*
GO MALL
Enables members to order products from over a hundred national retailers and catalogers. It is open 24 hours a day, seven days a week, and there are no connect-time charges, yearly membership fees or surcharges. *This Week's Mall News* (GO EMN) announces new merchants and special sales and promotions.

⑤ *Directory of Catalogs*
GO DTC
Listing of all catalogs from mall merchants in one directory.

⑤ *Shoppers Advantage Club*
GO SAC
A discount electronic shopping service containing more than 250,000 name-brand products—with savings up to 50 percent.

⑤ *SOFTEX Software Catalog*
GO SOFTEX

An electronic software catalog that enables users to purchase and receive commercial software.

⑤ *Business Dateline*
GO BUSDATE
A searchable database that provides a regional outlook with information on local economic conditions, retailing, real estate, people and management, financial institutions, transportation and electronics from 1985 to the present.

⑤ *Calculating Personal Finances*
GO FINTOL
Offers products that enable you to calculate your net worth and generate a loan amortization schedule.

⑤ *Citibank's Global Report*
GO GLOREP
Organizes financial news and data, foreign exchange rates, spot commodity prices, and market and industry news, including up to six months of historical news on many publicly held companies. Updated around the clock from sources around the world.

⑤ *Commodity Markets*
GO COMMODITIES
Offers members access to historical information on futures contracts and cash prices. Contains open, high, low, settling, and cash prices along with volume and open interest for every trading day over the past 12 years. Futures prices are generally available by 7:00 P.M. Eastern time (U.S.) (midnight GMT) with the cash price, volume and open interest available 24 hours later.

⑤ *Commodity Pricing*
GO CPRICE
Presents historical performance by day, week, or month for the requested commodity contract. Displays open, high, low, and settling prices along with volume and open interest. Also offers aggregated volume and open interest for all contracts for the requested commodity along with its cash market price.

⑤ *Commodity Symbol Lookup*
GO CSYMBOL
Displays available commodity groups including foods, grains, metals, financial, petroleum, fibers, currencies and indexes. Access symbols, active contracts, exchange where traded and commodity description are shown for each commodity.

⑤ Company Analyzer
GO ANALYZER

By entering a company name, ticker symbol, or CUSIP number, the *ANALYZER* will search various financial services to determine which ones contain data for the company selected. It then builds a customized menu of the services offering the information.

⑤ Company Information
GO COMPANY

Provides access to the various sources of information about specific companies.

⑤ Company Screening
GO COSCREEN

Enables users to screen the DISCLOSURE II database based on entered criteria and produce a list of companies that meet the criteria. The ticker symbols of the companies can be saved for use in other CompuServe programs. Updated weekly with market prices updated overnight.

⑤ Corporate Affiliations
GO AFFILIATIONS

Offers profiles and reference information on most of the large U.S. public companies and their affiliates. Includes organizations traded on the New York and American Stock Exchanges, their affiliates, and any company traded over-the-counter having affiliates.

⑤ Current Market SNAPSHOT
GO SNAPSHOT

Provides a picture of the current stock market by depicting key indicators in a concise one-page report of statistics. It highlights current trading trends by presenting the highest, lowest and latest values for the Dow Jones 30, Standard and Poor's 500 and NASDAQ Composite.

⑤ Current Quotes
GO QQUOTE

Enables users to retrieve the current market value of stocks, options, and market indexes. Quotes are delayed over 15 minutes, which is as soon as the exchanges will enable you to receive them without the payment of a monthly fee.

Major foreign currency exchange rates are updated twice each day, and current values for mutual funds and money market funds are available by 7 P.M. ET (midnight GMT).

⑤ D&B Dun's Market Identifiers
GO DUNS

Includes three searchable directories of business information online with its Market Identifiers databases. The companies are: D&B-Dun's Market Identifiers, D&B-Canadian Dun's Market Identifiers, and D&B-International Dun's Market Identifiers.

⑤ Detailed Issue Examination
GO EXAMINE

Offers a detailed description of a single issue including trading status, recent price, dividends, risk measures, and capitalization. Updated overnight.

⑤ DISCLOSURE II
GO DISCLOSURE

Compiled from the 10K's and other reports that publicly-owned companies file with the Securities and Exchange Commission. Updated every Sunday, with market prices updated every night. Ownership information is updated quarterly.

⑤ Dividends, Splits, Bond Interest
GO DIVIDENDS

Offers dividend, split and bond interest information for an issue over a given period. Hard-to-obtain mutual fund distributions are also available. Updated overnight.

⑤ Dun's Electronic Business Directory
GO DYP

Contains information on more than 8 million professionals and businesses in the U.S. includes information on the type of business, its SIC code, number of employees, the industry to which each entry belongs, the population of each entry's city and information about parent companies.

⑤ Earnings/Economic Projections
GO EARNINGS

Enables users to access information about different companies' earnings, projected earnings, and growth, and economic projections.

⑤ E*TRADE, America's Electronic Brokerage
GO ETRADE

Enables users to take complete control of their investments. Provided by Trade*Plus and available at base-connect rates.

⑤ E*TRADE Stock Market Game
GO ETGAME

Provides participants with $100,000 to invest in game accounts. Choose to play either the stocks-only game, the stocks and options game or both. Offers access to actual market data and prices, and computers even track commission costs to make the game realistic. At the end of every month, the player in each game with the largest percentage increase wins a cash prize.

⑨ European Company Library
GO EUROLIB

Contains directory and financial information on more than 2 million European companies. Information can be retrieved by entering the company name, industry codes, or a specific geographic location.

⑨ Financial Forums
GO FINFORUM

Enables users to ask specific questions about financial matters such as investments and the economy, or about technical matters such as running Lotus 1-2-3.

⑨ FundWatch Online
GO MONEYMAG

A comprehensive mutual fund database for screening and reporting on over 1,900 professionally managed investment alternatives.

⑨ Futures Focus
GO ACI

A weekly newsletter for the futures trader published by News-a-tron featuring the TSF trading system, a market overview, and tips on how to improve one's trading performance. Updated Fridays.

⑨ German Company Library
GO GERLIB

Offers financial and product information for more than 48,000 public and private German companies. Information can be retrieved by entering the company name, industry codes, or a specific geographic location.

⑨ Highlights—Previous Day
GO MARKET

Analyzes the most recent trading day for the New York Stock Exchange, American Stock Exchange and Over-The-Counter markets and prepares 19 different reports. Updated overnight.

⑨ Historical Stock/Fund Pricing
GO SECURITIES

Accesses the MicroQuote II historical database in a variety of ways.

⑨ I/B/E/S Earnings Estimates
GO IBES

This area is the Institutional Broker's Estimate System. It represents a consensus of annual and long-term forecasts from more than 2,500 analysts at 130 brokerage and institutional research firms. Updated every Sunday with market values updated daily.

⑨ Index Symbol Lookup
GO INDICATORS

Offers the ticker and the CUSIP number for all indexes included in the MicroQuote II database. Includes the time period for which each index has data.

⑨ Instructions/Fees
GO FINHELP

Provides immediate answers to commonly asked questions, information about session charges, product surcharges, and update times. Offers users an opportunity to give feedback on the financial service offerings.

⑨ International Company Information
GO COINTL

Contains information on millions of international companies. Each section offers its own databases to help users track information such as the countries' largest companies and their products for many public and private companies and leading businesses.

⑨ Investext
GO INVTEXT

Contains the full text of company and industry research reports compiled during the most recent 2 years by analysts in more than 50 Wall Street, regional, and international brokerage houses and research firms.

⑨ Investment Analysis
GO ANALYSIS

Contains selections that offer various methods of using MicroQuote II investment data.

⑨ Investors' Forum
GO INVFORUM

Provides a meeting place for users interested in the world of investing to discuss market trends, download investment software and participate in "real-time" conferences Conferences are scheduled regularly, and many feature experts speaking on specific areas of investing. Novice and expert investors are welcome.

⑨ IQINT—Company Information
GO IQINT

Designed for program-controlled downloading to your microcomputer. Retrieves descriptive items about the specified issue from MicroQuote II, company financial information from DISCLOSURE II, and earnings information from I/B/E/S. Updated weekly.

⑤ Issue/Symbol Lookup
GO SYMBOLS

Enables users to determine what securities and indexes are covered and the access symbol for each. Updated overnight.

⑤ List Bonds for Company
GO BONDS

Displays active bonds for the designated company. Includes the ticker symbols, CUSIP numbers, issue description, yield, current selling price for each bond, and the quality rating expressed by Standard & Poor's and Moody's. Updated overnight.

⑤ Market Quotes/Highlights
GO QUOTES

This area delivers CompuServe's current and historical quotes products via menus. Contains current market quotes on stocks, options and market indexes along with end-of-day foreign currency exchange rates, net asset values for mutual funds and current yields on money market funds. Stock quotes are delayed over 15 minutes. Most commodities data are available by 7:00 P.M. Eastern Time (midnight GMT), and MicroQuote II price and volume information for all securities is updated and available by 7:00 A.M. (noon GMT) the next morning.

⑤ MMS International Financial Reports
GO MMS

Specializes in financial and economic research. A schedule of updates is included online with the product.

⑤ MQDATA—Prices, Dividends, Security Descriptions
GO MQDATA

Creates files for transfer to your microcomputer and enables access to MicroQuote II data. Updated overnight.

⑤ MQINT—Securities Prices
GO MQINT

Designed to meet the needs of microcomputer software that automates the downloading process. Updated continually.

⑤ Multiple Issues—1 Day
GO QSHEET

Offers volume, close/average, high/ask, low/bid and CUSIP numbers for several issues for a given day. Updated overnight.

⑤ National Association of Investors Corporation Forum
GO NAIC

Educates long-term investors in how to find quality companies and buy stocks at good prices.

⑤ News-A-Tron Market Reports
GO NAT

Offers analysis and cash market prices on selected commodities, market indexes, financial instruments and foreign exchange information.

⑤ Options Profile
GO OPRICE

Lists all options currently trading on a given common stock or market index. Market prices updated continuously.

⑤ Personal Finance/Insurance
GO FINANCE

Includes many services and programs that are useful for making personal financial and insurance decisions.

⑤ Portfolio Valuation
GO PORT

Finds the value of a previously created portfolio for dates users select and displays unrealized gains and losses. Market prices updated continuously.

⑤ Price/Volume Graph
GO TREND

Provides graphic presentations of the traded price and the trading volume for the requested days, weeks, or months. The CompuServe Information Manager (CIM) software supports the graphics in the trend chart. Updated overnight.

⑤ Pricing History—1 Issue
GO PRICES

Offers over 12 years of historical prices by day, week, or month. It includes CUSIP, exchange code, volume, high/ask, low/bid, and close/average for a given security. Updated overnight.

⑤ Pricing Statistics
GO PRISTATS

Provides a snapshot of price and volume performance for a requested issue over a given period. Updated overnight.

⑤ Quick Way
GO QWK

Quick & Reilly offers all the functions of a traditional stockbroker including market and limit orders and trading on margin. For monthly exchange fees, you can get real-time quotes (otherwise quotes are delayed over 15 minutes). Can place, buy, or sell orders 24 hours per day.

◈ *RateGram Federally Insured CDs*
GO RATEGRAM

Provides a service for finding the highest yielding federally insured savings instruments available nationwide.

◈ *Return Analysis*
GO RETURN

Calculates the annualized returns for your securities. Updated overnight.

◈ *S&P Online*
GO S&P

Standard & Poor's Corporation offers recent information on approximately 5,600 companies including business summaries, earnings outlooks, historical earnings and dividends and product line summaries. All information is dated to indicate when it was last reviewed. Updated every Tuesday night.

◈ *Search for Company Name, Ticker Symbol or CUSIP*
GO LOOKUP

Offers searches by name, CUSIP number, ticker symbol, CNUM or SIC code, and lists all the issues for a selected company.

◈ *Securities Screening*
GO SCREEN

Enables users to select a type of investment and then screen the MicroQuote II database to see what securities meet their criteria. Updated overnight.

◈ *Spear Rees & Company*
GO SPEAR

Speer Rees & Company provides professional investment services to individual investors trading stocks, zero coupon bonds, options, index options, SEPs and IRAs, government securities, mutual funds, and insurance products. Around-the-clock availability.

◈ *Thomas Companies & Products Online*
GO THOMAS

Offers access to two databases—Thomas Register Online and Thomas New Industrial Products. Thomas Register Online contains company information on almost 150,000 U.S. and Canadian manufacturers and service providers. Updated annually. Thomas New Industrial Products contains the latest technical information on new industrial products introduced by the U.S. (and some non-U.S.) manufacturers and sellers.

◈ *TRW Business Profiles*
GO TRWREPORT

Provides credit and business information on more than 13 million organizations to help users find actual account information for over 70 million business account relationships as reported by participating corporations.

◈ *UK Company Library*
GO UKLIB

Contains directory, credit, and financial information on more than 1.2 million UK companies.

◈ *UK Historical Stock Quotes*
GO UKPRICE

Offers pricing information for over 5,000 United Kingdom equity issues and approximately 350 market indices. Most securities in the service have data dating back to July 1, 1990. Updated daily.

◈ *UK Issue Lookup*
GO SEDOL

Enables users to locate SEDOL (Stock Exchange Daily Official List) numbers, which provide a means of identifying issues traded on the UK exchanges.

◈ *Value Line Annual Reports*
GO VLANN

Lists summarized financial statements for industrial and service companies. Offers four annual statements. Updated every other Sunday.

◈ *Value Line Data Base II*
GO VLINE

Includes information for over 4,000 companies. Data is provided for the past 12 years where possible.

◈ *Value Line Quarterly Reports*
GO VLQTR

Summarizes information for the four quarters in any available fiscal year including sales, EPS, net income, dividend and stock price data. Updated every other Sunday.

◈ *Value Line 3-5 Year Projections*
GO VLFORE

Provides individual company forecasts of earnings, sales, dividends, book value, and anticipated high and low stock prices three to five years into the future.

The Business Wire
GO TBW

Provides press releases, news articles, and other information from the world of business. Updated continuously throughout the day and brings information on hundreds of different companies.

Executive News Service
GO ENS

Keeps members informed of news affecting their business and personal interests. Stories are clipped as they come across the wires and held in electronic folders for members to review at their convenience.

Business Management
GO MANAGEMENT

Contains information for the needs of managers of large and small businesses.

International Entrepreneurs' Forum
GO USEN

An information exchange for entrepreneurs and business resources.

IQuest Business Management InfoCenter
GO IQBUSINESS

An online reference tool to find information about business including management research, marketing studies, and specific companies.

Biz*File
GO BIZFILE or BIZ*FILE

Offers access to over 10 million U.S. and Canadian business establishments. Each business is listed by business name, address, telephone number and length of time it has been listed in the yellow pages. Available 24 hours a day.

Business Database Plus
GO BUSDB

Enables users to search for and retrieve full-text articles from more than 450 regional, national and international business and trade publications. For additional articles, access Magazine Database Plus (GO MAGDB), Computer Database Plus (GO COMPDB) and Health Database Plus (GO HLTDB).

Business Demographics
GO BUSDEM

Provides reports designed to help businesses analyze their markets. Two types of reports are available by various geographical units. The Business to Business Report details all major business categories by number of employees and state percentage. The Advertisers Service Reports provide employee counts and number of establishments by employee size for retail trade businesses.

CENDATA The Census BureauService
GO CENDATA

Provides Census Bureau data on manufacturing, housing starts, population, agriculture, and more to CompuServe members. Offers the latest press releases from the Census Bureau, and even lists the Census Bureau representative in your state.

Commerce Business Daily
GO COMBUS

Includes the full text of U.S. Commerce Department publications listing all significant Federal contracts, proposal requests, and data related to government contracts. Includes only listings from the most recent 90 days. Updated daily.

IQuest
GO IQUEST

CompuServe's online information retrieval service provides easy access to more than 850 databases from companies.

Marketing/Management Research Center
GO MGMTRC

Offers access to nine databases containing Indices and full text of major U.S. and international business, management and technical magazines, Indices to market and industry research reports, market studies and statistical reports, and U.S. and international company news releases.

Neighborhood Report
GO NEIGHBORHOOD

Provides a summary of the demographic makeup of any ZIP Code in the United States. An 80-column printer is needed for printing reports. Updated annually.

New Car Showroom
GO NEWCAR

Provides a comparison shopping guide for consumers making new vehicle purchases.

Phone*File
GO PHONEFILE

Contains names, addresses, and phone numbers of more than 75 million US households. Relatives and friends across the nation are easy to find by searching the database by name and address; surname plus state, city and ZIP code or telephone number.

SUPERSITE
GO SUPERSITE

Provides demographic information for the entire U.S. and every state, county, SMSA, Arbitron TV Market (ADI), Nielsen TV Market (DMA), Place, Census Tract, Minor Civil Division (MCD) and geometric definition by circle and ZIP Code in the United States. Each report in *SUPERSITE* is surcharged. Users are shown the cost of requested reports before they are run to give them the opportunity to abort the run before incurring any surcharges. An 80-column printer is needed for printing reports. Sample reports are available at no surcharge. Updated annually.

Trademark Research Center
GO TRADERC

Provides access to databases containing all textual-numeric (non-graphic) federal trademarks active in the U.S. and all non-graphic trademarks for Puerto Rico.

UK Marketing Library
GO UKMARKETING

Contains market research reports compiled by top marketing analysts. Most databases provide full-text articles. Updated regularly.

UK Trademark Library
GO UKTRADEMARK

This database contains information on technical standards and trademarks in the United Kingdom. BSI Standardline, , provides citations to data on current British technical standards. Updated monthly.

The British Trade Marks database contains all registered trademarks and pending applications, as well as lapsed trademarks and applications from 1976. Updated weekly.

US-State-County Reports
GO USSTCN

Provides summaries of the demographic makeup of the entire United States, any state or county. An 80-column printer is needed for printing reports. Updated annually.

VISTA Environmental Profiles
GO VISTA

Enables members to assess the major environmental risks associated with a company, site or area anywhere in the United States. An example of each report is available.

Working from Home Forum
GO WORK

Unites users who work from their homes with others who are in similar circumstances.

Basic Quotes
GO BASICQUOTES

Enables members to retrieve delayed quotes for items such as stocks, options, indexes, exchange rates, and mutual funds. Up to 20 quotes can be retrieved in a single session.

Brokerage Services
GO BROKERAGE

Enables users to choose among the various brokerage services on CompuServe.

PR and Marketing Forum
GO PRSIG

Provides a special interest group for professional communicators such as public relations, marketing, and communications directors or those holding related jobs in the public and private sector.

Demographics
GO DEMOGRAPHICS

Enables members to obtain demographic information for any area of the United States. Data is based on the 1990 Census and current year and five-year forecasts.

Patent Research Center
GO PATENT

Provides access to databases containing summaries of U.S. patents granted in chemical, mechanical, electrical and design categories, and summaries of patents granted internationally. Enables members to conduct research on patents listed in the Claims/U.S. Patent Abstracts (1950 to present) and the World Patents Index (1963 to present).

GEnie

Dr. Job
Keyword: DR.JOB or Page 395

Written by Sandra Pesmen, features editor of Crain's Chicago Business, DR.JOB is a weekly question and answer column covering career and employment issues ranging from corporate politics to communications to career decisions.

E-Span JobSearch
Keyword: ESPAN or Page 304

An employment advertising network that enables organizations to reach more than 3.5 million PC-literate professional, technical, and managerial candidates nationwide. Updated weekly and advertisements run for approximately two weeks.

◊ *Home Office/Small Business RT*
Keyword: HOSB or Page 370
An online resource for owners of small and home-based businesses, folks who want to start a business, or employed individuals who want career advancement

◊ *Home and Real Estate RT*
Keyword: HOME or Page 955
Offfers information about Real Estate and related issues.

◊ *The Business Resource Directory*
Keyword: DIRECTORY or Page 375
A searchable, electronic database where members can locate: small businesses, home workers (people who want to work at home but don't want to start their own business), job seekers who don't want to work at home, products, services, supplies, government offices that offer help to home offices and small businesses, trade magazines and associations, agencies, wholesalers, distributors, service bureaus, software for business and other business resources.

◊ *Dow Jones News/Retrieval*
Keyword: DOWJONES or Page 260
Provides access to over 50 databases containing company and industry news and information, as well as the full-text of hundreds of national and regional publications.

◊ *Trade Names Database*
Keyword: TRADENAMES or Page 1125
A database of more than 280,000 consumer brand names and their owners or distributors. It is the equivalent of *Brands and Their Companies* and *International Brands and Their Companies* published by the Gale Research, Inc.

◊ *Official Airline Guides*
Keyword: OAG or Page 761
Contains several travel-related databases that enables users to view schedules for over 600 airlines updated weekly, millions of fares updated daily, and over 37,500 hotels in North America, Europe, and the Pacific.

◊ *Air Force Small Business RoundTable*
Keyword: AFSB3 or Page 1035
Provides information about doing business with the Air Force and Department of Defense more accessible to: Small Businesses (SBs), Small Disadvantaged Businesses (SDBs), Section 8(a) Contractors, Historically Black Colleges and Universities, and Minority Institutions (HBCU/MIs), and large businesses looking for subcontractors

◊ *American Airlines EAASY SABRE*
Keyword: SABRE or Page 760
Enables users to retrieve flight, hotel, and weather information. You can set up an account on the EAASY SABRE system, and book flights, and make hotel reservations.

◊ *Traveler's Info. RoundTable*
Keyword: TIS or Page 560
For travellers who want to learn about new travel locations and travel bargains. Offers toll free 800 numbers for car rental agencies and cruise lines.

◊ *TRAVELSOURCE*
An online travel agency where users can book vacations at good prices.

◊ *The Investment ANALY$T*
Keyword: ANALYST or Page 781
Provides vital stock market information to investors: Current & Historical Quotes, Stock Performance Analysis, and Stock Screening & Selection.

◊ *Charles Schwab Brokerage Services*
Keyword: SCHWAB or Page 240
An online link to Charles Schwab Brokerage where users can trade in stocks, bonds, options, and mutual funds. Users can also cancel or change any outstanding trade orders, whether or not they were placed online.

◊ *Investors' RoundTable*
Keyword: INVEST or Page 290
Sponsored by Charles Schwab & Co., Inc, to provide the computerized investor with additional resources for investing.

◊ *SOS Registered Investment Advisors*
Keyword: SOS or Page 1295
A registered investment advisory company that offers investment advice to the general public via daily videotex publications.

◊ *GEnie Loan Calculator*
Keyword: LOAN or Page 790
Provides a handy program that calculates monthly payment tables, and produces amortization schedules for fixed-rate mortages.

◊ *D&B U.S. Company Profiles*
Keyword: D&BPROFILES or Page 1256

Enables users to quickly locate key statistics for millions of U.S. companies in D&B Company Profiles.

TRW Business Credit Profiles
Keyword: TRWPROFILES or Page 1262
Enables users to quickly locate credit information for millions of U.S. companies.

Corporate Affiliates Research Center
Keyword: AFFILIATES or Page 1252
Enables users to quickly locate information on the corporate hierarchy for thousands of companies and their affiliates.

Credentials
GEnieMall
Keyword: TRWCREDIT Aisle 1
Enables users to keep track of their credit profile for a fee.

Commerce Business Daily
Keyword: CBD or Page 1284
This is a searchable database that enables users to quickly find the latest announcements for product and service procurements from the U.S. Government. Announcements are posted here on the day before appearing in the printed publication.

Worldwide Patent Center
Keyword: PATENTS or Page 1268
Enables users to determine whether someone has registered a patent in the United States or any one of 30 other countries around the world. Full records show bibliographic information, an abstract, classification, and more. Updated weekly.

Thomas Register of North American Manufacturers
Keyword: TREGISTER or Page 1254
Enables users to locate information on manufacturers of a specific product, type of product, or providers of a service.

Trademark Center
Keyword: TRADEMARKS or Page 1266
Enables users to determine whether someone has registered a trademark at the Federal or State level.

The Well

Classifieds
`(g cla)`
Classifieds is an online version of the classified ads in your local paper.

Consultants
`(g consult)`
A forum for consultants of many industries, predominantly people who work in computer-related areas. Topics include marketing, taxes, running a small business, loneliness and collaboration.

Desktop Publishing & Presentation
`(g desk)`
For desktop publishing and presentation users.

Entrepreneurs
`(g entre)`
For entrepreneurs of all kinds.

Investment
`(g invest)`
Discusses investing stocks, mutual funds, options, and other issues.

Nonprofits Outreach
`(g non)`
Home of CompuMentor, where nonprofits and interested individuals can discuss the issues which affect nonprofit organizations.

One Person Business
`(g one)`
Offers information about running a one person business (OPB).

Periodical/Newsletter
`(g per)`
For publishers of newsletters and other small periodicals to share resources.

Restaurant
`(g rest)`
For discussions about restaurants.

Sustainable Economics
`(g sust)`
For discussing the development of practical, sustainable, economic, social, and political structures in North America.

Work
`(g work)`
Provides users with serious discussions of work-related issues.

Workers Conference
`(g workers)`
Provides users with discussions on Socialism, Utopian, and Scientific, Past, Present, and Future.

Network Discussions Lists

Internet (Includes Bitnet & UUCPNet)

Accounting

🜨 *Chargeback of computer resources*
For topics relating to chargeback of resources in the computing center. Discusses general issues as well as details pertaining to MVS and VM systems only.
```
BILLING@HDETUD1.BITNET
LISTSERV@HDETUD1.BITNET
```
Contact: Rob van Hoboken
```
<RCOPROB@HDETUD1.BITNET>
```

Activist

🜨 *Flexible Work Environment List.*
Discusses how people are handling flexible work situations. Archives of FLEXWORK back issues can be listed by sending the command INDEX FLEXWORK to LISTSERV@PSUHMC.BITNET.
```
FLEXWORK@PSUHMC.BITNET
LISTSERV@PSUHMC.BITNET
```
Contact: Maria Holcomb
```
<MHOLCOMB@PSUHMC.BITNET>
```

AWARDS

🜨 *Commerce Business Daily—Awards list*
```
AWARDS-B@OSUVM1.BITNET
LISTSERV@OSUVM1.BITNET
```

Business

🜨 *Boston Area Business Librarians Discussion List*
```
BABL-L@MITVMA.BITNET
LISTSERV@MITVMA.BITNET
```

Economics

🜨 *Association of Japanese business studies list.*
An international association of Japan scholars, students, government and business researchers, and executives interested in the Japanese economy and business systems
```
AJBS-L@NCSUVM.BITNET
LISTSERV@NCSUVM.BITNET
```
Contact: James W. Reese
```
<R505040@UNIVSCVM.CSD.SCAROLINA.EDU>
```

🜨 *Academy of Management International list.*
```
AMINT-L@PSUVM.BITNET
LISTSERV@PSUVM.BITNET
```

🜨 *Business school computing support list.*
```
BSCS-L@EMUVM1.BITNET
LISTSERV@EMUVM1.BITNET
```

🜨 *Business ethics computer network list.*
```
BUSETH-L@UBVM.BITNET
LISTSERV@UBVM.BITNET
```

🜨 *Cochran Research Center discussion list.*
```
BUSTALK@TEMPLEVM.BITNET
LISTSERV@TEMPLEVM.BITNET
```

🜨 *Caribbean economy list.*
```
CARECON@YORKVM1.BITNET
LISTSERV@YORKVM1.BITNET
```

🜨 *Caribbean Basin Economics*
Forum on the economies of the Caribbean Basin region. Compiled and distributed several times weekly.
```
CARIBBEAN-ECONOMY@VELA.ACS.OAKLAND.EDU
CARIBBEAN-ECONOMY-
REQUEST@VELA.ACS.OAKLAND.EDU
```
Contact: Addington Coppin
```
<coppin@oakland.bitnet>
```

🜨 *Canadian Associaton for the Study of International Development*
```
CASID-L@MCGILL1.BITNET
LISTSERV@MCGILL1.BITNET
```

🜨 *Faculty of Economics and Econometrics*
For researchers in the fields of Economics, Econometrics and Management.
```
CORRYFEE@HASARA11.BITNET
SARASERV@HASARA11.BITNET
```
Contact: Hans M. Amman
```
<amman@hasara5.BITNET>
```

🜨 *Research in Economic Education list.*
```
ECONED-L@UTDALLAS.BITNET
LISTSERV@UTDALLAS.BITNET
```

🜨 *Economic Problems in Less Developed Countries*
Discusses the economy and economic problems of less developed countries (LDCs) that have become real laboratories for both the economic discipline, and economic policy measures.
```
ECONOMY@TECMTYVM.BITNET
LISTSERV@TECMTYVM.BITNET
```
Contact: Alejandro Ibarra
```
5343TBIT@TECMTYVM.BITNET
```

🜨 *Eastern European Business Network*
For users doing business in Eastern Europe countries to help them in their transition to market economies and link business persons in Western Europe-Asia-North America with those in Eastern Europe.

E-EUROPE@NCSUVM.BITNET
LISTSERV@NCSUVM.BITNET
Contact: James W. Reese
<R505040@UNIVSCVM.BITNET>

🌀 *International Political Economy*
For users around the world interested in International Political Economy.
IPE@csf.colorado.edu
mailserv@csf.colorado.edu
Contact: Lev S. Gonick
<lgonick6@mach1.wlu.ca>

🌀 *North American Economics*
Focusses on the emerging North American Economy, from the perspective of labor in Canada, Mexico, and the United States
LABOR-L@YORKVM1.BITNET
LISTSERV@YORKVM1.BITNET

🌀 *Marketing*
For marketing academics and practitioners.
MARKET-L@UCF1VM.BITNET
LISTSERV@UCF1VM.BITNET
Contact: Charles Hofacker
CHofack@avm.cc.fsu.edu

🌀 *MBA Programs*
Provides users with information about MBA programs, their administration, problems, issues, questions.
MBA-L@MARIST.BITNET
LISTSERV@MARIST.BITNET

🌀 *National Business Education Association Discussion list*
NBEA-L@AKRONVM.BITNET
LISTSERV@AKRONVM.BITNET

🌀 *Pacific Business Researchers Forum (PCBR-L) list.*
PCBR-L@UHCCVM.BITNET
LISTSERV@UHCCVM.BITNET

🌀 *Real Estate Forum*
Discusses matters of general interest to real estate researchers and students.
RE-FORUM@UTARLVM1.BITNET
LISTSERV@UTARLVM1.BITNET
Contact: Hans Isakson
B581HRI@UTARLVM1.BITNET

Employment

🌀 *Employment Information*
bstring@mainz-emh2.army.mil

🌀 *Carolina Consortium for Human Development list.*
CCHD-L@UNCVM1.BITNET
LISTSERV@UNCVM1.BITNET

🌀 *Federal Employment Information*
For federal employees and others in the sharing of job opportunities as well as ideas on gaining employment.
employ@mainz-emh2.army.mil
employ-request@mainz-emh2.army.mil

🌀 *International Career and Employment News list.*
ICEN-L@IUBVM.BITNET
LISTSERV@IUBVM.BITNET

🌀 *Job Placement Issues*
For job search trainers, career educators, researchers looking at job search/labor market/ job placement issues, and private practice practitioners.
JOBPLACE@UKCC.BITNET
LISTSERV@UKCC.BITNET
Contact: Drema Howard
<DKHOWA01@UKCC.BITNET>

🌀 *Jobs and Employment Issues*
TESLJB-L@CUNYVM.BITNET
LISTSERV@CUNYVM.BITNET

🌀 *South Bend employment opportunities.*
For announcements of positions available in the South Bend area, and for statements of qualifications and interests of those
SBNJOBS@INDYCMS.BITNET
LISTSERV@INDYCMS.BITNET

Finance

🌀 *The Electronic Journal of Finance*
For academic researchers working in a variety of Finance related areas.
FINANCE@TEMPLEVM.BITNET
LISTSERV@TEMPLEVM.BITNET
Contact: Joseph Friedman
<JFRIED@TEMPLEVM.BITNET>

Geology

Mineral Economics and Management Society list.
MEMSNET@UABDPO.BITNET
LISTSERV@UABDPO.BITNET

Taxes

🌀 *Federal Taxation/Accounting Discussion*
Discusses federal taxation issues from a practical and academic viewpoint. FedTax-L is gatewayed to the USENET newsgroup misc.taxes.
FEDTAX-L@SHSU.BITNET
LISERV@SHSU.BITNET
Contact: Taylor Klett
<klett@SHSU.BITNET>

Fidonet

🌀 *Accounting/Tax*
ACCT_TAX
For professionals and businesspeople to discuss general areas of accounting and taxation.
Moderator: Larry Noah
1:280/333
Distribution: LOCAL-KCAREA

🌀 *Business Echo*
BUSINESS
Discusses starting/operating a business.
Moderator: Roy Tellason
1:270/716.23
Distribution: BACKBONE

🌀 *Commercial For Sale Message Area*
CFORSALE
A commercial buy and sell message area. Ads may be posted only by business, all may buy. No personal ads may be posted.
Moderator: Don Sands
1:203/601
Distribution: NATIONAL

🌀 *Consulting*
CONSULTING
An international forum for management and technology consultants with a variety of specialties.
Moderator: William Degnan
1:382/39
Distribution: BACKBONE

🌀 *Desktop Publishing*
DTP
A forum where users discuss all desktop publishing products, DOS, and Windows versions.
Moderator: Ed Lawyer
1:261/1056
Distribution: ECHONET BACKBONE (ZONE 50)

🌀 *Eastern Ontario Trade Echo*
EAST_ONT_TRADE
For users selling, trading, or buying for participating FidoNet systems in Eastern Ontario.
Moderator: Dean Laviolette
1:248/1
Distribution: NORTHSTAR

🌀 *Employment and Job Conference*
JOBS
Discusses employment related issues. Users can post a resume or job offerings.

Moderator: Ken Zwaschka
1:105/54
Distribution: BACKBONE
Gateways: RBBS NET VIA 1:10/8

🌀 *Entrepreneur Conference*
ENTREPRENEUR
For users who own their own business or who are self-employed, or would like to be.
Moderator: Chris Gunn
1:202/1008
Distribution: BACKBONE

🌀 *For Sale Conference*
4SALE
A general sales conference for personal items, an electronic "garage sale" type of setting. No commercial ads are allowed.
Moderator: Dave Reed
1:344/79
Distribution: ZONE-1 BACKBONE

🌀 *Forty Plus Job Transition Group New Member Info*
40_PLUS_INFO
For non-profit and member-staffed organizations that provide structured support for job placement and professional growth options for members.
Moderator: Chuck Cole
8:973/1
Restr: MOD-APVL
Distribution: 8:973/1, 1:282/78

🌀 *Forty Plus Network Support*
40_PLUS_NET
For non-profit and member-staffed organizations that provide structured support for job placement and professional growth for members. 40 Plus Network participation is restricted to members. Inquire via the 40_Plus_Info echo. Access requires a FAX from your 40 Plus group to 40 Plus of MN.
Moderator: Chuck Cole
8:973/1
Restr: MOD-APVL MEMBER
Distribution: 8:973/1, 1:282/78

🌀 *Home Office Echo*
HOME_OFFICE
For users who have elected to run their businesses or work on their jobs from their homes.
Moderator: Gary Hite
1:270/888
Distribution: BACKBONE

🌀 *Insurance*
INSURANCE
Offers conference on insurance topics.
Moderator: Dennis Volz
1:202/711.9
Distribution: BACKBONE, ZONE-2

🌀 *International Investor's Forum*
INVEST
A forum for investors who utilize personal computers
Moderator: Jack Williams
1:274/30
Distribution: BACKBONE

🌀 *Job & Employment offerings ONLY*
JOBS-NOW
Posts job offerings by individuals or companies with positions to offer. This is not a discussion group or a group for posting resumes.
Moderator: Ken Zwaschka
1:105/54
Distribution: BACKBONE (VIA REGION 17 REC TO PROTOSTAR)
Gateways: RBBS NET VIA 1:10/8

🌀 *Job Opportunities/Employment*
EMPLOY
For users seeking employment. Job openings are listed, as well as discussions about today's marketplace.
Moderator: Stan Hirschman
1:282/40.20
Distribution: ECHONET BACKBONE (ZONE 50)

🌀 *Multi-Level Marketing Conference*
MLM
For users engaged or interested in Multi-Level-Marketing (MLM).
Moderator: Chris Gunn
1:202/1008
Distribution: BACKBONE

🌀 *National For Sale Echo*
FOR-SALE
For the sale of personal items only. No commercial ads are permitted.
Moderator: Don Sands
1:203/601
Distribution: BACKBONE

🌀 *PC Consultants Echo*
PC_CONSULT
For users who offer PC based consulting services. Topics range from sources of products, solutions to common problems faced by consultants, dealing with clients and vendors, and ways to be more productive.

Moderator: Ken Levitt
1:16/390
Distribution: FIDONET BACKBONE

🌀 *Stock Market*
STOCK_MARKET
For the general discussion of stocks, mutual funds, investment strategies, and other investment related topics.
Moderator: Tom Cook
1:275/25.3
Distribution: BACKBONE

🌀 *The Real Estate Discussion Echo*
REAL
Discusses aspects of owning, buying, selling, renting, managing, and financing real estate
Moderator: Bob Germer
8:950/10
Distribution: FIDONET BACKBONE, RBBSNET
Gateways: FIDONET VIA 8:950/10, RBBSNET VIA 1:10/8

🌀 *Working out of your home.*
WORK-AT-HOME
For entrepreneurship.
Moderator: Al Thorley
1:387/301.1
Distribution: ECHONET BACKBONE (ZONE 50)

Usenet

🌀 *Discussion on operating a business.*
misc.entrepreneurs

🌀 *Short, tasteful postings about items for sale.*
misc.forsale

🌀 *Computers and computer equipment for sale.*
misc.forsale.computers

🌀 *Investments and the handling of money.*
misc.invest

🌀 *Property investments.*
misc.invest.real-estate

🌀 *Discussions about contract labor.*
misc.jobs.contract

🌀 *Discussion about employment, workplaces, careers.*
misc.jobs.misc

🌀 *Announcements of positions available.*
misc.jobs.offered

🌀 *Postings of resumes and "situation wanted" articles.*
misc.jobs.resumes

- *Tax laws and advice.*
  misc.taxes

- *The science of economics.*
  sci.econ

- *ClariNet UPI business news wiregroups.*
  clari.biz

- *Canadian Business Summaries. (Moderated)*
  clari.canada.biz

- *Commodity news and price reports. (Moderated)*
  clari.biz.commodity

- *Lawsuits and business related legal matters. (Moderated)*
  clari.biz.courts

- *Economic news and indicators. (Moderated)*
  clari.biz.economy

- *Economy stories for non-US countries. (Moderated)*
  clari.biz.economy.world

- *Business feature stories. (Moderated)*
  clari.biz.features

- *Finance, currency, Corporate finance. (Moderated)*
  clari.biz.finance

- *Earnings and dividend reports. (Moderated)*
  clari.biz.finance.earnings

- *Personal investing and finance. (Moderated)*
  clari.biz.finance.personal

- *Banks and financial industries. (Moderated)*
  clari.biz.finance.services

- *News for investors. (Moderated)*
  clari.biz.invest

- *Strikes, unions, and labor relations. (Moderated)*
  clari.biz.labor

- *General stock market news. (Moderated)*
  clari.biz.market

- *American Stock Exchange reports & news. (Moderated)*
  clari.biz.market.amex

- *Dow Jones NYSE reports. (Moderated)*
  clari.biz.market.dow

- *NYSE reports. (Moderated)*
  clari.biz.market.ny

- *NASDAQ reports. (Moderated)*
  clari.biz.market.otc

- *General market reports, S&P, and so on. (Moderated)*
  clari.biz.market.report

- *Mergers and acquisitions. (Moderated)*
  clari.biz.mergers

- *Other business news. (Moderated)*
  clari.biz.misc

- *Important new products & services. (Moderated)*
  clari.biz.products

- *Top business news. (Moderated)*
  clari.biz.top

- *Breaking business news. (Moderated)*
  clari.biz.urgent

- *General economic news. (Moderated)*
  clari.news.economy

- *Tax laws, trials, and so on. (Moderated)*
  clari.news.gov.taxes

- *Unions, strikes. (Moderated)*
  clari.news.labor

- *Strikes. (Moderated)*
  clari.news.labor.strike

- *Multi-level (network) marketing businesses.*
  alt.business.multi-level

- *Discussion about co-operatives.*
  alt.co-ops

- *Conference center management issues.*
  alt.conference-ctr

- *You locked your keys in *where*?*
  alt.locksmithing

- *Business Libraries List.*
  bit.listserv.buslib-l

- *Tourism Discussions.*
  bit.listserv.travel-l

Online Libraries

After Dark

- *ABI/Inform®*
Covers all phases of management, law, taxation, finance, data processing, advertising, human resources, and other areas of vital interest to the business community.
Coverage: 1971 to date
Updated: Weekly

⑤ Business Software Database
Descriptions of software products available for business professionals and systems users.
Coverage: Current information
Updated: Quarterly

⑤ Business Software Database
Descriptions of software products available for business professionals and systems users of microcomputers, minicomputers and mainframes, including information on the manufacturer availability, hardware and operating system compatibility, price, documentation and customer support.
Coverage: Current information
Updated: Quarterly

⑤ CAB: Economics, Development and Education
Contains all documents from three sections: l) World Agricultural Economics and Rural Sociology Abstracts; 2) Rural Development Abstracts, and 3) Rural Extension, Education and Training Abstracts.
Coverage: 1973 to pressent
Updated: Monthly

⑤ CAB: Leisure, Recreation and Tourism
A subset of CABA containing records from the Recreation and publication Leisure, Tourism Abstracts.
Coverage: 1980 to present
Updated: Monthly

⑤ Corporate and Industry Research Reports Online Index
Provides access to company and industry research reports issued by major U.S. and Canadian securities and institutional investment firms. Useful for tracking a company's research goals.
Coverage: 1982 to present
Updated: 1000-2000 records added monthly

⑤ Disclosure Database
Financial and textual data extracted from Securities and Exchange Commission filings and providing information on over 12,000 U.S. and non-U.S. public companies.
Coverage: Most recent 18 months of data available for a given company
Updated: Weekly (about 5000 records per update)

⑤ Disclosure/Health
A subset of Disclosure Database containing annual and quarterly financial and management information on companies publicly traded in the U.S. which deal with health care, pharmaceuticals and/or medical equipment.
Coverage: Current
Updated: Weekly

⑤ Federal Register Abstracts
A comprehensive abstracting and indexing system to the Federal Register, the daily government publication for legislative pronouncements.
Coverage: 1986 to present
Updated: Weekly

⑤ FINIS: Financial Industry Information Service
More than 250 financial industry newsletters, newspapers, and periodicals are reviewed for articles on all aspects of the industry with emphasis on marketing.
Coverage: 1982 to date
Updated: Bimonthly with approximately 500 records per update

⑤ Harvard Business Review/Online
The complete text of Harvard Business Review articles from 1976 to the present. Also offers bibliographic citations and extensive abstracts for articles from 1971 to 1975.
Coverage: 1971 to present with some earlier coverage
Updated: Concurrent with bimonthly HBR publication

⑤ Health Industry Research Reports
Index to research reports on health-related companies and the health industry issued by major U.S. and Canadian securities and institutional investment firms.
Coverage: 1982 to present
Updated: Quarterly

⑤ Investor's Daily
Abstracts of Investor's Daily, a financial newspaper with features such as Inside the Market, Today's News Digest, NYSE Stocks in the News, Stock Quotes (from all major exchanges), AMEX Stock in the News, Industries in the News, and At the Analysts.
Coverage: January 1986 to present
Updated: Monthly (400-500 records per update)

⑤ Management Contents™ and Backfile
Covers over 140 U.S. and international journals about management, administration, marketing, and personnel relations.
Coverage: 1974 to present
Updated: Monthly

PATDATA I
Information and abstracts for all utility patents issued by the U.S. Patent and Trademark Office since 1971, and all reissue patents issued since July 1, 1975.
Coverage: 1836 to date
Updated: Weekly about 1200 records per update

Wilson Business Peridoicals Index
Contains information from 345 of the key international English language business periodicals, offering all aspects of the contemporary business world.
Coverage: 1982 to present
Updated: Monthly

Knowledge Index

ABI/Inform®
Covers all phases of business management and administration.
Coverage: August 1971 to the present
Updated: Weekly

Business Dateline
Contains the full text of articles from regional business publications from throughout the US and Canada.
Coverage: 1985 to present
Updated: Weekly

BusinessWire
Contains the unedited text of news releases from over 10,000 different news sources.
Coverage: 1986 to present
Updated: Continuous

ICC British Company Directory
Covers 35,000 major German companies with sales exceeding 2.5 million DM or a minimum of 40 employees. Users can read the file in English or German.
Coverage: Current
Updated: Quarterly

PR NEWSWIRE
Contains the complete text of news releases prepared by sources covering the entire spectrum of the news. Major enterainment and media companies deliver information through entertainment. About 70% of the news is business related.
Coverage: May 1, 1987 to present
Updated: Continous

Standard & Poor's Corporate Descriptions plus News

This database provides comprehensive strategic and financial information and current news on about 12,000 publicly held companies.
Coverage: Current
Updated: Twice monthly

Trade & Industry Index ™
Provides current and comprehensive coverage of major trade journals and industry-related periodicals representing all Standard Industrial Classifications. Trade & Industry Index provides indexing and selective abstracting of over 300 trade and industry journals as well as comprehensive but selective coverage of business and trade information from nearly 1,200 additional publications. Indexing and abstracting for Trade & Industry Index is also included in Newsearch™ for daily updating during the current month.
Coverage: 1981 to the present
Updated: Weekly

Harvard Business Review
Covers the complete range of strategic management subjects of interest to managers and researchers.
Coverage: 1971 to the present
Updated: Bimonthly

Chemical Business Newsbase
Includes worldwide chemical news about chemicals, use, and production, with a particular emphasis on European news.
Coverage: October 1984 to the present
Updated: Weekly

Economic Literature Index
Covers journal articles and book reviews from 260 economics journals and approximately 200 monographs per year. The descriptive abstracts are approximately 100 words in length and are written by the author or editor of the journal article; all are in English. The database corresponds to the index section of the quarterly *Journal of Economic Literature*, and the annual *Index of Economic Articles*.
Coverage: 1969 to present
Updated: Quarterly

Standard & Poor's Register—Biographical
Provides extensive personal and professional data on key executives affiliated with public and private, U.S. and non-U.S. companies with sales of one million dollars and over.
Coverage: Current
Updated: Semiannual reloads

§ *Standard & Poor's Register—Corporate.*
Provides important business facts on over 45,000 leading public and private U.S. (and some non-U.S.) companies, usually with sales in excess of one million dollars. The file includes company records for parent companies plus subsidiaries, divisions, and affiliates.
Coverage: Current
Updated: Quarterly reloads

Orbit

§ *ABI/INFORM*
For business and management information. Contains citations to more than 800 publications.
Coverage: 1971 to present
Updated:L Weekly

§ *Accountants*
Provides international coverage on literature related to accounting, auditing, taxation, dataprocessing, investments, financial management, financial reporting, and related legal information. Only available On Orbit!
Coverage: 1974 to present
Updated: Quarterly

§ *API Energy Business Newss Index (APIBIZ)*
Includes twenty-four major news and economics publications as the primary sources for worldwide coverage of commercial, financial, marketing, and regulatory information affecting the petroleum and energy industries.
Coverage: 1975 to present
Updated: Weekly

§ *Chemical Economics Handbook*
Contains international supply/demand data for the chemical industry through the full text data base of the world's leading chemical market research service. Currently limited to hard copy subscribers.
Coverage: 1955-present
Updated: Monthly

§ *Chemical Industry Notes*
Contains citations to worldwide chemical business news. About 80 U.S. and non-U.S. publications are covered. Contains over 795,000 records.
Coverage: 1974 to present
Updated: Weekly

§ *Chinapats*
Covers all patent applications published under the patent law of the People's Republic of China. Contains English language. Information about equivalent non-Chinese patent publications provided by the European Patent Office is included as well.
Coverage: 1985 to present
Updated: Monthly

§ *CLAIMS*
Provides access to over 2 million United States patents issued by the U.S. Patent and Trademark Office. Chemical patents are covered from 1950 forward; mechanical and electrical patents from 1963 forward; design patents from 1980 forward.
Coverage: 1950 to present
Updated: Weekly

§ *CLAIMS Classification*
Provides a dictionary index to the U.S. Patent Office's classification code system. A full record contains the title of a pertinent subclass as well as the titles of its superior classes and subclasses.
Coverage: 1790 to present
Updated: Biannually

§ *CLAIMS Compound Registry*
Contains information for specific compounds that have been referenced in five or more patents contained in the CLAIMS/U database.
Coverage: 1950 to present
Updated: Quarterly

§ *CLAIMS Reassignments*
Provides information about more than 145,000 U.S. patents that have been reassigned since 1980, or reexamined since 1981. Reassignment occurs when ownership of a patent is transferred from the original owner to another individual or company. Also contains information about patents that have expired since 1985 because of non-payment of required maintenance fees, and patents that have been granted extension beyond their normal 17-year life since 1986.
Coverage: 1980 to present
Updated: Biomontly

§ *CorpTech*
Provides a comprehensive source of company information on over 35,000 U.S. manufacturers and developers of high-tech products. Ninety percent of the listed companies are private or operating units of larger corporations. Users can search by any combination of 20+ criteria including 3,000 high-tech product categories.
Coverage: Current
Updated: Quarterly

⑤ *Current Patents Evaluations*
Provides monthly in-depth, expert evaluations of pharmaceutical and biotechnology patents. Selected patents are examined in detail by specialists who provide English-language evaluations and commentaries in the context of the latest research findings. Approximately 35-40 patents are selected each month from patents appearing in the Current Patents: Fast Alert database.
Coverage : 1990 to present
Updated: Monthly

⑤ *Current Patents Fast Alert*
Provides weekly access to pharmaceutical, biotechnological, and agrochemical patent information. Approximately 250 patents are selected each week from published European, PCT, UK and German (for agrochemicals only) applications, and U.S.granted patents.
Coverage : July 1989 to most recent six weeks
Updated: Weekly

⑤ *Drug Patents International*
Provides evaluated product patent coverage for more than 800 pharmaceutical compounds, marketed or in active R&D. Data on 20 new compounds is added each month.
Coverage: Current
Updated: Monthly

⑤ *ENERGYLINE*
Provides comprehensive coverage of energy information. Contains more than 167,000 records with abstracts.
Coverage: 1971 to date
Updated: Monthly

⑤ *INPADOC/INPANEW*
Covers patent documents issued by more than fifty national and international patent offices. Bibliographic information is searchable. Contains approximately 18 million records.
Coverage: 1968 to present
Updated: Weekly

⑤ *JAPIO*
A comprehensive source of unexamined Japanese patent applications, with more than 2.8 million records in English covering all technologies.
Coverage: 1976 to present
Updated: Monthly

⑤ *LABORDOC*
Covers worldwide journal, report, and monographic literature on labor and labor-related areas. Contains more than 190,000 records.
Coverage: 1965 to present
Updated: Monthly

⑤ *Legal Status*
Contains types of actions that can affect the legal status of a patent document after it is published and after the patent is granted. Offers information about the disposition of patent applications published under the Patent Cooperation Treaty by the World Intellectual Property Organization.
Coverage: 1959 to present
Updated: Weekly

⑤ *LitAlert*
Offers notices of filing and subsequent action for patent and trademark infringement suits filed in the U.S. District Courts and reported to the Commissioner of Patents and Trademarks.. Only available on Orbit!
Coverage: 1970 to present
Updated: Weekly

⑤ *Materials Business File*
Covers all commercial aspects of iron and steel, non-ferrous metals and non-metallic materials, including ceramics, polymers, composites and plastics.
Coverage: 1985 to present
Updated: Monthly

⑤ *Patent Status File*
Provides a comprehensive alert to over 20 types of post-issue actions affecting U.S. patents. Includes actions since 1973 affecting over 200,000 patents dating back to 1969.
Coverage: 1973 to present
Updated: Monthly

⑤ *PIRA (Paper, Printing, and Publishing, Packaging, and Nonwovens Abstracts).*
Covers information on all aspects of paper, pulp, nonwovens, printing, publishing and packaging. As of January 1991, this file incorporates Electronic Publishing Abstracts (EPUB).
Coverage: 1975 to present
Updated: Biweekly

⑤ *Pharmaceutical News Index (PNI)*
A comprehensive resource for the latest U.S. and international news about the pharmaceuticals industry. Contains cover-to-cover indexing to 23 major industry newsletters.
Coverage: 1974 to present
Updated: Weekly

RAPRA Abstracts

Covers the world's polymer information, including journals, conference proceedings, books, specifications, reports and trade literature. Includes an adhesives subfile covering technical and commercial aspects of adhesives and sealants.
Coverage: 1972 to present
Updated: Biweekly

RAPRA Trade Names

Contains tradenames and trademarks used in the rubber and polymers industries around the world. Available only on Orbit
Coverage: 1976 to present
Updated: Biweekly

UK Trademarks

Contains information on registered UK trademarks, and marks for which application has been made since 1976. Information is also included for marks which have expired since January 1, 1976.
Coverage: 1976 to present
Updated: Weekly

US Classification

Contains all U.S. Classifications, Cross-Reference Classifications, and Unofficial Classifications for all patents issued from 1790 to date. Searching can be done by classification or by patent number.
Coverage: 1790 to present
Updated: Biannually

US Patents

Provides complete patent information, including complete front-page information, and claims of all U.S. patents issued since 1971 (claims are searchable prior to 1982). Available Only On Orbit,
Coverage: 1970 to present
Updated: Weekly

World Patents Index

A comprehensive and authoritative file of data relating to patent specifications issued by the patent offices of 31 major industrial countries.
Coverage: 1963 to present
Updated: Weekly and Monthly

WPIA/WPILA

Contains records for patents covering petroleum processes, fuels, lubricants, petro-chemicals, pipelines, tankers, storage, pollution control, synthetic fuels, synthetic gas, Cl chemistry and other technologies. Available only on Orbit.

Coverage: 1963 to present
Updated: Weekly and monthly

World Surface Coatings Abstracts

Provides international coverage of technical and commercial information on all aspects of paints and surface coatings. Available only on Orbit.
Coverage: 1976 to present
Updated: Monthly

NewsNet

Advertising and Marketing (AD)

Affluent Markets Alert
Frequency: Monthly
Earliest NewsNet Issue: 10/1/89
Covers consumer trends, demographics, lifestyle patterns, attitudes and priorities among the nation's affluent.

American Marketplace
Frequency: Biweekly
Earliest NewsNet Issue: 1/19/82
Covers new statistical data issued by the Census Bureau, other government statistical agencies, and private research firms with emphasis on demographic changes in the consumer marketplace.

The Boomer Report
Frequency: Monthly
Earliest NewsNet Issue: 11/1/89
Covers the attitudes and buying habits of "baby boomers."

Green Market Alert
Frequency: Monthly
Earliest NewsNet Issue: 12/1/91
Tracks the business impacts of environmental, or "green" consumerism.

Green Marketing Report
Frequency: Monthly
Earliest NewsNet Issue: 1/1/91
Reports on trends in "green" products and packaging, including environmentally-aware advertising, results of public opinion polls, green marketing case studies, government regulations, and health claims.

Marketing Research Review
Frequency: Monthly
Earliest NewsNet Issue: 10/1/85
Analyzes and evaluates commercially available marketing research and technology assessment reports. Helps readers identify, appropriate,

and adapt commercially available reports to their own special and particular needs.

🌎 *Marketing to Women*
Frequency: Monthly
Earliest NewsNet Issue: 9/1/91
Detailed guide to the latest women's market surveys. Includes interviews with experts on techniques for marketing to women, and book reviews.

🌎 *Minority Markets Alert*
Frequency: Monthly
Earliest NewsNet Issue: 10/1/89
Covers consumer trends, demographics, lifestyle patterns, attitudes and priorities among Hispanic, black, and Asian Americans.

🌎 *Research Alert*
Frequency: Biweekly
Earliest NewsNet Issue: 9/22/89
Offers users the latest information on consumer trends, lifestyles, demographics, attitudes, and shopping habits. Includes complete contact information for the reports covered.

🌎 *Sales & Marketing Digest*
Frequency: Monthly
Earliest NewsNet Issue: 4/1/91
Offers information on practical, profit-making sales and marketing strategies, tips, and techniques.

🌎 *Video Marketing News*
Frequency: Biweekly
Earliest NewsNet Issue: 1/4/88
An executive news service for marketers of consumer video programs and related hardware. Provides news, analysis, market research, statistics and forecasts of the U.S. and foreign home video and home entertainment markets.

🌎 *Youth Markets Alert*
Frequency: Monthly
Earliest NewsNet Issue: 10/1/89
Covers trends among young people, including lifestyles, attitudes, consumer patterns, and demographics.

Automotive (AU)

🌎 *The Autoparts Report*
Frequency: Biweekly
Earliest Issue Date: 1/15/90
Analyzes key sectors of the autoparts industry. Tracks consolidations and mergers, examines international joint ventures, offshore investing, and new autoparts ventures.

🌎 *Comline Japan Daily: Transportation*
Frequency: Daily
Earliest Issue Date: 1/5/90
Focuses on the auto and auto parts industries, including new product and model releases as well as new technologies.

Building and Construction (BC)

🌎 *The Construction Claims Citator*
Frequency: Monthly
Earliest NewsNet Issue: 7/1/90
A complete monthly listing of construction-related legal cases. Includes a small description.

🌎 *CPN: Contractor Profit News*
Frequency: Monthly
Earliest NewsNet Issue: 7/1/90
Covers marketing, management, and profits improvements for executives of construction companies.

🌎 *Energy Design Update*
Frequency: Monthly
Earliest NewsNet Issue: 1/1/90
Provides the latest information on energy-efficient building techniques to help builders keep up with technology, and to educate clients about the benefits of energy efficiency.

🌎 *Engineering News-Record*
Frequency: Weekly
Earliest NewsNet Issue: 9/30/91
A weekly magazine that provides business and technical news on all sectors of the construction industry, from buildings and highways to hazardous waste cleanups.

Business Wire (BW)

🌎 *Business Wire*
Frequency: Continuous wire feed with immediate up-dating; ten-week retention of articles.
Offers full-text press releases and announcements prepared and transmitted to Business Wire by over 10,000 U.S. companies. NewsNet monitors Business Wire on a 24-hour basis. Articles are immediately available for full-text retrieval in SCAN mode in hourly segments. Full-text searching of all articles is available within one hour of release.

🌎 *Electronic Provider: Mercury Computer Services Inc.*
Frequency: Daily
Earliest NewsNet Issue: 4 week retention

Commerce Business Daily (CB)

Offers six separate services comprising the full text of the printed edition of Commerce Business Daily, published each business day by the U.S. Department of Commerce. It is the official U.S. government publication listing all government procurement invitations over the amount of $25,000, contract awards, and sales of surplus property.

⑤ *CBD: Contract Awards—Services—CB03T*
Online equivalent of the services section of the Contract Award listings from the printed edition of Commerce Business Daily. Lists contract awards over $25,000 that are likely to result in any sub-contracts.

⑤ *CBD: Contract Awards—Supplies—CB04T*
Online equivalent of the services section of the Contract Award listings from the printed edition of Commerce Business Daily. Lists contract awards over $25,000 that are likely to result in any subcontracts.

⑤ *CBD: Foreign Government Standards—CB06*
Online equivalent of the Foreign Government Standards section of the printed edition of Commerce Business Daily. Lists notices of proposed changes in foreign standards and certification systems that could affect U.S. exports.

⑤ *CBD: Procurements—Services—CB0lT*
Lists all procurement invitations over $25,000, except those for classified services required within 15 days, services placed under existing contracts, certain utility services, and services not to be given advance publicity (as determined by the Small Business Administration).

⑤ *CBD: Procurements—Supplies—CB02T*
Online equivalent of the Supplies section of U.S. Government Procurements listings from the printed edition of Commerce Business Daily. All procurement invitations over $25,000 are listed, except for those for classified supplies, supplies required within 15 days, supplies placed under existing contracts, perishable supplies, or supplies not to be given advance publicity (as determined by the Small Business Administration).

⑤ *CBD: Special Notices—CBOS*
Online equivalent of the special notices section of the printed edition of Commerce Business Daily. Includes special notices of government actions affecting commerce and standards.

Dun & Bradstreet Information Services (DNB)

Gateway Access Rate: 40cts/min., plus transaction fees
Frequency: Continuous Updated
A gateway service that enables users to access premium commercial risk management information directly from the D&B database via NewsNet. Validation is required prior to access. D&B reports are separately priced according to the schedule posted in the gateway menus. Users will be charged $4 if a search is conducted without ordering a report. Each report costs $45.

FINANCE AND ACCOUNTING (FI)

⑤ *American Banker Full Text*
Frequency: Daily
Retention: Two years plus current year
Provides daily news coverage and analyses of events and trends in the financial-services industry, together with detailed examinations of selected topics on an annual basis.

⑤ *Asset Sales Report*
Frequency: Weekly
Earliest NewsNet Issue: 1/9/89
Provides market news and analysis, statistical features, and reports on regulatory and legal developments concerning several groups of financial assets, including commercial loans, mortgage credit, and consumer credit.

⑤ *Bank Automation News*
Frequency: Biweekly
Earliest NewsNet Issue: 6/6/89
Focuses on the selection and implementation of state-of-the-art technology in branch banking. Issues are discussed from a business management viewpoint, and practical advice on what to look for when installing a branch automation system is given.

⑤ *Bank Mergers & Acquisitions*
Frequency: Monthly
Reports, analyzes, and interprets the consolidation of the banking industry. Covers private bank and thrift deals, branch sales, RTC sales, and FDIC resolutions.

⑤ *Bank Network News*
Frequency: Biweekly
Earliest NewsNet Issue: 1/11/92
Reports and analyzes news in the electronic funds/transfer industry.

Bond Buyer Full Text
Frequency: Daily
Earliest NewsNet Issue: 1/4/88
Offers the complete editorial content of *The Bond Buyer*, including complete coverage of the municipal bond market. Other fixed income markets, including Treasury bonds, corporate bonds, futures, taxable issues, and mortgage-backed securities, are also extensively covered.

California Public Finance
Frequency: Weekly
Earliest NewsNet Issue: 3/25/g1
Provides in-depth coverage of California's municipal bond market, with reports on regulatory, legislative, and market developments.

Card News
Frequency: Biweekly
Earliest NewsNet Issue: 8/1/86
Presents information on changing transaction-card profit factors for banks and non-banks, profiles and status reports on new competitors, changes in costs of funds, operations, marketing, and services.

Corporate EFT Report
Frequency: Biweekly
Earliest NewsNet Issue: 1/11/84
Covers cash-management and money-transfer issues for treasurers and financial officers in the nation's leading companies.

Credit Card News
Frequency: Biweekly
Earliest NewsNet Issue: 11/1/91
Reports and analyzes events that affect the entire credit card industry. Includes marketing, legal issues, economics, and more.

Credit Risk Management Report
Frequency: Biweekly
Earliest NewsNet Issue: 1/7/91
Covers the consumer credit risk industry, with emphasis on hardware and software in evaluating consumer credit risk. Also offers current information on delinquency rates.

Dealing With Technology
Frequency: Biweekly
Earliest NewsNet Issue: 11/1/88
Reports on electronic information services and advanced technology applications in London's financial trading markets.

EFT Report
Frequency: Biweekly
Earliest NewsNet Issue: 1/5/84
Covers electronic funds-transfer issues for bankers and cash managers.

The FDIC Watch
Frequency: Weekly
Earliest NewsNet Issue: 12/6/91
Reports on developments at bank regulatory agencies that affect the nation's insured financial institutions.

Finance & Finland
Frequency: Quarterly
Earliest NewsNet Issue: 11/1/91
Provides business intelligence on industries and companies located in Finland.

Financial Services Report
Frequency: Biweekly
Earliest NewsNet Issue: 4/1/85
Provides a complete roundup of news and analysis on financial services.

FX Week
Frequency: Weekly
Earliest NewsNet Issue: 5/25/90
Provides weekly news coverage on currency trading. Reports on personnel, products, and strategies of major participants in the foreign exchange market.

Global Guaranty
Frequency: Weekly
Earliest NewsNet Issue: 3/25/91
Highlights important credit enhancement deals in public finance. Covers the U.S. public municipal and corporate bond markets, private placement markets, and Eurobond markets.

International Market Alert
Frequency: Daily
Earliest NewsNet Issue: 9/19/91
Offers comments and advice on the New York foreign exchange and credit markets. Includes analysis of major developments and economic releases and an assessment of their impact on interest and exchange rates.

Junk Bond Reporter
Frequency: Weekly
Earliest NewsNet Issue: 3/18/91
Provides in-depth analysis of the junk bond issues that investors and banks are tracking.

LDC Debt Report
Frequency: Weekly
Earliest NewsNet Issue: 1/9/89
Exclusively covers debts accrued by less developed countries (LDC). Offers help to anyone affected by this group of borrowers.

Also monitors all aspects of LDC debt, from the latest debt reduction programs to the effects that Third World borrowers have on bank earnings.

✌ MuniWeek
Frequency: Weekly
Earliest NewsNet Issue: 1/3/89
Offers information on the fixed-income securities market.

✌ POS News
Frequency: Monthly
Covers the use of debit cards and credit cards for electronic payment at the retail point of sale. Reports on strategic marketing, technology, and financial issues as they affect the use of cards at retail locations.

✌ Private Placement Reporter
Frequency: Weekly
Earliest NewsNet Issue: 3/18/91
Tracks the financing and underwriters of the major players in the largely unreported unregistered securities market. Provides reports on the structure and pricing of new deals, profiles of deal-makers, and the impact of Rule 144A.

✌ Public Finance/Washington Watch
Frequency: Weekly
Earliest NewsNet Issue: 1/9/89
Offers an insider's view of how Washington affects the financial marketplace for state and local government bonds.

✌ The Regulatory Compliance Watch
Frequency: Weekly
Earliest NewsNet Issue: 12/6/91
Reports on the changing federal regulatory environment for financial institutions. Lists important regulatory initiatives in Congress and the regulatory agencies involved in financial compliance.

✌ The RTC Watch
Frequency: Weekly
Earliest NewsNet Issue: 12/6/91
Covers the U.S. government bailout of the troubled savings and loan industry. Focuses on the operations and policies of the Resolution Trust Corporation, and on legislative and tax changes.

✌ Standard & Poor's Emerging & Special Situations
Earliest NewsNet Issue: 1/14/91
Serves aggressive investors who seek maximum capital gains through equity investments in emerging growth companies, new issues, and special situations.

✌ Standard & Poor's Review of Banking & Financial Services
Frequency: Biweekly
Earliest NewsNet Issue: 9/4/91
Offers practical analysis of regulations affecting banking and related industries.

✌ Standard & Poor's Review of Securities & Commodities Regulation
Frequency: Biweekly
Earliest NewsNet Issue: 7/1/91
Provides concise analysis of problems and developments in securities and commodities law.

✌ Thrift Liquidation Alert
Frequency: Weekly
Earliest NewsNet Issue: 10/2/89
Provides news, analysis, and listings that help users identify profit opportunities.

✌ Tokyo Financial Wire
Frequency: Daily
Earliest NewsNet Issue: 1/5/90
A daily English-language summary of news from Japan having an impact on financial markets.

✌ Trading Systems Technology
Frequency: Biweekly
Earliest NewsNet Issue: 1/4/88
Provides exclusive coverage of advanced technology applications in the financial trading arena.

✌ World Bank Watch
Frequency: Weekly
Earliest NewsNet Issue: 3/25/91
Provides news and information on projects slated for funding by the world's multilateral development banks.

General Business (GB)

✌ Corporate Giving Watch Newsletter
Frequency: Monthly
Earliest NewsNet Issue: 6/1/90
Covers trends in corporate philanthropy, new corporate funding opportunities, program changes and direct giving programs.

✌ Corporate Jobs Outlook!
Frequency: Bimonthly
Retention: One year plus current year
Publishes one hundred reports yearly, each covering one of the largest American corporations from an employee's point of view.

Foundation Giving Watch
Frequency: Monthly
Earliest NewsNet Issue: 6/1/90
Offers current information on trends in foundation philanthropy, new funding opportunities, and program changes.

German Business Scope
Frequency: Monthly
Earliest NewsNet Issue: 6/1/85
Business link between companies in Germany and the U.S., containing updated reports on German companies, as well as information on products and projects where international cooperation is sought. Contact names and addresses are included..

Incorporated News
Frequency: Monthly
Earliest NewsNet Issue: 1/1/89
Provides coverage of developments that affect the owners of small-to-medium-sized corporations.

Industries in Transition
Frequency: Monthly
Earliest NewsNet Issue: 9/1/89
Identifies and examines the markets where radical changes are taking place, as well as the causes and effects of such changes.

Nonprofit Insights
Frequency: Biweekly
Earliest NewsNet Issue: 12/16/91
Offers information for nonprofit executives on the latest management techniques, grantsmanship, fundraising, and IRS decisions.

Product Safety Letter
Frequency: Weekly
Earliest NewsNet Issue: 2/18/91
Monitors the U.S. Consumer Product Safety Commission and other key agencies. Includes coverage of industry developments, including major regulatory trends, actions, opinions, and ideas. Advance notice of new rules is a special feature.

Sales Prospector
Frequency: Monthly
Retention: One year plus current year
A monthly prospect research report for sales representatives and other business people interested in industrial, commercial, and institutional expansion, and relocation activity. The Sales Prospector reports on industrial, commercial and institutional expansions and relocations in 15 regional editions.

Insurance (IN)

Federal & State Insurance Week
Frequency: Weekly
Earliest NewsNet Issue: 2/27/87
Covers political and legislative developments affecting general insurance issues.

IMMS Weekly Marketeer
Frequency: Weekly
Earliest NewsNet Issue: 10/31/83
The week's news in the rapidly changing world of insurance and financial services.

International (IT)

Africa News
Frequency: Biweekly
Earliest NewsNet Issue: 7/4/83
Offers information on Africa's political, economic, and cultural developments, and its dealings with the U.S.

APS Diplomat
Frequency: Weekly
Earliest NewsNet Issue: 2/6/84
Covers internal and foreign policy, national defense, and regional security in the Middle East.

Asian Economic News
Frequency: Weekly
Earliest NewsNet Issue: 5/29/89
Reports on trade, debts and loans for the major players in the Far East, including South Korea, China, Taiwan, Thailand, the Philippines, Hong Kong, Singapore, and Malaysia.

Brazil Service
Frequency: Biweekly
Earliest NewsNet Issue: 1/9/91
Analyzes the political, social, and economic forces influencing Brazil's businesses.

Brazil Watch
Frequency: Biweekly
Earliest NewsNet Issue: 12/16/91
Reports on the political economy of Brazil, with briefings on economic and political developments. Each issue includes coverage of trade, finance, foreign debt, key industries, company news, and all topics of current interest.

Central America Update
Frequency: Weekly
Earliest NewsNet Issue: 1/31/86
Reports on political, economic, and social developments and U.S. policy in Central

America. Special attention is given to Nicaragua and El Salvador.

⑤ *Chronicle of Latin American Economic Affairs*
Frequency: Twice Weekly
Earliest NewsNet Issue: 1/24/86
Provides the latest on debt talks in the region, and country updates on the debt, balance of payments statistics, and political and economic developments bearing on the debt.

⑤ *Country Risk Guides*
Five separate services grouped by geographic areas.
Frequency: Monthly
Earliest NewsNet Issue: 1/1/91
Authoritative surveys of developments affecting political, economic, and financial risk regions throughout the world, providing guidance for evaluating direct investment and business opportunities. Each country is analyzed in-depth at least once a year with regular monthly updates as conditions require. The Country Risk Guides on NewsNet cover 5 separate regions: The Americas—ITll, Europe—IT12, Mid-East and North Africa—IT13, Sub-Saharan Africa—Irl4, Asia and The Pacific—IT16.

⑤ *East Asia Express Contracts—IT34*
Publisher: International Industrial Information Ltd.
Read Rate: $2.40/min. ($1.20/min.)
Frequency: Weekly
Retention: One year plus current year
Cross-referenced: FI, GB, Busops
Comprehensive catalog of opportunities for the western businessman. Lists opportunities in full, categorized by industry, with details of contacts, including telex, phone and address.

⑤ *EBRD Watch*
Frequency: Weekly
Earliest NewsNet Issue: 3/25/91
Provides advice, news and contacts to facilitate the expansion of Western business ventures into the new market economies of Eastern Europe.

⑤ *El Salvador On Line*
Frequency: Weekly
Earliest NewsNet Issue: 9/19/88
A comprehensive summary of newsbreaking events of the week dispatched from El Salvador. News is drawn from Salvadoran and U.S. dailies, church and university sources.

⑤ *European Community: Business Forecast*
Frequency: Semi-annually; Current Edition Only
A five-year forecast of the changes affecting international business, including facts and analyses aimed at helping businesses determine the right moves before and after the single market emerges in Europe.

⑤ *The Exporter*
Frequency: Monthly
Earliest NewsNet Issue: 5/1/83
Reports on the business of exporting. Functionally divided into operations, markets, training resources, and world trade information.

⑤ *Inter Press Service International News*
Frequency: Daily
Earliest NewsNet Issue: 9/5/89
Provides international, debt, human rights, environmental, and general news from the Inter Press Service (IPS) news wire. Concentrates on developing nations and international organizations. Compiled daily from the previous day's news.

⑤ *International Business Climate Indicators*
Frequency: Semiannually; Current Edition Only
A series of tables extracted from the fact sheets and forecasts of the PRS Forecast series (IT54IT60). Ranks 85 countries on political, social, and economic variables.

⑤ *The International Information Report*
Frequency: Monthly
Earliest NewsNet Issue: 9/1/88
Features about 40 news items that give descriptions of, and full contain information on, valuable information sources around the world. Widely used by company intelligence gatherers and analysts, as well as journalists, to aid them in getting information on foreign firms, multinationals, and U.S. firms with facilities overseas.

⑤ *International Reports*
Frequency: Weekly
Earliest NewsNet Issue: 1/4/91
Provides a summary and analysis of trends and developments in foreign exchange, interest rates, international debt and the economic and investment environment in important markets worldwide.

⑤ *International Travel Warning Service*
Frequency: Monthly

Retention: 26 weeks
Danger and disease warnings for international travelers, includes passport, visa, and vaccination requirements of all countries.

⑤ *Israel Commercial Economic Newsletter*
Frequency: Weekly
Earliest NewsNet Issue: 7/11/90
A synopsis of Israel's macro- and micro-economic news, categorized into 49 spheres of economic activity.

⑤ *Japan Free Press*
Frequency: Weekly
Earliest NewsNet Issue: 1/18/88
Covers a weekly synopsis of important issues, opinions, and analyses of Japan and the world, as seen and interpreted by the Japanese.

⑤ *Japan Weekly Monitor*
Frequency: Weekly
Earliest NewsNet Issue: 8/6/84
Provides a weekly recap of Japanese stock market activity, yen/dollar activity, economic indicators as released by government and industry associations, summaries of U.S.-Japan industry and government relations, and news highlights.

⑤ *Kyodo News Service*
Frequency: Daily
Cross-referenced: FI, GB, Iwires, Japan, Kyodo, Wires Transmitted from Japan Monday through Friday, this service carries major news developments in business, industries, and Japanese and Asian governments. Major market data are also included..

⑤ *Latin America Opportunity Report*
Frequency: Monthly
Earliest NewsNet Issue: 6/1/91
Provides business, investment, and economic news from the countries of the Caribbean and Latin America. Includes contact information for ventures seeking investors, and products and services seeking buyers.

⑤ *Mexico Service*
Frequency: Biweekly
Earliest NewsNet Issue: 1/2/91
Covers Mexico's financial, economic, and political climate.

⑤ *Mexico Trade and Law Reporter*
Frequency: Monthly
Earliest NewsNet Issue: 11/1/91
Practical advice on taking advantage of the

new opportunities of the Mexican market and how to avoid bad business decisions and costly mistakes. Covers the essentials of cross-border trade and investment.

⑤ *Mid-East Business Digest*
Frequency: Weekly
Earliest NewsNet Issue: 7/30/84
Summarizes the week's business stories from the regional and international press.

⑤ *Mideast Markets*
Frequency: Weekly
Earliest NewsNet Issue: 3/25/91
Reports on the commercial, financial, and governmental developments affecting business in the markets of the Middle East and North Africa.

⑤ *News From France*
Frequency: Biweekly
Earliest NewsNet Issue: 5/14/91
An English-language review of news and trends in the French press, emphasizing issues of particular interest to U.S. readers.

⑤ *North American Report on Free Trade*
Frequency: Weekly
Earliest NewsNet Issue: 12/2/91
Comprehensive analysis of all the issues affecting trade in North America. Focuses on the new trade and investment opportunities that are emerging as a result of negotiations to create a North American free trade zone.

⑤ *Northern Ireland News Service*
Frequency: Weekly
Earliest NewsNet Issue: 9/10/88
Provides coverage of social and political developments in Northern Ireland, including border disputes and contending political forces, and spokespersons.

⑤ *Opportunities Briefing: Central Europe*
Frequency: Bimonthly
Earliest NewsNet Issue: 6/1/91
Focuses on free-market trends and business opportunities in the reforming countries of eastern Europe. Provides news and analysis of political and economic developments in east-central Europe.

⑤ *Opportunities Briefing: Latin America*
Frequency: Bimonthly
Earliest NewsNet Issue: 5/1/91
Tracks economic reform and business activity in Latin America. Includes regular features on

monetary policy, commercial enterprise, law and economics, and U.S. Legislation affecting Latin America.

◐ Political Risk Services Forecasts
Frequency: Monthly—As reports are revised
Offers 18-month and 5-year forecasts of the most likely regimes and probabilities; risk ratings for turmoil, financial transfers, direct investments, and export market; as well as economic time series, social indicators, and governmental fact sheets. Each file on NewsNet summarizes one of 85 fifty-page country reports, revised annually. The Political Risk executive summaries on NewsNet cover 7 different regions: Asia & The Pacific—IT54, Eastern Europe—ITSS, Mid-East & North Africa—IT56, North & Central America—IT57, South America—IT58, Sub-Saharan Africa—IT59, Western Europe—IT60.

◐ PRS's Political Risk Letter
Frequency: Monthly
Retention: One year plus current year
Reports on political changes affecting the business environment of 70 countries. Covers export risk, manufacturing/extractive risk, and financial risk for the next 18 months, plus longer-term risk ratings.

◐ Russia Express
Frequency: Biweekly
Earliest NewsNet Issue: 4/3/89
Explores the current and future ramifications of perestroika with an eye toward opportunities for international businessmen.

◐ Russia Express Contracts
Frequency: Monthly
Earliest NewsNet Issue: 4/27/90
Lists projects for which Soviet businesses want western exports, expertise, or partnerships. Includes complete contact information.

◐ Security Intelligence Report
Frequency: Biweekly
Earliest NewsNet Issue: 11/16/87
Reports on worldwide terrorism incidents, defensive measures, government policy and regulation, business risks, new equipment and services, military activity, terror group analysis, trends in terrorism, and other security-related intelligence.

◐ SourceMex: Economic News on Mexico
Frequency: Biweekly
Earliest NewsNet Issue: ll/7/90

Covers economic conditions in Mexico, including coverage of private foreign and domestic investment, public sector finances and planning, foreign trade, foreign debt, and the oil industry.

◐ South African Focus
Frequency: Daily
Earliest NewsNet Issue: 1/8/89
A daily news summary compiled from various South African news sources, including all major newspapers in the Johannesburg/Pretoria metropolitan area.

◐ South American & Caribbean Political Affairs
Frequency: Biweekly
Earliest NewsNet Issue: 11/13/91
Provides up-to-date summary and analysis of diverse political conflicts and issues, such as military affairs, human rights, and multilateral initiatives for that region.

◐ SouthScan—Southern Africa
Frequency: Weekly
A weekly bulletin of southern African affairs, containing authoritative and timely reporting from correspondents in the field.

◐ Soviet Perspectives
Frequency: Monthly
Earliest NewsNet Issue: 3/1/91
Analyzes the movement toward free-market reform and the climate for continuing Western commercial relations with the Soviet Union.

◐ Sub-Saharan Monitor
Frequency: Monthly
Earliest NewsNet Issue: 2/1/91
Covers current political, military, and diplomatic developments in Angola and across the international spectrum with regard to the process of national reconciliation between Angola's MPLA government and UNITA's freedom fighters.

◐ Thomson International Banking Regulator
Frequency: Weekly
Earliest NewsNet Issue: 12/13/91
Provides analysis detailing the important regulatory and legislative decisions being made in key international financial centers.

◐ USSR Business
Frequency: Biweekly
Earliest NewsNet Issue: 6/190
Provides editorial commentary on Russia's economic system and how it is being prepared to

work with free-market societies. Names, addresses, and telephone numbers of contacts are included.

Washington Report: Latin America & Caribbean
Frequency: Biweekly
Earliest NewsNet Issue: 6/17/91
Describes the effect of U.S. policy on trade with, and investment in, Latin America and the Caribbean. Provides first-hand reporting of important policy decisions and interviews with key officials.

Washington Trade Daily
Frequency: Daily
Earliest NewsNet Issue: 4/29/91
Provides news on trade policy, the General Agreement on Tariffs and Trade, and import cases currently pending before the International Trade Commission and the Commerce Department.

The Week in Germany
Frequency: Weekly
Earliest NewsNet Issue: 10/2/87
Covers current events in the Federal Republic of Germany in politics, business and of general interest, compiled and edited by the German Information Center, New York, NY.

Investment

APS Review
Frequency: Weekly
Retention: One year plus current year
Divided into three sections: Oil Market Trends, Gas Market Trends, Downstream Trends.

Biotechnology Investment Opportunities
Frequency: Monthly
Retention: One year plus current year
Identifies and analyzes emerging investment opportunities in genetic engineering.

Boot Cove Economic Forecast
Frequency: Monthly
Earliest NewsNet Issue: 12/1/89
Provides information on the national economy. Includes major economic statistics.

Disclosure SEC Filings Index
Frequency: Three-Six Times Daily—Six-Week Retention
A listing of the reports filed with the U.S. Securities and Exchange Commission by over 18,000 publicly held companies issuing investment securities in the U.S. Updated continuously each weekday, excluding holidays.

International BusinessMan News Report
Frequency: Weekly
Retention: One year plus current year
Provides full contact information on and direct phone numbers to international moneymen and banks.

International Stocks Database
Frequency: Monthly
Retention: One year plus current year
Publishes current business data on corporations publicly traded on many worldwide securities exchanges. All data is edited monthly and, where applicable, updated.

Investment Management Technology
Frequency: Biweekly
Earliest NewsNet Issue: 9/20/91
Provides in-depth news and analysis on the information and technology concerns of the institutional investor marketplace.

MPT Review
Frequency: Monthly
Retention: 16 weeks
Extensive quantitative analysis on almost 100 stocks monthly, including commentary on selected stocks and market environment.

RateGram Online
Frequency: Weekly
Retention: 4 weeks
Provides an up-to-date directory of the nation's highest federally insured yields offered by banks and thrifts. Covers fixed net asset value investments, including CDs of all maturities, and money market funds.

Trendvest Ratings
Frequency: Weekly
Fully integrated market-timing and stock-selection system which provides a single numerical rating to summarize relative attractiveness of investment possibilities. No investment advice is given.

Surface Modification Technology News
Frequency: Monthly
Earliest NewsNet Issue: 6/1/91
Provides information on advanced engineered surface materials to help users keep up on the competition, examine investment opportunities, and follow production and process developments.

Office (OF)

⑤ *Advanced Office Technologies Report*
Frequency: Biweekly
Earliest NewsNet Issue: 12/14/90
Provides users and vendors with the latest office automation technology through news of products, technological breakthroughs, and industry developments.

Real Estate (RE)

⑤ *Real Estate & Venture Funding Directory*
Frequency: Annual
Provides buyers of real estate with the names, addresses, and telephone numbers of real estate lenders.

⑤ *Real Estate Buyers Directory*
Frequency: Annual
Provides sellers of real estate with the names, addresses, and telephone numbers of real estate buyers, including whether these buyers purchase for their own portfolio or for others, and the minimum and maximum amount they are investing.

⑤ *Real Estate For Sale Directory*
Frequency: Monthly
Earliest NewsNet Issue: 8/1/87
Contains a listing of real estate and businesses for sale for $500,000 and up.
Taxation (TX)

⑤ *Consolidated Returns Tax Report*
Frequency: Monthly
Earliest NewsNet Issue: 11/1/91
Offers strategies and techniques for planning the best tax results for this complex area of tax law. Also offers a look at what the IRS has in mind for consolidated returns.

⑤ *The Small Business Tax Review*
Frequency: Monthly
Earliest NewsNet Issue: 10/1/83
Provides small businesses with vital news on changes in the tax laws, IRS rulings, court cases, and pending legislation, in addition to in-depth analysis of changes that can help save taxes throughout the year.

⑤ *Tax Notes Today*
Frequency: Daily
Retention: One year plus current year
Provides comprehensive daily coverage of all federal tax developments, including Congressional hearings, court cases, IRS publications and rulings, and Treasury tax plans.

⑤ *Taxation of Mergers and Acquisitions*
Frequency: Monthly
Earliest NewsNet Issue: 11/1/91
Devoted to the tax consequences of mergers and acquisitions. Provides new tax planning strategies to reduce taxes for the buyer and the seller, the shareholders, the parent companies, and all parties to the deal.

Transport and Shipping (TS)

⑤ *Inside IVHS*
Frequency: Biweekly
Earliest NewsNet Issue: 1/21/91
Provides in-depth coverage of intelligent vehicle/highway systems development worldwide.

⑤ *Japan Transportation Scan*
Frequency: Weekly
Earliest NewsNet Issue: 1/2/89
Reports news in all areas of Japanese travel: air, land, and sea.

Travel and Tourism (TR)

⑤ *Business Travel News*
Frequency: Biweekly
Earliest NewsNet Issue: 2/25/91
Oriented toward corporate travel managers and business travel agents worldwide. Provides up-to-the-minute coverage of happenings in Washington, airline competition in Europe, hotel and rental car industries, and more.

⑤ *Tour & Travel News*
Frequency: Weekly
Earliest NewsNet Issue: 2/18/91
Tracks world conditions affecting travel, consumer trends that influence buying patterns, and new travel products, including new cruise ships, hotels, and resorts around the world.

TRW Business Profiles (TRW)

⑤ *TRW*
A premium gateway service available exclusively via NewsNet.
Producer: TRW Business Credit Services
Gateway Access Rate: 40cts/min., plus transaction fees
Frequency: Continuous Updates
TRW Business Profiles provides up-to-date payment histories on nearly 12 million business locations in the U.S. through a special gateway with NewsNet.

TRW access carries additional charges, as follows: each full report is billed at $36; TRW searches that yield a menu of matches or similar matches are billed at $5 when no report is selected from the menu. For details on using the TRW database, consult the Special Gateway Services section of the NewsNet Reference Guide.

VU/QUOTE STOCK AND COMMODITY QUOTES

◐ *(QUOTE)*
A special gateway service
Producer: Commodity News Services Inc., via Vu/Text
Gateway Access Rate: 80cts/min.
Frequency: Continuous updates during market hours
Provides information of 23 trading statistics on more than 5,200 NYSE, AMEX, and NASDAQ stocks on a 20-minute delay basis. Continuously updated reports track the biggest gainers, losers, and most active stocks.
For details on using the W/QUOTE database, consult the Special Gateway Services section of the NewsNet Reference Guide.

Bulletin Boards

CENSUS—BEA (Bureau of Economic Anaylsis) ELECTRONIC FORUM BBS

Provides census data in the form of bulletins and files that can be downloaded. Offers eight special interest groups: Open Forum, 1990 Census, TIGER, Census Economic, CD-ROM, Agriculture Census, Population Estimates & Projections, and Industry. They also offer 15 file libraries.
Availability: 24 hrs
Baud Rate: 300, 1200, 2400
BBS Number: (301) 763-7554
BBS Software: TBBS
Sysop: Nancy Smith & Jeff Newman
Help Line: (301) 763-1580 and ask for Nancy Smith, Kendall Oliphant, or John Rowe

Census Personnel BBS

Personnel Division's Electronic Bulletin Board
Displays Census Bureau vacancies from entry level to senior management. You can talk to a Personnel representative at (301) 763-5780.
Availability: 24 hrs
Baud Rate: 300, 1200, 2400
BBS Number: (301) 763-4574
BBS Software: RBBS-PC
Help Line: Ms. Sheila Ricks, College Relations, (301) 763-5780.

KIMBERELY

A public service electronic database from the Public Affairs Department of the Federal Reserve Bank in Minneapolis, Minnesota.
Baud Rate: 300, 1200, 2400
BBS Number: (612) 340-2489
BBS Software: RBBS-PC
Help Line: (612) 340-2443

FED FLASH BBS

Federal Reserve Bank of Dallas' Info Board. Contains financial information.
Baud Rate: 300, 1200, 2400, 9600
BBS Number: (214) 922-5199
BBS Software: RBBS-PC
Sysop: Linda Rueffer
Help Line: (214) 922-5173

OPM EXPRESS

A BBS for federal personnel agencies with special emphasis in training and development. Operated by the Office of Personnel Management, Human Resources Development Group, located in Dallas, Texas.
Baud Rate: 300, 1200, 2400, 9600
BBS Number: (214) 767-0565
BBS Software: PCBoard
Help Line: (214) 767-8245

W A S N E T

Office of personnel management SES openings.
Baud Rate: 300, 1200, 2400, 9600
BBS Number: (202) 606-1113
BBS Software: RBBS-PC
Help Line: (202) 606-2701

U.S. SMALL BUSINESS ADMINISTRATION SBA BBS

For the sole use of the small business administration and affiliated contractors.
Baud Rate: 300, 1200, 2400, 9600
BBS Number: (202) 205-6269 or (202) 205-6272
BBS Software: RBBS-PC

Sysop: Rick Butler & Ed Watkins
Help Line: (202) 205-6244 or (202) 205-6259

SBA Online

Helps small business men and women find information and discover resources that may help them start, maintain, expand, or operate a business.
Baud Rate: 300, 1200, 2400, 9600
BBS Number: (202) 205-7265 or 1 (800) 697-4636 (9600 bps),1 (800) 859-4636 (2400 bps)
Help Line: 1 (800) 827-5722

The CPA's BBS

Specializes in the delivery of accounting and financial information.
Availability: 24 hrs/7days
Baud Rate: 1200, 2400, 9600, 14.4
BBS Software: RBBS
BBS Number: (202) 882-9067 or (202) 882-9068
Sysop: Rob Richmond
Help Line: (202) 882-9063

BIZNET BBS

Offers special focus on business—small, home-based, and business opportunities.
Availability: 24 hours
Baud Rate: 300, 1200, 2400, 9600
BBS Number: (301) 297-9255
BBS Software: RBBS-PC
Sysop: Bob Norsworthy II,
Help Line: (301) 297-5371

The Economic Bulletin Board

A subscription based service—but new users can read 27 bulletins and download a couple of files—that offers current information produced by the Department of Commerce and other Federal government agencies. Annual subscription fee is $35 and includes 2 hours of free time. Calls made between 8 AM and noon are $12 per hour. Afternoon rates before 6PM are $9 per hours, and calls after 6PM and weekends are $3 per hour.
Availability: 24 hours/7 days
Baud Rate: 300, 1200, 2400
BBS Number: (202) 377-3870; (202) 377-0433
BBS Software: TBBS
Parameters: 8-0-1
Sysop: Ken Rogers
Help Line: (202) 377-1986
Comments: Use GUEST as your id when you first sign-on unless you are a paid member.

CD-ROM

Business Info

⑤ *American Business Disk*
American Business Informaton

⑤ *Business Indicators*
Slater Hall Information Products

⑤ *Business Lists*
American Business Information.

⑤ *Business Reference Directory*
PhoneDisc USA Corp

⑤ *Business Yellow Pages*
Innotech, Inc.

⑤ *Canadian Business & Current Affairs*
Dialog Informaton Services

⑤ *CD-Export*
Bourse de Commerce

⑤ *COMLINE*
SilverPlatter Information Inc.
One Newton Executive Park
Newton Lower Falls, MA 02162

⑤ *Corporate Affiliations*
Dialog Information Services

⑤ *County Business Patterns 86&87*
Bureau of the Census

⑤ *County Income and Employment*
Slater Hall Information Products.

⑤ *Dun's Million Dollar Discount*
Dun & Bradstreet

⑤ *European Business Guide*
Phillips International

⑤ *Federal Register Compact Disc*
Counterpoint Publishing

⑤ *Moody's 5000 Plus*
Moody's Investor Services

⑤ *Moody's Company Data*
Moody's Investor Services

⑤ *Moody's International Plus*
Moody's Investor Services

⑤ *PAIS International*
Silverplatter

⑤ *Standard & Poor's Corps.*
Standard & Poor's

⑤ *Thomas Register*
Dialog Information Services.

⑤ *US Exports of Merchandise*
Bureau of the Census

⑤ *US Exports of Merchandise*
Bureau of the Census

Construction

⑤ *Construction Criteria Base*
National Institute of Building Sciences.

⑤ *ICONDA*
SilverPlatter Information Inc.
One Newton Executive Park
Newton Lower Falls, MA 02162

Demographic

⑤ *American Profile*
Donnelley Marketing Information
70 Seaview Avenue
Stamford, CT 06904

⑤ *Cluster+ Workstation*
Donnelley Marketing Information
70 Seaview Avenue
Stamford, CT 06904

⑤ *Conquest/Canada*
Donnelley Marketing Information
70 Seaview Avenue
Stamford, CT 06904

⑤ *Consumer Lifestyles*
Donnelley Marketing Information
70 Seaview Avenue
Stamford, CT 06904

⑤ *County & City Databook*
Bureau of the Census

⑤ *County & City Statistics*
Slater Hall Information Products

⑤ *County Business Patterns 86&87*
Bureau of the Census

⑤ *Demographics Intelligence*
Strategic Intelligence System
404 Park Avenue S., Suite 1301
New York, NY 10016

⑤ *Economic Census 1987*
Bureau of the Census

⑤ *GraphicProfile*
Donnelley Marketing Information

70 Seaview Avenue
Stamford, CT 06904

⑤ *Income By Age*
Donnelley Marketing Information
70 Seaview Avenue
Stamford, CT 06904

⑤ *Market Potential*
Donnelley Marketing Information
70 Seaview Avenue
Stamford, CT 06904

⑤ *Population Statistics*
Slater Hall Information Products

⑤ *Supermap US Census Data*
Chadwyck-Healey, Inc

⑤ *TargetScan*
Donnelley Marketing Information
70 Seaview Avenue
Stamford, CT 06904

⑤ *Voter Lists*
Aristotle Industries.

Economics

⑤ *EconLit*
SilverPlatter Information Inc.
One Newton Executive Park
Newton Lower Falls, MA 02162

⑤ *Econ/Stats*
Hopkins Technology.

⑤ *Economic Census 1987*
Bureau of the Census

Health Safety

⑤ *CCINFOdisc*
CCOHS
250 Main Street, E.
Hamilton, ON L8N 1H6 Canada

Patents

⑤ *CASSIS*
NISC
3100 St. Paul Street, Suite 6
Baltimore, MD 21218

⑤ *Claims/Patent*
SilverPlatter Information Inc.
One Newton Executive Park
Newton Lower Falls, MA 02162.

❧ *Patent Information*
International Computaprint Corp.
475 Virginia Drive
Fort Washington, PA 19034

❧ *U.S. Patents*
MicroPatent
25 Science Park
New Haven, CT 06511

Safety

❧ *Material Safety Data*
National Safety Data Corp.
259 West Road
Salem, CT 06415

❧ *Material Safety Data*
Aldrich Chemical Co.
940 West St. Paul Avenue
Milwaukee, WI 53233

❧ *OHS MSDS on Disc*
Occupational Health Service
450 7th Avenue, Suite 2407
New York, NY 10123

Chemistry Resources

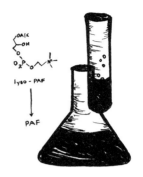

Forums & Databases

America Online (AOL)

No services available.

CompuServe (CIS)

No services available.

GEnie

No services available.

The Well

No services available.

Network Discussions Lists

Internet (Includes Bitnet & UUCPNet)

⑤ *Magyar Kemikusok Egyesuletenek Kibernetika list.*
```
CHEMCOMP@HUEARN.BITNET
LISTSERV@HUEARN.BITNET
```

⑤ *Chemistry list.*
```
CHEMCONF@UMDD.BITNET
LISTSERV@UMDD.BITNET
```

⑤ *Chemical Engineering list.*
An edited forum on the adaptation of chemical engineering in a changing world economy.
```
CHEME-L@PSUVM.BITNET
LISTSERV@PSUVM.BITNET
```
Contact: Raul Miranda
```
R0MIRA01@ULKYVM.BITNET
```

⑤ *Chemistry Education Discussion list.*
```
CHEMED-L@UWF.BITNET
LISTSERV@UWF.BITNET
```

⑤ *Chemistry in Israel list.*
Provides information on the local research activities in chemistry, including lectures, workshops, seminars, colloquia, and funding opportunities for academic investigators
```
CHEMIC-L@TAUNIVM.BITNET
ISTSERV@TAUNIVM.BITNET
```
Contact: Dr. Michael Wolff
```
WOLFF@ILNCRD.BITNET
```

⑤ *Computational Chemistry list.*
Maintained by the Ohio Supercomputer Center. Topics discussed include quantum chemistry, molecular mechanics/dynamics, molecular modeling, and molecular graphics.
```
Chemistry@osc.edu
CHEMISTRY-REQUEST@oscsunb.osc.edu
```
Contact: Jan Labanowski
```
<JKL@OHSTPY.BITNET>
```

⑤ *Chemical Information Sources*
Discusses topics related to chemistry and the sources used to find information about chemical compounds.
```
CHMINF-L@IUBVM.BITNET
LISTSERV@IUBVM.BITNET
```
Contact: Gary Wiggins
```
<WIGGINS@IUBACS.BITNET>
```

⑤ *Nitric Oxide/L-Arginine Discussion list.*
```
NO-L-ARG@UKACRL.BITNET
LISTSERV@UKACRL.BITNET
```

⑤ *Organic Chemistry*
For collaborative efforts (teaching and/or research activities) between specialists in Organic Chemistry and related areas.
```
ORGCHE-L@RPICICGE.BITNET
MSMITH@AMHERST.BITNET
```
Contact: Asuncion Valles
```
<D3Q0AVC0@EB0UB011.BITNET>
```

Fidonet

No services available.

Usenet

⑤ *Chemistry and related sciences.*
sci.chem

⑤ *All aspects of chemical engineering.*
sci.engr.chem

Online Libraries

After Dark

⑤ *Current Contents: Physical Chemical & Earth Sciences*
A subset of Current Contents Search™ corresponding to the *Current Contents: Physical, Chemical and Earth Sciences* edition.
Coverage: Most current 12 months
Updated: Weekly

⑤ *Kirk-Othmer Encyclopedia of Chemical Technology*
The online version of the 25-volume *Kirk-Othmer Encyclopedia of Chemical Technology* (3rd edition) and *Wiley's Encyclopedia of Polymer Science and Engineering* (2nd edition).
Coverage: Includes about 1,200 articles from the 24-volume Encyclopedia plus the 25th supplement.
Updated: Concurrent with the publication of each new volume.

⑤ *NTIS (National Technical Information Service) Bibliographic Database*
U.S. and foreign government-sponsored research reports and studies in the physical sciences, technology, engineering, biological sciences, medicine and health sciences, agriculture, and social sciences.
Coverage: 1970 to present
Updated: Monthly

Knowledge Index

⑤ *Agrochemicals Handbook*
Information on the active components of agrochemical products used worldwide.
Coverage: Current
Updated: Semiannually

⑤ *Analytical Abstracts*
Covers all aspects of analytical chemistry—any general application, inorganic chemistry,

organic chemistry, pharmaceutical chemistry, environmental agriculture, and more.
Coverage: 1980 to the present
Updated: Monthly

⑤ *Kirk-Othmer Online*
A comprehensive treatise of applied chemical science and industrial technology, its methods and materials, as well as the latest scientific advances in every branch of chemistry.
Coverage: 3rd edition of the Kirk-Othmer Encyclopedia of Chemical Technology
Updated: Irregular

Orbit

⑤ *Analytical Abstracts*
Abstracts on analytical chemistry, covering general, inorganic, organic, biochemical, pharmaceutical, food, agricultural, and environmental aspects, including computer and instrumental applications.
Coverage: 1980 to present
Updated: Monthly

⑤ *Beilstein*
Includes material on preparations and reactions, purification processes, chemical behavior, structure data, and physical data such as spectral, mechanical and electrical properties.
Coverage: 1779 to 1979
Updated: Periodically

⑤ *Biotechnology Abstracts*
Contains information on all technical aspects of biotechnology from genetic manipulation and biochemical engineering to fermentation and downstream processing, as well as industrial use of micro-organisms, inplant breeding, cell hybridization, industrial waste management, and related fields.
Coverage: July 1982 to present
Updated: Monthly

⑤ *Chemical Abstracts*
Worldwide coverage of chemical sciences literature from over 9,000 journals, patents from 27 countries, and more. Corresponds to the printed Chemical Abstracts.
Coverage: 1977 to present
Updated: Bimonthly

⑤ *Chemical Abstracts Service Source Index*
Bibliographic and library holdings information for scientific and technical primary literature in the chemical sciences.
Coverage: 1907 to present
Updated: Quarterly

Chemical Dictionary
A companion file to the Chemical Abstracts databases.
Coverage: 1957 to present
Updated: Monthly

Chemical Economics Handbook
International supply/demand data for the chemical industry through the full-text database of the world's leading chemical market research service.
Coverage: 1955 to present
Updated: Monthly

Chemical Engineering and Biotechnology Abstracts
Covers theoretical, practical, and commercial aspects of chemical engineering, plus process and reaction engineering, measurement and process control, environmental protection, plant design, and relevant equipment.
Coverage: 1971 to present
Updated: Monthly

Chemical Industry Notes
Contains worldwide chemical industry citations related to production, sales, pricing, facilities, products, processes, corporate/government activities, and people.
Coverage: 1974 to present
Updated: Weekly

Chemical Reactions Documentation Service
Current information on new developments in the field of synthetic organic chemistry. The monthly Journal of Synthetic Methods supplies data. Access limited to CRDS subscribers.
Coverage: 1942 to present
Updated: Monthly

Chemical Safety NewsBase
Covers information on the health and safety effects of hazardous chemicals encountered by employees in industry and laboratories.
Coverage: 1981 to present
Updated: Monthly

ChemQuest
Lists over 91,000 commercially important compounds, including organics, inorganics, biochemicals, dyes, and stains, plus suppliers.
Coverage: Current
Updated: Semi-annually

Corrosion
Over 24,000 records on the effects of widely-used metals, plastics, nonmetallics, and rubbers over a temperature range of 40 to 560 degrees Fahrenheit.
Coverage: Current
Updated: Periodically

PESTDOC
Covers worldwide literature on insecticides, herbicides, fungicides, molluscicides, and rodenticides as relative to analysis, biochemistry, chemistry, and toxicology.
Coverage: 1968 to present
Updated: Quarterly

RINGDOC
Covers worldwide pharmaceutical literature related to the needs of manufacturers.
Coverage: 1964 to present
Updated: Monthly

Standard Drug File
A companion to RINGDOC. Lists approximately 7,500 known drugs and compounds.
Coverage: Current
Updated: Periodically

Standard Pesticide File
A companion to PESTDOC. Lists approximately 3,900 known pesticides, including full name and standard registry name, chemical substructure terms, chemical ring codes, and other codes.
Coverage: Current
Updated: Periodically

VETDOC
Covers worldwide journal literature on veterinary applications of drugs, hormones, vaccines, and growth patterns for use in domestic and farm animals.
Coverage: 1968 to present
Updated: Quarterly

NewsNet

Chemical Engineering
Frequency: Monthly
Earliest NewsNet Issue: 9/1/91
Offers information on technologies used by worldwide chemical process industries.

The Chemical Monitor
Frequency: Monthly
Earliest NewsNet Issue: 5/1/86
Reviews technical and market information on chemical instrumentation. Focuses on new developments and applications in transducer systems.

◔ *Comline Japan Daily: Chemicals*
Frequency: Daily
Cross-referenced: IT, RD, Comline, Japan
Reports on new chemical materials and processes.

◔ *Hazardous Waste News*
Frequency: Weekly
Earliest NewsNet Issue: 1/4/82
Coverage of federal and state hazardous-waste management legislation, regulations, and litigation.

◔ *Hazmat Transport News*
Frequency: Biweekly
Earliest NewsNet Issue: 3/26/85
Covers legislation, regulations, investigations, and litigation concerning transport of hazardous materials by truck, rail, air, or barge.

◔ *Pesticide & Toxic Chemical News*
Frequency: Weekly
Covers pesticides, hazardous wastes, and toxic substances, including related regulatory decisions.

◔ *Plastics Business News*
Frequency: Biweekly
Earliest NewsNet Issue: 2/27/91
Provides news and information on new products, alternate uses of plastics, acquisitions and mergers, production and distribution processes, and environmental developments in light of "green" trends.

◔ *Platt's International Petrochemical Report*
Frequency: Weekly
Earliest NewsNet Issue: 9/12/91
For executives who manufacture, market, and distribute petroleum products. Coverage includes supply and demand trends.

◔ *State Environment Report*
Frequency: Biweekly
Earliest NewsNet Issue: 3/15/85
Covers toxic substance control and hazardous-waste management at the state level, as well as national developments from a state perspective.

◔ *Toxic Materials News*
Frequency: Weekly
Earliest NewsNet Issue: 1/6/82
Coverage of decisions pertaining to the Toxic Substances Control Act, as well as state and local activities, research and development, grants, contracts, publications and meetings.

Bulletin Boards
No services available.

CD-ROM

◔ *ADONIS*
Adonis B.V.

◔ *Analytical Abstracts*
SilverPlatter Information Inc.

◔ *CD-CHROM*
Preston Publications

◔ *CHEMBANK*
SilverPlatter Information Inc.
One Newton Executive Park
Newton Lower Falls, MA 02162

◔ *EI-CHEMDISC*
Dialog Information Services

◔ *EINECS Plus*
SilverPlatter Information Inc.

◔ *Encyclopedia of Chemical Technology*
John Wiley & Sons, Inc.
605 Third Avenue
New York, NY 10158

◔ *Kirk-Othmer Encyclopedia of Chemical Technology*
Dialog Information Service
3460 Hillview Avenue
Palo Alto, CA 94304

◔ *Mark Encyclopedia of Polymers*
John Wiley & Sons, Inc.
605 Third Avenue
New York, NY 10158

◔ *NIST/EPA/MSCE Mass Spectral Database*
Aldrich Chemical

◔ *OHS-ROM*
Occupational Health Services

◔ *Powder Diffraction*
International Center for Diffraction
2602 Park Lane
Swarthmore, PA 19801

◔ *Registry of Mass Spectral Data*
John Wiley & Sons

Communications Resources

Forums & Databases
America Online (AOL)

☙ *Communications/Networking Forum (Mac); Telecom & Networks (PC)*
Path: Computing & Software Department
Keywords: Mac Telecom, PC Telecom
For those interested in communications. The Mac forum is the richer in information. Special interest groups and public domain/shareware libraries are available.

☙ *Networker's Journal*
Path: News & Reference Department > Networker's Journal
Keyword: Networkers Journal
Every week, telecommunications expert Charlie Bown posts a synopsis of what's new on the commercial online services.

CompuServe (CIS)
No services available.

GEnie
No services available.

The Well
No services available.

Network Discussions Lists
Internet (Includes Bitnet & UUCPNet)

☙ *Blacksburg Electronic Village Open Discussion list.*
```
BEVPUB-L@VTVM1.BITNET
LISTSERV@VTVM1.BITNET
```

☙ *Communication & International Development list.*
```
COMDEV@RPIECS.BITNET
LISTSERV@RPIECS.BITNET
```

☙ *Communication Research and Theory Net list.*
Discusses all aspects of human communication.
```
CRTNET@PSUVM.BITNET
LISTSERV@PSUVM.BITNET
```
Contact: Tom Benson
```
T3B@PSUVM.BITNET
```

☙ *Disciplinary Practices in Communication Studies list.*
```
DISPRAC@RPICICGE.BITNET
COMSERVE@RPIECS.BITNET
```
Contact: Comserve Editorial Staff
```
PPORT@RPIECS.BITNET
```

☙ *Online Journal of Distance Education and Communication list.*
```
DISTED@UWAVM.BITNET
LISTSERV@UWAVM.BITNET
```
Contact: Paul J. Coffin
```
JXPJC@ALASKA.BITNET
```

☙ *Electronic Journal of Communication list.*
```
EJCREC@RPIECS.BITNET
LISTSERV@RPIECS.BITNET
```

☙ *List for Free-talking*
For talk about anything.
```
FREETALK@KRSNUCC1.BITNET
LISTSERV@KRSNUCC1.BITNET
```
Contact: Kim Eunkyung
```
<EGKIM@KRSNUCC1.BITNET>
```

☙ *Communication and Gender list.*
```
GENDER@RPICICGE.BITNET
COMSERVE@RPIECS.BITNET
```

☙ *Interpersonal/Small Group Communication list.*
```
INTERPER@RPICICGE.BITNET
COMSERVE@RPIECS.BITNET
```

☙ *LHU Forum list.*
```
LHU-L@ALBNYDH2.BITNET
LISTSERV@ALBNYDH2.BITNE
```

☙ *New Books in Communication list.*
```
NEWBOOKS@RPIECS.BITNET
LISTSERV@RPIECS.BITNET
```

☙ *South Bend (USA) Conversation lists.*
An experiment in networking for computer users in north central Indiana and southwest lower Michigan.
```
SBN@INDYCMS.BITNET
LISTSERV@IndyCMS.BITNET
```
Contact: John B Harlan
```
<JBHarlan@IndyVAX.BITNET>
```

☙ *Studies in Communication and Information Technology list.*
```
SCIT-L@QUCDN.BITNET
LISTSERV@QUCDN.BITNET
```
Contact: Elia Zureik
```
SCITDOC@QUCDN.BITNET
```

☙ *History of the Printed Word list.*
```
SHARP-L@IUBVM.BITNET
LISTSERV@IUBVM.BITNET
```
Contact: Patrick Leary
```
<pleary@IUBACS.BITNET>
```

☙ *Human Communication, Social Networks & Simulation list.*
For users interested in human communication, social networks, or simulation of complex phenomena.
```
SNET-L@ARIZVM1.BITNET
LISTSERV@ARIZVM1.BITNET
```
Contact: Ash Bose
```
<BOSE@ARIZVM1.BITNET>
```

☙ *Electronic Communications and Pen Pal list.*
```
TESLEC-L@CUNYVM.BITNET
LISTSERV@CUNYVM.BITNET
```

☙ *Intercultural Communication sublist.*
```
TESLIC-L@CUNYVM.BITNET
LISTSERV@CUNYVM.BITNET
```

☙ *Grupo de discussao e divulgacao da UNCED list.*
```
UNCE92-L@BRUFMG.BITNET
LISTSERV@BRUFMG.BITNET
```

Fidonet

☙ *Alpha-Omega Open Forum*
```
ALPHA
```

Viewpoints on all subjects, presented and discussed in a reasonably intelligent manner.
Moderator: E.A. Richards
```
1:154/414
```
Distribution: BACKBONE

☙ *Bitch Forum*
```
BITCH
```
A general chatter conference used as a forum to express a favorite complaint, or "bitch" in general.
Moderator: Ron Allard
```
8:954/401
```
Gateways: RBBS-NET VIA 8:8/8

☙ *Free-Form Free-Speech Forum*
```
CHAOS_LANDING
```
Moderator: Dale Springfield
```
1:124/5114
```
Distribution: BACKBONE

☙ *Mindless Chatter Conference*
```
CHATTER
```
A forum for utter nonsense, with no chance of seriousness.
Moderator: Joe Boburka
```
1:139/910
```
Distribution: BACKBONE

☙ *Gossip and Chit-Chat with Household Overtones*
```
COFFEE_KLATSCH
```
A general chatter conference for people interested in world and national events as well as what goes on in the home.
Moderator: Tia Darrow
```
1:128/68
```
Distribution: BACKBONE

☙ *Controversial Forum*
```
CONTROV
```
Discussions of controversial topics, current events, and contemporary attitudes, with no (or very few) holds barred.
Moderator: Charles Hill
```
1:147/61
```
Distribution: BACKBONE

☙ *Debate Conference*
```
DEBATE
```
For debate and discussion on a wide range of political, historical, contemporary, and philosophical topics. Forceful discussions are encouraged.
Moderator: Lester Garrett
```
1:125/101
```
Distribution: BACKBONE
Gateways: RBBS-NET

⑤ *Serious and Humorous SysOp Chatter*
ECHO50
A required conference for Echonet SysOps.
Moderator: John Radford
1:261/1083
Distribution: ECHONET BACKBONE (ZONE 50)

⑤ *National Flame! Echo*
FLAME
For heated, "no-holds-barred" debate on anything a user wants to flame (argue) about.
Moderator: John Clifton
1:153/6.4
Distribution: BACKBONE

⑤ *General Chitchat Conference for EchoNet Users*
FORUM
General conversation with participants throughout the U.S. and Canada.
Moderator: Ed Lawyer
1:261/1056
Distribution: ECHONET BACKBONE (ZONE 50)

⑤ *International General Conversation Forum*
INTERUSER
For the sharing of ideas, opinions, knowledge, and friendship with people worldwide. Any topic but computers. English-speaking only.
Moderator: Daan van Rooijen
2:512/1.2
Distribution: BACKBONE, TAP, TIPTOP, WORLD
Gateways: ZONE-2 VIA 1:260/1, ZONE-6 VIA 1:13/13

⑤ *Nostalgia*
MEMORIES
A forum about the good old days.
Moderator: Ronnie Toth
1:135/71
Distribution: BACKBONE

⑤ *Original and Highly Active Nostalgia/Trivia*
MEMORY_LANE
For users who enjoy looking to the future while cherishing the past.
Moderator: Ed Lawyer
1:261/1056
Distribution: ECHONET BACKBONE (ZONE 50)

⑤ *Chitchat for Modeming Moms*
MOM_TALK
A forum for mothers who enjoy chatting with other mothers on any topic.
Moderator: Bonnie Lind
1:369/18
Distribution: ECHONET BACKBONE (ZONE 50)

⑤ *Tough Debates Handled Gently, Almost*
PROS&CONS
A forum for users who enjoy robust debates without flaming one another—too much.
Moderator: James Ray
1:124/6002
Distribution: ECHONET BACKBONE (ZONE 50)

⑤ *The Serious Side*
SERIOUS_SIDE
A forum for non-inflammatory discussion of serious issues.
Moderator: Mike Riddle
1:285/27
Distribution: Primarily Great Plains And Colorado's Eastern Slope
Gateways: 1:104/424 1:285/2

⑤ *USA-Europe Link*
USA_EURLINK
A non-topical, non-political conference for enhancing the exchange of information between the U.S. and Europe.
Moderator: Brenda Donovan
1:202/701
Distribution: BACKBONE, ZONE-2
Gateways: 1:133/701 VIA 100:4000/503, 2:2/777 VIA 1:105/42

Usenet

⑤ *Communication education.*
bit.listserv.commed

Online Libraries
After Dark
No services available.

Knowledge Index
No services available.

Orbit

No services available.

NewsNet

No services available.

Bulletin Boards
Society For Technical Communication (STC) BBS

For members of STC. Access to the society mailing list, job leads, calendar of events, internships, and more.
Availability: 24 hours/ 7 days
Baud Rate: 300, 1200, 2400, 9600, 19.2
BBS Number: (703) 522-3299
BBS Software: WILDCAT
Sysop: Peter Herbst
Help Line: (703) 522-4114

CD-ROM

⚲ *Business Reference Directory*
PhoneDisc USA Corp.

⚲ *Business Yellow Pages CDROM*
Innotech, Inc.

⚲ *InfoDirect*
Compact Publications, Inc.

⚲ *National Directory Addresses/Phone Numbers*
General Information

⚲ *North American Facsimile (FAX) Book*
Quanta Press

⚲ *PhoneDisc USA*
PhoneDisc USA Corp.

⚲ *SpeedDial National Business Telephone Directory*
DataWare Technologies

Computer Resources

Forums & Databases
America Online (AOL)

🕙 *Newsbytes*
Keyword: Newsbytes
Path: News & Finance Department > Newsbytes
Covers the latest computer industry news. New issues appear daily.

🕙 *Networker's Journal*
Keyword: Networkers Journal
Path: News & Reference Department > Networker's Journal
Every week, telecommunications expert Charlie Bown posts a synopsis of what is new on the commercial on-line services.

🕙 *Home-Office Computing Magazine*
Path: News & Finance Department > Home-Office Computing
The on-line version of *Home Office Computing*. Includes access to the monthly Buyer's Guide (a roundup of comparison reviews).

🕙 *PC Novice/PC Today Magazines*
Path: News & Finance Department > PC Novice/PC Today Magazines
For novice computer users. Monthly articles explain the basics.

🕙 *PC Catalog*
Keyword: PC Catalog
Path: Travel & Shopping Department > PC Catalog
Lists thousands of hardware, software and other items available from price-competitive mail order vendors.

🕙 *Publications for Computers*
Keyword: bookstore
Path: Travel & Shopping Department > Publications for Computers
Lists hundreds of computer books from top publishers. Prices are discounted from list, and Publications for Computers promises shipment within two business days.

🕙 *Industry Connection*
Keyword: IC
Path: Computing & Software Department > Industry Connection
Offers on-line support from some of the leading hardware and software manufacturers. Over 140 PC, Windows, Mac, and Apple II companies support their products on-line, providing message boards for individual help, product information, frequently asked questions and answers, and software libraries full of upgrades, demos, utilities, and templates.

🕙 *Microsoft Knowledge Base*
Keyword: Microsoft
Path: Computing & Software Department > Microsoft Knowledge Base
This is the database the Microsoft customer support staff uses to answer questions. Searchable by keyword and phrase.

🕙 *Computing Forums*
Keyword: forums
Path: Computing & Software Department
Run by computing experts—forum leaders— each forum is a source of information about a given computer topic, a self-contained "special interest group" that includes message boards, live conferences, sub-groups, and software libraries. A plethora of topics are covered.

Contains over 30,000 each of DOS/Windows, Mac, and Apple II shareware and public domain files, searchable using "File Search."

⑤ Macworld Online
Keyword: Macworld
Path: Computing & Software Department > Macworld Online
The on-line version of the popular magazine. Contains recent reviews. Users may search past issues, discuss matters with other Mac users, and communicate with *Macworld's* editors.

⑤ Mac and Windows Shareware 500 Libraries
Keywords: Mac500, Windows500
Path: Computing & Software Department
Makes available high-quality shareware for the Mac and Windows. Files arranged by type—games, graphics, utilities, sounds, fonts, and so on.

CompuServe (CIS)

⑤ CompuServe Classifieds
GO CLASSIFIEDS
For browsing or posting an ad to sell unwanted items. National in scope. There is a surcharge for ad posting.

⑤ CompuServe Mail Hub
GO MHS or MHSADM
A global message exchange facility, giving NetWare MHS users the ability to communicate without having to dial each individual MHS site directly. Also allows message exchange with any CompuServe member and others.

⑤ Abacus
GO ABACUS
Provides technical support for Abacus utility applications.

⑤ Access Softek
GO WINAPA
Provides technical support for Access Softek applications.

⑤ Acer America
GO ACER
Provides technical support for Acer America's full line of computer systems.

⑤ ACIUS Forum
GO ACIUS
Supports all ACIUS products.

⑤ Activision (Tenpointo)
GO MACAVEN

Support for products such as Focal Point II and City to City in the Activision section of the Mac A Vendor Forum.

⑤ Adobe Forum
GO ADOBE
Operated by the Adobe technical support staff. For users, dealers, service bureaus, developers and other interested parties to discuss desktop publishing, especially of interest to users of Adobe products.

⑤ Advanced Gravis Computer Technology
GO PCVENB
For support of Advanced Gravis' full line of products.

⑤ AI Expert Forum
GO AIEXPERT
For information exchange in the artificial intelligence community and a supplement to *AI Expert* magazine. Makes available program listings and public domain expert systems software for downloading.

⑤ Aimtech
GO MULTIVEN
Supports IconAuthor, a Windows-based interactive multimedia authoring system.

⑤ Aladdin Systems, Inc.
GO MACCVEN
Supports Shortcut, StuffIt and StuffIt Deluxe.

⑤ Aldus Customer Services Forum
GO ALDSVC
Provides Aldus and Silicon Beach software users with upgrade and release information, as well as on-line support for customers with registered products. Libraries contain sneak previews of new and updated Aldus products. For technical questions, access the Silicon Beach/Aldus Public Forum, GO SBSALD.

⑤ Alpha Software
GO PCVENE
Presents product information and technical support from Alpha Software for Alpha Four, a networkable relational database management and application development system.

⑤ Altsys Corporation
GO MACBVEN
Offers technical support for Altsys products.

⑤ Alysis
GO MACCVEN
For technical support from Alysis.

⑤ *Amaze*
GO AMAZE

Supports Amaze's series of computer calendars.

⑤ *American Cybernetics*
GO CYBERNET

Provides support and information for American Cybernetics' line of products.

⑤ *American Power Conversion*
GO APCSUPPORT

Supplies information and technical support for American Power Conversion products.

⑤ *Amiga and Commodore Users Network*
GO CBMNET

Accesses seven forums devoted to Commodore computers.

⑤ *Amiga Arts Forum*
GO AMIGAARTS

For users at all levels with an interest in the creative aspects of the Amiga personal computer. Offers conference rooms, libraries, and message boards broken down by topic.

⑤ *Amiga File Finder*
GO AMIGAFF

Allows reference to some of the programs and files available in the Amiga Arts, Tech, User, and Vendor forums. Users can find the file they want using numerous search criteria.

⑤ *Amiga Tech Forum*
GO AMIGATECH

For all users interested in the technical aspects of the Amiga personal computer. Members have access to various sections of the message board, the on-line conferencing feature, libraries of public domain programs, and more—all free and available for downloading.

⑤ *Amiga User Forum*
GO AMIGAUSER

Dedicated to the use of Amiga computers. Offers message boards and classifieds.

⑤ *Amiga Vendor Forum*
GO AMIGAVENDOR

For discussions about Amiga products and finding support from selected product vendors. Vendors' individual descriptions and supported products included.

⑤ *APPC Info Exchange Forum*
GO APPCFORUM

Discusses topics related to the design and implementation of applications using Advanced Program-to-Program Communications (APPC).

⑤ *Apple Macintosh Forums*
GO MACINTOSH

Offers Macintosh users a variety of forums.

⑤ *Apple II Programmers' Forum*
GO APPROG

Teaches users how to create their own applications for their Apple II. Members exchange programming tips and application ideas.

⑤ *Apple II Users Forum*
GO APPUSER

Information on the Apple II and available programs. Offers message sections and libraries on choosing and using hardware and software programs. Many members are Apple II experts and can offer sound advice in purchasing and using products.

⑤ *Apple II Vendor Forum*
GO APIIVEN

Offers expert advice and support for Apple II purchasers. Manufacturer representatives answer questions about their products on-line.

⑤ *Apple II/III Forums*
GO APPLE II/III

Devoted to the Apple II, II+, IIe, IIc, IIGS and III.

⑤ *Aristosoft*
GO ARISTOSOFT

Provides support for Aristosoft products.

⑤ *Art Gallery Forum*
GO ARTGALLERY

Offers graphic images which push the upper limits of resolution, file size, and artistic ability.

⑤ *Articulate Systems*
GO MACAVEN

Provides support for Articulate Systems products.

⑤ *Artisoft Forum*
GO ARTISOFT

Provides support for Artisoft products.

⑤ *AdPro Forum*
GO AMIGAVENDOR

Provides support for the AdPro product.

⑤ *Ashlar Incorporated*
GO ADDVEN

Provides support for Ashlar applications.

⑤ *Ashton-Tate Support Library*
GO ASHTON

Provides support for Ashton-Tate products.

🍪 *Ask3Com*
GO ASK
Covers global data networking subjects.

🍪 *ASP/Shareware Forum*
GO ASPFORUM
For computer users who want to try software before buying it. You can communicate directly with ASP members or members of the forum knowledgeable about shareware.

🍪 *Asymetrix Corporation*
GO ASYMETRIX or MULTIVENDOR
Provides support for Asymetrix Corporation products.

🍪 *Atari 8-Bit Forum*
GO ATARI8
Not affiliated with Atari Corporation. Centers on the Atari 8-bit computer. Libraries contain programs, text files, help information, and more.

🍪 *Atari File Finder*
GO ATARIFF
A comprehensive, searchable database of files found in the Atari forums, including the Atari ST Productivity Forum, Atari ST Arts Forum, and Atari Vendors Forum.

🍪 *Atari Portfolio Forum*
GO APORTFOLIO
Provides support for Atari's hand-held Portfolio computer.

🍪 *Atari ST Arts Forum*
GO ATARIARTS
Supports and exchanges information on art and entertainment software for the Atari 16-bit (ST) series of computers.

🍪 *Atari ST Productivity Forum*
GO ATARIPRO
Connects members worldwide with an interest in the exchange of information and programs. Support and information for productivity software for the Atari 16-bit (ST) series of computers.

🍪 *Atari Users Network*
GO ATARINET
Forums for the 8-bit computer, the 16-bit computer, the Atari Portfolio, vendor support, and an electronic magazine.

🍪 *Atari Vendors Forum*
GO ATARIVEN
Provides access to Atari-related software and hardware vendors.

🍪 *ATI*
GO AMIGAVENDOR
Provides support for ATI's Whap! communications program.

🍪 *ATI Technologies Inc.*
GO ATITECH
Provides support for ATI products.

🍪 *Attitash*
GO ATTITASH
Provides support for Attitash utility products.

🍪 *Autodesk AutoCAD Forum*
GO ACAD
Hints and techniques for using various Autodesk products.

🍪 *Autodesk Retail Products Forum*
GO ARETAIL
Provides information and support for Autodesk or Generic Software products.

🍪 *Autodesk Software Forum*
GO ASOFT
Provides support for Autodesk multimedia and Science Series products.

🍪 *Automated Design Systems*
GO ADSINFO
Provides support for Windows Workstation.

🍪 *Avant-Garde Software Inc.*
GO AMIGAVENDOR
Provides support for Avant-Garde's product line.

🍪 *Avatar Corporation*
GO MACCVEN
Provides support for Avatar Corporation products.

🍪 *Banyan Forum*
GO BANFORUM
Provides support for Banyan network products and more.

🍪 *Banyan Systems*
GO BANYAN
Provides support and information for Banyan products. Members can send electronic feedback directly to Banyan.

🍪 *Baseline Publishing*
GO MACCVEN or WINAPD
Provides technical support for Baseline Publishing and Preferred Publishers products.

🍪 *BASIC Forum*
GO MSBASIC

Provides support for users of Microsoft's BASIC, QuickBasic and Visual Basic software.

⑤ *BASIS International Forum*
  GO BASIS
Provides support and information for BASIS software products.

⑤ *BCD Associates*
  GO MULTIVEN
Provides technical support for BCD Associates' interfaces.

⑤ *Bell Atlantic*
  GO THINX
Provides support for Bell Atlantic for Thinx.

⑤ *Bentley Systems*
  GO MSTATION
Provides support for the MicroStation product line.

⑤ *Berkeley Systems (Macintosh)*
  GO ADMAC
Provides technical support for After Dark, ScreenKeys, Stepping Out II, outSPOKEN, inLARGE and inTOUCH.

⑤ *Berkeley Systems (Windows)*
  GO ADWIN
Provides support for After Dark.

⑤ *Beyond, Inc.*
  GO BEYOND
Provides support for BeyondMail.

⑤ *Big Noise Software, Inc.*
  GO MIDIAVENDOR
Provides support for Big Noise's MIDI-based products.

⑤ *Black Belt Systems*
  GO AMIGAVENDOR
Provides support for Black Belt hardware and software.

⑤ *BLOC Publishing Corporation*
  GO BLOCPUB
Provides support for FormTool, FormFiller, Personal Law Firm, FastPak Mail and Diskvision.

⑤ *Blyth Software Forum*
  GO BLYTH
Provides technical support and user contacts for Blyth products.

⑤ *Borland Applications Forum*
  GO BORAPP
Technical support for Borland applications. Users can communicate with support personnel as well as other forum members.

⑤ *Borland Applications Forum B*
  GO BORAPB
Provides support for Borland products.

⑤ *Borland C++/DOS Forum*
  GO BCPPDOS
For programming information exchange among Borland International software users. For information about C and C++ for the Windows environment, see Borland C++/Windows Forum (GO BCPPWIN).

⑤ *Borland C++/Windows Forum*
  GO BCPPWIN
Provides support for Borland's C, C++, and related Windows programming tools. For information about C, C++ and Assembler for DOS environments, see Borland C++/DOS Forum (GO BCPPDOS).

⑤ *Borland Database Products Forum*
  GO BORDB
Provides technical support and information exchange for Borland database products.

⑤ *Borland GmbH Forum*
  GO BORGMBH
Provides technical support and information exchange for Borland's German-speaking customer base.

⑤ *Borland International*
  GO BORLAND
For users of Borland software; information about Borland International. Suggestion box and nine forums.

⑤ *Borland Programming Forum A*
  GO BPROGA
For exchange of tips, techniques, and information related to programming with Borland International software.

⑤ *Borland Quattro Pro Forum*
  GO QUATTROPRO
Provides technical support and information exchange for Borland's Quattro, Quattro Pro or Quattro Pro for Windows spreadsheet programs.

⑤ *Brightbill-Roberts*
  GO PCVENC
Provides support for HyperPAD and Show Partner F/X.

⑤ *Brightwork Development*
  GO BRIGHT
Provides support for Sitelock, PS-Print, NetRemote, LAN Support Center, and LAN Automatic Inventory.

Broderbund
GO MACAVEN or PCVENA
Provides support for Broderbund products.

ButtonWare, Inc.
GO PCVENA
Provides support for PC-File+, PC-Type II, Baker's Dozen, PC-Tickle, PC-Stylist, and PC-Dial.

CA Application Development Forum
GO CAIDEV
Provides support and information exchange for CA application development solutions. For information on additional CA products, see the CA Clipper Forum (GO CLIPPER), CA Productivity Solutions Forum (GO CAIPRO) and CA Vax/Unix Forum (GO CAIMINI).

CA Clipper Forum
GO CLIPPER
Offers tips and information to Clipper users. Members and CA representatives help you fine tune your projects. See also the CA Application Development Forum (GO CAIDEV), CA Productivity Solutions Forum (GO CAIPRO) and CA Vax/Unix Forum (GO CAIMINI).

CA Clipper Germany Forum
GO NANGMBH
Provides support for German-speaking Clipper users in Germany, Switzerland and Austria. For additional CA support, see the CA Clipper Forum (GO CLIPPER).

CA Productivity Solutions Forum
GO CAIPRO
Provides technical support and information for various CA products. See also the CA Application Development Forum (GO CAIDEV), CA Clipper Forum (GO CLIPPER) and CA VAX/Unix Forum (GO CAIMINI).

CA Vax/Unix Forum
GO CAMINI
Provides technical support and information exchange for Computer Associates Vax and Unix products. See also the CA Application Development Forum (GO CAIDEV), CA Clipper Forum (GO CLIPPER) and CA Productivity Solutions Forum (GO CAIPRO).

Cabletron Systems, Inc.
GO CTRON
Provides support for Cabletron LAN services and products.

CADD/CAM/CAE Vendor Forum
GO CADDVEN
Provides support and information for computer-aided design, manufacturing, and engineering software and hardware from various companies.

Cadkey, Inc.
GO CADKEY
Provides support for Cadkey's computer-aided design software.

Campbell Services
GO ONTIME
A support forum for OnTime for Windows, a personal information manager.

Canon Support Forum
GO CANON
Provides support and information exchange for Canon products.

CASE—DCI Forum
GO CASEFORUM
For software developers using CASE tools; members share information and tips.

CASEWORKS
GO CASEW
Provides support for Casework's applications development software, including CASE:W and CASE:PM.

Casio Inc.
GO PALMTOP
Provides support for Casio's B.O.S.S. line of electronic organizers.

CDROM Forum
GO CDROM
For information about CDROM technology.

CE Software
GO MACAVEN
Provides support for CE Software's line of Macintosh products.

Central Software
GO AMIGAVENDOR
Provides support for Central Software's Amiga utility titles.

Central Point Software DOS Forum
GO CPSDOS
Provides technical support for Central Point Software's DOS products. See also the Central Point Software Windows and Macintosh Forum (GO CPSWINMAC).

Central Point Software Windows and Macintosh Forum
GO CPSWINMAC

Provides information and support for Central Point software products for Windows and Macintosh. See also the Central Point Software DOS Forum (GO CPSDOS).

⑤ *ChipSoft*
GO MACAVEN, PCVENB or WINAPB
Provides support for TurboTax.

⑤ *The Clarion Tech Journal*
GO PCVEND
Provides support for users of Clarion Professional Developer.

⑤ *Claris Corporation*
GO MACAVEN
Provides support for File Maker II, MacDraw II, MacWrite II, Claris CAD, MacProject II, Claris Graphics Translator, and SmartForm

⑤ *Cobb Group Applications Forum*
GO ZNT:COBBAPP
Provides tips and downloadable software for users of Lotus 1-2-3, DOS and Microsoft Windows. Library includes downloadable text from Cobb Group journals, utilities, and shareware. Part of ZiffNet (GO ZIFFNET).

⑤ *Cobb Group Programming Forum*
GO ZNT:COBBPROG
Provides downloadable files and source codes from Cobb Programming journals for Pascal, C, C++, Paradox and dBase users. Part of ZiffNet (GO ZIFFNET).

⑤ *Coda Music Software*
GO MIDIBVEN
Provides technical support for Finale and MusicProse products.

⑤ *CodeHead Software*
GO ATARIVEN
Provides support for CodeHead Software Atari ST products.

⑤ *Cognetics*
GO COGNETICS
Provides technical support for Hyperties for the IBM-PC.

⑤ *Color Computer Forum*
GO COCO
Provides support and information exchange for the TRS-80 Color Computer and related peripherals.

⑤ *Command Software Systems*
GO PCVENF
Provides support for Command Software Systems' security and anti-virus software.

⑤ *Commodore Application Forum*
GO CBMAPP
Provides support and information for Commodore 8-bit computers.

⑤ *Commodore Arts and Games Forum*
GO CBMART
Dedicated to creative and entertainment applications for Commodore 8-bit computers.

⑤ *Commodore Newsletter*
GO CBMNEWS
Offers information and support for Commodore computers and other products direct from Commodore.

⑤ *Commodore Service Forum*
GO CBMSERVICE
Offers direct customer support for all Commodore computer models.

⑤ *Compaq Connection*
GO COMPAQ
Provides information on COMPAQ products. Access the Compaq Forum (GO CPQFORUM) for information on technical support and to download files for Compaq hardware products.

⑤ *Compaq Forum*
GO CPQFORUM
Provides technical support and information exchange for Compaq hardware components.

⑤ *Complementary Solutions Inc.*
GO PCVEND
Provides technical support for TELEMATE and its add-ons.

⑤ *CompuAdd Forum*
GO COMPUADD
Provides support and information for CompuAdd systems.

⑤ *Computer Art Forum*
GO COMART
Covers images generated by or created with a paint program. Libraries contain thousands of GIF images for downloading and display.

⑤ *Computer Club Forum*
GO CLUB
For users of computers no longer supported by their manufacturers, or who have no specific forum dedicated to their hardware on CompuServe.

⑤ *Computer Language Forum*
GO CLMFORUM
Contains source code, programs, articles mentioned in the magazine along with additional information on computer languages.

⑤ *Computer Presentations Inc.*
GO CPI

A forum for Computer Presentations Inc., which produces a series of image processing applications for Windows 3.0.

⑤ *Computer Shopper Forum*
GO ZNT:COMPSHOPPER

Information about buying computer products, plus opportunities to contact *Computer Shopper* editors and columnists. Part of ZiffNet (GO ZIFFNET).

⑤ *Connectix*
GO MACAVEN

Provides support for Connectix's HAND-Off II, MAXIMA, Mode32, MC73 PMMU, and Virtual.

⑤ *Contact Software International*
GO CONTACT

Provides support for Contact's ACT! software.

⑤ *Cool Shoes Software*
GO MIDIBVEN

A technical forum for Cool Shoes Software's DOS-based interactive music software.

⑤ *Corel Forum*
GO COREL

Provides information exchange and technical support for Corel graphics products.

⑤ *Corporate Computing Forum*
GO ZNT:CORPORATE

Provides information about issues facing MIS departments of Fortune 1000 companies. Part of ZiffNet (GO ZIFFNET).

⑤ *CoStar Corporation*
GO COSTAR

Provides support for CoStar printing products.

⑤ *CP/M Forum*
GO CPMFORUM

Information exchange and discussions regarding CP/M 8-bit and 16-bit computer operating systems and related software.

⑤ *Crosstalk Forum*
GO XTALK

Provides information and support for DCA/ Crosstalk Communications products.

⑤ *Ctrlalt Associates*
GO PCVENA

Provides support for Ctrlalt's full product line.

⑤ *Cumulus Corporation*
GO PCVEND

Provides support for Cumulus Corporation's line of PCs, custom memory products and mass storage devices.

⑤ *Custom Applications*
GO DTPVENDOR

Provides technical support for Freedom of Press.

⑤ *Custom Technologies*
GO PCVENA

Provides support for Custom Technologies' CheckMate series and Magic Menus.

⑤ *DacEasy*
GO PCVENB

Provides support for Lucid 3-D spreadsheet, Rolodex Live, Lightning Disk accelerating package, and Breakthru 286 accelerator cards.

⑤ *Data Access Corporation*
GO DAC

Provides support and information for Data Access products.

⑤ *Data Access Corporation Forum*
GO DACCESS

Provides technical support and information exchange for Data Access investigative software products.

⑤ *Data Based Advisor Forum*
GO DBADVISOR

A forum for discussions and product support of various database products.

⑤ *Databook Incorporated*
GO DATABOOK

Provides support for Databook Incorporated products.

⑤ *Datastorm Technologies Support Forum*
GO DATASTORM

Offers support for ProComm communications products.

⑤ *DaVinci*
GO DAVINCI

Provides support of DaVinci E-Mail for Windows 3.0.

⑤ *Daystar Digital*
GO MACAVEN

Provides technical support and product information on Daystar Digital products.

⑤ *DBMS Forum*
GO DBMSFORUM

Allows communication with authors and editors of *DBMS*, a magazine on database management issues, in addition to other forum members.

⑤ *Digital Equipment Corporation PC Forum*
GO DECPC
For exchange of information, ideas, and public domain programs concerning DEC PCs.

⑤ *Digital Equipment Corporation Users Network*
GO DECUNET
Contains four forums: the DEC PC Forum (GO DECPC), Digital's PC Integration Forum (GO DECPCI), the PDP-11 Forum (GO PDP11) and the VAX Forum (GO VAXFORUM).

⑤ *Dell Computer Corporation*
GO DELL
Provides information exchange and support for Dell desktop products.

⑤ *Delrina Technology*
GO DELRINA
Provides support for Delrina's form development and facsimile creation products.

⑤ *DeltaPoint*
GO MACAVEN
Provides support for DeltaPoint's MindWrite, Trapeze, Express, DeltaGraph, and Taste.

⑤ *Deneba Software*
GO MACBVEN
Provides support for Deneba Software's Canvas, UltraPaint, Spelling Coach Professional, Big Thesaurus, and Comment.

⑤ *Desktop Publishing Forum*
GO DTPFORUM
Provides information and tools for DTP users. Offers classified ads and libraries containing utilities, fonts, demos, reviews, templates, photos, and art.

⑤ *Deutsches Computer Forum*
GO GERNET
Provides a place for German-speaking CompuServe members to discuss sports, politics, games, travel, and computers. Libraries contain utilities, calendars of events, more.

⑤ *Digital Vision*
GO DIGVIS
Provides technical support Digital Vision's ComputerEyes line of digitizers.

⑤ *Digitalk Forum*
GO DIGITALK

Provides information and library files on the SmallTalk/V programming language and development environment.

⑤ *Digital's PC Integration Forum*
GO DECPCI
Provides support and information exchange for Digital's PC integration software and hardware, DECpc products, and the EtherWORKS family of network connectivity products.

⑤ *Disk-Count Software*
GO PCVENE
Provides support for Disk-Count Software's contact management products.

⑤ *Double Click Software*
GO ATARIVEN
Provides technical support for DC Desktop, DC Utilities, and Shadow products.

⑤ *Dr. Dobb's Journal*
GO DDJ
The electronic edition of *Dr. Dobb's Journal*, containing information about computer languages, tools, utilities, algorithms, programming techniques, and more.

⑤ *Dr. Neuhaus Forum*
GO NEUHAUS
Provides technical support and information for German-speaking users of Dr. Neuhaus communications products.

⑤ *DTP Vendor Forum*
GO DTPVENDOR
For DTP users to query specific vendors or engage in discussions with other members.

⑤ *Dvorak Development*
GO FORCE
Provides technical support and product information for Dvorak Development's FORCE.

⑤ *EETNet*
GO EETNET
Provides forums for electronic engineers to exchange information. Also provides headline news from the *EE Times* and information on jobs for electronic engineers.

⑤ *Eicon Forum*
GO EICON
Provides discussions, information, and technical support for Eicon products.

⑤ *E-Mu Systems*
GO MIDIAVENDOR
Provides support for E-Mu music products.

⑤ *Enable Software, Inc.*
GO PCVENA
Provides support for Enable Software's ENABLE/
OA and ENABLE/CE.

⑤ *Engineering Automation Productivity Forum*
GO LEAP
Hosts discussions and provides libraries
concerning CADD/CAM programs used by
professionals in computer-aided design.

⑤ *Epson Forum*
GO EPSON
Provides information and support for Epson
products.

⑤ *Eventide*
GO EVENTIDE
Provides technical support for Eventide
products.

⑤ *Evolution Computing*
GO EVOLUTION
Provides support for Evolution Computing's
DOS-based CAD products.

⑤ *Ex Machina, Inc.*
GO MACAVEN
Provides technical support for Notify!.

⑤ *Executives Online*
GO ZNT:EXEC
Gives members direct access to industry leaders
to discuss new products, company strategies
and industry issues. Part of ZiffNet (GO ZIFFNET).

⑤ *Farallon*
GO FARAPC or FARAMAC
Offers support for PhoneNET and Farallon PC
and Mac products.

⑤ *Federation of International Distributors (FID)*
Forum
GO FEDERATION
Discusses industry concerns and establishes
international business protocol standards with
members of the International Managers' Club
(IMC). Also aids developers and manufacturers
seeking international distributors for their
products.

⑤ *Fifth Generation Systems Forum*
GO FIFTH
Provides support for Fifth Generation Systems
Mac products.

⑤ *Finalsoft*
GO FINALSOFT
Provides support for Finalsoft Executive.

⑤ *The FocServices FocForum*
GO FOCSERVICES
Provides information on the FOCUS
programming language. See also FocWizards
FocForum (FOCWIZARDS), the FUSE Forum (FUSE),
and the FOCUS Connection (FOCUS).

⑤ *The FOCUS Connection*
GO FOCUS
Provides support services for the FOCUS
programming language. See also FocWizards
FocForum (GO FOCWIZARDS), the FocServices
FocForum (FOCSERVICES), and the FUSE Forum
(FUSE).

⑤ *FocWizards FocForum*
GO FOCWIZARDS
Supports users of the FOCUS programming
language. See also the FocServices FocForum
(FOCSERVICES), the FUSE Forum (FUSEFORUM) and
the FOCUS Connection (FOCUS).

⑤ *FontBank*
GO FONTBANK
Provides support for FontBank products.

⑤ *Foresight Corporation*
GO PCVENA
Provides support for Drafix Windows CAD,
Drafix CAD Ultra, Otto, and Drafix CAD
Overlay.

⑤ *Forth Forum/Creative Solutions*
GO FORTH
Provides support for Creative Solutions' Forth
products.

⑤ *Fox Software Forum*
GO FOXFORUM
Provides support for Fox database management
and graphics software.

⑤ *Funk Software*
GO PCVENF
Provides technical support for Funk products.

⑤ *FUSE Forum*
GO FUSE
For discussions about FOCUS and related topics.
See also FocWizards FocForum (GO FOCWIZARDS),
FocServices FocForum (GO FOCSERVICES) and the
FOCUS Connection (FOCUS).

⑤ *Future Soft Engineering*
GO DYNACOMM
Provides support for Future Soft Engineering's
software.

⑤ *Gadgets By Small, Inc.*
GO ATARIVEN

Provides support for Gadgets By Small's Macintosh Plus emulator for the Spectre 128.

⑤ *GammaLink*
GO PCVEND
Provides support for GammaLink products.

⑤ *Gateway 2000*
GATEWAY
Provides support for Gateway's line of IBM compatible microcomputers.

⑤ *GCC Technologies*
GO MACBVEN
Provides support for GCC Technologies products.

⑤ *Genus Inc.*
GO GENUS
Provides support for Genus Inc. graphics programming toolkits.

⑤ *Geographix*
GO WINAPA
Provides support for Geographix seismographic and geological analysis applications.

⑤ *GFA Software*
GO WINAPC
Provides support for GFA-BASIC for the Windows environment.

⑤ *Gilbert & Associates*
GO VIEWZ
Provides support for VIEWz for the Windows environment.

⑤ *Global Softworks Ltd.*
GO GSLSUPPORT
Provides support for Global Softworks' GeoClips clip art packages.

⑤ *Glockenspiel*
GO GLOCK
Provides support for the Glockenspiel C++ programming language.

⑤ *GO Corp.*
GO GOCORP
Provides support for GO's PenPoint operating system software.

⑤ *Gold Disk*
GO WINAPC
Provides support for Gold Disk products.

⑤ *Gold Hill*
GO WINAPC
Provides support for Gold Hill products.

⑤ *Graphics Corner*
GO CORNER
Devoted to the display of GIF images. Offers extensive image libraries.

⑤ *Graphics File Finder*
GO GRAPHFF
A comprehensive searchable database of files found in the Graphic forums.

⑤ *Graphics Forums*
GO GRAPHICS
Contains six forums: Art Gallery Forum (GO ARTGALLERY), Computer Art Forum (GO COMART), Graphics Corner Forum (GO CORNER), Graphics Support Forum (GO GRAPHSUPPORT), Graphics Vendor Forum (GO GRAPHVEN) and the Quick Pictures Forum (GO QPICS). An introduction to graphics is also provided, along with a Graphics File Finder (GO GRAPHFF).

⑤ *Graphics Software, Inc.*
GO BIGD
Provides support for Graphics Software's BIG-D.

⑤ *Graphics Support Forum*
GO GRAPHSUPPORT
Offers advice and discussions on GIF-related hardware and software support issues.

⑤ *Graphics Vendor Forum*
GO GRAPHVEN
Provides support from various manufacturers of graphics hardware and software products.

⑤ *Gribnif Software*
GO ATARIVEN
Provides support for Gribnif's line of Atari products.

⑤ *GRiD Systems*
GO GRID
Provides support for GRiD Systems' GRiDPad pen computer line and PenRight! graphical application development platform.

⑤ *Hardware Forums*
GO HARDWARE
Enables users of particular hardware to exchange ideas. Many forums provide interaction with hardware manufacturers and include extensive libraries of software programs.

⑤ *Harvard Associates, Inc.*
GO LOGOFORUM
Provides support for Harvard's Logo products.

⑤ *hDC Computer Corp.*
GO WINAPA

Provides support for hDC Computer Corporation utilities for the Windows 3.0 environment.

Hewlett-Packard Forums
GO HP
Provides support for HP products. The HP Peripherals Forum (GO HPPERIPHER) supports printers, plotters, scanners, fax units, and storage devices; the HP Systems Forum (GO HPSYSTEMS) provides support for HP systems.

Hilgraeve
GO HILGRAEVE
Provides technical support for Hilgraeve's HyperACCESS/5.

Hi-Q International
GO WINAPA
Provides support for Mission Control communications software.

Hooper International
GO PCVENC
Provides support for Hooper International's Takin' Care Of Business and Cheque-It-Out.

HP Handhelds Forum
GO HPHANDHELDS
Provides support, news, and discussions for users of HP handheld products.

HSC Software
GO HSCSOFTWARE
Provides support for HSC Software products.

Hybrid Arts
GO HYBRID
Provides support for Hybrid Arts' digital editing products.

Hyperkinetix, Inc.
GO PCVEND
Provides support for BUILDER, DeltaFile, DemoIT! and Warplink.

Hyperpress Publishing
GO MACBVEN
Provides support for Hyperpress Publishing products.

Hyphen
GO HYPHEN
Provides support for Hyphen's raster image processors.

IBM Applications Forum
GO IBMAPP
Discussions and information on core applications for the PC. Libraries contain thousands of downloadable programs.

IBM Bulletin Board Forum
GO IBMBBS
Provides information about bulletin boards for IBM PCs and compatibles.

IBM CAD
GO IBMCAD
Provides support for IBM CAD.

IBM Communications Forum
GO IBMCOM
Devoted to telecommunications on the IBM PC and compatibles. Supports public domain and commercial communications programs.

IBM European Users Forum
GO IBMEUROPE
Provides information on IBM PCs and compatibles for European users.

IBM File Finder
GO IBMFF
An on-line comprehensive searchable database of file descriptions found in the most popular IBM-related forums. Provides quick and easy reference to some of the best programs and files available in the many forums.

IBM Hardware Forum
GO IBMHW
Discusses the various products available for the PC. Libraries contain hardware-related programs and product reviews.

IBM LMU2 Forum
GO LMU2FORUM
Provides a direct communication route to the IBM LAN Management Utilities/2 development team. Provides information exchange and support for LMU/2 functions.

IBM New Users/Fun Forum
GO IBMNEW
Contains helpful hints from expert users and SysOps, plus many entertainment programs for the new IBM user.

IBM OS/2 Developers' Forums
GO OS2DF1 and OS2DF2
Provides two technical support forums for software developers for the OS/2 environment. The IBM OS/2 Developer 1 Forum (GO OS2DF1) hosts discussions about development tools, debugging techniques, and development products, while the IBM OS/2 Developer 2 Forum (GO OS2DF2) treats developing programs for LAN server, CD-ROM, database, and other applications.

✪ IBM OS/2 User and Support Forums
GO OS2USER and OS2SUPPORT

Provides two forums for information and support. The IBM OS/2 User Forum (GO OS2USER) discusses OS/2-related topics such as hardware requirements and applications. The IBM OS/2 Support Forum (GO OS2SUPPORT) provides support directly from IBM for OS/2 applications.

✪ IBM PC Users Network
GO IBMNET

Devoted to the IBM PC and compatibles. Includes many special-interest forums, addressing the needs of new and expert users.

✪ IBM Programming Forum
GO IBMPRO

For users interested in programming for the IBM PC or compatibles. Supplies assemblers and source codes in a variety of languages, plus help from other programmers. Experienced programmers will find valuable information and beginners will discover hints, tips, and tutorials.

✪ IBM Systems/Utilities Forum
GO IBMSYS

Information on utilities for IBM PC operating systems and environments. Libraries contain programs including DOS additions and improved DOS utilities, as well as resident desktop utilities. Download many popular shareware programs.

✪ IBM ThinkPad Forum
GO THINKPAD

Enables programmers to speak directly with IBM personnel and share information with one another.

✪ ICD, Inc.
GO ATARIVEN

Provides support for ICD products.

✪ ICOM Simulations
GO ICOM

Provides support for ICOM screen saver programs and utilities.

✪ Image-In Inc.
GO IMAGEIN

Provides support for Image-In-Color and Image-In-Color Professional.

✪ Impulse, Inc.
GO AMIGAVENDOR

Provides support for Impulse's Amiga product line.

✪ Infinite Technologies
GO PCVENF

Enables downloading of 30-day trial versions of Infinite Technologies products.

✪ Inline Design
GO MACCVEN

Provides support for Inline Design's Macintosh products.

✪ Innovative Data Concepts
GO PCVENC

Provides support for Innovative Data Concepts products.

✪ Inovatronics
GO AMIGAVENDOR

Provides support for Inovatronics products.

✪ Inset Systems Inc.
GO INSET

Provides support for Inset Systems products.

✪ Intel Forum
GO INTELFORUM

Provides support and product information for Intel products.

✪ Intel Software Developers Forum
GO INTELACCESS

Provides a place for developers to obtain support from Intel for its microprocessors and multimedia technologies. The iRMX User's Group (iRUG) hosts a message section where its members can find support and discuss iRUG issues.

✪ INTERSECT Software Corporation
GO ATARIVEN

Provides support for INTERSECT Software's Interlink ST and Deluxe Piano.

✪ Iomega Corporation
GO PCVENE or MACCVEN

Provides support for Iomega's Bernoulli Box items.

✪ ISD Marketing
GO ATARIVEN

Provides support for ISD Marketing's line of products for the Atari.

✪ ISICAD, Inc.
GO ISICAD

Provides support for ISICAD graphics and database systems.

✪ Jasik Designs
GO MACBVEN

Provides support for Jasik Designs' MacNosy and The Debugger.

⑤ *Javelin/EXPRESS Forum*
GO IRIFORUM
Information and demo programs for users of Javelin and EXPRESS software.

⑤ *Jensen-Jones*
GO JJSUPPORT
Provides support for Jensen-Jones's Commence.

⑤ *JLCooper Electronics*
GO MIDIAVENDOR
Provides support for JLCooper's MIDI accessories.

⑤ *Jovian Inc.*
GO JOVIAN
Provides support for Jovian Inc. products.

⑤ *J.P. Software*
GO JPSOFT
Provides technical support for J.P. Software's 4DOS program.

⑤ *Kidasa*
GO KIDASA
Provides support for Kidasa Software's Milestones, Etc.

⑤ *Knowledge Garden*
GO KNOWLEDGE
Provides support for Knowledge Garden's KnowledgePro for Windows.

⑤ *Korenthal Associates, Inc.*
GO PCVENB
Provides support for Webster's New World software series, 4PRINT and TAPMARK.

⑤ *Kurzweil Music Systems—Young Chang*
GO MIDIAVENDOR
Provides support for Kurzweil Music Systems' sampling equipment.

⑤ *Lan Technology Forum*
GO LANTECH
Provides users of LANs with information about various LAN products. Discussions of specific products, servers, internetworking and E-Mail.

⑤ *LDOS/TRSDOS 6 Forum*
GO LDOS
Provides support services and discussions for users of Radio Shack TRS-80 Models 1, 3, 4, 4P, 40 as well as 'work-alike' computers such as the LOBO MAX-80.

⑤ *Legato Systems, Inc.*
GO LEGATO

Provides support for Legato Systems networking products.

⑤ *Lexicor Software*
GO ATARIVEN
Provides technical support for Lexicor Software animation products.

⑤ *Logitech Forum*
GO LOGITECH
Provides product information and technical support for Logitech products.

⑤ *Logo Computer Systems, Inc.*
GO LOGOFORUM
Provides support for LogoEnsemble, The Phantom Fish Tank, Logo II, LogoExpress, and LogoWriter.

⑤ *Logo Forum*
GO LOGOFORUM
Uses a light-hearted approach to explore the Logo computer language. Cartoon characters keep interest high. Vendors are available on-line and provide support for their products.

⑤ *Lotus Spreadsheet Forum*
GO LOTUSA
Provides support and information exchange for Lotus 1-2-3, Lotus Symphony, HAL, and Jazz.

⑤ *Lotus Technical Library*
GO LTL
Offers an extensive library of technical bulletins about Lotus products and releases.

⑤ *Lotus Word Processing Forum*
GO LOTUSWP
Provides product support for users of Ami Pro, Ami, Lotus Manuscript, Samna Word IV, and SmarText word processing programs.

⑤ *Lotus Words & Pixels Forum*
GO LOTUSB
Discussions for users of non-spreadsheet Lotus products.

⑤ *Mac Applications Forum*
GO MACAP
Hosts discussions about Macintosh applications.

⑤ *Mac A Vendor Forum*
GO MACAVEN
Features various Macintosh vendors delivering on-line support to their customers.

⑤ *Mac B Vendor Forum*
GO MACBVEN

Features various Macintosh vendors delivering on-line support to their customers.

⑤ *Mac C Vendor Forum*
  GO MACCVEN
Offers on-line support from various Macintosh vendors.

⑤ *Mac File Finder*
  GO MACFF
An on-line searchable database of file descriptions of the most popular Macintosh-related forums.

⑤ *MacDonald Associates*
  GO ATARIVEN
Provides support for MacDonald Associates products.

⑤ *Macintosh Communications Forum*
  GO MACCOMM
Information on Macs communicating with other Macs and with other personal computers.

⑤ *Macintosh Community Clubhouse Forum*
  GO MACCLUB
Forum for Macintosh users to meet one another. Special conferences, parties, and updates on what's been recently uploaded in other Mac forums.

⑤ *Macintosh Developers Forum*
  GO MACDEV
Provides programming information for commercial Mac programmers, Mac developers, people who program for their own use, and new programmers.

⑤ *Macintosh Entertainment Forum*
  GO MACFUN
Helps users discover fun and creative new ways to use the Macintosh. Sections on games, music, sound, and more.

⑤ *Macintosh Hardware Forum*
  GO MACHW
Discusses and disseminates information regarding purchase of Mac hardware items.

⑤ *Macintosh Hypertext Forum*
  GO MACHYPER
Provides information and library files on Hypertext databases. Support provided for products by non-Apple developers.

⑤ *Macintosh New Users and Help Forum*
  GO MACNEW or MACHELP
Mac experts offer new Macintosh users answers to questions about their new computer.

⑤ *Macintosh System Software Forum*
  GO MACSYS
Information and discussion on Macintosh system software.

⑤ *Mackie Designs*
  GO MIDIBVEN
Provides support for Mackie Designs products.

⑤ *Macromedia Forum*
  GO MACROMEDIA
Provides support (check the libraries) and information exchange for Macromedia media products.

⑤ *MacUser Forum*
  GO ZMC:MACUSER
Part of Zmac (GO ZMAC). Enables interaction with *MacUser* editors, writers, columnists, and readers. Access to downloadable utilities and on-line *MacUser* indexes

⑤ *MacWEEK Forum*
  GO ZMC:MACWEEK
Part of Zmac (GO ZMAC). Enables interaction with *MacWEEK* editors and writers. Current headlines and news summaries available before publication; magazine indexes available on-line.

⑤ *Magee Enterprises, Inc.*
  GO MAGEE
Provides support for Magee Enterprises' Automenu, Treeview, and Screen Manager Professional.

⑤ *Magma Systems*
  GO MAGMA
Provides support for Magma Systems' MEWEL Window Library and ME Text Editor.

⑤ *Magnetic Music*
  GO MAGMUSIC
Provides support for Magnetic Music's Prism and Texture Classic.

⑤ *Mainstay*
  GO MACAVEN
Provides on-line support for Mainstay products.

⑤ *Mansfield Software Group*
  GO PCVENA
Provides support for KEDIT, REXX, and Personal REXX.

⑤ *Markt & Technik AG*
  GO MTD
Enables interaction with editors and readers of M&T publications. Forum and libraries in German.

Ⓢ Matesys Corp.
GO MATESYS
Provides support for Matesys Corp.'s graphical interface development tools.

Ⓢ Mathematica, Inc.
GO TEMPRA
Provides support for Mathematica Inc.'s Tempra Pro.

Ⓢ Maxwell CPU
GO ATARIVEN
Provides support for Megstender, GoGo-ST, and Fractal Fantasy.

Ⓢ McAfee Virus Forum
GO VIRUSFORUM
Libraries deal with detection and removal of computer viruses. Conferences, message boards, and technical support for virus-fighting products from Trend Micro Devices and McAfee Associates. The National Computer Security Association operates a section in the forum.

Ⓢ MECA Software Forum
GO MECA
Provides support for MECA products.

Ⓢ Media Vision
GO MEDIAVISION
Provides support for Pro-Audio Spectrum and ThunderBOARD.

Ⓢ Megahertz
GO MEGAHERTZ
Provides support for Megahertz products.

Ⓢ Metagraphics, Inc.
GO METAGRAPHICS
Provides support for Metagraphics products.

Ⓢ Metz Software
GO METZ
Provides technical support for Metz Software products.

Ⓢ Michtron
GO ATARIVEN
Provides supports for Michtron products.

Ⓢ Micro Engineering Solutions
GO MESOLUTIONS
Provides support for Micro Engineering Solutions software.

Ⓢ Micrografx.
GO MICROGRAFX
Provides support for Micrografx products.

Ⓢ Micropolis Corporation
GO PCVEND
Provides support for Micropolis products.

Ⓢ Microseeds Publishing
GO MACBVEN
Provides support for Microseeds Publishing's Rerdux, Rival, Initpicker, Screen Gems, and Astrix.

Ⓢ Microsoft Applications Forum
GO MSAPP
Provides information and support for all Microsoft application products.

Ⓢ Microsoft Basic Languages Forum
GO MSBASIC
Provides information exchange and support for BASIC, QuickBASIC, and Visual BASIC programming languages.

Ⓢ Microsoft C and Other Languages Forum.
GO MSLANG
Provides technical support for programming languages such as C, QuickC and QuickPascal MASM for Microsoft applications.

Ⓢ Microsoft Central Europe Forum
GO MSF
Provides support for Microsoft's German application software and programming languages, hosting discussions among Microsoft users and Microsoft Central Europe.

Ⓢ Microsoft Client Server Computing Forum
GO MSNETWORKS
Provides in-depth information about Client Server, the Microsoft LAN Manager network operating system, and the SQL Server database.

Ⓢ Microsoft Connection
GO MICROSOFT
Provides you with access to the Microsoft Forums. Communicate directly with Microsoft and other users of Microsoft software. Includes product information, sales and training information, support information, software libraries, and the Microsoft KnowledgeBase (GO MSKB) used by Microsoft support engineers.

Ⓢ Microsoft Developer Knowledge Base
GO MDKB
Contains technical information and articles about Microsoft developer-specific products.

Ⓢ Microsoft Developer Relations Forum
GO MSDR
Answers non-technical questions about development products and their usage. For

technical support, see the Microsoft Developer Services Area (GO MSDS).

🕭 *Microsoft Developer Services Area*
GO MSDS

Provides developers with technical support and information for Microsoft development products.

🕭 *Microsoft Developer Support Forums*
GO MSDEV

Provides the seven forums to support developers of Microsoft products: BASIC, Client Server Computing, C and Other Languages, Developer Relations, Windows Extentions, Windows SDK, and Win 32.

🕭 *Microsoft DOS 5.0 Forum*
GO MSDOS

Supports users of MS-DOS. Makes available message sections and conference areas.

🕭 *Microsoft End-User Support Forums*
GO MSUSER

Offers several forums in which users can access technical support directly from Microsoft and forum members.

🕭 *Microsoft Excel Forum*
GO EXCEL

Provides support for all versions of Microsoft Excel. Templates and spreadsheets are available for downloading.

🕭 *Microsoft Knowledge Base*
GO MSKB

A database providing access to information previously available only to Microsoft support engineers.

🕭 *Microsoft Service Request*
GO MSR

An optional, private (fee-based per incident) technical support service which helps solve complex development problems.

🕭 *Microsoft Software Library*
GO MSL

Uploaded binary files, samples, technical notes, and utilities for various Microsoft programs. Keyword-searchable and downloadable.

🕭 *Microsoft Win32 Forum*
GO MSWIN32

Offers information about the Microsoft Win32 Application Programming Interface.

🕭 *Microsoft Windows Advanced User Forum*
GO WINADV

Power users of Microsoft Windows communicate with one another to solve problems and share experiences. On-line support for questions and customer service.

🕭 *Microsoft Windows Extensions Forum*
GO WINEXT

Provides technical assistance and information for Microsoft development tools.

🕭 *Microsoft Windows New User Forum*
GO WINNEW

Provides information about Microsoft Windows fundamentals plus customer service support.

🕭 *Microsoft Windows SDK Forum*
GO WINSDK

For developers using the Windows Software Development Kit.

🕭 *Microsoft Word Forum*
GO MSWORD

Provides technical support and informative discussions for Microsoft Word for Windows, Macintosh, DOS or OS/2 environments.

🕭 *Microware Online Support*
GO MICROWARE

Provides information and technical support for Microware products.

🕭 *MIDI A Vendor Forum*
GO MIDIAVEN

Provides access and support for users from vendors in the MIDI industry. Professional musicians discuss their experiences with MIDI.

🕭 *MIDI B Vendor Forum*
GO MIDIBVEN

Provides access and support for users from vendors in the MIDI industry. Professional musicians discuss their experiences with MIDI.

🕭 *Midiman*
GO MIDIBVEN

Provides support for Midiman products.

🕭 *MIDI/Music Forum*
GO MIDIFORUM

Covers recording, synthesizers, samplers, music in different computing environments, more. Makes available downloadable files to play at your leisure.

🕭 *MIP Fund Accounting*
GO PCVENF

Information regarding the MIP Fund Accounting System.

↺ *Mirror Technologies*
GO MACCVEN
Provides technical support for Mirror products.

↺ *Model 100 Forum*
GO M100SIG
Share knowledge, experiences, programs and product information. Message boards and databases containing 1,000+ files not only of interest to TRS-80 Model 100 users, but also Tandy 102, 200, 600 and WP-2 users.

↺ *Modem Vendor Forum*
GO MODEMVENDOR
Provides information, libraries, and support from various vendors for modem users and potential buyers. Members share experience with different brands of modems.

↺ *Multimedia Forum*
GO MULTIMEDIA
Discussions for users interested in multimedia. Makes available conferences and message boards.

↺ *Multimedia Vendors Forum*
GO MULTIVENDOR
Provides information about leading multimedia hardware and software products. Members share purchasing advice; vendors on-line to help choose the right equipment.

↺ *Multisoft Corporation*
GO PCVENA
Provides support for Super PC-Kwik Power Pak, PC-Kwik Power Disk, and Super PC-Kwik Disk Accelerator.

↺ *M-USA Business Systems*
GO PCVENC
Offers support for M-USA's PACIOLI 2000 ACCOUNTING, PACIOLI 2000 PAYROLL, CashBIZ, and M-USA Video programs.

↺ *Music Quest*
GO MUSICQUEST
Provides support for Music Quest's MIDI Programmer's Toolkit and MIDI Starter System.

↺ *Mustang Software*
GO PCVENA
Provides support for Mustang Software's WILDCAT! Bulletin Board system, QMODEM, OFFR-LINE, wcMHS, and MIDNIGHT MAIL.

↺ *National Computer Security Association*
GO NCSA
Discussions and files on computer security, including computer viruses, encryption techniques, data center security, and more.

↺ *NBI, Inc.*
GO LEGACY
Provides support for NBI, Inc.'s Legacy.

↺ *NetFRAME Systems*
GO PCVENC
Provides support for NetFRAME's Network Server Systems.

↺ *New Horizons*
GO AMIGAVENDOR
Provides support for New Horizons products.

↺ *New Media Graphics*
GO MULTIVEN
Provides support for New Media Graphics products.

↺ *NewTek*
GO AMIGAVENDOR
Provides support for New Tek products.

↺ *NeXT Forum*
GO NEXTFORUM
Provides technical support for NeXT computers and products.

↺ *Northgate Computer Systems, Inc.*
GO NORTHGATE
Provides support for Northgate Computer Systems products.

↺ *Norton/Symantec Forums*
GO SYMANTEC
Hosts a Symantec Application Forum (GO SYMFORUM) for users of Symantec programs and a utilities forum (GO NORUTL) for both Norton and Symantec utilities software.

↺ *Novell Digital Research Forum*
GO DRFORUM
Provides support and information for Digital Research end users and software developers.

↺ *Novell Forums*
GO NOVFORUM
Provides support and technical information for Novell's local area network products. The Novell Library (GO NOVLIB) includes libraries and files.

↺ *Novell Forum A*
GO NOVA
Covers topics relating to NetWare operating systems and Novell's communication products.

↺ *Novell Forum B*
GO NOVB
Covers topics relating to network topologies, file servers and workstation issues.

⑤ *Novell Forum C*
    GO NOVC
Covers topics relating to NetWare Requester for OS/2 and development issues in the NetWare environment. Members can converse with Novell staff and prospective resellers. Support is also offered for users of Btrieve.

⑤ *Novell Library*
    GO NOVLIB
The distribution point for all files uploaded or downloaded in NetWire. A message section is available for questions about files that appear in the libraries.

⑤ *Novell NetWare 2.X Forum*
    GO NETW2X
Provides information relating to NetWare version 2.X.

⑤ *Novell NetWare 3.X Forum*
    GO NETW3X
Provides information relating to NetWare version 3.X.

⑤ *Novell NetWire*
    GO NOVELL
Provides 24-hour information and support for Novell products.

⑤ *nTergaid*
    GO NTERGAID
Provides support for nTergaid's HyperWriter.

⑤ *Olduvai Corporation*
    GO MACBVEN
Provides support for Olduvai products.

⑤ *Online Today*
    GO OLT
Provides daily updated computer and information industry news, CompuServe news, product announcements, reviews, and more.

⑤ *Online with Hayes*
    GO HAYES
Provides technical information on Hayes products.

⑤ *Online with Hayes Forum*
    GO HAYFORUM
Provides support and information exchange for Hayes products.

⑤ *Opcode Systems Incorporated (MIDI)*
    GO MIDIAVENDOR
Provides support for Opcode Systems' MIDI products.

⑤ *Oracle Forum*
    GO ORACLE
Provides support for Oracle users and maintains linkage with the International Oracle Users Group.

⑤ *OS-9 Forum*
    GO OS9
Supplies programs, utilities, data files, hints, tips, and discussions relating to the OS-9 operating system.

⑤ *Owl International (Windows)*
    GO WINAPB
Provides support for Owl International's Guide.

⑤ *Pacific Data Products, Inc.*
    GO PACDATA
Provides support for Pacific Data Products.

⑤ *Pacific Forum*
    GO PACFORUM
Discussions on Australian and New Zealand topics of interest such as recommended tourist sites, family connections with the U.S., and food. Encourages social interaction and access to some of Australia and New Zealand's hardware and software vendors.

⑤ *Packard Bell Forum*
    GO PACKARDBELL
Provides support for Packard Bell products.

⑤ *Palmtop Forum*
    GO PALMTOP
Provides information and discussions about palmtop computers. Several palmtop vendors provide on-line support.

⑤ *Paradigm Software, Inc.*
    GO LOGOFORUM
Provides support for Paradigm Software's Object Logo.

⑤ *Paragon Concepts*
    GO MACAVEN
Provides support for Paragon products.

⑤ *Parsons Technology, Inc.*
    GO PCVENC
Provides support for Parsons Technology products.

⑤ *Paul Mace Software*
    GO GRASP
Provides support for Paul Mace's GRASP.

⑤ *PC/Contact Forum from PC/Computing*
    GO ZNT:PCCONTACT
Part of ZiffNet (GO ZIFFNET). Coordinates discussions among PC/Computing's editors and

readers. Exchange information regarding problems or experiences with vendors.

◐ PC MagNet Forums from PC Magazine
GO ZNT:PCMAGNET

Part of ZiffNet (GO ZIFFNET). Makes available the best utilities from *PC Magazine* for downloading. Converse with the magazine staff.

◐ PC Plus/PC Answers Forum
GO PCPFORUM

Chat with the editorial staff and readers of the UK's *PC Plus* and *PC Answers* magazines. Download programs included in the magazines' cover disks.

◐ PC Plus/PC Answers Online
GO PCPLUS

Submit articles to PC Plus and PC Answers magazines and receive information about the programs on each SuperDisk. This area contains the PC Plus/PC Answers Forum (GO PCPFORUM).

◐ PC Sources Forum
GO ZNT:SOURCES

Provides information on computer-buying through discussions with editors, columnists, writers, industry experts, and so on. Part of ZiffNet (GO ZIFFNET).

◐ PC Vendor A Forum
GO PCVENA

Provides support from various vendors of PC products.

◐ PC Vendor B Forum
GO PCVENB

Provides support from various vendors of PC products.

◐ PC Vendor C Forum
GO PCVENC

Provides support from various vendors of PC products.

◐ PC Vendor D Forum
GO PCVEND

Provides support from various vendors of PC products.

◐ PC Vendor E Forum
GO PCVENE

Provides support from various vendors of PC products.

◐ PC Vendor F Forum
GO PCVENF

Provides support from various vendors of PC products.

◐ PC Week
GO ZNT:NEWS

Part of ZiffNet (GO ZIFFNET). Provides industry news—even headlines and summaries of news stories the Friday before they are published. Discuss industry issues with writers, editors, and readers.

◐ PC Week Extra! Forum from PC Week
GO ZNT:PCWEEK

Part of ZiffNet (GO ZIFFNET). Provides a platform for corporate buyers and *PC Week* writers and editors to discuss which products and services to buy, plus an opportunity to debate industry issues.

◐ PDP-11 Forum
GO PDP11

Encourages exchange of software for Digital Equipment Corporation's PDP/LSI computer systems. Covers languages used on PDPs. The PDP-11 Users Group facilitates communication among users of PDP-11, LSI-11 and PDP-10 computers.

◐ Peachtree Software
GO PEACHTREE

Provides support for Peachtree Software products.

◐ Pen Magazine
GO PENFORUM

Discusses articles published in *Pen Magazine*. Learn about new Pen products and communicate with the magazine staff.

◐ Pen Technology Forum
GO PENFORUM

Provides support for all aspects of pen-based computing. Various vendors provide support for their products.

◐ Personal File Area
GO PER

Enables CompuServe members to catalog and modify files stored on CompuServe.

◐ Personics Corporation
GO PCVENB

Provides technical support Personics' UltraVision, Look&Link, @Base, @Base Option Pac, SeeMore for 1-2-3, SeeMore for Symphony, SmartNotes, and Headmaster.

◐ PG Music
GO PGMUSIC

Provides support for PG Music products.

⑤ *PKWare*
    GO PKWARE
Provides support for PKWare's PC data-compression products.

⑤ *Playroom Software*
    GO PLAYROOM
Provides support for Playroom Software's environment enhancement products.

⑤ *Polaris Software*
    GO POLARIS
Provides support for Polaris Software's PackRat.

⑤ *Poqet Computer*
    GO POQET
Provides support for Poqet Computer's palmtop computers.

⑤ *Portable Programming Forum*
    GO CODEPORT
Supports programmers using various computer languages that are highly portable between different hardware platforms. Information on portable languages not supported by other CompuServe forums.

⑤ *Portfolio Systems*
    GO MACAVEN
Provides support for Portfolio Systems' Dynodex.

⑤ *Power Industries LP*
    GO LOGOFORUM
Provides support for Power Industries' Delta Drawing Today.

⑤ *Powercore, Inc.*
    GO PCVENB
Provides support and product information for Powercore products.

⑤ *Practical Peripherals Forum*
    GO PPIFORUM
Provides help, advice and technical support for Practical Peripherals products and users with an interest in computers and tele-communications.

⑤ *Precision Software (Atari)*
    GO ATARIVEN
Provides support for Precision products.

⑤ *Presidio Software*
    GO PRES
Provides support for Presidio's PC ANIMATE PLUS.

⑤ *Primavera Systems, Inc.*
    GO PCVENB
Provides support for Primavera Systems products.

⑤ *Prisma GmbH Forum*
    GO PRISMA
Provides technical support, discussions and information (in German) for users of Macintosh software and hardware, provided by the German distributor Prisma.

⑤ *PRO-C Corporation*
    GO PCVENB
Provides technical support for PRO-C Corporation products.

⑤ *Procom Technology, Inc.*
    GO PTINC
Provides support for Procom Technology products.

⑤ *Prolog Development Center*
    GO PCVENB
Provides support for PDC Prolog Compiler 3.2, PDC Prolog Toolbox, PDC Prolog Advanced Developer's Guide, and Turbo Prolog.

⑤ *Protoview*
    GO PROTOVIEW
Provides support for Protoview development tools.

⑤ *Psion, Inc.*
    GO PALMTOP
Provides support for Psion handheld computers.

⑤ *Public Brand Software Applications Forum*
    GO ZNT:PBS
Makes available the entire PBS catalog of downloadable shareware. Part of ZiffNet (GO ZIFFNET).

⑤ *Publishing Technologies*
    GO PUBTEC
Provides support for Publishing Technologies environment enhancement products.

⑤ *Pure Data, Limited*
    GO PUREDATA
Provides support for Pure Data products.

⑤ *QMS*
    GO QMSPRINT
Provides support for QMS non-impact print systems.

⑤ *Qualitas*
    GO PCVENA
Provides support for Qualitas 386MAX, BLUEMAX and MOVE'EM.

⑤ *Quality Assurance Institute (QAI)*
GO FORQAI
Discusses quality and productivity issues in the information technology industry. QAI seeks to improve quality and productivity in the information technology industry.

⑤ *Quarterdeck Forum*
GO QUARTERDECK
Provides technical support for Quarterdeck products.

⑤ *Quercus Systems*
GO QUERCUS
Provides technical support for Quercus Personal REXX and REXXTERM.

⑤ *Quick Pictures Forum*
GO QPICS
Stores low and medium resolution graphic images, provides discussion, and supports GIF files used elsewhere on CompuServe. Images ideal for low-end computers.

⑤ *Quicksoft, Inc.*
GO PCVENB
Provides support for Quicksoft's PC-Write and Font Selector.

⑤ *Radius Incorporated*
GO MACBVEN
Provides support and information for Radius products.

⑤ *REP Magazine*
GO REPMAGAZINE
Converse with subscribers and editors of *Recording Engineering Production*.

⑤ *Revelation Tech Forum*
GO REVELATION
Provides support and information exchange for the Advanced Revelation relational database.

⑤ *Right Answers*
GO AMIGAVENDOR
Provides technical support for Right Answers products.

⑤ *Rix Softworks*
GO RIXSOFT
Provides support for Rix Softworks paint programs.

⑤ *Roykore*
GO WINAPA
Provides support for Roykore products.

⑤ *Rupp Corporation*
GO RUPP

Provides support for Rupp's FastLynx, FastLock, and Plus FastLynx LapPack.

⑤ *Salient Software*
GO FIFTHGEN
Provides support for Salient Software's products.

⑤ *Saros*
GO SAROS
Provides support for Saros Corporation products.

⑤ *Schemers, Inc.*
GO LOGOFORUM
Provides support for Schemers Logo-based products.

⑤ *Scitex America Corp.*
GO SCITEX
Provides support for Scitex America's prepress products.

⑤ *SemWare*
GO SEMWARE
Provides support for SemWare's QEdit.

⑤ *Seybold Newsletters and Seminars*
GO ZNT:SEYBOLD
Enables users to order Seybold's computer industry newsletters. Part of ZiffNet (GO ZIFFNET).

⑤ *Sharp Electronics Corporation*
GO SHARP
Provides support for Sharp Electronics Corporation's Wizard handheld organizers and its PC-3000 products.

⑤ *Sigma Designs.*
GO SIGMA
Provides support for Sigma Designs products.

⑤ *Silicon Beach/Aldus Forum*
GO SBSALD
Provides support and information exchange for Silicon Beach and Aldus products. For non-technical questions, access the Aldus Customer Services Forum (GO ALDSVC).

⑤ *Sitka (DOS)*
GO PCVENA
Provides support Sitka's Network Bundle for DOS 3.0, FlashCard, and FlashCard MicroChannel.

⑤ *Sitka (TOPS) (Macintosh)*
GO MACAVEN
Provides supports for Sitka's Macintosh products.

⑤ *Slate Corp.*
GO SLATE

Provides support for Slate Corp.'s pen-based software applications.

⑤ *Softbridge*
GO SOFTBRIDGE
Provides support for Softbridge's products.

⑤ *SoftCraft*
GO WINAPB
Provides support for SoftCraft products.

⑤ *Soft-Logik Publishing (Amiga)*
GO AMIGAVENDOR
Provides support for Soft-Logik's PageStream for the Amiga.

⑤ *Soft-Logik Publishing (Atari)*
GO ATARIVEN
Provides support for Soft-Logik's PageStream for the Atari.

⑤ *Softsync, Inc.*
GO SOFTSYNC
Provides support for Softsync's Accountant, Inc. and Expert Color Paint.

⑤ *Software Forums*
GO SOFTWARE
Provides 24-hour information and support for the most popular software packages on the market, mostly sponsored by software publishers. Libraries with downloadable programs; electronic conferences; related software forums in the Hardware Forums section (GO HARDWARE).

⑤ *Software Publishers Association (SPA) Forum*
GO SPAFORUM
Keeps SPA members, developers, and users apprised of SPA activities and developments.

⑤ *Software Publishing Corporation*
GO SPC
Provides technical support for Software Publishing Corporation products, including international versions.

⑤ *Software Ventures*
GO MACBVEN
Provides support for Software Ventures' Microphone, Microphone II, and Microphone 4.0.

⑤ *Softwood*
GO AMIGAVENDOR
Provides support for Softwood products.

⑤ *Spectra Publishing*
GO PCVENB
Provides support for Spectra Publishing's PowerBASIC 2.0.

⑤ *Specular International*
GO MULTIVEN
Provides support for Specular International's Infini-D.

⑤ *Spinnaker Forum*
GO SPINNAKER
Provides support and information exchange for Spinnaker products.

⑤ *Stac Electronics*
GO STACKER
Provides support for Stac Electronics' STACKER.

⑤ *Standard Microsystems Forum*
GO SMC7
Provides support for SMF products.

⑤ *STB Systems*
GO STBSYS
Provides support for STB Systems PC-compatible boards.

⑤ *The Stirling Group*
GO STIRLING
Provides support for The Stirling Group's Shield software development tools.

⑤ *Storage Dimension*
GO PCVENF
Provides technical support for Storage Dimensions products.

⑤ *Super Mac Technology*
GO MACBVEN
Provides support for Super Mac Technology's Pixel Paint and Pixel Paint Professional here.

⑤ *Support On Site (SOS) Online*
GO ZNT:ONSITE
Makes available a database of technical support information on more than two dozen leading PC software applications. Part of ZiffNet (GO ZIFFNET).

⑤ *Supra Corporation*
GO ATARIVEN
Provides support for Supra Corporation products.

⑤ *Survivor Software*
GO MACAVEN
Provides support for Survivor's MacMoney, InvoicIt, and Sticky Notes+.

⑤ *SWFTE International*
GO SWFTE
Provides support for SWFTE International products.

○ *Symantec Forum*
GO SYMANTEC
Provides support, information exchange, and discussions for Symantec products.

○ *Syndesis*
GO AMIGAVENDOR
Provides support for Syndesis products.

○ *Tactic Software*
GO MACBVEN
Provides support for Tactic Software's Macintosh products.

○ *Tandy Corporation Newsletter*
GO TRS
Reports on current activities within the Tandy Corporation. Accesses Tandy technical information; questions can be sent directly to Tandy staff.

○ *Tandy Professional Forum*
GO TRS80PRO
Offers Tandy users information exchange with other users.

○ *Tandy Users Network*
GO TANDYNET
Accesses five Tandy product forums: the Color Computer Forum (GO COCO), the LDOS/TRSDOS6 Forum (GO LDOS), the Model 100/Portables Forum (GO M100SIG), the OS-9 Forum (GO OS9), the Tandy Professional Forum (GO TRS80PRO) and the Tandy Corporation Newsletter (GO TRS).

○ *TAPCIS Forum*
GO TAPCIS
Discusses the uses of TAPCIS.

○ *Tech III*
GO PCVEND
Provides support for Tech III products.

○ *TEGL Systems Corp.*
GO TEGL
Provides support for TEGL Systems' graphical interface programming toolkits.

○ *Telecommunication Issues Forum*
GO TELECO
Discussions for users interested in telecommunication services and products.

○ *Terrapin, Inc.*
GO LOGOFORUM
Provides support for Terrapin, Inc. products.

○ *Texas Instruments Forum*
GO TIFORUM
For anyone interested in any model of TI computer, especially the TI-99/4A and TI Pro-

fessional. Active message base; data libraries; weekly conferences.

○ *Texas Instruments Newsletter*
GO TINEWS
Provides the latest information about the TI Forum and TI world in general.

○ *Thomas-Conrad*
GO TCCFORUM
Provides technical support and information exchange for Thomas-Conrad products.

○ *3-D Visions*
GO STANFORD
Provides technical support for 3-D Visions products.

○ *Timeslips Corporation*
GO PCVEND
Provides support for Timeslips Corporation's Timeslips III.

○ *Timeworks*
GO TIMEWORKS
Provides support for Timeworks desktop publishing programs.

○ *T/Maker Company*
GO MACBVEN
Provides support for T/Maker products.

○ *TMS Peripherals*
GO MACCVEN
Provides support for TMS Peripherals products.

○ *Toshiba Forum*
GO TOSHIBA
Support and information for Toshiba. Information exchange for users interested in portable personal computer laptops and notebooks.

○ *Traveling Software, Inc.*
GO PALMTOP
Provides support for Traveling Software products.

○ *Trend Micro Devices*
GO TRENDMICRO
Provides support for Trend Micro Devices anti-virus products.

○ *Truevision*
GO TRUEVISION
Provides support for Truevision videographics boards.

○ *TurboPower Software*
GO PCVENB

Provides technical support for TurboPower Software's Turbo Professional, B-Tree Filer, Turbo Analyst, and Object Professional.

Turtle Beach Systems (MIDI)
GO TURBEACH

Provides support for Turtle Beach Systems' music software.

Turtle Beach Systems (Multimedia)
GO MULTIVENDOR

Provides support for Turtle Beach Systems' multimedia products.

Twelve Tone Systems
GO MIDIAVENDOR

Provides support for Twelve Tone Systems CAKEWALK.

UK Computing Forum
GO UKCOMP

Provides support for worldwide users of UK hardware and software products. Features several general computing sections managed by leading UK hardware and software vendors.

UK Forum
GO UKFORUM

Focuses on UK cultural and social themes. Includes the ever-popular "Rovers Return Pub," where members can participate in the kinds of forthright discussions associated with British pubs.

UK Shareware Forum
GO UKSHARE

Shareware enthusiasts exchange information, download upgrades, and more.

UK Shopper Forum
GO UKSHOPPER

Discusses the contents of the UK version of the magazine and other UK computer-related issues. Magazine staff actively take part in many discussions, which often lead to articles.

Universal Data Communications
GO UDCINC

Provides support for Universal Data Communications products.

Universal Technical Systems
GO UTSSUPPORT

Provides support for Universal Technical Systems products.

Unix Forum
GO UNIXFORUM

Users discuss Unix-related issues and exchange technical codes.

UserLand Software Forum
GO USERLAND

For Macintosh users interested in scripting using Userland Software's Frontier.

VAX Forum
GO VAXFORUM

Provides support and information exchange for VAX computer systems from Digital Equipment Corp.

Ventura Forum
GO VENTURA

Provides support and information exchange for Ventura software products. Converse with the publishers of *Ventura Professional!* magazine and find product reviews.

Vericomp
GO PCVENC

Provides technical support for Vericomp products.

VideoLogic
GO VIDEOLOGIC

Provides support for VideoLogic multimedia products.

Virtual Reality Laboratories, Inc.
GO VRLI

Provides support for VRLI's virtual reality products.

Virtus Corporation
GO VIRTUS

Provides support for Virtus WalkThrough.

The Voyager Company
GO VOYAGER

Provides support for Voyager products.

Wall Data
GO WALLDATA

Provides support for Wall Data's Rumba.

Wang Support Area
GO WANG

Provides support and information exchange for Wang computer systems and application programs. For additional support for Wang products, see Wang Support Forum (GO WANGFORUM).

Wang Support Forum
GO WANGFORUM

Provides support for users of Wang computer products. Message area hosts discussions. See also the Wang Support Area (GO WANG).

🌐 *What's New in the Atari Forums*
GO ATA
Gives useful information about all Atari forums including a What's New section and conference schedules.

🌐 *The Whitewater Group*
GO WHITEWATER
Provides support for The Whitewater Group products.

🌐 *Willies' Computer Software Co.*
GO WILLIES
Provides support for Willies' multitasking and utility products.

🌐 *Wilson WindowWare*
GO WILSON
Provides support for Wilson WindowWare products.

🌐 *Window Craft*
GO WINAPB
Provides support for Window Craft's Windowcraft.

🌐 *Window Users Group Network(WUGNET)*
GO WUGNET
Provides information to users and developers of software for the Windows 3.0 and OS/2 Presentation Manager environments. Includes a bimonthly WUGNET journal.

🌐 *Windows Vendor Forums*
GO WINVEN
Makes available four Windows vendor forums where users of non-Microsoft Windows applications can ask technical questions directly from Windows companies; each forum represents a different selection of vendors.

🌐 *Windows 3rd Party Applications A Forum*
GO WINAPA
Provides support from various companies for third-party applications designed to work with Microsoft Windows.

🌐 *Windows 3rd Party Applications B Forum*
GO WINAPB
Provides support from various companies for third-party applications designed to work with Microsoft Windows.

🌐 *Windows 3rd Party Applications C Forum*
GO WINAPC
Provides support from various companies for third-party applications designed to work with Microsoft Windows.

🌐 *Within Technologies*
GO WITHIN
Provides support for Within Technologies' Realizer.

🌐 *Wolfram Research Forum*
GO WOLFRAM
Provides information exchange relevant to Wolfram Research's Mathematica software.

🌐 *WordPerfect Users Forum*
GO WPUSERS
Provides support and discussions relevant to WordPerfect products. Sponsored by Support Group, Inc., a private company independent of WordPerfect Corporation.

🌐 *WordStar Forum*
GO WORDSTAR
Provides support and information exchange for WordStar products.

🌐 *Wordtech Systems*
GO WORDTECH
Provides support for Wordtech Systems' dBXL, Quicksilver, VP-expert, and VP-Graphics.

🌐 *Working Software*
GO MACBVEN
Provides support for Working Software's Quickletter, Findswell, Lookup, and Spellswell.

🌐 *The World of Lotus*
GO LOTUS
Provides information about Lotus products and services, access to electronic distribution of software, and the opportunity to 'talk' with fellow Lotus users.

🌐 *XChange*
GO XCHANGE
Provides support for developers of XTensions for QuarkXPress and other desktop publishing-related products.

🌐 *XTree Company*
GO XTREE
Provides support for XTree products.

🌐 *Zenith Forum*
GO ZENITH
For users interested in products from Zenith Data Systems and participating independent companies.

🌐 *Zenographics*
GO ZENO
Provides technical support for Zenographics' printing and image handling applications.

ⓢ *Zeos International*
GO ZEOS
Offers informational files and support for Zeos.

ⓢ *Ziff Buyers' Market*
GO BUYMARKET
Enables members to buy computer products directly from more than 130 companies. Provides product information in a searchable format.

ⓢ *ZiffNet*
GO ZIFFNET
Provides information on productivity-boosting software and advice to help you get the most from your PC. Access to shareware, utilities, technical tips, and current events in the computer industry.

ⓢ *ZiffNet European Services*
GO ZEUS
Offers a wide range of services for readers of *PC Magazine UK*. Connect with the editors and other users, download utilities and information, get UK computer industry news, and access magazine databases.

ⓢ *ZiffNet/Mac*
GO ZMAC
Dedicated to Macintosh users and their specific needs. Makes available reference databases, a buyer's guide, technical tips, and free downloadable utilities. Access to the leading industry news and opinions from *MacUser* and *MacWEEK*.

ⓢ *ZSoft Corporation (Windows)*
GO ZSOFT
Provides support for ZSoft Corporation's paint and imaging graphic tools.

ⓢ *The Electronic Frontier Foundation Forum*
GO EFFSIG
Enables users to discuss computer-based communication issues, including policy, social concerns, and innovation.

ⓢ *Apple News Clips*
GO APPLENEWS
Enables users to review the latest articles and reports about Apple from AP, UPI, Reuters, and other news wire services.

ⓢ *Computer Consultant's Forum*
GO CONSULT
For information exchange among computer consultants. Sponsored by the Independent Computer Consultants Association (ICCA).

ⓢ *Computer Training Forum*
GO DPTRAIN
For users with an interest in the computer learning process. Information on training techniques, office automation, careers, and computers in schools. Members can enroll in free on-line Professional Seminars taught by leading instructors.

ⓢ *Computer Database Plus*
GO COMPDB
Makes available computer-related article summaries and full texts. Includes nearly 200 magazine, paper, and journal titles; coverage for most starts with 1987. Searchable; updated weekly.

ⓢ *Computer Directory*
GO COMPDIR
Provides product and manufacturer information on over 69,000 computer-related items from more than 8,500 manufacturers.

ⓢ *Data-Processing Newsletters*
GO DPNEWS
Provides the full text of articles taken from several leading newsletters covering the computer, electronics, and telecommunications industries.

ⓢ *Personal Computer Support*
GO EUR-18
Lists forums containing information for European users of IBM, Borland, Nantucket, Microsoft, and shareware products.

GEnie

ⓢ *Jerry Pournelle RoundTable*
Keyword: JERRY or Page 245
Jerry Pournelle (a contributing editor to *Byte* and *InfoWorld*) discusses his views on computers, the state of science, politics, and sociology.

ⓢ *PC-VAN*
Keyword: PC-VAN or Page 315
Japan's number one on-line service. Boasts over 500,000 subscribers and features more than 140 special interest groups. Offers electronic mail, bulletin boards, on-line Japanese newspapers and magazines, shopping at 16 of Japan's most popular stores, and access to various Japanese commercial and professional databases.

꿈 *DTP RoundTable*
Keyword: DTP or Page 590
Serves the desktop publishing and electronic pre-press profession.

꿈 *E-Span JobSearch*
Keyword: ESPAN or Page 304
An employment advertising network reaching more than 3.5 million PC-literate professional, technical, and managerial candidates nationwide. Updated weekly.

꿈 *Adventures of the High-Tech Nomad*
Keyword: NOMAD or Page 320
Steve Roberts writes about his adventures.

꿈 *A Networker's Journal by Charles Bowen*
Keyword: BOWEN or Page 310
A regular computer column by Charles Bowen

꿈 *Computer Game Design RoundTable*
Keyword: JCGD or Page 935
Covers the design—but not the playing of—computer games.

꿈 *Apple II RoundTable*
Keyword: A2 or Page 645
Provides support for the Apple II computer and related items. Large file library for downloading.

꿈 *Apple II Programmers RoundTable*
Keyword: A2PRO or Page 530
For users interested in programming an Apple II, treating a variety of programming languages.

꿈 *GE-MUG (Macintosh) RoundTable*
Keyword: MAC or Page 605
Provides support for all flavors of Apple Macintosh computers. Library contains 30,000+ public domain files.

꿈 *Macintosh Developers RoundTable*
Keyword: MACPRO or Page 480
For users interested in programming and developing software for the Macintosh, or who want to learn about the technical side of the machine.

꿈 *Bulletin Board System (BBS) RoundTable*
Keyword: BBS or Page 610
For users who run computer bulletin boards in the U.S. Focus is on software, utilities, and discussion for IBM, Macintosh, and Amiga BBS Sysops.

꿈 *Borland RoundTable*
Keyword: BORLAND or Page 765
A forum for discussions dealing with Borland products.

꿈 *CE Software RoundTable*
Keyword: CESOFTWARE or Page 1005
Provides support for CE Software products.

꿈 *CP/M RoundTable*
Keyword: CPM or Page 685
Provides support for all varieties of CP/M, ZCPR3, ZSDOS, and Z3PLUS.

꿈 *Forth Interest Group RoundTable*
Keyword: FORTH or Page 710
Operated by the Forth Interest Group, a non-profit association of programmers, managers, and engineers who create "practical, Forth-based systems to meet real-world needs."

꿈 *Laptops RoundTable*
Keyword: LAPTOPS or Page 655
Provides support for various portable PC-compatibles.

꿈 *Microsoft RoundTable*
Keyword: MICROSOFT or Page 505
Managed and supported by the Product Support Services department at Microsoft. Answers questions on Microsoft retail products.

꿈 *Mini/Mainframe RoundTable*
Keyword: MAINFRAME or Page 1145
Facilitates exchange of information and ideas among programmers, analysts, and users of medium- to large-scale computer systems.

꿈 *Freesoft RoundTable*
Keyword: FREESOFT or Page 585
A support area available only to registered users of White Knight and Second Sight Mac software.

꿈 *Autodesk Retail Products RoundTable*
Keyword: CADD or Page 455
Facilitates exchange of information and files for Generic CADD users.

꿈 *ICD RoundTable*
Keyword: ICD or Page 1220
Provides support for ICD products.

꿈 *Softronics RoundTable*
Keyword: SOFTRONICS or Page 630
Provides technical support for Softronics products.

꿈 *WordPerfect RoundTable*
Keyword: WP or Page 521
Provides reviews, printer drivers, macros, graphics, models, templates, programs, tips, and all other kinds of information for WordPerfect Corporation products.

ChipSoft RoundTable
Keyword: CHIPSOFT or Page 170
Provides support for ChipSoft, Inc., products.

Database RoundTable
Keyword: DBMS or Page 485
For users of computer database management programs and systems (DBMS).

ENABLE RoundTable
Keyword: ENABLE or Page 465
Provides support for users of Enable Software's multi-windowed integrated package.

Gadgets By Small RoundTable
Keyword: GADGETS or Page 690
Provides support for Gadgets By Small products.

GeoWorks RoundTable by Tony Cuozzo
Keyword: GEOWORKS or Page 1050
Provides support for users of GeoWorks products.

Hayes RoundTable
Keyword: HAYES or Page 435
Answers questions on Hayes retail products. Also provides a worldwide list of bulletin boards.

Mustang Software RoundTable
Keyword: MUSTANG or Page 680
Provides support for Mustang Software products.

Soft Logik RoundTable
Keyword: SOFTLOGIK or Page 385
Provides support for SoftLogik products.

TimeWorks RoundTable
Keyword: TIMEWORKS or Page 1325
Provides support for TimeWorks products.

IBM PC RoundTable by Charles Strom
Keyword: IBMPC or Page 615
Discussions of all aspects of owning and operating IBM PCs.

Tandy RoundTable by Mike Hogan
Keyword: TANDY or Page 635
For all users of Tandy/Radio Shack computers.

PC Aladdin Support RoundTable
Keyword: PCALADDIN or Page 110
Provides support for GEnie PC Aladdin software.

Atari ST RoundTable
Keyword: ST or Page 475
Provides support for owners and users of Atari ST, STe, TT, and Falcon Computer systems.

Atari 8-Bit RoundTable
Keyword: ATARI8 or Page 665
Provides support for Atari 8-bit computers.

Portfolio RoundTable
Keyword: PORTFOLIO or Page 950
Provides support for Portfolio computer systems.

ST Aladdin RoundTable
Keyword: STALADDIN or Page 1000
Provides support for Aladdin telecommunications software.

Computer & Electronics NewsCenter
Keyword: COMPUTERS or Page 1282
A searchable database containing the product announcements, software and hardware reviews, editorials, and industry trends, plus articles from computer science journals and recent government reports.

PC Catalog
Keyword: PC-CATALOG or Page 1230
An on-line catalog of thousands of computer items for sale by some of the nation's most price-competitive mail-order vendors. Includes price and vendor information. Updated weekly.

TI RoundTable
Keyword: TI or Page 575
Provides support for users of Texas Instruments units and other computer "orphans."

PostScript RoundTable
Keyword: PSRT or Page 835
For users of the PostScript language, desktop publishing, or laser printers.

Unix RoundTable
Keyword: UNIX or Page 160
Provides support for users of Unix, Xenix, and Unix-like systems.

StarShip Amiga RoundTable
Keyword: AMIGA or Page 555
Provides support for users of Amiga computers.

StarShip Pro/Am RoundTable
Keyword: PRO/AM or Page 670
Provides support for users interested in Amiga programming.

FlagShip Commodore RoundTable
Keyword: CBM or Page 625
Provides support for users of C-64 and C-128 computers.

The Well

⑤ Apple Library User's Group
(g alug)

For all types of librarians who use Apples. Discussions of computers and information, copyright and intellectual freedom, networking, and electronic access to information.

⑤ Amiga
(g amiga)

Provided as a meeting place for developers, programmers and other users of the Commodore Amiga personal computer.

⑤ Computer Books
(g cbook)

An information forum for writers of computer books. Discusses the hottest topics for computer books, the best publishers, the worst subjects to write about, notices on new books looking for authors, and much more.

⑤ Consultants
(g consult)

For consultants who work in computers or computer-related areas. Discussions of such matters as marketing, taxes, running a small business, loneliness, and collaboration.

⑤ Computer Journalism
(g cpj)

Discusses how computers are covered by the media and general issues, as well as issues of special interest to computer journalists. Sponsored by The Computer Press Association.

⑤ CP/M
(g cpm)

Discussions concerning computers running the CP/M operating system.

⑤ Computer Professionals for Social Responsibility
(g cpsr)

Discussions about computers and society.

⑤ Computer Graphics
(g gra)

Dedicated to all aspects of graphics, from handmade to computer-generated, delivered via video, computer, and print.

⑤ Hacking / Cracking
(g hack)

Discussions about computer hacking.

⑤ IBM PC
(g ibm)

Features IBM PC-related discussions, including products to buy or sell, problems with equipment or software, and much more.

⑤ Internet
(g internet)

Teaches members how to use Internet from The Well.

⑤ LANs
(g lan)

Devoted to personal computer networks, with the focus on practical solutions available today—network operating systems, hardware, and multiuser applications—and the issues, standards, and products emerging from the industry.

⑤ Laptop
(g laptop)

Devoted to laptop computing. Discussions and information on all aspects of laptop models new and old.

⑤ Macintosh System 7
(g mac7)

For Macintosh users who have switched to System 7.0 (or may be thinking about it).

⑤ Macintosh Technical
(g mactech)

Discusses technical issues related to Apple Macintoshes, from basic programming to advanced features of the Mac operating system and the future of the industry.

⑤ MIDI
(g midi)

Hosted by Warren Sirota (warren), Carter Scholz (csz), and Larry Oppenheimer (toys). Discussions at all levels about MIDI and any issues pertaining to making music with electronics or computers.

⑤ The Matrix
(Private Conference)

A forum about computer networks.

⑤ Mondo 2000
(g mondo)

Covers cyberspace and cyberculture.

⑤ Muchomedia
(g mucho)

Discussions concerning the use of digital computer technology.

⑤ Programmer's Network
(g net)

For discussions between programmers and users.

Netweaver
(g netweaver)

The on-line monthly newsletter of the Electronic Networking Association (ENA).

NeXT
(g next)

For discussions pertaining to NeXT hardware and software.

Origin
(g origin)

Explores interdisciplinary topic linkage and integrated on-line networking.

OS/2
(g os2)

Disseminates user and technical information about OS/2.

Printers
(g print)

Provides information about printers.

Public (WELL) Software
(g public)

Provides suppport for user-contributed software.

Realtime
(g realtime)

For users interested in the design, construction, and programming of realtime or embedded systems, robots, expert systems, the Forth programming language or artificial intelligence.

Scientific Computing
(g scicomp)

Discussions concerning using computers to solve problems in science and engineering.

Software Design
(g sdc)

Facilitates discussions about the field of software design.

Software/Programming
(g soft)

Discussions for users interested in the principles of software design and coding.

Software Support
(g ssc)

Dedicated to the profession of software support—using shared experience and expertise to assist customers in effectively using software. Commentary on industry trends and influences in software support. This conference does NOT supply specific advice on how to use a particular product.

Telecommunicating
(g tele)

Discusses communications—electronic and otherwise. Topics range from engineering and technical ones to the legal and social impact that these technologies have on our lives.

Unix
(g unix)

Discussions relevant to the Unix community—public domain Unix software, Unix market penetration, new Unix machines (and old ones), more.

Virtual Communities
(g vc)

Explores the nature and variety of virtual communities, with an emphasis on social and cultural dynamics.

Virtual Reality
(g vr)

Discusses the technology, philosophy, ethics, psychology, politics, and business of virtual reality.

Windows
(g windows)

Discusses and supports of the use of Microsoft Windows.

Network Discussions Lists
Internet (Includes Bitnet & UUCPNet)

Turkish TeX

Discusses, disseminates, and exchanges information about TeX typesetting system and its variants.
    YUNUS@TRMETU.BITNET
    LISTSERV@TRMETU.BITNET
Contact: Mustafa Akgul
    akgul@trbilun.BITNET

Association for the Advancement of Computing

For all users interested in the Association for the Advancement of Computing in Education.
    AACE-L@AUVM.BITNET
    LISTSERV@AUVM.BITNET
Contact: Michael J. Strait
    <STRAIT@UMUC.BITNET>

AUTODIN Switch Interface

A series of programs that interface a data processing installation (DPI) with an AUTODIN switching center.

```
AAI@ST-LOUIS-EMH2.ARMY.MIL
AAI@ST-LOUIS-EMH2.ARMY.MIL
```
Contact: Jo Ann Bohnenstiehl
```
<jb1742@ST-LOUIS-EMH2.ARMY.MIL>
```

♫ *AAR Electronic Publication list.*
```
AARPUB-L@JPNIMRTU.BITNET
LISTSERV@JPNIMRTU.BITNET
```

♫ *Application Specific MICROprocessors*
For the interchange of information regarding all aspects of the design and use of Application Specific Microprocessors.
```
AASMICRO-L@VME131.LSI.USP.ANSP.BR
ASMICRO-REQUEST@VME131.LSI.USP.ANSP.BR
```
Contact: Pedro Luis Prospero Sanchez
```
<pl@vme131.lsi.usp.ansp.br>
```

♫ *Newsletter of the Association for Computers list.*
```
ACHNEWS@UCSBVM.BITNET
LISTSERV@UCSBVM.BITNET
```

♫ *ACM-L List for student chapters of ACM list.*
```
ACM-L@OHSTVMA.BITNET
LISTSERV@OHSTVMA.BITNET
```
Contact: Michael Clore
```
<CLORE@OHSTPHRM.BITNET>
```

♫ *ACM MEXICO list.*
```
ACMMEX-L@VMTECMEX.BITNET
LISTSERV@VMTECMEX.BITNET
```

♫ *ACM student chapters list.*
```
ACMSTCHP@SUVM.BITNET
LISTSERV@SUVM.BITNET
```

♫ *ACORN computers discussion list.*
```
ACORN-L@GREARN.BITNET
LISTSERV@GREARN.BITNET
```

♫ *IBM Advanced Control System discussion list.*
Discusses issues concerning IBM's "Advanced Control System," program number 5799-BEJ.
```
ACS-L@POLYGRAF.BITNET
LISTSERV@POLYGRAF.BITNET
```
Contact: Dave Rubin
```
<drubin@TASHA.BITNET>
```

♫ *Academic Software Development*
Discusses all aspects of academic software such as Courseware development, research tool development, institutional policies regarding development and use, development practices, Available resources (including grant sources).
```
ACSOFT-L@WUVMD.BITNET
LISTSERV@WUVMD.BITNET
```
Contact: Timothy Bergeron
```
<C09615TB@WUVMD.BITNET>
```

♫ *ADA Program Archive*
A mailing list for users who access and contribute software to the ADA Repository on SIMTEL20. Provides an information exchange medium between the repository users and to mail repository submissions to the coordinator for inclusion in the archives.
```
ADA-SW@WSMR-SIMTEL20.ARMY.MIL
ADA-SW-REQUEST@WSMR-SIMTEL20.ARMY.MIL
```
Contact: Rick Conn
```
<RCONN@WSMR-SIMTEL20.ARMY.MIL>
```

♫ *ADR Database products discussion list.*
For users of the ADR Database and related products from Applied Data Research, Inc. (ADR).
```
ADR-L@ALBNYVM1.BITNET
LISTSERV@ALBNYVM1.BITNET
```
Contact: Stephen T. Murphy
```
<asdstm@ALBNYVM1.BITNET>
```

♫ *Computing*
Enables users to find, comment, ask, and broadcast information about the latest advances on computing.
```
ADV-INFO@UTFSM.BITNET
LISTSERV@UTFSM.BITNET
```
Contact: Francisco Javier Fernandez
```
<FFERNAND@UTFSM.BITNET>
```

♫ *CC user support discussion list.*
```
ADVISORS@TECHNION.BITNET
LISTSERV@TECHNION.BITNET
```

♫ *AEDNET Mail Server*
```
AEDNET@SUVM.BITNET
LISTSERV@SUVM.BITNET
```

♫ *Applied Expert Systems research group list.*
```
AESRG-L@UMCVMB.BITNET
LISTSERV@UMCVMB.BITNET
```
Contact: Russ Meyer
```
<ENGLRUSS@UMCVMB.BITNET>
```

♫ *Information Technology and Africa*
Provide an electronic forum for sharing and exchanging information on the various activities going on in the field of information technology in Africa.
```
AFRICANA@WMVM1.BITNET
LISTSERV@WMVM1.BITNET
```
Contact: Paa-Bekoe Welbeck
```
<PBWELB@WMVM1.BITNET>
```

♫ *Ag Expert Systems*
This list is for the use of Expert Systems in Agricultural production and management. Primary emphasis is for practitioners, extension personnel and experiment station researchers in the land grant system.

```
AG-EXP-L@NDSUVM1.BITNET
LISTSERV@NDSUVM1.BITNET
```
Contact: Sandy Sprafka
```
<NU020746@NDSUVM1.BITNET>
```

🌀 *ASAE Knowledge systems discussion list.*
```
AGEN-KS@RUTVM1.BITNET
LISTSERV@RUTVM1.BITNET
```

🌀 *Association for History & Computing list.*
```
AHC-L@DGOGWDG1.BITNET
LISTSERV@DGOGWDG1.BITNET
```
Contact: Manfred Thaller
```
<MTHALLE1@DGOGWDG1.BITNET>
```

🌀 *Expert Systems and Education*
Discusses the application of artificial intelligence to education. Issues related to teaching AI are welcome. Topics may also include evaluation of tutoring systems.
```
AI-ED@SUN.COM
AI-Ed-Request@SUN.COM
```
Contact: J.R. Prohaska
```
<prohaska@SUN.COM>
```

🌀 *Artifical Intelligence & Medicine*
For computer scientists and engineers with and interest in biomedical and clinical research, and for physicians with and interest in medical informatics.
```
AI-MEDICINE@VUSE.VANDERBILT.EDU
ai-medicine-request@vuse.vanderbilt.edu
```
Contact: Serdar Uckun
```
MD <serdar@vuse.vanderbilt.edu>
```

🌀 *AICS discussion list.*
```
AICS-L@UBVM.BITNET
LISTSERV@UBVM.BITNET
```

🌀 *List for national membership of AIESEC.*
```
AIESEC-L@KENTVM.BITNET
LISTSERV@KENTVM.BITNET
```

🌀 *Artificial intelligence list.*
Discusses artificial intelligence and related topics. Contributions may be anything from tutorials to speculation.
```
AILIST@NDSUVM1.BITNET
LISTSERV@NDSUVM1.BITNET
```
Contact: Nick Papadakis
```
<Nick@AI.AI.MIT.EDU>
```

🌀 *IBM AIX discussion list.*
Discusses the AIX operating system, IBM's Unix solution for small and large computer systems.
```
AIX-L@PUCC.BITNET
LISTSERV@PUCC.BITNET
```
Contact: Michael R. Gettes
```
<CCMRG@BOSTONU.BITNET>
```

🌀 *AIX working group discussion list.*
```
AIXL@ICNUCEVM.BITNET
LISTSERV@ICNUCEVM.BITNET
```

🌀 *IBM AIX Unix Discussion*
A digested mail redistribution of the Usenet newsgroup comp.unix.aix, for sites that don't receive usenet news. About 90% of discussion focuses on the RS6000 platform. The remainder is mostly about PS2 AIX, with a rare posting about AIX/370.
```
AIXNEWS@PUCC.BITNET
LISTSERV@PUCC.BITNET
```
Contact: Doug Sewell
```
<doug@ysub.bitnet>
```

🌀 *AIX370 discussion list.*
```
AIX370-L@UWAVM.BITNET
LISTSERV@UWAVM.BITNET
```

🌀 *International ALEPH users list.*
```
ALEPHINT@TAUNIVM.BITNET
LISTSERV@TAUNIVM.BITNET
```

🌀 *ALL-IN-1 managers and users mailing list.*
For ALL-IN-1 managers and users to discuss problems and suggestions relating to the installation, management, and use of ALL-IN-1.
```
ALLIN1-L@SBCCVM.BITNET
LISTSERV@SBCCVM.BITNET
```
Contact: Sanjay Kapur
```
<SJKAPUR@CCMAIL.SUNYSB.EDU>
```

🌀 *Emory E-Mail general users list.*
```
ALLUSR-L@EMUVM1.BITNET
LISTSERV@EMUVM1.BITNET
```

🌀 *Amethyst Software*
For users of Amethyst, a software package of CP/M-80 programs: MINCE (an ersatz EMACS) and SCRIBBLE (an ersatz SCRIBE).
```
AMETHYST-USERS@SIMTEL20.ARMY.MIL
AMETHYST-USERS-REQUEST@SIMTEL20.ARMY.MIL
```
Contact: Frank Wancho
```
<WANCHO@WSMR-SIMTEL20.ARMY.MIL>
```

🌀 *Comp.Sys.Amiga.Hardware redistribution from Usenet.*
```
AMI-HARD@UMAINECS.BITNET
LISTSERV@UMAINECS.BITNET
```
Contact: Mark Nelson
```
<NELSON@UDEL.EDU>
```

🌀 *Csamiga Comp.Sys.Amiga.Tech Redistribution from Usenet*
```
AMI-TECH@UMAINECS.BITNET
LISTSERV@UMAINECS.BITNET
```

✪ *AMS Human Resource system discussion list.*
AMSHRS-L@UMDD.BITNET
LISTSERV@UMDD.BITNET

✪ *American Management Systems Student Forum*
Discusses topics related to the American Management System Student Information System (AMSSIS).
AMSSIS-L@UAFSYSB.BITNET
LISTSERV@UAFSYSB.BITNET
Contact: Allen Fields
<ALLENF@UAFSYSA.BITNET>

✪ *Andrew Software Demo*
Demonstrates the Andrew system software.
ANDREW-DEMOS@ANDREW.CMU.EDU
ANDREW-DEMOS-REQUEST@ANDREW.CMU.EDU
Contact: Nathaniel Borenstein
<nsb+@ANDREW.CMU.EDU>

✪ *Announcements of new ANSI and OSI draft standards list.*
ANNONSTD@BITNIC.BITNET
LISTSERV@BITNIC.BITNET

✪ *Documents from X3J18—ANSIREXX standards committee list.*
ANSIREXX@PSUVM.BITNET
LISTSERV@PSUVM.BITNET

✪ *Emory Computing Questions and Answers list.*
ANSWER-L@EMUVM1.BITNET
LISTSERV@EMUVM1.BITNET

✪ *AOS/VS Operating System Discussion list.*
AOSVS-L@TRMETU.BITNET
LISTSERV@TRMETU.BITNET

✪ *UCD APL Interest Group*
APL-ERS@IRLEARN.BITNET
LISTSERV@IRLEARN.BITNET
Contact: UCD Help Desk
<ADVISER@IRLEARN.BITNET>

✪ *APL Language discussion list.*
Discusses the APL language, its implementation, application and use.
APL-L@UNBVM1.BITNET
LISTSERV@UNBVM1.BITNET
Contact: David G. Macneil
<DGM%UNB.CA@VM1.NODAK.EDU>

✪ *APL in Education list.*
APLEDU-L@UNBVM1.BITNET
LISTSERV@UNBVM1.BITNET

✪ *Apollo Workstations*
For users of Apollo computers who are interested in sharing their experiences about Apollos.

apollo@UMIX.CC.UMICH.EDU
apollo-request@UMIX.CC.UMICH.EDU
Contact: Paul Killey
<paul@UMIX.CC.UMICH.EDU>

✪ *APPC discussion list.*
Discusses IBM's Advanced Program-to-Program Communication (APPC) as well as associated topics. To receive a list of files send the command INDEX APPC-L to LISTSERV@AUVM. These files are available from auvm.american.edu via ftp.
APPC-L@AUVM.BITNET
LISTSERV@AUVM.BITNET
Contact: Jim McIntosh
jim@american.edu>

✪ *Appletalk*
APPLENET@TECMTYVM.BITNET
LISTSERV@TECMTYVM.BITNET

✪ *Apple-2*
APPLE2-L@BROWNVM.BROWN.EDU
LISTSERV@BROWNVM.BROWN.EDU

✪ *Apple II List*
Discusses Apple II related topics and distributes Apple II software.
Contact: Christopher Chung
<CHRIS@BROWNVM.BROWN.EDU>

✪ *Applications under BITNET*
Discusses applications under BITNET. Includes material documents applications that run under BITNET. Examples of topics include file servers, package servers, and remote job entry.
APPLICAT@BITNIC.BITNET
LISTSERV@BITNIC.BITNET

✪ *Amiga REXX discussion list.*
AREXX-L@UCF1VM.BITNET
LISTSERV@UCF1VM.BITNET

✪ *American Society for Information Sciences list.*
ASIS-L@UVMVM.BITNET
LISTSERV@UVMVM.BITNET

✪ *askSam*
For users of askSam: A Free-form Information program.
ASKSAM-L@VTVM1.BITNET
LISTSERV@VTVM1.BITNET

✪ *IBM System/370*
Discusses programming in IBM System/370 Assembly Language.
ASM370@UCF1VM.BITNET
LISTSERV@UCF1VM.BITNET

⑤ *Discussion of AXL3 smallest resolvable cluster.*
ASRC-L@LEPICS.BITNET
LISTSERV@LEPICS.BITNET
Contact: David Stickland
<STICKLAN@LEPICS.BITNET>

⑤ *ASTRA users group discussion list.*
ASTRA-UG@ICNUCEVM.BITNET
LISTSERV@ICNUCEVM.BITNET
Contact: Patrizia Cecaloni
<ASTRA@ICNUCEVM.BITNET>

⑤ *Assembly for the IBM-PC*
For issues related to the PC Assembly languages
(Intel 8086/88/286/386/...).
ASSMPC@USACHVM1.BITNET
LISTSERV@USACHVM1.BITNET
Contact: Luis Valdivia P.
<LVALDIVI@USACHVM1.BITNET>

⑤ *ASUNOVEL list.*
ASUNOVEL@ASUACAD.BITNET
LISTSERV@ASUACAD.BITNET

⑤ *Portland Comm Col Redistribution of AS400 list.*
AS400-L@PCCVM.BITNET
LISTSERV@PCCVM.BITNET

⑤ *Campuswide Appletalk discussion list.*
ATALK-L@WUVMD.BITNET
LISTSERV@WUVMD.BITNET

⑤ *ATHENA Progetto polo UNIX list.*
ATHENA@ITOCSIVM.BITNET
LISTSERV@ITOCSIVM.BITNET

⑤ *Discussion about ATLAS-TI list.*
ATLAS-TI@DB0TUI11.BITNET
LISTSERV@DB0TUI11.BITNET

⑤ *BITNET BOF list; registration only.*
ATTENDBF@BITNIC.BITNET
LISTSERV@BITNIC.BITNET

⑤ *Autolog*
For problems from users that have accounts at
the Technion and work remotely through the
Remote Server (VMAUTOLG) located at the
Technion.
AUTO-L@TECHNION.BITNET
LISTSERV@TECHNION.BITNET
Contact: Robert (Al) Hartshorn
<CCSM1AL@TECHNION.BITNET>

⑤ *Autocad discussion list.*
AUTOCAD@OHSTVMA.BITNET
LISTSERV@OHSTVMA.BITNET
Contact: Bob Kalal
<KALAL@OHSTVMA.BITNET>

⑤ *AWARE-L*
Discusses dual platform authoring programs.
AWARE-L@UKANVM.BITNET
LISTSERV@UKANVM.BITNET

⑤ *Authorware Professional for Mac/Windows and related topics.*
Discussions for developers that use the program
Authorware Professional.
Aware-L@UKANVM.BITNET
LISTSERV@UKANVM.BITNET
Contact: Donald W. Tracia
<Tracia@UKANVM.BITNET>

⑤ *AWAY Package discussion list.*
Discussion list about the AWAY package which
is a combination of GONE, MSGTRAP, IPF's
VMUTIL, ECI, LISTSERV's LMON, reduced
CMSBATCH facility, and packages like these.
AWAY-L@TREARN.BITNET
LISTSERV@TREARN.BITNET
Contact: Bahri Bora Bali
<OPRJ36@TREARN.BITNET>

⑤ *AXIOM Computer Algebra System list.*
AXIOM@NDSUVM1.BITNET
LISTSERV@NDSUVM1.BITNET

⑤ *Student information system discussions.*
Discusses issues related to the SCT Student
Information System (BANNER).
BANNER-L@WVNVM.BITNET
LISTSERV@WVNVM.BITNET
Contact: Roxann Humbert
<U114C@WVNVM.BITNET>

⑤ *Banyan Networks discussion list.*
Discusses any aspect of Local Area Networks
(LANs) marketed by Banyan Systems Inc.
BANYAN-L@AKRONVM.BITNET
LISTSERV@AKRONVM.BITNET
Contact: Gary Sponseller
<SPONSELL@AKRONVM.BITNET>

⑤ *Visual Basic discussion list.*
Discusses Visual Basic software for PCs.
BAS-L@TAMVM1.BITNET
LISTSERV@TAMVM1.BITNET
Contact: Chris Barnes
<x005cb@tamvm1.tamu.edu>

⑤ *Purdue BATCH discussion list.*
BATCH-L@PURCCVM.BITNET
LISTSERV@PURCCVM.BITNET

⑤ *University Of Missouri*
BA275A@UMSLVMA.BITNET
LISTSERV@UMSLVMA.BITNET
Contact: Bill Meade
BA275A

🌀 *List for discussion about BBSs, creation, and usage.*
```
BBS-L@SAUPM00.BITNET
LISTSERV@SAUPM00.BITNET
```

🌀 *BEL-HD BelWue/HD-Net maintenance list.*
```
BEL-HD@DHDURZ1.BITNET
LISTSERV@DHDURZ1.BITNET
```

🌀 *Best North America Discussion group list.*
```
BEST-L@UTORONTO.BITNET
LISTSERV@UTORONTO.BITNET
```

🌀 *Buffalo Free Net committee list.*
```
BFN-L@UBVM.BITNET
LISTSERV@UBVM.BITNET
```

🌀 *Campus-Size LAN discussion group.*
Discusses issues in designing and operating Campus-Size Local Area Networks, especially complex ones utilizing multiple technologies and supporting multiple protocols.
```
BIG-LAN@SUVM.BITNET
LISTSERV@SUVM.BITNET
```
Contact: John Wobus
```
<JMWOBUS@SUVM.BITNET>
```

🌀 *BigmOuth/Powerline/Talking Technologies*
For users of BigmOuth and PowerLine voice mail PC cards, from Talking Technologies, Inc.
```
BIGM-L@VM.SAS.COM
LISTSERV@VM.SAS.COM
```
Contact: Dale Ingold
```
<snoddi@mvs.sas.com>
```

🌀 *Chargeback of (computer) resources list.*
```
BILLING@HDETUD1.BITNET
LISTSERV@HDETUD1.BITNET
```
Contact: Rob van Hoboken
```
<RCOPROB@HDETUD1.BITNET>
```

🌀 *BITLIB Distribution List.*
```
BITLIB-D@UTCVM.BITNET
LISTSERV@UTCVM.BITNET
```

🌀 *BITLIB Discussion List*
```
BITLIB-L@UTCVM.BITNET
LISTSERV@UTCVM.BITNET
```

🌀 *Discussion of BITNET II list.*
```
BITNET-2@TCSVM.BITNET
LISTSERV@TCSVM.BITNET
```

🌀 *BITNET Network news list.*
The official medium of the BITNET Network Information Center for distributing BITNET news and administrative developments.
```
BITNEWS@BITNIC.BITNET
LISTSERV@BITNIC.BITNET
```

🌀 *BITNET User's Group list.*
```
BITUSE-L@UMAB.BITNET
LISTSERV@UMAB.BITNET
```

🌀 *Barus Lab Interactive Speech System List*
```
BLISS-L@BROWNVM.BITNET
LISTSERV@BROWNVM.BITNET
```

🌀 *BITNET RFC discussion list.*
```
BRFC-L@PUCC.BITNET
LISTSERV@PUCC.BITNET
```

🌀 *BRS/Search Full Text Retrieval Software Discussion*
Discusses the BRS/Search Software product, available from BRS Information Technologies. BRS/Search is an inverted index, full-text storage and retrieval database which runs on a variety of platforms.
```
BRS-L@USCVM.BITNET
LISTSERV@USCVM.BITNET
```
Contact: Karl P. Geiger
```
<KARL@USCVM.BITNET>
```

🌀 *Database*
List for announcing and discussing BRS documents.
```
BRSDOC@LIVERPOOL.AC.UK
LISTSERV@LIVERPOOL.AC.UK
```

🌀 *Business school computing support list.*
```
BSCS-L@EMUVM1.BITNET
LISTSERV@EMUVM1.BITNET
```

🌀 *BSR Software discussion list.*
```
BSRUSERS@PUCC.BITNET
LISTSERV@PUCC.BITNET
```

🌀 *Bug reports for GNUISH MsDos Software*
```
bug-gnu-msdos@wugate.wustl.edu
bug-gnu-msdos-request@wugate.wustl.edu
```
Contact: Mr. David J. Camp
```
<david@wubios.wustl.edu>
```

🌀 *Faircom software*
Discusses FairCom's C-Tree, R-Tree, and D-Tree products. The list is not associated with FairCom.
```
C-TREE <oha!ctree@UUNET.UU.NET>
oha!ctree-request@UUNET.UU.NET
```
Contact: Tony Olekshy
```
<tony@OHA.UUCP>
```

🌀 *BITNET part of CA@Think.COM (Cellular Automata)*
For information on all aspects of cellular automata and their applications. The list is gatewayed to/from the Usenet group `comp.theory.cell-automata`.
```
CA-L@MITVMA.BITNET
LISTSERV@MITVMA.BITNET
```

🌀 *Canadian VMNET Backbone group list.*
```
CA-VMNET@UTORONTO.BITNET
LISTSERV@UTORONTO.BITNET
```

🖎 *Canadian Association of Campus Computer Store list.*
```
CACCS-L@UOGUELPH.BITNET
LISTSERV@UOGUELPH.BITNET
```

🖎 *CADAM guru forum*
For CADAM experts and maintainers, (micro and Professional CADAM too.)
```
CADAM-L@FINHUTC.BITNET
LISTSERV@FINHUTC.BITNET
```
Contact: Tony S. Dahbura
```
<DAHBURA@SUVM.BITNET>
```

🖎 *CAD General Discussion Group*
For general CAE/CAD/CAM/CIM discussion.
```
CADLIST@FINHUTC.BITNET
LISTSERV@FINHUTC.BITNET
```
Contact: Tony S. Dahbura
```
<DAHBURA@SUVM.BITNET>
```

🖎 *CAEDS guru forum*
For Structural Dynamic System Corporation's CAEDS finite analysis system experts and maintainers.
```
CAEDS-L@FINHUTC.BITNET
LISTSERV@FINHUTC.BITNET
```
Contact: Tony S. Dahbura
```
<DAHBURA@SUVM.BITNET>
```

🖎 *CAFSS-L is a list for members of the CAFSS.*
```
CAFSS-L@VTVM1.BITNET
LISTSERV@VTVM1.BITNET
```

🖎 *CAG_IBP Information Exchange list.*
```
CAG-IGBP@UOGUELPH.BITNET
LISTSERV@UOGUELPH.BITNET
```

🖎 *CANCHID: Canadian Network for Collaboration list.*
```
CANCHID@YORKVM1.BITNET
LISTSERV@YORKVM1.BITNET
```

🖎 *CANCHIDD is a digest for edited distributions list.*
```
CANCHIDD@YORKVM1.BITNET
LISTSERV@YORKVM1.BITNET
```

🖎 *Candle Products discussion list.*
Discusses Candle products.
```
CANDLE-L@UA1VM.BITNET
LISTSERV@UA1VM.BITNET
```
Contact: Darren Evans-Young
```
<DARREN@UA1VM.BITNET>
```

🖎 *CA*net Newsletter*
```
CANEWS@UVVM.BITNET
LISTSERV@UVVM.BITNET
```

🖎 *Columbia AppleTalk Protocol list.*
```
CAP-L@YALEVM.BITNET
LISTSERV@YALEVM.BITNET
```

🖎 *Canadian Association of Public Data Users*
For communication among members of the Canadian Association of Public Data Users.
```
CAPDU-L@UALTAVM.BITNET
LISTSERV@UALTAVM.BITNET
```

🖎 *Capital Notebook Advisory committee list.*
```
CAPNOTE@GWUVM.BITNET
LISTSERV@GWUVM.BITNET
```

🖎 *Computer Architecture International Group*
```
CARCH-L@IBACSATA.BITNET
LISTSERV@IBACSATA.BITNET
```
Contact: Professor Mario De Blasi
```
<DBCUM@IBACSATA.BITNET>
```

🖎 *Computer Aided Software Engineering*
Discusses the use of computer techniques in the systems development life cycle. Includes use of computers to aid in system analysis and design, description, coding, and documentation.
```
CASE-L@UCCVMA.BITNET
LISTSERV@UCCVMA.BITNET
```
Contact: Richard Hintz
```
<OPSRJH@UCCVMA.BITNET>
```

🖎 *CATIA guru forum.*
For Dassault's CATIA 3-D modeling system gurus.
```
CATIA-L@FINHUTC.BITNET
LISTSERV@FINHUTC.BITNET
```
Contact: Tony S. Dahbura
```
<DAHBURA@SUVM.BITNET>
```

🖎 *Chicago Area VM enthusiasts forum list.*
```
CAVMEN@UICVM.BITNET
LISTSERV@UICVM.BITNET
```

🖎 *CBDS guru forum.*
For Bell Northern Research's CBDS Circuit Board Design System experts and maintainers.
```
CBDS-L@FINHUTC.BITNET
LISTSERV@FINHUTC.BITNET
```
Contact: Tony S. Dahbura
```
<DAHBURA@SUVM.BITNET>
```

🖎 *ADP list.*
```
CCASD-L@NMSUVM1.BITNET
LISTSERV@NMSUVM1.BITNET
```

🖎 *Center for computational sciences list.*
```
CCS@UKCC.BITNET
LISTSERV@UKCC.BITNET
```

🖎 *Small systems group list.*
```
CCSSG-L@NMSUVM1.BITNET
LISTSERV@NMSUVM1.BITNET
```

🖎 *CDPLUS software user group list.*
```
CDPLUS-L@UTORONTO.BITNET
LISTSERV@UTORONTO.BITNET
```

🕉 *CD-ROM*
Discusses hardware and software issues related to the design, production, and use of CD-ROM.
```
CDROM-L@UCCVMA.BITNET
LISTSERV@UCCVMA.BITNET
```
Contact: Richard Hintz
```
<OPSRJH%UCCVMA.BITNET@VM1.NODAK.EDU>
```

🕉 *CDROM products in LAN environments.*
For information on all types of CDROM products. It also covers all types of LAN environments on all types of hardware.

🕉 *CD-ROM*
```
CDROMLAN@IDBSU.BITNET
LISTSERV@IDBSU.BITNET
```
Contact: Dan Lester
```
<ALILESTE@IDBSU.BITNET>
```

🕉 *Electronic user-group for Unesco's CDS/ISIS list.*
```
CDS-ISIS@HEARN.BITNET
LISTSERV@HEARN.BITNET
```

🕉 *Cellular Automata*
For the exchange of information on all aspects of cellular automata and their applications. The list is gatewayed to/from the Usenet group comp.theory.cell-automata.
```
CELLULAR-AUTOMATA@THINK.COM
LISTSERV@MITVMA.BITNET
```
Contact: Bruce Walker
```
<bruce@THINK.COM>
```

🕉 *Center availability information list.*
```
CENTINFO@INDYCMS.BITNET
LISTSERV@INDYCMS.BITNET
```

🕉 *CERN discussion list.*
```
CERN@PLEARN.BITNET
LISTSERV@PLEARN.BITNET
```

🕉 *Computer graphics education list.*
```
CGE@MARIST.BITNET
LISTSERV@MARIST.BITNET
```

🕉 *Chat*
Discusses problems related to a network user interface program called "Chat", which runs only under IBM's VM operating system.
```
CHAT-L@POLYGRAF.BITNET
LISTSERV@POLYGRAF.BITNET
```

🕉 *Procedures database list.*
```
CHEAT@TTUVM1.BITNET
LISTSERV@YYUVM1.BITNET
```

🕉 *CICS-Kermit discussion list.*
```
CICS-KER@LEHIIBM1.BITNET
LISTSERV@LEHIIBM1.BITNET
```

🕉 *IBM CICS software system discussion list.*
```
CICS-L@AKRONVM.BITNET
LISTSERV@MARIST.BITNET
```

🕉 *Cisco network products.*
Discusses network products from Cisco Systems, Inc; primarily the AGS gateway, but also the ASM terminal multiplexor and any other relevant products.
```
cisco@SPOT.COLORADO.EDU
cisco-request@SPOT.COLORADO.EDU
```
Contact: David Wood
```
<dcmwood@SPOT.COLORADO.EDU>
```

🕉 *Clarion Language and related tools. discussion list.*
```
CLARION@VMTECSLP.BITNET
LISTSERV@VMTECSLP.BITNET
```

🕉 *WordPerfect Corporation products discussion list.*
```
WPCORP-L@HEARN.BITNET
LISTSERV@HEARN.BITNET
```

🕉 *WordPerfect for Windows discussion list.*
```
WPWIN-L@UBVM.BITNET
LISTSERV@UBVM.BITNET
```

🕉 *WordPerfect 5.1 discussion group list.*
```
WP51-L@UOTTAWA.BITNET
LISTSERV@UOTTAWA.BITNET
```

🕉 *WS_T4_AU INET92 developing countries workshop list.*
```
WS_T4_AU@ICNUCEVM.BITNET
LISTSERV@ICNUCEVM.BITNET
```

🕉 *Computer lab management list.*
```
WSULAB-L@WSUVM1.BITNET
LISTSERV@WSUVM1.BITNET
```

🕉 *General list for Campuswide network users.*
```
WUNET-L@WUVMD.BITNET
LISTSERV@WUVMD.BITNET
```

🕉 *Washington University NIH guide distribution list.*
```
WUNIHG-L@WUVMD.BITNET
LISTSERV@WUVMD.BITNET
```

🕉 *Campuswide Novell Network discussion list.*
```
WUNOVELL@WUVMD.BITNET
LISTSERV@WUVMD.BITNET
```

🕉 *WX-MISC Miscellaneous WX products list.*
```
WX-MISC@UIUCVMD.BITNET
LISTSERV@UIUCVMD.BITNET
```

🕉 *WX-SUM summary weather products list.*
```
WX-SUM@UIUCVMD.BITNET
LISTSERV@UIUCVMD.BITNET
```

⑤ *WXMAP-L Program discussion list.*
WXMAP-L@UIUCVMD.BITNET
LISTSERV@UIUCVMD.BITNET

⑤ *WYLBUR system maintainers mailing list.*
WYLBUR-L@CUNYVM.BITNET
LISTSERV@CUNYVM.BITNET
Contact: Randi Robinson
RLRCU@CUNYVM.BITNET

⑤ *X Window ADA*
Discusses the uses of the X Window System with ADA.
X-ADA@EXPO.LCS.MIT.EDU
X-ADA-REQUEST@EXPO.LCS.MIT.EDU
Contact: X Staff
<LISTS-REQUEST@EXPO.LCS.MIT.EDU>

⑤ *x11 Protocol*
A mailing list for discussion on support of x11 across EIA232 (and other low bandwidth media).
X-SERIAL@LLL-CRG.LLNL.GOV
X-SERIAL-REQUEST@LLL-CRG.LLNL.GOV
Contact: Casey Leedom
<CASEY@GAUSS.LLNL.GOV>

⑤ *Effects of culture on instruction design list.*
XCULTINS@UNMVM.BITNET
LISTSERV@UNMVM.BITNET

⑤ *VM System Editor list.*
Mailing list for the discussion of the IBM VM System Editor (XEDIT).
XEDIT-L@MARIST.BITNET
LISTSERV@MARIST.BITNET

⑤ *The Xerox discussion list.*
A list for users of Xerox centralized and decentralized printing systems.
XEROX-L@TAMVM1.BITNET
LISTSERV@TAMVM1.BITNET

⑤ *X Window Image Processing*
Discusses image processing with the X Window System.
XIMAGE@EXPO.LCS.MIT.EDU
XIMAGE-REQUEST@EXPO.LCS.MIT.EDU
Contact: X Consortium staff
LISTS-REQUEST@EXPO.LCS.MIT.EDU

⑤ *Columbia Mailer*
The Columbia mailer list for BITNIC announcement of issues concerning sites that run the Crosswell MAILER.
XMAILER@BITNIC.BITNET
LISTSERV@BITNIC.BITNET

⑤ *CSNet x.25 Protocol*
For people who implement, install, or maintain CSNET X.25Net systems, which run TCP/IP

over x.25 protocols on public data networks or leased lines, connecting with CSNET's Internet gateway.
XNI-LIST@RELAY.CS.NET
XNI-LIST-REQUEST@RELAY.CS.NET
Contact: Leo Lanzillo
<leo@SH.CS.NET>

⑤ *X Window General Discussion*
For general discussion on the X window system, software running under X, and the like.
XPERT@ATHENA.MIT.EDU
XPERT-REQUEST@ATHENA.MIT.EDU
Contact: Keith Packard
<keith@ATHENA.MIT.EDU>

⑤ *X*Change Information Service*
For discussing the X*Change information service that X*Press Information Services Ltd. distributes over some cable television systems.
XPRESS-LIST@CSD.MOT.COM
xpress-list-request@csd.mot.com
Contact: Brian Smithson
<brian@csd.mot.com>

⑤ *Extropians—discussion/development of Extropy list.*
XTROPY-L@UBVM.BITNET
LISTSERV@UBVM.BITNET

⑤ *X Window Video Extensions*
Discusses possible extensions for using live and still video within the X Window System.
XVIDEO@EXPO.LCS.MIT.EDU
XVIDEO-REQUEST@EXPO.LCS.MIT.EDU
Contact: Consortium staff
<LISTS-REQUEST@EXPO.LCS.MIT.EDU>

⑤ *XVT developers' mailing list.*
A list for XVT Developers. XVT is a multi-platform window environment development tool. Interested parties should send mail with 'HELP XVTDEV' as the body of the letter to: listserv@qed.cts.com.
XVTDEV@qed.cts.com
LISTSERV@QED.CTS.COM
Contact: Tim Capps
<tim@qed.cts.com>

⑤ *X Window 3D Extensions*
Discusses 3D extensions to the X Window system.
X11-3D@ATHENA.MIT.EDU
X11-3D-REQUEST@ATHENA.MIT.EDU
Contact: X Consortium staff
LISTS-REQUEST@EXPO.LCS.MIT.EDU

⑤ *BITNET x.400 Discussion list.*
A discussion among BITNET technical representatives of the implications of a BITNET

migration to the CCITT's x.400 standards for message handling.

```
X400-L@BITNIC.BITNET
LISTSERV@BITNIC.BITNET
```

⑤ *x.400 List*
```
X400@CEARN.BITNET
LISTSERV@CEARN.BITNET
```

⑤ *Technical issues relating to the Yale people list.*
```
YP_TECH@YALEVM.BITNET
LISTSERV@YALEVM.BITNET
```

⑤ *Yale People project user discussion list.*
```
YP_USER@YALEVM.BITNET
LISTSERV@YALEVM.BITNET
```

⑤ *Yale Terminal Emulator Issues*
YTERM is a VT100 emulator that may be used with the IBM 7171 protocol converter and previous versions of the Yale ASCII terminal communication system. File transfer with YTERM is accomplished with PCTRANS host software. PC to PC file transfer over an asynch line is also possible with YTERM.
```
YTERM-L@YALEVM.BITNET
LISTSERV@YALEVM.BITNET
```

⑤ *Discussion list for NASK-KBN relations.*
```
ZIKBN@PLEARN.BITNET
LISTSERV@PLEARN.BITNET
```

⑤ *Marist Zwriter users group list.*
```
ZWSUG@MARIST.BITNET
LISTSERV@MARIST.BITNET
```

⑤ *Zeke/Zebb/Zack Project group list.*
```
ZZZ-L@UCSFVM.BITNET
LISTSERV@UCSFVM.BITNET
```

⑤ *1-Union: Industrial democracy and industrial list.*
```
1-UNION@UVMVM.BITNET
LISTSERV@UVMVM.BITNET
```

⑤ *2nd BNFNET Annual Computer Conference list.*
```
2BNFCC@SEARN.BITNET
LISTSERV@SEARN.BITNET
```

⑤ *3Com User interest group discussion list.*
Discusses 3Com products, such as 3+ Network, 3+Open LAN Manager, 3+Open TCP, 3+/3+Open Mail, NDIS, MultiConnect Repeater, LanScanner, Ethernet Cards and so on.
```
3COM-L@NUSVM.BITNET
LISTSERV@NUSVM.BITNET
```
Contact: Chandra Liem
```
(CCELC@NUSVM.BITNET)
```

⑤ *Graphics*
A list for discussion of 3D-Graphics.
```
3D-L@ARIZVM1.BITNET
LISTSERV@ARIZVM1.BITNET
```

⑤ *Intel 80386 Microprocessor*
For Intel 80386 topics, including hardware and software questions, reviews, rumors, and so on.
```
386USERS@UDEL.EDU
386USERS-REQUEST@UDEL.EDU
```
Contact: Bill Davidsen
```
<davidsen@CRDOS1.UUCP>
```

⑤ *IBM 9370 and VM/IS*
List for a discussion on topics to the IBM 9370 family and VM/IS.
```
9370-L@HEARN.BITNET
LISTSERV@HEARN.BITNET
```
Contact: Rob van Hoboken
```
<RCOPROB%HDETUD1@MITVMA.MIT.EDU>
```

⑤ *SIMULA for object-oriented programming and simulation.*
Discusses the ALGOL family. Topics may range from hints on programming techniques to information about available software, and questions and answers in general.
```
SIMULA@BITNIC.BITNET
LISTSERV@BITNIC.BITNET
```
Contact: Mats Ohlin
```
<MATSO@QZCOM.BITNET>
```

⑤ *Simulation software*
For all topics connected with simulation.
```
simulation@UFL.EDU
simulation-request@UFL.EDU
```
Contact: Paul Fishwick
```
<fishwick@FISH.CIS.UFL.EDU>
```

⑤ *Rochester Simulator Software*
A mailing list that enables users of the Rochester Connectionist Simulator to talk to one another.
```
simulator-users@CS.ROCHESTER.EDU
simulator-request@CS.ROCHESTER.EDU
```
Contact: Liudvikas Bukys
```
<bukys@CS.ROCHESTER.EDU>
```

⑤ *SIR/DBMS(r) software discussion list.*
```
SIR-L@UREGINA1.BITNET
LISTSERV@UREGINA1.BITNET
```
Contact: Melvin Klassen
```
KLASSEN@UVVM
```

⑤ *SUNY Student Information Systems list.*
```
SIS-L@UBVM.BITNET
LISTSERV@UBVM.BITNET
```

⑤ *Site Licensing at UC discussion list.*
```
SITE-LIC@UCSFVM.BITNET
LISTSERV@UCSFVM.BITNET
```

⑤ *Technical Services discussion group list.*
```
SLA-TECH@UKCC.BITNET
LISTSERV@UKCC.BITNET
```

⑤ *Symbolic Lisp*
To exchange information about the care and feeding, use and abuse, problems and pitfalls, wonders, and crocks of the Symbolics Lisp machines.
```
SLUG@AI.SRI.COM
SLUG-Request@AI.SRI.COM
```
Contact: Mabry Tyson
```
<Tyson@AI.SRI.COM>
```

⑤ *SmallTalk discussion list.*
```
SMALK@FINHUTC.BITNET
LISTSERV@FINHUTC.BITNET
```

⑤ *Standard ML language and its implementation list.*
```
sml-list@cs.cmu.edu
sml-list-request@cs.cmu.edu
```

⑤ *SNA Network management discussion list.*
```
SNAMGT-L@UMRVMB.BITNET
LISTSERV@UMRVMB.BITNET
```

⑤ *SNIFFER-Diskussions forum list.*
```
SNIFF-L@DEARN.BITNET
LISTSERV@DEARN.BITNET
```

⑤ *Systems and programming microcomputer list.*
```
SNPLAN-L@UKANVM.BITNET
LISTSERV@UKANVM.BITNET
```

⑤ *SNS/TCPaccess MVS*
For the discussion of questions and problems related to Interlink's SNS/TCPaccess product for IBM MVS systems.
```
SNSTCP-L@NIHLIST.BITNET
LISTSERV@NIHLIST.BITNET
```
Contact: Roger Fajman
```
<RAF@NIHCU.BITNET
```

⑤ *Software-Engineering Arpa Discussions*
Discusses software engineering and related topics.
```
SOFT-ENG@BYUVM.BITNET
LISTSERV@BYUVM.BITNET
```
Contact: Alok C. Nigam
```
<nigam@MWUNIX.MITRE.ORG>
```

⑤ *Software Engineering*
This is a list for discussion of software engineering and related topics.
```
SOFT-ENG@MWUNIX.MITRE.ORG
Soft-Eng-Request@MWUNIX.MITRE.ORG
```
Contact: Alok C. Nigam
```
<nigam@MWUNIX.MITRE.ORG>
```

⑤ *Software entrepreneur's mailing list.*
Devoted to the interests of entrepreneural software publishing, including (but not limited to) shareware.
```
softpub@toolz.uucptodd@toolz.uucp
softpub-request%toolz.uucp@mathcs.emory.edu
```

⑤ *Yale Project Eli Software Review Board*
Discussion list for the Yale BITNET users' group.
```
SOFTRB-L@YALEVM.BITNET
LISTSERV@YALEVM.BITNET
```
Contact: Doug Hawthorne
```
ELI@YALEVM
```

⑤ *SoftRevu Digest—small computer systems software list.*
```
SOFTREVD@BROWNVM.BROWN.EDU
LISTSERV@BROWNVM.BROWN.EDU
```

⑤ *Software Review*
For Cross-platform compatibility issues related to software and hardware, with an emphasis placed on software.
```
SOFTREVU@BROWNVM.BROWN.EDU
LISTSERV@BROWNVM.BITNET
```
Contact: Jamie Donnelly IV
```
<ENCSADM1@UCONNVM.BITNET>
```

⑤ *Solaris Operating Environment*
Discusses the Solaris operating system produced by SunSoft, a Sun Microsystems company. Completely independent of Solaris (the operating environment), SunSoft (the manufacturer) and Sun Microsystems (the parent corporation).
```
Solaris@INDYCMS.BITNET
LISTSERV@IndyCMS.BITNET
```
Contact: Phillip Gross Corporon
```
<phil@CSE.ND.Edu>
```

⑤ *AACRAO electronic transcript discussion list.*
```
SPEEDE-L@VTVM1.BITNET
LISTSERV@VTVM1.BITNET
```

⑤ *SPIRES Library discussion group list.*
```
SPILIB-L@SUVM.BITNET
LISTSERV@SUVM.BITNET
```

⑤ *SPIRES conference list.*
```
SPIRES-L@BITNIC.BITNET
LISTSERV@BITNIC.BITNET
```

⑤ *SPIRES technical personnel list.*
```
SPITEK-L@UNCVM1.BITNET
LISTSERV@UNCVM1.BITNET
```

⑤ *Borland Sprint word processor discussion.*
Discusses Borland's Sprint word processor: macros, problems, solutions, applications, and so on.

SPRINT-L@NDSUVM1.BITNET
LISTSERV@NDSUVM1.BITNET
Contact: David Dodell
ATW1H@ASUACAD.BITNET

🕙 *SPSSX-L Discussion*
SPSSX-L@MARIST.BITNET
LISTSERV@MARIST.BITNET
Contact: Duane Weaver
WEAVER@OHSTVMA.BITNET

🕙 *SPSS91 Conference List*
SPSS91-L@MCGILL1.BITNET
LISTSERV@MCGILL1.BITNET

🕙 *IBM database SQL/DS discussion list.*
SQL-L@DB0FUB11.BITNET
LISTSERV@DB0FUB11.BITNET

🕙 *UCLA Campus SQL users group list.*
SQL@UCLACN1.BITNET
LISTSERV@UCLACN1.BIT

🕙 *SQLINFO*
Discusses SQL/DS and general database topics.
SQLINFO@UICVM.BITNET
LISTSERV@UICVM.BITNET

🕙 *Server-Requester discussion list.*
Discusses LAN servers and requesters
(workstations), including OS/2 LAN Server, OS/
2 LAN Requester, DOS LAN Requester, PC LAN
Program, Novell Netware.
SRVREQ-L@INDYCMS.BITNET
LISTSERV@INDYCMS.BITNET
Contact: Manjit Trehan
<ITMS400@INDYCMS.BITNET>

🕙 *Discussion of SSC issues list.*
SSCLD0@UTDALLAS.BITNET
LISTSERV@UTDALLAS.BITNET

🕙 *SSSSINFO*
A list for dissemination of information between
members.
SSSSINFO@TAMVM1.BITNET
LISTSERV@TAMVM1.BITNET

🕙 *AT&T's StarServer*
A list for administrators, operators, and/or users
of StarServer systems.
STARSERVER@ENGR.UKY.EDU
starserver-request@engr.uky.edu
Contact: Wes Morgan
<starserver-owner@engr.uky.edu>

🕙 *K.U.Leuven Statistisch centrum list.*
STATKUL@BLEKUL11.BITNET
LISTSERV@BLEKUL11.BITNET

🕙 *STD-L*
Discusses BITNET "standard" environments and
software development projects required to
provide full functionality.
STD-L@BITNIC.BITNET
LISTSERV@BITNIC.BITNET

🕙 *STD-UNIX redistribution list.*
Discusses UNIX standards, particularly the IEEE
P1003 Portable Operating System Enviroment
draft standard. The list is moderated, and
corresponds to the newsgroup mod.std.unix on
USENET.
STD-UNIX@TCSVM.BITNET
LISTSERV@TCSVM.BITNET
Contact: John Quarterman
<jsq@UUNET.UU.NET>

🕙 *STKACS-L*
Discusses Storage Technology's ACS 4400
system.
STKACS-L@USCVM.BITNET
LISTSERV@USCVM.BITNET

🕙 *Structure Editors*
For users interested in structure editors and the
associated technology.
structure-editors+@andrew.cmu.edu
structure-editors-request+@andrew.cmu.edu
Contact: Ravinder Chandhok
chandhok+@andrew.cmu.edu

🕙 *IUPUI student activities information list.*
STUACTS@INDYCMS.BITNET
LISTSERV@INDYCMS.BITNET

🕙 *Student discussion on VM and EARN list.*
STUD-VM@HUEARN.BITNET
LISTSERV@HUEARN.BITNET

🕙 *USSR Computer Connections*
Discusses the ongoing work on connecting the
U.S.S.R. to international computer networks
(the internet) contributed by its readers, cross-
posted from other mailing lists, and retyped
(usually without permission) from the "real"
press.
SUEARN-L@UBVM.BITNET
LISTSERV@UBVM.BITNET
Contact: Mike Meystel
MEYSTMA@DUVM.BITNET

🕙 *RTPNC SAS users group list.*
SUG-L@UNCVM1.BITNET
LISTSERV@UNCVM1.BITNET

🕙 *SUGGEST*
Temple's mainframe discussion list.
SUGGEST@TEMPLEVM.BITNET
LISTSERV@TEMPLEVM.BITNET

☻ *Sun Workstation*
Discusses software and hardware issues relating to the Sun Workstation.
```
SUN-SPOTS@RICE.EDU
Sun-Spots-Request@RICE.EDU
```
Contact: Vicky Riffle
```
<rif@RICE.EDU>
```

☻ *Sun 386i*
Discusses issues specific to the Sun 386i system.
```
Sun-386i@RICE.EDU
sun-386i-request@RICE.EDU
```
Contact: Mike Cherry
```
<sun-386i-request@RICE.EDU>
```

☻ *Focus/Sun discussion group list.*
```
SUNIBI-L@YALEVM.BITNET
LISTSERV@YALEVM.BITNET
```

☻ *SUNY DEC local users group mailing list.*
```
SUNYDEC@UBVM.BITNET
LISTSERV@UBVM.BITNET
```

☻ *SUNY Educational Communications Centers list.*
```
SUNYEC-L@BINGVMB.BITNET
LISTSERV@BINGVMB.BITNET
```

☻ *Super computer users forum list.*
```
SUPER-L@MCGILL1.BITNET
LISTSERV@MCGILL1.BITNET
```

☻ *UNC/ACS super computer users list.*
```
SUPER-U@UNCVM1.BITNET
LISTSERV@UNCVM1.BITNET
```

☻ *Super list.*
```
SUPER@BLEKUL11.BITNET
LISTSERV@BLEKUL11.BITNET
```

☻ *Discussion of Supercomputing Issues*
For users of IBM equipment for high performance scientific applications (supercomputing).
```
SUPERIBM@UKCC.BITNET
LISTSERV@UKCC.BITNET
```
Contact: Bob Crovo
```
<Crovo@UKCC.BITNET>
```

☻ *Supercomputing in Europe (user's group) list.*
```
SUPEUR@FRMOP11.BITNET
LISTSERV@FRMOP11.BITNET
```

☻ *Super Steering Committee list.*
```
SUPSTEER@FRMOP11.BITNET
LISTSERV@FRMOP11.BITNET
```

☻ *SUS Software Consortium list.*
```
SUSCON-L@CFRVM.BITNET
LISTSERV@CFRVM.BITNET
```

☻ *SUT tool's discussion list.*
```
SUTTOOLS@JPNSUT00.BITNET
LISTSERV@JPNSUT00.BITNET
```

☻ *SUPER-UNIX user group list.*
```
SXUNIX-L@HEARN.BITNET
LISTSERV@HEARN.BITNET
```

☻ *Discussion of SYBASE Products, Platforms & Users list.*
```
SYBASE-L@UCSBVM.BITNET
LISTSERV@UCSBVM.BITNET
```

☻ *System programmers list.*
```
SYSPRG-L@TRITU.BITNET
LISTSERV@TRITU.BITNET
```

☻ *MacIntosh Operating System Version 7*
Discusses issues related to the installation, configuration, features, and product compatibilities of the Macintosh Operating System version 7.0. To receive a list of files send the command INDEX LISTNAME to LISTSERV@UAFSYSB.BITNET.
```
SYS7-L@UAFSYSB.BITNET
LISTSERV@UAFSYSB.BITNET
```
Contact: David Remington

☻ *Borland turbo assembler and debugger list.*
```
TASM-L@BRUFPB.BITNET
LISTSERV@BRUFPB.BITNET
```

☻ *TASP-L list.*
```
TASP-L@TTUVM1.BITNET
LISTSERV@TTUVM1.BITNET
```

☻ *THINK Class Library Digest list.*
```
TCL-DGST@BROWNVM.BITNET
LISTSERV@BROWNVM.BITNET
```

☻ *THINK Class Library list.*
```
TCL-TALK@BROWNVM.BITNET
LISTSERV@BROWNVM.BITNET
```

☻ *TCP/IP Services*
For the addition and expansion of TCP services.
```
TCP-IP@NIC.DDN.MIL
TCP-IP-REQUEST@NIC.DDN.MIL
```
Contact: Vivian Neou
```
<Vivian@NIC.DDN.MIL>
```

☻ *TCP-IP discussion redistribution list .*
```
TCP-IP@UTDALLAS.BITNET
LISTSERV@UTDALLAS.BITNET
```

☻ *TCPIP information distribution list.*
```
TCPIP-L@IRLEARN.BITNET
LISTSERV@IRLEARN.BITNET
```

☻ *TURBO C++ discussion group.*
Discusses the Borland product Turbo C++.

TCPLUS-L@UCF1VM.BITNET
LISTSERV@UCF1VM.BITNET
Contact: Lois Buwalda
<LOIS@UCF1VM.BITNET>

🌀 *TECH-L List*
TECH-L@BITNIC.BITNET
LISTSERV@BITNIC.BITNET

🌀 *TECH-LAN—Technion technical user group list.*
TECH-LAN@TECHNION.BITNET
LISTSERV@TECHNION.BITNET

🌀 *TECHMATH—Technion mathematics net list.*
TECHMATH@TECHNION.BITNET
LISTSERV@TECHNION.BITNET

🌀 *BITNET technical news list.*
TECHNEWS@BITNIC.BITNET
LISTSERV@BITNIC.BITNET

🌀 *TECNOMED database list.*
TECNOMED@ICNUCEVM.BITNET
LISTSERV@ICNUCEVM.BITNET

🌀 *SUN computer technical users list.*
TECSUN-L@MITVMA.BITNET
LISTSERV@MITVMA.BITNET

🌀 *Campus telephone directory discussion list.*
TELDIR-L@PUCC.BITNET
LISTSERV@PUCC.BITNET

🌀 *Network for the TELEMED project list.*
TELEMED@FRMOP11.BITNET
LISTSERV@FRMOP11.BITNET

🌀 *TELEX users list.*
TELEX@CEARN.BITNET
LISTSERV@CEARN.BITNET

🌀 *Telecom, competitiveness, and organizational change list.*
TELE290@GWUVM.BITNET
LISTSERV@GWUVM.BITNET

🌀 *Discussion on the TEMPUS list.*
TEMPUS@HUEARN.BITNET
LISTSERV@HUEARN.BITNET

🌀 *Test network mailing list.*
TESTMAIL@INDYCMS.BITNET
LISTSERV@INDYCMS.BITNET

🌀 *German TeX users communication list.*
TEX-D-L@DEARN.BITNET
LISTSERV@DEARN.BITNET

🌀 *TeX Education forum list.*
TEX-ED@UICVM.BITNET
LISTSERV@UICVM.BITNET

🌀 *TeX-Eur distribution list for European TeX list.*
TEX-EURO@DHDURZ1.BITNET
LISTSERV@DHDURZ1.BITNET

🌀 *TEX-IBM distribution list.*
TEX-IBM@DHDURZ1.BITNET
LISTSERV@DHDURZ1.BITNET

🌀 *The TeXnical topics list.*
A BITNET redistribution of the TeXhax digest, which is a moderated digest related to TeX, METAFONT, WEB, LaTeX, etc. Submissions to the digest should go to <TeXhax@cs.Washington.edu>.
TEX-L@BNANDP11.BITNET
LISTSERV@BNANDP11.BITNET
Contact: Pierre A MacKay
mackay@JUNE.CS.WASHINGTON.EDU

🌀 *TEX-NL List*
TEX-NL@HEARN.BITNET
LISTSERV@HEARN.BITNET

🌀 *TeX and Metafont*
For people interested in TeX and Metafont installation and maintanance.
TEXHAX-L@UWAVM.BITNET
LISTSERV@UWAVM.BITNET

🌀 *TEXMAG-L*
For users of TeXMaG, an electronic magazine available to anybody reachable by electronic mail.
TEXMAG-L@BYUADMIN.BITNET
LISTSERV@BYUADMIN.BITNET

🌀 *The TeXrox information list.*
TEXROX-L@TAMVM1.BITNET
LISTSERV@TAMVM1.BITNET
Contact: Tom Reid
X066TR@TAMVM1.BITNET

🌀 *Think C language list.*
think-c@ics.uci.edu
think-c-request@ics.uci.edu
Contact: Jason Bobier
<k059509@kzoo.edu>

🌀 *Thistle Discussion List*
THYST-L@BROWNVM.BROWN.EDU
LISTSERV@BROWNVM.BROWN.EDU

🌀 *Macintosh Computer News*
The TIDBITS list is a weekly electronic newsletter. Issues are released early each week and are occasionally supplemented by special issues focussing on a single topic or product.
TIDBITS@RICEVM1.BITNET
LISTSERV@RICEVM1.BITNET

Contact: Adam C. Engst
    <ace@tidbits.halcyon.com>

⑤ *Tierra*
A mailing list for Tierra users to get official announcements, updates, and bug-fixes.
    tierra-announce@life.slhs.udel.edu
    tierra-request@life.slhs.udel.edu

⑤ *Tierra*
A mailing list for Tierra users for official postings as well as discussion of Tierra by users.
    tierra-digest@life.slhs.udel.edu
    tierra-request@life.slhs.udel.edu

⑤ *Macintosh terminal emulator issues list.*
    TINCAN-L@YALEVM.BITNET
    LISTSERV@YALEVM.BITNET
Contact: Peter Furmonavicius
    Peter@YaleVM.BITNET

⑤ *Top information node covering all networking list.*
    TINCAN@YORKVM1.BITNET
    LISTSERV@YORKVM1.BITNET

⑤ *Computer help and tip exchange list.*
    TIPSHEET@WSUVM1.BITNET
    LISTSERV@WSUVM1.BITNET

⑤ *Thesaurus Musicarum Latinarum database for Latin list.*
    TML-L@IUBVM.BITNET
    LISTSERV@IUBVM.BITNET

⑤ *Tn3270 protocol discussion list.*
The BITNET redistribution of the tn3270@terminus.UMD.EDU list.
    TN3270-L@RUTVM1.BITNET
    LISTSERV@RUTVM1.BITNET
Contact: David R. Conrad
    davidc@terminus.umd.edu

⑤ *NewTek Video Toaster mailing list.*
Discussion list of the NewTek Video Toaster.
    @KARAZM.MATH.UH.EDU
    LISTSERV@KARAZM.MATH.UH.EDU
Contact: J. Eric Townsend
    <jet@uh.edu>

⑤ *ToolBook Application and Multimedia*
Provides a discussion of Asymetrix ToolBook software, application development, and its integration into a multimedia environment.
    TOOLB-L@UAFSYSB.BITNET
    LISTSERV@UAFSYSB.BITNET
Contact: Ken Schriner
    KS06054@UAFSYSB.BITNET

⑤ *TRACK Distribution List*
    TRACK-D@AWIIMC11.BITNET
    LISTSERV@AWIIMC11.BITNET

⑤ *Traffic Monitoring List*
    TRAFIC-L@BITNIC.BITNET
    LISTSERV@BITNIC.BITNET

⑤ *College and university computer trainer's list.*
    TRAIN-L@BROWNVM.BITNET
    LISTSERV@BROWNVM.BITNET

⑤ *TRANS-L*
Offers information about the transfer of files among VM, MVS and RSCS-emulating systems.
    TRANS-L@BITNIC.BITNET
    LISTSERV@BITNIC.BITNET

⑤ *Transputer Computer Systems*
For users interested in the Transputer and Transputer based systems.
    transputer@TCGOULD.TN.CORNELL.EDU
    transputer-request@TCGOULD.TN.CORNELL.EDU
Contact: Andy Pfiffer
    <andy@TCGOULD.TN.CORNELL.EDU>

⑤ *TRends in Angular Overlap Model*
    TRAOM-L@AEARN.BITNET
    LISTSERV@AEARN.BITNET
Contact: Svetozar R Niketic
    XPMFH01@YUBGSS21.BITNET

⑤ *TRDEV-L*
This list is for the exchange of information on the training and the development of human resources.
    TRDEV-L@PSUVM.BITNET
    LISTSERV@PSUVM.BITNET
Contact: David L. Passmore
    <DLP@psuvm.psu.edu>

⑤ *TSO REXX discussion list.*
    TSO-REXX@UCF1VM.BITNET
    LISTSERV@UCF1VM.BITNET

⑤ *TUG Conference question list.*
    TUG-Q@TAMVM1.BITNET
    LISTSERV@TAMVM1.BITNET

⑤ *TURBOC-L*
For Turbo C questions, tips, code, bug reports, and any other Turbo C related areas of interest.
    TURBOC-L@TREARN.BITNET
    LISTSERV@TREARN.BITNET

⑤ *TURBVIS discussion list.*
    TURBVIS@VTVM1.BITNET
    LISTSERV@VTVM1.BITNET

⑤ *TWNAD-L Taiwan BITNET NODE administration list.*
    TWNAD-L@TWNMOE10.BITNET
    LISTSERV@TWNMOE10.BITNET

⑤ *Texas BITNET issues list.*
    TXBITNET@UTDALLAS.BITNET
    LISTSERV@UTDALLAS.BITNET

🔊 *Typography discussion type list.*
TYPO-L@IRLEARN.BITNET
LISTSERV@IRLEARN.BITNET

🔊 *UA2 collaboration list.*
UA2PRIME@CERNVM.BITNET
LISTSERV@CERNVM.BITNET

🔊 *UB Libraries Distribution List*
UBLIB-L@UBVM.BITNET
LISTSERV@UBVM.BITNET

🔊 *UB Lists Owners List*
UBOWN-L@UBVM.BITNET
LISTSERV@UBVM.BITNET

🔊 *SIGUCCS 1992 Information List*
UCCS-92@AKRONVM.BITNET
LISTSERV@AKRONVM.BITNET

🔊 *LISTSERV User Directory Database*
Dedicated to the discussion of the LISTSERV
User Directory Database functions.
UDD-L@CEARN.BITNET
LISTSERV@CEARN.BITNET
Contact: Eric Thomas
ERIC@CEARN

🔊 *Network User Guide*
This list is for the discussion of the use and
abuse of the network, usage guidelines and
etiquette, local access policies, and enforcement
of guidelines.
UG-L@BITNIC.BITNET
LISTSERV@BITNIC.BITNET

🔊 *User Interfaces for Geographic Info Systems*
For topics related to the design and testing of
user interfaces for Geographic Information
Systems (GIS) and other geographic software.
UIGIS-L@UBVM.BITNET
LISTSERV@UBVM.BITNET
Contact: David M. Mark
<GISMGR@UBVMS.BITNET>

🔊 *Ukraine List*
UKRAINE@INDYCMS.BITNET
LISTSERV@INDYCMS.BITNET

🔊 *Chinese Student group list.*
ULCSS-L@ULKYVM.BITNET
LISTSERV@ULKYVM.BITNET

🔊 *ULGNET general discussion list.*
ULGNET@BLIULG11.BITNET
LISTSERV@BLIULG11.BITNET

🔊 *ULGNET Administrators List*
ULGNETAD@BLIULG11.BITNET
LISTSERV@BLIULG11.BITNET

🔊 *UL IDMS discussion list.*
ULIDMS12@ULKYVM.BITNET
LISTSERV@ULKYVM.BITNET

🔊 *Ultralite Computers*
For users of the original NEC UltraLite PC1701
and PC1702 computers (the V30-based
notebook computer with a 1MB or 2MB silicon
hard disk, not the newer 286- and 386-based
models).
ULTRALITE-LIST@STARNET.STARCONN.COM
ultralite-list-request@starnet.starconn.com
Contact: Brian Smithson
<brian@csd.mot.com>

🔊 *UNCC LISTSERV Discussion*
UNCC-L@UNCCVM.BITNET
LISTSERV@UNCCVM.BITNET

🔊 *UNC/ACS systems test list.*
UNCSYS-L@UNCVM1.BITNET
LISTSERV@UNCVM1.BITNET

🔊 *Unisys Computers*
This is a list for Unisys related topics.
unisys@TMC.EDU
unisys-request@TMC.EDU
Contact: Richard H. Miller
<rick@SVEDBERG.BCM.TMC.EDU>

🔊 *SUNY Unisys sites discussion list.*
UNISYS@UBVM.BITNET
LISTSERV@UBVM.BITNET
Contact: Marc Seybold
SEYBOLMP@SNYOLDBA.BITNET

🔊 *UNIVOC—NCRVE vocational education
university discussion group list.*
UNIVOC@UCBCMSA.BITNET
LISTSERV@UCBCMSA.BITNET

🔊 *EMACS Editors*
Discusses all EMACS type editors for UNIX. The
list is gatewayed both ways to usenet newsgroup
comp.emacs.
UNIX-EMACS@VM.TCS.TULANE.EDU
Unix-Emacs-Request@VM.TCS.TULANE.EDU

🔊 *John Voigt*
<sysbjav@vm.tcs.tulane.edu>

🔊 *PMDF Mailer on CSNet*
For users who implement, install or maintain
PMDF and CMDF mailers on UNIX hosts.
(PMDF= Pascal Message Distribution Facility
and CMDF = C-language Message Distribution
Facility).
UNIX-PMDF@RELAY.CS.NET
UNIX-PMDF-REQUEST@RELAY.CS.NET
Contact: Daniel Long
<long@SH.CS.NET>

⑤ *UNIX-SRC*
The ARPANET/MilNet gateway for distribution of the "UUCP net" Unix net.sources newslist.
```
UNIX-SRC@NDSUVM1.BITNET
LISTSERV@NDSUVM1.BITNET
```

⑤ *Unix Software Announcements*
A list for announcing the availability of new major packages of UNIX/'C' language software on the WSMR-SIMTEL20.ARMY.MIL repository.
```
UNIX-SW@WSMR-SIMTEL20.ARMY.MIL
UNIX-SW-REQUEST@WSMR-SIMTEL20.ARMY.MIL
```
Contact: Dave Curry
```
<DCURRY@WSMR-SIMTEL20.ARMY.MIL>
```

⑤ *Porting Tex82 to Unix*
Discusses matters involved in porting TeX82 to Unix.
```
UNIX-TeX@MIMSY.UMD.EDU
UNIX-TeX-REQUEST@MIMSY.UMD.EDU
```
Contact: Richard Furuta
```
<furuta@TOVE.UMD.EDU>
```

⑤ *Unix System Managers*
For users who maintain machines running the Unix operating system.
```
UNIX-WIZARDS@BRL.MIL
UNIX-WIZARDS-REQUEST@BRL.MIL
```
Contact: Mike Muuss
```
<mike@BRL.MIL>
```

⑤ *Unix applications mailing list.*
```
UNIXAPPL@LIVERPOOL.AC.UK
LISTSERV@LIVERPOOL.AC.UK
```

⑤ *UNIXPRGS—TECHNION CC Unix programmers list.*
```
UNIXPRGS@TECHNION.BITNET
LISTSERV@TECHNION.BITNET
```

⑤ *UN University millennium project discussion list.*
```
UNMETHOD@GWUVM.BITNET
LISTSERV@GWUVM.BITNET
```

⑤ *Discussion of UNIX CAFE Beta Testing list.*
```
UNXBTA-L@UTKVM1.BITNET
LISTSERV@UTKVM1.BITNET
```

⑤ *IBM upgrade discussions list.*
```
UPGRADE@IPFWVM.BITNET
LISTSERV@IPFWVM.BITNET
```

⑤ *UPSAC Discussion List*
```
UPSAC@GWUVM.BITNET
LISTSERV@GWUVM.BITNET
```

⑤ *UREAD-L Mailing List*
```
UREAD-L@MSU.BITNET
LISTSERV@MSU.BITNET
```

⑤ *UREP-L Mailing List*
```
UREP-L@BNLVMXA.BITNET
LISTSERV@BNLVMXA.BITNET
```

⑤ *Rexx under Unix*
```
UREXX-L@LIVERPOOL.AC.UK
LISTSERV@LIVERPOOL.AC.UK
```
Contact: Alan Thew
```
<QQ11@Liverpool.ac.uk>
```

⑤ *History of Usenet*
Discusses the socio-cultural,technical and political history of usenet.
```
usenet.hist@ucsd.edu
usenet.hist@ucsd.edu
```
Contact: Bruce Jones
```
bjones@ucsd.edu
```

⑤ *Vermont user services support group list.*
```
USERSERV@UVMVM.BITNET
LISTSERV@UVMVM.BITNET
```

⑤ *Universe Generation*
Discusses programs for various universe-generating software—accretion models, Traveller, Other Suns, and so on.
```
usml@HC.DSPO.GOV
usml-request@HC.DSPO.GOV
```
Contact: Josh Siegel
```
<usml-request@HC.DSPO.GOV>
```

⑤ *User Directory List*
```
USRDIR-L@BITNIC.BITNET
LISTSERV@BITNIC.BITNET
```

⑤ *GWU's USERGRP Discussion List*
```
USRGROUP@GWUVM.BITNET
LISTSERV@GWUVM.BITNET
```

⑤ *CICS Conference List*
```
UT-CICS@UTORONTO.BITNET
LISTSERV@UTORONTO.BITNET
```

⑤ *UT System Information Technology Council List*
```
UTS-ITC@UTXVM.BITNET
LISTSERV@UTXVM.BITNET
```

⑤ *Amdahl UTS discussion list.*
Discusses Amdahl's UTS/580 implementation of Unix and for software running in the UTS environment.
```
UTS-L@YSUB.BITNET
LISTSERV@YSUB.BITNET
```
Contact: Lou Anschuetz
```
TEMNGT23@YSUB.BITNET
```

⑤ *BITNIC Update program administration list.*
```
UVP-A@BITNIC.BITNET
LISTSERV@BITNIC.BITNET
```

⑤ *BITNIC Update program development list.*
UVP-D@BITNIC.BITNET
LISTSERV@BITNIC.BITNET

⑤ *UVTERM users list.*
UVTERM-L@UVVM.BITNET
LISTSERV@UVVM.BITNET

⑤ *Mailing list for UW DECUS group.*
UWDECUS@UWAVM.BITNET
LISTSERV@UWAVM.BITNET

⑤ *University of Washington distribution list.*
UWNSF-L@UWAVM.BITNET
LISTSERV@UWAVM.BITNET

⑤ *UW Reference Library List*
UWREFLIB@UWAVM.BITNET
LISTSERV@UWAVM.BITNET

⑤ *VAX user account request/changes from consult list.*
VAXSYS@INDYCMS.BITNET
LISTSERV@INDYCMS.BITNET

⑤ *VAX Toolbox BITNET Magazine for VAX users.*
This list is for VAX users. Send all article submissions to <BOAG@MUVMS1>.
VAXTOOLS@DEARN.BITNET
LISTSERV@DEARN.BITNET

⑤ *Ege University remote vector processor users list.*
VECSRV-L@TREARN.BITNET
LISTSERV@TREARN.BITNET

⑤ *IBM 3090 Vector Processors list.*
VECTOR-L@UNBVM1.BITNET
LISTSERV@UNBVM1.BITNET

⑤ *VETE-ULG general discussion list.*
VETE-ULG@BLIULG11.BITNET
LISTSERV@BLIUG11.BITNET

⑤ *Virginia Educational Vax Association List*
VEVA-L@VTVM2.BITNET
LISTSERV@VTVM2.BITNET

⑤ *VS-Fortran discussion list.*
VFORT-L@EB0UB011.BITNET
LISTSERV@EB0UB011.BITNET

⑤ *ARPA Videotech relay list.*
VIDEOTEC@VTVM1.BITNET
LISTSERV@VTVM1.BITNET

⑤ *VIDNET-L*
Discusses mutual problems and concerns which face all who are involved in the operation of a campus-wide video network.
VIDNET-L@UGA.BITNET
LISTSERV@UGA.BITNET

⑤ *VIGIS-L list.*
VIGIS-L@UWAVM.BITNET
LISTSERV@UWAVM.BITNET

⑤ *Virtual Worlds*
This list is a bi-directional gateway for the Usenet newsgroup scientific virtual-worlds and is a discussion of all aspects of virtual reality.
VIRTU-L@UIUCVMD.BITNET
LISTSERV@UIUCVMD.BITNET
Contact: Greg Newby
<gbnewby@uiucvmd.bitnet>

⑤ *Virus Alert List*
VALERT-L@LEHIIBM1.BITNET
LISTSERV@LEHIIBM1.BITNET

⑤ *Virus Discussion List*
A forum specifically for the discussion of computer virus experiences, protection software, and other virus related topics.
VIRUS-L@LEHIIBM1.BITNET
LISTSERV@LEHIIBM1.BITNET
Contact: Kenneth R. van Wyk
LUKEN@LEHIIBM1.BITNET

⑤ *Discussion for Microsoft Visual Basic list.*
VISBAS-L@TAMVM1.BITNET
LISTSERV@TAMVM1.BITNET

⑤ *Vision research group list.*
VISION-L@PSUVM.BITNET
LISTSERV@PSUVM.BITNET

⑤ *BITNET part of Info-VLSI@Think.COM*
For the exchange of information on all aspects of integrated circuit (IC) design. The list is gatewayed to and from the Usenet group comp.lsi.
VLSI-L@MITVMA.BITNET
LISTSERV@MITVMA.BITNET

⑤ *VLSI CAD interest list (CADinterest)*
Discusses issues and exchanges ideas pertaining to VLSI computer aided design and layout.
VLSICAD@EB0UB011.BITNET
LISTSERV@EB0UB011.BITNET
Contact: Craig Anderson
<ANDERSON.ES@XEROX.COM>

⑤ *VM/SP REXX Language Discussion List*
VM-REXX@OHSTVMA.BITNET
LISTSERV@OHSTVMA.BITNET
Contact: Duane Weaver
<WEAVER@OHSTVMA.BITNET>

⑤ *VM Utilities Discussion List*
For the discussion and redistribution of useful and interesting utilities for use by the VM/SP and CMS operating systems.

VM-UTIL@MARIST.BITNET
LISTSERV@MARIST.BITNET
Contact: David Young
DYOUNG@TRINITY.BITNET

☙ *VM Maintenance discussions.*
VMAINT-L@UIUCVMD.BITNET
LISTSERV@UIUCVMD.BITNET

☙ *GWU's VMARCHIVE discussion list.*
VMARCHL@GWUVM.BITNET
LISTSERV@GWUVM.BITNET

☙ *GWU's VMBATCH Discussion List*
VMBATL@GWUVM.BITNET
LISTSERV@GWUVM.BITNET

☙ *VM Consultants discussion list.*
VMCONS@MIAMIU.BITNET
LISTSERV@MIAMIU.BITNET

☙ *VIP Media discussion group list.*
VMEDIA-L@UOTTAWA.BITNET
LISTSERV@UOTTAWA.BITNET

☙ *VM/ESA discussions list.*
VMESA-L@UAFSYSB.BITNET
LISTSERV@UAFSYSB.BITNET

☙ *VM GOPHER discussion list.*
VMGOPHER@PUCC.BITNET
LISTSERV@PUCC.BITNET

☙ *VM low-key Tech-staff discussion list.*
VMKIDS-L@DEARN.BITNET
LISTSERV@DEARN.BITNET

☙ *VM Performance list.*
VMPR-L@MCGILL1.BITNET
LISTSERV@.BITNET

☙ *VM Release 6 (SP and HPO) discussions list.*
Discusses topics relating to IBM VM/SP and
VM/HPO Release 6 CP, CMS, and related
components (e.g. TSAF, AVS, APPC services,
and so on.).
VMREL6-L@UAFSYSB.BITNET
LISTSERV@UAFSYSB.BITNET

☙ *Swedish EARN Node Administrators—VMS
system list.*
VMS-SE@SEARN.BITNET
LISTSERV@SEARN.BITNET

☙ *VAX/VMS LISTSERV discussion list.*
Offers ideas related to the development of a
LISTSERV package for VAX/VMS systems.
VMSLSV-L@UBVM.BITNET
LISTSERV@UBVM.BITNET
Contact: Brian Nelson
<BRIAN@UOFT02.BITNET>

☙ *VMSTEX-L list*
VMSTEX-L@UICVM.BITNET
LISTSERV@UICVM.BITNET

☙ *VM Systems Programmers List*
VMSYS-L@UGA.BITNET
LISTSERV@UGA.BITNET

☙ *GWU's VMTAPE Discussion List*
VMTAPEL@GWUVM.BITNET
LISTSERV@GWUVM.BITNET

☙ *VM Tools discussions list.*
VMTOOL-L@UIUCVMD.BITNET
LISTSERV@UIUCVMD.BITNET

☙ *IBM soft and hard discussion list.*
VMUSER-L@JPNSUT00.BITNET
LISTSERV@JPNSUT00.BITNET

☙ *VMUTIL-A (archive files only).*
VMUTIL-A@UIUCVMD.BITNET
LISTSERV@UIUCVMD.BITNET

☙ *VM viruses and worms discussion list.*
VMVIRUS@PCCVM.BITNET
LISTSERV@PCCVM.BITNET

☙ *VM VTAM discussions list.*
VMVTAM-L@UIUCVMD.BITNET
LISTSERV@UIUCVMD.BITNET

☙ *VM/XA Discussion List*
Discusses issues in installation, operation, and
maintenance of VM/XA systems.
VMXA-L@UGA.BITNET
LISTSERV@UGA.BITNET

☙ *VMXA list: Testing VMXA*
VMXA@BLEKUL10.BITNET
LISTSERV@BLEKUL10.BITNET

☙ *VM 3800 printer discussions list.*
VM3800-L@UIUCVMD.BITNET
LISTSERV@UIUCVMD.BITNET

☙ *VNEWS Discussion List*
VNEWS-L@UBVM.BITNET
LISTSERV@UBVM.BITNET

☙ *Single User Unix Discussion*
Supports discussion about the idea of running
a single-user configured Unix on private virtual
machines as an alternative to CMS.
VNIX-L@TAMCBA.BITNET
LISTSERV@TAMCBA.BITNET
Contact: Rick Troth
TROTH@RICE.EDU

☙ *VOX Humanities List*
VOXHUM-L@EMUVM1.BITNET
LISTSERV@EMUVM1.BITNET

© *VISUAL-L Discussion List*
```
VISUAL-L@VTVM1.BITNET
LISTSERV@VTVM1.BITNET
```

© *Visual Programming Languages*
Discusses topics related to the study, design, development, implementation, and evaluation of visual programming languages (VPLs).
```
VPLLIST@SUSHI.STANFORD.EDU
VPLLIST-REQUEST@SUSHI.STANFORD.EDU
```
Contact: Marvin M. Zauderer
```
<ZAUDERER@SUSHI.STANFORD.EDU>
```

© *Virtual Storage Access Method Discussion List*
Discusses the features of VSAM.
```
VSAM-L@TREARN.BITNET
LISTSERV@TREARN.BITNET
```
Contact: Dr. Ozel Ergen
```
BILMOE@TREARN.BITNET
```

© *Virginia Tech Computer Aided Design Discussion list*
```
VTCAD-L@VTVM2.BITNET
LISTSERV@VTVM2.BITNET
```

© *VTLSLIST.*
Discussion list for VTLS, a Virginia Tech Library System, online public access catalog for libraries.
```
VTLSLIST@VTVM1.BITNET
LISTSERV@VTVM1.BITNET
```

© *Virginia Tech NOVELL users.*
```
VTNOVELL@VTVM1.BITNET
LISTSERV@VTVM1.BITNET
```

© *Virginia Tech Single System Image Mail Discussion list.*
```
VTSSI-L@VTVM2.BITNET
LISTSERV@VTVM2.BITNET
```

© *Virginia Tech Women List*
```
VTWOMEN@VTVM1.BITNET
LISTSERV@VTVM1.BITNET
```

© *DEC VideoText Discussion List*
```
VTX-L@NCSUVM.BITNET
LISTSERV@NCSUVM.BITNET
```

© *VUGMAIL List*
```
VUGMAIL@UKACRL.BITNET
LISTSERV@UKACRL.BITNET
```

© *Pronet Token Ring*
For people who use Pronet/V2LNI Ring networks.
```
V2LNI-PEOPLE@MC.LCS.MIT.EDU
LWA@MC.LCS.MIT.EDU
```

© *Washington Area Academic Computing Centers list.*
```
WAACC-L@UMDD.BITNET
LISTSERV@UMDD.BITNET
```

© *LocalTalk on IP Networks*
Discusses the issues associated with the technology and administration of an AppleTalk network across the Internet.
```
WAAN@NISC.NYSER.NET
WAAN-REQUEST@NISC.NYSER.NET
```
Contact: Craig A. McGowan
```
<MCGOWAN@MAPLE-LEAF.NYSER.NET>
```

© *Wellfleet Communications Inc. routers user group.*
Engineers and users around the world discuss problems of all types. Also posts announcements of interest to users.
```
wellfleet-l@nstn.ns.ca
wellfleet-l-request@nstn.ns.ca
```
Contact: Daniel MacKay
```
<daniel@nstn.ns.ca>
```

© *CREN White Pages List*
```
WHITE-PG@BITNIC.BITNET
LISTSERV@BITNIC.BITNET
```

© *Expert Systems*
Discusses subjects related to AI applications to human-computer interface design.
```
wiley!ai-chi@LLL-LCC.LLNL.GOV
wiley!ai-chi-request@LLL-LCC.LLNL.GOV
```
Contact: Dr. Sherman Tyler
```
<wiley!sherman@LLL-LCC.LLNL.GOV>
```

© *MS-Windows interfaces to VAX-Rdb list.*
```
WIN-VAX@UMDD.BITNET
LISTSERV@UMDD.BITNET
```

© *Wollongong Incorporated TCP/IP products.*
Offers archives of WINTCP-L and related files that are stored in the WINTCP-L FILELIST. Also gatewayed into the vmsnet.networks.tcp-ip.wintcp news group of USENET News.
```
WINTCP-L@UBVM.BITNET
LISTSERV@UBVM.BITNET
```
Contact: Jim Gerland
```
<gerland@ubvms>
```

© *Microsoft Windows 3 discussion list.*
A forum for the discussion about Microsoft Windows and related issues.
```
WIN3-L@UICVM.BITNET
LISTSERV@UICVM.BITNET
```

© *WISCNET interested party list.*
```
WISCNET@DB0TUI11.BITNET
LISTSERV@DB0TUI11.BITNET
```

© *Workshop on Information Systems Ecosystem*
```
WISE@UICVM.BITNET
LISTSERV@UICVM.BITNET
```

๑ *Endometriosis Treatment and Support.*
WITSENDO@DARTCMS1.BITNET
LISTSERV@DARTCMS1.BITNET

๑ *Windowing korn shell discussion list.*
WKSH-L@UCSFVM.BITNET
LISTSERV@UCSFVM.BITNET

๑ *Macintosh Microsoft Word*
For users of Microsoft Word running on
Macintosh computers.
WORD-MAC@ACC.HAVERFORD.EDU.BITNET
MAILSERV@ACC.HAVERFORD.EDU.BITNET

๑ *DOS Microsoft Word*
For users of Microsoft Word running under
DOS and Windows.
WORD-PC@ufobi1.uni-forst.gwdg.de
LISTSERV@ufobi1.uni-forst.gwdg.de
Contact: Reinhold Meyer
<rmeyer@ufobi2.uni-forst.gwdg.de>

๑ *Personal work station discussion list.*
Discusses personal work station computers,
such as the Sun2, Sun3, Apollo, Silicon Graphics,
and AT&T Workstations.
WORKS@RUTVM1.BITNET
LISTSERV@RUTVM1.BITNET

๑ *JES3 Systems Programmers List*
JES3-L@UGA.BITNET
LISTSERV@UGA.BITNET

๑ *JNET Discussion Group*
Discusses Jnet running under VAX VMS.
JNET-L@BITNIC.BITNET
LISTSERV@BITNIC.BITNET
Contact: Jim Gerland
<GERLAND@UBVM.BITNET>

๑ *Job offers from EARN Institute members*
For posting job offers at institutions that are
full EARN members.
JOB-LIST@FRORS12.BITNET
LISTSERV@FRORS12.BITNET
Contact: Hans Deckers
DECK@FRORS12

๑ *Discussion about Japan and the BITNET list.*
JPBIT-L@JPNSUT00.BITNET
LISTSERV@JPNSUT00.BITNET

๑ *Japan HEP/SPAN DECnet meeting list.*
JPDECNET@JPNKEKVM.BITNET
LISTSERV@JPNKEKVM.BITNET

๑ *JP Software products (4DOS/4OS2 et al) list.*
JPSOFT@INDYCMS.BITNET
LISTSERV@INDYCMS.BITNET

๑ *KAIROS E-Mail Distribution Service list.*
KAIROS@UTCVM.BITNET
LISTSERV@UTCVM.BITNET

๑ *KEKMAC-L MAC user's list.*
KEKMAC-L@JPNKEKVM.BITNET
LISTSERV@JPNKEKVM.BITNET

๑ *Kermit discussion list.*
KERMIT-L@JPNSUT30.BITNET
LISTSERV@JPNSUT30.BITNET

๑ *List for users of Kleio-Software list.*
KLEIO-L@DGOGWDG1.BITNET
LISTSERV@DGOGWDG1.BITNET

๑ *The KNET discussion list.*
KNET-L@TAMVM1.BITNET
LISTSERV@TAMVM1.BITNET
Contact: David Lippke
LIPPKE@UTDALLAS.BITNET

๑ *The Kent network users group list.*
KNUG@KENTVM.BITNET
LISTSERV@KENTVM.BITNET

๑ *Kent State University lists owners discussion
list.*
KSUOWN-L@KENTVM.BITNET
LISTSERV@KENTVM.BITNET

๑ *WAIS Initiative for North Carolina list.*
KUDZU-L@NCSUVM.BITNET
LISTSERV@NCSUVM.BITNET

๑ *K.U.Leuven RISC/6000 users list.*
KUL6000@BLEKUL11.BITNET
LISTSERV@BLEKUL11.BITNET

๑ *Canadian History Association Conference on
Computers*
For members of the CHA to discuss issues
related to computing in history.
L-CHA@UQAM.BITNET
LISTSERV@UQAM.BITNET
Contact: Jose Igartua
R12270@UQAM.BITNET

๑ *L-OHACAD*
Discusses academic topics and concerns within
the OHECC group—Ohio Higher Education
Computer Council.
L-OHACAD@AKRONVM.BITNET
LISTSERV@AKRONVM.BITNET

๑ *Database*
Discusses all issues relevant to the ORACLE
database management system.
L-ORACLE@UQAM.BITNET
LISTSERV@UQAM.BITNET

๑ *Ohio Super Computing*
Discusses Ohio SuperComputing.
L-OSC@AKRONVM.BITNET
LISTSERV@AKRONVM.BITNET

🐍 *Virus List*
```
L-VIRUS@PSUVM.BITNET
LISTSERV@PSUVM.BITNET
```

🐍 *VMCENTER Components Discussion List*
Discusses any VMCENTER components.
Includes all components in the VMCENTER
and VMCENTER II product lines.
```
L-VMCTR@AKRONVM.BITNET
LISTSERV@AKRONVM.BITNET
```
Contact: Gary Sponseller
```
SPONSELL@AKRONVM.BITNET
```

🐍 *Academic Microcomputer Lab Management*
Discusses issues concerning the management
of microcomputer labs in academic settings.
```
LABMGR@UKCC.BITNET
LISTSERV@UKCC.BITNET
```
Contact: Mary Molinaro
```
<MOLINARO@ukcc.uky.edu>
```

🐍 *Microsoft LAN Manager*
For LAN Manager and its variants, including
LAN Manager for Unix, DEC Pathworks, and
IBM LAN Server.
```
LANMAN-L@NIHLIST.BITNET
LISTSERV@NIHLIST.BITNET
```
Contact: Chris Ohlandt
```
<CJO@helix.nih.gov>
```

🐍 *Laser Printer Information Distribution List*
```
LASER-L@IRLEARN.BITNET
LISTSERV@IRLEARN.BITNET
```

🐍 *Printing*
Discusses topics related to the design and use of
laser printer hardware, software, and fonts.
```
LASER@BNANDP11.BITNET
LISTSERV@BNANDP11.BITNET
```

🐍 *FORUM LATEX list*
```
LATEX-L@BRUFSC.BITNET
LISTSERV@BRUFSC.BITNET
```

🐍 *LaTeX users group list.*
```
LATEX-UG@SAUPM00.BITNET
LISTSERV@SAUPM00.BITNET
```

🐍 *Listserve Database Search Facility*
For the in depth investigation of the power of
the Listserve Database Search facility.
```
LDBASE-L@UKANVM.BITNET
LISTSERV@UKANVM.BITNET
```
Contact: Phil Endacott
```
<ENDACOTT@UKANVAX.BITNET>
```

🐍 *International seminar list.*
```
LECTU-L@BRUFSC.BITNET
LISTSERV@BRUFSC.BITNET
```

🐍 *LEPICS Parallel Processing Project Group list*
```
LEPICSP3@LEPICS.BITNET
LISTSERV@LEPICS.BITNET
```

🐍 *LEXX editor discussions.*
Discusses IBM's LEXX Live Parsing Editor for
VM.
```
LEXX-L@IRISHVMA.BITNET
LISTSERV@IRISHVMA.BITNET
```
Contact: Nick Laflamme
```
<NLAFLAMM@IRISHVMA>
```

🐍 *Network Site Liaisons*
A forum for communications among user
services people at BITNET sites.
```
LIAISON@BITNIC.BITNET
LISTSERV@BITNIC.BITNET
```

🐍 *Software Licensing*
For issues related to software licensing:
experiences, comments, and ideas.
```
LICENSE@BITNIC.BITNET
LISTSERV@BITNIC.BITNET
```

🐍 *Linda*
For users and potential users of Linda based
parallel programming systems. Linda is a set of
operators that are added to various conventional
programming languages to produce a parallel
programming language.
```
linda-users@cs.yale.edu
linda-users-request@cs.yale.edu
```

🐍 *GSU Wells Computer Center newsletter*
discussion list.
```
LINK-L@GSUVM1.BITNET
LISTSERV@GSUVM1.BITNET
```

🐍 *Mailing Lists*
Discusses issues related to managing Internet
mailing lists, including (but not limited to)
software, methods, mechanisms, techniques,
and policies.
```
List-Managers-Digest@GreatCircle.COM
Majordomo@GreatCircle.COM
```
Contact: Brent Chapman
```
<Brent@GreatCircle.COM>
```

🐍 *Literate Programming*
For dealing with topics related to Literate
Programming.
```
LITPROG@SHSU.BITNET
LISTSERV@SHSU.BITNET
```
Contact: George D. Greenwade
```
<BED_GDG@SHSU.BITNET>
```

🐍 *LMAN interface of LISTMAN discussion list*
```
LMAN-L@GREARN.BITNET
LISTSERV@GREARN.BITNET
```

⑤ *Lojban: Artificial language (also called Loglan)*
About the language that has been recently completed after 35 years of work, and is spoken by a few people, and growing steadily.
```
lojban-list@snark.thyrsus.com
lojban-list-request@snark.thyrsus.com
```
Contact: John Cowan
```
(cowan@snark.thyrsus.com)
```

⑤ *Lojban List*
```
LOJBAN@CUVMA.BITNET
LISTSERV@CUVMA.BITNET
```

⑤ *LOLA users list.*
```
LOLA-L@LSUVM.BITNET
LISTSERV@LSUVM.BITNET
```

⑤ *LISTEARN BETA test sites, discussion list.*
```
LSTBETA@TREARN.BITNET
LISTSERV@TREARN.BITNET
```

⑤ *LSTERN Server*
Discusses issues related to the LISTEARN server.
```
LSTERN-L@FRMOP11.BITNET
LISTSERV@FRMOP11.BITNET
```

⑤ *Interactive Access Facility Discussion*
To define and formalize the LISTEARN Interactive Access Facility development.
```
LSTIAF-L@TAUNIVM.BITNET
LISTSERV@TAUNIVM.BITNET
```
Contact: Turgut Kalfaoglu
```
<TURGUT@FRORS12.BITNET>
```

⑤ *Forum on LISTSERV Release 1.6*
```
LSTSRV-L@POLYGRAF.BITNET
LISTSERV@POLYGRAF.BITNET
```

⑤ *Revised LISTSERV maintainers list.*
```
LSTSRV-M@SEARN.BITNET
LISTSERV@SEARN.BITNET
```

⑤ *Language testing research and practice list.*
```
LTEST-L@UCLACN1.BITNET
LISTSERV@UCLACN1.BITNET
```

⑤ *LANWatch*
For the technical discussion among users of the LANWatch Local Area Network Analyzer for the IBM Personal Computer from FTP Software, Inc.
```
LWUSERS@NDSUVM1.BITNET
LISTSERV@NDSUVM1.BITNET
```

⑤ *Mac-Conf: The Macintosh computer in the university list.*
```
MAC-CONF@UVMVM.BITNET
LISTSERV@UVMVM.BITNET
```
Contact: Steve Cavrak
```
sjc@uvmvm.BITNET
```

⑤ *Macintosh news and information list.*
```
MAC-L@YALEVM.BITNET
LISTSERV@YALEVM.BITNET
```

⑤ *Macintosh Security*
Discusses existing security problems and solutions in Macintosh applications and harware.
```
mac-security@eclectic.com
mac-security-request@eclectic.com
```
Contact: David C. Kovar
```
<kovar@eclectic.com>
```

⑤ *EARN Macintosh Users List—Extension for Mac*
```
MAC-TEL@IRLEARN.BITNET
LISTSERV@IRLEARN.BITNET
```

⑤ *EARN Macintosh Users List*
```
MAC-USER@IRLEARN.BITNET
LISTSERV@IRLEARN.BITNET
```

⑤ *Mac Applications News and Tips*
For the exchange of questions and advice concerning usage of Macintosh application software of all kinds at Dartmouth.
```
MACAPPLI@DARTCMS1.BITNET
LISTSERV@DARTCMS1.BITNET
```
Contact: David Avery
```
DAVID@DARTCMS1.BITNET
```

⑤ *McGill Macintosh Users Group*
```
MACGIL-L@MCGILL1.BITNET
LISTSERV@MCGILL1.BITNET
```

⑤ *Macintosh Hardware*
For the posting of alerts about hardware problems, availability and repairs for Macintosh hardware and related items from other vendors.
```
MACHRDWR@DARTCMS1.BITNET
LISTSERV@DARTCMS1.BITNET
```

⑤ *Macintosh IRC Client Design List*
```
MACIRC-L@BROWNVM.BITNET
LISTSERV@BROWNVM.BITNET
```

⑤ *MAC Mail Discussion List*
```
MACMAIL@UTORONTO.BITNET
LISTSERV@UTORONTO.BITNET
```

⑤ *Macintosh Multimedia Discussion List*
```
MACMULTI@FCCJ.BITNET
LISTSERV@FCCJ.BITNET
```

⑤ *Macintosh Networking Issues*
```
MACNET-L@YALEVM.BITNET
LISTSERV@YALEVM.BITNET
```

⑤ *Macintosh Programming*
The Internet answer to the Usenet programming forum.

```
MACPROG@WUVMD.BITNET
LISTSERV@WUVMD.BITNET
```
Contact: Bill Brandt
```
<WBRANDT@WAYNEST1.BITNET>
```

🕥 *Missouri Association of Collegiate Registrars*
```
MACRAO@UMVMA.BITNET
LISTSERV@UMVMA.BITNET
```

🕥 *Macintosh System Software*
For the Macintosh system software, including advice about the topics of "which system?" and "which finder?"
```
MACSYSTM@DARTCMS1.BITNET
LISTSERV@DARTCMS1.BITNET
```

🕥 *Turkish Macintosh Users Group list*
```
MACTURK@TREARN.BITNET
LISTSERV@TREARN.BITNET
```

🕥 *University of Ottawa's Mac users discussion group list.*
```
MACUO-L@UOTTAWA.BITNET
LISTSERV@UOTTAWA.BITNET
```

🕥 *Interleaf*
For discussions on all aspects related to the Interleaf publishing environment.
```
mail.interleaf
<leaf%TEKSCE.SCE.TEK.COM@RELAY.CS
leafrequest%TEKSCE.SCE.TEK.COM@RELAY.CS.NET
```

🕥 *Electronic Mail future developements list.*
```
MAIL-ITA@IBACSATA.BITNET
LISTSERV@IBACSATA.BITNET
```

🕥 *Mail*
For the discussion about programs and protocols used for the transfer of mail such as Crosswell MAILER and BSMTP; internet gateways; local campus networks; VM end-user mail interfaces, such as MIT MAIL and BITNOTE, and campatibility of their formats with non-VM user agents; "mail handling" programs, such as NMENU and MAILBOOK; and mail formats.
```
MAIL-L@BITNIC.BITNET
LISTSERV@BITNIC.BITNET
```

🕥 *Zilog Computers*
For communications among Zilog users. Open to end users and systems houses.
```
Mail-Zilog <cbmvax!mail-
zilog@SEISMO.CSS.GOV>
cbmvax!mail-zilog@SEISMO.CSS.GOV or UUCP
```
Contact: George Robbins
```
<cbmvax!grr@SEISMO.CSS.GOV>
```

🕥 *MAIL/MAILBOOK Subscription List*
```
MAILBOOK@CLVM.BITNET
LISTSERV@CLVM.BITNET
```

🕥 *Discussion on MAPLE software list.*
```
MAPLE-L@IRLEARN.BITNET
LISTSERV@IRLEARN.BITNET
```

🕥 *Marcha-L Distribution List*
```
MARCHA-L@YALEVM.BITNET
LISTSERV@YALEVM.BITNET
```

🕥 *GLDV-AK fuer TEI-Guideline-Anpassung list.*
```
MARKUP-L@DGOGWDG1.BITNET
LISTSERV@DGOGWDG1.BITNET
```

🕥 *TECHMATI: Technion Mathematics Net— International list.*
```
MATHDEPT@TECHNION.BITNET
LISTSERV@TECHNION.BITNET
```

🕥 *List on Micro Cluster*
```
MCLUSTER@JPNIMRTU.BITNET
LISTSERV@JPNIMRTU.BITNET
```

🕥 *MDS32 Discussion List*
For the discussion of creative ideas and techniques using MDS32, Menu Design System from Ergodic, Inc., for VAX/VMS systems.
```
MDS32-L@INDYCMS.BITNET
LISTSERV@INDYCMS.BITNET
```

🕥 *Info-DEC-Micro Mailing List*
For the exchange of information concerning Digital Equipment Corp's microcomputers, including the VAXmate, the Professional Series, the DECmate, and the Rainbow.
```
MD4J@UGA.BITNET
LISTSERV@UGA.BITNET
```
Contact: Rob Locke
```
RALII@DRYCAS.BITNET
```

🕥 *Mossbauer Effect Data Center*
```
MEDC-L@NCSUVM.BITNET
LISTSERV@NCSUVM.BITNET
```

🕥 *BITNET MENTOR referral list.*
For referrals of BITNET problems to list members from new listserve members and to provide distributed support.
```
MENTOR-L@BITNIC.BITNET
LISTSERV@BITNIC.BITNET
```
Contact: Lisa M. Covi, BITNET Support
```
COVI@BITNIC
```

🕥 *MEX-ENP6*
Bulletin Board for the student exchange of Mexico list.
```
MEX-ENP6@UNAMVM1.BITNET
LISTSERV@UNAMVM1.BITNET
```

🕥 *MH Mail System*
A discussion group which focuses on the UCI version of the Rand Message Handling (MH) system; a list for MH maintainers and experts.

```
MH-WORKERS@ICS.UCI.EDU
MH-Workers-Request@ICS.UCI.EDU
```
Contact: John L. Romine (JLR3)
```
<Bug-MH@ICS.UCI.EDU>
```

⑤ *MHS News*
For anyone interested in implementing the CCITT X.400 (MHS) message handling protocols.
```
MHSNEWS@IBACSATA.BITNET
LISTSERV@IBACSATA.BITNET
```
Contact: Tim Kehres
```
<kehres@TIS.LLNL.GOV>
```

⑤ *x.400 Protocols*
For anyone seriously interested in implementing the CCITT X.400 (MHS) message handling protocols.
```
MHSnews@ICS.UCI.EDU
mhsnews-request@ICS.UCI.EDU
```
Contact: Tim Kehres
```
<kehres@TIS.LLNL.GOV>
```

⑤ *McGill Information Access list*
```
MIA-L@MCGILL1.BITNET
LISTSERV@MCGILL1.BITNET
```

⑤ *UCLA Micro Information Center News*
```
MICNEWS@UCLACN1.BITNET
LISTSERV@BRUSPVM.BITNET
```

⑤ *Microcomputer Coordination Committee list*
```
MICROC-L@YALEVM.BITNET
LISTSERV@YALEVM.BITNET
```

⑤ *Morino's MVS Information Control System*
A technical discussion about the MCS Information Control System from Morino Inc.
```
MICS-L@HDETUD1.BITNET
LISTSERV@HDETUD1.BITNET
```
Contact: Rob van Hoboken
```
RCOPROB@HDETUD1.BITNET
```

⑤ *MIDAS Progetto ESPRIT list.*
```
MIDAS@ITOCSIVM.BITNET
LISTSERV@ITOCSIVM.BITNET
```

⑤ *MIDnet Discussion Group*
```
MIDNET-L@KSUVM.BITNET
LISTSERV@KSUVM.BITNET
```

⑤ *MIDnet Reconfiguration Discussion Group*
```
MIDNET-R@KSUVM.BITNET
LISTSERV@KSUVM.BITNET
```

⑤ *MIDnet User Services Discussion Group*
```
MIDNET-U@KSUVM.BITNET
LISTSERV@KSUVM.BITNET
```

⑤ *Midnet Executive Committee list*
```
MIDNET-X@KSUVM.BITNET
LISTSERV@KSUVM.BITNET
```

⑤ *MINITEL list*
```
MINITEL@STLAWU.BITNET
LISTSERV@STLAWU.BITNET
```

⑤ *Minix operating system*
For the discussion of the Minix Operating system. This a Version 7 Unix clone written for IBM Compatible PCs by Andy Tanenbaum (`minix@vu44.uucp` or `minix@cs.vu.nl`). This list is gatewayed to the arpanet list `info-minix@udel.edu`.
```
MINIX-L@DEARN.BITNET
LISTSERV@DEARN.BITNET
```
Contact: Glen Overby
```
minix@Plains.NoDak.EDU
```

⑤ *MMDF2 Mailer*
A mailing list for people who implement, install or maintain the MMDF2 mailer on UNIX hosts. MMDF is widely used in many environments including the Internet and CSNET's PhoneNet.
```
MMDF2@SH.CS.NET
MMDF2-REQUEST@SH.CS.NET
```
Contact: David Herron
```
<david@MS.UKY.EDU>
```

⑤ *Multimedia Discussion*
Discusses this growing field in education and training.
```
MMEDIA-L@VMTECMEX.BITNET
LISTSERV@VMTECMEX.BITNET
```
Contact: Alejandro Kurczyn S.
```
<499229@VMTECMEX.BITNET>
```

⑤ *MMEDIA Multi Media List*
```
MMEDIA@ICNUCEVM.BITNET
LISTSERV@ICNUCEVM.BITNET
```

⑤ *Multimedia Mail*
For users who are active or interested in multimedia mail.
```
MMM-PEOPLE@ISI.EDU
MMM-PEOPLE-REQUEST@ISI.EDU
```
Contact: Ann Westine
```
WESTINE@ISI.EDU
```

⑤ *Mid-Missouri Network Users Group*
```
MMNUG-L@UMCVMB.BITNET
LISTSERV@UMCVMB.BITNET
```

⑤ *MEDIANET Discussion List*
```
MNET-L@AKRONVM.BITNET
LISTSERV@AKRONVM.BITNET
```

⑤ *MOD-IETF*
A moderated redistribution of the IETF list.
```
MOD-IETF@SEARN.BITNET
LISTSERV@SEARN.BITNET
```

⑤ *Macintosh modeling package ModelShop.*
Discusses software from San Francisco-based MacroMind. Paracomp is used primarily to

quickly create three-dimensional models, produce low-quality rendered views, and generate animated "walk-thrus" or "fly-bys" of models.

```
MODLSHOP@IRISHVMA.BITNET
LISTSERV@IRISHVMA.BITNET
```
Contact: Mike W. Miller
```
<MWMILLER@IRISHVMA>
```

⑤ *Modula-2 (language) discussions list.*
```
MODULA-L@UALTAVM.BITNET
LISTSERV@UALTAVM.BITNET
```

⑤ *Network Traffic*
Discusses issues related to monitoring network traffic, controlling local access to BITNET, and system security.
```
MON-L@BITNIC.BITNET
LISTSERV@BITNIC.BITNET
```

⑤ *Yale MultiProtocol Gateway discussion group list.*
```
MPG-L@YALEVM.BITNET
LISTSERV@YALEVM.BITNET
```

⑤ *Microsoft Mail Discussion List*
Discusses Microsoft mail.
```
MSMAIL-L@YALEVM.BITNET
LISTSERV@YALEVM.BITNET
```
Contact: Peter Furmonavicius
```
<PETER@YALEVM.BITNET>
```

⑤ *Communication*
Hosts participating in NJE/RSCS-based networks provide their users with a messaging command that enables them to communicate one-on-one in "real time." Capability is not standard in TCP/IP-based networks. RFC-1312 (Message Send Protocol 2) is an experimental protocol that proposes a method to provide this feature under TCP/IP.
```
MSP-L@ALBANY.BITNET
LISTSERV@ALBANY.BITNET
```

⑤ *Middle States Steering list.*
```
MSSC-L@UBVM.BITNET
LISTSERV@UBVM.BITNET
```

⑤ *Microsoft SQL Server Discussion List*
Deals with Microsoft's SQL Server for OS/2.
```
MSSQL-L@DUKEFSB.BITNET
LISTSERV@DUKEFSB.BITNET
```
Contact: Brian Eder
```
<Eder@dukefsb.BITNET>
```

⑤ *MAPPA Trainers Network*
```
MTN@IUBVM.BITNET
LISTSERV@IUBVM.BITNET
```

⑤ *MT3270-L*
For discussing test versions of TN3270 for the Macintosh.
```
MT3270-L@BROWNVM.BROWN.EDU
LISTSERV@BROWNVM.BROWN.EDU
```

⑤ *The MUDA List*
```
MUDA-L@GREARN.BITNET
LISTSERV@GREARN.BITNET
```

⑤ *ADA Compiler*
For users of Meridian Software Systems's Ada compilers.
```
mug@meridian.com
mug-request@MERIDIAN.COM
```
Contact: Jerry N. Sweet
```
<jns@ARRAKIS.MERIDIAN.COM>
```

⑤ *Multitasking for PC Programmers*
For PC programers interested in multitasking programing The list is intended for primarily Turbo Pascal and Turbo C users.
```
MULTAS-L@TREARN.BITNET
LISTSERV@TREARN.BITNET
```

⑤ *MULTILIS users discussion list.*
```
MULTILIS@ALBNYVM1.BITNET
LISTSERV@ALBNYVM1.BITNET
```

⑤ *L3 Muon Reconstruction Software Forum*
```
MUL3-L@LEPICS.BITNET
LISTSERV@LEPICS.BITNET
```

⑤ *Miami University mail exchange discussion list.*
```
MUMAIL-L@MIAMIU.BITNET
LISTSERV@MIAMU.BITNET
```

⑤ *MUMPS List*
MUMPS Operating System Discussion list. Created January 4, 1987.
```
MUMPS-L@UGA.BITNET
LISTSERV@UGA.BITNET
```
Contact: Harold Pritchett
```
HAROLD@UGA.BITNET
```

⑤ *Missouri University NeXT User's Group*
```
MUNUG-L@UMCVMB.BITNET
LISTSERV@UMCVMB.BITNET
```

⑤ *Masscomp Computer Systems*
The Masscomp Users Society (MUS) mailing list for people who are interested in the Masscomp line of computers.
```
MUS@TMC.EDU
mus-request@TMC.EDU
```
Contact: Stan Barber
```
<sob@BCM.TMC.EDU>
```

⑤ *MuTeX and MusicTeX*
For the discussion of MuTeX and MusicTeX related issues.

```
mutex@stolaf.edu
mutex-request@stolaf.edu
```

🌜 *Swedish EARN Node ADministrators—MVS system list*
```
MVS-SE@SEARN.BITNET
LISTSERV@SEARN.BITNET
```

🌜 *MVS Utilities*
For the discussion on utility programs for MVS sites.
```
MVS-UTIL@OHSTVMA.BITNET
LISTSERV@OHSTVMA.BITNET
```
Contact: Duane Weaver
```
<WEAVER@OHSTVMA>
```

🌜 *MVS/ESA List*
```
MVSESA-L@NMSUVM1.BITNET
LISTSERV@NDSUVM1.BITNET
```

🌜 *MVS LPD and MVS NJE-over-IP discussion list.*
```
MVSLPD-L@USCVM.BITNET
LISTSERV@USCVM.BITNET
```

🌜 *Discussion Group for Marshall-Wythe Law School*
```
MWL-L@WMVM1.BITNET
LISTSERV@WMVM1.BITNET
```

🌜 *Model 204 Database Discussion*
For the discussion of any aspect of the Model 204 Database System, a software package from Computer Corporation of America.
```
M204-L@AKRONVM.BITNET
LISTSERV@AKRONVM.BITNET
```
Contact: Gary Sponseller
```
SPONSELL@AKRONVM.BITNET
```

🌜 *BITNET/NetNorth/EARN redistribution list.*
A BITNET/NetNorth/EARN Redistribution list for Usenet Newsgroup to announce.conferences and post calls for papers. Contributions should be submitted to mcmi!news-announce-conferences@uunet.uu.net.
```
NAC@NDSUVM1.BITNET
LISTSERV@NDSUVM1.BITNET
```

🌜 *National Association of Educational Buyers*
```
NAEB-L@RITVM.BITNET
LISTSERV@RITVM.BITNET
```

🌜 *Network Architecture Focus Group*
```
NAF@NRCVM01.BITNET
LISTSERV@NRCVM01.BITNET
```

🌜 *North American Fuzzy Information Processing*
```
NAFIPS-L@GSUVM1.BITNET
LISTSERV@GSUVM1.BITNET
```

🌜 *Domain Naming Conventions*
For the discussion of the concepts, principles, design, and implementation of the domain style names.
```
NAMEDROPPERS@NIC.DDN.MIL
NAMEDROPPERS-REQUEST@NIC.DDN.MIL
```

🌜 *NaNet list*
```
NANET@FINHUTC.BITNET
LISTSERV@FINHUTC.BITNET
```

🌜 *Nanny for the VAX*
For people using the Nanny package written for VAX using VMS.
```
Nanny-Users@XHMEIA.CALTECH.EDU
Nanny-Users-Request@XHMEIA.Caltech.Edu
```
Contact: Perfect Tommy
```
<zar@IAGO.CALTECH.EDU>
```

🌜 *North American Service Industries Research Network list.*
```
NASIRN-L@UBVM.BITNET
LISTSERV@UBVM.BITNET
```

🌜 *NASK discussion list.*
```
NASK@PLEARN.BITNET
LISTSERV@PLEARN.BITNET
```

🌜 *National Association of Sigma Users Conference*
```
NASU-L@MSU.BITNET
LISTSERV@MSU.BITNET
```

🌜 *NATURAL NEWS Distribution List*
```
NATUSR-L@MAINE.BITNET
LISTSERV@MAINE.BITNET
```

🌜 *Hayao Miyazaki Discussion list*
```
NAUSICAA@BROWNVM.BROWN.EDU
LISTSERV@BROWNVM.BROWN.EDU
```

🌜 *Navigating The Internet Workshop*
```
NAVIGATE@UBVM.BITNET
LISTSERV@UBVM.BITNET
```

🌜 *Network Architecture Working Group*
```
NAWG-L@UNBVM1.BITNET
LISTSERV@UNBVM1.BITNET
```

🌜 *National Communication Chairs Discussion List*
```
NCC-L@TAMVM1.BITNET
LISTSERV@TAMVM1.BITNET
```

🌜 *NCSU Multimedia User Groups*
```
NCSU-MUG@NCSUVM.BITNET
LISTSERV@NCSUVM.BITNET
```

🌜 *NCSU Digitized Document Transmission Project*
```
NCSUDDTP@NCSUVM.BITNET
LISTSERV@NCSUVM.BITNET
```

⑤ *North Carolina DEC VTX Discussion List*
```
NCVTX-L@NCSUVM.BITNET
LISTSERV@NCSUVM.BITNET
```

⑤ *NEARnet Regional Technical Network*
A list for technical discussions about NEARnet, the New England Academic and Research Network.
```
nearnet-tech@NIC.NEAR.NET
nearnet-tech-request@NIC.NEAR.NET
```
Contact: NEARnet Staff
```
<nearnet-staff@NIC.NEAR.NET>
```

⑤ *NEARnet Regional General Network*
For the general discussion of NEARnet, the New England Academic and Research Network, its services, growth, policies, and so on.
```
nearnet@NIC.NEAR.NET
nearnet-request@NIC.NEAR.NET
```
Contact: NEARnet Staff
```
<nearnet-staff@NIC.NEAR.NET>
```

⑤ *Northeast Notis Users Group*
```
NENUG-L@YALEVM.BITNET
LISTSERV@YALEVM.BITNET
```

⑤ *NorthEast SAS Users Group*
```
NESUG-L@UMAB.BITNET
LISTSERV@UMAB.BITNET
```

⑤ *LISTEARN Net-L Student's Internet/BITNET list.*
```
NET-L@PLTUMK11.BITNET
LISTSERV@PLTUMK11.BITNET
```

⑤ *Notre Dame National Networking News*
```
NET-NATL@IRISHVMA.BITNET
LISTSERV@IRISHVMA.BITNET
```

⑤ *Notre Dame Networking News list.*
```
NET-ND@IRISHVMA.BITNET
LISTSERV@IRISHVMA.BITNET
```

⑤ *Operation and Management of Computer Networks list*
```
NET-OPS@NSC.DEC.COM
NET-OPS-REQUEST@NSC.DEC.COM
```

⑤ *Network Team Discussion List*
```
NET-TEAM@GREARN.BITNET
LISTSERV@GREARN.BITNET
```

⑤ *Bitnet/Internet Trainers List*
For users are involved in the training or support of others using the resources available on Bitnet and Internet.
```
NET-TRAIN@CORNELL.BITNET
LISTSERV@CORNELL.BITNET
```
Contact: James Milles
```
<MILLESJG@SLUVCA.BITNET>
```

⑤ *Network Licensing List*
```
NET_LIC@SUVM.BITNET
LISTSERV@SUVM.BITNET
```

⑤ *Network Advisory Committee*
```
NETADV-L@MCGILL1.BITNET
LISTSERV@MCGILL1.BITNET
```

⑤ *Netblazer*
A list for discussions among users of Telebit NetBlazer products.
```
netblazer-users@telebit.com
netblazer-users-request@telebit.com
```

⑤ *NETDATAK discussion list.*
Discusses the NETDATA-K , in technical issues and in managing issues. Any opinions, ideas, views, suggestions, advices, and information are welcome.
```
NETDATAK@JPNKEKVM.BITNET
LISTSERV@JPNKEKVM.BITNET
```
Contact: Yoshiaki Banno/KEK
```
BANNO@JPNKEKVM.BITNET
```

⑤ *Netnorth Directors List*
```
NETDIR-L@UTORONTO.BITNET
LISTSERV@UTORONTO.BITNET
```

⑤ *NETDOC-L List*
```
NETDOC-L@VTVM1.BITNET
LISTSERV@VTVM1.BITNET
```

⑤ *WSU Network Information List*
```
NETINFO@WSUVM1.BITNET
LISTSERV@WSUVM1.BITNET
```

⑤ *Net Managers Discussion List*
```
NETMGR-L@WUVMD.BITNET
LISTSERV@WUVMD.BITNET
```

⑤ *Discussion of NETMON list.*
```
NETMON-L@BITNIC.BITNET
LISTSERV@BITNIC.BITNET
```

⑤ *NetMonth/Bitnet Services Library Staff*
For NetMonth, a network service publication distributed free of charge to students and professionals in BITNET and other networks.
```
NETMONTH@MARIST.BITNET
LISTSERV@MARIST.BITNET
```
Contact: Chris Condon
```
<BITLIB%YALEVM.BITNET@CUNYVM.CUNY.EDU>
```

⑤ *NETNWS-L Netnews List*
For operators and developers of various Netnews programs on non-UUCP networks.
```
NETNWS-L@NDSUVM1.BITNET
LISTSERV@NDSUVM1.BITNET
```
Contact: Bill Verity
```
WHV@PSUVM.BITNET
```

⑤ *U-B Net_One Discussion Group*
```
NETONE@UKCC.BITNET
LISTSERV@UKCC.BITNET
```

⑤ *Network Operations List*
```
NETOPS@YORKVM1.BITNET
LISTSERV@YORKVM1.BITNET
```

⑤ *Netnorth Mail Application Technical Contacts List*
```
NETPST-L@UTORONTO.BITNET
LISTSERV@UTORONTO.BITNET
```

⑤ *Netnorth Representatives List*
```
NETREP-L@UTORONTO.BITNET
LISTSERV@UTORONTO.BITNET
```

⑤ *Network accessible Servers, FTP sites, Filelists, lists, and toolslis.*
This list is for finding files.
```
NETSCOUT@VMTECMEX.BITNET
LISTSERV@VMTECMEX.BITNET
```
Contact: Alejandro Kurczyn S.
```
<499229@VMTECMEX.BITNET>
```

⑤ *NETSRV-L LIST*
```
NETSRV-L@CEARN.BITNET
LISTSERV@CEARN.BITNET
```

⑤ *Teaching Network Use*
For librarians, computer support personnel, computer jocks—all users who are involved in teaching others how to use Bitnet and Internet.
```
NETTRAIN@UBVM.BITNET
LISTSERV@UBVM.BITNET
```
Contact: Jim Milles
```
<MILLESJG@SLUVCA.BITNET>
```

⑤ *View discussion list.*
```
NETV-L@MARIST.BITNET
LISTSERV@MARIST.BITNET   IBM'sNET
```

⑤ *Net3270 Forum List*
```
NET3270@MCGILL1.BITNET
LISTSERV@MCGILL1.BITNET
```

⑤ *Artificial Neural Networks discussion.*
```
NEURAL-N@ANDESCOL.BITNET
LISTSERV@ANDESCOL.BITNET
```

⑤ *NEWLIST*
This list is a central address to post announce-ments of new public mailing lists.
```
NEW-LIST@NDSUVM1.BITNET
LISTSERV@NDSUVM1.BITNET
```

⑤ *Network Organizing Executive List*
```
NEWEXE-L@UNBVM1.BITNET
LISTSERV@UNBVM1.BITNET
```

⑤ *Network Organizing Conference*
```
NEWNET-L@UNBVM1.BITNET
LISTSERV@UNBVM1.BITNET
```

⑤ *CANARIE Network Organizing Conference List*
```
NEWNEW-L@UNBVM1.BITNET
LISTSERV@UNBVM1.BITNET
```

⑤ *Texas A & I University computer newsletter list.*
```
NEWS-L@TAIVM1.BITNET
LISTSERV@TAIVM1.BITNET
```

⑤ *NeWS Windows*
Discusses NeWS: the Network/extensible Window System. NeWS is an extensible multitasking window system environment, consisting of a network based display server that is controlled and programmed in PostScript.
```
NeWS-makers@BRILLIG.UMD.EDU
NeWS-makers-request@BRILLIG.UMD.EDU
```

⑤ *NeXT Computer List*
Discusses the NeXT computers.
```
NEXT-L@BROWNVM.BROWN.EDU
LISTSERV@BROWNVM.BROWN.EDU
```
Contact: Atul Butte
```
ATUL@BROWNVM.BROWN.EDU
```

⑤ *System managers of NeXt Systems*
For quick-turnaround trouble shooting aid for users who administer and manage NeXT systems.
```
next-managers@stolaf.edu
next-managers-request@stolaf.edu
```
Contact: Craig D. Rice
```
<cdr@acc.stolaf.edu>
```

⑤ *NeXT Computer Announcement Digest List*
```
NEXTAN-D@BROWNVM.BROWN.EDU
LISTSERV@BROWNVM.BROWN.EDU
```

⑤ *Development for NeXT computers Shareware,Bugs list.*
```
NEXTDE-L@TECMTYVM.BITNET
LISTSERV@TECMTYVM.BITNET
```

⑤ *NeXT Computer Programmer Digest List*
```
NEXTPR-D@BROWNVM.BROWN.EDU
LISTSERV@BROWNVM.BROWN.EDU
```

⑤ *NeXTstep Operating Environment*
For the discussion of the NeXTstep operating environment produced by NeXT Computer, Inc. NeXTstep is bidirectionally gatewayed to the INET newsgroup.
```
NeXTstep@INDYCMS.BITNET
LISTSERV@IndyCMS.BITNET
```
Contact: Phillip Gross Corporon
```
<phil@CSE.ND.Edu>
```

❺ *NeXT Campus Support List*
NEXTSUPP@RICEVM1.BITNET
LISTSERV@RICEVM.BITNET

❺ *NeXT Computer Sysadmin Digest List*
NEXTSY-D@BROWNVM.BROWN.EDU
LISTSERV@BROWNVM.BROWN.EDU

❺ *Nordisk Forum List*
NFDL-L@SEARN.BITNET
LISTSERV@SEARN.BITNET

❺ *Numerically Intensive Computing (general info) list.*
NIC-INFO@FRMOP11.BITNET
LISTSERV@FRMOP11.BITNET
Contact: Jean-Loic Delhaye
DELHAYE@FRMOP11

❺ *NIH Guide Primary Distribution List*
NIHGDE-L@JHUVM.BITNET
LISTSERV@JHUVM.BITNET

❺ *NIH Listing of Available Grants and Contracts*
NIHGUIDE@UMAB.BITNET
LISTSERV@UMAB.BITNET

❺ *The National Indian Policy Research Institute*
NIPRI@GWUVM.BITNET
LISTSERV@GWUVM.BITNET

❺ *GARR NIS REPORT List*
NIS-REP@ICNUCEVM.BITNET
LISTSERV@ICNUCEVM.BITNET

❺ *National Information Standards Organization*
NISO-L@NERVM.BITNET
LISTSERV@NERVM.BITNET

❺ *NISS discussion list.*
NISS@PLEARN.BITNET
LISTSERV@PLEARN.BITNET

❺ *NKI Electronic Bulletin Board List*
NKI-BBS@NKI.BITNET
LISTSERV@NKI.BITNET

❺ *Natural Language & Knowledge Represe*
For the discussion and announcements related to the fields of Natural Languange and Knowledge Representation. Postings should be sent to nl-kr@cs.rpi.edu.
NL-KR-L@TAUNIVM.BITNET
LISTSERV@TAUNIVM.BITNET
Contact: Chris Welty
nl-kr-request@CS.RPI.EDU

❺ *NLSNEWS NLS Newsletter Subscription List*
NLSNEWS@OHSTVMA.BITNET
LISTSERV@OHSTVMA.BITNET

Contact: Peter A. Tomasek
TOMASEK@OHSTHR.BITNET

❺ *NLSUPDAT NLS Data Update Service List*
NLSUPDAT@OHSTVMA.BITNET
LISTSERV@OHSTVMA.BITNET
Contact: Peter A. Tomasek
TOMASEK@OHSTHR.BITNET

❺ *Novell Netware Master's Group*
NMG@NRCVM01.BITNET
LISTSERV@NRCVM01.BITNET

❺ *Netnorth Directors in Ontario (NNDIRONT)*
NNDIRONT@UTORONTO.BITNET
LISTSERV@UTORONTO.BITNET

❺ *MVS/TSO NNTP News Reader (NNMVS)*
Informs users on how to obtain the NNMVS software for their site.
NNMVS-L@USCVM.BITNET
LISTSERV@USCVM.BITNET
Contact: Steve Bacher (Batchman)
<seb@draper.com>

❺ *Network News Reader Protocol List*
NNRP-L@BROWNVM.BITNET
LISTSERV@BROWNVM.BITNET

❺ *Discussion of NNR/VM (News Client Software)*
NNRVM-L@VMTECQRO.BITNET
LISTSERV@VMTECQRO.BITNET

❺ *National Network List*
NNSP-L@UNCVM1.BITNET
LISTSERV@UNCVM1.BITNET

❺ *NODMGT-L*
Discusses format and content of the primary node information database; collection, processing and distribution of node information; local access to and use of the node database; tools to perform the previous functions.
NODMGT-L@BITNIC.BITNET
LISTSERV@BITNIC.BITNET

❺ *NOMAD2 Discussion List*
For users of MUST Software PRODUCTS. Topics for discussion include the base product, tools, and any interfaces.
NOMAD2-L@TAMVM1.BITNET
LISTSERV@TAMVM1.BITNET
Contact: Mark Oliveri
X043MO@TAMVM1.BITNET

❺ *NOMINATE—CREN Nominating Committe List*
NOMINATE@BITNIC.BITNET
LISTSERV@BITNIC.BITNET

☙ *Networking between Nordic and Baltic countries list.*
NORDBALT@SEARN.BITNET
LISTSERV@SEARN.BITNET

☙ *North Bay ITS Commuter Information Exchange List*
NORTHBAY@UCSFVM.BITNET
LISTSERV@UCSFVM.BITNET

☙ *Northstar Computers*
Discussions for Northstar microcomputer users.
NORTHSTAR-USERS@WSMR-SIMTEL20.ARMY.MIL
NORTHSTAR-USERS-REQUEST@SIMTEL20.ARMY.MIL
Contact: Frank J. Wancho
<WANCHO@WSMR-SIMTEL20.ARMY.MIL>

☙ *Archives & Manuscripts Discussion List*
NOTIS-AR@UMINN1.BITNET
LISTSERV@UMINN1.BITNET

☙ *NOTIS/DOBIS discussion group list.*
NOTIS-L@TCSVM.BITNET
LISTSERV@TCSVM.BITNET

☙ *NOTIS Acquisitions Discussion Group*
NOTISACQ@ULKYVM.BITNET
LISTSERV@ULKYVM.BITNET
Contact: Joyce G. McDonough
JGMCDO01@ULKYVM.BITNET

☙ *NOTIS Music Library List*
NOTMUS-L@UBVM.BITNET
LISTSERV@UBVM.BITNET
Contact: Chuck Dunn
CHUCK@UBVM.BITNET

☙ *Novell Discussion Group*
For people in higher education who use the Novell Netware (c) Network Operating System (NOS).
NOVELL@SUVM.BITNET
LISTSERV@SUVM.BITNET

☙ *Novell Technology Operations List*
NOVOPS@SUVM.BITNET
LISTSERV@SUVM.BITNET

☙ *Novell Technology Transfer Partners List*
NOVTTP@SUVM.BITNET
LISTSERV@SUVM.BITNET

☙ *Moderated discussion list of the Pathways Technology list.*
NP-DETA@UMUC.BITNET
LISTSERV@UMUC.BITNET

☙ *Moderated discussion list of the Pathways Topics list.*
NP-RSRCH@UMUC.BITNET
LISTSERV@UMUC.BITNET

☙ *National Reserach Education Network*
Discusses the NREN (National Research and Education Network).
NREN-Disc@psi.com
nren-discuss-request@psi.com
Contact: Jim Cerny
<j_cerny@unhh.unh.edu>

☙ *Niedersaechsischer Rechnerverbund List*
NRV@DCZTU1.BITNET
LISTSERV@DCZTU1.BITNET

☙ *Nsn/News List*
NSNNEWS@FINHUTC.BITNET
LISTSERV@FINHUTC.BITNET

☙ *NTS-L Distribution List*
NTS-L@DHDURZ1.BITNET
LISTSERV@DHDURZ1.BITNET

☙ *Support for Nuntius Newsreader for the Mac.*
Discusses the Macintosh NNTP client Nuntius
NUNTIUS-L@CORNELL.EDU
LISTSERV@cornell.edu
Contact: Aaron Freimark
<abf1@cornell.edu>
Contact: Peter Speck
<speck@ruc.dk>.

☙ *NUTN Member List*
NUTN-L@OSUVM1.BITNET
LISTSERV@OSUVM1.BITNET

☙ *NetView Access Services session manager discussion list.*
Discusses issues related to IBM's NetView Access Services session manager.
NVAS-L@CUVMC.BITNET
LISTSERV@CUVMC.BITNET
Contact: Terrence Ford
<TFOCU@CUVMC.BITNET>

☙ *NYSERNet Technical List*
NYSERTEC@POLYGRAF.BITNET
LISTSERV@POLYGRAF.BITNET

☙ *Organizing Committee—Med Info 95 list.*
OC-L@UMAB.BITNET
LISTSERV@UMAB.BITNET

☙ *OHECC Administrative Discussion List*
OH-ADMN@AKRONVM.BITNET
LISTSERV@AKRONVM.BITNET

☙ *OMR Scanner Discussion List*
OMRSCAN@UOGUELPH.BITNET
LISTSERV@UOGUELPH.BITNET

☙ *Ontario Academic Computer Lab Administration list*
ONACLABS@HUMBER.BITNET
LISTSERV@HUMBER.BITNET

❧ *Emory One Card list*
```
ONECRD-L@EMUVM1.BITNET
LISTSERV@EMUVM1.BITNET
```

❧ *Mainframe Operations*
Offers discussions about MAINFRAME Computer Operations for computer operators, lead operators and supervisors, and so on.
```
OPERS-L@AKRONVM.BITNET
LISTSERV@AKRONVM.BITNET
```
Contact: Tom Evert
```
<01EVERT@AKRONVM.BITNET>
```

❧ *University of California operations managers list.*
```
OPMAN-L@UCSBVM.BITNET
LISTSERV@UCSBVM.BITNET
```

❧ *Optical Computing and Holography List*
Offers discussions on holography and its applications.
```
OPT-PROC@TAUNIVM.BITNET
LISTSERV@TAUNIVM.BITNET
```
Contact: Shelly Glaser
```
GLASER@USCVM.BITNET
```

❧ *University Of Toronto ORACLE Issue List*
```
ORACL-UT@UTORONTO.BITNET
LISTSERV@UTORONTO.BITNET
```

❧ *Oracle*
Discusses issues relevant to the ORACLE database management system.
```
ORACLE-L@SBCCVM.BITNET
LISTSERV@SBCCVM.BITNET
```

❧ *Questions/Answers List*
This list is for answerering all of your questions. Send mail to `oracle@iuvax.cs.indiana.edu` with the word "help" in the subject line for complete details. There is a distribution list for compilations of the Oracle's best answers.
```
ORACLE@IUVAX.CS.INDIANA.EDU
oracle-request@iuvax.cs.indiana.edu
```

❧ *Operations Research/Management Science and Computer Science*
This list is for researchers, practitioners, and graduate students working in OR/CS interface.
```
ORCS-L@OSUVM1.BITNET
LISTSERV@OSUVM1.BITNET
```
Contact: Ramesh Sharda
```
<MGMTRSH@OSUVM1>
```

❧ *Oregon Banner List*
```
OREBAN-L@PSUORVM.BITNET
LISTSERV@PSUORVM.BITNET
```

❧ *OSI Management Application Project List*
```
OSIMA-L@DEARN.BITNET
LISTSERV@DEARN.BITNET
```

❧ *OS2*
For issues regarding OS/2, including user queries, Workplace, programming, OS/2 2.0, and other related issues.
```
OS2-L@FRORS12.BITNET
LISTSERV@FRORS12.BITNET
```

❧ *Moderated discussion list on OS/2.*
```
OS2@BLEKUL11.BITNET
LISTSERV@BLEKUL11.BITNET
```

❧ *Operating Systems OS/2 for IBM Compatible PCs*
Discusses the operating systems OS/2 for IBM Compatible PCs.
```
OS2@CC1.KULEUVEN.AC.BE
LISTSERV@cc1.kuleuven.ac.be
```

❧ *Ontario University Registrar's Association Discussion list.*
```
OURASG-L@RYERSON.BITNET
LISTSERV@RYERSON.BITNET
```

❧ *Ontario University Systems Software Support Group*
```
OUSSS-L@UTORONTO.BITNET
LISTSERV@UTORONTO.BITNET
```

❧ *ObjectVision Application Development*
```
OVISION@VTVM1.BITNET
LISTSERV@VTVM1.BITNET
```

❧ *PACS-L*
Deals with all computer systems that libraries make available to their patrons, including CD-ROM databases, computer-assisted instruction (CAI and ICAI) programs, expert systems, hypermedia programs, library microcomputer facilities, and local databases.
```
PACS-L@UHUPVM1.BITNET
LISTSERV@UHUPVM1.BITNET
```

❧ *Public-Access Computer Systems Publications*
```
PACS-P@UHUPVM1.BITNET
LISTSERV@UHUPVM1.BITNET
```

❧ *PACV-L Discussions List*
```
PACV-L@DEARN.BITNET
LISTSERV@DEARN.BITNET
```

❧ *IBM 3812/3820 Tips and Problems Discussion List*
A mailing list for IBM 3812 and IBM 3820 Page Printer discussions, problems, and tips.
```
PAGE-L@UCF1VM.BITNET
LISTSERV@UCF1VM.BITNET
```
Contact: Jim Ennis
```
<JIM@UCF1VM.BITNET>
```

❧ *Discussion list for the CEC RARE II PAGEIN printer list.*

```
PAGEIN-L@HEARN.BITNET
LISTSERV@HEARN.BITNET
```

✏ *PageMaker for Desktop Publishers*
For PageMaker users to share their ideas and
problems.
```
PAGEMAKR@INDYCMS.BITNET
LISTSERV@INDYCMS.BITNET
```
Contact: Cindy Stone
```
<stonec@GOLD.UCS.INDIANA.EDU>
```

✏ *Library Automation*
Deals will all aspects of the MSUS/Unisys/PALS
Library Automation application, and the Unisys
1100/2200 series computers it runs on.
```
PALS-L@KNUTH.MTSU.EDU
LISTSERV@KNUTH.MTSU.EDU PALS
```
Contact: David Robinson
```
<robinson@mtsu.edu>
```

✏ *The P.A.O.K. fans discussion list.*
```
PAOK-L@GREARN.BITNET
LISTSERV@GREARN.BITNET
```

✏ *Parallel Computing Taskforce*
```
PAR-L@UTORONTO.BITNET
LISTSERV@UTORONTO.BITNET
```

✏ *Parallel computing/AMT DAP mailing list.*
For massive SIMD processing architectures and
techniques and all topics related to the AMT
DAP (SIMD) machine.
```
PARA-DAP@IRLEARN.BITNET
LISTSERV@IRLEARN.BITNET
```
Contact: Rotan Hanrahan
```
HANRAH88@IRLEARN.BITNET
```

✏ *Borland Paradox*
```
PARADOX@BRUFPB.BITNET
LISTSERV@BRUFPB.BITNET
```

✏ *Pathalias Routing Mailing List*
```
PAROUTE@BITNIC.BITNET
LISTSERV@BITNIC.BITNET
```

✏ *Pascal Language Discussion List*
```
PASCAL-L@TREARN.BITNET
LISTSERV@TREARN.BITNET
```

✏ *Paradigms for Boosting Development—
Networklist*
```
PBDLIST@SUVM.BITNET
LISTSERV@SUVM.BITNET
```

✏ *Personal Computer Evaluation*
For the exchange of personal computer
evaluations between and among computer
centre personnel in Irish third-level educational
institutions.
```
PC-EVAL@IRLEARN.BITNET
LISTSERV@IRLEARN.BITNET
```

✏ *Tel Aviv University PC forum list.*
```
PC-FORUM@TAUNIVM.BITNET
LISTSERV@TAUNIVM.BITNET
```

✏ *Rexx*
For discussions of personal REXX.
```
PC-REXX@UCF1VM.BITNET
LISTSERV@UCF1VM.BITNET
```

✏ *PC Arabization List*
Discusses various researches and problems
related to personal computer arabization tools
such as Nafitha, Musaad Alarabi, Sakhr, or any
new researches.
```
PCARAB-L@SAKFU00.BITNET
LISTSERV@SAKFU00.BITNET
```
Contact: Yasser Ahmed Zaki
```
<DEVYAZ69@SAKFU00.BITNET>
```

✏ *GeoWorks Ensemble*
For users of PC/GEOS products, including
GeoWorks Ensemble, GeoWorks Pro,
GeoWorks POS, and third party products.
```
PCGEOS-LIST@CSD.MOT.COM
PCGEOS-list-request@csd.mot.com
```
Contact: Brian Smithson
```
<brian@csd.mot.com>
```

✏ *PC-IP Arpa Discussion List*
```
PCIP-L@BYUADMIN.BITNET
LISTSERV@BYUADMIN.BITNET
```

✏ *TCP/IP Protocol Implementations for PC
Discussion*
For the various sets of TCP/IP implementations
for personal computers.
```
PCIP@IRLEARN.BITNET
LISTSERV@IRLEARN.BITNET
```
Contact: Gary Delp
```
<delp@HUEY.UDEL.EDU>
```

✏ *BITNET Public domain software servers list.*
```
PCSERV-L@RPICICGE.BITNET
COMSERVE@RPIECS.
```

✏ *Forum for the discussion of PC user support
issues.*
Discusses approaches to providing coordinated
PC user support within the institutional context,
and for resolving specific problems, as well as
keeping user support professionals up to date.
```
PCSUPT-L@YALEVM.BITNET
LISTSERV@YALEVM.BITNET
```
Contact: Richard Crane
```
MCSC@YALEVM.BITNET
```

✏ *MS-DOS Compatibles discussion list.*
```
PCTECH-L@TREARN.BITNET
LISTSERV@TREARN.BITNET
```

🐌 *PCTrans Issues List*
```
PCTRAN-L@YALEVM.BITNET
LISTSERV@YALEVM.BITNET
```

🐌 *NEC PC-9800 series discussion list.*
```
PC9801@JPNSUT30.BITNET
LISTSERV@JPNSUT30.BITNET
```
Contact: Masamichi Ute
```
UTE@JPNSUT30.BITNET
```

🐌 *PDP 8 DEC Computers*
```
PDP8-LOVERS@AI.MIT.EDU
PDP8-LOVERS-REQUEST@AI.MIT.EDU
```
For mailing communication and cooperation between owners of vintage DEC computers, but not limited to, the PDP-8 series of minicomputers.
Contact: Robert Seastrom
```
<PDP8-LOVERS-REQUEST@AI.MIT.EDU>
```

🐌 *UNCC PENPAL-L Discussion List*
```
PENPAL-L@UNCCVM.BITNET
LISTSERV@UNCCVM.BITNET
```

🐌 *PERL Language*
For the discussion of PERL, Larry Wall's Practical Extraction and Report Language. This list is bi-directionally gatewayed with the USENET newsgroup comp.lang.perl. It is distributed as a digest that is created and distributed at least once per day.
```
PERL-USERS@VIRGINIA.EDU
Perl-Users-Request@Virginia.EDU
```
Contact: Marc Rouleau
```
<mer6g@VIRGINIA.EDU>
```

🐌 *Perseus Discussion List*
```
PERSEUS@BROWNVM.BROWN.EDU
LISTSERV@BROWNVM.BROWN.EDU
```

🐌 *Personal and Micro computer users distribution list.*
```
PERSON-L@IRLEARN.BITNET
LISTSERV@IRLEARN.BITNET
```

🐌 *PFUG-L*
Distributes "Parallel Dispatches", the newsletter of the IBM Parallel FORTRAN Users'Group (PFUG).
```
PFUG-L@JHUVM.BITNET
LISTSERV@JHUVM.BITNET
```

🐌 *PHIGS-L*
For PHIGS 3-D graphigs standard library maintainers and experts. Products like IBM's graPHIGS and Personal graPHIGS, TEMPLATE's FIGARO or other PHIGS implementations and their applications.
```
PHIGS-L@FINHUTC.BITNET
LISTSERV@FINHUTC.BITNET
```

🐌 *CMS Pipelines Design List*
```
PIPDSGN@PUCC.BITNET
LISTSERV@PUCC.BITNET
```

🐌 *BITNET2 Mid-Eastern U.S. List*
```
PITSREG2@UBVM.BITNET
LISTSERV@UBVM.BITNET
```

🐌 *Polish EARN Topics Discussion*
Discusses possible Poland <-> EARN network traffic.
```
PLEARN-L@UBVM.BITNET
LISTSERV@UBVM.BITNET
```
Contact: Jerzy Pawlowski
```
v132nrea@ubvms.BITNET
```

🐌 *PLNTINFO—a private conference on plant information list.*
```
PLNTINFO@SIVM.BITNET
LISTSERV@SIVM.BITNET
```

🐌 *PL1 (language) Discussion List*
```
PL1-L@UIUCVMD.BITNET
LISTSERV@UIUCVMD.BITNET
```

🐌 *Pegasus Mail Technical Discussion*
For bug reports, questions, and update announcements for the Pegasus Mail electronic mail program and the Charon internet gateway.
```
pmail-updates@splicer.cba.hawaii.edu
pmail-request@splicer.cba.hawaii.edu
```
Contact: John D. Hopkins
```
<jhopkins@cbacc.cba.uga.edu>
```

🐌 *PMC-Talk list*
```
PMC-TALK@NCSUVM.BITNET
LISTSERV@NCSUVM.BITNET
```

🐌 *PMDF Distribution List*
```
PMDF-L@IRLEARN.BITNET
LISTSERV@IRLEARN.BITNET
```

🐌 *GARR-PMN NET management list.*
```
PMN-MGR@ITOCSIVM.BITNET
LISTSERV@ITOCSIVM.BITNET
```

🐌 *POD POD Network List*
```
POD@OHSTVMA.BITNET
LISTSERV@OHSTVMA.BITNET
```

🐌 *PODCORE POD Core Committee*
```
PODCORE@OHSTVMA.BITNET
LISTSERV@OHSTVMA.BITNET
```

🐌 *PODIUM-L LIST*
```
PODIUM-L@UKCC.BITNET
LISTSERV@UKCC.BITNET
```

🐌 *Discussion list for Polish Crystallography.*
```
POL$CRYS@PLEARN.BITNET
LISTSERV@PLEARN.BITNET
```

✆ *POLICY-L*
For proposed and present BITNET policies discussion.
```
POLICY-L@BITNIC.BITNET
LISTSERV@BITNIC.BITNET
```

✆ *POLPAL-L Discussion List*
```
POLPAL-L@UOGUELPH.BITNET
LISTSERV@UOGUELPH.BITNET
```

✆ *ADA under POSIX*
For working group members of IEEE 1003.5, the group that is involved in developing the Ada binding to the IEEE POSIX specification.
```
posix-ada@GREBYN.COM
posix-ada-request@GREBYN.COM
```
Contact: Karl Nyberg
```
<karl@GREBYN.COM>
```

✆ *Fortran under Posix*
For working group members of IEEE 1003.9, the group that is involved in developing the FORTRAN binding to the IEEE POSIX specification.
```
posix-fortran@SANDIA.GOV
posix-fortran-request@SANDIA.GOV
```
Contact: Michael J. Hannah
```
<mjhanna@SANDIA.GOV>
```

✆ *Postmast Standard List*
```
POST-STD@BITNIC.BITNET
LISTSERV@BITNIC.BITNET
```

✆ *Postmasters list*
```
POSTMAST@PURCCVM.BITNET
LISTSERV@PURCCVM.BITNET
```

✆ *IBM R6000 RISC Processors*
Discusses the IBM RISC System/6000 (tm IBM) family based on the Performance Optimization With Enhanced RISC (POWER) Architecture (also known as RIOS in the rumor mill) announced on February 15, 1990.
```
POWER-L@NDSUVM1.BITNET
LISTSERV@NDSUVM1.BITNET I
```
Contact: Marty Hoag
```
NU021172@NDSUVM1.BITNET
```

✆ *PowerHouse 4GL*
Discusses any topic (vaguely) related to PowerHouse, the 4GL package from COGNOS.
```
POWERH-L@UNB.CA
LISTSERV@UNB.CA
```
Contact: Georges M. Bourgeois
```
<BOURGEG@UMONCTON.CA>
```

✆ *Discussion list for the PowerHouse Software.*
```
POWERH-L@UNBVM1.BITNET
LISTSERV@UNBVM1.BITNET
```

✆ *PENPAGES project between Penn State and Wisconsion list.*
```
PPAGES-L@PSUVM.BITNET
LISTSERV@PSUVM.BITNET
```

✆ *Payroll technical information exchange list.*
```
PPSINF-L@UCSFVM.BITNET
LISTSERV@UCSFVM.BITNET
```

✆ *UK's Prime-NJI Emulator list.*
```
PRIMENJI@UKCC.BITNET
LISTSERV@UKCC.BITNET
```

✆ *EARN policy and basic non-technical EARN matters list.*
```
PRINCIPL@FRMOP11.BITNET
LISTSERV@FRMOP11.BITNET
```

✆ *CPT Primary Promotions Sub-Committee*
```
PRIPROM@PURCCVM.BITNET
LISTSERV@PURCCVM.BITNET
```

✆ *Principia Cybernetica List*
```
PRNCYB-L@BINGVMB.BITNET
LISTSERV@BINGVMB.BITNET
```

✆ *Printing Task Discussion Group*
```
PRNTNG-L@YALEVM.BITNET
LISTSERV@YALEVM.BITNET
```

✆ *ProComm Terminal Emulation*
For discussion among users of the ProComm 2.4.2, 2.4.3, and ProComm Plus terminal emulators on PCs and PC clones.
```
PROCOM-L@ATSUVAX1.BITNET
MAILSERV@ATSUVAX1.BITNET
```
Contact: Bill Bailey
```
<BAILEYB@ATSUVAX1.BITNET>
```

✆ *Commerce Business Daily—Procurement list*
```
PROCUR-B@OSUVM1.BITNET
LISTSERV@OSUVM1.BITNET
```

✆ *PROFS Discussion*
```
PROFS-L@DEARN.BITNET
LISTSERV@DEARN.BITNET
```
Contact: Harold C. Pritchett
```
HAROLD@UGA.UGA.EDU
```

✆ *PROFS Alternatives*
For tips and techniques for Profs sites who wish to investigate converting to office automation facilities which make more sense given today's network realities.
```
PROFSALT@PCCVM.BITNET
LISTSERV@PCCVM.BITNET
```
Contact: R N Hathhorn
```
<sysmaint@PCCVM.BITNET>
```

✆ *INFO-ATARI16 Programs List*
```
PROG-A16@UOGUELPH.BITNET
LISTSERV@UOGUELPH.BITNET
```

Progress Relational Database Management System

For the discussion of all relevant aspects of the PROGRESS(tm) RDBMS.

progress-list@uunet.UU.NET
progress-list-request@uunet.UU.NET

Contact: Ethan A. Lish
(ethan@thinc.UUCP)

PROGRESS(tm) RDBMS

For discussion of all relevant aspects of the PROGRESS(tm) RDBMS.

PROGRESS@THINC.COM
PROGRESS@THINC.COM

Contact: Ethan A. Lish
(Ethan.Lish@THINC.COM)

Prolog and logic programming mailing lists.

For general Prolog and logic programming information. PROLOG-HACKERS will provide a direct mailing for more deatiled information and bugs..

PROLOG-HACKERS@SUSHI.STANFORD.EDU
PROLOG-REQUEST@SUSHI.STANFORD.EDU

Contact: Chuck Restivo
<Restivo@SUSHI.STANFORD.EDU>

PROP-L

Discusses problems, suggestions, and helpful information about the Programmable Operator component of IBM CMS.

PROP-L@UTARLVM1.BITNET
LISTSERV@UTARLVM1.BITNET

Prosody Discussion List

PROSODY@PURCCVM.BITNET
LISTSERV@PURCCVM.BITNET

Computer Protocol

Discusses all kinds of computer protocols.

PROTOCOL@UIUCVMD.BITNET
LISTSERV@UIUCVMD.BITNET

Postscript Forum List

PSCRIPT@BNANDP11.BITNET
LISTSERV@BNANDP11.BITNET

Psion Handheld Computer

For the discussion and exchange of information and software for Psion computers.

psion@csd4.csd.uwm.edu
psion-request@csd4.csd.uwm.edu

Contact: Anthony Stieber
anthony@csd4.csd.uwm.edu

Domain Application Technical Contacts

PST-L@UTORONTO.BITNET
LISTSERV@UTORONTO.BITNET

Discussion of the programs in PSUTOOLS list.

PSUTOOLS@PSUVM.BITNET
LISTSERV@PSUVM.BITNET

National Network (.pt) Link Failures Annoucements list.

PTFAIL@PTEARN.BITNET
LISTSERV@PTEARN.BITNET

PTM-L List

PTM-L@ASUACAD.BITNET
LISTSERV@ASUACAD.BITNET

A.S.A. PD Graphics Repository Discussion list.

PUBGRF-L@NCSUVM.BITNET
LISTSERV@NCSUVM.BITNET

Media

Discusses the role of computers, specifically workstations, in book, magazine, newspaper, and other types of publishing.

publish@chron.com
publish-request@chron.com

Unix

Discusses public access UNIX systems.

pubnet@chinacat.unicom.com
chip@chinacat.Unicom.COM

PUMP Discussion List

PUMP-L@UVVM.BITNET
LISTSERV@UVVM.BITNET

Pass-Through Virtual Machines discussion list.

PVM-L@DB0FUB11.BITNET
LISTSERV@DB0FUB11.BITNET

Power Users Group

PWRUSR-L@MCGILL1.BITNET
LISTSERV@MCGILL1.BITNET

Proteon

Discusses Proteon's P4200-series gateway products.

P4200@COMET.CIT.CORNELL.EDU
P4200-REQUEST@COMET.CIT.CORNELL.EDU

Contact: Scott Brim
<SWB@COMET.CIT.CORNELL.EDU>

P4200-series Gateway Products Discussion Group

P4200@IRLEARN.BITNET
LISTSERV@IRLEARN.BITNET

QuickMail (CESoftware) Users

Enables users to talk to other QuickMail users, to discuss common experiences, problems, configurations, and so on.

QM-L@YALEVM.BITNET
LISTSERV@YALEVM.BITNET

Contact: Peter Furmonavicius
Peter@YaleVM.BITNET

🕉 *QMail Information List*
Distributes information about the QMail mail user agent.
QMAIL-L@NCSUVM.BITNET
LISTSERV@NCSUVM.BITNET

🕉 *QUAKE-L*
Discusses the ways various national and international computer networks can help in the event of an earthquake, or the help can be enhanced.
QUAKE-L@NDSUVM1.BITNET
LISTSERV@NDSUVM1.BITNET

🕉 *Wordcrunchers—Microcomputer Analysis List*
QUALNET@SUVM.BITNET
LISTSERV@SUVM.BITNET

🕉 *Quark Express*
For express desktop publishers.
QUARKEXP@IUBVM.BITNET
LISTSERV@IUBVM.BITNET
Contact: Cindy Stone
<STONEC@IUBACS.BITNET>

🕉 *The Quark Express List*
QUARKXPR@IUBVM.BITNET
LISTSERV@IUBVM.BITNET

🕉 *QUASI-L Quasiperiodicity—Theory and Application List*
QUASI-L@DEARN.BITNET
LISTSERV@DEARN.BITNET

🕉 *Borland Quattro discussion group at Yale list.*
QUATRO-L@YALEVM.BITNET
LISTSERV@YALEVM.BITNET

🕉 *QUIDNOVI: What's New—Computer Applications List*
QUIDNOVI@ASUACAD.BITNET
LISTSERV@ASUACAD.BITNET

🕉 *RACF Security Discussion List*
For discussions and questions on the IBM security product, RACF (Resource Access Control Facility.) It is for the MVS and VM versions of RACF and is open to anyone with an interest in security on IBM mainframe computers.
RACF-L@UGA.BITNET
LISTSERV@UGA.BITNET
Contact: Harold Pritchett
<HAROLD@UGA>

🕉 *RADIS-L List*
RADIS-L@UWAVM.BITNET
LISTSERV@UWAVM.BITNET

🕉 *Radiology Special Interest Group*
RADSIG@UWAVM.BITNET
LISTSERV@UWAVM.BITNET

🕉 *RAMIS-4GL Discussion List*
RAMIS-L@CFRVM.BITNET
LISTSERV@CFRVM.BITNET

🕉 *RANDOM Meeting Group List*
RANDOM@IBACSATA.BITNET
LISTSERV@IBACSATA.BITNET

🕉 *The RARE Broadband Task Force*
RARE-BTF@HEARN.BITNET
LISTSERV@HEARN.BITNET

🕉 *Reevaluation Co-counseling discussion list.*
RC-LIST@UCF1VM.BITNET
LISTSERV@UCF1VM.BITNET

🕉 *Real COKE Users Group*
RCUG@IRLEARN.BITNET
LISTSERV@IRLEARN.BITNET
Contact: Tom Wade
T_WADE@CCVAX.BITNET

🕉 *RDM Discussion List*
RDM-L@UVVM.BITNET
LISTSERV@UVVM.BITNET

🕉 *Research in Education discussion list.*
RED-NET@IVEUNCC.BITNET
LISTSERV@IVEUNCC.BITNET

🕉 *Coordination internet projet REDALC list.*
REDINT@FRMOP11.BITNET
LISTSERV@FRMOP11.BITNET

🕉 *ARPA Re-Distribution List*
REDIST-L@EB0UB011.BITNET
LISTSERV@EB0UB011.BITNET

🕉 *REG List*
REG@MCGILL1.BITNET
LISTSERV@MCGILL1.BITNET

🕉 *Title 10 rules and regulations list.*
REGS-L@ALBNYDH2.BITNET
LISTSERV@ALBNYDN2.BITNET

🕉 *Relay Users Forum List*
RELUSR-L@NCSUVM.BITNET
LISTSERV@NCSUVM.BITNET

🕉 *L3 reconstruction software forum list.*
REL3-L@LEPICS.BITNET
LISTSERV@LEPICS.BITNET

⑤ *Domain Representatives List*
    REP-L@UTORONTO.BITNET
    LISTSERV@UTORONTO.BITNET

⑤ *Research Computing Forum*
Covers information on computing issues in research environments.
    RES-COMP@NKI.BITNET
    LISTSERV@NKI.BITNET
Contact: Bill Alexander
    <ALEX@NKI.BITNET>

⑤ *RESCOMP—Research Computer Architecture Group*
    RESCOMP@UTORONTO.BITNET
    LISTSERV@UTORONTO.BITNET

⑤ *VMRESMON Maintainers List*
Provides a distribution and communication mechanism for maintainers of the University of Arkansas VM Resource Limiter (VMRESMON).
    RESMON-L@UAFSYSB.BITNET
    LISTSERV@UAFSYSB.BITNET
Contact: Daniel P. Martin
    DMARTIN@UAFSYSB.BITNET

⑤ *Response to KIDS-91 List*
    RESPONSE@NDSUVM1.BITNET
    LISTSERV@NDSUVM1.BITNET

⑤ *Rexx (language) Discussion List*
    REXX-L@UIUCVMD.BITNET
    LISTSERV@UIUCVMD.BITNET

⑤ *REXXCOMP*
Discusses all aspects of the CMS REXX Compiler, including installation, maintenance, and use.
    REXXCOMP@UCF1VM.BITNET
    LISTSERV@UCF1VM.BITNET

⑤ *REXXLIST*
Discusses the REXX command language.
    REXXLIST@DEARN.BITNET
    LISTSERV@DEARN.BITNET

⑤ *RFC's*
Distributes announcements of new Requests for Comments. These are the publications of the Internet protocol development community, and include the specifications of protocol standards for the Internet, as well as policy statements and informational memos.
    RFC@NIC.DDN.MIL
    RFC-REQUEST@NIC.DDN.MIL

⑤ *RFMH Electronic Bulletin Board List*
    RFMH-BBS@NKI.BITNET
    LISTSERV@NKI.BITNET

⑤ *GA Regents' Global Center Information List*
    RGC-L@GSUVM1.BITNET
    LISTSERV@GSUVM1.BITNET

⑤ *Rice CWIS Discussion List*
    RICECWIS@RICEVM1.BITNET
    LISTSERV@RICEVM1.BITNET

⑤ *Rights and Responsibilities List*
    RIGHTS-L@AUVM.BITNET
    LISTSERV@AUVM.BITNET

⑤ *Networks*
For visualising computer networks.
    ripe-map@nic.eu.net
    ripe-map-request@nic.eu.net

⑤ *Risk and Insurance Issues list*
    RISK@UTXVM.BITNET
    LISTSERV@UTXVM.BITNET

⑤ *Risks of Computers*
Discusses issues related to risks to the public in the use of computer systems.
    RISKS@CSL.SRI.COM
    RISKS-REQUEST@CSL.SRI.COM
Contact: Peter G. Neumann
    <NEUMANN@CSL.SRI.COM>

⑤ *RNA is a Neural Net list in spanish.*
This list is for people interested in the development and investigation in the field of Artificial Neural Nets. The official language is Spanish, though contributions in English are accepted.
    RNA@UTFSM.BITNET
    LISTSERV@UTFSM.BITNET
Contact: Douglas Sargent (The Bug)
    <DSARGENT@UTFSM.BITNET>

⑤ *Robotech Mecha Listserv Group*
    ROBOTECH@USCVM.BITNET
    LISTSERV@USCVM.BITNET

⑤ *ROUTTAB Test Sites List*
    ROUTTAB@BITNIC.BITNET
    LISTSERV@BITNIC.BITNET

⑤ *RSAREF users interest group.*
Discusses topics related to the free reference implementation of RSA public-key cryptography for use in Internet Privacy-Enhanced Mail (PEM). For information about the RSAREF product, send mail to rsaref-info@rsa.com.
    rsaref-users@rsa.com
    rsaref-users-request@rsa.com

⑤ *RSCSMODS*
Discusses modifications to IBM's RSCS system product.

```
RSCSMODS@EB0UB011.BITNET
LISTSERV@EB0UB011.BITNET
```

✧ *RSCS Transparent Line Drivers for IBM 7171*
*Fo*r RSCS systems programmers who are interested in the Yale Transparent linedrivers for RSCS Version 2 on an IBM 7171.
```
RSTRAN-L@YALEVM.BITNET
LISTSERV@YALEVM.BITNET
```
Contact: Susan Bramhall
```
Susan@YaleVM.BITNET
```

✧ *RS1-L RS/1 List*
For the discussion of RS/1, a research and data analysis package put out by BBN.
```
RS1-L@NDSUVM1.BITNET
LISTSERV@NDSUVM1.BITNET
```
Contact: Brian McMahon
```
MCMAHON@GRIN1.BITNET
```

✧ *Russian TeX and Cyrillic Text Processing*
*F*acilitates the work on the Russian language version of the TeX typesetting system, but related technical topics are often discussed.
```
RUSTEX-L@UBVM.BITNET
LISTSERV@UBVM.BITNET
```
Contact: Dimitri Vulis
```
DLV@CUNYVMS1.BITNET
```

✧ *rxIRC Discussion List*
Discusses all technical and usage aspects of the rxIRC client software for communicating with Internet Relay Chat servers on the Internet.
```
RXIRC-L@VMTECQRO.BITNET
Listserv@VMTECQRO.BITNET
```
Contact: Carl von Loesch
```
<Carl.von.Loesch@arbi.informatik.uni-
oldenburg.de>
```

✧ *BITNET II Region 2 Information List*
```
R2B2@UBVM.BITNET
LISTSERV@UBVM.BITNET
```

✧ *SuperComputers List (MARIST)*
```
S-COMPUT@MARIST.BITNET
LISTSERV@MARIST.BITNET
```

✧ *Software AG Discussion List*
Discusses topics relating to Software AG products (such as ADABAS and NATURAL). Although it is intended for topics of a technical nature, topics concerning applications and applications programming are encouraged.
```
SAG-L@UAFSYSB.BITNET
LISTSERV@UAFSYSB.BITNET
```
Contact: David L. Merrifield
```
DM06900@UAFSYSB.BITNET
```

✧ *SAS Discussion List*
```
SAS-L@MARIST.BITNET
LISTSERV@MARIST.BITNET
```

✧ *SAS JOBS-SAS Classes/Seminars List*
```
SASJOB-L@ALBNYDH2.BITNET
LISTSERV@ALBNYDH2.BITNET
```

✧ *K.U.Leuven SAS kerngroep users mailing list.*
```
SASKERN@BLEKUL11.BITNET
LISTSERV@BLEKUL11.BITNET
```

✧ *K.U.Leuven SAS users mailing list.*
```
SASKUL@BLEKUL11.BITNET
LISTSERV@BLEKUL11.BITNET
```

✧ *SAS Public Access Consortium-S ASP AC-L List*
```
SASPAC-L@UMSLVMA.BITNET
LISTSERV@UMSLVM A.BITNET
```

✧ *SAS Performance Testing*
```
SASTUN-L@NCSUVM.BITNET
LISTSERV@NCSUVM.BITNET
```

✧ *Marist SAS Users Group*
```
SASUG@MARIST.BITNET
LISTSERV@MARIST.BITNET
```

✧ *'SAVEIT' software discussion list.*
```
SAVEIT-L@USCVM.BITNET
LISTSERV@USCVM.BITNET
```

✧ *SAW Discussion List*
```
SAW-L@UBVM.BITNET
LISTSERV@UBVM.BITNET
```

✧ *SUNY/Stony Brook IEEE Local Chapter list.*
```
SBIEEE-L@SBCCVM.BITNET
LISTSERV@SBCCVM.BITNET
```

✧ *South Bend Help*
An electronic cross between a library reference desk, a community information and referral center, and a computing center help desk—for all South Bend residents, and anyone else.
```
SBNHELP@INDYCMS.BITNET
LISTSERV@INDYCMS.BITNET
```

✧ *SUNY/Stony Brook Statistical Software Interest*
```
SBSTAT-L@SBCCVM.BITNET
LISTSERV@SBCCVM.BITNET
```

✧ *Stony Brook Supercomputer Mailing List*
```
SBSUPER@SBCCVM.BITNET
LISTSERV@SBCCVM.BITNET
```

✧ *SUNY Student Computing Access Program List*
```
SCAP-L@UBVM.BITNET
LISTSERV@UBVM.BITNET
```

✧ *SUNY Student Access to Computing Technology*
```
SCAPCOM@UBVM.BITNET
LISTSERV@UBVM.BITNET
```

◐ *Scheme Language*
Discusses anything related to the Scheme programming language(s), with particular emphasis on the use of Scheme in education.
```
SCHEME@MC.LCS.MIT.EDU
Scheme-Request@MC.LCS.MIT.EDU
```
Contact: Jonathan Rees
```
<JAR@MC.LCS.MIT.EDU>
```

◐ *SCRIB-L—Handwriting production, recognition, list.*
```
SCRIB-L@HEARN.BITNET
LISTSERV@HEARN.BITNET
```

◐ *Scribe Software*
For users who perform the role of Scribe Database Administrator at their installation. Discussion is about Scribe features, bugs, enhancements, performance, support, and other topics of interest to Scribe DBAs.
```
SCRIBE-HACKS@CS.UTAH.EDU
SCRIBE-HACKS-REQUEST@CS.UTAH.EDU
```
Contact: Dan Reading
```
<reading@CS.UTAH.EDU>
```

◐ *IBM vs Waterloo SCRIPT discussion group list.*
```
SCRIPT-L@DEARN.BITNET
LISTSERV@DEARN.BITNET
```

◐ *The SCRIPT/9700 Distribution List*
```
SCR97-D@TAMVM1.BITNET
LISTSERV@TAMVM1.BITNET
```
Contact: Tom Reid
```
X066TR@TAMVM1.BITNET
```

◐ *The SCRIPT/9700 Information List*
```
SCR97-L@TAMVM1.BITNET
LISTSERV@TAMVM1.BITNET
```

◐ *The SCT-INFO Distribution List*
```
SCT-INFO@POLYVM.BITNET
LISTSERV@POLYVM.BITNET
```

◐ *BannerSystem Implementation List*
```
SCT-L@LLUVM.BITNET
LISTSERV@LLUVM.BITNET
```

◐ *Mid-Altantic SCUP Newsletter*
```
SCUPMA-L@AUVM.BITNET
LISTSERV@AUVM.BITNET
```

◐ *SDS-L List*
```
SDS-L@AUVM.BITNET
LISTSERV@AUVM.BITNET
```

◐ *Security*
Discusses the field of security in general—electronic, physical, or computer-related.
```
SECURITY@AIM.RUTGERS.EDU
SECURITY-REQUEST@AIM.RUTGERS.EDU
```

Contact: *Hobbit*
```
<Hobbit@AIM.RUTGERS.EDU>
```

◐ *Serpent Software*
For technical discussions about Serpent, the user interface management system developed at the Software Engineering Institute.
```
serpent-list@sei.cmu.edu
serpent-list-request@sei.cmu.edu
```
Contact: Erik Hardy
```
<erik@sei.cmu.edu>
```

◐ *EARNTECH Servers Discussion List*
```
SERVER-L@IRLEARN.BITNET
LISTSERV@IRLEARN.BITNET
```

◐ *Servers Machine Discussion List*
```
SERVERS@BNANDP11.BITNET
LISTSERV@BNANDP11.BITNET
```

◐ *GU Computing/Networking Service Providers*
```
SERVPROV@GUVM.BITNET
LISTSERV@GUVM.BITNET
```

◐ *Shared File System*
Discusses the VM shared file system.
```
SFS-L@SEARN.BITNET
LISTSERV@SEARN.BITNET
```

◐ *BBS for ShadowRun list*
```
SHADOWTK@HEARN.BITNET
LISTSERV@HEARN.BITNET
```

◐ *SHAPE-L*
Discusses issues concerning the shape-toolkit ("shapetools"), and provides assistance to users and maintainers of shape. It integrates the functionalities of revision control systems (such as SCCS or RCS) and Make.
```
SHAPE-L@DB0TUI11.BITNET
LISTSERV@DB0TUI11.BITNET
```

◐ *Microcomputer Users Forum list.*
```
SHOPTALK@MCGILL1.BITNET
LISTSERV@MCGILL1.BITNET
```

◐ *History of Computing*
```
SHOTHC-L@SIVM.BITNET
LISTSERV@SIVM.BITNET
```
Discusses topics of interest to the Society for History of Technology (SHOT) Special Interest Group on Information, Computing and Society.

◐ *IRC Course Showcase list.*
```
SHOWCASE@IBACSATA.BITNET
LISTSERV@IBACSATA.BITNET
```

◐ *SICHAT-L: Smithsonian Internal Group list.*
```
SICHAT-L@SIVM.BITNET
LISTSERV@SIVM.BITNET
```

🖐 *History of Computers list.*
SIGPAST@List.Kean.EDU
SIGPAST-Request@List.Kean.EDU
Discusses research into the history of computers.
Contact: StanL@TURBO.Kean.EDU

🖐 *Special Interest Group/Tel (SIG/Tel) list.*
SIGTEL-L@UNMVM.BITNET
LISTSERV@UNMVM.BITNET

🖐 *Sig/Tel Board of Directors list.*
SIGTELBD@UNMVMA.BITNET
LISTSERV@UNMVMA.BITNET

🖐 *SIGUCCS Board of Directors discussion list.*
SIGUCCSB@UMDD.BITNET
LISTSERV@UMDD.BITNET

🖐 *Excel Developers list.*
clay=xldev@cs.cmu.edu
clay=xldev-add@cs.cmu.edu
For advanced Microsoft Excel users, treating topics such as executive information systems, numerical simulations, financial forecasts, and stock analysis programs.
Contact: Clay Bridges
<clay+@cs.cmu.edu>

🖐 *Forum for Clipper and DBMS systems for the IBM PC list.*
CLIPPER@BRUFPB.BITNET
LISTSERV@BRUFPB.BITNET

🖐 *Concurrent Logic Programming.*
CLP.X@XEROX.COM
CLP-REQUEST.X@XEROX.COM
Discusses concurrent logic programming languages.
Contact: Jacob Levy
<jlevy.PA@XEROX.COM>

🖐 *CLU Software Exchange*
clu-sw@cs.utu.fi.UUCP
clu-sw-request@cs.utu.fi
Facilitates exchange of CLU software and technical discussion of related topics. This list is identical to the USENET mailing list mail.clu.
Contact: Matti Jokinen
<mcvax!cs.utu.fi!jokine>

🖐 *CMIS Project list.*
CMIS-L@UMAB.BITNET
LISTSERV@UMAB.BITNET

🖐 *Computer Engineering list.*
CMPENET@PSUVM.BITNET
LISTSERV@PSUVM.BITNET

🖐 *CMSAPPL list.*
CMSAPPL@UKACRL.BITNET
LISTSERV@UKACRL.BITNET

🖐 *VM/SP CMS Pipelines discussion list.*
CMSPIP-L@AWIIMC11.BITNET
LISTSERV@AWIIMC11.BITNET
Discussions for users of VM/SP CMS Pipelines (5785-RAC in Europe and 5799-DKF in America).
Contact: Christian Reichetzeder
<REICHETZ@AWIIMC11.BITNET>

🖐 *CMS Release 4 discussion list.*
CMSR4-L@UIUCVMD.BITNET
LISTSERV@UIUCVMD.BITNET

🖐 *CMS Release 5 discussion list.*
CMSR5-L@UIUCVMD.BITNET
LISTSERV@UIUCVMD.BITNET

🖐 *CMS list.*
CMSUG-L@NDSUVM1.BITNET
LISTSERV@NDSUVM1.BITNET
Discussions of topics relating to CMS.
Contact: Gary Samek
<C133GES@UTARLVM1.BITNET>

🖐 *Lista de Pruebas y Paltas de VM.*
CMSUSER@UTFSM.BITNET
LISTSERV@UTFSM.BITNET

🖐 *TCP/IP for VAX list.*
CMU-TEK-TCP@CS.CMU.EDU
CMU-TEK-TCP-REQUEST@CS.CMU.EDU
Discussions of the CMU-TEK TCP/IP package for VAX/VMS.
Contact: Dale Moore
<Dale.Moore@PS1.CS.CMU.EDU>

🖐 *International Centre Communication Network list.*
CNETIE-L@UALTAVM.BITNET
LISTSERV@UALTAVM.BITNET

🖐 *Coalition for Networked Information list.*
CNIDIR-L@UNMVM.BITNET
LISTSERV@UNMVM.BITNET

🖐 *Networked Information Discovery and Retrieval list.*
CNIDR-L@UNCCVM.BITNET
LISTSERV@UNCCVM.BITNET

🖐 *Grupo de discussao do CNPQ list.*
CNPQ-L@BRUFMG.BITNET
LISTSERV@BRUFMG.BITNET

🖐 *Cornell Supercomputing Facility list.*
CNSF-L@UBVM.BITNET
LISTSERV@UBVM.BITNET
Facilitates distribution of information regarding activities and events at the Cornell National Supercomputing Facility (CNSF).
Contact: Tom Britt
<BRITTT@SNYSYRV1.BITNET>

CNUCE Commissione Consuntiva list.
CNUCE-CC@ICNUCEVM.BITNET
LISTSERV@ICNUCEVM.BITNET

COCO—Tandy Co. list.
COCO@PUCC.BITNET
LISTSERV@PUCC.BITNET

Coherent Operating System list.
COHERENT@INDYCMS.BITNET
LISTSERV@INDYCMS.BITNET
Discussions of the Coherent operating system produced by the Mark Williams Company.
Contact: John B. Harlan
<IJBH200@IndyVAX.BITNET>

FORUM COINF-L—Comite de Informaticalist.
COINF-L@BRUFSC.BITNET
LISTSERV@BRUFSC.BITNET

Commercialization of Internet discussion list.
com-priv@psi.com
com-priv-request@uu.psi.com

Library and Information Services list.
COMENIUS@CSEARN.BITNET
LISTSERV@CSEARN.BITNET
Discussions on the development of library and information services through computing technology and networking.
Contact: Alexandra Cernochova
Alexaprg@<CSEARN.BITNET>

Commodore Computers discussion list.
COMMODOR@UBVM.BITNET
LISTSERV@UBVM.BITNET

COMMUNE Protocol discussion list.
commune-list@STEALTH.ACF.NYU.EDU
commune-request@STEALTH.ACF.NYU.EDU
Contact: Dan Bernstein
<brnstnd@STEALTH.ACF.NYU.EDU>

Si les communications t'interessent list.
COMMUNIK@UQUEBEC.BITNET
LISTSERV@UQUEBEC.BITNET

Computer Center Managers list.
COMP-CEN@UCCVMA.BITNET
LISTSERV@UCCVMA.BITNET
Discussion of issues related to planning and managing a mid- to large-scale computing center.
Contact: Richard Hintz
<SPGRJH@UCCVMA.BITNET>

Computer Privacy list.
comp-privacy@pica.army.mil
comp-privacy-request@pica.army.mil
Discussions of how technology impacts privacy. Gatewayed into the moderated USENET newsgroup comp.society.privacy.
Contact: Dennis G. Rears
<drears@pilot.njin.net>

Comp-Sci Distribution list.
COMP-SCI@TAUNIVM.BITNET
LISTSERV@TAUNIVM.BITNET
A BITNET newsletter on computer science in Israel.
Contact: Joseph van Zwaren de Zwarenstein
<JO@ILNCRD.BITNET>

Redistribution of comp.compilers USENET group list.
COMPIL-L@AUVM.BITNET
LISTSERV@AUVM.BITNET

Computers and Society ARPA Digest list.
COMSOC-L@BYUVM.BITNET
LISTSERV@BYUVM.BITNET

Networking discussion list.
COMTEN-L@UCSBVM.BITNET
LISTSERV@UCSBVM.BITNET
Discusses software, hardware, LAN/WAN attachments, workstations, problems, and other networking topics.
Contact: Dwight M. McCann
<DWIGHT@UCSBVM.BITNET>

COM 338 discussion list.
COM338@PUCC.BITNET
LISTSERV@PUCC.BITNET

Ken Hacker's Class list.
COM470-L@NMSUVM1.BITNET
LISTSERV@NMSUVM1.BITNET

IETF ISN WG Subcommittee on Connectivity Mode list.
CONNECT@UNMVM.BITNET
LISTSERV@UNMVM.BITNET

Consultants Forum.
CONS-L@MCGILL1.BITNET
LISTSERV@MCGILL1.BITNET
For university computing center consultants to discuss such issues as problem tracking, resource management, training, and consulting strategies.
Contact: Sander Wasser
<CCSW@MCGILLA.BITNET>

Consulting list.
CONSULT@NERVM.BITNET
LISTSERV@VERBM.BITNET

RARE and EARN Cooperation list.
COOPRARE@FRORS12.BITNET
LISTSERV@FRORS12.BITNET

🖙 *Lista para troca de informacoes entre os coor.*
COORBR-L@BRUFMG.BITNET
LISTSERV@BRUFMG.BITNET

🖙 *Consortium for School Networking Discussion Forum list.*
COSNDISC@BITNIC.BITNET
LISTSERV@BITNIC.BITNET

🖙 *COSW-L list.*
COSW-L@ASUACAD.BITNET
LISTSERV@ASUACAD.BITNET

🖙 *Research and Ideas discussion list.*
COURTSHP@TAMVM1.BITNET
LISTSERV@TAMVM1.BITNET

🖙 *Computer Performance Evaluation list.*
CPE-LIST@UNCVM1.BITNET
LISTSERV@UNCVM1.BITNET
Communication concerning performance evaluation issues involved in the use large-scale computing engines.
Contact: Lyman A. Ripperton III
<Lyman@unchmvs.unch.unc.edu>

🖙 *CPI-L: College Preparatory Initiative list.*
CPI-L@CUNYVM.BITNET
LISTSERV@CUNYVM.BITNET

🖙 *CP Release 4 discussion list.*
CPR4-L@UIUCVMD.BITNET
LISTSERV@UIUCVMD.BITNET

🖙 *CP Release 5 discussion list.*
CPR5-L@UIUCVMD.BITNET
LISTSERV@UIUCVMD.BITNET

🖙 *CPS-L: Centre for Pacific Studies Discussion list.*
CPS-L@HEARN.BITNET
LISTSERV@HEARN.BITNET

🖙 *Computer Professionals for Social Responsibility (CPSR) list.*
CPSR@GWUVM.BITNET
LISTSERV@GWUVM.GWU.EDU
Archives CPSR-related materials and disseminates CPSR-related announcements. Accessible via Internet and Bitnet E-mail.
Contact: Paul Hyland
<phyland@GWUVM.BITNET>

🖙 *CPT Co-op discussion list.*
CPTCOOP@PURCCVM.BITNET
LISTSERV@PURCCVM.BITNET

🖙 *CREATE-L list.*
CREATE-L@ASUACAD.BITNET
LISTSERV@CREATE-L.BITNET

🖙 *CREN Board and Staff Principals list.*
CRENBDST@BITNIC.BITNET
LISTSERV@BITNIC.BITNET

🖙 *CREN Documentation Review list.*
CRENDOC@BITNIC.BITNET
LISTSERV@BITNIC.BITNET

🖙 *CREN Technical Committee list.*
CRENTECH@BITNIC.BITNET
LISTSERV@BITNIC.BITNET

🖙 *Planning and Communications Studio list.*
CRP510@UNMVMA.BITNET
LISTSERV@UNMVMA.BITNET

🖙 *Mizzou Student ACM Chapter discussion list.*
CSACM-L@UMCVMB.BITNET
LISTSERV@UMCVMB.BITNET

🖙 *Society of Computer Science in Economics & Management list.*
CSEMLIST@HASARA11.BITNET
LISTSERV@HASARA11.BITNET
Supplies information for researchers in the field of computer science in economics and management science.
Contact: Hans M. Amman
A608HANS@HASARA11.BITNET

🖙 *Control Systems Group Network (CSGnet) list.*
CSG-L@UIUCVMD.BITNET
LISTSERV@UIUCVMD.BITNET

🖙 *Carolina SIS User discussion list.*
CSISU-L@UNCCVM.BITNET
LISTSERV@UNCCVM.BITNET

🖙 *Regional DEC CSLG/ESL discussion list.*
CSLESL@PSUVM.BITNET
LISTSERV@PSUVM.BITNET

🖙 *Planning for ACM/SIGUCCS CSMS XX list.*
CSMS93-L@UMSLVMA.BITNET
LISTSERV@UMSLVMA.BITNET

🖙 *CSNet Interests list.*
CSNET-FORUM@SH.CS.NET
CSNET-FORUM-REQUEST@SH.CS.NET
Topics of interest to the CSNET community. Informal announcements, current news, and special features. New issues appear several times a year.
Contact: Charlotte Mooers
<CSNET-FORUM-REQUEST@SH.CS.NET>

🖙 *Cross System Product discussion list.*
CSP-L@TREARN.BITNET
LISTSERV@TREARN.BITNET

Discusses problems in maintenance, installation, and administration of Cross System Product (CSP).
Contact: Esra Delen
    ESRA@TREARN.BITNET

↺ *University of Alberta Center for Systems Research list.*
    CSR-L@UALTAVM.BITNET
    LISTSERV@UALTAVM.BITNET
Communication among the Research Associates and Affiliates of the University of Alberta Center for Systems Research and among participants in projects supported by the Center.
Contact: Richard Jung
    CSR@UALTAVM.BITNET

↺ *BYU Customer Support Rep discussion list.*
    CSRADM-L@BYUVM.BITNET
    LISTSERV@BYUVM.BITNET

↺ *CSTG-L discussion list.*
    CSTG-L@VTVM1.BITNET
    LISTSERV@VTVM1.BITNET

↺ *Usenet comp.sys.smiga.graphics redistribution list.*
    CSYS-AMI@UMAINECS.BITNET
    LISTSERV@UMAINECS.BITNET

↺ *COPPUL Systems Group list.*
    CSYS-L@UALTAVM.BITNET
    LISTSERV@UALTAVM.BITNET

↺ *Using Object Oriented C for a 1st Computer Compiler list.*
    CS1OBJ-L@PSUVM.BITNET
    LISTSERV@PSUVM.BITNET

↺ *FORUM CTC-L—Divulgacao de eventos*
    CTC-L@BRUFSC.BITNET
    LISTSERV@BRUFSC.BITNET

↺ *Computer Literacy in Higher Education*
    CTI-Complit@durham.ac.uk
    mailbase@newcastle.ac.uk
For users interested in computer literacy in higher education and related issues.
Contact: Audrey McCartan
    <Audrey.McCartan@durham.ac.uk>

↺ *Using Computers to Learn list.*
    CTI-L@IRLEARN.UCD.IE
    LISTSERV@IRLEARN.UCD.IE
Discusses issues in the use of computers in teaching.
Contact: Claron O'Reilly
    <CLARON@IRLEARN.UCD.IE>

↺ *comp.text.tex list.*
    CTT-DIGEST@SHSU.BITNET
    LISTSERV@SHSU.BITNET

A digest of the activity on the comp.text.tex newsgroup.
Contact: George D. Greenwade
    <BED_GDG@SHSU.BITNET>

↺ *All Virginia Cities and Towns On LGNET list.*
    CTYTWN-L@VTVM1.BITNET
    LISTSERV@VTVM1.BITNET

↺ *Comite des Utilisateurs du CIRCE list.*
    CUC-L@FRORS12.BITNET
    LISTSERV@FRORS12.BITNET

↺ *CUFS System discussion list.*
    CUFS-L@MIAMIU.BITNET
    LISTSERV@MIAMIU.BITNET

↺ *CUFSTECH list.*
    CUFSTECH@CUVMC.BITNET
    LISTSERV@CUVMC.BITNET

↺ *College Administration Computer Use list.*
    CUMREC-L@NDSUVM1.BITNET
    LISTSERV@NDSUVM1.BITNET
For users involved with computer use in college and university administration, especially for non-technical administrators.

↺ *CPT Curriculum Mailing list.*
    CURRICUL@PURCCVM.BITNET
    LISTSERV@PURCCVM.BITNET

↺ *Campus-Wide Electronic Mail Systems Discussion list.*
    CW-EMAIL@TECMTYVM.BITNET
    LISTSERV@TECMTYVM.BITNET
Discussions of unified E-mail systems.
Contact: Juan M. Courcoul
    POSTMAST@TECMTYVM.BITNET

↺ *Computers And Writing list.*
    CW-L@TTUVM1.BITNET
    LISTSERV@TTUVM1.BITNET

↺ *Campus-Wide Information Systems list.*
    CWIS-L@WUVMD.BITNET
    LISTSERV@WUVMD.BITNET
Discusses the creation and implimentation of campus-wide information systems.
Contact: Timothy Bergeron
    C09615TB@WUVMD.BITNET

↺ *CYBER list.*
    CYBER-L@BITNIC.BITNET
    LISTSERV@BITNIC.BITNET
For BITNET users interested in CDC online support systems, announcement and review of new CYBER products, sharing of installation experiences, and access to server machines.

❧ *The Law and Policy of Computer Networks list.*
CYBERLAW@WMVM1.BITNET
LISTSERV@WMVM1.BITNET

❧ *Utilisateurs C3NI list.*
C3NI-L@FRMOP11.BITNET
LISTSERV@FRMOP11.BITNET

❧ *C/370 Discussion list.*
C370-L@NCSUVM.BITNET
LISTSERV@NCSUVM.BITNET
Discussion of the C programming language on 370-architecture machines.
Contact: Chuck Kesler
CHUCK@NCSUVM.BITNET

❧ *Data Access Language List*
DAL-L@MITVMA.BITNET
LISTSERV@MITVMA.BITNET

❧ *TUVAKA Servisleri Danisma Listesi.*
DANISMAN@TRITU.BITNET
LISTSERV@TRITU.BITNET

❧ *UB Distributed Application Support Discussion list.*
DAS-L@UBVM.BITNET
LISTSERV@UBVM.BITNET

❧ *DATPERS—Dalit and Tribal Peoples Electronic list.*
DATPERS@YORKVM1.BITNET
LISTSERV@YORKVM1.BITNET

❧ *DATUS Anwendergruppe.*
DATUS-L@DEARN.BITNET
LISTSERV@DEARN.BITNET
Contact: Helmut Woehlbier
C0033001@DBSTU1.BITNET

❧ *dBase Language and Dialects Discussion list.*
DBASE-L@TECMTYVM.BITNET
LISTSERV@TECMTYVM.BITNET
Discussions on the use of the dBase language for manipulating databases and how to build and maintain working systems using dialects.
Contact: Agustin Gonzalez Tuchmann
PL155880@TECMTYV

❧ *Database & Free Text Mail list.*
DBFT@LIVERPOOL.AC.UK
LISTSERV@LIVERPOOL.AC.UK

❧ *GARR-PE Data Database Test list.*
DBGARRPE@ICNUCEVM.BITNET
LISTSERV@ICNUCEVM.BITNET

❧ *DBIPNET Data Database list.*
DBIPNET@ICNUCEVM.BITNET
LISTSERV@ICNUCEVM.BITNET

❧ *Open Forum on L3 Databases list.*
DBL3-L@LEPICS.BITNET
LISTSERV@LEPICS.BITNET

❧ *DB2 Data Base Discussion list.*
DB2-L@AUVM.BITNET
LISTSERV@AUVM.BITNET
Discussions of IBM's DB2 Data Base Product (5740-XYR and 5665-DB2), and associated topics.
Contact: Patty Burke
PBURKE@AUVM.BITNET

❧ *Forum do Depto. de Ciencia da Computacao da*
DCCFUA-L@BRLNCC.BITNET
LISTSERV@BRLNCC.BITNET

❧ *Probleme der verteilten Datenverarbeitung*
DCEAK-L@DGOGWDG1.BITNET
LISTSERV@DGOGWDG1.BITNET

❧ *Display Device Management System (DDMS) Discussion list.*
DDMS-L@UCSBVM.BITNET
LISTSERV@UCSBVM.BITNET

❧ *Defect Tracking list.*
DDTs-Users@BigBird.BU.EDU
Majordomo@BigBird.BU.EDU
Discussions related to DDT defect-tracking software.
Contact: Joe Wells
<jbw@cs.bu.edu>

❧ *EARN Directors Open Submission list.*
DEAR-BOD@IRLEARN.BITNET
LISTSERV@IRLEARN.BITNET

❧ *DEC Enterprise Network Management list.*
decmcc@ralph.rtpnc.epa.gov
listserv@ralph.rtpnc.epa.gov
Discussions about network management using the DEC Enterprise Management Architecture product-set named DECmcc.
Contact: Bob Boyd
<rbn@ralph.rtpnc.epa.gov>

❧ *Monthly Newsletter of DEC's Education/ Science Unit.*
DECNEWS@UBVM.BITNET
LISTSERV@UBVM.BITNET
Provide a single source of information about digital to users in educational institutions and research organizations.
Contact: Mary Hoffmann
<hoffmann@mr4dec.enet.dec.com>

❧ *DEC's Relational Database Products list.*
DECRDB-L@SBCCVM.BITNET
LISTSERV@SBCCVM.BITNET

Discusses issues related to Rdb or any associated software and competing products.
Contact: Sanjay Kapur
`<Sanjay.Kapur@sunysb.edu>`

✒ *DEC's The Education Initiative discussion list.*
`DECTEI-L@UBVM.BITNET`
`LISTSERV@UBVM.BITNET`

✒ *Decus Hellas Members list.*
`DECUS_M@GREARN.BITNET`
`LISTSERV@GREARN.BITNET`

✒ *DEFINITY Call Center Products Group list.*
`DEF-CC@UMDD.BITNET`
`LISTSERV@UMDD.BITNET`

✒ *Definity User Group's Education Focus Group list.*
`DEF-EDU@UMDD.BITNET`
`LISTSERV@UMDD.BITNET`

✒ *DEFINITY Generic 3 Group list.*
`DEF-G3@UMDD.BITNET`
`LISTSERV@UMDD.BITNET`

✒ *DEFINITY Service and Maintenance Group list.*
`DEF-SERV@UMDD.BITNET`
`LISTSERV@UMDD.BITNET`

✒ *DEFINITY System Management Products Group list.*
`DEF-SYSM@UMDD.BITNET`
`LISTSERV@UMDD.BITNET`

✒ *DEFINITY Voice Processing Products Group list.*
`DEF-VP@UMDD.BITNET`
`LISTSERV@UMDD.BITNET`

✒ *DEFINITY Voice Terminal Products Group list.*
`DEF-VT@UMDD.BITNET`
`LISTSERV@UMDD.BITNET`

✒ *DEFINITY Generic 1 and System 75 Group list.*
`DEF-75G1@UMDD.BITNET`
`LISTSERV@UMDD.BITNET`

✒ *DEFINITY Generic 2 and System 85 Group list.*
`DEF-85G2@UMDD.BITNET`
`LISTSERV@UMDD.BITNET`

✒ *Definity/System85 User Group discussion list.*
`DEFINITY@UMDD.BITNET`
`LISTSERV@UMDD.BITNET`

✒ *Definity User Group Self-Maintenance Discussion list.*
`DEFMAINT@UMDD.BITNET`
`LISTSERV@UMDD.BITNET`

✒ *Degas Network list.*
`DEGAS@UQUEBEC.BITNET`
`LISTSERV@UQUEBEC.BITNET`

✒ *The W. Edwards Deming Forum list.*
`DEMING-L@UHCCVM.BITNET`
`LISTSERV@UHCCVM.BITNET`

✒ *Gemi Insaati/Makinalari ve Deniz Bilimleri list.*
`DENIZ-L@TRITU.BITNET`
`LISTSERV@TRITU.BITNET`

✒ *Desqview and Qemm Systems list.*
`DESQVIEW@BRUFPB.BITNET`
`LISTSERV@BRUFPB.BITNET`

✒ *DEVCIT: Development and CIT Group list.*
`DEVCIT@UVMVM.BITNET`
`LISTSERV@UVMVM.BITNET`

✒ *X.400 Postmaster list.*
`DFNMHSPW@DEARN.BITNET`
`LISTSERV@DEARN.BITNET`

✒ *DFN-Software Diskussionsforum MVS.*
`DFNMVS@DEARN.BITNET`
`LISTSERV@DEARN.BITNET`
Contact: Manfred Bogen
`MABOGEN@DEARN.BITNET`

✒ *DFN-Software Diskussionsforum VM.*
`DFNVM@DEARN.BITNET`
`LISTSERV@DEARN.BITNET`
Contact: Jochen Bruening
`RZBNG@DKNKURZ1.BITNET`

✒ *Dial in Access to IPX Network list.*
`DIAL-IPX@EMUVM1.BITNET`
`LISTSERV@EMUVM1.BITNET`

✒ *Usuarios remotos via linha discada list.*
`DIAL-L@BRLNCC.BITNET`
`LISTSERV@BRLNCC.BITNET`

✒ *Biosym Technologies Software Users list.*
`DIBUG@AVOGADRO.BARNARD.COLUMBIA.EDU`
`dibug-request@avogadro.barnard.columbia.edu`
Contact: Peter S. Shenkin
`<shenkin@avogadro.barnard.columbia.edu>`

✒ *DIGIT list.*
`DIGIT-L@CFRVM.BITNET`
`LISTSERV@CFRVM.BITNET`

✒ *Computer and Video Game Reviews and discussion list.*

digital-games-submissions@DIGITAL-
GAMES.INTUITIVE.COM
digital-games-request@Digital-
Games.Intuitive.Com

For computer and video game reviews, Also covers games for the portable market.
Contact: Dave Taylor
<taylor@LIMBO.INTUITIVE.COM>

❦ *DINI-L Mailliste fuer die Diplomanden-und Dok.*
DINI-L@DEARN.BITNET
LISTSERV@DEARN.BITNET

❦ *CSNet Dial-up Maintenance list.*
DIP-PEOPLE@RELAY.CS.NET
DIP-PEOPLE-REQUEST@RELAY.CS.NET

For users who implement, install, or maintain CSNET Dial-Up IP systems.
Contact: Leo Lanzillo
<leo@SH.CS.NET>

❦ *MacroMind Director (Macintosh) list.*
DIRECT-L@UAFSYSB.BITNET
LISTSERV@UAFSYSB.BITNET
Contact: C.B. Lih
<CBLIH@UAFSYSB.BITNET>

❦ *DISSPLA list.*
DISSPLA@TAUNIVM.BITNET
LISTSERV@TAUNIVM.BITNET

Discussions of Display Integrated Software System and Plotting Language (DISSPLA), a high-level FORTRAN graphics subroutine library.
Contact: Zvika Bar-Dero
AER7101@TECHNION.BITNET

❦ *INFO-CPM Mailing list.*
DIST-CPM@RPICICGE.BITNET
COMSERVE@RPIECS.BITNET

❦ *VCES District Director User IDs list.*
DISTDIR@VTVM1.BITNET
LISTSERV@VTVM1.BITNET

❦ *Distributed Systems list.*
DISTOBJ@HPLB.HPL.HP.COM
distobj-request@hplb.hpl.hp.com

Discussions of large-scale distributed-object systems.
Contact: Harry Barman
<hjb@hplb.hpl.hp.com>

❦ *IBM Data Interfile Transfer, Testing, and Operations Utility list.*
DITTO-L@AWIIMC12.BITNET
LISTSERV@AWIIMC12.BITNET

❦ *Rich Wener DIV34 Distribution list.*
DIV34@POLYVM.BITNET
LISTSERV@POLYVM.BITNET

❦ *DKB Ray Tracer list.*
DKB-L@TREARN.BITNET
LISTSERV@TREARN.BITNET

Discusses the DKB Ray Tracer developed by David Buck.
Contact: Turgut
<TURGUT@TREARN.BITNET>

❦ *DKB Graphical User Interface list.*
DKBGUI@TREARN.BITNET
LISTSERV@TREARN.BITNET

Discusses work on a graphical interface for DKB
Contact: Turgut
<TURGUT@TREARN.BITNET>

❦ *DKB Ray Tracer Porting list.*
DKBPORT@TREARN.BITNET
LISTSERVTREARN.BITNET

Discusses porting DKB Ray Tracer to other platforms.
Contact: Turgut
<TURGUT@TREARN.BITNET>

❦ *DNC-L list.*
DNC-L@DEARN.BITNET
LISTSERV@DEARN.BITNET

❦ *Documentation Coordinators list.*
DOC-COOR@IRISHVMA.BITNET
LISTSERV@IRISHVMA.BITNET

❦ *Data Database Documentazione Sala Macc list.*
DOCSM@ICNUCEVM.BITNET
LISTSERV@ICNUCEVM.BITNET

❦ *Domains Discussion Group list.*
DOMAIN-L@BITNIC.BITNET
LISTSERV@BITNIC.BITNET

❦ *CNUCE Gestione Domini Posta Elettronica.*
DOMAIN@ICNUCEVM.BITNET
LISTSERV@ICNUCEVM.BITNET

❦ *University of Maryland/IBM MS-DOS TCP/IP Discussion list.*
dosip-list@terminus.umd.edu
dosip-request@terminus.umd.edu
Contact: Billy Taylor
<billy@terminus.umd edu>

❦ *MS-DOS Probleme (lokale Liste, Uni Osnabruec).*
DOSRZ-L@DOSUNI1.BITNET
LISTSERV@DOSUNI1.BITNET

❦ *bb Delphi Asymmetry Group list.*
DPASYM-L@FRCPN11.BITNET
LISTSERV@FRCPN11.BITNET

❦ *Purdue chapter of DPMA discussion list.*
DPMA-L@PURCCVM.BITNET
LISTSERV@PURCCVM.BITNET

⑤ *Data Processing Management Association list.*
DPMAST-L@CMSUVMB.BITNET
LISTSERV@CMSUVMB.BITNET

⑤ *Data Protection Review Board Correspondence list.*
DPRB-L@ALBNYDH2.BITNET
LISTSERV@ALBNYDH2.BITNET

⑤ *TUG DVI Driver Standards discussion list.*
DRIV-L@TAMVM1.BITNET
LISTSERV@TAMVM1.BITNET
Contact: Don Hosek
DHOSEK@HMCVAX.BITNET

⑤ *Network Programmers list.*
driver-workers@sun.soe.clarkson.edu
listserv@sun.soe.clarkson.edu

⑤ *Disaster Recovery Plan for Computing Services list.*
DRP-L@UOGUELPH.BITNET
LISTSERV@UOGUELPH.BITNET
Contact: Pearl Bower
<OPPEARL@UOGUELPH>

⑤ *Genel Amacli Tartisma Listesi.*
DUVAR-L@TRITU.BITNET
LISTSERV@TRITU.BITNET

⑤ *UNC/ACS Dynamic Systems list.*
DYNSYS-L@UNCVM1.BITNET
LISTSERV@UNCVM1.BITNET
Exchange of information among people working in ergodic theory and dynamical systems.
Contact: Karl Petersen
<UNCKEP@UNC.BITNET>

⑤ *E-mail Course Planning Conference list.*
E-COURSE@WMVM1.BITNET
LISTSERV@WMVM1.BITNET

⑤ *EAESP Forum list.*
EAESPNET@BNANDP11.BITNET
LISTSERV@BNANDP11.BITNET

⑤ *Network Operations Group list.*
EARN-NOG@FRMOP11.BITNET
LISTSERV@FRMOP11.BITNET

⑤ *EARN Operating Procedures Group list.*
EARN-OPG@IRLEARN.BITNET
LISTSERV@IRLEARN.BITNET

⑤ *Noeuds EARN Region Ile de France list.*
EARN-RIF@FRULM11.BITNET
LISTSERV@FRULM11.BITNET

⑤ *EARN RTC Users Group list.*
EARN-RTC@IRLEARN.BITNET
LISTSERV@IRLEARN.BITNET

⑤ *EARN-SNA Coordination list.*
EARN-SNA@FRMOP11.BITNET
LISTSERV@FRMOP11.BITNET

⑤ *EARN Users Group discussion list.*
EARN-UG@IRLEARN.BITNET
LISTSERV@IRLEARN.BITNET
Contact: Hans Deckers
DECK@FRORS12.BITNET

⑤ *EARN X.25 Project Coordination and Technical list.*
EARN-X25@IRLEARN.BITNET
LISTSERV@IRLEARN.BITNET

⑤ *EARN Users in Norway list.*
EARNBRUK@NOBIVM.BITNET
LISTSERV@NOBIVM.BITNET

⑤ *EARN Newsletter Broadcasting list.*
EARNEST@FRORS12.BITNET
LISTSERV@FRORS12.BITNET

⑤ *EARN News list.*
EARNEWS@FRMOP11.BITNET
LISTSERV@FRMOP11.BITNET

⑤ *EARN Executive list.*
EARNEXEC@IRLEARN.BITNET
LISTSERV@IRLEARN.BITNET

⑤ *EARN Working Group on Information Services list.*
EARNINFO@FRMOP11.BITNET
LISTSERV@FRMOP11.BITNET

⑤ *EARN Statistics Group list.*
EARNSTAT@DEARN.BITNET
LISTSERV@DEARN.BITNET
Contact: Manfred Bogen
MABOGEN@DEARN.BITNET

⑤ *EARN Technical Group list.*
EARNTECH@BITNIC.BITNET
LISTSERV@BITNIC.BITNET

⑤ *EASInet Project Committee list.*
EASI-EPC@DEARN.BITNET
LISTSERV@DEARN.BITNET

⑤ *Computers in Biotechnology, Research, and Education list.*
EBCBBUL@HDETUD1.BITNET
LISTSERV@HDETUD1.BITNET
Stimulate and facilitates the use of computers in biotechnological training and research in Europe.
Contact: Arie Braat
RCSTBRA@HDETUD1.BITNET

⑤ *Catalogue of Biotechnological software.*
EBCBCAT@HDETUD1.BITNET
LISTSERV@HDETUD1.BITNET

Information about public-domain and commercial software for use in biotechnological research and teaching.
Contact: Arie Braat
    RCSTBRA@HDETUD1.TUDELFT.NL

✆ *ECAPS Research Projects discussion list.*
    ECAPS@GWUVM.BITNET
    LISTSERV@GWUVM.BITNET

✆ *Open Forum on the ECL3 Program.*
    ECL3-L@LEPICS.BITNET
    LISTSERV@LEPICS.BITNET
Contact: Bob Clare
    BOBCLARE@LEPICS.BITNET

✆ *Electronic Communal Temporal Lobe.*
    ectl@snowhite.cis.uoguelph.ca
    ectl-request@snowhite.cis.uoguelph.ca
Users doing research (or who are simply interested in) computer speech interfaces.
Contact: David Leip
    <david@snowhite.cis.uoguelph.ca>

✆ *Educational Administration discussion list.*
    EDAD-L@WVNVM.BITNET
    LISTSERV@WVNVM.BITNET

✆ *EDD Data Editor List, rev 0.*
    DD-L@KENTVM.BITNET
    LISTSERV@KENTVM.BITNET

✆ *Electronic Data Interchange Issues list.*
    EDI-L@UCCVMA.BITNET
    LISTSERV@UCCVMA.BITNET
Discussions of electronic transmission and receipt of business documentation.
Contact: Richard Hintz
    SPGRJH@UCCVMA.BITNET

✆ *DECUS EDUSIG Executive and Steering Committees list.*
    EDU-EXEC@UBVM.BITNET
    LISTSERV@UBVM.BITNET

✆ *Chercheurs en education list.*
    EDUC@UQUEBEC.BITNET
    LISTSERV@UQUEBEC.BITNET

✆ *Education and Digital Equipment Corporation Discussion list.*
    EDUSIG-L@UBVM.BITNET
    LISTSERV@UBVM.BITNET

✆ *Diskusjon om Norge, EF og EOES (Norwegian).*
    EF-L@NOBIVM.BITNET
    LISTSERV@NOBIVM.BITNET

✆ *Greek TeX list.*
    ELLHNIKA@DHDURZ1.BITNET
    LISTSERV@DHDURZ1.BITNET

For linguists who typeset ancient Greek, as well as for people using Greek as their everyday language. Languages of the list are English and Greek.
Contact: Yannis Haralambous
    <YANNIS@FRCITL81.BITNET>

✆ *Unix-EMACS Distribution list.*
    EMACS@BNANDP11.BITNET
    LISTSERV@BNANDP11.BITNET
Discussions of all EMACS-type editors for Unix.
Contact: Richard Miller
    RICK@SVEDBERG.BCM.TMC.EDU

✆ *UNIX-EMACS Distribution list.*
    EMACS@TCSVM.BITNET
    LISTSERV@TCSVM.BITNET
Contact: Manole Calamari
    SYSBJAV@TCSVM.BITNET

✆ *Accessing Electronic Information Learning list.*
    EMAILMAN@VTVM1.BITNET
    LISTSERV@VTVM1.BITNET

✆ *Greek EMBL Management list.*
    EMBLGR@GREARN.BITNET
    LISTSERV@GREARN.BITNET

✆ *EMPACT! News.*
    EMPACT@UCSFVM.BITNET
    LISTSERV@UCSFVM.BITNET

✆ *Emergency Information List Server for UCSB.*
    EMRG-L@UCSBVM.BITNET
    LISTSERV@UCSBVM.BITNET

✆ *Emory FOCUS Discussion Group list.*
    EMUFOC-L@EMUVM1.BITNET
    LISTSERV@EMUVM1.BITNET

✆ *Emulation SW & HW on the IBM-PC.*
    EMULPC@USACHVM1.BITNET
    LISTSERV@USACHVM1.BITNET
Discusses PC Emulation software and hardware.
Contact: Gonzalo Rojas C.
    GROJASCO@USACHVM1

✆ *Enterprise Network Data Interconnectivity list.*
    ENDIF-L@WVNVM.BITNET
    LISTSERV@WVNVM.BITNET

✆ *EndNote/EndLink Users Forum list.*
    ENDNOTE@UCSBVM.BITNET
    LISTSERV@UCSBVM.BITNET

✆ *Forum de Debates do PROTEM—RJ.*
    EPISTEMO@UFRJ.BITNET
    LISTSERV@UFRJ.BITNET

☙ *Ad-Hoc UB Electronic Publications Task Force list.*
EPUBS-L@UBVM.BITNET
LISTSERV@UBVM.BITNET

☙ *Equipe Reseau du CNUSC.*
ERC@FRMOP11.BITNET
LISTSERV@FRMOP11.BITNET

☙ *ERIS Discussion list.*
ERIS-L@VTVM1.BITNET
LISTSERV@VTVM1.BITNET

☙ *ERUDITIO: Knowledge Through Electronic Communication list.*
ERUDITIO@ASUACAD.BITNET
LISTSERV@ASUACAD.BITNET

☙ *Expert Systems Environment Mailing list.*
ESE-L@SBCCVM.BITNET
LISTSERV@SBCCVM.BITNET
Discusses the development of expert systems knowledge bases.
Contact: Sanjay Kapur
SK@SBCCVM.BITNET

☙ *Lista para troca de informacoes entre os esta.*
ESTAG-L@BRUFMG.BITNET
LISTSERV@BRUFMG.BITNET

☙ *Ethical Issues in Software Engineering list.*
ETHCSE-L@UTKVM1.BITNET
LISTSERV@UTKVM1.BITNET
Deals with ethical issues for professional software engineers.
Contact: Don Gotterbarn
<I01GBARN@ETSU.BITNET>

☙ *Ethics in Computing Discussion list.*
ETHICS-L@DEARN.BITNET
LISTSERV@DEARN.BITNET

☙ *Routers in Europe: Discussion on Interworking list.*
EU-ROUTE@HEARN.BITNET
LISTSERV@HEARN.BITNET

☙ *Kerberized Eudora list.*
EUDKRB-L@BROWNVM.BITNET
LISTSERV@BROWNVM.BITNET

☙ *Eudora on the PC list.*
EUDPC-L@BROWNVM.BITNET
LISTSERV@BROWNVM.BITNET

☙ *EURO-LEX (All EUROpean Legal Information EXchange) list.*
EURO-LEX@DS0RUS1I.BITNET
LISTSERV@DS0RUS1I.BITNET

☙ *Reseau Junior Enterprise list.*
EXPECT@FRECP12.BITNET
LISTSERV@FRECP12.BITNET

☙ *Experiences on Viral Attacks list.*
EXPER-L@TREARN.BITNET
LISTSERV@TREARN.BITNET
Collates information on network security leakages.
Contact: Esra Delen
NAD <ESRA@TREARN.BITNET>

☙ *Explorer Modular Visualisation Environment (MVE) Discussion list.*
Virtual Explorer@CASTLE.ED.AC.UK
explorer-request@castle.ed.ac.uk
Contact: <gordonc@epcc.ed.ac.uk>

☙ *EXPRESS Information Modeling Language Discussion list.*
express-users@cme.nist.gov
express-users-request@cme.nist.gov
Contact: Steve Clark
<express-users-request@cme.nist.gov>

☙ *EZTrieve Discussion Group list.*
EZTRV-L@ULKYVM.BITNET
LISTSERV@ULKYVM.BITNET

☙ *SUNY Faculty Access to Computing Technology list.*
FACT-L@UBVM.BITNET
LISTSERV@UBVM.BITNET

☙ *BTI/K200/NECU Driver Distribution list.*
FALBTI-L@UTDALLAS.BITNET
LISTSERV@UTDALLAS.BITNET

☙ *Subcommittee of ISN/IETF WG list.*
FAQ@UNMVMA.BITNET
LISTSERV@UNMVMA.BITNET

☙ *FASTBUS Discussion list.*
FASTBS-L@UALTAVM.BITNET
LISTSERV@UALTAVM.BITNET

☙ *Virginia Tech Computing Center News list.*
FASTLN-L@VTVM1.BITNET
LISTSERV@VTVM1.BITNET

☙ *Fiber Distributed Data Interface Technology Discussion list.*
FDDI@List.Kean.EDU
FDDI-subscribe@List.Kean.EDU

☙ *Federal Electronic Data Special Interest Group list.*
FEDSIG-L@WVNVM.BITNET
LISTSERV@WVNVM.BITNET

☙ *Forth Interest Group International list.*
FIGI-L@SCFVM.BITNET
LISTSERV@SCFVM.BITNET
Discussions about the Forth programming language.

Contact: Lee E. Brotzman
ZMLEB@SCFVM.BITNET

✎ *VCES Satellite Training for Financial Volunteers list.*
FINVOL-L@VTVM1.BITNET
LISTSERV@VTVM1.BITNET

✎ *Internet Security Firewall Systems list.*
Firewalls@GreatCircle.COM
Majordomo@GreatCircle.COM

✎ *Florida Artificial Intelligence Research Symposium list.*
FLAIRS@UCF1VM.BITNET
LISTSERV@UCF1VM.BITNET
Communications among AI researchers in Florida.
Contact: Owner
<UCFOWN@UCF1VM.BITNET>

✎ *FLITSERV list.*
FLITSERV@SIUCVMB.BITNET
LISTSERV@SIUCVMB.BITNET

✎ *FOCUS-L list.*
FOCUS-L@ASUACAD.BITNET
LISTSERV@ASUACAD.BITNET

✎ *FORAGE Discussion list.*
FORAGE-L@UNLVM.BITNET
LISTSERV@UNLVM.BITNET

✎ *Forum de Engenharia Quimica list.*
FORBEQ@UFRJ.BITNET
LISTSERV@UFRJ.BITNET

✎ *On-line Form Templates discussion list.*
FORMS-L@UCSFVM.BITNET
LISTSERV@UCSFVM.BITNET

✎ *Fortran Programlama Dili.*
ORTRAN@TRITU.BITNET
LISTSERV@TRITU.BITNET

✎ *FOTA Tiedollisen kasva.*
FOTA@FINHUTC.BITNET
LISTSERV@FINHUTC.BITNET

✎ *Franz Lisp Language list.*
FRANZ-FRIENDS@BERKELEY.EDU
FRANZ-FRIENDS-REQUEST@BERKELEY.EDU
Discusses all versions of the Franz Lisp Language.
Contact: Charley Cox
(cox@BERKELEY.EDU)

✎ *FRIEND Server discussion list.*
FRIEND-L@TREARN.BITNET
LISTSERV@TREARN.BITNET

✎ *Userland's Frontier Script Language list.*
FRONTIER@DARTCMS1.BITNET
LISTSERV@DARTCMS1.BITNET

Exchange of information on Userland's Frontier.
Contact: Andy Williams
<andy.j.williams@dartmouth.edu>

✎ *Field Service Steering Committee NAFSA list.*
FSSC-L@GSUVM1.BITNET
LISTSERV@GSUVM1.BITNET

✎ *FTPSEGI Program Information list.*
FTPSEGI@BLIULG11.BITNET
LISTSERV@BLIULG11.BITNET

✎ *The Foundation of the Search and Academic list.*
FUNDACJA@PLEARN.BITNET
LISTSERV@PLEARN.BITNET

✎ *BITNET Futures list.*
FUTURE-L@BITNIC.BITNET
LISTSERV@BITNIC.BITNET

✎ *GAMS User list.*
GAMS-L@DEARN.BITNET
LISTSERV@DEARN.BITNET

✎ *BITNET GARR Piemonte.*
GARR-PMN@ITOCSIVM.BITNET
LISTSERV@ITOSIVM

✎ *Cornell's GateDaemon Software discussion list.*
GATED-PEOPLE@DEVVAX.TN.CORNELL.EDU
GATED-PEOPLE-REQUEST@DEVVAX.TN.CORNELL.EDU
A Unix daemon supporting multiple routing protocols, including RIP, EGP and BGP.
Contact: Jeffrey C Honig
<JCH@DEVVAX.TN.CORNELL.EDU>

✎ *GCS discussion list.*
GCS-L@UIUCVMD.BITNET
LISTSERV@UIUCVMD.BITNET

✎ *GDDM discussion list.*
GDDM-L@POLYGRAF.BITNET
LISTSERV@POLYGRAF.BITNET
Contact: Tony Monteiro
MONTEIRO@POLYGRAF.BITNET

✎ *Forum de discussao do GEEE-L.*
GEEE-L@BRUFMG.BITNET
LISTSERV@BRUFMG.BITNET

✎ *Gemini Project list.*
GEMINI@NRCVM01.BITNET
LISTSERV@NRCVM01.BITNET

✎ *BITNET User's Guide list.*
GGUIDE@BITNIC.BITNET
LISTSERV@BITNIC.BITNET

✎ *GIF Graphics and Applications list.*
GIF-L@VMTECMEX.BITNET
LISTSERV@VMTECMEX.BITNET

❧ *GIGA—GMD Internet GMD Ankuendigung list.*
GIGA-L@DEARN.BITNET
LISTSERV@DEARN.BITNET

❧ *Leserforum des Informationsdienstes GIGA.*
GIGA@DEARN.BITNET
LISTSERV@DEARN.BITNET

❧ *Graphics Interface Kit/2 discussion list.*
GIK2-L@AWIIMC12.BITNET
LISTSERV@AWIIMC12.BITNET
Contact: Christian Reichetzeder
<REICHETZ@AWIIMC12.IMC.UniVie.AC.AT>

❧ *GI-ABS Mailing list.*
GI3ABS-L@DHDURZ1.BITNET
LISTSERV@DHDURZ1.BITNET

❧ *Great Lakes Economic Development Research Group list.*
GLED@UICVM.BITNET
LISTSERV@UICVM.BITNET

❧ *The Global Modeling Forum list.*
GLOMOD-L@UHCCVM.BITNET
LISTSERV@UHCCVM.BITNET

❧ *Global Systems Analysis and Simulation list.*
GLOSAS-L@UOTTAWA.BITNET
LISTSERV@UOTTAWA.BITNET

❧ *Global Systems Analysis and Simulation Association list.*
GLOSAS@MCGILL1.BITNET
LISTSERV@MCGILL1.BITNET

❧ *Great Lakes Research Consortium Information list.*
GLRC@SUVM.BITNET
LISTSERV@SUVM.BITNET

❧ *Global Nomads list.*
GNI-L@BROWNVM.BITNET
LISTSERV@BROWNVM.BITNET

❧ *GONE Program discussion list.*
GONE-L@TAUNIVM.BITNET
LISTSERV@TAUNIVM.BITNET

❧ *Gopher Glossary Item Submission list.*
GOPHGLOS@MSU.BITNET
LISTSERV@MSU.BITNET

❧ *Gould CSD User's list.*
GOULDBUG@CS.UTAH.EDU.BITNET
LISTSERV@CS.UTAH.EDU.BITNET
Reporting bugs and problems with the GOULD UTX/32 (Unix) operating system and software.
Contact: Valdis Kletnieks
VALDIS@CS.UTAH.EDU.BITNET

❧ *CAS Gradref Information list.*
GRADREF@TEMPLEVM.BITNET
LISTSERV@TEMPLEVM.BITNET

❧ *OSP Funding Alert list.*
GRANT-L@UA1VM.BITNET
LISTSERV@UA1VM.BITNET

❧ *Yale University Graphics Users list.*
GRAPH-L@YALEVM.BITNET
LISTSERV@YALEVM.BITNET

❧ *GRAPH-TI Texas Instruments Graphing Calculato list.*
GRAPH-TI@OHSTVMA.BITNET
LISTSERV@OHSTVMA.BITNET

❧ *KFUPM Graphics Users Group list.*
GRAPH-UG@SAUPM00.BITNET
LISTSERV@SAUPM00.BITNET

❧ *GRAPHICS OSU Computer Graphics Discussion list.*
GRAPHICS@OHSTVMA.BITNET
LISTSERV@OHSTVMA.BITNET
Contact: Bob Kalal
KALAL@OHSTVMA.BITNET

❧ *Computer Graphics list.*
GRAPHIX@UTFSM.BITNET
LISTSERV@UTFSM.BITNET
Discussion of formats, documents, and archives relative to graphics oriented to PC/PS and compatibles users.
Contact: Hernan Lobos
<HLOBOS@UTFSM.BITNET>

❧ *Aspects of Computer Graphics discussion list.*
GraphUK%graphics.computerscience.manchester.
ac.uk@NSS.CS.UCL.AC.UK
GraphUK%graphics.computerscience.manchester.
ac.uk@NSS.CS.UCL.AC.UK
Contact: Toby Howard
<THOWARD%graphics.computerscience.manchester.
ac.uk@NSS.CS.UCL.AC.UK>

❧ *GRiD Compass Computers list.*
GRiD@STALLER.SPT.TEK.COM
jans@TEKCRL.TEK.COM
Contact: Jan Steinman
<jans@STALLER.SPT.TEK.COM>

❧ *Forum GRUDES-L list.*
GRUDES-L@BRUFSC.BITNET
LISTSERV@BRUFSC.BITNET

❧ *Gruppenforschung/Forum list.*
GRUFO-L@DGOGWDG1.BITNET
LISTSERV@DGOGWDG1.BITNET

❧ *Gruppenforschung/Initiatorengruppe.*
GRUPIN-L@DGOGWDG1.BITNET
LISTSERV@DGOGWDG1.BITNET

- *Gruppenforschung/Initiatorengruppe*
  GSDSP@OCF.BERKELEY.EDU
  gsdsp-request@ocf.berkeley.edu

- *GS/DSP discussion list.*
Discussions of the GS/DSP co-processor board for the Apple II family of computers currently being developed by Pete Snowberg.
Contact: Pete Snowberg
  <pets@abacus.com>

- *Genesil and Related Tools discussion list.*
  gug-sysadmin@vlsivie.tuwien.ac.at
  gug-sysadmins-requiest@vlsivie.tuwien.ac.at

- *Forum Grupo de Usuarios MUSIC do Brasil (GUM).*
  GUM@BRUFMG.BITNET
  LISTSERV@BRUFMG.BITNET

- *Groupe francophone des Utilisateurs TeX*
  GUT@FRULM11.BITNET
  LISTSERV@FRULM11.BITNET

- *Machine Readable Texts E-mail list.*
  GUTNBERG@UIUCVMD.BITNET
  LISTSERV@UIUCVMD.BITNET

- *GWU's GWCOMM discussion list.*
  GWCOMM@GWUVM.BITNET
  LISTSERV@GWUVM.BITNET

- *Mitteilungen der GWDG*
  GWDG-NEU@DGOGWDG1.BITNET
  LISTSERV@DGOGWDG1.BITNET

- *E-mail/OA Task Force list.*
  GWEMAIL@GWUVM.BITNET
  LISTSERV@GWUVM.BITNET

- *Handheld computers list.*
  HANDHELDS@CSL.SRI.COM
  HANDHELDS-REQUEST@CSL.SRI.COM
For users interested in handheld computers or programmable calculators.
Contact: David Edwards
  <DLE@CSL.SRI.COM>

- *HARNET Technical Group list.*
  HARNTECH@HKUVM1.BITNET
  LISTSERV@HKUVM1.BITNET

- *HASAFRAN: The AJL discussion Forum list.*
  HASAFRAN@OHSTVMA.BITNET
  LISTSERV@OHSTVMA.BITNET

- *Help Desks discussion list.*
  HDESK-L@WVNVM.BITNET
  LISTSERV@WVNVM.BITNET

- *Header-People discussion list.*
  HDR-PPL@MARIST.BITNET
  LISTSERV@MARIST.BITNET

- *Mail Headers discussion list.*
  HEADER-PEOPLE@MC.LCS.MIT.EDU
  HEADER-PEOPLE-REQUEST@MC.LCS.MIT.EDU
For users with an interest in the format of message headers and related issues.
Contact: Pandora B. Berman
  <CENT@AI.AI.MIT.EDU>

- *Zenith Computers discussion list.*
  Heath-People@MC.LCS.MIT.EDU
  HEATH-PEOPLE-REQUEST@MC.LCS.MIT.EDU
Discussion of the construction, use, and modification of Heath or Zenith terminals, computers, and related products.
Contact: Michael A. Patton
  <MAP@AI.AI.MIT.EDU>

- *GNUISH MS-DOS Software discussion list.*
  help-gnu-msdos@wugate.wustl.edu
  help-gnu-msdos-request@wugate.wustl.edu
Contact: Mr. David J. Camp
  david@wubios.wustl.edu

- *Network Problems discussion list.*
  HELP-NET@TEMPLEVM.BITNET
  LISTSERV@TEMPLEVM.BITNET
Seeks to solve user problems with utilities and software related to the Internet and BITNET networks.
Contact: Jeff Linder
  V5057U@TEMPLEVM.BITNET

- *Preprint server for Computational and Lattice list.*
  HEP-LATL@JPNYITP.BITNET
  LISTSERV@JPNYITP.BITNET

- *HEPDB distribution list.*
  HEPDB@CERNVM.BITNET
  LISTSERV@CERNVM.BITNET

- *HEPHIN discussion list.*
  HEPHIN@ICNUCEVM.BITNET
  LISTSERV@ICNUCEVM.BITNET

- *HEP Unix France list.*
  HEPIX-F@FRCPN11.BITNET
  LISTSERV@FRCPN11.BITNET

- *Japanese HEPnet discussion list.*
  HEPNET-J@JPNKEKVM.BITNET
  LISTSERV@JPNKEKVM.BITNET
Discusses technical and managing issues related to the Japanese HEPnet. All input is welcome.
Contact: Yukio Karita
  KARITA@JPNKEKVX.BITNET

- *HEPTHS-L Preprint Distributor for String list.*
  HEPTHS-L@JPNRIFP.BITNET
  LISTSERV@JPNRIFP.BITNET

🕙 *HL-7 (Health Level Seven) Conference list.*
HL-7@VIRGINIA.EDU
HL-7-REQUEST@VIRGINIA.EDU
Communication concerning technical, operational, and business issues involved in the use of the HL-7 interface protocol.
Contact: David John Marotta
<djm5g@virginia.edu>

🕙 *HELP Commands for VM/CMS list.*
HLPCMD-L@BROWNVM.BROWN.EDU
LISTSERV@BROWNVM.BROWN.EDU
Discusses HELP commands for VM/CMS, including (but not limited) to Brown's HELP command replacement.
Contact: Peter DiCamillo
CMSMAINT@BROWNVM.BROWN.EDU

🕙 *HP-48 Hand-Held Systems discussion list.*
HP-48@NDSUVM1.BITNET
LISTSERV@NDSUVM1.BITNET

🕙 *Hewlett-Packard 9000 Series MiniComputer Discussion list.*
HPMINI-L@UAFSYSB.BITNET
LISTSERV@UAFSYSB.BITNET
Discusses topics relating to hardware and software for HP9000 computers.
Contact: Christopher C. Corke
CHRISC@UAFSYSB.BITNET

🕙 *HP-3000 discussion list.*
HP3000-L@UTCVM.BITNET
LISTSERV@UTCVM.BITNET

🕙 *IA HRS IDMS discussion list.*
HRS-IDMS@UNMVMA.BITNET
LISTSERV@UNMVMA.BITNET

🕙 *Hospital Computer Network discussion list.*
HSPNET-D@ALBNYDH2.BITNET
LISTSERV@ALBNYDH2.BITNET
Emphasizes restoration and extension of consulting for rural hospitals by connection to major medical centers.
Contact: Donald F. Parsons MD
DFP10@ALBNYVM1

🕙 *Staff computacional do Hospital Universitari list.*
HUCFF-L@BRLNCC.BITNET
LISTSERV@BRLNCC.BITNET

🕙 *Hungarian EARN discussion list.*
HUEARN-L@HUEARN.BITNET
LISTSERV@HUEARN.BITNET

🕙 *Hyperchannel and IP list.*
HY-PEOPLE@ORVILLE.ARC.NASA.GOV
HY-PEOPLE-REQUEST@ORVILLE.ARC.NASA.GOV

Discusses hyperchannel networks in the context of an IP network.
Contact: John Lekashman
<lekash@ORVILLE.ARC.NASA.GOV>

🕙 *Mutual Assistance list.*
hyperami@archive.oit.unc.edu
listserv@archive.oit.unc.edu
For discussion and mutual assistance concerning: AmigaVision, InterActor, CanDo, PILOT, DeluxeVideo III, ShowMaker, Director 2, TACL, Foundation, Thinker, Hyperbook, and VIVA.

🕙 *Macintosh Hypercard discussion list.*
HYPERCRD@PURCCVM.BITNET
LISTSERV@PURCCVM.BITNET
Contact: George D. Allen
<allenge@ecn.purdue.edu>

🕙 *Biomedical Hypermedia Instructional Design list.*
HYPERMED@UMAB.BITNET
LISTSERV@UMAB.BITNET

🕙 *Integrated Technologies Hypermedia Conference list.*
HYPER93@INDYCMS.BITNET
LISTSERV@INDYCMS.BITNET

🕙 *Archive of I-AMIGA list.*
I-AMIGA@UIUCVMD.BITNET
LISTSERV@UIUCVMD.BITNET

🕙 *VAX Bboard discussion list.*
I-BBOARD@SPCVXA.BITNET
I-BBoard@SPCVXA.SPC.EDU
Contact: Benjamin Cohen
<BEN@SPCVXA.SPC.EDU>

🕙 *Finger Software list.*
I-FINGER@SPCVXA.BITNET
I-FINREQ@SPCVXA.BITNET
Discusses the Finger program and related utilities.
Contact: Terry Kennedy
<terry@SPCVXA.BITNET>

🕙 *IBM PC Discussions*
I-IBMPC@UIUCVMD.BITNET
LISTSERV@UIUCVMD.BITNET

🕙 *INFO-KERMIT Digest*
I-KERMIT@CUVMA.BITNET
LISTSERV@CUVMA.BITNET
Contact: Christine Gianone
KERMIT@CUVMA.BITNET

🕙 *Info-Pascal list.*
I-PASCAL@UTFSM.BITNET
LISTSERV@UTFSM.BITNET

Contact: Hernan Lobos
```
<HLOBOS@UTFSM.BITNET>
```

☙ *Info-Unix Distribution list.*
```
I-UNIX@TCSVM.BITNET
LISTSERV@TCSVM.BITNET
```

☙ *VideoTech discussion list.*
```
I-VIDTEK@UIUCVMD.BITNET
LISTSERV@UIUCVMD.BITNET
```
Discusses home satellite, teletext, cable television, stereo television, video disc technology, HighRes television, and video tape recorders.

☙ *IA ADS discussion list.*
```
IA-ADS@MARIST.BITNET
LISTSERV@IA-ADS.BITNET
```

☙ *SCT Acquesion of IA discussion list.*
```
IA-SCT@MARIST.BITNET
LISTSERV@MARIST.BITNET
```

☙ *Irish Academic Computing list.*
```
IAC-L@IRLEARN.BITNET
LISTSERV@IRLEARN.BITNET
```

☙ *Informatics Advisory Committee list.*
```
IAC@NRCVM01.BITNET
LISTSERV@NRCVM01.BITNET
```

☙ *IDMS-based I/A Software discussion list.*
```
IAIMU-L@ULKYVM.BITNET
LISTSERV@ULKYVM.BITNET
```

☙ *Artificial Intelligence discussion list.*
```
IAMEX-L@TECMTYVM.BITNET
LISTSERV@TECMTYVM.BITNET
```
Contact: Juana Maria Gomez Puertos
```
PL500368@TECMTYVM.BITNET
```

☙ *International AIX Users Group list.*
```
IAUG-L@PSUVM.BITNET
LISTSERV@PSUVM.BITNET
```

☙ *IBM Higher Education Consortium Discussion list.*
```
IBM-HESC@PSUORVM.BITNET
LISTSERV@PSUORVM.BITNET
```
Contact: Fred Dayton
```
FRED@PSUORVM.BITNET
```

☙ *IBM Mainframe KERMIT Developers list.*
```
IBM-KERM@CUVMA.BITNET
LISTSERV@CUVMA.BITNET
```
For discussion of IBM 370 Series KERMIT development.
Contact: John Chandler
```
PEPMNT@CFAAMP.BITNET
```

☙ *IBMMAIL Facilities discussion list.*
```
IBM-MAIL@FRORS13.BITNET
LISTSERV@FRORS13.BITNET
```

☙ *IBM Mainframe discussion list.*
```
IBM-MAIN@AKRONVM.BITNET
LISTSERV@AKRONVM.BITNET
```
Contact: Darren Evans-Young
```
DARREN@UA1VM.BITNET
```

☙ *BITNIC IBM-NETS list.*
```
IBM-NETS@BITNIC.BITNET
LISTSERV@BITNIC.BITNET
```
Discussion of IBM mainframes and networking.
Contact: Henry Nussbacher
```
HANK@BARILVM.BITNET
```

☙ *IBM Screen Reader Product discussion list.*
```
IBM-SRD@NDSUVM1.BITNET
LISTSERV@NDSUVM1.BITNET
```
Contact: Brett G. Person
```
<NU079509@NDSUVM1.BITNET>
```

☙ *IBM Field Television Network Schedule Distribution list.*
```
IBMFTN@UCLACN1.BITNET
LISTSERV@UCLACN1.BITNET
```

☙ *INFO-IBMPC Digest*
```
IBMPC-L@POLYGRAF.BITNET
LISTSERV@POLYGRAF.BITNET
```
Discusses the IBM Personal Computer and compatible micro-computers.
Contact: Gregory Hicks
```
GHICKS@SIMTEL20.ARMY.MIL
```

☙ *IBM TCP/IP Software Products discussion list.*
```
IBMTCP-L@PUCC.BITNET
LISTSERV@PUCC.BITNET
```

☙ *International Business School Computing list.*
```
IBSCG@MIAMIU.BITNET
LISTSERV@MIAMIU.BITNET
```
Contact: Rajkumar
```
RAJKUMAR@MIAMIU.BITNET
```

☙ *ICOM User list.*
```
ICOMALL@JPNIMRTU.BITNET
LISTSERV@JPNIMRTU.BITNET
```

☙ *Icon Language list.*
```
Icon-Group@ARIZONA.EDU
Icon-Group-Request@ARIZONA.EDU
```
Discusses topics related to the Icon programming language.
Contact: Bill Mitchell
```
<whm@ARIZONA.EDU>
```

☙ *Cullinet IDMS discussion list.*
```
IDMS-L@UGA.BITNET
LISTSERV@UGA.BITNET
```

☙ *CSS Community Leaders Group list.*
```
IFCSS-L@ULKYVM.BITNET
LISTSERV@ULKYVM.BITNET
```

✪ *IFCSS Newsletter Mailing list.*
IFCSS-NL@PSUORVM.BITNET
LISTSERV@PSUORVM.BITNET

✪ *IFIP WG 6.5 Task Group discussion list.*
IFIP-DIALUP@ics.uci.edu
ifip-dialup-request@ics.uci.edu
Supports an open task group of volunteers to work under the aegis of IFIP Working Group 6.5 in the Pre-Standards Development Mode.
Contact: Einar Stefferud
<stef@nma.com>

✪ *X.400 Gateways.*
IFIP-GTWY@UCS.UCI.EDU
<IFIP-GTWY-REQUEST@ICS.UCI.EDU>
For the IFIP 6.5 Task Group on Gateways (gateways and interworking between X.400 and non-X.400 MHS environments and between 1984 and 1988 X.400 conformant systems).
Contact: Tim Kehres
<Kehres@TIS.LLNL.GOV>

✪ *IFIP Multimedia Multimode Messaging list.*
IFIP-MMM@IBACSATA.BITNET
LISTSERV@IBACSATA.BITNET

✪ *IIF felhsznalok levelezese list.*
IIF-FELH@HUEARN.BITNET
LISTSERV@HUEARN.BITNET

✪ *IIF koordinator lista.*
IIF-KOOR@HUEARN.BITNET
LISTSERV@HUEARN.BITNET

✪ *Illinois ACRAO Speede discussion list.*
ILSPEEDE@UIUCVMD.BITNET
LISTSERV@UIUCVMD.BITNET

✪ *IMAGEN Laser Printer discussion list.*
IMAGEN-L@UOGUELPH.BITNET
LISTSERV@UOGUELPH.BITNET
Discusses all aspects of the IMAGEN XP series of laser printers.
Contact: Scotty
SCOTTY@UOGUELPH.BITNET

✪ *Digital Image Processing of Remote Sensing list.*
IMAGRS-L@CSEARN.BITNET
LISTSERV@CSEARN.BITNET

✪ *Compatability of Multimedia Applications list.*
IMAMEDIA@UMDD.BITNET
LISTSERV@UMDD.BITNET

✪ *INCENTER—International Center list.*
INCENTER@UNMVM.BITNET
LISTSERV@UNMVM.BITNET

✪ *NOTIS Implementation Within the IU Library System list.*
INDNOTIS@INDYCMS.BITNET
LISTSERV@INDYCMS.BITNET

✪ *IUPUI Mainframe discussion list.*
INDYMAIN@INDYCMS.BITNET
LISTSERV@INDYCMS.BITNET

✪ *SAS at IUPUI list.*
INDYSAS@INDYCMS.BITNET
LISTSERV@INDYCMS.BITNET

✪ *SPSSx at IUPUI list.*
INDYSPSS@INDYCMS.BITNET
LISTSERV@INDYCMS.BITNET

✪ *INET92 Workshop for Developing Countries list.*
INET92WD@ICNUCEVM.BITNET
LISTSERV@ICNUCEVM.BITNET

✪ *Heath/Zenith Z100 Information Mailing list.*
INF-Z100@CLVM.BITNET
LISTSERV@CLVM.BITNET
Discusses topics related to the Zenith Z-100 (Heath H-100) family of professional desktop computers.
Contact: Gern
<GERN@TOPS20.RADC.AF.MIL>

✪ *ADA Programming Language (INFO-ADA) discussion list.*
INFO-ADA@FINHUTC.BITNET
LISTSERV@FINHUTC.BITNET
Contact: Edward E. Cragg
<ECRAGG@GMUVAX.GMU.EDU>

✪ *Alliant Computer System discussion list.*
Alliant info-alliant@MCS.ANL.GOV
info-alliant-request@MCS.ANL.GOV
Discusses Alliant computer systems.
Contact: Gene Rackow
<rackow@MCS.ANL.GOV>

✪ *Andrew Software Bugs list.*
Info-Andrew-Bugs@ANDREW.CMU.EDU
Info-Andrew-Bugs-Request@ANDREW.CMU.EDU
For reporting bugs/problems.
Contact: Adam Stoller
<ghoti+@ANDREW.CMU.EDU>

✪ *Andrew Environment list.*
Info-Andrew@ANDREW.CMU.EDU
Info-Andrew-Request@ANDREW.CMU.EDU
A joint project of Carnegie Mellon University and IBM, Andrew is a prototype computing environment for academic and research use under the Unix operating system.
Contact: Adam Stoller
<ghoti+@ANDREW.CMU.EDU>

🖐 *INFO-APP Info-Apple list.*
```
INFO-APP@NDSUVM1.BITNET
LISTSERV@NDSUVM1.BITNET
```
Contact: Brint Cooper
```
<abc@BRL.MIL>
```

🖐 *Applebus developers list.*
```
INFO-APPLETALK@ANDREW.CMU.EDU
INFO-APPLETALK-REQUEST@ANDREW.CMU.EDU
```
For communication between Applebus hardware and software developers and other interested parties.
Contact: Tom Holodnik
```
<tjh+@ANDREW.CMU.EDU>
```

🖐 *IBM AS/400 discussion list.*
```
INFO-AS400@JOINER.BITNET
Info-AS400-Request@Joiner.COM
```
Discussion on IBM AS/400 architecture, systems, and software.
Contact: Stephen L. Arnold
```
Arnold@Joiner.COM
```

🖐 *Atari ST Users Forum (INFO-ATARI16).*
```
INFO-ATARI16@NAUCSE.CSE.NAU.EDU
INFO-ATARI16-REQUEST@SCORE.STANFORD.EDU
```
Discussions of 16-bit Atari computers and related topics.
Contact: Peter Jasper-Fayer
```
<sofpjf@UOGUELPH.BITNET>
```

🖐 *INFO-ATARI8 discussion list.*
```
INFO-ATARI8@NAUCSE.CSE.NAU.EDU
INFO-ATARI8-REQUEST@SCORE.STANFORD.EDU
```
Contact: John Voigt
```
<sysbjav@TCSVM.BITNET>
```

🖐 *A/UX discussion and software list.*
```
INFO-AUX@PUCC.BITNET
LISTSERV@PUCC.BITNET
```

🖐 *Info-C list.*
```
INFO-C@NDSUVM1.BITNET
LISTSERV@NDSUVM1.BITNET
```
Discusses C programming and the C programming language.
Contact: Mark Plotnick
```
<info-c-request@RESEARCH.ATT.COM>
```

🖐 *CCMD Software Package list.*
```
Info-CCMD@CUNIXF.CC.COLUMBIA.EDU
INFO-CCMD-REQUEST@CUNIXF.CC.COLUMBIA.EDU
```
Deals with the CCMD package (TOPS-20 COMND% JSYS emulation written in C).
Contact: Fuat Baran
```
fuat@columbia.edu
```

🖐 *Convex Minisupercomputers list.*
```
INFO-CONVEX@PEMRAC.SPACE.SWRI.EDU
info-convex-request@PEMRAC.SPACE.SWRI.EDU
```

For sharing ideas, questions, bug fixes, and so forth for Convex Corp. products. Unmoderated.
Contact: Karen Birkelbach
```
karen@pemrac.space.swri.edu
```

🖐 *CP/M Operating System.*
```
INFO-CPM@WSMR-SIMTEL20.ARMY.MIL
INFO-CPM-REQUEST@WSMR-SIMTEL20.ARMY.MIL
```
For information and discussion on both 8 and 16-bit versions of the CP/M microcomputer operating system.
Contact: Keith Petersen
```
<W8SDZ@WSMR-SIMTEL20.ARMY.MIL>
```

🖐 *Databasix Information Systems Software Discussion list.*
```
info-databasix@blx-a.prime.com
listserver@blx-a.prime.com
```
Contact: Ronald van der Meer
```
<ronald@dcs.prime.com>
```

🖐 *DEC Microcomputers list.*
```
INFO-DEC-MICRO@ANDREW.CMU.EDU
Info-DEC-Micro-Request@ANDREW.CMU.EDU
```
For users to ask questions and share answers about various topics concerning DEC microcomputers.
Contact: Rob Locke
```
<rl1b+@ANDREW.CMU.EDU>
```

🖐 *DSEE Software list.*
```
INFO-DSEE@APOLLO.COM
info-dsee-request@apollo.com
```
Contact: David Lubkin
```
<lubkin@APOLLO.COM>
```

🖐 *Encore Computers list.*
```
INFO-ENCORE@UB.D.UMN.EDU
INFO-ENCORE-REQUEST@UB.D.UMN.EDU
```
For users of the Encore MultiMax computers and Encore Annex terminal servers.
Contact: Dan Burrows
```
<dburrows@CS-GW.D.UMN.EDU>
```

🖐 *Frameworks Software list.*
```
info-frame@AEROSPACE.AERO.ORG
info-frame-request@AEROSPACE.AERO.ORG
```
Information for software tool developers responsible for integrating heterogenous software products.
Contact: Louis McDonald
```
<louis@AEROSPACE.AERO.ORG>
```

🖐 *Announcements About GNUISH MS-DOS Software.*
```
info-gnu-msdos@wugate.wustl.edu
info-gnu-msdos-request@wugate.wustl.edu
```
Contact: David J. Camp
```
<david@wubios.wustl.edu>
```

⑤ *Computer graphics discussion list.*
```
INFO-GRAPHICS@ADS.COM
INFO-GRAPHICS-REQUEST@ADS.COM
```
Contact: Andy Cromarty
```
<andy@ADS.COM>
```

⑤ *IBM RT Workstation discussion list.*
```
INFO-IBMRT@POLYA.STANFORD.EDU
INFO-IBMRT-REQUEST@POLYA.STANFORD.EDU
```
Contact: James Wilson
```
<jwilson@POLYA.STANFORD.EDU>
```

⑤ *IDL Language list.*
```
INFO-IDL@SEI.CMU.EDU
INFO-IDL-REQUEST@SEI.CMU.EDU
```
Discussion of issues relating to IDL (Interface Description Language) and IDL-like technologies.
Contact: Don Stone
```
ds@SEI.CMU.EDU
```

⑤ *Silicon Graphics Computers list.*
```
INFO-IRIS@BRL.MIL
Info-Iris-Request@BRL.MIL
```
For communication and sharing between computer science research groups using or interested in using Silicon Graphics Iris workstations and software.
Contact: Chuck Kennedy
```
<kermit@BRL.MIL>
```

⑤ *Macintosh Labview list.*
```
info-labview@pica.army.mil
info-labview-request@pica.army.mil
```
For discussion of National Instruments' LabVIEW package for the Apple Macintosh.
Contact: Tom Coradeschi
```
<tcora@pica.army.mil>
```

⑤ *Macintosh Research and Instructional Developers/Users list.*
```
INFO-MAC@SUMEX-AIM.STANFORD.EDU
INFO-MAC-REQUEST@SUMEX-AIM.STANFORD.EDU
```
Contact: Lance Nakata
```
<nakata@JESSICA.STANFORD.EDU>
```

⑤ *Mach Operating System discussion list.*
```
INFO-MACH@CS.CMU.EDU
INFO-MACH-REQUEST@CS.CMU.EDU
```
Contact: Doug Orr
```
<Doug.Orr@CS.CMU.EDU>
```

⑤ *General Microcomputers discussion list.*
```
INFO-MICRO@WSMR-SIMTEL20.ARMY.MIL
INFO-MICRO-REQUEST@WSMR-SIMTEL20.ARMY.MIL
```
For questions/discussions on a particular operating system.
Contact: Keith Petersen
```
<W8SDZ@WSMR-SIMTEL20.ARMY.MIL>
```

⑤ *Columbia Mailer.*
```
Info-MM@COLUMBIA.EDU
MM-Request@COLUMBIA.EDU
```
For Columbia-MM maintainers and sites to communicate, distribute patches, get bug reports, comment, and so on.
Contact: Fuat Baran
```
<fuat@columbia.edu>
```

⑤ *Modems list.*
```
Info-Modems@WSMR-SIMTEL20.ARMY.MIL
Info-Modems-Request@WSMR-SIMTEL20.ARMY.MIL
```
Discussions of special interest to modem users. Gatewayed to/from Usenet newsgroup comp.dcom.modems.
Contact: Keith Petersen
```
<W8SDZ@WSMR-SIMTEL20.ARMY.MIL>
```

⑤ *Modula-2 Programming Language discussion list.*
```
INFO-M2@UCF1VM.BITNET
LISTSERV@UCF1VM.BITNET
```
Contact: Thomas Habernoll
```
HABERNOL@DB0TUI11
```

⑤ *Office Document Architecture list.*
```
info-oda+@ANDREW.CMU.EDU
info-oda-request+@ANDREW.CMU.EDU
```
For discussions about the ISO standard 8613 "Office Document Architecture."
Contact: Mark Sherman
```
<mss+@ANDREW.CMU.EDU>
```

⑤ *Pascal discussion list.*
```
INFO-PASCAL@BRL.MIL
INFO-PASCAL-REQUEST@BRL.MIL
```

⑤ *PC Mail Systems list.*
```
Info-PCNet@AI.AI.MIT.EDU
Info-PCNet-Request@AI.AI.MIT.EDU
```
Seeks to discuss and begin implementing a network of personal computers to extend the advantages of net-mail.
Contact: Michael A. Patton
```
<MAP@AI.AI.MIT.EDU>
```

⑤ *PDP-11 discussion list.*
```
info-pdp11@TRANSARC.COM
info-pdp11-request@TRANSARC.COM
```
Discusses issues related to Digital's PDP-11 series minicomputers and their operating systems.
Contact: Pat Barron
```
<pat@TRANSARC.COM>
```

⑤ *Prime list.*
```
Info-Prime@Blx-A.Prime.COM
ListServer@Blx-A.Prime.COM
```
Discussions and information regarding Prime machines.

Contact: Toni van de Wiel
<Toni@Blx-S.Prime.COM>

☙ *Prime Computer Discussion list.*
INFO-PRIME@LIST.KEAN.EDU
Info-Prime-Request@LIST.KEAN.EDU
Discussions of Prime computers. Discussion on Primos, Prime Information, and Primix are all welcome.
Contact: Al Costanzo
<AL@TURBO.KEAN.EDU>

☙ *Printers list.*
INFO-PRINTERS@EDDIE.MIT.EDU
INFO-PRINTERS-REQUEST@EDDIE.MIT.EDU
For information on printers.
Contact: Jon Solomon
<jsol@EDDIE.MIT.EDU>

☙ *Prograph Programming Language list.*
info-prograph@grove.iup.edu
info-prograph-request@grove.iup.edu
Discussions of Prograph, an icon-based object-oriented programming language.
Contact: Mark Nutter
<manutter@grove.iup.edu>

☙ *Pyramid Computer list.*
INFO-PYRAMID@MIMSY.UMD.EDU
INFO-PYRAMID-REQUEST@MIMSY.UMD.EDU
Discussion of Pyramid (the manufacturer, not the shape) computers.
Contact: Mark Weiser
<mark@MIMSY.UMD.EDU>

☙ *Solbourne Computer list.*
INFO-SOLBOURNE@ACSU.BUFFALO.EDU
info-solbourne-request@acsu.buffalo.edu
Discussions about Solbourne computers, multiprocessor Sun-4 compatible workstations and servers.
Contact: Paul Graham
<pjg@acsu.buffalo.edu>

☙ *Unisys Computer list.*
INFO-SPERRY-5000@WSMR-SIMTEL20.ARMY.MIL
INFO-SPERRY-5000-REQUEST@WSMR-
SIMTEL20.ARMY.MIL
Contact: Frank Wancho
<WANCHO@WSMR-SIMTEL20.ARMY.MIL>

☙ *Stratus Computer discussion list.*
Info-Stratus@mike.lrc.edu
Info-Stratus-Request@mike.lrc.edu
Contact: Richard S. Shuford
<shuford@cs.utk.edu>

☙ *Tahoe Systems list.*
INFO-TAHOE@CSD1.MILW.WISC.EDU
INFO-TAHOE-REQUEST@CSD1.MILW.WISC.EDU

Discussions pertaining to Tahoe-type CPUs.
Contact: Jim Lowe
<james@CSD4.MILW.WISC.EDU>

☙ *Terminals Information list.*
INFO-TERMS@EDDIE.MIT.EDU
INFO-TERMS-REQUEST@EDDIE.MIT.EDU
Contact: Jon Solomon
<jsol@EDDIE.MIT.EDU>

☙ *TI Explorer list.*
INFO-TI-EXPLORER@SUMEX-AIM.STANFORD.EDU
INFO-TI-EXPLORER-REQUEST@SUMEX-
AIM.STANFORD.EDU
For information exchange among DARPA-sponsored projects using TI Explorers.
Contact: Richard Acuff
<ACUFF@SUMEX-AIM.STANFORD.EDU>

☙ *TMODEM list.*
INFO-TMODEM@WSMR-SIMTEL20.ARMY.MIL
INFO-TMODEM-REQUEST@WSMR-SIMTEL20.ARMY.MIL
Contact: Frank J. Wancho
<WANCHO@WSMR-SIMTEL20.ARMY.MIL>

☙ *TOPs to Unix Migration list.*
Info-TOPSUX@CUNIXF.CC.COLUMBIA.EDU
Info-TOPSUX-Request@CUNIXF.CC.COLUMBIA.EDU
For discussion of topics related to the migration from a TOPS20 environment to a Unix one.
Contact: Ken Rossman
<ken@cunixf.cc.columbia.edu>

☙ *Unix System Managers discussion list.*
INFO-UNIX@BRL.MIL
INFO-UNIX-REQUEST@BRL.MIL
Contact: Mike Muuss
<mike@BRL.MIL>

☙ *V-System list.*
INFO-V@PESCADERO.STANFORD.EDU
INFO-V-REQUEST@PESCADERO.STANFORD.EDU
For the V-distributed operating system (V-System), developed by the Distributed Systems Group of Stanford University.
Contact: Keith A. Lantz
<LANTZ@GREGORIO.STANFORD.EDU>

☙ *INFO-VAX discussion list.*
INFO-VAX@MARIST.BITNET
LISTSERV@MARIST.BITNET
Discussion of the Digital Equipment Corporation VAX series of computers.
Contact: Harold Pritchett
HAROLD@UGA.BITNET

☙ *INFO-VAX DEC VAX Computer list.*
INFO-VAX@SRI.COM
INFO-VAX-REQUEST@SRI.COM
Discussion of the Digital Equipment Corporation VAX series of computers.

Gatewayed to the usenet group COMP.OS.VMS.
Contact: Ramon Curiel
    <Ray@SRI.COM>

✎ *View Mail Mode discussion list.*
    Info-VM@uunet.uu.net
    Info-VM-Request@UUNET.UU.NET

✎ *Xenix on Intel 310s discussion list.*
    INFO-XENIX310@WSMR-SIMTEL20.ARMY.MIL
    INFO-XENIX310-REQUEST@WSMR-
    SIMTEL20.ARMY.MIL
Contact: John Mitchener
    JMITCHENER@WSMR-SIMTEL20.ARMY.MIL

✎ *Xmodem File Transfer list.*
    INFO-XMODEM@WSMR-SIMTEL20.ARMY.MIL
    INFO-XMODEM-REQUEST@WSMR-SIMTEL20.ARMY.MIL
Discussion of XMODEM Christensen protocol
file transfer programs.
Contact: Keith Petersen
    <W8SDZ@WSMR-SIMTEL20.ARMY.MIL>

✎ *ZIP Software list.*
    Info-ZIP@WSMR-SIMTEL20.ARMY.MIL
    Info-ZIP-Request@WSMR-SIMTEL20.Army.Mil
For the developers of ZIP-related programs for
mainframe use.
Contact: Keith Petersen
    w8sdz@WSMR-SIMTEL20.Army.Mil

✎ *Xerox Lisp Environment list.*
    INFO-1100@TUT.CIS.OHIO-STATE.EDU
    Info-1100-Request@TUT.CIS.OHIO-STATE.EDU
Discussion on the Xerox/Envos Lisp
environment and the associated protocols.
Contact: Arun Welch
    <welch@TUT.CIS.OHIO-STATE.EDU>

✎ *68000 Systems list.*
    INFO-68K@BERKELEY.EDU
    Info-68K-Request@BERKELEY.EDU
For OS users capable of running on small 68000
systems.
Contact: Mike Meyer
    <mwm@BERKELEY.EDU>

✎ *INFOCHIM—Chimica Computazionale e
Information list.*
    INFOCHIM@ICINECA.BITNET
    LISTSERV@ICINECA.BITNET

✎ *CP/M Operating System Distribution list.*
    INFOCPM@FINHUTC.BITNET
    LISTSERV@FINHUTC.BITNET

✎ *Grupo de interes en la red earn espanyola.*
    INFOEARN@EBCESCA1.BITNET
    LISTSERV@EBCESCA1.BITNET

✎ *Network discussion list (focusing on inter-
network connectivity).*
    INFONETS@BITNIC.BITNET
    LISTSERV@BITNIC.BITNET

✎ *Informix E-mail discussion list.*
    Informix@rmy.emory.edu
    informix-list-request@rmy.emory.edu
Discussion of Informix software and related
subjects.
Contact: Walt Hultgren
    <walt@rmy.emory.edu>

✎ *Information Systems Mailing list.*
Discussions, postings, and announcements
relevant to practitioners and researchers in
information systems.
    INFOSYS@HDETUD1.BITNET
    LISTSERV@HDETUD1.BITNET

✎ *Xerox 1100 Workstation/Protocol discussion
list.*
    INFO1100@FINHUTC.BITNET
    LISTSERV@FINHUTC.BITNET

✎ *Information Graphics list.*
    INGRAFX@PSUVM.BITNET
    LISTSERV@PSUVM.BITNET
Discussions on the interdisciplinary areas of
cartography, information graphics, and
scientific visualization.
Contact: Jeremy Crampton
    <ELE@PSUVM.BITNET>

✎ *INGRES RDBMS discussion list.*
    INGRES-L@HDETUD1.BITNET
    LISTSERV@HDETUD1.BITNET

✎ *Rotterdam/Delft INGRES list.*
    INGRESNL@HDETUD1.BITNET
    LISTSERV@HDETUD1.BITNET

✎ *International Health Communication list.*
    INHEALTH@RPIECS.BITNET
    LISTSERV@RPIECS.BITNET

✎ *Discussao da Situacao Criada pela sua
Extinca.*
    INIC@PTEARN.BITNET
    LISTSERV@PTEARN.BITNET

✎ *International Neural Network Society list.*
    INNS-L@UMDD.BITNET
    LISTSERV@UMDD.BITNET

✎ *University Internal Audit (Canada) list.*
    INTAUD-L@UALTAVM.BITNET
    LISTSERV@UALTVM.BITNET

✎ *Internet Chile list.*
    INTER-CH@PUCING.BITNET
    LISTSERV@PUCING.BITNET

⑨ *BITNET Cross-cultural communication list.*
INTERCUL@RPICICGE.BITNET
COMSERVE@RPIECS.

⑨ *User-System Interfaces discussion list.*
interfaces-p-m@crim.ca
interfaces-p-m-request@crim.ca

⑨ *ARPA-Internet News list.*
INTERNET@ICNUCEVM.BITNET
LISTSERV@ICNUCEVM.BITNET

⑨ *CDNet Internet Gateway.*
IP-PEOPLE@RELAY.CS.NET
IP-PEOPLE-REQUEST@RELAY.CS.NET
Contact: Leo Lanzillo
<leo@SH.CS.NET>

⑨ *Interpersonal Computing and Technology list.*
IPCT-L@GUVM.BITNET
LISTSERV@GUVM.BITNET
For pedagogical issues involving teaching with technology, and especially with connectivity and networking.
Contact: Zane Berge
<BERGE@GUVAX.BITNET>

⑨ *IPN Information list.*
IPNINF-L@FRCPN11.BITNET
LISTSERV@FRCPN11.BITNET

⑨ *iPSC/1 and 2 list.*
iPSC <ipsclist@TCGOULD.TN.CORNELL.EDU>
ipsclist@TCGOULD.TN.CORNELL.EDU:
For iPSC/1 and iPSC/2 users and systems administrators to communicate easily and directly.

⑨ *Information Retrieval list.*
IR-L@UCCVMA.BITNET
LISTSERV@UCCVMA.BITNET
Discussion of any topic related to information retrieval.
Contact: Clifford Lynch
<lynch@POSTGRES.BERKELEY.EDU>

⑨ *Information Retrieval Distribution list.*
IR-LIST@IRLEARN.BITNET
LISTSERV@IRLEARN.BITNET

⑨ *IRC Rete Interregionale IATINET list.*
IRCRETE@IBACSATA.BITNET
LISTSERV@IBACSATA.BITNET

⑨ *TQM Implementation in IS discussion list.*
IS-TQM@MITVMA.BITNET
LISTSERV@MITVMA.BITNET

⑨ *International Simulation and Gaming Association Forum list.*
ISAGA-L@UHCCVM.BITNET
LISTSERV@UHCCVM.BITNET

⑨ *FORUM ISAPL-L list.*
ISAPL-L@BRUFSC.BITNET
LISTSERV@BRUFSC.BITNET

⑨ *Informatics Steering Committee list.*
ISC@NRCVM01.BITNET
LISTSERV@NRCVM01.BITNET

⑨ *Computer Assisted Management and Manipulation list.*
ISCAMI@GREARN.BITNET
LISTSERV@GREARN.BITNET

⑨ *ISDN list.*
isdn@teknologi.agderforskning.no
isdn-request@teknologi.agderforskning.no
Discusses all aspects of ISDN (protocols, services, applications, experiences, status, and so on).

⑨ *ISETL Language discussion list.*
ISETL-L@CLVM.BITNET
LISTSERV@CLVM.BITNET

⑨ *ISN Data Switch Technical Discussion Group list.*
ISN@RITVM.BITNET
LISTSERV@RITVM.BITNET

⑨ *ISO WG4 Messaging list.*
ISO-MSGS@IBACSATA.BITNET
LISTSERV@IBACSATA.BITNET

⑨ *ISO Protocol Stack discussion list.*
ISO@NIC.DDN.MIL
ISO-REQUEST@NIC.DDN.MIL

⑨ *ISO Development Environment discussion list.*
ISODE@IRLEARN.BITNET
LISTSERV@IRLEARN.BITNET

⑨ *Multibyte Coded-Character Set discussion list.*
ISO10646@JHUVM.BITNET
LISTSERV@JHUVM.BITNET
For information on and discussion of multi-byte coded-character sets.

⑨ *ASCII/EBCDIC Character Set discussion list.*
ISO8859@JHUVM.BITNET
LISTSERV@JHUVM.BITNET
Contact: Ed Hart
HART@APLVM.BITNET

⑨ *ISPF Discussion list.*
ISPF-L@DB0FUB11.BITNET
LISTSERV@DB0FUB11.BITNET

⑨ *Italian Student/Young Pugwash list.*
ISYP@ICNUCEVM.BITNET
LISTSERV@ICNUCEVM.BITNET

꙳ *Integrated Technologies Help list.*
```
IT-HELP@INDYCMS.BITNET
LISTSERV@INDYCMS.BITNET
```

꙳ *Instructional Technology Advisory Committee list.*
```
ITAC-L@UTKVM1.BITNET
LISTSERV@UTKVM1.BITNET
```

꙳ *ITALIC-L—The Irish Tex And Latex Interest Conference.*
```
ITALIC-L@IRLEARN.BITNET
LISTSERV@IRLEARN.BITNET
```
Contact: Brendan Dixon
```
<BDIXON@IRLEARN.BITNET>
```

꙳ *Israel Technology Exchange (ITEX) Discussion list.*
```
ITEX-L@TAUNIVM.BITNET
LISTSERV@TAUNIVM.BITNET
```
Enables Israeli scientists to utilize effort and investment already made in R&D.
Contact: Dr. Menachem Fishbein
```
FISHB@ILJCT.BITNET
```

꙳ *ITS Management list.*
```
ITSMGMT@UCSFVM.BITNET
LISTSERV@UCSFVM.BITNET
```

꙳ *Information Technology Services Newsletter list.*
```
ITSNEWS@UCSFVM.BITNET
LISTSERV@UCSFVM.BITNET
```

꙳ *I.T.U. Mezunlari Listesi.*
```
ITU-L@TRITU.BITNET
LISTSERV@TRITU.BITNET
```

꙳ *Journal of Computers in Mathematics and Science list.*
```
JCMST-L@PURCCVM.BITNET
LISTSERV@PURCCVM.BITNET
```

꙳ *Networking for Universities in Central Slovak list.*
```
JEP-BB@CSEARN.BITNET
LISTSERV@CSEARN.BITNET
```

꙳ *The Jericho Project list.*
```
JERICHO@BITNIC.BITNET
LISTSERV@BITNIC.BITNET
```

꙳ *JES2 Discussion Group.*
```
JES2-L@CEARN.BITNET
LISTSERV@CEARN.BITNET
```
Contact: Jan Gibb
```
Gibb@VTVM1.BITNET
```

꙳ *ANU-NEWS discussion list.*
```
ANU-NEWS@NDSUVM1.BITNET
LISTSERV@NDSUVM1.BITNET
```

Discussion of uses, bugs, and fixes for ANU-NEWS software.
Contact: Tim Russell
```
<russell@zeus.unl.edu>
```

꙳ *Japanese Animedia and Other Animation News list.*
```
ANIME-L@VTVM1.BITNET
LISTSERV@VTVM1.BITNET
```

꙳ *VT ANIMATIONS list.*
```
ANMI-L@RMCS.CRANFIELD.AC.UK
ANIM-L@rmcs.cranfield.ac.uk
```
For the distribution and discussion of VT/ANSI ANIMATION files.
Contact: Tim Kimber
```
<TJK@RMCS.CRANFIELD.AC.UK>
```

꙳ *BMDP Software Users Discussion Group.*
```
BMDP-L@MCGILL1.BITNET
LISTSERV@MCGILL1.BITNET
```
Contact: Michael Walsh
```
<CCMW@MCGILLA.BITNET>
```

꙳ *Chinese Computing/Word Processing list.*
```
CCNET-L@UGA.BITNET
LISTSERV@UGA.BITNET
```
Discussions on technology relating to the use of Chinese on computers.
Contact: Weihe Guan
```
<INR@UGA.BITNET>
```

꙳ *CHINANET: Networking In China list.*
```
CHINANET@TAMVM1.BITNET
LISTSERV@TAMVM1.BITNET
```
Contact: Butch Kemper
```
<X040BK@TAMVM1.BITNET>
```

꙳ *Turkish Electronic Mail list.*
```
TEL@USCVM .BITNET
LISTSERV@USCVM .BITNET
```
Facilitates communication among Turkish scientists around the world.
Contact: Dr. Sitki Aytac
```
BILSAY@TREARN.BITNET
```

꙳ *TESLCA-L: Computer Assisted Language Learning list.*
```
TESLCA-L@CUNYVM.BITNET
LISTSERV@CUNYVM.BITNET
```

꙳ *TPrint Issues list.*
```
TPRINT-L@YALEVM.BITNET
LISTSERV@YALEVM.BITNET
```

꙳ *UCLAMAIL TSO MAIL Interested Parties list.*
```
UCLAMAIL@OHSTVMA.BITNET
LISTSERV@OHSTVMA.BITNET
```
Contact: Pete Nielsen
```
CSYSPCN@UCLAMVS
```

🖙 *University Computing Project Mailing list.*
UCP-L@UBVM.BITNET
LISTSERV@UBVM.BITNET

🖙 *Vital Statistics at Albnydh2 list.*
VSTAT-L@ALBNYDH2.BITNET
LISTSERV@ALBNYDH2.BITNET

🖙 *NORDUnet Network Project Information list.*
NDNNET-I@FINHUTC.BITNET
LISTSERV@FINHUTC.BITNET

🖙 *RARE Working Group 1 Multi Media Environment list.*
RARE-MME@IBACSATA.BITNET
LISTSERV@IBACSATA.BITNET

🖙 *RARE Working Group 1 list.*
RARE-WG1@IBACSATA.BITNET
LISTSERV@IBACSATA.BITNET

🖙 *RARE Working Group 8 list.*
RARE-WG8@HEARN.BITNET
LISTSERV@HEARN.BITNET

🖙 *Comp-Sci Distribution list.*
COMP-SCI@TAUNIVM.BITNET
LISTSERV@TAUNIVM.BITNET
A BITNET newsletter on computer science in Israel.
Contact: Joseph van Zwaren de Zwarenstein
<JO@ILNCRD.BITNET>

🖙 *American Psychological Association Division 28 Executive Board Discussion list.*
EXEC28@GWUVM.BITNET
LISTSERV@GWUVM.BITNET

🖙 *Fractal discussion list.*
FRAC-L@GITVM1.BITNET
LISTSERV@GITVM1.BITNET
Discussion of computer graphical generation of fractals.
Contact: David D. Lester
CC100DL@GITVM1.BITNET

🖙 *GARR list.*
GARR-PE@IBACSATA.BITNET
LISTSERV@IBACSATA.BITNET

🖙 *L3 Analysis Group Beta Resource Commitment list.*
GBRC-L@LEPICS.BITNET
LISTSERV@LEPICS.BITNET

🖙 *Network Gateway Software list.*
gwmon@SH.CS.NET
gwmon-request@SH.CS.NET
Discusses the development of a monitoring suite for gateways.
Contact: Craig Partridge
<craig@LOKI.BBN.COM>

🖙 *Worldnet list.*
HUMAN-NETS@RED.RUTGERS.EDU
HUMAN-NETS-REQUEST@ARAMIS.RUTGERS.EDU
For discussion on the theme of a worldwide computer and telecommunications network.
Contact: Charles McGrew
<MCGREW@RED.RUTGERS.EDU>

🖙 *ION Associates of Texas Users Group list.*
IATEX-L@TAMVM1.BITNET
LISTSERV@TAMVM1.BITNET INFORMAT

🖙 *Celerity Computer discussion list.*
INFO-CELERITY@DOLPHIN.BU.EDU
INFO-CELERITY-REQUEST@DOLPHIN.BU.EDU.
Discussions pertaining to superminicomputer systems manufactured by Celerity.
Contact: Glenn Bresnahan
<glenn@DOLPHIN.BU.EDU>

🖙 *IETF WG on Internet School Networking (ISN) list.*
ISN-WG@UNMVM.BITNET
LISTSERV@UNMVM.BITNET

🖙 *VERnet Users list.*
VERN-USR@VTVM1.BITNET
LISTSERV@VTVM1.BITNET

🖙 *Lodz$L Users Distribution List*
LODZ$L@PLEARN.BITNET
LISTSERV@PLEARN.BITNET

🖙 *Microelectronics in Israel list.*
MICRO-EL@TAUNIVM.BITNET
LISTSERV@TAUNIVM.BITNET
For information for the Israeli research community involved in microelectronics.
Contact: Dr Michael Wolff
WOLFF@ILNCRD.BITNET

🖙 *COCHCOSH discussion list.*
COCHCOSH@UTORONTO.BITNET
LISTSERV@UTORONTO.BITNET

🖙 *Corpora list.*
CORPORA@X400.HD.UIB.NO
CORPORA-REQUEST@X400.HD.UIB.NO
For information and questions about text corpora such as availability, aspects of compiling and using corpora, software, tagging, parsing, bibliography, and so on.
Contact: Knut Hofland
<knut@x400.hd.uib.no>

🖙 *UCLA CWIS Abstracts list.*
INFOINDX@UCLACN1.BITNET
LISTSERV@UCLACN1.BITNET

🖙 *TACT-L discussion list.*
TACT-L@UTORONTO.BITNET
LISTSERV@UTORONTO.BITNET

§ Netnorth Administrative Secretary list.
ADMINSEC@UTORONTO.BITNET
LISTSERV@UTORONTO.BITNET

Fidonet

*§ *N*X (UNIX, XENIX, MINIX, QNX, COHERENT, and so on)*
UNIX
Deals with Unix and related OSs, systems, networks, and software.
Moderator: Thomas Lynch
1:273/225
Distribution: BACKBONE, WORLDWIDE, MULTI-ZONE
Gateways: MULTI-ZONE

§ 4DOS ECHO
4DOS
For users interested in the COMMAND.COM replacement 4DOS and 4DOS related programs such as NDOS and 4OS2, the corresponding program for OS/2. Excludes general software and hardware discussions/problems.
Moderator: Jean Hart
1:130/21
Distribution: BACKBONE
Gateways: RBBS-NET VIA 1:10/8

§ Adam International Computer Conference
ADAM
For the discussion and exchange of information concerning the Coleco Adam computer. All topics of interest to Adam owners and users including hardware, software, user groups, and meetings are welcome.
Moderator: James Young
1:3608/1
Distribution: BACKBONE

§ ADAnet International Technical Topics Forum
ADATECH
Discusses network technical administration. Originates within ADAnet (tm).
Moderator: ADAnet
94:94/1
Distribution: ADANET INTERNATIONAL DISABILITY NETWORK
Gateways: ADANET (94:94/1)

§ ADAnet International Topics Forum
ADANET
Discusses disability topics. Has also been used Discusses the ADAnet International Disability Network. Originating within ADAnet (tm).
Moderator: Bill Freeman
94:2050/1

Distribution: ADANET INTERNATIONAL DISABILITY NETWORK

§ Adlib and Compatible Sound Cards Discussion
ADLIB
Discusses all types of sound cards.
Moderator: Todd Toles
1:396/1.4
Distribution: BACKBONE

§ ALLFIX—File Request Echo
ALLFIX
Supports the ALLFIX utility to locate filenames and possible file request locations. Sysops must install ALLFIX on their end in order for this to work. ALLFIX checks for a valid Filename, Size, System Location, Baud Rate/Speed, System Name, and Telephone Number.
Moderator: Greg Edwards
1:133/520
Distribution: CHATEAUNET FIDONET
Gateways: 100:4000/501<>1:133/520

§ Amiga Assembly Language Programming Echo
AMIGA_ASM
For programmers to discuss, give example code, and share useful information related to writing 680x0 and custom chip code in assembler.
Moderator: John Preston
1:283/310
Distribution: BACKBONE

§ Amiga CDROM & CDTV Discussion/Sales
AMIGA_CDROM
For discussion and information on CDROM, CDTV, CD Sales, and varies CD titles for Amiga Users to get help with Amiga installations, available Amiga titles, and the sale of used or new equipment for the Amiga.
Moderator: Mario Bonelli
1:273/934

§ Amiga Communications Software and Hardware Discussions
AMIGA_COMMS
Covers programs such as JrCOMM, Term, and Ncomm, plus communications hardware such as modems and multi-port serial cards.
Moderator: Robert Williamson
1:167/104
Distribution: BACKBONE

§ Amiga Fidonet Point and Node Software Support
AMY_POINT
Offers assistance and information to users of Amiga-based Fidonet Software. Configuration,

installation, and other setup problems are covered, as well discussions of anything else relating to the Amiga within Fidonet.
Moderator: Robert Williamson
1:167/104.1
Distribution: BACKBONE

✆ *AMIGA For Sale Echo*
AMIGA_SALE
Facilitates the selling items of interest for the Amiga.
Moderator: Joe Mollica
1:273/50
Distribution: 1:114/52, 1:273/912, 1:232/301, 1:102/747

✆ *Amiga Gaming*
AMIGAGAMES
For game reviews, hints, tips, tricks, backdoors, solutions, comparisons, and general discussions of games for Amiga computers. Aimed at anyone who enjoys gaming on the Amiga.
Moderator: Adam Sternberg
1:209/700
Distribution: BACKBONE

✆ *Amiga International Echo*
AMIGA
Discusses all models of the Commodore Amiga computer system; answers users' questions about the Amiga; provides information about new Amiga products offered by Commodore and by third party vendors.
Moderator: Joyce Divina
1:3612/42
Distribution: BACKBONE

✆ *Amiga Language C programming & SAS/C Conference*
AMIGA_LC
For users who dabble in the C language. Emphasis on the SAS/C compiler. Hints, tips, tricks, questions, and programmings ideas are covered.
Moderator: Gary Gulliver
1:2608/27
Distribution: BACKBONE & NATIONAL

✆ *Amiga Music/sound topics*
AMIGA_MUSIC
For Commodore Amiga owners using their computers for music, composing, sampling, and the like.
Moderator: Nathan Barber
1:366/3
Distribution: BACKBONE

✆ *Amiga Network Developers*
AMIGA_NET_DEV

Discussions for developers of Amiga software, in a similar vein as NET_DEV. This forum is Amiga-specific and not a user support area.
Moderator: Russell McOrmond
1:1/109
Distribution: BACKBONE

✆ *Amiga Noncommercial Items for Sale*
AMIGASALE
For Commodore Amiga computers and equipment that can be used on them.
Moderator: Nathan Barber
1:366/3
Distribution: BACKBONE

✆ *Amiga Operating Systems and Emulators*
AMIGA_OS&EM
Offers assistance and information to users of Amiga-based operating systems (Releases 1 and 2, Amix, Unix, Minix, and OS-9000) and emulators (CP/M, MSdos, Macintosh, Atari, C64, and so on). Covers configuration, installation, and other setup problems
Moderator: Robert Williamson
1:167/104
Distribution: BACKBONE
Gateways: NEC240

✆ *Amiga Programming Discussions*
AMIGA_PROG
Discusses issues relating to programming Amiga computers. Users of all languages are welcome; novice and expert users alike are welcomed. Code snippets, discussions of algorithms, questions and answers to programming problems, discussions of various compilers, and so on are appropriate topics.
Moderator: Tim Aston
1:247/192
Distribution: BACKBONE

✆ *Amiga Public Domain and Requests*
AMIGA_PDREVIEW
For Amiga users around the world to get a better idea of all the PD/Shareware programs available. Users can give their own reviews of PD/SW programs. Allows general requests for specific types of shareware program. Reviews/requests of commercial programs or discussions on piracy/illegal actions not allowed.
Moderator: Gary Gulliver
1:2608/27
Distribution: BACKBONE & NATIONAL
Gateways: ZONE-2 VIA 1:232/301, ZONE-3 VIA 1:232/301

✆ *Amiga SilverBox Mail Reader Support*
SILVERBOX

Offers assistance and information to sysops and users of the SilverBox Mail Reader by David Lebel. Covers configuration, installation, and other setup problems.
Moderator: Robert Williamson
1:167/104
Distribution: REGION 12, REGION 20

✎ *Amiga Sysop General Discussions*
AMIGA_SYSOP
For Amiga sysops only. Discussions include system configurations, BBS and file distribution, and assistance to other Amiga sysops.
Moderator: John Preston
1:283/310
Restr: SYSOP
Distribution: BACKBONE

✎ *Amiga Technical/Hardware Conference*
AMY_TECH
Discusses the hardware of the Commodore-Amiga computer, ranging from accelerator cards to hard disks.
Moderator: David Jones
1:163/109.8
Distribution: BACKBONE

✎ *Amiga User Groups*
AMIGA_UG
Helps Amiga user groups share information and supply tips on running and promoting their group. Affiliated with ADS area CBNWS for the exchange of user group newsletters; if your group is interested in exchanging newsletters with other groups, contact your regional ADSHUB.
Moderator: Joe Mollica
1:273/50
Distribution: 1:273/912, 1:232/301, 1:102/747

✎ *Amiga Video/Graphics and Desktop Video Echo*
AMIGA_VIDEO
Pertains to Amiga video and graphics, mainly Desktop Video, Video Toaster, Lightwave 3D, and more.
Moderator: Ron Kramer
1:228/13
Distribution: BACKBONE

✎ *Amiga Worldwide*
AMIGA_INT
For general Amiga information.
Moderator: Kevin Vahey
1:101/475
Distribution: ZONE 1, ZONE 2, ZONE 3

✎ *ARJ Support Echo*
ARJ

Discusses the ARJ file compression program. Covers bug reports, usage tips, new release announcements, new feature suggestions, and general help. Robert Jung, ARJ's author, reads and responds to messages in this area.
Moderator: Ken Levitt
1:16/390
Distribution: FIDONET BACKBONE

✎ *Artificial Intelligence forum*
AI
Discusses artificial intelligence and related subjects such as expert systems, knowledge base design, natural language interfaces, artificial life, genetic algorithms, and so on
Moderator: Steve Rainwater
1:124/2206
Distribution: BACKBONE, RBBS-NET
Gateways: RBBS-NET VIA 1:10/8

✎ *Association of Shareware Professionals (ASP)*
ASP
Provides information about ASP and its members, serving as an announcement area for programs, new releases of the ASP catalog, and changes to ASP application procedures. Acts as a point of contact for shareware authors, vendors, and BBSs who want more information on becoming part of ASP. Open to all users.
Moderator: Charles Schell
1:231/290
Distribution: BACKBONE

✎ *Assembly Language Programming (Intel CPUs mainly)*
80XXX
Discusses assembly language programming. Discussion of programming of embedded systems and other CPU families also discretionarily allowed.
Moderator: Ed Beroset
1:3641/1.250
Distribution: BACKBONE
Gateways: ZONE-2 ISRAEL VIA 2:396/1; ZONE-2 EUROPE VIA 2:2405/100 RBBS-NET VIA 1:10/8; ZONE-3 VIA 3:290/627

✎ *AT&T PC Support Conference*
AT&T
Advice, suggestions, and information exchange for AT&T PCs.
Moderator: Bob Haberkost
1:129/125
Distribution: BACKBONE

✎ *Atari 8-bit Computers Topic*
ATARI

For users interested in the Atari 8-bit computer; discusses advantages, abilities and associated chit-chat.
Moderator: Larry Black
1:3608/121

✎ *Atari ST Echo*
ATARI_ST
For Atari ST owners and those interested in the Atari ST. This includes the ST, Mega ST, and TT—not the 8-bits.
Moderator: Mark Corona
1:124/1016
Distribution: BACKBONE

✎ *BASIC and Related Topics*
QUIK_BAS
For QuickBASIC programmers and users who would like to share their experiences using QuickBASIC and other extensions to QuickBASIC.
Moderator: Rick Haburne
1:116/2
Distribution: NO POSTIT ECHO FILE TRANSFERS BACKBONE

✎ *BASIC PDS Programmers Conference*
BASIC7
For programmers using the Microsoft BASIC Professional Development System.
Moderator: Chris Wagner
1:273/202

✎ *Batch Languages Programming*
BATPOWER
For batch file programming. Emphasis on MS-DOS and PC-DOS, but OS is welcomed. Tricks, tips, techniques, and external utilities to enchance the power of BAT.
Moderator: Marek Majewski
1:109/541
Distribution: BACKBONE

✎ *BBS Software Running in OS/2 DOS Boxes*
OS2DOSBBS
Discusses running DOS BBS software and utilities in OS/2 Dos Boxes.
Moderator: Howie Ducat
1:278/0
Distribution: SOON-TO-BE-BACKBONE

✎ *BBSLIST Discussions*
BBSLIST
A place for bbslist authors to exchange ideas on creating, maintaining, distributing, and improving their bbslist publications. Users and sysops are welcome to comment and make suggestions.

Moderator: Paul Knupke Jr.
1:3603/750
Distribution: ZONE 1 BACKBONE

✎ *BinkleyTerm Support Conference*
BINKLEY
A support conference for users of the BinkleyTerm
Moderator: Bob Juge
1:106/2000
Distribution: BACKBONE

✎ *Blue Wave Reader and Door Support Echo*
BLUEWAVE
Discusses the Blue Wave Offline Mail System and compatible updates.
Moderator: George Hatchew
1:2240/176
Distribution: BACKBONE

✎ *BNU FOSSIL Support*
BNU
For covering BNU usage, problems, beta testing, and other general FOSSIL-related topics.
Moderator: David Nugent
3:632/348
Distribution: ZONE-3, ZONE-1, ZONE-2
Gateways: ZONE-3 VIA 1:290/4, ZONE-2 VIA 2:281/603

✎ *BOI Doors and Utils*
BOI-DOORS
Discusses on-line doors and utilities written with the BBS Onliner Interface. Programmers, sysops, and users are welcome.
Moderator: Andrew Mead
1:3641/417

✎ *BOI Programming*
BOI-PROG
Discusses programming with the BBS Onliner Interface. Code fragments, bug reports, and related materials are welcome.
Moderator: Andrew Mead
1:3641/417

✎ *Bulletin Board Advertising—Promote your BBS!*
BBS_ADS
Discusses BBSs; sysops can promote features which they believe make their system unique.
Moderator: Bob Johnstone
42:1001/24
Distribution: BACKBONE AND GROUPMAIL

✎ *Bulletin Board Legal Issues Conference*
BBSLAW
Discusses legal issues, case histories, and legislative actions which affect sysops and BBS operation.

Moderator: Danny Burdick
1:374/17
Distribution: BACKBONE-BBSLAW

✎ *Canada Sysop Echo*
CANADA
Discusses affairs as pertaining to sysops in Canada. All Canadian Fidonet sysops are welcome, as are others with permission of the Moderator.
Moderator: Dixon Kenner
1:243/5
Distribution: BACKBONE

✎ *Canadian Government Computer Systems and Vendor Chat*
GOVT_CS
Discusses issues in the Canadian Federal computing industry.
Moderator: Raymond Ouellette
1:163/125
Distribution: CROSS CANADA. MAINLY IN OTTAWA-TORONTO AREA.
Gateways: IMEX, FEDNET

✎ *CD ROM Items For Sale*
CDROM_SALE
Posts notice of items of interest for sale by individuals or companies.
Moderator: Jim Oxford
1:147/20
Distribution: NET-147 BACKBONE

✎ *Checkfree Software Support Conference*
CHEKFREE
A support conference for Checkfree Software. Pay your bills electronically using the U.S. Federal Reserve System.
Moderator: David Pointer
1:226/5200
Distribution: ZONE 1

✎ *Chitchat About the Hobby of Modeming*
MODEMERS
For PC-ers addicted to modeming; chitchat is restricted to topics specifically related to modeming being addictive...and fun.
Moderator: Judy Proctor
1:361/12
Distribution: ECHONET BACKBONE (ZONE 50)

✎ *Classified Advertising Echo*
CLASSIFIEDS
Allows users to advertise items for sale, wanted, for trade, and so on. Noncommercial only.
Moderator: Jean Cody
1:260/250
Distribution: BACKBONE

✎ *CNet Amiga BBS Software Support For CNet Sysops*
CNET
Discussions for users who would like to expand their knowledge of the CNet program, be able to search for help with a problem, and offer suggestions for improvement.
Moderator: Mario Bonelli
1:273/934
Distribution: ZONE 1 BACKBONE

✎ *Commodore 128 Conference*
CBM-128
Discusses the Commodore C-128/C-128D computer, related hardware and software, new products, programming, news, and information.
Moderator: Jim Speerbrecher
1:154/92
Distribution: FIDONET ZONE 1 BACKBONE
Gateways: RBBS-NET VIA 1:10/8

✎ *Commodore Computer Conference*
CBM
For users of Commodore 8-bit computers.
Moderator: Russell Prater
1:3608/1
Distribution: BACKBONE

✎ *Communications Echo*
COMM
Discusses communications; topics include: modems and protocols, terminal emulation, BBS software, telephone equipment/services, more. Discussions are primarily technical.
Moderator: Bat Lang
1:382/91.3
Distribution: BACKBONE, INTERNATIONAL

✎ *COMNET BBS Software Development*
CNETDEV
For Beta testers and anyone else interested int the development of COMNET BBS software.
Moderator: Paul Di Novo
1:267/113
Distribution: 1:267/200

✎ *Compression Software Discussion*
COMPRESS
Discusses compression software of all types. General discussion as well as product comparisons, tips, tricks, and traps.
Moderator: Michael Crosson
1:203/49
Distribution: BACKBONE, INTERNATIONAL

Computer Addicts Conference
PC_ADDICT

For the true computer addict/schizoid with often humorous discussion, chat, assistance, and so on. Anything relating to computers (not too technical) or computer addiction, problems with spouses or companions and the like, is acceptable.
Moderator: Michele Stewart
   1:369/21
Distribution: BACKBONE

🖑 *Computer-Aided Design (Drafting)—
Computer-Aided Manufacturing*
   CAD-CAM
Supports Computer-Aided Design/Drafting and Computer-Aided Manufacturing.
Moderator: Stan Bimson
   1:116/32
Distribution: BACKBONE, INTERNATIONAL, RBBSNET
Gateways: RBBS VIA 1:10/8

🖑 *Computer Related Sales*
   COMPUSALE
For the advertisment and negotiation of sales of computer hardware, software, and peripherials. Non-commercial and commercial posts allowed.
Moderator: Tom Jeffrey
   1:124/2118
Distribution: NET124, NET130

🖑 *Computer RPGs and Adventure Games*
   CRPGS
For general discussion, support, reviews, hints, and so on, of computer role-playing games and adventure games.
Moderator: Steve Derby
   1:161/414
Distribution: NETMAIL REQUEST TO 1:161/414

🖑 *Computer Users in the Social Sciences*
   CUSS
For students, professionals, and interested individuals to discuss issues involving computers in the social sciences.
Moderator: Bill Allbritten
   1:11/301
Distribution: BACKBONE, 1:11/301

🖑 *Coordinator's Chatter Conference*
   COORD
For coordinators and moderators to discuss Echomail-related subjects.
Moderator: Butch Walker (ZEC)
   1:1/200
Distribution: BACKBONE

🖑 *CP/M Technical Echoconference*
   CPMTECH
Discusses and supports the CP/M family of operating systems from Digital Research, as well as emulators, work-alikes, and clones. Covers the various system software and hardware, and Fidonet and UUCP mailers for CP/M.
Moderator: Jack Winslade
   1:285/666
Distribution: BACKBONE
Gateways: ZONE 2 VIA 1:260/1; ZONE 3 VIA 1:1/3; METRONET VIA 1:104/424; THE NETWORK VIA 1:11/50

🖑 *CyberSpace and Virtual Reality*
   CYBER
Discusses cyberspace and current virtual reality news.
Moderator: Zak Smith
   1:154/736
Gateways: ZONE-2 VIA 2:253/513; ZONE-3 VIA 3:635/553

🖑 *D'Bridge Support Echo*
   DBRIDGE
Discusses the D'Bridge Electronic Mail package.
Moderator: Arthur Greenberg
   1:3601/14
Distribution: BACKBONE
Gateways: 1:105/3 >2: 3:

🖑 *Dallas/Fort Worth BBS Ads*
   DFW_BBS
For BBS sysops and users to share information on their favorite BBS.
Moderator: Christopher Molnar
   1:124/1025
Distribution: LOCAL-DFW

🖑 *Database topics, techniques, & advice*
   DBASE
For users of all database products in the dBASE language.
Moderator: John Vukovic
   1:129/26
Distribution: BACKBONE

🖑 *DEC RAINBOW Conference on Digital's
Personal Computer*
   RAINBOW
For Rainbow-relevant topics, techniques, resources, and discussion.
Moderator: David Strickler
   1:101/45
Distribution: BACKBONE, 102/138, 129/15, 101/45, 132/777, 141/491, 101/115, 360/8

🖑 *Desktop Publishing*
   DTP

Discusses all desktop publishing products.
Moderator: Ed Lawyer
1:261/1056
Distribution: ECHONET BACKBONE (ZONE 50)

↺ *DESQview Tech Conference*
DESQVIEW
Discusses DESQview and other Quarterdeck DESC products as well as how they work with different hardware and DESC software combinations.
Moderator: Mike Exner
1:204/9.234
Distribution: BACKBONE

↺ *Direct PCBoard Support Echo*
PCBSUPPORT
For direct support of PCBoard from CDC. Only those with current Salt-Air support licenses will be answered. CDC monitors all PCB licensees for compliance.
Moderator: Michele Stewart
1:369/21
Distribution: RIME,BACKBONE

↺ *Disability Sysop Forum within ADAnet*
ADASYSOP
Discusses disability topics by ADAnet system operators. Originating within ADAnet (tm).
Moderator: ADAnet
94:94/1
Distribution: ADANET INTERNATIONAL DISABILITY NETWORK
Gateways: ADANET (94:94/1)

↺ *DLG Professional Information*
DLG_INFO
For discussing topics related to the DLG Professional Bulletin Board Operating system for the Amiga.
Moderator: Mike Oliphant
1:202/503
Distribution: BACKBONE
Gateways: ZONE-2 VIA 1:140/90

↺ *Doctor Debug's Laboratory*
DR_DEBUG
For computer-related information, help, and humor for all makes of computers and all computer languages.
Moderator: Stu Turk
1:129/26.2
Distribution: BACKBONE

↺ *Domain-Gating Support Conference*
DMNGATES
For the support of the DOMAIN gating program originally written by Jim Nutt.

Moderator: Burt Juda
1:107/1
Distribution: BACKBONE 107/1 107/10 107/583 107/3 107/323 107/557 13/13
Gateways: GROUPMAIL VIA 1:107/3; USENET VIA 1:107/10

↺ *Door Games Discussion Echo*
DOORGAMES
Discusses and supports door games for door game authors, sysops, and users.
Moderator: Steve Derby
1:161/414
Distribution: BACKBONE

↺ *East Coast Programmer's Echo*
ECPROG
Open to programmers throughout the world. C, Pascal, Assembler, BASIC, RPG, are all supported.
Moderator: Brian Dunworth
1:267/54
Distribution: BACKBONE

↺ *Echo Requests*
ECHO_REQ
Announce your echos here! Not limited to just Fidonet echos.
Moderator: Aaron Schmiedel
1:124/4104
Distribution: FIDONET

↺ *EchoDor Users*
ECHODOR
Provides information about EchoDor.
Moderator: Robert Mccullough
1:116/1000
Distribution: BACKBONE

↺ *Echomail Technology Conference*
ECHO_TECH
For general, non-product-specific support and discussions relating to Echomail and other conference mail technologies. Discusses how to integrate conference mail programs.
Moderator: Joshua Lee
1:109/542
Distribution: VIA 1:109/6

↺ *EchoNet *C conference*
STARC_ECHO
An administrative conference restricted to EchoNet *Cs.
Moderator: Ed Lawyer
1:261/1056
Distribution: ECHONET BACKBONE (ZONE 50)

💲 *EchoNet's "For Sale" Conference*
FLEA_MARKET
For bargain hunting.
Moderator: Bob Tarallo
1:3603/70
Distribution: ECHONET BACKBONE (ZONE 50)

💲 *Electronic Data Interchange Conference*
EDI
For users, managers, and programmers of EDI software.
Moderator: George Dahlco
1:102/138
Distribution: USA

💲 *Electronic Publishing*
E_PUB
Discusses the writing, distribution, and reading of publications entirely on computer. Current and future trends, the tools (Hypertext), and what is needed to advance the field.
Moderator: Kief Morris
1:3603/210
Distribution: NET 3603, 377, 363

💲 *eXpress Response System support*
QMX_XRS
For User and Sysop support for XRS/XRSDoor and all XRS related programs.
Moderator: Mike Ratledge
1:372/666.1
Distribution: BACKBONE

💲 *Ezycom Development Echo*
EC_DEV
The Ezycom third-party development conference.
Moderator: Peter Davies
3:633/152
Gateways: 3:633/152 VIA 1:387/635

💲 *Ezycom Support Echo*
EC_SUPPORT
The Ezycom support conference.
Moderator: Peter Davies
3:633/152
Gateways: 3:633/152 VIA 1:387/635

💲 *FastEcho Support and Help Echo*
FE_HELP
For the FastEcho program and related programs.
Moderator: Dave Rasche
1:2380/300
Distribution: REG-11, 1:2607/103

💲 *Female Sysops Echo*
FEMALE_SYSOP
For female sysops and "wannabees." Subjects range from sysop problems to general chit-chat.

Moderator: Cyndi Collins
1:260/236
Distribution: NATIONAL

💲 *FidoBBS Topics*
FIDO
For FidoBBS sysops. Discusses all aspects of FidoBBS, current version 12U. Latest techniques, upgrades, utilities, and doors are all valid subjects. NOT a conference for discussion of Fidonet (tm); restricted to sysop participation only, although sysops of other systems are encouraged to participate.
Moderator: Ray Brown
1:135/70
Restr: SYSOP
Gateways: ZONE 8 VIA 1:10/8

💲 *FIDOBILL Software Support*
FIDOBILL
Support echo for the FIDOBILL billing/accounting program. Contains inter-user discussion and general program release announcements.
Moderator: Craig Steiner
1:104/332
Distribution: ZONE-1-BACKBONE

💲 *FIDOdoor & Utility Discussions*
FIDODOOR
Discusses FIDOdoor, FIDOdoor utilities, and support programs.
Moderator: Bill Jones
1:231/370
Distribution: BACKBONE

💲 *Fidonet & Net Problem Discussion Area*
NET-POL
Discusses and aims to correct problems within Fidonet.
Moderator: Wilma Morgel
1:105/77
Distribution: BACKBONE

💲 *Fidonet News Chat Conference*
NEWSCHAT
For users and sysops to read the Fidonet News on-line and chat about what's happening in Fidonet. No article submissions accepted. Topics limited to two weeks.
Moderator: Michele Stewart
1:369/21
Distribution: BACKBONE

💲 *Fidonet Yellow Pages*
YELLOWPAGES
Provides a place for commercial systems to place brief ads for products or services.
Moderator: Christopher Molnar
1:124/1025

⑤ *File Distribution Networks Files, Information and Links*
FILE_REQ
Files announcements from FDN Headquarter's system. Sysops only may post; users may use as read-only.
Moderator: Kevin Snively
1:116/29
Restr: SYSOP
Distribution: BACKBONE

⑤ *Filebone Hubs Conference*
FILE_MOVERS
Filebone is a file Distribution system; this echo is used to coordinate it.
Moderator: John Souvestre
1:396/1
Distribution: FILEBONE HUBS
Gateways: ZONE 2 VIA 1:107/230

⑤ *Florida Sysops Net*
FLA_NET
Sysops-only echo for Florida. Get assistance, chat, meet new sysops.
Moderator: Larry Squire
1:3620/9
Restr: SYSOP
Distribution: REGION-18 BACKBONE

⑤ *Fmail Support Echo*
FMAIL_HELP
Discusses the mail processor FMail. The author, Folkert Wijnstra, is an active participant of this echo.
Moderator: Karen Maynor
1:3640/5
Distribution: BACKBONE
Gateways: TIPTOP LINK

⑤ *For and About Amiga Computers*
AMIGA_TALK
Deals with any subject of interest to the Amiga computer operator.
Moderator: Dan McCarriar
1:261/1056.6
Distribution: ECHONET BACKBONE (ZONE 50)

⑤ *FoxPro & Fox Database Products*
FOXPRO
Discusses the FOXPRO database products and related topics.
Moderator: Mike Huntzinger
1:159/850
Distribution: BACKBONE, ZONE-1, ZONE-2, ZONE-3
Gateways: ZONE 3 VIA 1:124/4210

⑤ *FrontDoor/TosScan Support Conference*
FDECHO
For users of FrontDoor, TosScan, and related utilities.
Moderator: Joaquim Homrighausen 2:270/17
Distribution: TIPTOP, TAP, BACKBONE, ZONE-1, ZONE-2, ZONE-3, ZONE-6
Gateways: 2:310/11 VIA 1:260/340, 3:690/625 VIA 1:260/340

⑤ *Game Programmer's Support Conference*
GAME_DESIGN
Enables game programmers and players to work together to create the ultimate game. BASIC, Assembly, C, C++, Pascal, and other language programmers and players are all welcome to join in discussions about graphics, image manipulation, modeX, and more.
Moderator: Matthew Hudson
1:3622/801.4
Distribution: LOCAL-R18

⑤ *GEcho/MBUTIL Support Conference*
GECHO_HELP
For the GEcho E-Mail Processor, MBUTIL Message Base Utility and utilities related to these programs.
Moderator: Gerard van.der.Land
2:283/15
Distribution: BACKBONE

⑤ *Genealogy Software*
GENSOFT
Deals with genealogy software, hardware, utilities, more.
Moderator: Richard Pence
1:109/302
Distribution: WORLD-WIDE

⑤ *Genealogy Sysop Echo*
GENSYSOP
For sysops and co-sysops of genealogy-oriented systems.
Moderator: Wayne Silsbee
1:105/223.1
Distribution: Z1 BACKBONE; Z2

⑤ *General programming*
GEN_PROG
Discusses programming. Short routines may be shared as well. Popular languages include C, Pascal, BASIC, Assembly Language, Prolog, ADA, COBOL, and Fortran.
Moderator: Mike Wilson
1:130/28
Distribution: ECHONET BACKBONE (ZONE 50)

↺ GeoWorks Ensemble Help Echo
GEOWORKS

Provides update info, support file info, tips, and tricks concerning Geoworks Ensemble.
Moderator: Jack Cross
1:3805/13.3

↺ GoldED Help & Information Conference
GOLDED

Provides help and info on Odinn Sorensen's GoldED message reader/editor. Discussions for beginning and advanced users.
Moderator: Michael Ernst
1:115/653
Distribution: BACKBONE

↺ Golden HorseShoe File Network Administration
HS-FILE

Discusses new file networks, distribution topologies, and so on.
Moderator: Glen Hawley
1:244/101
Distribution: PRIVATE

↺ Golden HorseShoe File Network Notices
RFP

For notifying participating nodes of inbound files, new file conferences, and more.
Moderator: Glen Hawley
1:244/101
Distribution: NET244/247/250/259

↺ Great Valley Products (GVP)
GVP_ECHO

Provides support for Great Valley Products for the Amiga.
Moderator: Joe Mollica
1:273/50
Distribution: BACKBONE
Gateways: 3:633/351 VIA 1:232/301 8:7705/2 VIA 1:232/301

↺ Grunged Message Detector User Forum
GMD

For users of the Grunged Message Detector program. Discusses how to effectively use GMD; users share experiences, successes, and failures using the program.
Moderator: John Souvestre
1:396/1
Distribution: BACKBONE, INTERNATIONAL

↺ GSBBS Support Echo
GSBBS

Supports the GSBBS integrated BBS and message processing package, as well as other Jones Data Systems freeware and shareware products.

Moderator: Michelangelo Jones
1:1/124
Distribution: LOCAL-ROCHESTER-NY

↺ Help with Multi-Zone Technical Problems
ENET_TECH

The EchoNet technical sysop conference. The forum is conversational, not didactic, in nature.
Moderator: John Radford
1:261/1083
Distribution: ECHONET BACKBONE (ZONE 50)

↺ Hermes Sysops Support
HERMES_SYSOPS

For sysops using Hermes BBS software. All aspects of Hermes are discussed, including external development and use of Hermes in conjunction with Tabby.
Moderator: Steve Ebener
1:152/42

↺ Hi-Powered (i.e. Hewlett-Packard) Handhelds
HPHH

Discusses the HP handheld computers.
Moderator: Maynard Riley
1:115/678
Distribution: 1:115/678, 2:512/106, 3:711/401

↺ High-Speed Modems
HS_MODEMS

For users who need help setting up and running high-speed modems.
Moderator: Tony Wagner
1:1/92
Distribution: BACKBONE
Gateways: 1:105/2 > 2: 3: 4: 5: 6:

↺ High-Speed Transfer Modems 4-Sale
HST-SALE

For the buying and selling of used high-speed modems. Businesses are welcome to read but not advertise.
Moderator: Kris Lewis
1:202/613
Distribution: BACKBONE

↺ HST Modems from US Robotics
HST

Assists users of the US Robotics Courier HST model modem. Provides technical support for modems based on this model.
Moderator: Stephen Hendricks
1:3630/90
Distribution: BACKBONE

↺ IBM PC Discussions
PC_TECH

A technical and informative conference for users interested in the IBM-type personal computer.

Moderator: Ted Rosenberg
1:261/1056
Distribution: ECHONET BACKBONE (ZONE 50)

↺ *Information Power!*
LIBRARY
For librarians exploring technological access to information. Includes, but is not limited to, on-line databases, CD-ROM, cable access news, interactive media, automated circulation and on-line public access systems.
Moderator: Janet Murray
1:105/23
Distribution: NATIONAL BACKBONE

↺ *Interactive Video Systems Support*
IVS
For users of Interactive Video Systems' Amiga-compatible computer peripherals.
Moderator: Bart Kaplan
1:103/180
Distribution: NATIONAL
Gateways: 8:8/0 (AKA 1:10/8) RBBS NET

↺ *InterMail Support Echo*
INTERMAIL
For InterMail and other InterZone software products.
Moderator: Michele Stewart
1:369/21
Distribution: BACKBONE

↺ *International Sysop Conference (the original one)*
SYSOP
For use by sysops all over the world.
Moderator: Bob Moravsik
1:2606/583
Restr: SYSOP
Distribution: WORLDWIDE

↺ *International AutoCAD/CAD Conference*
A_CAD
Discusses AutoCAD software and related topics. Open to all levels of user. Advertisements of any type are not welcome. Users may discuss their use of any CAD-related software/hardware product or service.
Moderator: Stan Bimson
1:116/32
Distribution: BACKBONE, INTERNATIONAL, RBBSNET
Gateways: RBBS VIA 1:10/8

↺ *International C Echo*
C_ECHO
Discusses the C programming language.

Moderator: Jon Guthrie
1:106/2000.25
Distribution: BACKBONE

↺ *International CSP Sysop Echo*
CSPSYSOP
For all Fido and Non-Fido CSP sysops to chat. Provides an area to build a CSP file library for all.
Moderator: Danny Burdick
1:374/17
Distribution: BACKBONE-CSPSYSOP

↺ *International Fidonet Sysop Echo*
FN_SYSOP
For Fidonet sysops all over the world.
Moderator: Graham Broadbridge
3:711/907
Restr: SYSOP
Distribution: WORLDWIDE

↺ *International Fidonet Sysop Echo*
FNSYSOP
For Fidonet sysops all over the world.
Moderator: Matt Whelan
3:712/627
Restr: SYSOP
Distribution: WORLDWIDE

↺ *International Personal Computer Gaming*
GAMING
Discusses games for personal computers. If there is already an echo for games of a particular computer (such as Mac or Amiga), participants are encouraged to participate there to cut down traffic.
Moderator: Clint Adams
1:2607/401
Distribution: BACKBONE, ZONE-2, ZONE-3, ZONE-4, ZONE-6
Gateways: ALTERNET VIA 107/3, RBBSNET VIA 10/8

↺ *International Renegade Support*
RENEGADE
For Renegade BBS software.
Moderator: Cott Lang
1:133/501
Distribution: FIDONET

↺ *International Wordstar Users Forum*
WORDSTAR
For users of Wordstar International word processing software. General Wordstar-related conversation, tips, tricks, and tracks are emphasized for beginning and advanced users.
Moderator: Michael Crosson
1:203/49

Distribution: BACKBONE, INTERNATIONAL

🖙 *IOWA Echo*
IOWA_ECHO
For IOWA Fidonet BBS's and anyone else interested in maintaining contact with IOWA.
Moderator: Dan Buda
1:290/627
Distribution: REGION 14 HUBS, IOWA & OUT-OF-STATE

🖙 *K12net Academic Computing Conference*
K12_COMP_LIT
Curriculum-oriented discussions dealing with hardware, software, and instructional methodologies in academic and instructional computing at the elementary and secondary school levels. Not available singly. Moderators are appointed by K12net Council and coordinated by Jack Crawford. See K12.SYSOP for details.
Moderator: Jack Crawford
1:260/620

🖙 *K12net Sysops Conference*
K12.SYSOP
For K12net sysops only. <<GENERAL INFO>> K12net is privately distributed to hundreds of school-based BBS's within Fidonet zones 1, 2, and 3 as well as in USEnet and other networks. Oriented to curriculum/classroom use for introducing kindergarten thru 12th-grade students—plus teachers and administrators—to the "global village" of telecommunications. To prevent fragmentation of this community, K12net echoes are not available singly.
Moderator: Jack Crawford
1:260/620

🖙 *Laser Publishing*
LASERPUB
Focuses on typesetting and the graphic arts, both traditional and computerized, including publishing hardware and software, design techniques and aesthetics, the PostScript language, and related subjects such as multimedia publishing.
Moderator: Margo Schulter
1:203/289.7227
Distribution: BACKBONE
Gateways: ZONE-2 VIA 1:109/519

🖙 *Linux Software Discussions*
LINUX
Discusses the operating system and utilities of Linux.
Moderator: Greg Naber
1:343/34

Distribution: BACKBONE
Gateways: INTERNET VIA 1:343/94

🖙 *LNXNET Management Echoid*
LNXMANAGE
For the Management of Linux Net. File Announcements, questions concerning the distribution of Linux files, and general operational concerns. For downstream sysop use.
Moderator: Greg Naber
1:343/34
Restr: SYSOP
Distribution: BACKBONE

🖙 *Macintosh Hardware*
MACHW
For Macintosh Hardware topics.
Moderator: Norm Goodger
1:204/555
Distribution: FIDONET ZONE 1 BACKBONE

Macintosh Entertainment & Education Echo
MAC_GAMES
Dedicated to the transmission of information about the entertainment and educational qualities of the Mac.
Moderator: Bob Nordling
1:396/1
Distribution: BACKBONE, GATE ZONE-2 VIA 1:107/412, GATE RBBS VIA 1:129/34

🖙 *Macintosh For Sale/Wanted*
MACFSALE
Posts noncommercial ads for Macintosh and NeXT (and related) equipment, hardware, and software.
Moderator: Brian Hall
1:106/6268
Distribution: BACKBONE, ZONE 1

🖙 *Macintosh Items for Sale/Wanted*
MAC4SALE
Promotes hardware and software sales of any Macintosh-related item. Minimal rules, wide latitude, friendly atmosphere.
Moderator: John Gillett
1:114/27.1
Distribution: BACKBONE,ZONE-1

🖙 *Macintosh Network Communications Echo*
MACNETCOM
Discussions about LAN, WAN, modem and connectivity issues (hardware and software) as they impact use with the Macintosh computer. Encryption, decryption, and data security are also addressed.

Moderator: Scott Christensen
1:282/24
Distribution: 1:2605/611 AND 1:282/105

⑤ *Macintosh Sysop Discussion Forum*
MACSYSOP
Discusses topics that are related to the Macintosh sysop.
Moderator: Ralph Merritt
1:2605/611
Distribution: FIDONET ZONE 1 BACKBONE

⑤ *Macintosh System 7 Support*
SYSTEM7
Discusses use and programming of Macintosh System 7-specific features, software compatability, and hardware recommendations.
Moderator: Eric Larson
1:260/330
Distribution: BACKBONE

⑤ *Macintosh Telefinder BBS Forum*
MAC_TELEFINDER
Discusses TeleFinder Group Edition Host, TeleFinder/User, and TeleFinder/Pro.
Moderator: Russ Jacobson
1:233/11
Distribution: BACKBONE

⑤ *Macintosh Software Topics*
MACSW
For Macintosh software topics.
Moderator: Norm Goodger
1:204/555
Distribution: FIDONET ZONE 1 BACKBONE

⑤ *Mainframe Computing Technical Topics*
MAINFRAME
Discusses mainframe computers, operating systems, databases, program language, and third-party products.
Moderator: Bob Rudolph
1:261/999
Distribution: WORLDWIDE

⑤ *Mansion BBS & Copernicus Support Echo*
MANSION
Provides support for the Mansion BBS, Copernicus, Caprica, TagIt and other products of Software Design and ZSys Software.
Moderator: Mark Toland
1:290/2
Distribution: BACKBONE

⑤ *Maximus Developers Conference*
MAXDEV

Discusses technical aspects of Maximus, third-party utilities, message base formats, and more.
Moderator: Jesse Hollington
1:225/1.1
Restr: SYSOP
Distribution: BACKBONE
Gateways: MAXNET VIA 1:249/106

⑤ *Maximus MECCA Language Conference*
MECCA
Discusses sharing of Maximus Embedded Command Language Scripts.
Moderator: Jesse Hollington
1:225/1.1
Restr: SYSOP
Distribution: BACKBONE
Gateways: MAXNET VIA 1:249/106

⑤ *Maximus-CBCS SysOp Conference*
MUFFIN
Discusses the Maximus Computer-Based Conversation System (BBS) and related utilities.
Moderator: Jesse Hollington
1:225/1.1
Restr: SYSOP
Distribution: BACKBONE
Gateways: IMEXNET VIA 1:229/414 MAXNET VIA 1:249/106

⑤ *Meadow Opus Sysops Conference*
MEADOW
Discusses technical matters related to Opus CBCS.
Moderator: Bev Freed
1:129/104
Restr: SYSOP
Distribution: BACKBONE

⑤ *MEBBS Support Echo*
MEBBS
Official support echo for MEBBS products released by and thru by William Bowling.
Moderator: Joe Mollica
1:273/50
Gateways: 1:273/50 VIA 2:204/455

⑤ *Microsoft Windows*
WINDOWS
Discusses tips, techniques, and problems with Microsoft Windows and Windows applications.
Moderator: Tim Carter
1:142/222

⑤ *MIDI Software Programmer's Conference*
MIDI-PROGRAMMING

Discusses MIDI technical issues.
Moderator: Rick Ashworth
1:108/90.96
Distribution: INTERNATIONAL

↘ *MIDI-NET(tm) International MIDI
Conference*
MIDI-NET
For discussion of MIDI, computer music, and synthesizers.
Moderator: Rick Ashworth
1:108/90.96
Distribution: INTERNATIONAL

↘ *Midrange Systems*
MIDRANGE
Discusses the IBM Midrange Family of minicomputers, including the System/34, System/36, System/38, Application System/400, and Risc System/6000.
Moderator: David Gibbs
1:115/439
Distribution: BACKBONE
Gateways: ALTERNET VIA 1:107/583

↘ *MM/1 Users*
MM1_TECH
Enables MM/1 users to exchange ideas and get help.
Moderator: Warren Hrach
1:202/343
Distribution: BACKBONE

↘ *Modem Users of Minnesota*
MUM
For modem users in Minnesota and those interested in MUM to discuss events, activities. and chit-chat. Notices of meetings are posted.
Moderator: Erik Jacobson
1:282/31
Distribution: LOCAL-NET282

↘ *Moderator's Echo*
MODERATOR
For conference moderators to exchange ideas and information pertaining to conference operation.
Moderator: William Degnan
1:382/39
Restr: MOD-APVL
Distribution: BACKBONE

↘ *Modula-2 Programming Language*
MODULA-2
For the programming language Modula-2. Intended for programmers and implementors. Emphasis on language and standards, not particular products.

Moderator: Randy Bush
1:105/6
Distribution: WORLD
Gateways: USENET COMP.LANG.MODULA2

↘ *MPC (Multimedia for Personal Computers)*
MPC
For multimedia hardware/software discussions.
Moderator: Rick Ashworth
1:108/90
Distribution: INTERNATIONAL

↘ *MS-DOS to CBM-DOS Porting and CBM
Publications*
PCWRITE
Discusses the porting of programs from MS-DOS to CS-DOS, and more.
Moderator: Jack Vanderwhite
1:203/999
Distribution: BACKBONE

↘ *Multitasking Products and Problems*
MTASK
Deals with multitasking and multiuser OSs, systems, networks, and software.
Moderator: Thomas Lynch
1:273/225
Distribution: BACKBONE, WORLDWIDE, MULTI-ZONE
Gateways: MULTI-ZONE

↘ *Mythical Kingdom Support Echo*
MK
For all Mythical Kingdom software, including MKQwk, MKRead, MKDraw, and MKBBS.
Moderator: Andy Harris
1:3625/457
Distribution: 1:110/290, 1:3625/457, 1:151/1000, 1:151/1003
Gateways: CHATEAUNET

↘ *NAPLPS BBS VGA/EGA/CGA/Apple/etc On-
Line Graphics*
NAPLPS
For NAPLPS (North American Presentation Level Protocol Syntax) Vidotex Graphics, and how it compares with other graphical standards.
Moderator: Shawn Rhoads
1:362/614
Distribution: NET362

↘ *National DEC PDP-11 Echo*
PDP-11
Discusses the hardware and software of the Digitial Equipement Corporation PDP-11. This includes the operating systems RSTS/E, RT11, RSX, and TSX, along with third party hardware.

Moderator: Mark Buda
1:132/777
Distribution: BACKBONE

✎ *National General Technical Discussion Conference*
TECH
Discusses all technical subjects, including but not limited to computers and software, electronics, automotive technology, and all general technological and scientific subjects.
Moderator: Jim Gifford
1:203/289
Distribution: INTERNATIONAL

✎ *Net 325/VSA Discussion Area*
VT_SYSOP
A sysop discussion area for local sysops. Help with new software setups, debugging, more.
Moderator: John Antram
1:325/0

✎ *Networking and OS/2*
OS2LAN
Technical discussions on connectivity in the OS/2 environment. All aspects of connectivity and OS2 are discussed.
Moderator: Gerry Rozema
1:153/905
Distribution: BACKBONE

✎ *Networking for a Purpose General Forum*
NET_PURPOSE
Discusses networking between professionals in Forty Plus of MN and members of affiliated professional associations. Participation is restricted to members. Regional emphasis in the Upper Midwest, but no geographic limits.
Moderator: Chuck Cole
8:973/1
Restr: MOD-APVL MEMBER
Distribution: 8:973/1, 1:282/78

✎ *Networking with Novell Netware*
INTER_NOVELL
Linked to the NOVELL@SUVM.BITNET mailing list. A high-quality BITNET mailing list with many professional subscribers. Definitive answers to questions regarding Novell Netware can be found in this echo.
Moderator: Hector Mandel
1:233/15
Restr: MOD-APVL
Distribution: 1:233/15
Gateways: BITNET VIA 1:233/13

✎ *New Opus Sysop Echo*
NEWOPUS

For the new Opus Sysop who may require extra assistance in getting her/his Opus BBS running in top form.
Moderator: Christopher Baker
1:374/14
Distribution: ZONE1 BACKBONE, ZONE2, ZONE3

✎ *Odyssey Members Sysop Echo*
ODYSSEUS
Designed specifically for Odyssey sysops.
Moderator: Jerry Woody
1:3607/20
Restr: MEMBER
Distribution: FIDONET ECHOMAIL

✎ *Odyssey New File Arrival Echo. Read Only*
OD_FREQ
Designed specifically for Odyssey new file announcements.
Moderator: Jerry Woody
1:3607/20
Restr: MEMBER
Distribution: FIDONET ECHOMAIL

✎ *Odyssey Sysop Family Support Echo*
SYSOP_ORPHAN
Designed specifically for support of Odyssey sysops.
Moderator: Kathy Puckett
1:3607/20
Restr: MEMBER
Distribution: FIDONET ECHOMAIL

✎ *Official EchoNet InterMail Support Conference*
IM-SUPPORT
For InterZone products, particularly InterMail.
Moderator: Michele Stewart
1:369/21
Distribution: ECHONET BACKBONE (ZONE 50)

✎ *Offline Mail (Readers, Doors, Utils, and so on)*
OFFLINE
Discusses reading mail off-line. Topics include off-line mail readers, mail doors, formats, and the basics of running a point. Network mail-transfer mechanism discussions are also welcome. Numerous programmers of related software participate.
Moderator: Paul Knupke, Jr.
1:3603/750
Distribution: ZONE 1 BACKBONE, RBBS-NET, PLANONET (VIA QWK), ZONES 2, 3, 6
Gateways: PLANONET VIA 1:124/6300, RBBSNET VIA 1:10/8

⤷ *Online Games*
ON_LINE_GAMES
For discussion, help, and release informatio on new or updated on-line games, including fixes and other useful utilities.
Moderator: Mike Samczak
1:226/390

⤷ *OpenDoors and BBS Door/Utility Programming Conference*
OPENDOORS
Devoted to the OpenDoors C programming library, and BBS utility and door programming in general. Covers help in writing BBS door/utilitty programs, sharing of program ideas/source code, and suggestions, bug reports and information pertaining to future versions of OpenDoors.
Moderator: Brian Pirie
1:243/8

⤷ *Operating System Debate*
OS-DEBATE
Discussions and comparisons of various operating systems and systems software such as DOS, Windows, OS/2, NT, and Unix.
Moderator: Craig Swanson
1:202/514
Distribution: ZONE-1, ZONE-2
Gateways: ZONE-2 VIA 1:13/13

⤷ *OS-9 Operating System Conference*
OS9
Discusses OS-9 hardware and software on the COCO and other computers, help to new users, RiBBS, multitasking, windows, and any other discussion of OS-9.
Moderator: John Wight
1:345/200
Distribution: BACKBONE

⤷ *OS/2 BBS'ing*
OS2BBS
Discusses the operation of a BBS under the OS/2 operating system.
Moderator: Steve Lesner
1:141/261
Distribution: BACKBONE

⤷ *OS/2 Conference*
OS2
Discusses the OS/2 operating system and related topics.
Moderator: Jim Gilliland
1:141/209.3
Distribution: BACKBONE

⤷ *OS/2 Hardware*
OS2HW

Discusses hardware issues relating to the OS/2 operating system such as device drivers, hardware compatibility, installation difficulties, and hardware performance.
Moderator: Craig Swanson
1:202/514
Distribution: BACKBONE, ZONE-1, ZONE-2, ZONE-3
Gateways: ZONE-2 VIA 1:141/209

⤷ *OS/2 Programming Echo*
OS2PROG
Discusses programming under the OS/2 operating system.
Moderator: Peter Fitzsimmons
1:250/292
Distribution: BACKBONE

⤷ *OtherNets: Information on Networks Other than Fidonet*
OTHERNETS
Disseminates information about OtherNets, the multiple alternatives to Fidonet.
Moderator: Adam Michlin
1:143/313
Distribution: FIDONET ZONE 1 BACKBONE, VERVAN'S GAMING NETWORK (ZONE 45)
Gateways: ZONE 45 VIA 1:100/375

⤷ *Paragon/Star-Net Sysop Support Echo*
PARAGON_SYSOP
Provides support for Paragon/StarNet BBS software for the Amiga Computer. Also shares helpful ideas between sysops. Restricted to registered Paragon/StarNet sysops. Moderator approval required for access to this echo.
Moderator: Joe Mollica
1:273/50
Restr: MOD-APVL
Distribution: BACKBONE
Gateways: 3:633/351 VIA 1:280/314 8:7705/2 VIA 1:280/314

⤷ *PARish COMputing: Computers in the Church*
PARCOM
For authors and users of church management, bible, and Christian education/games software. Users share tricks and tips on automating elements of the Church's work, and much more.
Moderator: Lou Pascazi
1:129/75
Distribution: NON-BACKBONE
Gateways: GT:001/060 VIA 1:106/960 NETWORK:70/0 VIA 1:11/50

🖙 *Pascal*
PASCAL
Discusses the Pascal language (any dialect).
Moderator: Trevor Carlsen 3:690/644

🖙 *Pascal Programming Lessons*
PASCAL_LESSONS
For those interested in learning the Pascal programming language.
Moderator: Roger Cherry
1:3617/10
Distribution: ZONE-1

🖙 *PC Consultants Echo*
PC_CONSULT
Exchange of ideas and information between persons engaged in PC-based consulting work. This includes hardware, software, and technical writing.
Moderator: Ken Levitt
1:16/390
Distribution: FIDONET BACKBONE

🖙 *PC User Groups*
PCUG
Discussions for users who particapate in or are interested in PC user groups.
Moderator: Derek Oldfather
1:282/62
Distribution: BACKBONE

🖙 *PCTools*
PCTOOLS
Discusses and supports Central Point Software's PCTools Deluxe. Topics range from fundamental operations like simple shell and backup operations, to advanced and esoteric applications.
Moderator: John Nelson
1:105/107
Distribution: BACKBONE

🖙 *PCBComm Support Echo*
PCBCOMM
Provides support for PCBComm.
Moderator: Dean Laviolette
1:248/1
Distribution: FIDONET BACKBONE
Gateways: NANET VIA 1:248/1

🖙 *PCBoard Sysops Conference*
PCBNET
Restricted to sysops. For PCBoard BBS software; technical and basic help on setting up PCBoard with Fidonet Mailers and more.
Moderator: Michele Stewart
1:369/21

Distribution: BACKBONE, EGGNET

🖙 *PCjr Conference*
JR-MSG
Dedicated to the users of the IBM PCjr computer. Discussions are about enhancements and modifications to the PCjr.
Moderator: John Knox
1:147/7

🖙 *Piracy and Computer Crime Prevention Forum*
NOPIRACY
Discusses the various types of computer crimes and how to prevent them. The major subject is software piracy, but discussions of any type of computer crime are permitted. This echo is available to all users.
Moderator: Dan McCarriar
1:261/1056.6
Distribution: BACKBONE

🖙 *Pirating, Hacks, Trojan, and Virus Alerts*
DIRTY_DOZEN
Discussions which alert the personal computing community.
Moderator: Rick Haburne
1:116/2
Distribution: BACKBONE

🖙 *Policy 5 Assimilation, Discussion, and Implementation*
POLICY_5
For users interested in seeing a new Fidonet policy (Policy 5).
Moderator: Chip Kukuk
1:3636/3
Distribution: REQUEST
Gateways: ZONE 3 VIA 1:291/11

🖙 *Practical Peripherals Modem Support*
PPI_MODEMS
For owners and users of Practical Peripherals brand modems.
Moderator: Paul Dyer
1:203/90
Distribution: PRIVATE

🖙 *Prevention of software piracy*
PIRATES_BEWARE
Discussions on preventing software piracy and related topics.
Moderator: Dan McCarriar
1:261/1056.6
Distribution: ECHONET BACKBONE (ZONE 50)

🕈 *ProBBS Support Conference*
PROBBS
Provides support for ProBBS and related utilities, as well as other software titles from Bill Rathbone Software.
Moderator: Bill Rathbone
1:124/7002
Distribution: WORLDWIDE MULTI-ZONE ECHOMAIL

🕈 *ProBoard BBS Support Echo*
PROBOARD
A ProBoard BBS support echo. For help with running Proboard, PEX files, and general information on Proboard.
Moderator: Jim Biggs
1:282/30
Distribution: BACKBONE

🕈 *Programmers Distribution Network Echo*
PDNECHO
General messages about the Programmers Distribution Network, regarding policy changes and information.
Moderator: Janis Kracht
1:272/38
Distribution: BACKBONE

🕈 *Public Domain and Shareware Software Chatter*
PDREVIEW
Discusses software without its own echo.
Moderator: Art Hunter
1:163/131

🕈 *Public-Key Distribution Echo*
PKEY_DROP
A companion conference to PUBLIC_KEYS Echo. For the specific purpose of entering and gathering public-keys in one place within the Fidonet Echo structure.
Moderator: Christopher Baker
1:374/14
Distribution: LOCAL, ZONE1 BACKBONE, ZONE2
Gateways: 2:253/513

🕈 *Public-Key Encryption and Distribution Echo*
PUBLIC_KEYS
Discusses public-key privacy techniques and programs and the distribution of public-keys in Fidonet and other BBS and E-mail networks. Privacy issues related to encryption are also germane.

Moderator: Christopher Baker
1:374/14
Distribution: LOCAL, ZONE1 BACKBONE, ZONE2
Gateways: 2:253/513

🕈 *QEdit Echo*
QEDIT
Discusses QEdit. Q&A from SemWare (the makers of QEdit).
Moderator: Richard Blackburn
1:133/314

🕈 *QTACH2 Multiuser, Multitasking BBS and Utilities*
QTACH2
Deals with the multitasking and multiuser BBS program QTACH2 written by Sector Technologies.
Moderator: Thomas Lynch
1:273/225
Distribution: BACKBONE, WORLDWIDE, MULTI-ZONE
Gateways: MULTI-ZONE

🕈 *Quantum Software Systems LTD QNX OS*
QNX
Deals with the multitasking and multiuser OS called QNX by Quantum Software Systems.
Moderator: Thomas Lynch
1:273/225
Distribution: BACKBONE, WORLDWIDE, MULTI-ZONE
Gateways: MULTI-ZONE

🕈 *Quick-Clone BBS Support Conference*
QUIKLONE
Provides sysop support for all Hudson-style message bases, including QuickBBS, Remote Access, and SuperBBS. Material includes suggestions for and discussions about proposed advancements on the Hudson-style format for future derivations.
Moderator: Jason Steck
1:104/424
Restr: SYSOP
Distribution: METRONET
Gateways: FIDONET VIA 1:104/424

🕈 *QuickBBS Professional Sysop Forum*
QUICKPRO
For sysops only; topics related to QuickBBS or compatible programs and utilities.
Moderator: George Vandervort

1:382/8
Restr: SYSOP
Distribution: BACKBONE

⍉ *QuickBBS Support*
QUICKBBS
Supports QuickBBS sysops, new and experienced; discussions of external utilities.
Moderator: Jim Westbrook
1:382/29
Restr: SYSOP
Distribution: BACKBONE

⍉ *RAIMA Data/Object Manager Programmers Support*
RAIMA
Exchange of ideas, bug fixes, program fragments, and so on using Raima Corporation's Raima Data Manager or Raima Object Manager on any platform.
Moderator: Lawrence Chen
1:134/3002

⍉ *RBBS-PC Maple Merges Support*
RBBS_MAPLE
A support forum for RBBS-PC sysops using the Maple Merges to enhance their RBBS-PC system.
Moderator: Eddie Rowe
1:19/124
Distribution: 1:380/5

⍉ *Region 11 Operator's Conference*
REGION11
Discusses all relevant BBS/Network ideas and issues.
Moderator: Region Coordinator
1:11/0
Restr: SYSOP MOD-APVL
Distribution: REGION-11-ONLY

⍉ *Region 12 Policy Creation/Update Conference*
R12POLICY
For Region 12 policy discussions.
Moderator: Glen Hawley
1:244/101
Distribution: REGION 12

⍉ *Region 14 Echo Coordinator Conference*
14_REC
Exchanges information between Fidonet Region 14 RC/REC and NC's/NEC's and the working sysops.
Moderator: Dan Buda
1:1/214
Distribution: FIDONET REGION 14 ONLY

⍉ *Region 18 Election Discussion & Candidate Statement Echo*
R18ELECT
A sysop-only forum for discussion of election mechanics and procedures in Region 18. Gives office candidates a place to meet the voters, make platform statements, and answer voter questions.
Moderator: Christopher Baker
1:374/14
Distribution: REGION18

⍉ *Region 18 For Sale*
4SALE18
Region 18's echo for buying and selling merchandise. Commercial ads are tolerated at moderator's discretion. Prohibited ads include firearms and explosives, pornography and multi-level marketing schemes.
Moderator: Jeff Cochran
1:371/26
Distribution: REGION 18 BACKBONE

⍉ *Region 19 Coord Conference*
R19COORD
For discussion among Region 19 coordinators regarding the distribution of Echomail and voting procedures within the Region. Only Region 19 coordinators (RC, REC, Region Hubs,NCs, NECs, Net Hubs) are allowed access.
Moderator: Bob Davis
1:19/0
Restr: MOD-APVL MEMBER
Distribution: REGION-19

⍉ *Region 19 Sysops*
R19SYSOP
For Fidonet Region 19 sysops. Region 19 events and happenings, as well as policies and politics are discussed here.
Moderator: Bob Davis
1:19/0
Restr: SYSOP
Distribution: REGION 19

⍉ *Remote Access Multi-Node Sysops Echo*
RA_MULTI
Dedicated to sharing technical know-how on running a multi-node Remote Access BBS.
Moderator: Ed Borghi
1:260/224
Distribution: NATIONAL

◆ *Remote Access Support Echo*
RA_SUPPORT
Deals with the RemoteAccess BBS system and its interaction with related utilities.
Moderator: Bruce Bodger
1:170/400
Distribution: BACKBONE, SIGNET, RBBSNET, NETWORK, TAP, AND SO ON

◆ *Remote Echo Control Software Support*
REC_SUPPORT
Questions, problems, suggestions, and any other comments for the support and improvement of Remote Echo Control.
Moderator: Dan Fitch
1:104/435
Distribution: BACKBONE, FIDONET
Gateways: METRONET VIA 1:104/424

◆ *RemoteAccess Utilities Echo*
RA_UTIL
Discusses programs designed to work with the RemoteAccess Bulletin Board System.
Moderator: Karen Maynor
1:3640/5
Distribution: BACKBONE

◆ *Required Conference for EchoNet Moderators*
ECHOMOD
An administrative conference for EchoNet moderators.
Moderator: Michele Stewart
1:369/21
Distribution: ECHONET BACKBONE (ZONE 50)

◆ *RiBBS (CoCo/OS9) Sysop Support*
RIBBS
Deals with RiBBS software. Popular topics include help in setup, finding solutions to operating difficulties, and exchanging ideas concerning new utilities and games made to augment RiBBS.
Moderator: Charles West
1:147/61
Distribution: BACKBONE,ZONE-1

◆ *RoboBoard EGA/VGA BBS Support Echo*
ROBO
For RoboBoard users, sysops, and third-party developers using the RBO Interface. Covers any mailers/echotossers in the RBO interface.
Moderator: Jason Dever
1:163/420
Distribution: ZONE-1

◆ *Rybbs Sysop Echo*
RYBBSOP

For support of Rybbs BBS software.
Moderator: John Steele
1:273/910
Restr: SYSOP

◆ *Searchlight BBS Support Echo*
SEARCHLIGHT
Supports Searchlight BBS and related software. Searchlight sysops, users, and third-party software authors are welcome.
Moderator: Wayne Robinson
1:2604/269
Distribution: BACKBONE
Gateways: SL_NET VIA 1:3632/4 FAMILY_NET VIA 1:11/50

◆ *Shareware Products Discussion Forum*
SHAREWRE
For users interested in discussing the various software programs distributed as shareware as well as the moral, ethical and philosophical issues surrounding shareware and its distribution.
Moderator: Kent Anderson
1:382/91
Distribution: BACKBONE, INTERNATIONAL

◆ *Sirius Support*
SIRIUS
Provides support for the Sirius Fidonet Message Base Manager (current Sirius version: 1.0ya), and a forum for all those interested in influencing its future.
Moderator: Maynard Riley
1:115/678
Distribution: BACKBONE

◆ *Solutions for Setting Up On-Line Games*
GAMES_SETUP
Discusses problems for EchoNet sysops in attempting to set up on-line games.
Moderator: Mike Gurski
1:261/1062
Distribution: ECHONET BACKBONE (ZONE 50)

◆ *Spitfire BBS Support Echo*
SPITFIRE
Discusses the Spitfire BBS by Mike Woltz and relevant programs.
Moderator: Ira Lichtenstein
1:272/43
Distribution: BACKBONE

◆ *SquishMail Users*
TUB

Discusses the SquishMail conference processor and related utilities.
Moderator: Jesse Hollington
1:225/1
Restr: SYSOP
Distribution: BACKBONE
Gateways: MAXNET VIA 1:249/106

✒ *Star-Net Sysop Support Echo*
STAR-NET
Supports StarNet BBS software for the Amiga Computer. Also facilitates sharing helpful ideas between sysops. This echo restricted to registered StarNet sysops.
Moderator: Joe Mollica
1:273/50
Gateways: 1:273/50 VIA 2:204/455

✒ *Steel City Buy and Sell Forum*
BNSFORUM
For local network buy and sell activities.
Moderator: Glen Hawley
1:244/101
Distribution: NET244

✒ *Steel City Local Users Echo*
STEELCITY
For local network user chatter.
Moderator: Glen Hawley
1:244/101
Distribution: NET244

✒ *Steel City Net Sysop Conference*
SYSOP244
For local network announcements, elections, and chatter.
Moderator: Glen Hawley
1:244/101
Distribution: NET244-ONLY

✒ *Support Echo and General Door Development Forum*
DOORWARE
Support for door development.
Moderator: Ronnie Toth
1:135/71
Distribution: BACKBONE

✒ *Support Echo for the FidoPCB, PCBoard-Fido Interface*
FIDOPCB
For the FidoPCB Mail Tosser/Scanner. Serves as a forum for discussing the program, troubleshooting, tips, ideas for future releases, and some talk about interaction with the Front Ends supported by the program.
Moderator: George Silberstern
1:273/214
Gateways: ZONE-2 VIA 1:273/214

✒ *Suprafax Modem Conference*
SUPRAFAX
For information pertaining to the Suprafax modem v.32 and v.32b, internal and external, init strings fax, BBS mailer information, and so on.
Moderator: Wayne Boyd
1:153/763
Gateways: ZONE-2 VIA 1:153/763

✒ *SURVNET Sysop Conference*
SURVNET_SYSOP
A restricted-access conference for SURVNET sysops.
Moderator: Dave Skinner
1:105/711
Distribution: SURVNET

✒ *Sysops Interested in Disability Advances*
HANDY.SYSOP
"The Sysops Who Care." For sysops to discuss disability-accessibility issues related and unrelated to BBS's.
Moderator: Les Barr
1:147/41
Restr: SYSOP
Distribution: FIDO BACKBONE
Gateways: ADANET

✒ *T.A.G. BBS (Multinode) Support Echo*
TAGMULTI
A support Echo for T.A.G. BBS (Multinode).
Moderator: Randy Goebel
1:120/36
Distribution: BACKBONE

✒ *T.A.G. BBS Support Echo*
TAG
A support Echo for T.A.G. BBS software.
Moderator: Randy Goebel
1:120/36
Distribution: BACKBONE

✒ *T.A.G. Doors Support Echo*
TAGDOORS
A support Echo for T.A.G. BBS external doors.
Moderator: Debra Ackley
1:159/100
Distribution: BACKBONE

✒ *Tandy Color Computer Conference*
COCO
Discusses COCO hardware and software, technical advice, help to new COCO users, COCO related companies, COCO club, the COCO in Fidonet, and anything else regarding the COCO.
Moderator: John Wight
1:345/200
Distribution: BACKBONE

⑤ Tandy Model 1000 Personal Computers Users Conference
MOD1000

For the Tandy 1000 owner. Discussions include hardware upgrades, software compatibility, and general problems encountered in the everyday use of the Tandy Computer.
Moderator: Paul Casey
1:343/117
Distribution: BACKBONE

⑤ Tandy Model 2000 Echomail Conference
TAND2000

Discusses Tandy's discontinued Model 2000.
Moderator: Bob Juge
1:106/2000
Distribution: BACKBONE

⑤ Tandy TRS-80 Conference
TRS-MOD134

Discusses the TRS-80 Models I, III, 4x computers, related hardware, software, and TRSLink TRS-80 Magazine.
Moderator: Jim Howard
1:363/18
Distribution: BACKBONE, FAMILYNET
Gateways: FAMILYNET VIA 1:11/50

⑤ TBBS Sysops Support
TBBS

For TBBS sysops. Conference topics include TBBS and associated utilities, including applications support from third-party vendors.
Moderator: Steve Sherwick
1:282/7
Restr: SYSOP
Distribution: BACKBONE

⑤ Technical Q&A GroupMail Conference
ASKATECH

For technical Q&A GroupMail and any related topics.
Moderator: Burt Juda
1:107/1
Distribution: 107/1 107/10 107/583 107/323 107/517 107/557

⑤ TeleBit Modem & PEP Topics
PEP

Centers on the use and applications of modems produced by or using the PEP modulation scheme of the TeleBit Corporation.
Moderator: Nolan Lee
1:390/5
Distribution: BACKBONE
Gateways: CAAMORA VIA 3:711/453

⑤ Telegard BBS Support
TG_SUPPORT

Support for the Telegard BBS.
Moderator: Martin Pollard
1:120/187
Restr: SYSOP MOD-APVL
Distribution: RESTRICTED

⑤ Telemate
TM

Discusses the Telemate communications program.
Moderator: Kerry Pierce
1:2202/0
Distribution: FIDONET

⑤ Telix Users Information Exchange
TELIX

For users of the TELIX communications program produced by deltaComm Development.
Moderator: Zack Jones
1:387/641.1
Distribution: BACKBONE, INTERNATIONAL

⑤ Texas Instruments Topics
TI-ECHO

Discusses the TI-99/4A computer and related clones. Issues include programming, hardware hacking, material sources, and general 99'er topics.
Moderator: Walter Tietjen
1:151/114
Distribution: BACKBONE
Gateways: RBBS-NET VIA 1:10/8 WWIVNET VIA 1:376/94

⑤ The Amiga AMOS Programming Echo
AMIGA_AMOS

For AMOS programmers and users.
Moderator: Bruce Berna
1:154/77
Distribution: REGION 11

⑤ The Amiga Desktop Publishing Conference
AMIGA_DESKTOP

Discusses the various Amiga desktop publishing programs.
Moderator: Michael DeBerg
1:232/301
Distribution: BACKBONE

⑤ The Amiga Distribution System Announcements
ADS_ANNOUNCE

A support network for Amiga. ADS provides support for the Amiga with File Echos Message Echos.
Moderator: Michael DeBerg
1:232/301
Distribution: ADS, FILEBONE
Gateways: ***E-2 VIA 1:232/301, ZONE-3 VIA 1:232/301

⑨ *The Amiga Distribution System Coordinators Discussion Conference*
ADS_COORD
For ADS coordinators only.
Moderator: Michael DeBerg
1:232/301
Restr: MOD-APVL
Distribution: ADS
Gateways: ZONE-2 VIA 1:232/301, ZONE-3 VIA 1:232/301

⑨ *The Amiga Distribution System Discussion Conference*
ADS_CHAT
A message echo for general discussion.
Moderator: Michael DeBerg
1:232/301
Distribution: ADS
Gateways: ZONE-2 VIA 1:232/301, ZONE-3 VIA 1:232/301

⑨ *The Region 11 Chat Echo*
R11CHAT
For Fidonet Region 11.
Moderator: REC Region 11
1:1/211
Distribution: REGION 11

⑨ *TransAmiga BBS Support Conference*
TRANSAMIGA
Support for TransAmiga, a shareware BBS package for the Amiga.
Moderator: Tim Aston
1:247/192
Distribution: NORTH AMERICA, EUROPE, AUSTRALIA

⑨ *Turbo Pascal For Windows (Borland) Technical/Programming*
TPWTECH
Covers technical topics for TPW programmers—an advanced echo for established programmers.
Moderator: Scott Samet
1:135/990
Restr: MOD-APVL
Distribution: Z1 BACKBONE

⑨ *TurBoard BBS Support and Suggestions*
TURBOARD
A technical ideas and support forum for the TurBoard BBS system.
Moderator: Shawn Rhoads
1:362/614
Distribution: NET362
Gateways: 362/614 260/216 286/705 387/1201

⑨ *UltraBBS Support Conference*
ULTRASUP

Support for UltraBBS.
Moderator: Jon Hutto
1:124/6016
Distribution: ECHOMAIL

⑨ *Unicorn Software Support Conference*
UNICORN
Provides support of the shareware programs produced by Unicorn Software Ltd.
Moderator: Charles Schell
1:231/290
Distribution: 1:231/290

⑨ *Usenet-Fidonet Gating Conference*
UFGATE
Supports systems gating mail and newsgroups between Fidonet and RFC-822 technologies.
Moderator: Hostmaster
1:1/31
Distribution: BACKBONE NNTP
Gateways: GROUPMAIL VIA 1:107/3, USENET VIA 1:107/10

⑨ *VAX conference for users and managers of Digital's VAX*
VAX
For users and managers of VAX, VMS, and other DEC topics.
Moderator: GEORGE DAHLCO
1:102/138
Distribution: BACKBONE, 102/138, 129/15, 101/45, 132/777, 141/491, 101/115, 360/8

⑨ *Video Making! Video Toaster, and home and semi-pro video.*
VIDEO
Pertains to desktop video-making. Camcorders, VCRs, genlocks, computerized edit controllers, and other video-making equipment are discussed.
Moderator: Ron Kramer
1:228/13
Distribution: BACKBONE

⑨ *Visual Basic Programming Echo*
VISUAL_BASIC
Visual Basic programmers exchange information on techniques for Microsoft Visual Basic. Discussions concerning both the Windows and DOS versions are encouraged. Open to all user levels.
Moderator: Margaret Romao
1:3603/150
Distribution: BACKBONE

⑨ *Welmat Support Echo*
WELMAT
Provides technical support for this CopyLeft product. Bug reports, suggestions, and

difficulties. Much of the discussion relates to future development of the package.
Moderator: Russell McOrmond
1:1/139.1
Distribution: BACKBONE

↺ *Wide-Area Network Distributed Database Applications*
WAN_DBASE
Development and implementation of a Wide-area (FTN) database environment supporting a distributed database.
Moderator: Bill Freeman
94:2050/1
Distribution: ADANET INTERNATIONAL DISABILITY NETWORK
Gateways: ADANET (94:94/1)

↺ *WILDCAT! BBS Sysop Conference*
WILDCAT
For WILDCAT! sysops to get help and to discuss WILDCAT! and third-party utility issues with other sysops.
Moderator: Derek Koopowitz
1:161/502
Restr: SYSOP
Distribution: BACKBONE

↺ *Windows/NT and Win32 Discussions Echo*
WIN32
Dedicated to the discussion of Windows/NT and the Win32 Application Programming Interface.
Moderator: Mark Ryland
1:109/170
Distribution: WORLD

↺ *WoodyWare Door Support Echo*
WOODYWARE
For bulletin board doors written by Jerry Woody.
Moderator: Jerry Woody
1:3607/20
Restr: MOD-APVL
Distribution: FIDONET ECHOMAIL, DOORNET

↺ *WordPerfect Corporation Products Advanced Echo*
PERFECT_MACRO
Advanced questions in regard to WPC programs, shareware utilities, macros, third-party programs, and so on.
Moderator: Bob Germer
8:950/10
Distribution: FIDONET BACKBONE, RBBSNET
Gateways: FIDONET VIA 8:950/10, RBBSNET VIA 1:10/8

↺ *WordPerfect Corporation Products Basic Echo*
PERFECT
Discusses basic questions in regard to WPC programs.
Moderator: Bob Germer
8:950/10
Distribution: FIDONET BACKBONE, RBBSNET
Gateways: FIDONET VIA 8:950/10, RBBSNET VIA 1:10/8

↺ *Wordperfect TOOL Development Support for Anyone!*
WP-TOOLS
Provides TOOL development support for extensions and customizations. For the novice, accomplished artist, instructor, student, technical writer, or other user.
Moderator: Chuck Cole
8:973/1
Distribution: BACKBONES OF RBBS-NET, FIDO ZONES 1 & 2
Gateways: RBBS-NET VIA 8:8/0, ZONE 1 VIA 1:13/13, ZONE 2 VIA 2:2/508

↺ *Wordperfect WRITERS Support for Anyone!*
WP-CRAFT
For the novice, accomplished artist, technical writer, clerk, author, student, instructor, or other word crafter. The topic includes using Wordperfect products, or anything compatible with their files.
Moderator: Chuck Cole
8:973/1
Distribution: BACKBONES OF RBBS-NET, FIDO ZONES 1 & 2
Gateways: RBBS-NET VIA 8:8/0, ZONE 1 VIA 1:13/13, ZONE 2 VIA 2:2/508,

↺ *WorldPol Development Echo*
WORLDPOL
For discussion about the Worldwide Fidonet Policy Proposal. All Fidonet sysops welcome.
Moderator: Pablo Kleinman
1:102/631
Restr: SYSOP
Distribution: BACKBONE, ZONE 2 BACKBONE, ZONE 6 BACKBONE, ZONE 4

↺ *WorldWide Opus Consortium Software Developers Forum*
WOC-AIDS
For users of software compatible with the Opus CBCS program Wynn Wagner III.
Moderator: Steve Shapiro
1:101/440
Distribution: BACKBONE, INTERNATIONAL

X00 FOSSIL User Echomail Conference
X00_USER
Discusses Ray Gwinn's X00 DOS FOSSIL driver,
Moderator: Bob Juge
1:106/2000
Distribution: BACKBONE

**YaleBBS Advanced Graphic-Style BBS
Support and YES Emulation**
YALEBBS_SUPPORT
Support for YaleBBS.
Moderator: Ernest Yale
1:167/125

ZMail Support Conference
ZMAIL
Supports all versions of the ZMail Echomail
processor.
Moderator: Jason Steck
1:104/424
Distribution: FIDONET, METRONET,
FMLYNET
Gateways: METRONET VIA 1:104/
424@FIDONET.ORG, FMLYNET VIA 1:104/
424@FIDONET.ORG

**Zone 1 Echomail Coordinator Echo
Conference**
ZEC
For Fidonet sysops to discuss Echomail-related
subjects with the Z1EC.
Moderator: Butch Walker (ZEC)
1:1/200
Distribution: BACKBONE

Zone 1 Election Echo
Z1_ELECTION
Discusses Zone 1 ZC/ZEC elections, policy
elections, and elections in Fidonet in general.
Moderator: Dan Buda
1:290/627
Distribution: BACKBONE

ZyXEL Modem Echo
ZYXEL
Covers ZyXEL modem basics.
Moderator: Honlin Lue
6:720/13
Distribution: WORLDWIDE (ZONE 1, ZONE 2
AND ZONE 6)

\{Commo\} Program
\{COMMO\}
Discusses Fred Brucker's \{Commo\},comms
program.
Moderator: Tim Spofford
1:105/99
Distribution: ZONE 1

A Telephone Industry Watchdog Conference
PHONES
Keeps abreast of the proposed tariffs and
regulatory agencies affecting the BBS
community.
Moderator: John Summers
1:124/4103
Distribution: USA & CANADA

Dogfight Echomail Conference
DOGFIGHT
For users of Dogfight and programs interfaced
with Spitfire bulletin board software.
Moderator: Vernon Merck
1:161/306
Distribution: BACKBONE

Usenet

Discussions of site administration policies.
comp.admin.policy

Artificial intelligence discussions.
comp.ai

All aspects of neural networks.
comp.ai.neural-nets

**Natural language and knowledge
representation. (Moderated)**
comp.ai.nlang-know-rep

Philosophical aspects of artificial intelligence.
comp.ai.philosophy

**Artificial intelligence applied to shells.
(Moderated)**
comp.ai.shells

Spreadsheets on various platforms.
comp.apps.spreadsheets

Computer architecture.
comp.arch

**Storage system issues, both hardware and
software.**
comp.arch.storage

**Descriptions of public access archives.
(Moderated)**
comp.archives

**Issues relating to computer archive
administration.**
comp.archives.admin

**All aspects of computer bulletin board
systems.**
comp.bbs.misc

- The Waffle BBS and USENET system on all platforms.
  `comp.bbs.waffle`

- Discussion of benchmarking techniques and results.
  `comp.benchmarks`

- Binary-only postings for Acorn machines. (Moderated)
  `comp.binaries.acorn`

- Encoded public domain programs in binary. (Moderated)
  `comp.binaries.amiga`

- Binary-only postings for the Apple II computer.
  `comp.binaries.apple2`

- Binary-only postings for the Atari ST. (Moderated)
  `comp.binaries.atari.st`

- Binary-only postings for IBM PC/MS-DOS. (Moderated)
  `comp.binaries.ibm.pc`

- Announcements related to IBM PC archive sites.
  `comp.binaries.ibm.pc.archives`

- Discussions about IBM PC binary postings.
  `comp.binaries.ibm.pc.d`

- Requests for IBM PC and compatible programs.
  `comp.binaries.ibm.pc.wanted`

- Encoded Macintosh programs in binary. (Moderated)
  `comp.binaries.mac`

- Binaries for use under the OS/2 ABI. (Moderated)
  `comp.binaries.os2`

- Reports of Unix version 2BSD related bugs.
  `comp.bugs.2bsd`

- Reports of Unix version 4BSD related bugs.
  `comp.bugs.4bsd`

- Bug reports/fixes for BSD Unix. (Moderated)
  `comp.bugs.4bsd.ucb-fixes`

- General Unix bug reports and fixes (incl V7, uucp).
  `comp.bugs.misc`

- Reports of USG (System III, V, etc.) bugs.
  `comp.bugs.sys5`

- Users of Cadence Design Systems products.
  `comp.cad.cadence`

- Cognitive engineering.
  `comp.cog-eng`

- Compiler construction, theory, and so on. (Moderated)
  `comp.compilers`

- Data compression algorithms and theory.
  `comp.compression`

- Discussions about data compression research.
  `comp.compression.research`

- Database and data management issues and theory.
  `comp.databases`

- Informix database management software discussions.
  `comp.databases.informix`

- Issues relating to INGRES products.
  `comp.databases.ingres`

- The SQL database products of the Oracle Corporation.
  `comp.databases.oracle`

- Discussing advances in database technology.
  `comp.databases.theory`

- Forum for discussion of Cell Relay-based products.
  `comp.dcom.cell-relay`

- Fax hardware, software, and protocols.
  `comp.dcom.fax`

- The Integrated Services Digital Network (ISDN).
  `comp.dcom.isdn`

- Discussions of the Ethernet/IEEE 802.3 protocols.
  `comp.dcom.lans.ethernet`

- Discussions of the FDDI protocol suite.
  `comp.dcom.lans.fddi`

- Local area network hardware and software.
  `comp.dcom.lans.misc`

🖑 *Data communications hardware and software.*
comp.dcom.modems

🖑 *Selecting and operating data communications servers.*
comp.dcom.servers

🖑 *Info on Cisco routers and bridges.*
comp.dcom.sys.cisco

🖑 *Telecommunications digest. (Moderated)*
comp.dcom.telecom

🖑 *Archived public-domain documentation. (Moderated)*
comp.doc

🖑 *Lists of technical reports. (Moderated)*
comp.doc.techreports

🖑 *Digital Signal Processing using computers.*
comp.dsp

🖑 *Computer science education.*
comp.edu

🖑 *EMACS editors of different flavors.*
comp.emacs

🖑 *Typefonts—design, conversion, use, and so on.*
comp.fonts

🖑 *Computer graphics, art, animation, image processing.*
comp.graphics

🖑 *The Application Visualization System.*
comp.graphics.avs

🖑 *The Explorer Modular Visualisation Environment (MVE).*
comp.graphics.explorer

🖑 *Highly technical computer graphics discussion. Moderated.*
comp.graphics.research

🖑 *Info on scientific visualization.*
comp.graphics.visualization

🖑 *Software and hardware for shared interactive environments.*
comp.groupware

🖑 *Issues related to human-computer interaction (HCI).*
comp.human-factors

🖑 *Any discussion about information systems.*
comp.infosystems

🖑 *All aspects of Geographic Information Systems.*
comp.infosystems.gis

🖑 *The Z39.50-based WAIS full-text search system.*
comp.infosystems.wais

🖑 *Discussing electronic libraries. (Moderated)*
comp.internet.library

🖑 *Interactive videodiscs—uses, potential, etc.*
comp.ivideodisc

🖑 *Discussion about ADA.*
comp.lang.ada

🖑 *Discussion about APL.*
comp.lang.apl

🖑 *Discussion about C.*
comp.lang.c

🖑 *The object-oriented C++ language.*
comp.lang.c++

🖑 *Common Lisp Object System discussions.*
comp.lang.clos

🖑 *The object-oriented Eiffel language.*
comp.lang.eiffel

🖑 *Discussion about Forth.*
comp.lang.forth

🖑 *Discussion about FORTRAN.*
comp.lang.fortran

🖑 *Discussion about functional languages.*
comp.lang.functional

🖑 *The Hermes language for distributed applications.*
comp.lang.hermes

🖑 *IDL and PV-Wave language discussions.*
comp.lang.idl-pvwave

🖑 *Discussion about LISP.*
comp.lang.lisp

🖑 *Discussing Apple's Macintosh Common Lisp.*
comp.lang.lisp.mcl

🖑 *Different computer languages not specifically listed.*
comp.lang.misc

🖑 *Discussion about Modula-2.*
comp.lang.modula2

🖑 *Discussion about the Modula-3 language.*
comp.lang.modula3

- *The Objective-C language and environment.*
  `comp.lang.objective-c`

- *Discussion about Pascal.*
  `comp.lang.pascal`

- *Discussion of Larry Wall's Perl system.*
  `comp.lang.perl`

- *The PostScript Page Description Language.*
  `comp.lang.postscript`

- *Discussion about PROLOG.*
  `comp.lang.prolog`

- *The Scheme programming language.*
  `comp.lang.scheme`

- *Info & announcements from ACM SIGPLAN. (Moderated)*
  `comp.lang.sigplan`

- *Discussion about Smalltalk 80.*
  `comp.lang.smalltalk`

- *The Tcl programming language and related tools.*
  `comp.lang.tcl`

- *Discussing Verilog and PLI.*
  `comp.lang.verilog`

- *VHSIC Hardware Description Language, IEEE 1076/87.*
  `comp.lang.vhdl`

- *Laser printers, hardware & software. (Moderated)*
  `comp.laser-printers`

- *Large scale integrated circuits.*
  `comp.lsi`

- *Testing of electronic circuits.*
  `comp.lsi.testing`

- *Discussion and fixes for ELM mail system.*
  `comp.mail.elm`

- *Gatewayed from the Internet header-people list.*
  `comp.mail.headers`

- *Various maps, including UUCP maps. (Moderated)*
  `comp.mail.maps`

- *The UCI version of the Rand Message Handling system.*
  `comp.mail.mh`

- *General discussions about computer mail.*
  `comp.mail.misc`

- *The Mail User's Shell (MUSH).*
  `comp.mail.mush`

- *Configuring and using the BSD sendmail agent.*
  `comp.mail.sendmail`

- *Mail in the uucp network environment.*
  `comp.mail.uucp`

- *General topics about computers not covered elsewhere.*
  `comp.misc`

- *Interactive multimedia technologies of all kinds.*
  `comp.multimedia`

- *Announcements of new products of interest. (Moderated)*
  `comp.newprod`

- *Object-oriented programming and languages.*
  `comp.object`

- *Topics about the Association for Computing Machinery.*
  `comp.org.acm`

- *Digital Equipment Computer Users' Society newsgroup.*
  `comp.org.decus`

- *FidoNews Digest, official news of FidoNet Assoc. (Moderated)*
  `comp.org.fidonet`

- *Issues and announcements about the IEEE and its members.*
  `comp.org.ieee`

- *The International Student Society for Neural Networks.*
  `comp.org.issnnet`

- *Talk about/for the The Sun User's Group.*
  `comp.org.sug`

- *USENIX Association events and announcements.*
  `comp.org.usenix`

- *Finding lodging during Usenix conferences.*
  `comp.org.usenix.roomshare`

- *Discussion and support of the Coherent operating system.*
  `comp.os.coherent`

- *Discussion about the CP/M operating system.*
  `comp.os.cpm`

꙳ *The free Unix-clone for the 386/486, LINUX.*
comp.os.linux

꙳ *The MACH OS from CMU & other places.*
comp.os.mach

꙳ *Discussion of Tanenbaum's MINIX system.*
comp.os.minix

꙳ *General OS-oriented discussion not carried elsewhere.*
comp.os.misc

꙳ *Speculation and debate about Microsoft Windows.*
comp.os.ms-windows.advocacy

꙳ *Announcements relating to Windows. (Moderated)*
comp.os.ms-windows.announce

꙳ *Applications in the Windows environment.*
comp.os.ms-windows.apps

꙳ *General discussions about Windows issues.*
comp.os.ms-windows.misc

꙳ *Programming Microsoft Windows.*
comp.os.ms-windows.programmer.misc

꙳ *Development tools in Windows.*
comp.os.ms-windows.programmer.tools

꙳ *32-bit Windows programming interfaces.*
comp.os.ms-windows.programmer.win32

꙳ *Installing and configuring Microsoft Windows.*
comp.os.ms-windows.setup

꙳ *Discussion of applications that run under MS-DOS.*
comp.os.msdos.apps

꙳ *QuarterDeck's Desqview and related products.*
comp.os.msdos.desqview

꙳ *Miscellaneous topics about MS-DOS machines.*
comp.os.msdos.misc

꙳ *GeoWorks PC/GEOS and PC/GEOS-based packages.*
comp.os.msdos.pcgeos

꙳ *Programming MS-DOS machines.*
comp.os.msdos.programmer

꙳ *Supporting and flaming OS/2.*
comp.os.os2.advocacy

꙳ *Discussions of applications under OS/2.*
comp.os.os2.apps

꙳ *Miscellaneous topics about the OS/2 system.*
comp.os.os2.misc

꙳ *Networking in OS/2 environments.*
comp.os.os2.networking

꙳ *Programming OS/2 machines.*
comp.os.os2.programmer

꙳ *Discussions about the os9 operating system.*
comp.os.os9

꙳ *Operating systems and related areas. (Moderated)*
comp.os.research

꙳ *DEC's VAX line of computers & VMS.*
comp.os.vms

꙳ *The VxWorks real-time operating system.*
comp.os.vxworks

꙳ *The XINU operating system from Purdue (D. Comer).*
comp.os.xinu

꙳ *Massively parallel hardware/software. (Moderated)*
comp.parallel

꙳ *Discussing patents of computer technology. (Moderated)*
comp.patents

꙳ *Peripheral devices.*
comp.periphs

꙳ *Discussion of SCSI-based peripheral devices.*
comp.periphs.scsi

꙳ *Programming issues that transcend languages and OSs.*
comp.programming

꙳ *Applebus hardware & software.*
comp.protocols.appletalk

꙳ *Networking with IBM mainframes.*
comp.protocols.ibm

꙳ *The ISO protocol stack.*
comp.protocols.iso

꙳ *The Kerberos authentication server.*
comp.protocols.kerberos

- *Info about the Kermit package. Moderated.*
  `comp.protocols.kermit`
- *Various forms and types of FTP protocol.*
  `comp.protocols.misc`
- *Discussion about the Network File System protocol.*
  `comp.protocols.nfs`
- *Discussion of the Internet Point to Point Protocol.*
  `comp.protocols.ppp`
- *TCP and IP network protocols.*
  `comp.protocols.tcp-ip`
- *TCP/IP for IBM(-like) personal computers.*
  `comp.protocols.tcp-ip.ibmpc`
- *Issues related to real-time computing.*
  `comp.realtime`
- *The nature of research in Japan. (Moderated)*
  `comp.research.japan`
- *Risks to the public from computers & users. (Moderated)*
  `comp.risks`
- *All aspects of robots and their applications.*
  `comp.robotics`
- *Security issues of computers and networks.*
  `comp.security.misc`
- *Simulation methods, problems, uses. (Moderated)*
  `comp.simulation`
- *The impact of technology on society. (Moderated)*
  `comp.society`
- *Computer technology in developing countries.*
  `comp.society.development`
- *Computer folklore & culture, past & present. (Moderated)*
  `comp.society.folklore`
- *Events in technology affecting future computing.*
  `comp.society.futures`
- *Effects of technology on privacy. (Moderated)*
  `comp.society.privacy`
- *The Khoros X11 visualization system.*
  `comp.soft-sys.khoros`
- *Software engineering and related topics.*
  `comp.software-eng`
- *Source code-only postings for the AT&T 3b1. (Moderated)*
  `comp.sources.3b1`
- *Source code-only postings for the Acorn. (Moderated)*
  `comp.sources.acorn`
- *Source code-only postings for the Amiga. (Moderated)*
  `comp.sources.amiga`
- *Source code and discussion for the Apple II. (Moderated)*
  `comp.sources.apple2`
- *Source code-only postings for the Atari ST. (Moderated)*
  `comp.sources.atari.st`
- *Bug reports, fixes, discussion for posted sources.*
  `comp.sources.bugs`
- *For any discussion of source postings.*
  `comp.sources.d`
- *Postings of recreational software. (Moderated)*
  `comp.sources.games`
- *Bug reports and fixes for posted game software.*
  `comp.sources.games.bugs`
- *Programs for the HP48 and HP28 calculators. (Moderated)*
  `comp.sources.hp48`
- *Software for the Apple Macintosh. (Moderated)*
  `comp.sources.mac`
- *Posting of software. (Moderated)*
  `comp.sources.misc`
- *Source code evaluated by peer review. (Moderated)*
  `comp.sources.reviewed`
- *Software for Sun workstations. (Moderated)*
  `comp.sources.sun`
- *Postings of complete, Unix-oriented sources. (Moderated)*
  `comp.sources.unix`

꙳ *Requests for software and fixes.*
comp.sources.wanted

꙳ *Software for the X windows system.*
Moderated.
comp.sources.x

꙳ *Languages and methodologies for formal*
specification.
comp.specification

꙳ *Discussion about the formal specification*
notation Z.
comp.specification.z

꙳ *Discussion about C language standards.*
comp.std.c

꙳ *Discussion about C++ language, library,*
standards.
comp.std.c++

꙳ *Discussion about international standards.*
comp.std.internat

꙳ *Discussion about various standards.*
comp.std.misc

꙳ *Discussion for the X11.1 committee on*
Mumps. (Moderated)
comp.std.mumps

꙳ *Discussion for the P1003 committee on Unix.*
(Moderated)
comp.std.unix

꙳ *Software components and related technology.*
comp.sw.components

꙳ *Discussion and support of AT&T 7300/3B1/*
UnixPC.
comp.sys.3b1

꙳ *Discussion on Acorn and ARM-based*
computers.
comp.sys.acorn

꙳ *Info and discussion about Alliant computers.*
comp.sys.alliant

꙳ *Why an Amiga is better than XYZ.*
comp.sys.amiga.advocacy

꙳ *Announcements about the Amiga.*
(Moderated)
comp.sys.amiga.announce

꙳ *Miscellaneous applications.*
comp.sys.amiga.applications

꙳ *Music, MIDI, speech synthesis, other sounds.*
comp.sys.amiga.audio

꙳ *Methods of getting bytes in and out.*
comp.sys.amiga.datacomm

꙳ *Various hardware & software emulators.*
comp.sys.amiga.emulations

꙳ *Discussion of games for the Commodore*
Amiga.
comp.sys.amiga.games

꙳ *Charts, graphs, pictures, and so on.*
comp.sys.amiga.graphics

꙳ *Amiga computer hardware, Q&A, reviews,*
etc.
comp.sys.amiga.hardware

꙳ *Group for newcomers to Amigas.*
comp.sys.amiga.introduction

꙳ *Where to find it, prices, and so on.*
comp.sys.amiga.marketplace

꙳ *Discussions not falling in another Amiga*
group.
comp.sys.amiga.misc

꙳ *Animations, video, & multimedia.*
comp.sys.amiga.multimedia

꙳ *Developers & hobbyists discuss code.*
comp.sys.amiga.programmer

꙳ *Reviews of Amiga software, hardware.*
(Moderated)
comp.sys.amiga.reviews

꙳ *Apollo computer systems.*
comp.sys.apollo

꙳ *Discussion about Apple II micros.*
comp.sys.apple2

꙳ *Discussion about 8-bit Atari micros.*
comp.sys.atari.8bit

꙳ *Discussion about 16-bit Atari micros.*
comp.sys.atari.st

꙳ *Technical discussions of Atari ST hard/*
software.
comp.sys.atari.st.tech

꙳ *Discussions about AT&T microcomputers.*
comp.sys.att

꙳ *Discussion about Commodore micros.*
comp.sys.cbm

꙳ *The Concurrent/Masscomp line of computers.*
(Moderated)
comp.sys.concurrent

꙳ *Discussions about DEC computer systems.*
comp.sys.dec

- *DEC Micros (Rainbow, Professional 350/380).*
  comp.sys.dec.micro
- *Encore's MultiMax computers.*
  comp.sys.encore
- *Discussion about Hewlett-Packard equipment.*
  comp.sys.hp
- *Hewlett-Packard's HP48 and HP28 calculators.*
  comp.sys.hp48
- *The IBM PC, PC-XT, and PC-AT. (Moderated)*
  comp.sys.ibm.pc.digest
- *Games for IBM PCs and compatibles.*
  comp.sys.ibm.pc.games
- *XT/AT/EISA hardware, any vendor.*
  comp.sys.ibm.pc.hardware
- *Discussion about IBM personal computers.*
  comp.sys.ibm.pc.misc
- *Topics related to IBM's RT computer.*
  comp.sys.ibm.pc.rt
- *Hardware and software aspects of PC sound cards.*
  comp.sys.ibm.pc.soundcard
- *Microchannel hardware, any vendor.*
  comp.sys.ibm.ps2.hardware
- *Discussions about Intel systems and parts.*
  comp.sys.intel
- *The ISIS distributed system from Cornell.*
  comp.sys.isis
- *Laptop (portable) computers.*
  comp.sys.laptops
- *Discussion about 6809s.*
  comp.sys.m6809
- *Discussion about 68k's.*
  comp.sys.m68k
- *Discussion about 68k-based PCs. (Moderated)*
  comp.sys.m68k.pc
- *Discussion about 88k-based computers.*
  comp.sys.m88k
- *Important notices for Macintosh users. (Moderated)*
  comp.sys.mac.announce
- *Discussions of Macintosh applications.*
  comp.sys.mac.apps
- *Discussion of Macintosh communications.*
  comp.sys.mac.comm
- *Database systems for the Apple Macintosh.*
  comp.sys.mac.databases
- *Apple Macintosh: info & uses, but no programs. Moderated.*
  comp.sys.mac.digest
- *Discussions of games on the Macintosh.*
  comp.sys.mac.games
- *Macintosh hardware issues & discussions.*
  comp.sys.mac.hardware
- *The Macintosh Hypercard: info & uses.*
  comp.sys.mac.hypercard
- *General discussions about the Apple Macintosh.*
  comp.sys.mac.misc
- *Discussion by people programming the Apple Macintosh.*
  comp.sys.mac.programmer
- *Discussions of Macintosh system software.*
  comp.sys.mac.system
- *Postings of "I want XYZ for my Mac."*
  comp.sys.mac.wanted
- *Mentor Graphics products & the Silicon Compiler System.*
  comp.sys.mentor
- *Systems based on MIPS chips.*
  comp.sys.mips
- *Discussion about computers of all kinds.*
  comp.sys.misc
- *Discussion about NCR computers.*
  comp.sys.ncr
- *The NeXT religion.*
  comp.sys.next.advocacy
- *Announcements related to the NeXT computer system. (Moderated)*
  comp.sys.next.announce
- *Discussing the physical aspects of NeXT computers.*
  comp.sys.next.hardware

𝔖 *NeXT hardware, software and jobs.*
comp.sys.next.marketplace

𝔖 *General discussion about the NeXT computer system.*
comp.sys.next.misc

𝔖 *NeXT related programming issues.*
comp.sys.next.programmer

𝔖 *Function, use, and availability of NeXT programs.*
comp.sys.next.software

𝔖 *Discussions related to NeXT system administration.*
comp.sys.next.sysadmin

𝔖 *Discussion of Novell Netware products.*
comp.sys.novell

𝔖 *National Semiconductor 32000 series chips.*
comp.sys.nsc.32k

𝔖 *Super-powered calculators the palm of your hand.*
comp.sys.palmtops

𝔖 *Interacting with computers through pen gestures.*
comp.sys.pen

𝔖 *Prime Computer products.*
comp.sys.prime

𝔖 *Proteon gateway products.*
comp.sys.proteon

𝔖 *Pyramid 90x computers.*
comp.sys.pyramid

𝔖 *Ridge 32 computers and ROS.*
comp.sys.ridge

𝔖 *Sequent systems (Balance and Symmetry).*
comp.sys.sequent

𝔖 *Silicon Graphics's Iris workstations and software.*
comp.sys.sgi

𝔖 *Sun system administration issues and questions.*
comp.sys.sun.admin

𝔖 *Sun announcements and Sunergy mailings. Moderated.*
comp.sys.sun.announce

𝔖 *Software applications for Sun computer systems.*
comp.sys.sun.apps

𝔖 *Sun Microsystems hardware.*
comp.sys.sun.hardware

𝔖 *Miscellaneous discussions about Sun products.*
comp.sys.sun.misc

𝔖 *People looking for Sun products and support.*
comp.sys.sun.wanted

𝔖 *CCI 6/32, Harris HCX/7, & Sperry 7000 computers.*
comp.sys.tahoe

𝔖 *Discussion about Tandy computers: new & old.*
comp.sys.tandy

𝔖 *Discussion about Texas Instruments.*
comp.sys.ti

𝔖 *The Transputer computer and OCCAM language.*
comp.sys.transputer

𝔖 *Sperry, Burroughs, Convergent and Unisys systems.*
comp.sys.unisys

𝔖 *Xerox 1100 workstations and protocols.*
comp.sys.xerox

𝔖 *The Zenith Z-100 (Heath H-100) family of computers.*
comp.sys.zenith.z100

𝔖 *All sorts of terminals.*
comp.terminals

𝔖 *Text processing issues and methods.*
comp.text

𝔖 *Technology & techniques of desktop publishing.*
comp.text.desktop

𝔖 *Desktop publishing with FrameMaker.*
comp.text.frame

𝔖 *Applications and use of Interleaf software.*
comp.text.interleaf

𝔖 *ISO 8879 SGML, structured documents, markup languages.*
comp.text.sgml

𝔖 *Discussion about the TeX and LaTeX systems & macros.*
comp.text.tex

𝔖 *Information Retrieval topics. (Moderated)*
comp.theory.info-retrieval

❧ *Administering a Unix-based system.*
comp.unix.admin

❧ *IBM's version of Unix.*
comp.unix.aix

❧ *Minix, SYSV4 and other *nix on an Amiga.*
comp.unix.amiga

❧ *The version of Unix for Apple Macintosh II computers.*
comp.unix.aux

❧ *Discussion of Berkeley Software Distribution Unix.*
comp.unix.bsd

❧ *Discussions on hacking Unix internals.*
comp.unix.internals

❧ *Unix on mainframes and in large networks.*
comp.unix.large

❧ *Various topics that don't fit other groups.*
comp.unix.misc

❧ *MS-DOS running under Unix by whatever means.*
comp.unix.msdos

❧ *Q&A for people programming under Unix.*
comp.unix.programmer

❧ *Unix neophytes group.*
comp.unix.questions

❧ *Using and programming the Unix shell.*
comp.unix.shell

❧ *Unix System V (not XENIX) on the 286.*
comp.unix.sysv286

❧ *Versions of System V (not XENIX) on Intel 80386-based boxes.*
comp.unix.sysv386

❧ *Discussions about DEC's Ultrix.*
comp.unix.ultrix

❧ *Questions for only true Unix wizards.*
comp.unix.wizards

❧ *General discussions regarding XENIX (except SCO).*
comp.unix.xenix.misc

❧ *XENIX versions from the Santa Cruz Operation.*
comp.unix.xenix.sco

❧ *Computer viruses & security. (Moderated)*
comp.virus

❧ *The InterViews object-oriented windowing system.*
comp.windows.interviews

❧ *Various issues about windowing systems.*
comp.windows.misc

❧ *Window systems under MS-DOS.*
comp.windows.ms

❧ *Writing apps for MS Windows.*
comp.windows.ms.programmer

❧ *Sun Microsystems' NeWS window system.*
comp.windows.news

❧ *Discussion about the Open Look GUI.*
comp.windows.open-look

❧ *Discussion about the X Window System.*
comp.windows.x

❧ *Getting and using, not programming, applications for X.*
comp.windows.x.apps

❧ *Discussion of the X toolkit.*
comp.windows.x.intrinsics

❧ *The PHIGS extension of the X Window System.*
comp.windows.x.pex

❧ *Computers and computer equipment for sale.*
misc.forsale.computers

❧ *Discussing the legal climate of the computing world.*
misc.legal.computing

❧ *For testing of network software.*
misc.test

❧ *Comments directed to news administrators.*
news.admin

❧ *Calls for papers and conference announcements. (Moderated)*
news.announce.conferences

❧ *General announcements of interest to all. (Moderated)*
news.announce.important

❧ *Calls for newgroups & announcements of same. (Moderated)*
news.announce.newgroups

❧ *Explanatory postings for new users. (Moderated)*
news.announce.newusers

❧ *Repository for periodic USENET articles. (Moderated)*
news.answers

❧ *Postings of system down times and interruptions.*
news.config

❧ *The future technology of network news systems.*
news.future

❧ *Discussions and lists of newsgroups.*
news.groups

❧ *News-related statistics and lists. (Moderated)*
news.lists

❧ *Maps relating to USENET traffic flows. (Moderated)*
news.lists.ps-maps

❧ *Discussions of USENET itself.*
news.misc

❧ *Postings of new site announcements.*
news.newsites

❧ *Q & A for users new to the Usenet.*
news.newusers.questions

❧ *VMS B-news software from Australian National University.*
news.software.anu-news

❧ *Discussion about B-news-compatible software.*
news.software.b

❧ *Discussion about the "nn" news reader package.*
news.software.nn

❧ *Notesfile software from the University of Illinois.*
news.software.notes

❧ *Discussion of software used to read network news.*
news.software.readers

❧ *Comments directed to system administrators.*
news.sysadmin

❧ *Different methods of data en/decryption.*
sci.crypt

❧ *Administration of the VMSnet newsgroups.*
vmsnet.admin

❧ *General announcements of interest to all. (Moderated)*
vmsnet.announce

❧ *Orientation info for new users. (Moderated)*
vmsnet.announce.newusers

❧ *Discussion of DECUS Local User Groups and related issues.*
vmsnet.decus.lugs

❧ *Jobs sought/offered, workplace and employment related issues.*
vmsnet.employment

❧ *VMS internals, MACRO-32, Bliss, and so on, gatewayed to MACRO32 list.*
vmsnet.internals

❧ *Other electronic mail software.*
vmsnet.mail.misc

❧ *PMDF email system, gatewayed to ipmdf mailing list.*
vmsnet.mail.pmdf

❧ *MX email system from RPI, gatewayed to MX mailing list.*
vmsnet.mail.mx

❧ *General VMS topics not covered elsewhere.*
vmsnet.misc

❧ *Other desktop integration software.*
vmsnet.networks.desktop.misc

❧ *DEC Pathworks desktop integration software.*
vmsnet.networks.desktop.pathworks

❧ *DECmcc and related software.*
vmsnet.networks.management.decmcc

❧ *Other network management solutions.*
vmsnet.networks.management.misc

❧ *General networking topics not covered elsewhere.*
vmsnet.networks.misc

❧ *CMU-TEK TCP/IP package, gatewayed to* cmu-tek-tcp+@andrew.cmu.edu.
vmsnet.networks.tcp-ip.cmu-tek

❧ *Other TCP/IP solutions for VMS.*
vmsnet.networks.tcp-ip.misc

❧ *TGV's Multinet TCP/IP, gatewayed to info-multinet.*
vmsnet.networks.tcp-ip.multinet

⑨ DEC's VMS/Ultrix Connection (or TCP/IP services for VMS) product.
vmsnet.networks.tcp-ip.ucx

⑨ The Wollongong Group's WIN-TCP TCP/IP software.
vmsnet.networks.tcp-ip.wintcp

⑨ PDP-11 hardware and software, gatewayed to info-pdp11.
vmsnet.pdp-11

⑨ Source code postings ONLY. (Moderated)
vmsnet.sources

⑨ Discussion about or requests for sources.
vmsnet.sources.d

⑨ Recreational software postings.
vmsnet.sources.games

⑨ VMS system management.
vmsnet.sysmgt

⑨ Test messages.
vmsnet.test

⑨ TPU language and applications, gatewayed to info-tpu.
vmsnet.tpu

⑨ DECUS uucp software, gatewayed to vmsnet mailing list.
vmsnet.uucp

⑨ 3B Distribution configuration.
u3b.config

⑨ 3B Miscellaneous Discussions.
u3b.misc

⑨ Sources for AT&T 3B systems.
u3b.sources

⑨ B Technical Discussions.
u3b.tech 3

⑨ 3B Distribution Testing.
u3b.test

⑨ Applications of Artificial Intelligence to Education.
comp.ai.edu

⑨ Artificial Intelligence Vision Research. (Moderated)
comp.ai.vision

⑨ Hyperchannel networks within an IP network.
comp.dcom.lans.hyperchannel

⑨ Topics related to computerized text editing.
comp.editors

⑨ Writing instruction in computer-based classrooms.
comp.edu.composition

⑨ News from the Electronic Frontiers Foundation. (Moderated)
comp.org.eff.news

⑨ Discussion of EFF goals, strategies, etc.
comp.org.eff.talk

⑨ Programming in IBM System/370 Assembly Language.
comp.lang.asm370

⑨ The CLU language & related topics.
comp.lang.clu

⑨ The CSI MacForth programming environment.
comp.lang.forth.mac

⑨ Topics related to the ICON programming language.
comp.lang.icon

⑨ IDL (Interface Description Language) related topics.
comp.lang.idl

⑨ The Franz Lisp programming language.
comp.lang.lisp.franz

⑨ The XLISP language system.
comp.lang.lisp.x

⑨ The REXX command language.
comp.lang.rexx

⑨ The Scheme language environment.
comp.lang.scheme.c

⑨ Visual programming languages.
comp.lang.visual

⑨ Electrical computer-aided design.
comp.lsi.cad

⑨ Multimedia Mail.
comp.mail.multi-media

⑨ Applications of computers in music research.
comp.music

⑨ Topics related to Data General's AOS/VS.
comp.os.aos

⑨ Discussion of Amethyst, CP/M-80 software package.
comp.os.cpm.amethyst

❧ *The 4DOS command processor for MS-DOS.*
comp.os.msdos.4dos

❧ *Topics related to the PDP-11 RSTS/E operating system.*
comp.os.rsts

❧ *The V distributed operating system from Stanford.*
comp.os.v

❧ *Information on printers.*
comp.periphs.printers

❧ *The ISO Development Environment.*
comp.protocols.iso.dev-environ

❧ *X400 mail protocol discussions.*
comp.protocols.iso.x400

❧ *X400 mail gateway discussions. (Moderated)*
comp.protocols.iso.x400.gateway

❧ *Topics related to PCNET (a personal computer network).*
comp.protocols.pcnet

❧ *The Simple Network Management Protocol.*
comp.protocols.snmp

❧ *Topics related to Domain Style names.*
comp.protocols.tcp-ip.domains

❧ *The network time protocol.*
comp.protocols.time.ntp

❧ *Announcements from CERT about security. (Moderated)*
comp.security.announce

❧ *The Andrew system from CMU.*
comp.soft-sys.andrew

❧ *The NeXTstep computing environment.*
comp.soft-sys.nextstep

❧ *Announcements about standards activities. (Moderated)*
comp.std.announce

❧ *Control Data Corporation Computers (for example, Cybers).*
comp.sys.cdc

❧ *Handheld computers and programmable calculators.*
comp.sys.handhelds

❧ *Anything related to the Intel 310.*
comp.sys.intel.ipsc310

❧ *Northstar microcomputer users.*
comp.sys.northstar

❧ *Supercomputers.*
comp.sys.super

❧ *The Texas Instruments Explorer.*
comp.sys.ti.explorer

❧ *Heath terminals and related Zenith products.*
comp.sys.zenith

❧ *The BB&N BitGraph Terminal.*
comp.terminals.bitgraph

❧ *AT&T Dot Mapped Display Terminals (5620 and BLIT).*
comp.terminals.tty5620

❧ *Theoretical Computer Science.*
comp.theory

❧ *Discussion of all aspects of cellular automata.*
comp.theory.cell-automata

❧ *Ergodic Theory and Dynamical Systems.*
comp.theory.dynamic-sys

❧ *Topics related to self-organization.*
comp.theory.self-org-sys

❧ *Cray computers and their operating systems.*
comp.unix.cray

❧ *Discussions about the Solaris operating system.*
comp.unix.solaris

❧ *X Consortium announcements. (Moderated)*
comp.windows.x.announce

❧ *The Motif GUI for the X Window System.*
comp.windows.x.motif

❧ *The Network News Transfer Protocol.*
news.software.nntp

❧ *The Vectrex game system.*
rec.games.vectrex

❧ *A science fiction "fanzine." (Moderated)*
rec.mag.fsfnet

❧ *Any topic relating to biotechnology.*
sci.bio.technology

❧ *Numerical analysis.*
sci.math.num-analysis

- *Discussions within the scope of metaphilosophy.*
  sci.philosophy.meta
- *The neutral international language Esperanto.*
  soc.culture.esperanto
- *The DDN Management Bulletin from NIC.DDN.MIL. (Moderated)*
  ddn.mgt-bulletin
- *The DDN Newsletter from NIC.DDN.MIL (Moderated)*
  ddn.newsletter
- *Status and announcements from the Project. (Moderated)*
  gnu.announce
- *Bourne Again SHell bug reports and suggested fixes. (Moderated)*
  gnu.bash.bug
- *Announcements about the GNU Chess program.*
  gnu.chess
- *Announcements about GNU Emacs. (Moderated)*
  gnu.emacs.announce
- *GNU Emacs bug reports and suggested fixes. (Moderated)*
  gnu.emacs.bug
- *News reading under GNU Emacs using Weemba's Gnews.*
  gnu.emacs.gnews
- *News reading under GNU Emacs using GNUS (in English).*
  gnu.emacs.gnus
- *User queries and answers.*
  gnu.emacs.help
- *ONLY (please!) C and Lisp source code for GNU Emacs.*
  gnu.emacs.sources
- *Bug reports on the Emacs VM mail package.*
  gnu.emacs.vm.bug
- *Information about the Emacs VM mail package.*
  gnu.emacs.vm.info
- *VMS port of GNU Emacs.*
  gnu.emacs.vms
- *The Epoch X11 extensions to Emacs.*
  gnu.epoch.misc
- *Announcements about the GNU C++ Compiler. (Moderated)*
  gnu.g++.announce
- *g++ bug reports and suggested fixes. (Moderated)*
  gnu.g++.bug
- *GNU C++ compiler (G++) user queries and answers.*
  gnu.g++.help
- *g++ library bug reports/suggested fixes. (Moderated)*
  gnu.g++.lib.bug
- *Announcements about the GNU C Compiler. (Moderated)*
  gnu.gcc.announce
- *GNU C Compiler bug reports/suggested fixes. (Moderated)*
  gnu.gcc.bug
- *GNU C Compiler (gcc) user queries and answers.*
  gnu.gcc.help
- *gcc/g++ DeBugger bugs and suggested fixes. (Moderated)*
  gnu.gdb.bug
- *GNU Ghostscript interpreter bugs. (Moderated)*
  gnu.ghostscript.bug
- *GNU's Not Usenet administration and configuration.*
  gnu.gnusenet.config
- *GNU's Not Usenet alternative hierarchy testing.*
  gnu.gnusenet.test
- *Bugs in the GNU roff programs. (Moderated)*
  gnu.groff.bug
- *Serious discussion about GNU and freed software.*
  gnu.misc.discuss
- *Bugs in GNU Smalltalk. (Moderated)*
  gnu.smalltalk.bug
- *GNU utilities bugs (e.g., make, gawk. ls). (Moderated)*
  gnu.utils.bug

🕲 *To discuss software on gnu.emacs.sources*
gnu.emacs.help

🕲 *ClariNet Newsbytes Information service Newsgroups.*
clari.nb

🕲 *Computer industry, applications and developments. (Moderated)*
clari.tw.computers

🕲 *Regular reports on computer & technology stock prices. (Moderated)*
clari.tw.stocks

🕲 *Weekly summary of Newsbytes computer news. (Moderated)*
clari.nb.index

🕲 *Newsbytes Apple/Macintosh news. (Moderated)*
clari.nb.apple

🕲 *Newsbytes business & industry news. (Moderated)*
clari.nb.business

🕲 *Newsbytes general computer news. (Moderated)*
clari.nb.general

🕲 *Newsbytes legal and government computer news. (Moderated)*
clari.nb.govt

🕲 *Newsbytes IBM PC World coverage. (Moderated)*
clari.nb.ibm

🕲 *Newsbytes new product reviews. (Moderated)*
clari.nb.review

🕲 *Newsbytes telecom & online industry news. (Moderated)*
clari.nb.telecom

🕲 *Newsbytes new developments & trends. (Moderated)*
clari.nb.trends

🕲 *Newsbytes Unix news. (Moderated)*
clari.nb.unix

🕲 *Three-dimensional imaging.*
alt.3d

🕲 *Computer BBS systems & software.*
alt.bbs

🕲 *Ads for various computer BBSs.*
alt.bbs.ads

🕲 *For BBS operators*
alt.bbs.allsysop

🕲 *BBS systems accessible via the Internet.*
alt.bbs.internet

🕲 *Postings of regional BBS listings.*
alt.bbs.lists

🕲 *Discussion about regional BBS listings.*
alt.bbs.lists.d

🕲 *Sort of an oxymoron.*
alt.best.of.internet

🕲 *Sound, text and graphics data rolled in one.*
alt.binaries.multimedia

🕲 *Discussions about picture postings.*
alt.binaries.pictures.d

🕲 *Gigabytes of copyright violations.*
alt.binaries.pictures.erotica

🕲 *Discussing erotic copyright violations.*
alt.binaries.pictures.erotica.d

🕲 *Copyright violations featuring mostly males.*
alt.binaries.pictures.erotica.male

🕲 *Copyright violations featuring mostly females.*
alt.binaries.pictures.erotica.female

🕲 *Discussion about huge image files. (Moderated)*
alt.binaries.pictures.fine-art.d

🕲 *Postings of huge image files. (Moderated)*
alt.binaries.pictures.fine-art.graphics

🕲 *Even more huge files. (Moderated)*
alt.binaries.pictures.fine-art.digitized

🕲 *Cheaper just to send the program parameters.*
alt.binaries.pictures.fractals

🕲 *Have we saturated the network yet?*
alt.binaries.pictures.misc

🕲 *"Eccchh, that last one was sick..."*
alt.binaries.pictures.tasteless

🕲 *Sounding off.*
alt.binaries.sounds.d

🕲 *Ngghhh! MMMMMMM! uuuhhhnnnnnOOOOOHHHhhhhh...*
alt.binaries.sounds.erotica

🕲 *Computer-aided design.*
alt.cad

- CAD as practiced by customers of Autodesk.
  alt.cad.autocad

- Discussions of optical storage media.
  alt.cd-rom

- Relationship between programming and stone axes.
  alt.cobol

- Academic freedom issues related to computers. (Moderated)
  alt.comp.acad-freedom.news

- Academic freedom issues related to computers.
  alt.comp.acad-freedom.talk

- Alternative subnet discussions and connectivity.
  alt.config

- Council of Sysops & Users Against Rate Discrimination.
  alt.cosuard

- Cybernetics and systems.
  alt.cyb-sys

- High-tech low-life.
  alt.cyberpunk

- Literary virtual reality in a cyberpunk hangout.
  alt.cyberpunk.chatsubo

- Cybernizing the universe.
  alt.cyberpunk.movement

- Cyberspace and cyberpunk technology.
  alt.cyberpunk.tech

- Cyberspace and how it should work.
  alt.cyberspace

- Cyberpunk epic.
  alt.cybertoon

- The ultimate in moderated newsgroups. (Moderated)
  alt.dev.null

- A computer fantasy environment (like Usenet is).
  alt.dragons-inn

- Discussion of the gopher information service.
  alt.gopher

- Usenet spraypainters and their documenters.
  alt.graffiti

- Some prefer this to comp.graphics.
  alt.graphics

- Discussion of pixmap utilities.
  alt.graphics.pixutils

- Descriptions of projects currently under development. (Moderated)
  alt.hackers

- Discussion of hypertext—uses, transport, etc.
  alt.hypertext

- The Industrial Computing Society.
  alt.industrial

- Internet Relay Chat material.
  alt.irc

- Assembly languages of various flavors.
  alt.lang.asm

- The language That Would Not Die.
  alt.lang.basic

- Discussion of the future of the C programming language
  alt.lang.cfutures

- A joke language with a real compiler.
  alt.lang.intercal

- The ML and SML symbolic languages.
  alt.lang.ml

- The TECO editor language.
  alt.lang.teco

- For people who don't like to rmgroup/ newgroup things.
  alt.newgroup

- Privacy issues in cyberspace.
  alt.privacy

- People who believe computing is "real life."
  alt.religion.computers

- Emacs. Umacs. We all macs.
  alt.religion.emacs

- For the people who like to rmgroup/newgroup things.
  alt.rmgroup

- Programming the Sound Blaster card for IBM PC clones.
  alt.sb.programmer

- Postings about the Computer Underground. (Moderated)
  alt.society.cu-digest

⑨ *Alternative source code, unmoderated. Caveat Emptor.*
alt.sources

⑨ *Technically-oriented Amiga PC sources.*
alt.sources.amiga

⑨ *Discussion of posted sources.*
alt.sources.d

⑨ *Pointers to source code in alt.sources. (Moderated)*
alt.sources.index

⑨ *Reposted patches from non-bugs groups.*
alt.sources.patches

⑨ *Requests for source code.*
alt.sources.wanted

⑨ *Code and talk to show off the Amiga.*
alt.sys.amiga.demos

⑨ *AmigaUUCP.*
alt.sys.amiga.uucp

⑨ *Patches for AmigaUUCP.*
alt.sys.amiga.uucp.patches

⑨ *Support for Intergraph machines.*
alt.sys.intergraph

⑨ *The X windows XView toolkit.*
alt.toolkits.xview

⑨ *Reupholster your news reader.*
alt.usenet.recovery

⑨ *Bit Newgroups discussions.*
bit.admin

⑨ *Discussions Relating to BitNet/Usenet.*
bit.general

⑨ *User services list.*
bit.listserv.advise-l

⑨ *IBM AIX discussion list.*
bit.listserv.aix-l

⑨ *APPC discussion list.*
bit.listserv.appc-l

⑨ *Apple II list.*
bit.listserv.apple2-l

⑨ *Applications under BITNET.*
bit.listserv.applicat

⑨ *IBM 370 Assembly Programming discussions.*
bit.listserv.asm370

⑨ *Banyan Vines Network Software Discussions.*
bit.listserv.banyan-l

⑨ *Campus-Size LAN Discussion Group. (Moderated)*
bit.listserv.big-lan

⑨ *Chargeback of computer resources.*
bit.listserv.billing

⑨ *Computer and Health Discussion List.*
bit.listserv.c+health

⑨ *Candle Products Discussion List.*
bit.listserv.candle-l

⑨ *CD-ROM on Local Area Networks.*
bit.listserv.cdromlan

⑨ *VM/SP CMS Pipelines Discussion List.*
bit.listserv.cmspip-l

⑨ *Control System Group Network.*
bit.listserv.csg-l

⑨ *CUMREC-L Administrative computer use.*
bit.listserv.cumrec-l

⑨ *Campus-Wide E-mail discussion List.*
bit.listserv.cw-email

⑨ *Campus-Wide Information Systems.*
bit.listserv.cwis-l

⑨ *CDC Computer discussion.*
bit.listserv.cyber-l

⑨ *C/370 Discussion List.*
bit.listserv.c370-l

⑨ *Database Administration.*
bit.listserv.dasig

⑨ *Discussion on the use of the dBase IV.*
bit.listserv.dbase-l

⑨ *DB2 Data Base discussion list.*
bit.listserv.db2-l

⑨ *Digital Equipment Corporation News List.*
bit.listserv.decnews

⑨ *DECUS Education Software Library Discussions.*
bit.listserv.dectei-l

⑨ *Domains Discussion Group.*
bit.listserv.domain-l

⑨ *EARN Technical Group.*
bit.listserv.earntech

⑨ *Electronic Data Interchange Issues.*
bit.listserv.edi-l

⑨ *Discussion of Ethics in Computing.*
bit.listserv.ethics-l

✋ *FRACTAL Discussion List.*
  `bit.listserv.frac-l`

✋ *Computer Games List.*
  `bit.listserv.games-l`

✋ *BITNIC GGUIDE List.*
  `bit.listserv.gguide`

✋ *Info-Amiga List.*
  `bit.listserv.i-amiga`

✋ *IBM Higher Education Consortium.*
  `bit.listserv.ibm-hesc`

✋ *IBM Mainframe Discussion List.*
  `bit.listserv.ibm-main`

✋ *BITNIC IBM-NETS List.*
  `bit.listserv.ibm-nets`

✋ *IBM TCP/IP List.*
  `bit.listserv.ibmtcp-l`

✋ *Protocol Converter List.*
  `bit.listserv.ibm7171`

✋ *Infonets Redistribution.*
  `bit.listserv.infonets`

✋ *Innovative Interfaces Online Public Access.*
  `bit.listserv.innopac`

✋ *ISN Data Switch Technical Discussion Group.*
  `bit.listserv.isn`

✋ *JES2 Discussion group.*
  `bit.listserv.jes2-l`

✋ *BITNIC JNET-L List.*
  `bit.listserv.jnet-l`

✋ *VMCENTER Components Discussion List.*
  `bit.listserv.l-vmctr`

✋ *BITNIC LIAISON.*
  `bit.listserv.liaison`

✋ *Software Licensing List.*
  `bit.listserv.license`

✋ *Link failure announcements.*
  `bit.listserv.linkfail`

✋ *Forum on LISTSERV.*
  `bit.listserv.lstsrv-l`

✋ *BITNIC MAIL-L List.*
  `bit.listserv.mail-l`

✋ *MAIL/MAILBOOK subscription List.*
  `bit.listserv.mailbook`

✋ *NETNWS-L Netnews List.*
  `bit.listserv.netnws-l`

✋ *NEW-LIST - New List Announcements. (Moderated)*
  `bit.listserv.new-list`

✋ *NeXT Computer List.*
  `bit.listserv.next-l`

✋ *Node Management.*
  `bit.listserv.nodmgt-l`

✋ *Novell LAN Interest Group.*
  `bit.listserv.novell`

✋ *OMR Scanner Discussion.*
  `bit.listserv.omrscan`

✋ *Public-Access Computer System Forum. (Moderated)*
  `bit.listserv.pacs-l`

✋ *IBM 3812/3820 Tips and Problems Discussion List.*
  `bit.listserv.page-l`

✋ *PageMaker for Desktop Publishers.*
  `bit.listserv.pagemakr`

✋ *PMDF Distribution List.*
  `bit.listserv.pmdf-l`

✋ *Relay Users Forum.*
  `bit.listserv.relusr-l`

✋ *REXX Programming Discussion List.*
  `bit.listserv.rexxlist`

✋ *VM/RSCS Mailing List.*
  `bit.listserv.rscs-l`

✋ *The RSCS modifications List.*
  `bit.listserv.rscsmods`

✋ *SuperComputers List.*
  `bit.listserv.s-comput`

✋ *IBM vs Waterloo SCRIPT Discussion Group.*
  `bit.listserv.script-l`

✋ *VM Shared File System Discussion List.*
  `bit.listserv.sfs-l`

✋ *Student Government Global Mail Network.*
  `bit.listserv.sganet`

✋ *The SIMULA Language List.*
  `bit.listserv.simula`

✋ *SPSSX Discussion.*
  `bit.listserv.spssx-l`

✋ *Forum for SQL/DS and Related Topics.*
  `bit.listserv.sqlinfo`

꙳ *Statistical Consulting.*
bit.listserv.stat-l

꙳ *BITNIC TECH-L List.*
bit.listserv.tech-l

꙳ *Test Newsgroup.*
bit.listserv.test

꙳ *The TeXnical topics List.*
bit.listserv.tex-l

꙳ *tn3270 protocol Discussion List.*
bit.listserv.tn3270-l

꙳ *BITNIC TRANS-L List.*
bit.listserv.trans-l

꙳ *UREP-L Mailing List.*
bit.listserv.urep-l

꙳ *User Directory List.*
bit.listserv.usrdir-l

꙳ *Virus Alert List. (Moderated)*
bit.listserv.valert-l

꙳ *VS-Fortran Discussion List.*
bit.listserv.vfort-l

꙳ *VM Utilities Discussion List.*
bit.listserv.vm-util

꙳ *VM/ESA Mailing List.*
bit.listserv.vmesa-l

꙳ *VAX/VMS LISTSERV Discussion List.*
bit.listserv.vmslsv-l

꙳ *VM/XA Discussion List.*
bit.listserv.vmxa-l

꙳ *VNEWS Discussion List.*
bit.listserv.vnews-l

꙳ *Electronic Publishing Discussion List.*
bit.listserv.vpiej-l

꙳ *Microsoft Windows Version 3 Forum.*
bit.listserv.win3-l

꙳ *VM System Editor List.*
bit.listserv.xedit-l

꙳ *The Xerox Discussion List.*
bit.listserv.xerox-l

꙳ *Crosswell Mailer.*
bit.listserv.xmailer

꙳ *Extopian List.*
bit.listserv.xtropy-l

꙳ *x.400 Protocol List.*
bit.listserv.x400-l

꙳ *IBM 9370 and VM/IS specific topics List.*
bit.listserv.9370-l

꙳ *Word Processing on the Macintosh.*
bit.mailserv.word-mac

꙳ *Word Processing on the IBM PC.*
bit.mailserv.word-pc

꙳ *Generic commercial hardware postings.*
biz.comp.hardware

꙳ *Generic commercial service postings.*
biz.comp.services

꙳ *Generic commercial software postings.*
biz.comp.software

꙳ *Support of the Telebit modem.*
biz.comp.telebit

꙳ *The Telebit Netblazer.*
biz.comp.telebit.netblazer

꙳ *Biz Usenet configuration and administration.*
biz.config

꙳ *Control information and messages.*
biz.control

꙳ *DEC equipment & software.*
biz.dec

꙳ *IP networking on DEC machines.*
biz.dec.ip

꙳ *DEC workstation discussions & info.*
biz.dec.workstations

꙳ *Position announcements.*
biz.jobs.offered

꙳ *Miscellaneous postings of a commercial nature.*
biz.misc

꙳ *SCO and related product announcements. (Moderated)*
biz.sco.announce

꙳ *Q&A, discussions and comments on SCO products.*
biz.sco.general

꙳ *ODT environment and applications technical info, Q&A.*
biz.sco.opendesktop

꙳ *Biz newsgroup test messages.*
biz.test

꙳ *Postings about stolen merchandise.*
biz.stolen

꙳ *University Computing Project Mailing List.*
bit.listserv.ucp-l

꙳ *Usage Guidelines.*
bit.listserv.ug-l

- *User Interface for Geographical Info Systems.*
  `bit.listserv.uigis-l`

- *WordPerfect for Windows.*
  `bit.listserv.wpwin-l`

- *WordPerfect Corporation Products Discussions.*
  `bit.listserv.wpcorp-l`

- *SNA Network Management Discussion.*
  `bit.listserv.snamgt-l`

- *POWER-L IBM RS/6000 POWER Family.*
  `bit.listserv.power-l`

- *Information Graphics.*
  `bit.listserv.ingrafx`

- *Discussion of Ethics in Computing.*
  `bit.listserv.ethics-l`

- *BITNET News.*
  `bit.listserv.bitnews`

- *Alternative subnetwork testing.*
  `alt.test`

- *Discussion of the AT&T Documenter's WorkBench.*
  `alt.text.dwb`

- *1/2 an OS for 1/2 a computer, twice as late.*
  `alt.half.operating.system.delay.delay.delay`

- *Fractals in math, graphics, and art.*
  `alt.fractals`

- *Stories & anecdotes about computers (some true!).*
  `alt.folklore.computers`

- *A postscript comic strip.*
  `alt.comics.buffalo-roam`

Online Libraries
After Dark

- *Business Software Database*
  Descriptions of software products available for business and systems users, including information on availability, compatibility, price, documentation, and support.
  Coverage: Current information
  Updated: Quarterly

- *Computer & Mathematics Search®*
  A citation index to articles from journals and multi-authored books on general and applied mathematics, computer science, statistics, operations research, and management science.
  Coverage: 1980 to present
  Updated: Biweekly

- *Computer Database™*
  An index to over 360 major computer industry journals containing articles on computer-related hardware, software, applications, companies, services, and products.
  Coverage: 1983 to present
  Updated: Semi-monthly

- *Computer Retrieval of Information on Scientific Projects*
  Documents data on research projects supported by the U.S. Public Health Service, the largest organization supporting biomedical research in the world.
  Coverage: 1986 to present
  Updated: Monthly

- *SOFT—Online Microcomputer Software Guide and Directory*
  Current microcomputer software descriptions plus related information on costs, applications, purchasing, hardware requirements, and more.
  Coverage: Currently available microcomputer software
  Updated: Monthly

Knowledge Index

- *Business Software Database*
  Contains descriptions of business software packages for use with micro and minicomputers.
  Coverage: Current
  Updated: Quarterly

- *Buyers Guide to Micro Software (Soft)*
  A directory of business and professional software available in the U.S. Provides directory, product, technical, and bibliographic information on leading software packages.
  Coverage: Current
  Updated: Monthly

- *Computer Database™*
  Abstracts and indexes journals on almost every aspect of computers, telecommunications, and electronics. Answers questions about hardware, software, peripherals, and services. Includes product evaluations and financial information on related firms. In addition to indexing, makes available full-text records from more than 50 magazines from 1983 to present.

Coverage: January 1983 to present
Updated: Weekly

Computer News Fulltext
Contains full-text articles from *Computerworld* and *Networld World*, IDG publications.
Coverage: 1989 to present
Updated: Weekly

INSPEC
Scans approximately 3,900 journals in physics, electrotechnology, computers and control, and information technology; over 730 abstracted completely. Journal papers, conference proceedings, technical reports, books, and university theses are abstracted and indexed. Corresponds to the printed *Physics Abstracts, Electrical and Electronics Abstracts, Computer and Control Abstracts*, and *IT Focus.*
Coverage: 1969 to present
Updated: Monthly

Microcomputer Index™
A subject and abstract guide to magazine articles from 50 microcomputer journals. Includes general articles, reviews, descriptions of new products, and more. Corresponds to the print work of the same name.
Coverage: 1981 to present
Updated: Monthly

Microcomputer Software Guide
Contains infomation on virtually every microcomputer software program and hardware system available or produced in the U.S. Records include ordering information and other data.
Coverage: Current
Updated: Monthly

Orbit

MICROSEARCH
Covers more than 50,000 reviews from microcomputer-related literature—specifically, the availability, applications, compatibility, and comparative evaluations of hardware and software products. Provides information on products from over 7,000 hardware and software manufacturers and over 170 trade journals.
Coverage: 1983 to present
Updated: Periodically

NewsNet

AD/Solutions Report
Frequency: Biweekly
Earliest NewsNet Issue: 2/1/91
Covers the ways in which IBM's SAA-based AD/Cycle framework shapes the applications development environment. Evaluates the effectiveness of AD/Cycle tools in real-life situations.

AIX Age
Frequency: Bimonthly
Earliest NewsNet Issue: 6/1/91
Covers operating systems designed to the specifications of the Advanced Interactive Executive (AIX) Family Definitions, IBM's unified version of Unix.

The Business Computer
Frequency: Twice weekly
Earliest NewsNet Issue: 2/6/83
Expanded from weekly newspaper columns; features user-oriented tests of equipment and software and innovative answers to problems facing most computer users.

Byte
Frequency: Monthly
Earliest NewsNet Issue: 10/1/91
On-line magazine for professional users and buyers of microcomputers and related products. Includes reviews, evaluations, and features on new computer technology and applications.

CASE Strategies
Frequency: Monthly
Earliest NewsNet Issue: 1/1/90
Provides information to help integrate computer-aided systems engineering into your organization, including market and product developments and their implications for business.

CD Computing News
Frequency: Monthly
Earliest NewsNet Issue: 6/1/87
Developments, applications, and business ventures in compact optical discs and associated products used in computing. Covers CD-ROM, CD-I, and all other optical media.

⑨ *CD-ROM Databases*
Frequency: Monthly
Earliest NewsNet Issue: 9/1/87
Provides titles, prices, and vendor information for available CD-ROM databases.

⑨ *Comline Japan Daily: Computers*
Frequency: Daily
Earliest NewsNet Issue: 1/5/90
Monitors hardware and software developments in Japan, emphasizing products likely to have the most international impact.

⑨ *Computer Book Review*
Frequency: Monthly
Earliest NewsNet Issue: Two years plus current year
Critical reviews of the latest computer-related books. Also includes a trade news section.

⑨ *Computer Protocols*
Frequency: Monthly
Earliest NewsNet Issue: 6/1/88
Covers developments in computer communication protocols (including international developments) and related products. Also monitors software interfaces between personal computers and mainframes.

⑨ *Computer Reseller News*
Frequency: Weekly
Earliest NewsNet Issue: 3/4/91
Covers issues that impact high-end resellers of microcomputer hardware and software. Focus is on channels of distribution.

⑨ *Computer Workstations*
Frequency: Monthly
Earliest NewsNet Issue: 8/1/88
News and information on computer workstations used in business and industrial applications. Covers the products, people, and companies using and making workstations, with an emphasis on product marketing strategies.

⑨ *Computergram International*
Frequency: Daily
Earliest NewsNet Issue: 11/25/87
A London-based daily newspaper for data processing, communications, and micro-electronics professionals and investors. Reporters in Europe, Japan, and the U.S. contribute daily.

⑨ *Computerized Processes*
Frequency: Monthly
Earliest NewsNet Issue: 10/1/88
Information on emerging computer and electronic technologies designed to increase productivity in manufacturing.

⑨ *The DataTrends Report on DEC and IBM*
Frequency: Monthly
Earliest NewsNet Issue: 11/1/89
Analyzes the latest technology and market strategies of DEC and IBM. Studies the issues and activities of these computing environments, both from a competitive and systems integration standpoint.

⑨ *Edge: Work Group Computing Report*
Frequency: Weekly
Earliest NewsNet Issue: 5/28/90
Reports on the major aspects of today's work-group computing environment, with emphasis on new products, applications, people, and events affecting global information movement and management.

⑨ *Electronic Imaging Report*
Frequency: Biweekly
Earliest NewsNet Issue: 6/19/91
Provides image-management executives with news and analysis on imaging strategies, applications, and case studies. Reporters analyze user implementation, vendor marketing strategies, industry trends, and more.

⑨ *GUI Program News*
Frequency: Monthly
Earliest NewsNet Issue: 11/1/90
A monthly update on graphical user interfaces and associated applications for personal computers and workstations.

⑨ *IDB Online—The Computing Industry Daily*
Frequency: Daily
Earliest NewsNet Issue: 1/3/86
Provides the latest background stories, financial news, and business deals in hardware, software, telecommunications, and CAD/CAM. Provides a link to the European computing industry, as well as a sounding board for the performance of U.S. companies and products.

⑨ *Imaging Update*
Frequency: Monthly
Earliest NewsNet Issue: 2/1/90

Covers the digitized image and computer graphics industry. Analyzes new hardware and software products, offering articles on research and development.

Intelligent Software Strategies
Frequency: Monthly
Earliest NewsNet Issue: 1/1/90
Information for systems professionals on combining methods of expert-systems development with software innovations such as neural networks, object-oriented programming, CASE, and natural language.

Item Processing Report
Frequency: Biweekly
Earliest NewsNet Issue: 2/15/90
Devoted to the area of remittance and check-processing. Reports on new technologies and strategies in image processing, optical character recognition, check truncation, and hardware and software advances.

Japan Computer Industry Scan
Frequency: Weekly
Earliest NewsNet Issue: 1/1/84
Covers the Japanese computer market. News on major breakthroughs, research and development, and Japanese computer marketing techniques, plus feature articles.

Japan Semiconductor Scan
Frequency: Weekly
Earliest NewsNet Issue: 6/1/84
Discusses U.S./Japan relations in high technology and electronic fields. Examines and analyzes major trends.

LAN Product News
Frequency: Monthly
Earliest NewsNet Issue: 1/1/90
Covers the fast-growing Local AreaNetwork (LAN) industry, including new hardware and software, research and development, applications, and industry standards developments.

LAN Times
Frequency: Biweekly
Earliest NewsNet Issue: 9/16/91
A network-computing trade magazine covering PC-based networking, including network design, installation, configuration, applications, and management.

Mainframe Communications Report
Frequency: Biweekly
Earliest NewsNet Issue: 2/11/88
Provides news and analysis of Systems Network Architecture (SNA) products, services, and trends. Covers IBM and other vendors providing SNA products.

Mainframe Computing
Frequency: Monthly
Earliest NewsNet Issue: 12/1/88
News and information on computer mainframes, including supercomputers. Covers new hardware, peripherals, applications software, operating systems, and network systems, with special emphasis on the marketing strategies of mainframe and peripheral vendors.

Microcomputer Resources
Frequency: Monthly
Earliest NewsNet Issue: 9/1/86
Studies the rapid advances being made in the fields of data processing, telecommunications, and fiber optics.

Modem Users News
Frequency: Monthly
Earliest NewsNet Issue: 10/1/89
News and information on software, hardware, supplies, and services for modem users.

Multimedia & Videodisc Monitor
Frequency: Monthly
Earliest NewsNet Issue: 9/1/87
Covers industrial applications of video-disc, interactive video, compact disc, and related technologies. Features product news, analysis, market statistics, and in-depth articles.

NASA Software Directory
Frequency: Annual
An encyclopedic listing of program abstracts describing more than 1,300 NASA-sponsored and developed computer programs.

Netline
Frequency: Monthly
Earliest NewsNet Issue: 9/30/88
Concentrates on local area networking of microcomputers and workstations. Coverage includes profiles of computer network vendors and their products and strategies, detailed discussions of networking solutions, and timely analysis of important news.

⑤ Network Computing
Frequency: Monthly
Earliest NewsNet Issue: 5/1/91
For users who build and manage computing applications in a network environment. Reports on which technologies work and how.

⑤ Network Management Systems & Strategies
Frequency: Biweekly
Earliest NewsNet Issue: 7/31/89
The manager's guide to new products, technologies, and management techniques in computer networking. Provides latest news, user innovations, and previews of future network management solutions.

⑤ Networks Update
Frequency: Monthly
Earliest NewsNet Issue: 9/1/89
News and information on the computer network industry, including national, international, public, private, and military networks.

⑤ Newsbytes News Network
Frequency: Daily
Earliest NewsNet Issue: 3/14/89
Highlights and analysis of the most significant microcomputer and consumer technology news. Coverage includes hardware, software, corporate movements, new product offerings, more.

⑤ Object-Oriented Strategies
Frequency: Monthly
Earliest NewsNet Issue: 10/1/91
For managers and developers of object-oriented systems. Provides reports, forecasts, and analysis to help organizations devise the best strategy for acquiring and applying technology.

⑤ OPEN: OSI Product and Equipment News
Frequency: Biweekly
Earliest NewsNet Issue: 5/12/88
News and analysis regarding product and equipment developments for networks conforming to Open Systems Interconnect (OSI) international standards. Covers vendor strategies, product conformance, standards development, and user experiences.

⑤ Open Systems Communication
Frequency: Biweekly
Earliest NewsNet Issue: 10/5/90

Focuses on computer interoperability and interconnection, including news and analysis of the latest strategic business plans and standards-based, vendor-neutral information technology products.

⑤ Optical & Magnetic Report
Frequency: Monthly
Earliest NewsNet Issue: 12/1/89
Monitors technologies, strategies, applications, and opportunities in the field of storage media, including digital audio tape, recordable videodiscs, and more.

⑤ Optical Information Systems Update
Frequency: Monthly
Covers of the interactive videodisc, digital optical disk, and CD-ROM marketplaces. Discusses recent technical developments, software announcements, courseware, executive movements, calendar items, and conferences.

⑤ Optical Memory News
Frequency: Biweekly
Earliest NewsNet Issue: 11/13/91
News and analysis from a vendor's perspective on the optical storage marketplace. Covers industry trends, new product releases, alliances, and partnerships.

⑤ Outlook on IBM
Frequency: Not currently updated.
Earliest NewsNet Issue: 1/1/85-7/31/87
Provides in-depth news and analysis to make you a better-informed IBM competitor, customer, client, or supplier.

⑤ PC Business Products
Frequency: Monthly
Earliest NewsNet Issue: 7/1/89
A practical guide to the use of personal computers in business. Contains detailed product information to help select the best equipment.

⑤ Productivity Software
Frequency: Monthly
Earliest NewsNet Issue: 9/1/88
News and information on productivity-enhancing business software. Covers vendors as well as end users. Also evaluates products, applications, and marketing strategies.

The Report on IBM
Frequency: Weekly
Earliest NewsNet Issue: 11/6/85
News and analysis regarding IBM products, services, and corporate strategy. Includes latest information on new technologies, marketing and distribution strategy, research and development. Also covers the computer industry relative to IBM's market position.

Semiconductor Industry & Business Survey
Frequency: Biweekly
Earliest NewsNet Issue: 9/26/83
Provides business and marketing intelligence on over 200 semiconductor firms worldwide. Analyzes various industry financial indicators.

Strategic Systems
Frequency: Monthly
Earliest NewsNet Issue: 3/1/88
Timely reports and commentary on IBM's new software technology, Systems Application Architecture.

Systems & Network Integration
Frequency: Biweekly
News and analysis of events affecting systems integrators, VARs, and OEMs, including coverage of products, technologies, companies, and people.

Technical Computing
Frequency: Monthly
Earliest NewsNet Issue: 1/1/88
Abstracts and reports on news of interest to scientists and engineers who use computers. Intended as a digest of computer news for professionals unable to keep up with all the sources.

Unix Today
Frequency: Biweekly
Earliest NewsNet Issue: 5/13/91
Supplies managers and builders of business information systems with news, analysis, and product information on open systems.

Unix Update
Frequency: Monthly
Earliest NewsNet Issue: 10/1/90
Provides news and information on Unix computer systems and products, including new hardware and software, enhancements, and research and development. Special emphasis on marketing strategies of Unix vendors.

UnixWorld
Frequency: Monthly
Earliest NewsNet Issue: 7/1/91
Reports on multiuser, multitasking open-systems computing and Unix-based operating systems.

VARBusiness
Frequency: Monthly
Earliest NewsNet Issue: 7/1/91
Business, technology, and industry information for value-added resellers. Analysis of industry trends, market advice on established and emerging technologies, and tips and insights on business management.

Worldwide Databases
Frequency: Monthly
Earliest NewsNet Issue: 2/1/90
Provides information on on-line computer databases around the world. Features on new database products and enhancements, user applications and accessing requirements, and news on products in development.

Worldwide Videotex Update
Frequency: Monthly
Earliest NewsNet Issue: 12/1/82
News and information on videotex/teletext products, services, and projects around the world. Emphasis on material of interest to marketers.

On-line Libraries and Microcomputers
Frequency: Monthly
Earliest NewsNet Issue: 1/15/89
Reports developments in the field of library and information science, including new technology, applications, and evaluation of library-oriented software and hardware.

On-line Newsletter
Frequency: Monthly
Earliest NewsNet Issue: 1/1/88
Covers major aspects of on-line and CD-ROM development, including mergers and acquisitions, forthcoming databases, and people making news in the industry. Editorials analyze events and product developments affecting on-line users.

Bulletin Boards

The North American ISDN Users BBS

Operated by the National Institute of Standards and Technology, National Computer Sytems Laboratory, Advanced Systems Division. Discusses North America ISDN networking issues. Makes available bulletins and documents as well as areas for workgroups.
Availability: 24 hours/ 7 days
Baud Rate: 300, 1200, 2400
BBS Number: (301) 869-7281
BBS Software: TEAMate
Help Line: (301) 975-2937

ADA Language System/Navy BBS

Devoted to the ADA programming language.
Baud Rate: 300, 1200, 2400
BBS Number: (202) 342-4568
BBS Software: PCBoard

ADA Technical Support BBS

Operated by the Naval Computer and Telecommunications Area Master Tele-communications Command. Offers technical support for the ADA programming language
Availability: 24 hours/ 7 days
Baud Rate: 300, 1200, 2400, 9600, 16.8
BBS Number: (804) 444-7841
Sysop: Dave Parker
Help Line: (804) 444-4680

ATI Technologies Online

Provides support and the latest drivers and diskettes, as well as a variety of information on ATI products.
Availability: 24 hours/ 7 days
Baud Rate: 9600
BBS Number: (416) 756-4591
BBS Software: PCBoard
Sysop: SYSOP
Help Line: (416) 756-0711

Central Point Software Online Support Center

Provides support for CPS Software products.
Availability: 24 hours/ 7 days
Baud Rate: 2400, 9600
BBS Number: (503) 690-6650 (2400); (503) 690-4777 (9600)
Help Line: (503) 690-8080

INTEL PC & LAN Enhancements Support BBS

Provides support for INTEL-based products.
Availability: 24 hours/ 7 days
Baud Rate: 300, 19.2
BBS Number: (503) 645-6275
BBS Software: TBBS
Sysop: Jim Willing
Help Line: (503) 629-7000

Microsoft Download Service

Provides support for Microsoft application notes, drivers, and other files for Windows, DOS, Word, Excel, Works, Basic, and more, for both PC and Macintosh environments.
Availability: 24 hours/ 7 days
Baud Rate: 9600
BBS Number: (206) 936-6735
BBS Software: TBBS
Sysop: SYSOP

Online with Hayes

Provides technical support for Hayes modems. Also contains the complete Darwin BBS list, which allows users to search for bulletin boards around the country.
Availability: 24 hours/ 7 days
Baud Rate: 300, 2400
BBS Number: (404) 446-6336
BBS Software: Bread Board

Practical Peripherals BBS

Serves the customers of PPI products.
Availability: 24 hours/ 7 days

Baud Rate: 14.4
BBS Number: (805) 496-4445
BBS Software: WILDCAT!
Help Line: (818) 991-8200

US Robotics Customer Support and Sales BBS

Provides support for US Robotics modems.
Availability: 24 hours/ 7 days
Baud Rate: 14.4
BBS Number: (708) 982-5092
Sysop: Adam Strack

WordPerfect Customer Support BBS

Provides support for WordPerfect products. Drivers are available for download as well.
Availability: 24 hours/ 7 days
Baud Rate: 14.4
BBS Number: (801) 225-4444
BBS Software: PCBoard
Help Line: (801) 228-9904

CD-ROM

✸ *Computing Archives: Bibliography & Reviews from AC*
ACM Press

✸ *Computer Library*
OCLC
6565 Franz Road
Dublin, OH 43017

✸ *Computer Products*
GML Corp.

✸ *ICP/Software Information Database*
ICP

✸ *Newsbytes News Network*
Wayzata Technology

✸ *Software Du Jour*
ALDE Publishing

✸ *Software Users Year Book*
VNV Business Publications

Ecological Science Resources

Forums & Databases
America Online (AOL)
Services not available.

CompuServe (CIS)
Services not available.

GEnie
Services not available.

The Well
Services not available.

Network Discussions Lists
Internet (Includes Bitnet & UUCPNet)
Services not available.

Fidonet

⑤ *Ecology, Problems, and Potential Solutions*
ECOLOGY
Focuses on ecological problems and problem resolution.
Moderator: Lon Levy
1:154/11
Distribution: BACKBONE

⑤ *Ecology Network*
ECONET
For all who want to learn what can be done to protect the planet and its resources.

Moderator: David Dickerson
1:109/70.921
Distribution: BACKBONE

Usenet
Services not available.

Online Libraries

After Dark
Services not available.

Knowledge Index
Services not available.

Orbit
Services not available.

NewsNet
Services not available.

Bulletin Boards
National Ecology Research Center BBS
Run by the U.S. Fish and Wildlife Service, NERC. For people working on ecological modeling techniques.
Availability: 24 hours/ 7 days
Baud Rate: 300, 1200, 2400
BBS Name/Sponsor: NERC (National Ecology Research Center) Bulletin Board System (formerly the HMRL BBS).

BBS Number: (303) 226-9365
BBS Software: RBBS-PC
Sysop: Gene Whitaker
Help Line: (202) 343-3245.
Comments: Call (303) 226-9335 for a hardcopy
user's guide.

CD-ROM

⟨S⟩ *Aquatic Sciences & Fisheries Abstracts*
Cambridge Scientific Abstracts

⟨S⟩ *Arctic & Antarctic Regions*
National Information Services Corp.

⟨S⟩ *Biological Abstracts*
SilverPlatter Information Inc.

⟨S⟩ *Natural Resources Megabase*
National Information Services Corp.

⟨S⟩ *Wildlife & Fish Worldwide*
National Information Services Corp.

Education Resources

Forums & Databases
America Online (AOL)

⑤ *Academic Assistance Center*
Keyword: homework
Path: Learning & Reference Department > Academic Assistance Center
Offers live, nightly homework help services in a variety of subjects for secondary-school students. Also offers exam preparation and study skills development materials for students and teachers. Students may post research questions on a message board and within 72 hours receive a brief overview of the subject matter and body of research available, as well as a bibliography.

⑤ *Association for Supervision and Curriculum Development*
Keyword: ASCD
Path: Learning & Reference Department > ASCD Online
Seeks to develop better methods of assessing student learning, and to strengthen and expand early childhood education. Features articles from Educational Leadership, catalogs of information about new ASCD products and services, an Ask ASCD research service, and more.

⑤ *Cable News Network (CNN) Online*
Keyword: CNN
Path: Learning & Reference Department > CNN Online
Provides lesson plans and activity guides for teachers to use in conjunction with CNN's Newsroom and Democracy in America television programs. The programs—which teach students about current events and the political process—can be videotaped and shown to students during the school day. Message boards enable students to share ideas with students across the country.

⑤ *College Board Online*
Keyword: college board
Path: Learning & Reference Department > College Board Online
Provides information about the SAT, including test dates and preparation materials. Other resources—such as books about writing your college application essay and finding financial aid—can be ordered on-line from the College Board Store. The searchable College Handbook contains information for over 3,000 universities and colleges, including majors offered, admissions standards, and program details

⑤ *Compton's Encyclopedia*
Keyword: Encyclopedia
Path: Learning & Reference Department > Compton's Encyclopedia
Searchable using keywords, phrases, and Boolean delimiters. Uses multitasking Mac and Windows software, enabling users to cut and paste entries into documents or save them to refer to off-line.

⑤ *Educational Magazines Database*
Path: Learning & Reference > Teacher's Information Network > Educational Magazines Database
Provides contact and publication information on over 3OO educational publications.

⑤ *Educational Television & Radio Listings Database*
Path: Learning & Reference Department > Teacher's Information Network > TV & Radio Listings Database
A database of television and radio programs of educational value for children. Provided by KidsNet. Text-searchable and updated monthly. Also makes available a regularly updated list of upcoming television movies of interest to children and families.

⑤ *Interactive Education Services*
Keyword: IES
Path: Learning & Reference Department > Interactive Education Services
Offers live, on-line classes in a variety of subjects: English/Languages, History/Social Sciences, Math/Science, Computer Science, Arts, and Professional Studies. Classes are at the college level; students download course materials and attend classes in real time. A few colleges offer for-credit courses as well.

⑤ *Library of Congress Online*
Path: Learning & Reference Department > Library of Congress Online
On-line versions of Library of Congress exhibits. Currently available is "Revelations from the Russian Archives," which includes translated excerpts from the documents, graphic (GIF) images of the actual documents, message board discussions, and on-line conferences with experts. The Library of Congress and America Online are working to develop future exhibits.

⑤ *National Education Association Online*
Keyword: NEA
Path: Learning & Reference Department > NEA Online
Here the national union for teachers communicates with their computer-using members and provides general education information to the general public. Access NEA's Educational Issues Database, a source of benchmark information concerning education in America today. NEA members can access private on-line areas to use NEA's Attorney Referral Program and its Affiliate Newsletter Service.

⑤ *National Geographic Online*
Keyword: NGS
Path: Learning & Reference Department > National Geographic Online
Makes available feature articles from *National Geographic* magazine, as well as *National Geographic's World and Traveler* magazines. Access broadcast schedules and descriptions of *National Geographic* television programs and specials, and the geographic film and video catalog. The on-line Geographic Store enables users to subscribe to various magazines, and order CD-ROM programs, books, software, and board games; the Geographic Interactive on-line area helps teachers exchange ideas on integrating geography into school curricula.

⑤ *Parents' Information Network*
Keyword: Parents
Path: Learning & Reference Department > Parent's Information Network
Offers interactive forums on issues of importance to parents, timely articles from major educational periodicals, databases of useful information, real-time conferencing opportunities, and parent-oriented guides to other parts of America Online.

⑤ *Student Access Online*
Keyword: Student Access
Path: Learning & Reference Department > Student Access Online
Sponsored by Princeton Review. Resources for students, including message board exchange; members can access private areas providing admissions counseling, job placement services, and financial and internship planning.

⑤ *Teachers' Information Network*
Keyword: TIN
Path: Learning & Reference Department > Teacher's Information Network
Devoted to the needs and interests of educators. Educators can discuss issues on message boards and in live weekly conferences; makes available articles from Scholastic's *Electronic Learning Magazine* and the *American School Board Journal*, as well as software reviews and a searchable database of over 300 relevant magazines; provides seminars where educators can learn new skills and techniques; facilitates exchange of lesson plans, exams, and public domain educational software.

CompuServe (CIS)

⑤ *Academic American Encyclopedia*
GO ENCYCLOPEDIA
The on-line edition of Grolier's *Academic American Encyclopedia*, a general reference source of over 33,000 articles, updated and revised quarterly.

Books in Print
GO BOOKS

Enables users to find books distributed in the U.S. for purchase, books currently in print, books to be published in the next six months, and books gone out of print or out of stock in the last two years. Searchable by subject, author, and title.

Book Review Digest
GO BOOKREVIEW

Provides references to over 26,000 fiction and nonfiction English-language books. Reviews are drawn from over 80 American, Canadian, and British periodicals. Maintains a full citation and abstract for each book; updated twice weekly.

Consumer Reports
GO CONSUMER

Provides reports which outline desirable features, brand ratings, and recommendations from Consumers Union for automobiles, appliances, electronics, cameras and products for the home. Reports are added monthly.

Dissertation Abstracts
GO DISSERTATION

Provides information on dissertations for academic doctoral degrees at accredited U.S. institutions since 1861, selected masters theses, and dissertations accepted at Canadian and many other non-U.S. institutions. Abstracts are available for dissertations added to the database after July 1980.

Education Forum
GO EDFORUM

Designed to meet the needs of users involved in the teaching and learning process, including teachers, parents, students, faculty, and other professionals in education. The increasing use of microcomputers and other technologies in schools and homes is a natural topic of discussion.

Educational Research Forum
GO EDRESEARCH

For users interested in research about the process and products of education. The latest research findings are shared and compared, and dialogue is established between researchers and educators. Sponsored by the American Educational Research Association.

ERIC—Education Research
GO ERIC

Contains abstracts of articles and other educational resources covering all aspects of education. Information extends back to 1966 and is updated monthly. Published by the U.S. Department of Education.

IQuest
GO IQUEST

Provides access to more than 850 databases. Contains fully indexed historical data, updated daily. Both bibliographic and full-text documents are available. Source materials include magazines, newspapers, indexes, conference proceedings, directories, books, newsletters, government documents, dissertations, encyclopedias, patent records, and reference guides. On-line help is available by typing SOS.

IQuest Education InfoCenter
GO IQEDUCATION

Enables users to find information on education theory and research, testing, and vocational training. Provides access to information extracted from published sources such as journals, books, and government publications about education.

Mensa Forum
GO MENSA

Sponsored by American Mensa, Ltd. Provides a place for Mensa members and non-members to discuss the development and application of human intelligence. Message and library sections cover topics such as scholarships, gifted children, and puzzles.

Peterson's College Database
GO PETERSON

Offers a comprehensive database containing detailed descriptions of over 4,000 accredited or approved U.S. and Canadian colleges that grant associate or bachelor degrees. Members may search colleges by characteristics or name/location.

Students' Forum
GO STUFO

For students who want to share their ideas and interests with other students around the world.

GEnie

Computer-Assisted Learning Center
Keyword: CALC or Page 175

Provides live on-line tutoring and education. Non-Credit courses for adult continuing education, professional development and self-enrichment, middle school, high school, home school, and GED/CLEP preparation.

College Aid Sources for Higher Education
Keyword: CASHE or Page 408
A sophisticated scholarship database retrieval system containing information on sources of college financial aid, including leads on scholarships, fellowships, loans, internships, and work cooperative programs. Covers both undergraduate and graduate assistance.

Education RoundTable
Keyword: ERT or Page 405
Discussion and information exchange for members of the educational community, professional trainers, and the public.

Educator's Center
Keyword: EDUCATORS or Page 1286
Covers education research, psychology, child abuse studies, and even directories. Enter a question and the computer will quickly search thousands of journals, magazines, and reports to let you know where information can be found.

Grolier's Electronic Encyclopedia
Keyword: GROLIERS or Page 365
The electronic edition of Grolier's Academic American Encyclopedia, with more than 33,000 articles. Searchable.

Rensselaer Polytechnic Roundtable
Keyword: RPI or Page 265
Helps students and their parents explore the many opportunities available to them at Rensselaer Polytechnic Institute.

The Well

Interpersonal Communication
`(g in)`
Discusses the various ways that communication between people is assisted or blocked.

KidLink
`(g kids)`
A global computer network for youth ages 10-15.

Unity
`(g unity)`
A place for discussion of issues affecting minorities in a supportive atmosphere.

Network Discussions Lists Internet (Includes Bitnet & UUCPNet)

Association for the Advancement of Computing in Education list.
AACE-L@AUVM.BITNET
LISTSERV@AUVM.BITNET
For all persons interested in AACE.
Contact: Michael J. Strait
<STRAIT@UMUC.BITNET>

UCLA Academic Leadership list.
ACADLEAD@UCLACN1.BITNET
LISTSERV@UCLACN1.BITNET

Ag Communicators in Education list.
ACEWEST@WSUVM1.BITNET
LISTSERV@WSUVM1.BITNET

Canadian Adult Education Network list.
ADLTED-L@UREGINA1.BITNET
LISTSERV@UREGINA1.BITNET

American Education Research Association—Med list.
AERAMC-L@UAFSYSB.BITNET
LISTSERV@UAFSYSB.BITNET

African American Issues in Higher Education list.
AFROAM-L@TEMPLEVM.BITNET
LISTSERV@TEMPLEVM.BITNET
For discussion of African-American issues in higher education.
Contact: Lee Baker
V1328G@<TEMPLEVM.BITNET>

Alternative Approaches to Learning Discussion list.
ALTLEARN@SJUVM.BITNET
LISTSERV@SJUVM.BITNET

AMIA Education PSG Administrative Committee list.
AMIEDC-L@UBVM.BITNET
LISTSERV@UBVM.BITNET

Association of Discussion Groups and Electronic Journals for Scholars list.
ARACHNET@UOTTAWA.BITNET
LISTSERV@UOTTAWA.BITNET
Keeps track of more than 600 discussion groups, newsletters, digests, and electronic journals devoted to topics of scholarly interest.
Contact: Diane Kovacs
<dkovacs@kentvm.BITNET>

🕲 *Association for the Study of Higher Education list.*
ASHE-L@UMCVMB.BITNET
LISTSERV@UMCVMB.BITNET
Contact: Irv Cockriel
<EDRSR438@UMCVMB.BITNET>

🕲 *Assessment in Higher Education list.*
ASSESS@UKCC.BITNET
LISTSERV@UKCC.BITNET
Informal discussions of assessment issues and policies, as well as information on current practices in higher education.
Contact: Thomas Kunselman
<VAATEK@UKCC.BITNET>

🕲 *Quality of Education list.*
BGEDU-L@UKCC.BITNET
LISTSERV@UKCC.BITNET

🕲 *Secondary Biology Teacher Enhancement list.*
BIOPI-L@KSUVM.BITNET
LISTSERV@KSUVM.BITNET

🕲 *Capital Area Researchers in Educational Technology list.*
CARET@GWUVM.BITNET
LISTSERV@GWUVM.BITNET

🕲 *Liste MTP Spring School of the Caribbean*
CARIB-L@FRCPN11.BITNET
LISTSERV@FRCPN11.BITNET

🕲 *Catalyst*
CATALYST@VTVM1.BITNET
LISTSERV@VTVM1.BITNET
A quarterly, refereed journal serving community college educators. Published by the National Council on Community Services and Continuing Education.
Contact: Lon Savage
<SAVAGE@VTVM1.BITNET>

🕲 *Canadian University Continuing Education Policy list.*
CAUCE-PP@UREGINA1.BITNET
LISTSERV@UREGINA1.BITNET

🕲 *Causerie list.*
CAUSERIE@UQUEBEC.BITNET
LISTSERV@UQUEBEC.BITNET
A list for communication in French.
Contact: Pierre J. Hamel
<HAMEL@INRS-URB.UQUEBEC.CA>

🕲 *Computers in Education list.*
CBEHIGH@BLEKUL11.BITNET
LISTSERV@BLEKUL11.BITNET
Discusses the use of computers as an educational tool in higher education.
Contact: Peter Arien
<laaaa43@blekul11.bitnet>

🕲 *College on Location list.*
COLA-L@UALTAVM.BITNET
LISTSERV@UALTAVM1.BITNET

🕲 *International Two-Year College Educators' Discussion list.*
COMMCOLL@UKCC.BITNET
LISTSERV@UKCC.BITNET
A global network of two-year college educators who recognize the importance of teaching in communicating knowledge to the next generation.
Contact: Anne Kearney
<JCCANNEK@UKCC.BITNET>

🕲 *Electronic Network for Distance Education list.*
CREAD-D@YORKVM1.BITNET
LISTSERV@YORKVM1.BITNET
The Sam Lanfranco Digest of the Electronic Network for Distance Education Across Latin America and the Caribbean.

🕲 *Computing Strategies Across the Curriculum list.*
CSAC@UVMVM.BITNET
LISTSERV@UVMVM.BITNET

🕲 *Center for the Study of Reading Contact list.*
CSRNOT-L@UIUCVMD.BITNET
LISTSERV@UIUCVMD.BITNET

🕲 *Computer Literacy in Higher Education list.*
CTI-Complit@durham.ac.uk
mailbase@newcastle.ac.uk
Discusses computer literacy in higher education and related issues.
Contact: Audrey McCartan
<Audrey.McCartan@durham.ac.uk>

🕲 *Using Computers to Learn*
CTI-L@IRLEARN.UCD.IE
LISTSERV@IRLEARN.UCD.IE
Discusses issues in the use of computers in teaching.
Contact: Claron O'Reilly
<CLARON@IRLEARN.UCD.IE>

🕲 *DEOSNEWS—The Distance Education Online Symposium*
DEOS-L@PSUVM.BITNET
LISTSERV@PSUVM.BITNET
For professionals and students in the field of distance education.
Contact: Morten Flate Paulsen
<MFP101@PSUVM.BITNET>

🕲 *On-line Journal of Distance Education and Communication list.*
DISTED@UWAVM.BITNET
LISTSERV@UWAVM.BITNET
Contact: Paul J. Coffin
JXPJC@ALASKA.BITNET

❧ *Early Childhood Education/Young Children (0-8) list.*
ECENET-L@UIUCVMD.BITNET
LISTSERV@UIUCVMD.BITNET

❧ *Educacion a Distancia list.*
EDISTA@USACHVM1.BITNET
LISTSERV@USACHVM1.BITNET
For discussion on distance education.
Contact: Jorge Urbina Fuentes
<UNIDIS@USACHVM1.BITNET>

❧ *Use of Networks in Education list.*
EDNET@nic.umass.edu
listserv@nic.umass.edu
For users interested in exploring the educational potential of Internet. Discussion ranges from K-12 to adult higher education.
Contact: pgsmith@ucsvax.ucs.umass.edu

❧ *Educational Development Network of New York list.*
EDNETNY@SUVM.BITNET
LISTSERV@SUVM.BITNET

❧ *Professionals and Students Discussing Education list.*
EDPOLYAN@ASUACAD.BITNET
LISTSERV@ASUACAD.BITNET

❧ *Educational Technology Discussion list.*
EDTECH@OHSTVMA.BITNET
LISTSERV@OHSTVMA.BITNET EDTECH

❧ *Women's Issues in Technology and Education Discussion list.*
EDUCOM-W@BITNIC.BITNET
LISTSERV@BITNIC.BITNET

❧ *Education and Information Technologies list.*
EDUTEL@RPIECS.BITNET
LISTSERV@RPIECS.BITNET

❧ *Educational Research list.*
ERL-L@TCSVM.BITNET
LISTSERV@TCSVM.BITNET
Disseminates updates from Washington. News about requests for proposals, grant reviewers, comments on programs, and so on.
Contact: Jean Pierce
P30JWP1@NIU.BITNET

❧ *Global Classroom list.*
GLOBALED@UNMVM.BITNET
LISTSERV@UNMV.BITNET

❧ *Research & Teaching in Global Information Technology list.*
GTRTI-L@GSUVM1.BITNET
LISTSERV@GSUVM1.BITNET

❧ *GWUs Honors Program Discussion list.*
GWHONORS@GWUVM.BITNET
LISTSERV@GWUVM.BITNET

❧ *HOLMES ED School Reform list.*
HOLMES@OHSTVMA.BITNET
LISTSERV@OHSTVMA.BITNET

❧ *Informatica y Computacion en Educacion list.*
IEDUCOM@USACHVM1.BITNET
LISTSERV@USACHVM1.BITNET

❧ *Interdisciplinary Studies Discussion list*
INTERDIS@MIAMIU.BITNET
LISTSERV@MIAMU.BITNET

❧ *Interpersonal Computing and Technology list.*
IPCT-L@GUVM.BITNET
LISTSERV@GUVM.BITNET
For pedagogical issues important to higher education involving teaching with technology, especially connectivity and networking.
Contact: Zane Berge
<BERGE@GUVAX.BITNET>

❧ *Worldwide Irish-Interest Research Net list.*
IRL-NET@IRLEARN.BITNET
LISTSERV@IRLEARN.BITNET
For research among those working in Ireland and elsewhere.
Contact: Fionn Murtagh
FIONN@DGAES051.BITNET

❧ *Indiana University MultiMedia Discussion list.*
IUMMEDIA@IUBVM.BITNET
LISTSERV@IUBVM.BITNET

❧ *Kids-91 Dialog list.*
KIDCAFE@NDSUVM1.BITNET
LISTSERV@NDSUVM1.BITNET KIDCAFE

❧ *KIDFORUM KidLink Coordination list.*
KIDFORUM@NDSUVM1.BITNET
LISTSERV@NDSUVM1.BITNET

❧ *KIDLEADR KidLink Coordination list.*
KIDLEADR@NDSUVM1.BITNET
LISTSERV@NDSUVM1.BITNET

❧ *KidLink Project list.*
KIDLINK@NDSUVM1.BITNET
LISTSERV@NDSUVM1.BITNET

❧ *KIDPLAN2 KidLink Work Group list.*
KIDPLAN2@NDSUVM1.BITNET
LISTSERV@NDSUVM1.BITNET

❧ *Special KidLink Projects list.*
KIDPROJ@NDSUVM1.BITNET
LISTSERV@NDSUVM1.BITNET

🕉 KIDS-ACT: What can I do list.
KIDS-ACT@NDSUVM1.BITNET
LISTSERV@NDSUVM1.BITNET

🕉 Kindergarten, Primary and Secondary-school Computing list.
KIDSNET@VMS.CIS.PITT.EDU
KIDSNET-REQUEST@VMS.CIS.PITT.EDU
Provides a global network for the use of children and teachers in grades K-12.
Contact: Bob Carlitz
<carlitz@VMS.CIS.PITT.EDU>

🕉 KIDZMAIL: Kids Exploring Issues And Interests list.
KIDZMAIL@ASUACAD.BITNET
LISTSERV@ASUACAD.BITNET

🕉 KINDEX—KidLink Subject Summaries list.
KINDEX@NDSUVM1.BITNET
LISTSERV@NDSUVM1.BITNET

🕉 Weekly KidLink Subject Summaries list.
KINDEXW@NDSUVM1.BITNET
LISTSERV@NDSUVM1.BITNET

🕉 Kentucky Honors Students list.
KYHONORS@UKCC.BITNET
LISTSERV@UKCC.BITNET
For members of the Kentucky Honors Roundtable, a group of eight schools whose Honors programs attempt to share in the Honors experience.
Contact: Jason Griffey
<GRIFJM@MOREKYPR.BITNET>

🕉 College of Education list.
L-EDUC@PSUVM.BITNET
LISTSERV@PSUVM.BITNET

🕉 L-HCAP list.
L-HCAP@NDSUVM1.BITNET
LISTSERV@NDSUVM1.BITNET
Discusses issues related to handicapped people in education.
Contact: Bill McGarry
wtm@bunker.BITNET

🕉 Networking Lead Teachers list.
LEADTCHR@PSUVM.BITNET
LISTSERV@PSUVM.BITNET

🕉 Dual Degree Programs Discussion list.
MDPHD-L@UBVM.BITNET
LISTSERV@UBVM.BITNET

🕉 MUSIC-ED: Music Education list.
MUSIC-ED@UMINN1.BITNET
LISTSERV@UMINN1.BITNET

🕉 Non-profit Academic Centers Council Discussion list.
NACC@INDYCMS.BITNET
LISTSERV@INDYCMS.BITNET

🕉 NAT-EDU Educational Issues Pertaining to Abortion list.
NAT-EDU@INDYCMS.BITNET
LISTSERV@INDYCMS.BITNET

🕉 New Paradigms in Education list.
NEWEDU-L@USCVM.BITNET
LISTSERV@USCVM.BITNET
Dedicated to experimenting with and exploring the way we educate.

🕉 Nordic Initiative for Research and Education list.
NORDREN@SEARN.BITNET
LISTSERV@SEARN.BITNET

🕉 Assessment of Student Learning Discussion list.
NP-ASSAY@UMUC.BITNET
LISTSERV@UMUC.BITNET

🕉 Open Forum on New Pathways to a Degree list.
NP-FORUM@UMUC.BITNET
LISTSERV@UMUC.BITNET
Helps colleges use technologies to open degree programs to new students and new academic resources.
Contact: Michael Strait
<Strait@UMUC.BITNET>

🕉 The New Pathways to a Degree News Service list.
NP-NEWS@UMUC.BITNET
LISTSERV@UMUC.BITNET
Information on "New Pathways to a Degree," the Annenberg/CPB funded initiative to help colleges use technologies to open degree programs to new students and new academic resources.
Contact: Michael Strait
<Strait@UMUC.BITNET>

🕉 PACE Degree Audit System Discussion list.
PACE-L@GSUVM1.BITNET
LISTSERV@GSUVM1.BITNET

🕉 Prison Teacher's Discussion list.
PRISON-L@DARTCMS1.BITNET
LISTSERV@DARTCMS1.BITNET
Promotes exchange among users who have taught or currently teach in prisons.
Contact: Patricia B. McRae
<T350134@UNIVSCVM.BITNET>

🌀 *Problem Solving Across the Curriculum Conference list.*
PSATC-L@UBVM.BITNET
LISTSERV@UBVM.BITNET

🌀 *Qualitative Research in Education list.*
QUALRSED@UNMVM.BITNET
LISTSERV@UNMVM.BITNET

🌀 *Research and Educational Applications of Computing list.*
REACH@UCSBVM.BITNET
LISTSERV@UCSBVM.BITNET

🌀 *Resident Hall Association Discussion list.*
RHA-L@TAMVM1.BITNET
LISTSERV@TAMVM1.BITNET

🌀 *Daily Report Card News Service list.*
RPTCRD@GWUVM.BITNET
LISTSERV@GWUVM.BITNET

🌀 *Science Awareness and Promotion list.*
SAIS-L@UNB.CA
LISTSERV@UNB.ca
Exchange of innovative ideas about making science more appealing to students.
Contact: Keith W. Wilson
<SAIS@UNB.ca>

🌀 *Student Affairs Officers Discussion list.*
SAO-L@UHCCVM.BITNET
LISTSERV@UHCCVM.BITNET

🌀 *Primary and Post-Primary Schools list.*
SCHOOL-L@IRLEARN.BITNET
LISTSERV@IRLEARN.BITNET

🌀 *Swedish Initiative for Research and Education list.*
SIREN@SEARN.BITNET
LISTSERV@SEARN.BITNET

🌀 *Subject Matter, Knowledge, Conceptual Change list.*
SMKCC-L@QUCDN.BITNET
LISTSERV@QUCDN.BITNET

🌀 *SUNY Buffalo Special Education (Students) Discussion list.*
SPCEDS-L@UBVM.BITNET
LISTSERV@UBVM.BITNET

🌀 *Teaching & Learning in Higher Education list.*
STLHE-L@UNBVM1.BITNET
LISTSERV@UNBVM1.BITNET
Exchange of ideas, views, and experiences on the subject of teaching and learning in higher education.
Contact: Esam Hussein
Hussein@UNB

🌀 *Talented and Gifted Education Discussion list.*
TAG-L@NDSUVM1.BITNET
LISTSERV@NDSUVM1.BITNET
Teaching Effectiveness list.
TEACHEFT@WCU.BITNET
LISTSERV@WCU.BITNET

🌀 *TESLIT-L: Adult Education and Literacy list.*
TESLIT-L@CUNYVM.BITNET
LISTSERV@CUNYVM.BITNET

🌀 *TQM in Higher Education list.*
TQM-L@UKANVM.BITNET
LISTSERV@UKANVM.BITNET
Discusses all aspects of total quality management and how these concepts can be implemented in institutions of higher education.
Contact: Phil Endacott
<ENDACOTT@UKANVAX.BITNET>

🌀 *TRIO Program Educators list.*
TRIO@NDSUVM1.BITNET
LISTSERV@NDSUVM1.BITNET

🌀 *VOCNET—Vocational Education Practitioners' Discussion list.*
VOCNET@UCBCMSA.BITNET
LISTSERV@UCBCMSA.BITNET

🌀 *Visual Resources Association list.*
VRA-L@UAFSYSB.BITNET
LISTSERV@UAFSYSB.BITNET

🌀 *VT K-12 School Network list.*
VT-HSNET@VTVM1.BITNET
LISTSERV@VTVM1.BITNET

🌀 *Western Cooperative for Educational Television list.*
WCETALL@UNMVM.BITNET
LISTSERV@UNMVM.BITNET

Fidonet

🌀 *Education and Related Discussions*
EDUCATION
General discussion about public and private education.
Moderator: Steve Winter
98:98/1
Distribution: 98:98/1
Gateways: PRIME NETWORK

🌀 *Educator*
EDUCATOR
For educators, parents, and others. Discusses issues of interest to teachers.
Moderator: Morton Sternheim
1:321/109
Distribution: BACKBONE

⟲ *Homeschooling Support*
HOMESCHL
Discusses curricula choices for those interested in home education.
Moderator: C. Lee Duckert
1:139/600
Distribution: BACKBONE

⟲ *K12net Art Education Conference*
K12_ART_ED
A curriculum-oriented discussion relating to elementary and secondary-school "art class". Not available singly.
Moderator: Jack Crawford
1:260/620

⟲ *K12net Business Education Conference*
K12_BUS_ED
A curriculum-oriented discussion relating to typical elementary and secondary "business ed" classrooms. Not available singly.
Moderator: Jack Crawford
1:260/620

⟲ *K12net Channel 0*
K12.CH0
For K12net Channel 0. See the K12.PROJECTS area for a weekly listing of current teacher/school-initiated projects.
Moderator: Helen Sternheim
1:321/109
Restr: MEMBER
Distribution: K12NET PRIVATE NETWORK; BACKBONE NODES LISTED BELOW

⟲ *K12net Channel 1*
K12.CH1
For K12net Channel 1. See the K12.PROJECTS area for a weekly listing of current teacher/school-initiated projects.
Moderator: Helen Sternheim
1:321/109
Restr: MEMBER
Distribution: K12NET PRIVATE NETWORK; BACKBONE NODES LISTED BELOW

⟲ *K12net Channel 2*
K12.CH2
For K12net Channel 2. See K12.PROJECTS area for a weekly listing of current teacher/school-initiated projects.
Moderator: Helen Sternheim
1:321/109
Restr: MEMBER
Distribution: K12NET PRIVATE NETWORK; BACKBONE NODES LISTED BELOW

⟲ *K12net Channel 3*
K12.CH3
For K12net Channel 3. See the K12.PROJECTS area for a weekly listing of current teacher/school-initiated projects.
Moderator: Helen Sternheim
1:321/109
Restr: MEMBER
Distribution: K12NET PRIVATE NETWORK; BACKBONE NODES LISTED BELOW

⟲ *K12net Channel 4*
K12.CH4
For K12net Channel 4. See the K12.PROJECTS area for a weekly listing of current teacher/school-initiated projects.
Moderator: Helen Sternheim
1:321/109
Restr: MEMBER
Distribution: K12NET PRIVATE NETWORK; BACKBONE NODES LISTED BELOW

⟲ *K12net Channel 5*
K12.CH5
For K12net Channel 5. See the K12.PROJECTS area for a weekly listing of current teacher/school-initiated projects.
Moderator: Helen Sternheim
1:321/109
Restr: MEMBER
Distribution: K12NET PRIVATE NETWORK; BACKBONE NODES LISTED BELOW

⟲ *K12net Channel 6*
K12.CH6
For K12net Channel 6. See the K12.PROJECTS area for a weekly listing of current teacher/school-initiated projects.
Moderator: Helen Sternheim
1:321/109
Restr: MEMBER
Distribution: K12NET PRIVATE NETWORK; BACKBONE NODES LISTED BELOW

⟲ *K12net Channel 7*
K12.CH7
For K12net Channel 7. See the K12.PROJECTS area for a weekly listing of current teacher/school-initiated projects.
Moderator: Helen Sternheim
1:321/109
Restr: MEMBER
Distribution: K12NET PRIVATE NETWORK; BACKBONE NODES LISTED BELOW

⟲ *K12net Channel 8*
K12.CH8
For K12net Channel 8. See the K12.PROJECTS area for a weekly listing of current teacher/school-initiated projects.

Moderator: Helen Sternheim
1:321/109
Restr: MEMBER
Distribution: K12NET PRIVATE NETWORK; BACKBONE NODES LISTED BELOW

🌎 *K12net Channel 9*
K12.CH9
For K12net Channel 9. See the K12.PROJECTS area for a weekly listing of current teacher/school-initiated projects.
Moderator: Helen Sternheim
1:321/109
Restr: MEMBER
Distribution: K12NET PRIVATE NETWORK; BACKBONE NODES LISTED BELOW

🌎 *K12net Channel 10*
K12.CH10
For K12net Channel 10. See the K12.PROJECTS area for a weekly listing of current teacher/school-initiated projects.
Moderator: Helen Sternheim
1:321/109
Restr: MEMBER
Distribution: K12NET PRIVATE NETWORK; BACKBONE NODES LISTED BELOW

🌎 *K12net Channel 11*
K12.CH11
For K12net Channel 11. See the K12.PROJECTS area for a weekly listing of current teacher/school-initiated projects.
Moderator: Helen Sternheim
1:321/109
Restr: MEMBER
Distribution: K12NET PRIVATE NETWORK; BACKBONE NODES LISTED BELOW

🌎 *K12net Channel 12*
K12.CH12
For K12net Channel 12. See the K12.PROJECTS area for a weekly listing of current teacher/school-initiated projects.
Moderator: Helen Sternheim

1:321/109
Restr: MEMBER
Distribution: K12NET PRIVATE NETWORK; BACKBONE NODES LISTED BELOW

🌎 *K12net Academic Computing Conference*
K12_COMP_LIT
A curriculum-oriented discussion dealing with hardware, software, and instructional methodologies relating to academic and instructional computing at the elementary and secondary-school levels. Not available singly. See K12.SYSOP for details.
Moderator: Jack Crawford
1:260/620

🌎 *K12net Elementary School "Chat" Conference*
K12_ELE_CHAT
For students in grades K-6 only. Not available singly; see K12.SYSOP for details.
Moderator: Jack Crawford
1:260/620

🌎 *K12net French Language Education Conference*
K12_FRANCAIS
For curriculum-oriented discussion promoting use of French as a second language by elementary and secondary-school students. Not available singly; see K12.SYSOP for details.
Moderator: Jack Crawford
1:260/620

🌎 *K12net German Language Education Conference*
K12_GERM_ENG
Similar to K12_FRANCAIS. Not available singly; see K12.SYSOP for details.
Moderator: Jack Crawford
1:260/620

🌎 *K12net Health and Physical Education Conference*
K12_HLTH_PE
Curriculum-oriented discussion relating to typical elementary and secondary-school health and physical education classes. Not available singly; see K12.SYSOP for details.
Moderator: Jack Crawford
1:260/620

🌎 *K12net Junior High/Middle School "Chat" Conference*
K12_JR_CHAT
This forum is for all-purpose area for students in the middle grades only. Not available singly; see K12.SYSOP for details.
Moderator: Jack Crawford
1:260/620

🌎 *K12net Language Arts Education Conference*
K12_LANG_ART
Curriculum-oriented discussion relating to reading, writing, literature, composition at the elementary and secondary-school levels. Not available singly; see K12.SYSOP for details.
Moderator: Jack Crawford
1:260/620

🌎 *K12net Life Skills Education Conference*
K12_LIF_SKIL
Curriculum-oriented discussion relating to home economics, safety, career development, and other life skills as applicable to elementary

and secondary schools. Not available singly; see K12.SYSOP for details.
Moderator: Jack Crawford
1:260/620

S *K12net Mathematics Education Conference*
K12_MATH_ED
Curriculum-oriented discussion relating to mathematics at the elementary and secondary-school levels. Not available singly; see K12.SYSOP for details.
Moderator: Jack Crawford
1:260/620

S *K12net Performing Arts Education Conference*
K12_MUSIC_ED
Curriculum-oriented discussion relating to elementary and secondary-school performing arts education. Not available singly; see K12.SYSOP for details.
Moderator: Jack Crawford
1:260/620

S *K12net News Conference*
K12_NEWS
This forum is a read-only conference and provides news pertinent to K12net and education. Current features include the Daily Report Card, a newsfeed which chronicles educational reform in the U.S. Not available singly; see K12.SYSOP for details.
Moderator: Jack Crawford
1:260/620

S *K12net Projects Conference*
K12.PROJECTS
For project descriptions, rules, and discussion for the 13 channels (message areas) of K12net.
Moderator: Helen Sternheim
1:321/109
Restr: MEMBER
Distribution: K12NET PRIVATE NETWORK; BACKBONE NODES LISTED BELOW

S *K12net Russian Language Education Conference*
K12_RUSSIAN
Similar to K12_FRANCAIS. Not available singly; see K12.SYSOP for details.
Moderator: Jack Crawford
1:260/620

S *K12net Science Education Conference*
K12_SCI_ED
Curriculum-oriented discussion relating to elementary and secondary-school science education. Not available singly; see K12.SYSOP for details.

Moderator: Jack Crawford
1:260/620

S *K12net Social Studies Education Conference*
K12_SOC_STUD
Curriculum-oriented discussion relating to elementary and secondary-school social studies education. Not available singly; see K12.SYSOP for details.
Moderator: Jack Crawford
1:260/620

S *K12net Spanish Language Education Conference*
K12_SPAN_ENG
Similar to K12_FRANCAIS. Not available singly; see K12.SYSOP for details.
Moderator: Jack Crawford
1:260/620

S *K12net Compensatory Education Conference*
K12_SPEC_ED
Curriculum-oriented discussion relating to the education of elementary and secondary-school children with disabilities or other special needs. Not available singly; see K12.SYSOP for details.
Moderator: Jack Crawford
1:260/620

S *K12net Senior High School "Chat" Conference*
K12_SR_CHAT
An all-purpose area for students in senior high school grades only. Not available singly; see K12.SYSOP for details.
Moderator: Jack Crawford
1:260/620

S *K12net Sysops Conference*
K12.SYSOP
Restricted to K12net sysops only. Not available singly. K12net is privately distributed to hundreds of school-based/oriented BBS's. Oriented to curriculum/classroom use in introducing kindergarten through 12th-grade students (and their teachers and administrators) to the "global village" of telecommunications. To prevent fragmentation of this community, K12net echoes are not available singly. For more information file request K12_INFO.ZIP from any of these members of the K12net Council of Coordinators: Gordon Benedict, Calgary, Alberta @1:134/49; Jack Crawford, Stanley, New York @ 1:260/620; John Feltham, Queensland, Australia @ 3:640/706; Janet Murray, Portland @ 1:105/23; Rob Reilly, Lanesboro, Mass @ 1:321/218; Gleason Sackman, Bottineau, North Dakota @ 1:288/5;

Helen Sternheim, Amherst, Mass. @ 1:321/110; Mort Sternheim, Amherst, Mass. @ 1:321/109; Andy VanDuyne, Norwood, New York @ 1:2608/75; Louis Van Geel, Antwerp, Belgium @ 2:295/3.
Moderator: Jack Crawford
    1:260/620

⑤ *K12net Talented and Gifted Education Conference*
    K12_TAG
Curriculum-oriented discussion relating to the education of elementary and secondary-school children capable of advanced academic challenges. Not available singly; see K12.SYSOP for details.
Moderator: Jack Crawford
    1:260/620

⑤ *K12net Professional Educators "Chat" Conference*
    K12.TCH_CHAT
An all-purpose area for the discussion of pedagogical philosophies, methods and materials, school reform, and other educational issues relating to elementary and secondary schools. Not available singly; see K12.SYSOP for details.
Moderator: Jack Crawford
    1:260/620

⑤ *K12net Technology and Vocational Education Conference*
    K12_TECH_ED
Curriculum-oriented discussion broadly relating to educating elementary and secondary-school students about robotics, engineering, industrial, and manufacturing technologies, drafting, CAD/CAM, all forms of skilled trades, and so on. Not available singly; see K12.SYSOP for details.
Moderator: Jack Crawford
    1:260/620

⑤ *Mensa, Intelligence, Education, Other High-IQ Groups*
    MENSA
For current and potential members of Mensa (a high-IQ society) and anyone else to discuss Mensa, intelligence, education, and other related matters.
Moderator: Dave Aronson
    1:109/120
Distribution: Z1-BACKBONE, RBBSNET, METRONET, USENET?

⑤ *Mensans Only Echo for Members Only*
    MENSANS_ONLY

A non-Backbone echo for general discussion between members only. Anyone may read the echo but only verified members of American Mensa, Ltd., or any other official Mensa organization may post messages.
Moderator: Christopher Baker
    1:374/14
Restr: MEMBER
Distribution: LOCAL, ZONE1, ZONE2

⑤ *Non-Traditional Student*
    NON_TRAD_STU
Discusses the adult returning to college. Topics include costs, schedules, credit for prior experience, competing with the "kids", study habits, more.
Moderator: Butch Walker
    1:157/2
Distribution: BACKBONE

⑤ *Special Education Topics*
    SPECIAL_ED
Discusses special education. Although created for parents, other interested users are welcome to contribute.
Moderator: Hector Mandel
    1:233/15
Restr: MOD-APVL
Distribution: 1:233/15

Usenet

⑤ *Academic freedom issues related to computers. Moderated.*
    alt.comp.acad-freedom.news

⑤ *Academic freedom issues related to computers.*
    alt.comp.acad-freedom.talk

⑤ *Learning over nets and so on.*
    alt.education.distance

⑤ *A place for the pre-college set on the net.*
    alt.kids-talk

⑤ *Higher education policy and research.*
    bit.listserv.ashe-l

⑤ *Communication education.*
    bit.listserv.commed

⑤ *DECUS education software library discussions.*
    bit.listserv.dectei-l

⑤ *Professionals and students discuss education.*
    bit.listserv.edpolyan

◈ EDTECH—educational technology. Moderated.
`bit.listserv.edtech`

◈ Educational research.
`bit.listserv.erl-l`

◈ IBM higher education consortium.
`bit.listserv.ibm-hesc`

◈ MBA student curriculum discussion.
`bit.listserv.mba-l`

◈ NOTIS/DOBIS discussion group.
`bit.listserv.notis-l`

◈ Stories involving universities & colleges. Moderated.
`clari.tw.education`

◈ Informal discussion among elementary students, grades K-5.
`k12.chat.elementary`

◈ Informal discussion among students, grades 6-8.
`k12.chat.junior`

◈ Informal discussion among high school students.
`k12.chat.senior`

◈ Informal discussion among teachers, grades K-12.
`k12.chat.teacher`

◈ Art curriculum in K-12 education.
`k12.ed.art`

◈ Business education curriculum, grades K-12.
`K12.ed.business`

◈ Teaching computer literacy, grades K-12.
`k12.ed.comp.literacy`

◈ Health and physical education curriculum, grades K-12.
`k12.ed.health-pe`

◈ Home economics and career education, grades K-12.
`k12.ed.life-skills`

◈ Mathematics curriculum, grades K-12.
`k12.ed.math`

◈ Music and performing arts curriculum, grades K-12.
`k12.ed.music`

◈ Science curriculum, grades K-12.
`k12.ed.science`

◈ Social studies and history curriculum, grades K-12.
`k12.ed.soc-studies`

◈ K-12 education for students with handicaps or special needs.
`k12.ed.special`

◈ K-12 education for talented and gifted students.
`k12.ed.tag`

◈ Industrial arts and vocational education, grades K-12.
`k12.ed.tech`

◈ Language arts curriculum, grades K-12.
`k12.lang.art`

◈ Bilingual German/English practice with native speakers.
`k12.lang.deutsch-eng`

◈ Bilingual Spanish/English practice with native speakers.
`k12.lang.esp-eng`

◈ Bilingual French/English practice with native speakers.
`k12.lang.francais`

◈ Bilingual Russian/English practice with native speakers.
`k12.lang.russian`

◈ Discussion of the educational system.
`misc.education`

◈ Discussion about employment, workplaces, careers.
`misc.jobs.misc`

◈ The science of education.
`sci.edu`

Online Libraries
After Dark

◈ *Academic Index™*
A bibliographic database indexing more than 400 publications of primary importance in undergraduate research.
Coverage: 1985 to present
Updated: Monthly

◈ *Dissertation Abstracts*
Citations on virtually every doctoral dissertation accepted at North American universities since 1861. Abstracts are included for dissertations added since 1980.

Coverage: 1861 to present
Updated: Monthly; Quarterly for Masters records

⑤ *Educational Resources Information Center (ERIC)*
Over 576,000 citations covering research findings, project and technical reports, speeches, unpublished manuscripts, books, and journal articles in the field of education.
Coverage: 1966 to present
Updated: Monthly

⑤ *Educational Testing Service Test Collection*
Current information on many types of tests used in education, psychological services, business, and health science.
Coverage: Current and past assessment devices
Updated: Quarterly

⑤ *Exceptional Child Education Resources*
Citations and abstracts of English-language print and non-print materials dealing with the education and development of individuals who are gifted or disabled.
Coverage: 1966 to present
Updated: Monthly

⑤ *Knowledge Industry Publications Database*
Descriptions of databases publicly available on-line in North America, including producer, vendor, and price information.
Coverage: Current
Updated: Monthly

⑤ *Mental Measurements Yearbook*
Contains factual information, critical reviews, and reliability-validity information on test materials covered by the Mental Measurements Yearbook.
Coverage: 1972 to present
Updated: Monthly

⑤ *Ontario Education Resources Information System*
A bilingual (English-French) bibliographic database comprised of four subfiles whose records include educational research, curriculum guidelines, reports and position papers, and learning materials of all types for elementary and secondary schools.
Coverage: 1974 to present (selected older coverage)
Updated: Bimonthly

⑤ *Resources in Vocational Education*
Information on state and federally administered research, curriculum development, and professional development projects in vocational education.
Coverage: 1978 to present
Updated: Quarterly

⑤ *Vocational Education Curriculum Materials*
Records of current print and non-print vocational and technical education curriculum materials.
Coverage: 1977 to present (selected older coverage)
Updated: Quarterly

⑤ *Wilson Education Index*
Covers over 350 English-language periodicals in all areas of education.
Coverage: 1983 to present
Updated: Monthly

Knowledge Index

⑤ *Academic Index*
Covers more than 400 scholarly and general interest publications, including the most commonly held titles in over 120 college and university libraries.
Coverage: 1976 to present
Updated: Monthly

⑤ *A-V Online*
Comprehensive coverage of non-print educational materials. Preschool to professional level materials are covered.
Coverage: 1964 to present
Updated: Irregular

⑤ *Dissertation Abstracts Online*
A guide to virtually every American dissertation accepted at an accredited institution since 1861. Masters abstracts from spring 1988 to present are also included.
Coverage: 1861 to present
Updated: Monthly

⑤ *The Educational Directory*
A specialized business directory providing information on public and private schools, public school districts, and public libraries in the U.S. Records contains extensive economic and demographic information.
Coverage: Current
Updated: Semiannual

⑤ *ERIC*
Available as an on-line database and in compact disc format. Identifies the most significant and

timely education research reports; indexes more than 700 periodicals of interest to the education profession. Many items can be purchased from the ERIC Document Reproduction Service in paper copy or microfiche.
Coverage: 1966 to present
Updated: Monthly; Quarterly on disc

⑤ *Everyone's Encyclopedia*
A reference work providing detailed articles covering the full range of human knowledge.
Coverage: Current
Updated: Closed

⑤ *Marquis Who's Who*
Detailed biographies of over 77,000 individuals. Top professionals in business, sports, government, the arts, entertainment, science, and technology are included.
Coverage: Current
Updated: Quarterly

⑤ *Peterson's College Database*
Lists colleges and universities with two- and four-year degree programs in the U.S., the territories of Guam and the Virgin Islands, and Canada.
Coverage: Current
Updated: Annual

⑤ *Peterson's Gradline*
Covers all accredited institutions in the U.S. and Canada offering post-baccalaureate degrees.
Coverage: Current
Updated: Annual

Orbit

No services available.

NewsNet

⑤ *Education Daily*
Frequency: Daily
Earliest NewsNet Issue: 1/4/88
Provides current reports every business day on national, state, and local events pertinent to top-level education officials. Includes news from Congress, the Education Department, the White House and the courts, and reports on the latest education research, civil rights, special education, and higher education news.

⑤ *Heller Report on Educational Technology and Telecommunications Markets*
Frequency: Monthly
Earliest NewsNet Issue: 5/1/90

Provides coverage and analysis of the K-12, higher education, corporate/industrial training, and home education markets. A wide range of technology and telecommunications products and services are covered, including educational software, distance learning, and integrated learning systems.

⑤ *Report on Literacy Programs*
Frequency: Biweekly
Earliest NewsNet Issue: 12/7/89
A guide for education and business leaders to legislation, funding, programs, and resources in the vital field of adult education. Special emphasis is placed on corporate literacy and basic-skills training programs.

Bulletin Boards

Federal Information Exchange (FEDIX) BBS

For colleges, universities, and other research organizations. Contains news releases, speeches, legal issues, and other information of use to higher education.
Baud Rate: 300, 1200, 2400, 9600
BBS Number: (800) 783-3349 or (301) 258-0953
Help Line: (301) 975-0103
Comments: logon as FEDIX; Internet E-Mail to comments@fedix.fie.com

The Laboratory—Hackensack High School

For the use of students, teachers, and others interested in the free exchange of ideas.
Availability: 24 hours/ 7 days
Baud Rate: 300, 1200, 2400, 9600, 14.4
BBS Number: (201) 342-5659
BBS Software: RBBS-PC
Sysop: Robert Curtis

Minority On-Line Information Service (MOLIS) BBS

Provides current information about historically Black and Hispanic colleges and universities.
Baud Rate: 300, 1200, 2400, 9600
BBS Number: (800) 783-3349 or (301) 258-0953

Help Line: (301) 975-0103
Comments: logon as FEDIX; Internet E-Mail to `comments@fedix.fie.com`

U.S. Department of Education National Education BBS

Provides individuals and organizations interested in education access to research and statistical findings of the U.S. Department of Education's Office of Educational Research and Improvement (OERI). Obtain research reports, statistical tables, and other items; share information with other educators; discuss education topics and issues through an electronic messaging system; distribute research papers, announcements, and software.
Availability: 24 hours/ 7 days
Baud Rate: 300, 2400
BBS Number: (800) 222-4922
BBS Software: RBBS-PC

W-FL Teacher Resource Center BBS

Home of the K12Net.
Availability: 24 hours/ 7 days
Baud Rate: up to 14.4
BBS Number: (716) 526-6495
Sysop: Jack Crawford
Help Line: (716) 526-6431

CD-ROM

🌐 *Education Index*
H.W. Wilson

🌐 *EMIL*
OCLC
6565 Franz Road
Dublin, OH 43017

🌐 *ERIC*
SilverPlatter Information Inc.
One Newton Executive Park
Newton Lower Falls, MA 02162

🌐 *ERIC/EMIL*
OCLC
6565 Franz Road
Dublin, OH 43017

🌐 *ERIC Retrospective*
OCLC
6565 Franz Road
Dublin, OH 43017

🌐 *International Encyclopedia of Education*
Pergamon Compact Solution

🌐 *New Electronic Encyclopedia*
Grolier Electronic Publishing
Sherman Turnpike
Danbury, CT 06816

🌐 *Science & Tech Reference*
McGraw-Hill Book Co.
11 West 19th Street
New York, NY 10011

🌐 *Science Helper*
PC-SIG
1030D East Duane Avenue
Sunnyvale, CA 94086

Electronics Resources

Forums & Databases
America Online (AOL)
No services available.

CompuServe (CIS)

🕥 *Consumer Electronics Forum*
GO CEFORUM
Dedicated to exchange of information about electronic consumer products and current issues facing the industry. Interactive conferences feature guests from manufacturers such as Sony, Pioneer, and Panasonic.

GEnie

🕥 *Radio & Electronics RoundTable*
Keyword: RADIO or Page 345
For all electronics and radio hobbyists; covers amateur radio, shortwave, CB, audio and video, and so on.

The Well
No services available.

Network Discussions Lists
Internet (Includes Bitnet & UUCPNet)

🕥 *Electronics Advances list.*
For discussions and information about the leading edge of electronics.
ADV-ELO@UTFSM.BITNET
LISTSERV@UTFSM.BITNET

Contact: Francisco Javier Fernandez
<FFERNAND@UTFSM.BITNET>

🕥 *Circuit Analysis list.*
Discussions of all aspects of introductory courses in circuit analysis for electrical engineering undergraduates.
CIRCUITS-L@UWPLATT.EDU
CIRCUITS-REQUEST@UWPLATT.EDU
Contact: <GRAY@UWPLATT.EDU>

🕥 *Microelectronics in Israel list.*
Information list for the Israeli research community involved in microelectronics.
MICRO-EL@TAUNIVM.BITNET
LISTSERV@TAUNIVM.BITNET
Contact: Dr. Michael Wolff
WOLFF@ILNCRD.BITNET

Fidonet
No services available.

Usenet

🕥 *Circuits, theory, electrons, and discussions.*
sci.electronics

Online Libraries
After Dark
No services available.

Knowledge Index
No services available.

Orbit
No services available.

NewsNet

⑨ *Comline Japan Daily: Electronics.*
Frequency: Daily
Earliest NewsNet Issue: 1/5/90
News from the semiconductor and consumer electronics industries on new technologies and consumer electronic goods.

⑨ *Consumer Electronics.*
Frequency: Weekly
Earliest NewsNet Issue: 3/15/82
Information on all aspects of consumer electronics. Includes current industry news in sales, marketing, new technologies, personnel changes, and more.

⑨ *Electronic Buyers' News.*
Earliest NewsNet Issue: 4/1/91
Buyer-oriented news related to procurement of electronic components, materials, instruments, and systems. Coverage is nontechnical.

⑨ *Electronic Engineering Times*
Frequency: Weekly
Earliest NewsNet Issue: 12/24/90
News and analysis of the electronics industry, including technology and business, current design practices, and professional development.

⑨ *Electronic Trade and Transport News.*
Frequency: Biweekly
Earliest NewsNet Issue: 6/12/90
Analyzes the news, trends, issues, business strategies, and equipment in today's trade and transport industry.

⑨ *Electronic World News.*
Frequency: Biweekly
Earliest NewsNet Issue: 4/22/91
Worldwide coverage of the electronics industry, focusing on information of interest to professionals in Europe and Asia.

⑨ *Japan Consumer Electronics Scan.*
Frequency: Weekly
Earliest NewsNet Issue: 1/2/89
Covers the electronics and electrical appliance industry in Japan.

Bulletin Boards
No services available.

CD-ROM

⑨ *ACEL Electronic Device Finder*
ACEL Information Pty. Ltd.

⑨ *COMPENDEX PLUS*
Dialog Information Services

⑨ *The Electronic Encyclopedia*
Grolier Electronic Publishing

Engineering Resources

Forums & Databases
America Online (AOL)
No services available.

CompuServe (CIS)

⑤ *IQuest Engineering InfoCenter*
   GO IQENGINEER
InfoCenter databases provide users with access to information extracted from published sources such as journals, books, and government publications about engineering.

⑤ *Compendex—Engineering Index*
   GO COMPENDEX
Contains abstracts of articles taken from significant engineering and technical literature. Topics include properties and testing of materials, fluid flow, pollution, ocean technology, applied physics, food technology, and measurement.

GEnie
No services available.

The Well
No services available.

Network Discussions Lists
Internet (Includes Bitnet & UUCPNet)

⑤ *Electrical Engineering*
Enables users to comment, ask/answer questions, and broadcast information about electrical engineering.
   ADV-ELI@UTFSM.BITNET
   LISTSERV@UTFSM.BITNET

Contact: Francisco Javier Fernandez
   <FFERNAND@UTFSM.BITNET>

⑤ *Electronics Advances*
Enables users to comment, ask/answer questions, and broadcast information about electric engineering.
   ADV-ELO@UTFSM.BITNET
   LISTSERV@UTFSM.BITNET
Contact: Francisco Javier Fernandez
   <FFERNAND@UTFSM.BITNET>

⑤ *Industrial Engineering Division of ASEE*
   ASEE-IED@ETSUADMN.BITNET
   LISTSERV@ETSUADMN.BITNET

⑤ *Congress of Canadian Engineering Students*
   CCES-L@UNBVM1.BITNET
   LISTSERV@UNBVM1.BITNET

⑤ *Civil Engineering Reasearch & Education*
   CIVIL-L@UNBVM1.BITNET
   LISTSERV@UNBVM1.BITNET

⑤ *Engineering Committee on Computing*
   ECC-L@MCGILL1.BITNET
   LISTSERV@MCGILL1.BITNET

⑤ *CSO Electrical Engineering Online Logbook*
   EELOG@UIUCVMD.BITNET
   LISTSERV@UIUCVMD.BITNET

⑤ *Engineering and Public Policy Discussion List*
   EPPD-L@UNBVM1.BITNET
   LISTSERV@UNBVM1.BITNET

⑤ *IEEE Ege list student branch discussion and announcements.*
   IEEE-EGE@TREARN.BITNET
   LISTSERV@TREARN.BITNET

⑤ *IEEE-L officers/members list.*
For all IEEE student branch officers and members.
   IEEE-L@BINGVMB.BITNET
   LISTSERV@BINGVMB.BITNET

Contact: Paul D. Kroculick
<TJW0465@BINGTJW.BITNET>

IEEE Turkish Section Communication List
IEEE-TR@TRITU.BITNET
LISTSERV@TRITU.BITNET

Spanish IEEE Discussions
A discussion list on Bitnet, devoted to the interchange of ideas, discussions, and meeting announcements in the field of electronic, electrical, and computer engineering in Spanish.
IEEE@USACHVM1.BITNET
LISTSERV@USACHVM1
Contact: Eric A. Soto-Lavin
<IEEESB@USACHVM1.BITNET>

Illuminating Engineering Society (IES)
IES-L@PSUVM.BITNET
LISTSERV@PSUVM.BITNET

Interfacial Phenomena Interest List
Discusses meetings, articles, software, theories, materials, methods, and tools on interfacial phenomena.
IFPHEN-L@WSUVM1.BITNET
LISTSERV@WSUVM1.BITNET

McGill Engineering AdHoc Committee on Computing
MEACC-L@MCGILL1.BITNET
LISTSERV@MCGILL1.BITNET

Mechanical Engineering
Discusses any topics pertinent to the mechanical engineering communities such as meeting announcements, software evaluation, and composite material research.
MECH-L@UTARLVM1.BITNET
LISTSERV@UTARLVM1.BITNET

Pre-Engineering Curriculum
PREENG-L@RPIECS.BITNET
LISTSERV@RPIECS.BITNET

Society of Women Engineers—Student Section
SBSWE-L@SBCCVM.BITNET
LISTSERV@SBCCVM.BITNET

Transportation and traffic engineering discussion list.
TRANSP-L@ASUACAD.BITNET
LISTSERV@ASUACAD.BITNET

Fidonet

Institute of Electrical and Electronics Engineers Conference
IEEE
Helps disseminate information to local IEEE members and to promote discussions among the engineering community. It is available in EchoMail and GroupMail formats.
Moderator: Burt Juda
1:107/10
Distribution: BACKBONE 107/10 13/13 107/323 107/3 260/206 107/1 107/516 107/210 107/211 107/323 107/3
Gateways: GROUPMAIL VIA 1:107/3

Biomedical and Clinical Engineering Topics
BIOMED
For employees of hospitals, clinics, and biomedical service organizations that work on medical equipment, or for biomedical equipment technicians, clinical engineers, or for for all others to learn what BMET/CBET/CE's are and what they do.
Moderator: Ray Brown
1:135/70
Distribution: BACKBONE

Usenet

General Announcements for IEEE community.
ieee.announce

Postings about managing the ieee. groups.*
ieee.config

IEEE—General discussion.
ieee.general

Discussion and tips on PC-NFS.
ieee.pcnfs

Regional Activities Board—Announcements.
ieee.rab.announce

Regional Activities Board—General discussion.
ieee.rab.general

Region 1 Announcements.
ieee.region1

Technical Activities Board—Announcements.
ieee.tab.announce

Technical Activities Board—General discussion.
ieee.tab.general

USAB—Announcements.
ieee.usab.announce

USAB—General discussion.
ieee.usab.general

- *Technical discussions about engineering tasks.*
  sci.engr
- *Biomedical engineering discussions.*
  sci.engr.biomed
- *Aspects of chemical engineering.*
  sci.engr.chem
- *Civil engineering topics.*
  sci.engr.civil
- *Mechanical engineering topics.*
  sci.engr.mech
- *Aspects of materials engineering.*
  sci.materials

Online Libraries
After Dark

- *Cambridge Scientific Abstracts Engineering*
Brings together information from five separate CSA abstracting services: Computer & Information Systems Abstracts, Electronics & Communications Abstracts, ISMEC: Mechanical Engineering Abstracts, Health & Safety Science Abstracts and Solid State/Superconductivity Abstracts.
Coverage: 1981 to present
Updated: Monthly

- *Current Contents: Engineering, Technology & Applied Sciences*
A subset of Current Contents Search™ corresponding to the Current Contents: Engineering, Technology & Applied Sciences print edition.
Coverage: Most current 12 months
Updated: Weekly

Knowledge Index

- *CompendexPlus*
Contains information on soil contamination, groundwater, pollution control equipment, and water treatment.
Coverage: Current
Updated: Monthly

- *Aerospace Database*
Provides references, abstracts, and controlled-vocabulary indexing of key scientific and technical documents, as well as books, reports, and conferences, covering aerospace research and development in over 40 countries. Available only in the United States and Canada. Access by non-U.S. governments, organizations, or persons acting on their behalf is not allowed without written approval of the American Institute of Aeronautics and Astronautics, Technical Information Service.
Coverage: 1962 to the present
Updated: Twice a month

Orbit

- *Aqualine*
Covers the literature on water and wastewater technology and environmental protection. Only available on Orbit.
Coverage: 1960 to present
Updated: Biweekly

- *Biotechnology Abstracts*
Covers all technical aspects of biotechnology from genetic manipulation and biochemical engineering to fermentation and downstream processing.
Coverage: July 1982 to present
Updated: Monthly

- *Chemical Abstracts*
Covers chemical sciences literature from over 9,000 journals, patents from 27 countries and 2 industrial property organizations, new books, conference proceedings, and government research reports.
Coverage: 1977 to present
Updated: Bimonthly

- *Chemical Engineering and Biotechnology Abstracts*
Covers theoretical, practical and commercial material on all aspects of chemical engineering as well as articles covering chemically-related aspects of processing, safety, and the environment.
Coverage: 1970 to present
Updated: Monthly

- *COLD*
Covers all disciplines dealing with the Arctic, Antarctica, the Antarctic Ocean, and sub-Antarctic islands: snow, ice, and frozen ground; navigation on ice; civil engineering in cold regions; and behavior and the operation of materials and equipment in cold temperatures. Only available on Orbit.
Coverage: 1951 to present
Updated: Quarterly

COMPENDEX PLUS
Provides the coverage of the COMPENDEX and EI Engineering meetings databases, journal articles, and individual conference papers without duplicate coverage.
Coverage: 1970 to present
Updated: Monthly

CORROSION
Contains records on the effects of over 600 agents on the most widely used metals, plastics, nonmetallics, and rubbers over a temperature range of 40-560 degrees fahrenheit. Also provides information useful in avoiding corrosion problems in the initial design state, in solving existing corrosion problems, and in determining what corrosion problems exist. Only available on Orbit.
Coverage: Current
Updated: Periodically

Engineered Materials Abstracts
Covers journal articles, conference papers, reviews, technical reports, books, dissertations, government reports and U.S., British, and European patents in the fields of material engineering and related subjects.
Coverage: 1986 to present
Updated: Monthly

GeoMechanics Abstracts
Contains bibliographic data covering published literature on the mechanical performance of geological materials relevant to the extraction of raw materials for mankind from the earth, and construction of structures on or in the earth for civil engineering projects or energy generation.Only available on Orbit.
Coverage: 1977 to present (some pre 1977)
Updated: Bimonthly

GEOREF
Covers geo-sciences literature from journals, books, conference proceedings, government documents, maps, and theses. Subscription costs or surcharges may apply to GEOREF.
Coverage: 1785 to present
Updated: Monthly

ICONDA- The CIB International Construction Database
Contains bibliographic references to articles published worldwide on construction, civil engineering, architecture, and town planning.
Coverage: 1976 to present
Updated: Monthly

INSPEC
Provides worldwide coverage on physics, electrical and electronics engineering, computers and control, and information technology.
Coverage: 1969 to present
Updated: Biweekly

MICROSEARCH
Provides coverage of reviews from microcomputer-related literature; specifically, the availability, applications, compatibility, and comparative evaluations of hardware and software products.
Coverage: 1983 to present
Updated: Periodically

Remote Sensing
Contains bibliographic references to studies, technical reports, papers, symposia, and conference proceedings covering the instrumentation, techniques, and applications of remote sensing technology.
Coverage: 1973 to present
Updated: Monthly

SAE Global Mobility Database
Provides access to technical papers presented at Society of Automotive Engineers (SAE) meetings and conferences.
Coverage: 1906 to present
Updated: varies

Supertech
Combines the following high-tech files from Bowker Electronic Publishing: Artificial Intelligence, CAD/CAM, and Robotics. Each file may also be accessed separately. Covers a wide variety of areas within the subject scope of the three files.
Coverage: 1973 to present
Updated: Monthly

Weldasearch
Contains citations with abstracts covering international literature such as journal articles, research reports, books, conference papers, standards, patents, theses, and special publications in the areas of joining of metals and plastics, metal spraying and thermal cutting. Only available on Orbit.
Coverage: 1967 to present
Updated: Monthly

NewsNet

No services available.

Bulletin Boards
MechEng

The BBS of the American Society of Mechanical Engineers

A free service of the American Society of Mechanical Engineers and Mechanical Engineering Magazine. The system is open to the public and supports technical and scientific software specializing on mechanical engineering software.
Baud Rate: 300, 1200, 2400, 9600
BBS Number: (608) 233-3378 or (608) 233-5378 (9600 bps)
BBS Software: PCBoard
Sysop: Greg Jackson

Engineering Bulletin Board System (EBBS)

Offers the engineering professional instant access to a variety of civil and structural engineering programs as well as CADD utilities for the IBM-PC/XT/AT, PS/2, 80386, 80486 and 80586 computers. Also offers conferences.
Baud Rate: 300, 1200, 2400
BBS Number: (805) 253-2917
BBS Software: dBBS
Help Line: (805) 259-6902

The IEEE (San Diego) BBS

The Institute of Electrical and Electronics Engineers, Inc.
Availability: 24 hrs/7days
Baud Rate: 300, 1200, 2400, 9600, 14.4Kbps
BBS Number: (619) 452-3131
Sysop: Larry Hamerman
Help Line: (619) 535-7618
Comments: InterNet: ieee@ucsd.edu

ENGINET ONLINE

ENGINET is owned and operated by a licensed professional engineer and is maintained by a group of technical professionals. Provide an environment where technical professionals may encounter new associates and share resources.
Availability: 24hrs/7days
Baud Rate: 300, 1200, 2400, 9600, 38.4 kbps
BBS Number: (513) 858-2688
BBS Software: PCBoard
Help Line: (513) 858-2483

The Biomedical Engineering Computer Bulletin Board Service
Baud Rate: 300, 1200, 2400, 9600
BBS Software: Searchlight
BBS Number: (201) 596-5679
Sysop: John F. Andrews

The Professional Surveyor.

A board devoted to the profession of surveying.
Baud Rate: 300, 1200, 2400, 9600
BBS Number: (703) 979-9103
BBS Software: WILDCAT!

CD-ROM

❧ *Civil Engineering*
CITIS CD-ROM CITIS Ltd.
210 Fifth Avenue, Suite 1102
New York, NY 10010

❧ *ACEL Electronic Device Finder*
ACEL Information PTy. LTD

❧ *ACEL Engineering Index Plus*
ACEL Information PTy. LTD

❧ *Compendex Plus*
Dialog Information Service
3460 Hillview Avenue
Palo Alto, CA 94304

❧ *Ei EE Disc*
Dialog Information Services

❧ *METADEX Collections: Metals Polymers Ceramics*
Dialog Information Services

❧ *NTIS*
Dialog Information Services

❧ *MOVE-SAE Mobility Engineering Technology*
Society of Automotive Engineers

❧ *The Electronic Encyclopedia*
Groiler Electronic Publishing

❧ *Your Engineering Sourcebook*
Y.E.S.
8922 E. 59th Street
Tulsa, OK 74145

Environment Resources

Forums & Databases
America Online (AOL)

⑤ *Environmental Forum*
Keyword: Earth
Path: Lifestyles & Interests Department
>Environment Club
Hosted by the author of this book and contains many areas for posting and reading environmental information, covering all aspects of the environment.

⑤ *Network Earth*
Keyword: Network Earth
Path: Lifestyles & Interests Department > Network Earth
An online supplement to CNN's Network Earth weekly environmental series. Users can ask questions to the producers of the show, discuss shows, and get more information on the subject of each show.

CompuServe (CIS)

No services available.

GEnie

No services available.

The Well

⑤ *Environment*
(g env)
Discusses all facets of the global environment.

⑤ *Energy*
(g power)
Covers issues on energy. The conference addresses three sides of the energy question: resources, technology, and policy.

⑤ *Flora and Fauna*
(g wild)
Discusses flora and fauna; threats to their habitats, plans for helping to save endangered species, and alerts to new animal conservation activities in regional areas.

Network Discussions Lists

Internet (Includes Bitnet & UUCPNet)

⑤ *Activist*
ANIMAL-RIGHTS@CS.ODU.EDU
Animal-Rights-Request@XANTH.CS.ODU.EDU

⑤ *Animal Rights*
Discusses animal rights.
Contact: Chip Roberson
<csrobe@CS.WM.EDU>

⑤ *Aquaculture Discussion List*
For users interested in the science, technology, and the business of rearing aquatic species.
AQUA-L@UOGUELPH.BITNET
LISTSERV@UOGUELPH.BITNET
Contact: Ted White
<ZOOWHITE@UOGUELPH.BITNET>

⑤ *Pollution and Groundwater Recharge*
Discusses water issues particularly on aquifers.
AQUIFER@IBACSATA.BITNET
LISTSERV@IBACSATA.BITNET
Contact: Professor S. Troisi
<1026TRO@ICSUNIV.BITNET>

○ *Bee Biology*
Discusses research and information about the biology of bees.
```
BEE-L@ALBNYVM1.BITNET
LISTSERV@ALBNYVM1.BITNET
```
Contact: Mary Jo Orzech
```
<MJO@BROCK1P.BITNET>
```

○ *Biosphere and Ecology*
Discusses topics related to the biosphere, pollution, CO-2 effect, ecology, habitats, climate, and so on.
```
BIOSPH-L@UBVM.BITNET
LISTSERV@UBVM.BITNET
```
Contact: Dave Phillips
```
davep@acsu.buffalo.edu
```

○ *National Birding Hotline Cooperative Expands Again*
For discussions among users who provide hotline transcripts to the first three lists.
```
BIRD_RBA@ARIZVM1.BITNET
LISTSERV@ARIZVM1.BITNET
```
Contact: Charles B. Williamson (Chuck)
```
<CHUCKW@ARIZEVAX.BITNET>
```

○ *National Birding Hotline Cooperative Expands Again*
Provides information for bird banders to discuss their trade.
```
BIRDBAND@ARIZVM1.BITNET
LISTSERV@ARIZVM1.BITNET
```
Contact: Charles B. Williamson (Chuck)
```
<CHUCKW@ARIZEVAX.BITNET>
```

○ *National Birding Hotline Cooperative Expands Again*
Discusses birding experiences, birding hotspots, and just about anything else of interest regarding wild birds.
```
BIRDCHAT@ARIZVM1.BITNET
LISTSERV@ARIZVM1.BITNET
```
Contact: Charles B. Williamson (Chuck)
```
<CHUCKW@ARIZEVAX.BITNET>
```

○ *National Birding Hotline Cooperative Expands Again*
Offers transcripts of current Central U.S. Hotlines.
```
BIRDCNTR@ARIZVM1.BITNET
LISTSERV@ARIZVM1.BITNET
```
Contact: Charles B. Williamson (Chuck)
```
<CHUCKW@ARIZEVAX.BITNET>
```

○ *National Birding Hotline Cooperative Expands Again*
Offers transcripts of current Eastern U.S. hotlines.

```
BIRDEAST@ARIZVM1.BITNET
LISTSERV@ARIZVM1.BITNET
```
Contact: Charles B. Williamson (Chuck)
```
<CHUCKW@ARIZEVAX.BITNET>
```

○ *NBHC Birding Trip Reports*
```
BIRDTRIP@ARIZVM1.BITNET
LISTSERV@ARIZVM1.BITNET
```

○ *National Birding Hotline Cooperative Expands Again*
Offers transcripts of current Western U.S. hotlines.
```
BIRDWEST@ARIZVM1.BITNET
LISTSERV@ARIZVM1.BITNET
```
Contact: Charles B. Williamson (Chuck)
```
<CHUCKW@ARIZEVAX.BITNET>
```

○ *Discussion of beliefs and practices of conservation list.*
```
CJ-L@ALBNYVM1.BITNET
LISTSERV@ALBNYVM1.BITNET
```

○ *The Energy and Climate Information Exchange*
A project of EcoNet aimed at educating the environmental community and the general public on the potential of energy efficiency and renewable energy to reduce the use of fossil fuels and their contribution to climate change.
```
ecixfiles@igc.org
ecixfiles@igc.org
```
Contact: Lelani Arris
```
<larris@igc.org>
```

○ *Ecological Society of America: Grants and Jobs*
```
ECOLOG-L@UMDD.BITNET
LISTSERV@UMDD.BITNET
```

○ *Ecological and Environmental Issues*
```
ECONET@MIAMIU.BITNET
LISTSERV@MIAMIU.BITNET
```

○ *Ecosystem Theory and Models*
```
ECOSYS-L@DEARN.BITNET
LISTSERV@DEARN.BITNET
```

○ *Enviornmental Studies*
Exchanges information about environmental studies (ES) programs, generally—course designs, successful student projects, important information sources, and so on.
```
ENVST-L@BROWNVM.BROWN.EDU
LISTSERV@BROWNVM.BROWN.EDU
```
Contact: Sandra Baptista
```
<ST802218@BROWNVM>
```

🖑 *Ecology of Nitrogen Fixing Bacteria*
Eng-Leong Foo <eng-leong_foo_mircen-
ki%micforum@mica.mic.ki.se>
A mailing list for BNFNET's—Biological
Nitrogen Fixation Electronic Network—2nd
BNFNET Annual Computer Conference on the
Ecology of Nitrogen Fixing Bacteria.

🖑 *Green Organizations*
Discusses strategic and tactical issues facing
Green organizations worldwide.
GreenOrg@INDYCMS.BITNET
ListServ@IndyCMS.BITNET
Contact: John B Harlan
<JBHarlan@IndyVAX.BITNET>

🖑 *Organization and the Natural Environment*
ONE-L@CLVM.BITNET
LISTSERV@CLVM.BITNET

🖑 *Recycling in Practice*
RECYCLE@UMAB.BITNET
LISTSERV@UMAB.BITNET

🖑 *Max Scott Southwest Center for the
Environment*
SCERP-L@NMSUVM1.BITNET
LISTSERV@NMSUVM1.BITNET

🖑 *South Florida Environmental Reader*
For environmental issues related to South
Florida.
SFER-L@UCF1VM.BITNET
LISTSERV@UCF1VM.BITNET

🖑 *Flordia Environmental Reader*
Offers environmental information for people
in South Florida.
SFER@MTHVAX.CS.MIAMI.EDU
sfer-request@MTHVAX.CS.MIAMI.EDU
Contact: A.E. Mossberg
<aem@MTHVAX.CS.MIAMI.EDU>

🖑 *Sino-Ecologists Club Overseas Forum*
SINOECOL@MIAMIU.BITNET
LISTSERV@MIAMIU.BITNET

🖑 *UNCEDGEN—Public discussion list about
the environment list.*
UNCEDGEN@UFRJ.BITNET
LISTSERV@UFRJ.BITNET

Fidonet

🖑 *Sahara Club Discussion Area*
SAHARA
Discusses environmental-radical tactics, land
closures caused by them, businesses and
recreation attacked by them, and what Sahara
Club is doing to prohibit these tactics.
Moderator: Patrick Martin

1:102/825
Restr: MOD-APVL
Distirbution: PRIVATELY DISTRIBUTED

🖑 *Sierra Club Echo*
SIERRAN
Offers information on Sierra DESC Club
campaigns, events, and outings, as well as
general DESC environmental topics.
Moderator: Eddie Rowe
1:19/124
Distirbution: BACKBONE

🖑 *World Talk Conference & United Nations
News*
WORLDTLK
Contains United Nations proceedings from the
General Assembly; includes UN press releases,
global environmental news, news flashes from
UNICEF, World Health Organization, and other
related UN organizations.
Moderator: James Waldron
1:2604/401
Distirbution: BACKBONE (ZONE-1, ZONE-2,
ZONE-3 AND ZONE-4)
Gateways: FREDMAIL AND RBBSNET.
INTERNET MAILING LIST.

🖑 *Environmental Issues*
For environmental discussions where topics
range from diapers to Nuclear power plants.
ENVIRON
Moderator: James Farrow
1:163/242
Distirbution: BACKBONE

🖑 *Save Our Sealife Committee Echo for FLorida*
S.O.S.
A grassroots petition campaign to amend the
Constitution of FLorida to prohibit the use of
gill nets and other entangling nets. Also, to
prohibit the use of large seines and food-shrimp
nets from the Florida nearshore and inshore.
Moderator: Christopher Baker
1:374/14
Distirbution: LOCAL, FLORIDA

🖑 *Alternative Energy Systems and Homemade
Power*
Offers information on small scale alternative
energy systems and personal power production.
HOMEPOWR
Moderator: Don Kulha
1:125/7
Distirbution: BACKBONE

Usenet

- *Environmental news, hazardous waste, forests. (Moderated)*
  `clari.tw.environment`

- *Discussions of the Great Lakes and adjacent places.*
  `alt.great-lakes`

- *Environmentalist causes.*
  `alt.save.the.earth`

- *Biosphere and ecology, discussion list.*
  `bit.listserv.biosph-l`

- *Forum on Environment and Human Behavior.*
  `bit.listserv.envbeh-l`

- *List for the Discussion of Buckminster Fuller.*
  `bit.listserv.geodesic`

- *OZONE Discussion List.*
  `bit.listserv.ozone`

- *Hobbyists interested in bird watching.*
  `rec.birds`

- *Discussions about the environment and ecology.*
  `sci.environment`

Online Libraries
After Dark

- *BIOSIS Previews,® Backfile and Merged File*
  Offers international coverage of journal articles, research reports, reviews, conference papers, symposia, books and other sources in biology, medicine, and other life sciences.
  Coverage: 1970 to date
  Updated: Monthly

- *Current Contents: Physical Chemical & Earth Sciences*
  A subset of Current Contents Search™ corresponding to the Current Contents: Physical, Chemical, and Earth Sciences edition.
  Coverage: Most current 12 months
  Updated: Weekly

- *TOXLINE*
  Contains bibliographic files from the National Library of Medicine, with citations from 1965 to the present, covering the pharmacological biomedical, physiological and toxicological effects of drugs, and other chemicals.

Coverage: Pre-1965 to present
Updated: Monthly with about 5000 documents per update

- *TOXLINE Subset*
  A subset of TOXLINE containing documents from all TOXLINE subfiles except the MEDLINE-derived subfile, TOXBIB.
  Coverage: pre-1965 tpo present
  Updated: Monthly

Knowledge Index

- *Pollution Abstracts*
  Pollution Abstracts is a source of references to literature on pollution, its sources, and its control.
  Coverage: 1970 to present
  Updated: Bimonthly

Orbit

- *Aqualine*
  Covers literature on water and wastewater technology and environmental protection. Only available on Orbit.
  Coverage: 1960 to present
  Updated: Biweekly

- *Chemical Safety NewsBase*
  Covers a range of information on the health and safety affects of hazardous chemicals encountered by employees in industry and laboratories.
  Coverage: 1981 to present
  Updated: Monthly

- *CISDOC*
  Provides international coverage of all topics related to general safety, health, and conditions at work.
  Coverage: 1972 to present
  Updated: Bimonthly

- *ENVIROLINE*
  Provides abstracts on air environment, environmental health, land environment, resource management, and water environment.
  Coverage: 1971 to present
  Updated: Monthly

- *Food Science and Technology Abstracts*
  Covers literature on food science and technology. FSTA includes articles on the basic food sciences, food safety, engineering, packaging, food products, and food processes.
  Coverage: 1969 to present
  Updated: Monthly

Health and Safety Executive
Contains bibliographic references from journals, books, pamphlets, government publications, and conference proceedings on occupational health and safety aspects
Coverage: 1977 to present
Updated: Monthly

National Institute for Occupational Saftey and Health Technical information Center (NIOSHTIC)
Contains records covering all aspects of occupational safety and health from the National Institute for Occupational Safety and Health.
Coverage: 19th century to present
Updated: Quarterly

Pharmaceutical News Index (PNI)
A comprehensive resource for the latest U.S. and international news about the pharmaceuticals industry. Contains cover-to-cover indexing to 23 major industry newsletters.
Coverage: 1974 to present
Updated: Weekly

Safety Science Abstracts
Covers the broad interdisciplinary science of safety—identifying, evaluating and eliminating or controlling hazards.
Coverage: 1981 to present
Updated: Monthly

WasteInfo
Contains bibliographic references on all aspects of non-radioactive waste management. Only available on ORBIT.
Coverage: 1973 to present
Updated: Monthly

NewsNet

Energy

Clean-Coal/Synfuels Letter
Frequency: Weekly
Earliest NewsNet Issue: 9/9/91
Provides worldwide coverage of clean-coal technologies and synthetic fuels, including private industry and government developments.

Coal Outlook
Frequency: Weekly
Earliest NewsNet Issue: 8/13/90
Covers coal market and price information, legislation, transportation, regulation, coal exports, trends, and business opportunities.

Coal & Synfuels Technology
Frequency: Weekly
Earliest NewsNet Issue: 8/13/90
Reports on advances in major clean coal technologies and synthetic fuels, the U.S. Department of Energy's Clean Coal Program, acid rain legislation, demonstration projects, subcontracting and sales opportunities, and new publications.

Coal Week
Frequency: Weekly
Earliest NewsNet Issue: 9/9/91
Weekly intelligence report for executives in the coal industry, covering prices, markets, legislation, news reports, and analyses of industry events.

Coal Week International
Frequency: Weekly
Earliest NewsNet Issue: 9/10/91
Market management intelligence service for executives concerned with world trade in metallurgical and steam coal.

Eastern European Energy Report
Frequency: Monthly
Earliest NewsNet Issue: 6/1/91
Covers developing opportunities in the energy and environmental sectors of Eastern Europe for U.S. energy and environmental firms.

Electric Utility Week
Frequency: Weekly
Earliest NewsNet Issue: 9/9/91
Provides news and analysis of developments affecting the electric utility industry, including legislation, litigation, rates, environmental regulation, and fuel price changes.

Energy Conservation News—
Frequency: Monthly
Earliest NewsNet Issue: 9/1/89
Focuses on the technology and economics of energy conservation at industrial, commercial, and institutional facilities.

The Energy Daily
Frequency: Daily
Earliest NewsNet Issue: 4/10/89
Reports on the energy industry and its regulators. Areas covered include natural gas, nuclear power, electric utilities, oil, energy technology, and environmental issues.

Energy, Economics, and Climate Change
Frequency: Monthly
Earliest NewsNet Issue: 10/1/91

Focuses on the economic implications of climate change policies and how these will affect the energy industry worldwide.

☉ *The Energy Report*
Frequency: Weekly
Earliest NewsNet Issue: 8/28/89
Provides news on all energy sources: oil, natural gas, coal, nuclear, alternative fuels, and so on.

☉ *Enhanced Energy Recovery News*
Frequency: Monthly
Earliest NewsNet Issue: 9/1/89
Covers the technology and trends of enhanced recovery, including summaries of research and demonstration, and patents, company and product profiles.

☉ *HydroWire*
Frequency: Biweekly
Earliest NewsNet Issue: 11/30/87
Provides timely reports on the North American hydroelectric industry.

☉ *Independent Power Report*
Frequency: Biweekly
Earliest NewsNet Issue: 9/13/91
Tracks changes in rates and regulations affecting the small power production industry.

☉ *Industrial Energy Bulletin*
Frequency: Biweekly
Earliest NewsNet Issue: 9/13/91
Covers the new market forces reshaping the relationship between industrial energy consumers and their utility and fuel suppliers.

☉*Inside Energy/With Federal Lands*
Frequency: Weekly
Earliest NewsNet Issue: 9/9/91
Covers U.S. government policy on energy, land use, and development.

☉ *Inside F.E.R.C.*
Frequency: Weekly
Earliest NewsNet Issue: 9/9/91
Offers policy-oriented, in-depth coverage of US. federal regulation of natural gas, electric utility and oil pipelines, the U.S. Department of Energy, and state governments.

☉ *Inside F.E.R.C.'s Gas Market Report*
Frequency: Biweekly
Earliest NewsNet Issue: 9/13/91
Reports on the natural gas market, including deregulation, spot market, prices paid or received, contract terms, brokering, and futures trading.

☉ *Inside N.R.C.*
Frequency: Biweekly
Earliest NewsNet Issue: 9/9/91
Focuses exclusively on the U.S. Nuclear Regulatory Commission.

☉ *Japan Energy Scan*
Frequency: Weekly
Earliest NewsNet Issue: 1/2/89
Covers the Japanese oil industry, nuclear energy applications, utilities usage, and forecasting, in addition to reporting on advances in geothermal energy techniques and alternate fuels.

☉ *Nuclear Fuel*
Frequency: Biweekly
Earliest NewsNet Issue: 9/16/91
Combines news reports from around the world on the nuclear fuel cycle with detailed coverage of regulatory agencies.

☉ *Nucleonics Week*
Frequency: Weekly
Earliest NewsNet Issue: 9/12/91
Covers all aspects of international commercial nuclear power, including plant construction, low-level waste, government policies, plant performance, and statistics.

☉ *Platt's Oilgram News*
Frequency: Daily
Earliest NewsNet Issue: 9/3/91
An international news report serving all branches of the petroleum industry with coverage of government agencies, industry, and financial institutions.

☉ *Platt's Oilgram Price Report*
Frequency: Daily
Earliest NewsNet Issue: 9/3/91
A daily report on world oil prices, including all major fields worldwide and all principal wholesale centers.

☉ *Purpa Lines*
Frequency: Biweekly
Earliest NewsNet Issue: 11/23/87
Provides timely reports on the small-power production market.

☉ *U.S. Oil Week*
Frequency: Weekly
Retention: One year plus current year
Provides information on profit-making strategies for petroleum marketers across the country, as well as the latest regulations and updates on storage tanks.

⑤ Utility Reporter—Fuels, Energy & Power
Frequency: Monthly
Earliest NewsNet Issue: 6/1/84
Covers worldwide activities dealing with energy and power, systems and components, transmission and distribution, resources and fuels, research and development, management and economics, regulatory and legislative, software, innovations, and more—activities of interest to technologists, managers, and operating personnel.

⑤ Worldwide Energy
Frequency: Monthly
Earliest NewsNet Issue: 11/1/90
Reports on all types of energy sources and applications, including oil, gas, coal, nuclear, electric, solar and the latest energy alternatives.

Environment

⑤ Air/water Pollution Report
Frequency: Weekly
Earliest NewsNet Issue: 1/4/82
Coverage of federal environmental legislation, regulation and litigation, as well as state and local developments, business and technology news, grants and contracts, publications and meetings.

⑤ Asbestos Control Report
Frequency: Biweekly
Covers matters of interest to asbestos industry professionals, including control techniques, worksite health and safety, new federal standards, medical research efforts, state and local regulations, and more.

⑤ Business and the Environment
Frequency: Monthly
Earliest NewsNet Issue: 9/1/90
Covers regulation innovations by "green" companies, global news and analysis, investment trends and venture deals, and tracks important market deals related to the environment.

⑤ California Planning & Development Report
Frequency: Monthly
Earliest NewsNet Issue: 6/1/88
Covers local growth and development issues in California and throughout the country.

⑤ Environment Watch: Latin America
Frequency: Monthly
Earliest NewsNet Issue: 11/1/91
Offers on developments in environmental regulation, law, and enforcement in Latin America.

⑤ Environment Week
Frequency: Weekly
Earliest NewsNet Issue: 2/23/89
Reports on a host of pressing environmental issues, from acid rain and the greenhouse effect to nuclear and hazardous waste disposal.

⑤ Environmental Compliance Update
Frequency: Monthly
Earliest NewsNet Issue: 10/1/85
Identifies and analyzes the issues, business, and economic impact of environmental compliance law, and monitors the relevant changes due to legislation, court decisions, private rulings, and technology.

⑤ Global Environmental Change Report
Frequency: Biweekly
Earliest NewsNet Issue: 1/12/90
Provides coverage of global change, including scientific findings, policy trends, and industry actions worldwide, reporting in the areas of global warming, ozone depletion, deforestation, and acid precipitation.

⑤ Golob's Oil Pollution Bulletin
Frequency: Biweekly
Earliest NewsNet Issue: 1/18/91
Provides in-depth news and analysis on developments in oil pollution prevention, control, and cleanup.

⑤ Greenhouse Effect Report
Frequency: Monthly
Earliest NewsNet Issue: 12/1/89
Covers Congressional, regulatory, business, technological, and international actions on global warming and the greenhouse effect.

⑤ Hazardous Materials Intelligence Report
Frequency: Weekly
Earliest NewsNet Issue: 9/2/88
Contains news and analysis on hazardous waste and hazardous materials management, state and federal legislation, litigation, new products and services, and so on.

⑤ Hazardous Materials Transportation
Frequency: Biweekly
Earliest NewsNet Issue: 2/20/91
Covers the latest rulings and regulations at federal, state, and local levels, plus international regulatory actions.

⑤ Hazardous Waste Business
Frequency: Biweekly
Earliest NewsNet Issue: 1/2/92

Devoted to the business of the hazardous waste market as contrasted to the regulatory side. Complements McGraw-Hill's Integrated Waste Management (EV40).

Indoor Air Quality Update
Frequency: Monthly
Earliest NewsNet Issue: 1/1/90
Provides practical solutions to indoor air problems.

Industrial Environment
Frequency: Monthly
Earliest NewsNet Issue: 1/1/91
Discusses products, procedures, and processes being developed or in operation to improve the environment, in industry and in business.

Integrated Waste Management
Frequency: Biweekly
Earliest NewsNet Issue: 9/18/91
Offers worldwide coverage of waste to energy, recycling, composting, source reduction, landfilling, and related subjects involving the handling of municipal, agricultural, and industrial solid wastes.

Medical Waste News
Frequency: Biweekly
Earliest NewsNet Issue: 11/15/89
Provides comprehensive coverage of the field of medical and infectious waste, including regulation, legislation, and business.

Nuclear Waste News
Frequency: Weekly
Earliest NewsNet Issue: 6/9/83
Covers major developments in the field of nuclear waste, including legislation and regulations, research and development activities, and economic and technical reports.

Oil Spill Intelligence Report
Frequency: Weekly
Earliest NewsNet Issue: 5/3/90
Covers oil-spill cleanup, prevention, and control world-wide.

Oil Spill U.S. Law Report
Frequency: Monthly
Earliest NewsNet Issue: 3/1/91
Reports on U.S. Legislation, regulation, and litigation. Covers emerging regulations and agency interpretations, industry compliance efforts, and the latest court decisions.

Plastic Waste Strategies
Frequency: Monthly
Earliest NewsNet Issue: 5/1/91
Focuses on recycling, degradability, incineration, and alternative methods of handling solid waste.

Report on Defense Plant Wastes
Frequency: Biweekly
Earliest NewsNet Issue: 12/8/89
Covers environmental laws, regulations, cleanups, contracting, and court action affecting U.S. defense, weapons production, and other government facilities.

Solid Waste Report
Frequency: Weekly
Earliest NewsNet Issue: 1/12/87
Covers processing, disposal, recycling, and collection of nonhazardous waste.

Superfund
Frequency: Biweekly
Earliest NewsNet Issue: 8/13/90
Covers Superfund cleanup and litigation, the latest developments in federal and state hazardous-waste cleanup programs, remedial technologies, EPA action involving the Superfund program, potentially responsible parties, penalties, and settlements.

Utility Environment Report
Frequency: Biweekly
Earliest NewsNet Issue: 1/11/91
Covers environmental issues that impact the utility and independent power industries.

Waste Treatment Technology News
Frequency: Monthly
Earliest NewsNet Issue: 9/1/89
Examines the technologies, reports on critical developments, and analyzes the new concepts necessary for the effective handling and management of all types of hazardous waste.

World Environment Report
Frequency: Biweekly
Earliest NewsNet Issue: 1/5/81
Coverage of environmental news from Europe, Asia, Africa, and Latin America, including air and water pollution, waste management, toxic-substances control, land-use planning, and alternative energy.

Bulletin Boards

GULFLINE BBS

Gulf of Mexico Program (GMP) Electronic Information System

Contains a comprehensive list of chemicals released into the environment by industry. Option 1 lists Chemicals, Option 2 lets you search for Companies by location, zip code, and many other variables.

Availability: 24 hrs
Baud Rate: 1200, 2400, 9600
BBS Numbers: (800) 235-4662 or (601) 688-2677; (800) 235-4662: 3 lines, toll-free in the United States; (601) 688-2677: 3 lines; (601) 688-7018: 2 lines; (FTS) 494-2677: 3 lines; (FTS) 494-7018: 2 lines
BBS Software: RBBS-PC
Sysop: Kay Mcgovern
Help Line: (601) 688-1065
Comment: Once registered, more access is granted.

EPA DRIPSS BBS

(Drinking Water Information Processing Support System)

Facilitates the exchange of information and programs between EPA and other drinking water professionals.

BBS Number: (800) 229-3737
Availability: 24 hrs
Baud Rate: 300, 1200, 2400
BBS Software: PCBoard
Sysop: Barry Gates
Help Line: (703) 339-0420

ATTIC

Alternative Treatment Technology Information Center BBS

The latest version of the RREL Treatability Database has been adapted for use online. The database includes soil and water treatability data .

Baud Rate: 300, 1200, 2400, 9600
BBS Number: (301) 670-3808, (301) 670-3813, or (301) 670-3813 or 14 (both 9600)
BBS Software: PCBoard
Help Line: (301) 670-6294

PIN BBS

The Pesticide Information Network

The Pesticide Information Network (PIN) is a collection of files containing up-to-date pesticide information. Currently, PIN has three databases: THE PESTICIDE MONITORING INVENTORY (PMI); THE RESTRICTED USE PRODUCTS FILE (RUP); THE CHEMICAL INDEX.

Baud Rate: 300, 1200, 2400,
BBS Number: (703) 305-5919
Help Line: (703) 305-7499
Comments: Set CAPSLOCK on before calling the BBS.

SWICH BBS

Solid Waste Information Clearinghouse (SWICH) BBS

Provides updated information on solid waste issues including: meeting and conference information, message inquiries, case studies, new technologies, new publications, expert contact information, and state and federal legislative and regulatory changes. The SWICH EBB is a subscription service as of November 1, 1992.

Baud Rate: 300, 1200, 2400
BBS Number: (301) 585-0204
BBS Software: PCBoard
Help Line: (800)-67-SWICH

Commission Issuance Posting System (CIPS) BBS

Provides access to Commission information and daily issuances. Lots of bulletins.

Availability: 23 hours every day. Not available between 8:00 a.m. and 9:00 a.m. Monday through Friday.
Baud Rate: 300, 1200, 2400, 9600
BBS Number: (202) 208-1397 or (202) 208-1781
BBS Software: RBBS-PC

OEA BBS

Office of Environmental Affairs, Dept of Interior

Offers information for users with an interest in, or business with, the Department of the Interior's Office of Environmental Affairs.

Baud Rate: 300, 1200, 2400, 9600
BBS Number: (202) 208-7119
BBS Software: WILDCAT

EarthNet Environmental Information Service: EEIS BBS

Offers the latest environmental news and forums for discussions on environmental topics.

Baud Rate: 300, 1200, 2400, 9600
BBS Number: (516) 321-4893
BBS Software: RemoteAccess
Sysop: BAI computers & Networking, Byron Arnao
Help Line: (516) 669-0138 or (516) 691-3689

ENVIRO

Contains information on environmental protection, ecology, wildlife, endangered species, natural resources and other topics.
Baud Rate: 300, 1200, 2400
BBS Number: (703) 524-1837
BBS Software: RBBS-PC
Sysop: Kurt Riegel
Help Line: (703) 522-5427
Comment: riegel_k@seaa.navsea.navy.mil

DOE'S FE TELENEWS

The Office of Fossil Energy's Online Information Service
Provides up-to-date information about or related to the Office of Fossil Energy, including news releases, speeches, Congressional testimony, and other information .
Availability: 24 hrs/7 days
Baud Rate: 300, 1200, 2400, 9600
BBS Number: (202) 586-6496
BBS Software: RBBS-PC
Sysop: Bob Porter,
Help Line: (202) 586-6503

WTIE—Wastewater Treatment Information Exchange BBS

National Small Flows Clearinghouse
Concentrates on wastewater treatment technologies, financing, operation and maintenance, wastewater and water equipment exchange.
Availability: 24 hrs/7 days
Baud Rate: 300, 1200, 2400, 9600
BBS Number: (800) 544-1936
BBS Software: PCBoard
Sysop: Harry Kidder and Loukis Kissonergis
Help Line: (800) 624-8301 or (304) 293-4191

WI-Lakes BBS

Wisconsin Department of Natural Resources
Concentrates on the lake resources of Wisonsin.
Availability: 5 PM - 9 AM M-F 24 Hrs Sat & Sun

Lake Professionals Only 9 AM - 5 PM M-Friday
Baud Rate: 300, 1200, 2400, 9600
BBS Number: (608) 267-7551
BBS Software: PCBoard
Sysop: James Vennie
Help Line: (608) 266-2212

EPA Region IV Water Management Division Bulletin Board

Provides information on wastewater treatment plants, their design, operation, maintenance, and Government Regulations.
Baud Rate: 300, 1200, 2400
BBS Number: (404) 347-1767
BBS Software: RBBS-PC
Sysop: John Harkins
Help Line: (404) 347-3633

CLU-IN: Cleanup Information Bulletin Board

United States Environmental Protection Agency Office of Solid Waste and Emergency Response Technology Innovation Office
Availability: 24 hours
Baud Rate: 300, 1200, 2400, 9600
BBS Number: (301) 589-8366
BBS Software: PCBoard
Sysop: Environmental Management Support
Help Line: (301) 589-8368

EnviroNet

Sponsored by Greenpeace for anyone interested in peace and ecological issues. Seven conferences titled gossip, disarmament, energy, forests, general, stepping lightly, and toxics are each moderated by different individuals and files for each subject area are available for downloading. On-line discussion with members is available in a special on-line chat area. Grassroots groups can get access to Environet through a special 800 number if they qualify.
Availability: 24 hrs/7 days
Baud Rate: 300, 1200, 2400
BBS Name/Sponsor: EnviroNet
BBS Number: (415) 512-9108
Parameters: 8-0-1
Sysop: Dick Dillman.

MNS ONLINE

MNS ONLINE is the run by the author. Supports the Apple User Group Community worldwide.

MNS (Mug News Service) is a UPI-like news service but it has a special environmental section.
Availability: 24 hrs/7 days
Baud Rate: 200, 2400, 9600
BBS Number: (518) 381-4430
BBS Software: FirstClass
Parameters: 8-0-1
Sysop: Don Rittner

Southeastern Software And Message Exchange (Sesame)

Offers discussions on hunting and fishing, ecology and natural resources, law enforcement, employment opportunities, and a private section for other cooperative wildlife biologists.
Availability: 24 hrs/7 days
Baud Rate: 300, 1200
BBS Name/Sponsor: SESAME
BBS Number: (919) 737-3990
BBS Software: RBBS-PC
Parameters: 8-0-1
Sysop: Wayne Cornelius
Help Line: (919) 737-2531.

Florida FishLINE

For anyone interested in fishing or fresh water fish of Florida, it is operated by the Florida Game and Fresh Water Fish Commission.
Availability: 24 hrs/7 days
Baud Rate: 300, 1200, 2400
BBS Name/Sponsor: Florida FishLINE
BBS Number: (904) 488-3773
BBS Software: Opus-CBCS
Parameters: 8-N-1
Sysop: Steven Atran
Help Line: (904) 488-4069 (business hours only)

Hazardous Materials Information Exchange (HMIX)

Provides a centralized database for federal, state, local and private sector users to share information pertaining to hazard materials emergency management, training, resources, technical assistance and regulations.
Availability: 24 hrs/7 days
Baud Rate: 300, 1200, 2400, 9600
BBS Name/Sponsor: Hazardous Materials Information Exchange (HMIS) BBS

BBS Number: (800) 874-2884
BBS Software: PCBoard
Parameters: 8-N-1
Sysop: Lessie Graves
Help Line: 1(800) 752-6367, 1(800) 367-9592 (IN ILLINOIS)

FireNet Leader

Contains reports and files on hazardous wastes, toxic information, how to handle toxics in case of a fire, federal and state laws regulating them, hazardous handling contingency plans, training plans, and so on.
Baud Rate: 300, 1200, 2400, 9600
BBS Name/Sponsor: FireNet Leader BBS
BBS Number: (719) 591-7415
BBS Software: Maximus-CBCS

Rachel

Contains information on a wide range of problems associated with hazardous materials. It is sponsored by the Environmental Research Foundation of Princeton, NJ.
Availability: 24 hrs/7 days
Baud Rate: 1200, 2400
BBS Name/Sponsor: Remote Access Chemical Hazards Electronic Library
BBS Number: (410) 263-8903
BBS Software: BRS/Search UNIX
Parameters: 8-0-1
Sysop: Dr. Peter Montague
Comments: Call ERF for a four page users guide and a user's account. Also you need to sign a form for free accounts.

W&WNET

Covers water and waste issues. Includes the Federal Register Abstracts online. Five bulletin areas contain discussion on Water, wastewater, Laboratories, and Water research,
Availability: 24 hrs/7 days
BBS Name/Sponsor: WATER & WASTEWATER NETWORK (W&WNET)
BBS Number: (517) 686-4055
BBS Software: PCBoard
Parameters: 8-0-1
Baud Rate: 300, 1200, 2400
Sysop: John DeKam and Randall Fisher

OSWER BBS

Encourages the transfer of data, information, activities and technological assistance to

regional hazardous waste and Superfund permitting and enforcement personnel.
Availability: 24 hrs/7 days
Baud Rate: 1200, 2400
BBS Name/Sponsor: OSWER BBS (Office of Solid and Hazardous Waste Technology Transfer Electronic Bulletin Board)
BBS Number: (301) 5890-8366
BBS Software: PCBoard
Parameters: 8-N-1
Help Line: (301) 589-8368

Center for Exposure Assessment Modeling (CEAM) BBS

Designed and used for the distribution of various environmental exposure assessment models supported by the CEAM and for interactive user support.
Availability: 24 hrs/7 days
Baud Rate: 1200-9600
BBS Number: (404) 546-3402
Parameters: 8-0-1
Sysop: Shawn Turk
Help Line: (404) 546-3549

PIES

Pollution Prevention Information Clearinghouse (PPIC)

Pollution Prevention Information Exchange System (PIES)
Provides a preliminary source of information on pollution prevention programs and options that may save money, reduce liabilities, and reduce derogatory effects on the environment.
Available: 24 hours/7 days
Baud Rate 1200-2400
BBS Number: (703) 506-1025
BBS Software: PC Board
Parameter: 8-0-1
Help Line: Myles Morse, EPA Technical Representative - (202) 475-7161, or EIES Technical Support - (703) 821-4800

Nonpoint Source Information Exchange BBS

Provides state and local agencies, private organizations, businesses, and concerned individuals with timely NPS information, a forum for open discussion, and the ability to exchange computer text and program files.
Availability: 24 hrs/7 days
Baud Rate: 1200, 2400, 9600 bps
BBS Number: (301) 589-0205
BBS Software: PCBoard
Sysop: Judy Trimarchi
Help Line: (301) 589-5318
Comments: You can call the help line to request a complete user manual and telecommunications fact sheet.

Occupational Safety and Health BBS

Enables organizations and individuals with occupational health and safety concerns to exchange information and ideas, get technical assistance with occupational health problems, and gain access to a variety of information resources.
Availability: 24 hrs/7 days
Baud Rate: 2400
BBS Number: (212) 385-2034
BBS Software: PCBoard
Sysop: Michael McCann
Help Line: (212) 227-6220

EARTH ART BBS

This BBS is the main hub of Greennet and the host board of Rime's outdoors conference. The board is considered the "stock market" of all official federal, state and international government limited edition conservation prints. Maintains a list of environmental bulletin boards.
Availability: 24 hrs/ 7 days
Baud Rate: 300, 57.6
BBS Number: (803) 552-4389
BBS Software: PCBoard
Sysop: Bob Chapman

PENCYCLE BBS

PA Resources Council Information Exchange

It is is a service of the Pennsyvania Resources Council. The board has many conferences on reycling topics, a searchable database on product and companies that recycle, and more.
Availability: 24 hrs/7 days
Baud Rate: 2400
BBS Number: (215) 892-9940
BBS Software: The Major BBS

The Energy & Regulatory Matters BBS

Established to speed the information transfer and communications among state agencies and individuals interested in energy and regulatory issues in Michigan.
Availability: 24 hrs/7 days
Baud Rate: 300, 2400
BBS Number: (517) 882-1421
BBS Software: The Major BBS
Help Line: (517) 334-6264

CD-ROM

Energy

❧ *Energy*
OCLC
6565 Franz Road
Dublin, OH 43017

Environment

❧ *Aquatic Sciences & Fisheries Abstracts*
Cambridge Scientific Abstracts

❧ *Arctic & Antarctic Regions*
National Information Services Corp.

❧ *Biological Abstracts*
SilverPlatter Information Inc.
One Newton Executive Park
Newton Lower Falls, MA 02162.

❧ *Enviro/Energyline*
R.R. Bowker Electronic Publishing
245 West 17th Street
New York, NY 10011

❧ *Environment*
OCLC
6565 Franz Road
Dublin, OH 43017

❧ *Environmental Bibliography*
NISC
3100 St. Paul Street, Suite 6
Baltimore, MD 21218

❧ *Natural Resources Metabase*
National Information Services Corp.

❧ *OCLC Environment Library*
SilverPlatter Information Inc.

❧ *OSH-ROM*
SilverPlatter Information Inc.
One Newton Executive Park
Newton Lower Falls, MA 02162.

❧ *Pest-Bank*
PolTox
Compact Cambridge
7200 Wisconsin Avenue
Bethesda, MD 20814

❧ *TOMES Plus*
Micromedex Inc.
660 Bannock Street, 3rd Flr.
Denver, CO 80204

❧ *TOXLINE*
SilverPlatter Information Inc.
One Newton Executive Park
Newton Lower Falls, MA 02162.

❧ *Water Resources Abstracts*
SilverPlatter Information Inc.
One Newton Executive Park
Newton Lower Falls, MA 02162.

Nature

❧ *Birds of America*
CMC ReSearch, Inc.
7150 SW Hampton, Suite C-120
Portland, OR 97223

❧ *MutiMedia Audubon's Mammals*
CMC ReSearch, Inc.

❧ *Northern Great Plains AVHRR*
National Mapping Program
Department of Interior
Call EROS data center at (605) 594-6507

❧ *Urban Phytonarian*
Quanta Press Inc.
2550 University Avenue,W.,#245N
St. Paul, MN 55114

❧ *Wildlife & Fish Worldwide*
National Information Services Corp.

Games/ Hobbies Resources

Forums & Databases

America Online (AOL)

🔇 Advanced Dungeons & Dragons
Keyword: OGF
Path: Entertainment Department > Advanced Dungeons & Dragons
PC-using members can play an on-line version of Neverwinter Nights, a Dungeons & Dragons adventure in real time with friends from across the country. Members must purchase a software kit online for $14.95.

🔇 Critic's Choice
Keyword: Critic's Choice
Path: Entertainment Department > Critic's Choice
Synopses and reviews of current movies, books, videos, games, and music. Members post their own reviews of entertainment products.

🔇 Trivia Club
Keyword: Trivia
Path: Entertainment Department > Trivia Club
Real-time triva games on a variety of topics, held nightly. Brain-busters are posted daily on the club's very active message boards. Members can participate in casual games, or in scored activities for prizes.

🔇 Comedy Club
Keyword: Comedy
Path: Entertainment Department > Comedy Club
Jokes of every variety are posted on the message boards by members. Schedules of events for the various improv clubs are posted here, and club discount tickets are available to AOL members.

🔇 Bulls & Bears
Path: Entertainment Department > Bulls & Bears
A stock market simulation game in which players buy and sell stocks and options, using real market prices in a race to accumulate the most wealth before the end of the game. Users can buy and sell stocks online through America Online's StockLink service (see Business & Finance).

🔇 HAM Radio Club
Keyword: Ham Radio
Path: Lifestyles & Interests > HAM Radio Club
For amateur radio enthusiasts. Offers Q&A with radio professionals, a Swap & Sell message board, and weekly live conferences are all offered.

🔇 Radio Control Club
Keyword: Radio Control
Path: Lifestyles & Interests Department > Radio Control Club
For radio control hobbyists and all users interested in learning more about radio controlled cars, helicopters, boats, and planes.

🔇 Wine & Dine Online
Keyword: Wine
Path: Lifestyles & Interests Department > Wine & Dine Online
Offers restaurant, winery, and merchant guides, wine ratings, a beer and brewing message board, a travel guide, and plenty of resources for people who love good food and spirits.

🔇 Games Forum
Path: Computing & Software Department > Games Forum

Keywords: Mac Games, PC Games
Offers thousands of public domain and shareware games.

CompuServe (CIS)

⑤ *Air Traffic Controller*
GO ATCONTROL
Makes users responsible for clearing planes for arrival and landing while keeping track of those arriving from other sectors; neighboring sectors may be controlled by other ATC players.

⑤ *Biorhythm Charting*
GO BIORHYTHM
Plots personalized biorhythm charts for any month or series of months within a given year and provides a written analysis of each month.

⑤ *BlackDragon*
GO BLACKDRAGON
A multi-level fantasy adventure game.

⑤ *British Legends*
GO LEGENDS
The goal of the game is to collect treasures, score points, and reach the honorable status of "Wizard."

⑤ *CastleQuest*
GO CQUEST
The goal of this game is to thoroughly explore a castle, kill the master, loot the castle of its treasures, and accumulate points.

⑤ *Chess Forum*
GO CHESSFORUM
Members play games of electronic postal chess. Earn your own CompuServe rating or a rating from the U.S. Chess Federation.

⑤ *Classic Adventure*
GO CLADVENT
The goal of this game is to explore a cave and collect its numerous treasures.

⑤ *The Electronic Gamer Archives(TM)*
GO TEG
An online source of reviews and step-by-step "walk-throughs" for popular computer games.

⑤ *Enhanced Adventure*
GO ENADVENT
Enhanced Adventure is much like Classic Adventure; the setting is the same, but there are more treasures to be found.

⑤ *The Entertainment Center*
GO ECENTER
Offers a variety of PC computer games ranging from combat in outer space to familiar board games such as backgammon. (ECENTER games require EGA or better graphics.)

⑤ *Flight Simulation Forum*
GO FSFORUM
Offers discussions about civilian, space, combat, and air traffic control simulations.

⑤ *Game Publishers Forum*
GO GAMPUB
Supports a variety of games and game-related products for all types of computers. Selected publishers have their own message section for direct correspondence with customers.

⑤ *The Gamers' Forum*
GO GAMERS
Dedicated to the communications, support, and entertainment needs of the general computer game-playing community. Tips, hints, reviews, and instructions for the latest computer games on the market.

⑤ *Hangman*
GO HANGMAN
The computerized version of the famous game.

⑤ *Island of Kesmai*
GO ISLAND
Consists of two segments: the Basic Game, includes the regions of Kesmai, Leng, Oakvael, and Axe Glacier; and the Advanced Game includes the regions of Torii, Annwn, Rift Glacier and Shukumei.

⑤ *MegaWars I: The Galactic Conflict*
GO MEGA1
In this game you try to capture planets and build an empire before the enemy destroys you.

⑤ *MegaWars III: The New Empire*
GO MEGA3
MegaWars III is a multi-player game of planetary domination which consists of two separate phases: an interactive phase and an economic phase.

⑤ *The Modem Games Forum*
GO MODEMGAMES
Owners of modem-capable computer games meet here. Members play in head-to-head tournaments organized by forum staffers and run in the Modem-To-Modem Gaming Lobby(TM).

⑤ The Modem-To-Modem Challenge Board
GO MTMCHALLENGE

Owners of selected modem-capable games can locate worldwide opponents to play through the use of the MTM Challenge Board.

⑤ The Modem-To-Modem Gaming Lobby
GO MTMLOBBY

Enables users to play PC computer games in head-to-head competition with players from around the world.

⑤ Multi-Players Games Forum
GO MPGAMES

Supports the entertainment needs of members who play any of the multiple-player games via the CompuServe online environment.

⑤ The Multiple Choice
GO TMC

Offers a host of on-line games and tests to challenge, amuse and even train you. Trivia games are available in versions for kids, teens and all ages. Offers two achievement tests: One tests high school competency similarly to the New York State Board of Regents Tests for grades 9 - 12. The other is a simulation of the "Miller Analogies Test" used as an entrance test to many graduate schools.

⑤ Role-Playing Games Forum
GO RPGAMES

Users discuss and play all types of board/paper/text role-playing games including AD&D, Rune Quest, Gamma World, Traveller, Champions and Justice, Inc. Role-playing games are conducted in the conference area every evening.

⑤ Science Trivia Quiz
GO SCITRIVIA

Test your knowledge of biology, chemistry and physics through the Science Trivia Quiz. Questions and comments can be discussed in the Science/Math Education Forum (GO SCIENCE).

⑤ SHOWBIZQUIZ
GO SBQ

A trivia game that tests your knowledge of the entertainment world in a variety of categories such as Frank Sinatra, the Twilight Zone, or the Rolling Stones.

⑤ SNIPER!
GO SNIPER

Set in 1943 on the battlegrounds of World War II, SNIPER! is the multi-player war game that pits your squad of soldiers against others in a realistic simulation of wartime conditions.

⑤ Stage II — Two Stage Trivia
GO STAGEII

Stage II is a trivia game where you answer three trivia questions and then look for a common theme in the answers.

⑤ The Whiz Quiz
GO WHIZ

Sponsored by Grolier's Academic American Encyclopedia, it will test your knowledge in a variety of categories.

⑤ You Guessed It!
GO YGI

A real-time, multi-player game show simulation in which players form teams, answer general information, and trivia questions and vie for bonus points.

⑤ Aquaria Fish Forums
GO FISHFORUMS

Aquarium professionals and hobbyists alike can find information and friends in FISHFORUMS. Questions to the forum administrator (SysOp) will be answered within 24 hours; a voice line is also available.

⑤ Model Aviation Forum
GO MODELNET

For the model hobbyist. Builders of model airplanes, rockets, cars and boats will find all these disciplines covered in the forum.

⑤ TrainNet Forum
GO TRAINNET

This is the railroad forum. If you are a model railroader or railfan, TrainNet offers something for anyone interested in anything that runs on flanged wheels from Amtrak to Z Scale.

⑤ CARS
GO CARS

Covers all facets of the automotive world from buying, selling and fixing cars to dreaming about what future cars will be like. You can find answers to your questions or demonstrate your own knowledge about car finance, insurance, safety and problems.

⑤ Automotive Information
GO AUTO

Provides information on a variety of automotive products, including car showrooms, an auto racing forum, and automotive equipment.

🌐 *Bacchus Wine Forum*
`GO WINEFORUM`
Presents information on many wine-related and home beer brewing topics.

🌐 *Collectibles Forum*
`GO COLLECT`
For philatelists, numismatics, and other collectors to price and trade information, and to check out the Collectors' and Dealers' Network. Baseball cards and other collectibles are also included.

🌐 *Comics/Animation Forum*
`GO COMICS`
Features news, reviews and conferences with some of the greats of comic books and animations.

🌐 *Cooks Online*
`GO COOKS`
Enables users to share their enthusiasm for cooking and gourmet food. Fine restaurants are discussed, and members can consult with cooking experts online.

🌐 *Crafts Forum*
`GO CRAFTS`
Enables members to compare techniques, swap project ideas, and describe projects they are working on now or have done in the past. The libraries are stuffed with downloadable patterns and articles about crafts.

🌐 *Food/Wine*
`GO FOOD`
Contains forums for people who enjoy good food and wine.

🌐 *Gardening Forum*
`GO GARDENING`
Contains over a decade's worth of gardening knowledge and experience from green-thumbed experts.

🌐 *Worldwide Car Network*
`GO WCN`
Provides information about the exotic- and collectible-car market, this forum hosts discussions on everything about cars from driving the latest Ferrari to finding parts for that old Ford.

🌐 *New Car Showroom*
`GO NEWCAR`
A comparison shopping guide for consumers making new vehicle purchases. Enables users to calculate their monthly payments after selecting a vehicle.

GEnie

🌐 *Games RoundTable by Scorpia*
Keyword: SCORPIA or Page 805
Offers reviews and product information on adventure, action/arcade, sports, strategy/war, D&D, and board games.

🌐 *GEnie Multi-player Games*
Keyword: MPGAMES or Page 801

🌐 *The Multiplayer Games RoundTable*
Keyword: MPGRT or Page 1045
Enables users to learn about, discuss, and make suggestions for the multi-player games and on-line single player games available on GEnie.

🌐 *Computer Game Design RT*
Keyword: JCGD or Page 935
Covers the design of computer games, but does not cover the playing of computer games.

🌐 *Sports Pool Games*
Keyword: POOL or Page 419

🌐 *TSR Online RoundTable*
Keyword: TSR or Page 125
A support forum for role playing products created by TSR and to promoting fantasy gaming and role playing.

🌐 *Classic Games*
Keyword: CLASSIC or Page 803

🌐 *The Software Club by SoftClub*
Keyword: SOFTCLUB or Page 1115
Offers a selection of excellent games for the Commodore Amiga, Atari ST, and IBM PC and compatibles. Each month new games and special offers are made for each of these computers.

The Well

🌐 *Antiques and Collectibles*
`(g collect)`
Enables users to discuss all aspects of collecting from antiques to more modern things.

🌐 *Conference: Motoring*
`(g car)`
A forum about cars.

🌐 *Chess*
`(g chess)`
An informal conference about and for chess.

🌐 *Comics*
`(g comics)`

Enables users to have four-color fun in a two-color medium. Share your views on the past, present, and future of favorite funnybooks.

🍥 *Cooking*
(g cook)
Discusses cooking, recipes, foods, and other topics related to things the family does in the kitchen.

🍥 *The Corner Pub*
(g corner)
A forum where pub talk occurs.

🍥 *Drinks*
(g drinks)
A forum about everything from beer to wine and scotch to soda.

🍥 *Flying*
(g flying)
Covers aircraft (all kinds), balloons, kites, RC models, birds—and pilots and flight crew, passengers, aircraft designers, controllers, the FAA.

🍥 *Games*
(g games)
Discusses all types of games

🍥 *Gardening*
(g gard)
Discusses the ins and outs of gardening.

🍥 *Jokes*
(g jokes)
Discusses humor.

🍥 *Motorcycling*
(g ride)
This forum is the place for cyclists to meet, swap info on products, bikes, and good rides.

Network Discussions Lists

Internet (Includes Bitnet & UUCPNet)

🍥 *Advanced Dungeons and Dragons discussion*
Discusses the Dungeons & Dragons and Advanced Dungeons & Dragons role-playing games.
ADND-L@UTARLVM1.BITNET
LISTSERV@UTARLVM1.BITNET
Contact: Faustino Cantu
<FGC82B1@OANAM.BITNET>

🍥 *Ars Magica*
For players of the Ars Magica roleplaying game Shannon Appel & Mark Phaedrus.
ARS-MAGICA@OCF.BERKELEY.EDU
ars-magica-request@ocf.berkeley.edu

🍥 *Beer*
Discusses the making and tasting of beer, ale, and mead. Related issues, such as breweries, books, judging, commercial beers, beer festivals, and so on, are also discussed.
BEER-L@UA1VM.BITNET
LISTSERV@UA1VM.BITNET

🍥 *Backgammon strategy list*
BKGAMMbit.listserv.dipl-l
ON@INDYCMS.BITNET

🍥 *BONSAI DISCUSSION LIST*
Discusses the art and craft of bonsai and related art forms.
BONSAI@WAYNEST1.BITNET
LISTSERV@WAYNEST1.BITNET
Contact: Daniel Cwiertniewicz
<DCWIERT@WAYNEST1.BITNET>

🍥 *Cards (Sportscards, that is...)*
For users interested in collection, speculation and investing in baseball, football, basketball, hockey and other trading cards and/or memoribilia.
cards@tanstaafl.uchicago.edu
cards-request@tanstaafl.uchicago.edu
Contact: Keane Arase
<kean@tanstaafl.uchicago.edu>

🍥 *The Chess Discussion List*
Provides chess players with a way to communicate through e-mail. Announces tournaments and shares ideas about chess problems and interesting chess games.
CHESS-L@GREARN.BITNET
LISTSERV@GREARN.BITNET
Contact: Theodore J. Soldatos
<SYSTU003@GRCRUN11.BITNET>

🍥 *COMICS Discussion List*
COMICS-L@UNLVM.BITNET
LISTSERV@UNLVM.BITNET

🍥 *Rubik's Cube*
CUBE-LOVERS@AI.AI.MIT.EDU
CUBE-LOVERS-REQUEST@AI.AI.MIT.EDU
Contact: Alan Bawden
ALAN@AI.AI.MIT.EDU

🍥 *Computer and video game reviews and discussion*
For computer and video game reviews, with interest in any games that run on computers. Also covers games for the portable market.

digital-games-submissions@DIGITAL-
GAMES.INTUITIVE.COM
digital-games-request@Digital-
Games.Intuitive.Com
Contact: Dave Taylor
<taylor@LIMBO.INTUITIVE.COM>

🌕 *10 Player Diplomacy Game List*
D20A-L@MITVMA.BITNET
LISTSERV@MITVMA.BITNET

🌕 *Famous (in Italy) horror comic Dylan Dog*
Dedicated to the famous comic DylanDog.
Also deals with the world of Horror fiction in
general.
DYLANDOG@IGECUNIV.BITNET
LISTSERV@IGECUNIV.BITNET
Contact: Davide Bianchini
<DAVIDE@IGECUNIV.BITNET>

🌕 *Computer Games List*
Discusses games that can be played by using
any type of computer from micro to mainframe.
GAMES-L GAMES-L@BROWNVM.BROWN.EDU
LISTSERV@BROWNVM.BROWN.EDU
Contact: Spyros Bartsocas
SCB@BROWNVM.BROWN.EDU

🌕 *Gardens and gardening*
Promotes and exchanges information about
home gardening.
GARDENS@UKCC.BITNET
LISTSERV@UKCC.BITNET
Contact: Bob Crovo
<Crovo@UKCC>

🌕 *UCF-IST GISMO Game List*
GISMO-L@UCF1VM.BITNET
LISTSERV@UCF1VM.BITNET

🌕 *Gamemasters Interest Group*
Discusses adventure game programming..
GMAST-L@UTCVM.BITNET
LISTSERV@UTCVM.BITNET
Contact: Jeff Kell
<JEFF@UTCVM.BITNET>

🌕 *The game of GO*
For players interested in the game of GO.
GO-L@SMCVAX.BITNET
MAILSERV%SMCVAX.BITNET@VM1.NODAK.EDU

🌕 *Beer and ale making (homebrew)*
Discusses the making and tasting of beer, ale,
and mead.
homebrew%hpfcmr@HPLABS.HP.COM
homebrew-request%hpfcmr@HPLABS.HP.COM
Contact: Rob Gardner
<rdg%hpfcmr@HPLABS.HP.COM>

🌕 *Live role play games*
For playing all forms of live-role-playing
games.
KILLER@UMASS.BITNET
CEREBUS%UMASS.BITNET@CUNYVM.CUNY.EDU
Contact: David Kovar
<dk1z#@ANDREW.CMU.EDU>

🌕 *Master Gardeners list*
MGARDEN@WSUVM1.BITNET
LISTSERV@WSUVM1.BITNET

🌕 *Traditional Nutty Stuff*
NUTS@FINHUTC.BITNET
LISTSERV@FINHUTC.BITNET
Contact: Joe Desbonnet
PHYDESBONNET@VAX1.ucg.ie ()

🌕 *Redistribution list for the NETNEWS
newsgroup rec.humor.funny.*
NUTWORKS@TCSVM.BITNET
LISTSERV@TCSVM.BITNET

🌕 *Orchid growers*
Shares and discusses information and
experiences of orchid growers.
ORCHIDS@SCU.BITNET
MAILSERV@SCU.BITNET
Contact: Willis Dair
<DAIR@SCU.BITNET>

🌕 *Origame (paper folding) discussion*
Discusses all facets of origami, the Japanese art
of paper folding.
ORIGAMI@CS.UTEXAS.EDU
origami-request@CS.UTEXAS.EDU
Contact: Brad Blumenthal
(brad@CS.UTEXAS.EDU)

🌕 *Paintball discussion list*
PAINTBOL@TCSVM.BITNET
LISTSERV@TCSVM.BITNET

🌕 *Exchanging and collecting postcards*
For exchanging or collecting picture postcards
of all types and eras.
POSTCARD@IDBSU.BITNET
LISTSERV@IDBSU.BITNET
Contact: Dan Lester
<ALILESTE@idbsu.BITNET>

🌕 *Quilting and Related Topics Discussions*
Discusses quilting: questions, answers, book
reports, tips, mail order sources, patterns, and
favorite stores.
QUILT@cornell.edu
listserv@cornell.edu
Contact: Anne Louise Gockel
<alg@cs.cornell.edu>

✆ *Discussion of Remote Control Hobbies list*
REMOTE-L@SUVM.BITNET
LISTSERV@SUVM.BITNET

✆ *ShadowRun Fantasy Game*
SHADOWRN@HEARN.BITNET
LISTSERV@HEARN.BITNET
Contact: Brett Barnhart
<BARNHART@KNOX.BITNET>

✆ *The Shogi Discussion List*
Discusses Shogi, a Japanese board game played by two players. The object of the game is to capture the opponent's King.
SHOGI-L@TECHNION.BITNET
LISTSERV@TECHNION.BITNET

✆ *The list for people who love philately!*
For users who collect, or just have a passing interest in, stamps and related items.
STAMPS@CUNYVM.BITNET
LISTSERV@CUNYVM.BITNET
Contact: Geert K. Marien
<GKMQC@CUNYVM.CUNY.EDU>

✆ *The Stamps List*
A weekly digest of discussions on philatelic matters of all kinds, new issues announcements, and news items.
STAMPS@PCCVM.BITNET
LISTSERV@PCCVM.BITNET
Contact: Geert K. Marien
<GKMCU@CUNYVM.CUNY.EDU>

✆ *STARTREK Role Playing game list*
Discusses the Star Trek role-playing game .
STARGAME@PCCVM.BITNET
LISTSERV@PCCVM.BITNET
Contact: Brian Hartsfield
bh@eng.auburn.edu

✆ *The Theatre Discussion List*
For users who are or want to be involved with theatre as a hobby, and as a way to communicate and share ideas and experiences.
THEATRE@GREARN.BITNET
LISTSERV@GREARN.BITNET
Contact: Theodore J. Soldatos
SYSTU003@GRCRUN11.BITNET

✆ *Vectrex Game*
Discusses the Vectrex game.
VECTREX-PEOPLE@C.CS.CMU.EDU
VECTREX-PEOPLE-REQUEST@C.CS.CMU.EDU
Contact: Vince Fuller
<VAF@C.CS.CMU.EDU>

Fidonet

✆ *AD&D Discussions*
AD&D_CHAT

Discusses topics related to the Advanced Dungeons and Dragons game as published by TSR, Inc.
Moderator: Ralph Merritt
1:2605/611
Restr: MEMBER
Distribution: FIDONET, VERVAN'S GAMING NETWORK (ZONE 45)
Gateways: VNET VIA 1:100/375

✆ *Advanced Dungeons and Dragons*
AD&D
Discusses and playes the Advanced Dungeons and Dragons (tm) Fantasy Role-Playing Game, published by TSR, Inc.
Moderator: Scott Royall
1:106/357
Distribution: FIDONET, BACKBONE
Gateways: GROUPMAIL VIA 1:107/3

✆ *Airgunners' Information Exchange*
AIRGUN
For airgunners to discuss current and collectible model airguns, upcoming shows and matches, and anything to do with airguns.
Moderator: Jim Henry
1:273/408
Distribution: ECHONET BACKBONE (ZONE 50)

✆ *Amiga Gaming*
AMIGAGAMES
For game reviews, hints, tips, tricks, backdoors, solutions, comparisons, and general discussions of games for the Amiga line of personal computers.
Moderator: Adam Sternberg
1:209/700
Distribution: BACKBONE

✆ *Fishkeeping, fresh and marine tanks*
AQUARIUM
For all aspects of keeping fish, in either salt or marine tanks, small to large.
Moderator: Vern Faulkner
1:340/44
Distribution: BACKBONE

✆ *For The Automotive Enthusiast*
AUTOMOTIVE
For automotive conversation on all levels from restoration to racing
Moderator: John Pummill
1:123/30
Distribution: BACKBONE

✆ *Auto Racing*
AUTORACE

For Auto racing enthusiasts; Winston Cup, Drag Racing, Busch Grand National, and World of Outlaws.
Moderator: Pete Farias
1:321/210
Distribution: BACKBONE

🌎 *Baseball Card Conference*
BB-CARDS
Discusses baseball cards, baseball card collection software, and listing of cards wanted, for sale, or trade.
Moderator: Jay Brown
1:264/167
Distribution: BACKBONE

🌎 *Battletech echo Ltd.*
BATTLETECH
Discusses FASAs Battletech game.
Moderator: Mark Wandrey
1:231/340
Distribution: LIMITED

🌎 *British Car Echo*
BRIT_CAR
Discusses British automobiles, their problems, sources for parts, and various remedies in keeping them running.
Moderator: Dixon Kenner
1:243/5
Distribution: BACKBONE

🌎 *Chatter about cars, old and new.*
CARS
For automobile enthusiasts.
Moderator: Dave Overton
1:203/988
Distribution: ECHONET BACKBONE (ZONE 50)

🌎 *Craft and Needlework Hobbies of All Kinds*
Discusses craft hobbies and shares pointers.
Moderator: Tandika Star
1:308/10
Distribution: BACKBONE

🌎 *Computer RGPs & Adventure Games*
CRPGS
For the discussion, support, reviews, and hints of computer role playing games and adventure games of any sort.
Moderator: Steve Derby
1:161/414
Distribution: NETMAIL REQUEST TO 1:161/414

🌎 *National Cooking Echo*
COOKING
Discusses cooking and food and related topics.
Moderator: Joann Pierce
1:105/81
Restr: MOD-APVL
Distribution: ALL

🌎 *Disney Discussions*
DISNEY
For Disney enthusiasts, from the theme parks, to the classic motion pictures, to the Disney stores, and Disney television.
Moderator: Chris Harrower
1:270/417
Distribution: ZONE ONE BACKBONE

🌎 *Door Games Discussion Echo*
DOORGAMES
For the discussion and support of door games by door game authors, sysops, and users.
Moderator: Steve Derby
1:161/414
Distribution: BACKBONE

🌎 *All hobbies except modeming and computers.*
ENET_HOBBIES
For users who want to chat about their hobbies such as stamp collecting, fishing, model railroading, bicycling, and the like.
Moderator: John Radford
1:261/1083

🌎 *Dungeons & Dragons Discussion Base*
DND
For the discussion of "Dungeons & Dragons" type mediaeval game systems.
Moderator: Rodney Barnes
1:347/6
Distribution: BACKBONE

🌎 *Home Electronics and Appliances Discussions*
ELECTRONICS
Discusses home electronic equipment, as well as occasional forays into theoretical electronics.
Moderator: Alan Hess
1:261/1000
Distribution: BACKBONE

🌎 *Florida Cooking and Eating Echo*
FLA_COOKS
Discusses the Florida cuisine, restaurants, and cooking with local ingredients. FLA_COOKS is available to any FidoNet system in Florida via the North, Central or South Hubs at 1:3620/9, 1:374/14, or 1:135/71, respectively. 1:135/71 is PC Pursuitable.
Moderator: Christopher Baker
1:374/14
Distribution: LOCAL, FLORIDA, REGION18

🕭 *Game Programmer's Support Conference*
GAME_DESIGN
Enables game programmers and players to work together to create the ultimate game.
Moderator: Matthew Hudson
1:3622/801.4
Distribution: LOCAL-R18

🕭 *Solutions for setting up online games.*
GAMES_SETUP
Helps users resolve problems for EchoNet with Sysops attempting to set up their online games.
Moderator: Mike Gurski
1:261/1062
Distribution: ECHONET BACKBONE (ZONE 50)

🕭 *International Personal Computer Gaming*
GAMING
Discusses games for personal computers.
Moderator: Clint Adams
1:2607/401
Distribution: BACKBONE, ZONE-2, ZONE-3, ZONE-4, ZONE-6
Gateways: ALTERNET VIA 107/3, RBBSNET VIA 10/8

🕭 *Gourmet Cooking*
GOURMET
Discusses lighter, leaner, and healthier ways of cooking.
Moderator: Perry Lowell
1:322/359
Restr: MOD-APVL
Distribution: BACKBONE

🕭 *All Hobbies*
HOBBIES
For all legitimate hobbies.
Moderator: Harvey Smith
1:100/519
Distribution: ECHOMAIL

🕭 *Home Automation*
HOMEAUT
Discusses control, wireless remote controls, pre-scheduled control, and energy saving controls.
Moderator: Rick Ellis
1:103/208
Distribution: CONTACT MODERATOR FOR A FEED

🕭 *The Home and Garden Echo*
HOME-N-GRDN
Discusses all aspects of gardening and lawn care home maintenance.
Moderator: Bob Germer

8:950/10
Distribution: FIDONET BACKBONE, RBBSNET
Gateways: FIDONET VIA 8:950/10, RBBSNET VIA 1:10/8

🕭 *The Home Repair Echo*
HOME_REPAIR
Discusses all types of do-it-yourself projects at home.
Moderator: Bob Germer
8:950/10
Distribution: FIDONET BACKBONE, RBBSNET
Gateways: FIDONET VIA 8:950/10

🕭 *House and Garden.*
HOUSE_GARDEN
Offers information about house fix-ups, paint-ups, repairs; house and garden hints, tips, questions, and answers.
Moderator: John Radford
1:261/1083
Distribution: ECHONET BACKBONE (ZONE 50)

🕭 *International Chess Echo*
CHESS
Enbales users to discuss current chess topics and encourages them to participate in tournaments..
Moderator: Tim Eichman
1:2607/107
Distribution: ZONE-1 BACKBONE, ZONE-3 BACKBONE, FAMILYNET LIMITED, RBBSNET LIMITED, WWIVNET LIMITED
Gateways: ZONE-3 VIA 1:105/42, FAMILYNET VIA 1:11/5, RBBSNET VIA 1:10/8, WWIVNET VIA 1:396/11

🕭 *Macintosh Entertainment & Education Echo*
MAC_GAMES
Offers information about the entertainment and educational qualities of the Mac
Moderator: Bob Nordling
1:396/1
Distribution: BACKBONE, GATE ZONE-2 VIA 1:107/412, GATE RBBS VIA 1:129/34

🕭 *MELEE and Banzai Software Support Conference*
MELEE
For support and player interaction for MELEE, the Sci-Fi gladiatorial combat role playing door game by Kevin Higgins.
Moderator: Kevin Higgins
1:128/74
Distribution: ZONE-1, ZONE-2, DOORNET, V-NET

Gateways: V-NET VIA 1:229/2, DOORNET VIA 75:75/1

🕈 *NEO-GEO Video Game System*
NEO-GEO
For general chatter for NEO-GEO owners and those interested in purchasing one.
Moderator: Kevin Bass
1:19/107
Distribution: BACKBONE

🕈 *Operation: Overkill II Players/Discussion*
OKILLERS
For avid (and not so avid) players discuss their experiences in the wastelands of Operation: Overkill II.
Moderator: Dustin Nulf
1:124/6304
Distribution: BACKBONE

🕈 *Old Cars and Related Topics*
OLDCARS
For talking about old cars, parts for older cars, and stories about old cars.
Moderator: Gerry Calhoun
1:102/1304
Distribution: BACKBONE

🕈 *Online Games*
ON_LINE_GAMES
For the discussion/help/release notices of new or updated online games including fixes or other useful utilities.
Moderator: Mike Samczak
1:226/390

🕈 *Operation: Overkill II Sysop/Development*
OOII
For the discussion on Operation: Overkill II installation and configuration of programs .
Moderator: Dustin Nulf
1:124/6304
Distribution: BACKBONE

🕈 *OTHER SUNS Science Fiction Role Playing Game*
OTHER_SUNS
Devoted to the SFRPG OTHER SUNS, published by Fantasy Games Unlimited.
Moderator: Nicolai Shapero
1:102/524
Restr: MOD-APVL

🕈 *Radio Controlled Modeling*
RC_MODEL
For radio control modelers to discuss their hobby, ask and answer questions, share tips, and more.

Moderator: John Nelson
1:105/107
Distribution: BACKBONE

🕈 *Radio Controlled Models*
RCM
For the advancement of radio controlled models and the people and events surrounding them.
Moderator: John Bierrie
1:232/39
Distribution: ZONE-1

🕈 *Role Playing Games*
RECFRP
For the discussion of role playing games, board games, war games, science fiction, fantasy, and the like.
Moderator: Brion Lienhart
1:213/700
Distribution: BACKBONE

🕈 *Down-home and gourmet cooking.*
RECIPE_CORNER
Enables users to exchange recipes, talk about kitchen techniques, and share humorous epicurean experiences.
Moderator: Fred Peters
1:261/1056
Distribution: ECHONET BACKBONE (ZONE 50)

🕈 *Stamp & Cover Collectors' Echo*
STAMPS
For stamp and cover Collectors.
Moderator: Clarence Moore
8:7309/1
Distribution: INTERNATIONAL, NATIONAL, BACKBONE
Gateways: INTO FAMILYNET VIA 1:115/887 (REQUIRES FAMILYNET NODE NUMBER)

🕈 *Startrek Role-Playing-Game Echo*
STARTREK
For anyone who wants to take place in RPGS' (Role-Playing-Games) based on the popular StarTrek, StarTrek Movies and the TNG theme.
Moderator: Mike Shepherd
1:151/2395
Distribution: BACKBONE

🕈 *Solar Realms Support Echo*
SRGAMES
Devoted to questions and discussions about Door games from The Solar Realm.
Moderator: Harold Weiss
1:106/478

🕈 *Trade Wars*
TRADE_WARS

Offers tips, tricks, and hints for any space-war-trading game of the TradeWars genre, particularly TW2002.
Moderator: Kris Lewis
    1:202/613
Distribution: BACKBONE

🌀 *Videogame System Discussion Echo*
    VID_GAME
Discusses videogame systems such as the SEGA Genesis, SEGA Master System, SEGA Game Gear, NEC TurboGrafx, NEC TurboExpress, SNES, Nintendo, NES Game Boy, Atari Lynx, and SNK Neo Geo machines.
Moderator: Bob Nordling
    1:396/1
Distribution: BACKBONE

🌀 *Home Wine Makers' Conference*
    VIN_MAISON
For the home wine maker.
Moderator: Chris Grainger
    1:163/518
Distribution: BACKBONE

🌀 *Beer Homebrewing*
    ZYMURGY
Discusses making homemade brew.
Moderator: Wayne Hamilton
    1:233/5

Usenet

🌀 *Discussion of all facets of older automobiles.*
    alt.autos.antique

🌀 *Good for what ales ya.*
    alt.beer

🌀 *Fishing as a hobby and sport.*
    alt.fishing

🌀 *The Galactic Bloodshed conquest game.*
    alt.games.gb

🌀 *The Atari Lynx.*
    alt.games.lynx

🌀 *Discussion of the Crescent game, and playing.*
    alt.games.mornington.crescent

🌀 *The computer game Omega.*
    alt.games.omega

🌀 *The video game Street Fighter 2.*
    alt.games.sf2

🌀 *Gateway for TORG mailing list.*
    alt.games.torg

🌀 *All about a Star Trek game for X.*
    alt.games.xtrek

🌀 *For discussion about stage magic.*
    alt.magic

🌀 *Model building, design, etc.*
    alt.models

🌀 *Hog heaven.*
    alt.motorcycles.harley

🌀 *Working with needle and thread.*
    alt.sewing

🌀 *Eponymy.*
    alt.silly.group.names.d

🌀 *Discussion of all apsects of skate-boarding.*
    alt.skate-board

🌀 *Diplomacy Game Discussion List.*
    bit.listserv.dipl-l

🌀 *Discussing antiques and vintage items.*
    rec.antiques

🌀 *Keeping fish and aquaria as a hobby.*
    rec.aquaria

🌀 *Discussion of various kinds of animation.*
    rec.arts.animation

🌀 *Japanese animation fen discussion.*
    rec.arts.anime

🌀 *Tattoos and body decoration discussions.*
    rec.arts.bodyart

🌀 *Comic books, graphic novels, sequential art.*
    rec.arts.comics

🌀 *Reviews, convention information and other comics news. Moderated.*
    rec.arts.comics.info

🌀 *The exchange of comics and comic-related items.*
    rec.arts.comics.marketplace

🌀 *Comic books, graphic novels, sequential art.*
    rec.arts.comics.misc

🌀 *Discussion of short-form comics.*
    rec.arts.comics.strips

🌀 *The Mutant Universe of Marvel Comics.*
    rec.arts.comics.xbooks

🌀 *Automobiles, automotive products and laws.*
    rec.autos

🌀 *Discussion of any Disney-related subjects.*
    rec.arts.disney

🌀 *Driving automobiles.*
rec.autos.driving

🌀 *Discussion of organized, legal auto competitions.*
rec.autos.sport

🌀 *Technical aspects of automobiles, et. al.*
rec.autos.tech

🌀 *Issues pertaining to Volkswagen products.*
rec.autos.vw

🌀 *Bicycles, related products and laws.*
rec.bicycles

🌀 *Hobbyists interested in boating.*
rec.boats

🌀 *Hobbyists interested in bird watching.*
rec.birds

🌀 *Talk about any boats with oars, paddles, etc.*
rec.boats.paddle

🌀 *Climbing techniques, competition announcements*
rec.climbing

🌀 *Discussion among collectors of many things.*
rec.collecting

🌀 *The art of making beers and meads.*
rec.crafts.brewing

🌀 *Handiwork arts not covered elsewhere.*
rec.crafts.misc

🌀 *Sewing, weaving, knitting and other fiber arts.*
rec.crafts.textiles

🌀 *Discussion of things equestrian.*
rec.equestrian

🌀 *Folk dances, dancers, and dancing.*
rec.folk-dancing

🌀 *Food, cooking, cookbooks, and recipes.*
rec.food.cooking

🌀 *Wines and spirits.*
rec.food.drink

🌀 *Recipes for interesting food and drink. (Moderated)*
rec.food.recipes

🌀 *Discussion of dining out.*
rec.food.restaurants

🌀 *Vegetarians.*
rec.food.veg

🌀 *Articles on games of chance & betting.*
rec.gambling

🌀 *Discussion of the game of backgammon.*
rec.games.backgammon

🌀 *Discussion and hints on board games.*
rec.games.board

🌀 *The Cosmic Encounter board game.*
rec.games.board.ce

🌀 *Hobbyists interested in bridge.*
rec.games.bridge

🌀 *Chess & computer chess.*
rec.games.chess

🌀 *The Core War computer challenge.*
rec.games.corewar

🌀 *Discussions of cyberpunk related games. (Moderated)*
rec.games.cyber

🌀 *Discussion of game design related issues.*
rec.games.design

🌀 *Discussion and hints about Empire.*
rec.games.empire

🌀 *Discussion about Role Playing games.*
rec.games.frp

🌀 *Flames and rebuttals about various role-playing systems.*
rec.games.frp.advocacy

🌀 *Announcements of happenings in the role-playing world. (Moderated)*
rec.games.frp.announce

🌀 *Archivable fantasy stories and other projects. (Moderated)*
rec.games.frp.archives

🌀 *Fantasy role-playing with TSR's Dungeons and Dragons.*
rec.games.frp.dnd

🌀 *Role-playing game materials wanted and for sale.*
rec.games.frp.marketplace

🌀 *General discussions of role-playing games.*
rec.games.frp.misc

🌀 *Discussion about Go.*
rec.games.go

🌀 *Discussion, hints, etc. about the Hack game.*
rec.games.hack

⑤ *Games and computer games.*
rec.games.misc

⑤ *Comments, hints, and info about the Moria game.*
rec.games.moria

⑤ *Various aspects of multi-users computer games.*
rec.games.mud

⑤ *Admnistrative issues of multiuser dungeons.*
rec.games.mud.admin

⑤ *Informational articles about multiuser dungeons. (Moderated)*
rec.games.mud.announce

⑤ *All about DikuMuds.*
rec.games.mud.diku

⑤ *Discussions of the LPMUD computer role playing game.*
rec.games.mud.lp

⑤ *Various aspects of multiuser computer games.*
rec.games.mud.misc

⑤ *Discussion about Tiny muds, like MUSH, MUSE and MOO.*
rec.games.mud.tiny

⑤ *Discussion of the X window system game Netrek (XtrekII).*
rec.games.netrek

⑤ *Discussion about Play by Mail games.*
rec.games.pbm

⑤ *Discussing pinball-related issues.*
rec.games.pinball

⑤ *Discussion of adventure game programming.*
rec.games.programmer

⑤ *Discussion and hints about Rogue.*
rec.games.rogue

⑤ *Discussion about trivia.*
rec.games.trivia

⑤ *Discussion about video games.*
rec.games.video

⑤ *Discussions about coin-operated video games.*
rec.games.video.arcade

⑤ *Strategy and tactics for the distributed game Xtank.*
rec.games.xtank.play

⑤ *Coding the Xtank game and its robots.*
rec.games.xtank.programmer

⑤ *Gardening, methods and results.*
rec.gardens

⑤ *Discussions about firearms. (Moderated)*
rec.guns

⑤ *Jokes and the like. May be somewhat offensive.*
rec.humor

⑤ *Discussions on the content of rec.humor articles.*
rec.humor.d

⑤ *Jokes that are funny (in the moderator's opinion). (Moderated)*
rec.humor.funny

⑤ *Sagacious advice from the USENET Oracle. (Moderated)*
rec.humor.oracle

⑤ *Comments about the USENET Oracle's comments.*
rec.humor.oracle.d

⑤ *Discussions about hunting. (Moderated)*
rec.hunting

⑤ *Juggling techniques, equipment and events.*
rec.juggling

⑤ *Talk about kites and kiting.*
rec.kites

⑤ *Discussion of the various martial art forms.*
rec.martial-arts

⑤ *General topics about recreational/participant sports.*
rec.misc

⑤ *Model railroads of all scales.*
rec.models.railroad

⑤ *Radio-controlled models for hobbyists.*
rec.models.rc

⑤ *Model rockets for hobbyists.*
rec.models.rockets

⑤ *Motorcycles and related products and laws.*
rec.motorcycles

⑤ *Riding motorcycles and ATVs off-road.*
rec.motorcycles.dirt

⑤ *Discussion of all aspects of racing motorcycles.*
rec.motorcycles.racing

⑤ *Hobbyists interested in naturist/nudist activities.*
rec.nude

- *Pets, pet care, and household animals in general.*
  `rec.pets`

- *The culture and care of indoor birds.*
  `rec.pets.birds`

- *Discussion about domestic cats.*
  `rec.pets.cats`

- *Any and all subjects relating to dogs as pets.*
  `rec.pets.dogs`

- *Reptiles, amphibians and other exotic vivarium pets.*
  `rec.pets.herp`

- *Puzzles, problems, and quizzes.*
  `rec.puzzles`

- *Making and playing gridded word puzzles.*
  `rec.puzzles.crosswords`

- *Fireworks, rocketry, safety, & other topics.*
  `rec.pyrotechnics`

- *Real and model train fans' newsgroup.*
  `rec.railroad`

- *Roller coasters and other amusement park rides.*
  `rec.roller-coaster`

- *Scouting youth organizations worldwide.*
  `rec.scouting`

- *Hobbyists interested in SCUBA diving.*
  `rec.scuba`

- *Ice skating and roller skating.*
  `rec.skate`

- *Hobbyists interested in snow skiing.*
  `rec.skiing`

- *Hobbyists interested in skydiving.*
  `rec.skydiving`

- *Riding the waves as a hobby.*
  `rec.windsurfing`

- *Hobbyists interested in woodworking.*
  `rec.woodworking`

Online Libraries

After Dark

No services available.

Knowledge Index

No services available.

Orbit

No services available.

NewsNet

- *Hollywood Hotline*
  Frequency: Daily
  Earliest NewsNet Issue: One year plus current year
  Reports on the latest entertainment news from Hollywood.

- *The Fearless Taster*
  Frequency: Daily
  Earliest NewsNet Issue: 8/15/82
  Accompanies a fully rated wine, described in detail, and written for enjoyable reading Often contains many shorter notes on recent wine releases.

Bulletin Boards

Rapid Transit BBS.

Dedicated to Chrysler enthusiasts for discussing Chrysler Corp (Mopar) cars, and for advertising Mopar cars and parts. The bulletin board is divided into many separate message boards for different types of Mopars.
Baud Rate: 300, 1200, 2400, 9600
BBS Number: (703) 771-1315
Sysop: Tom Cardwell

SCORPIO RISING III BBS

A board for games and poetry.
Baud Rate: 300, 1200, 2400, 9600
BBS Number: (703) 620-2827
BBS Software: MAXIMUS-CBCS

NumisNet

A special BBS for coin collectors.
Availability: 24 hrs/7 days
Baud Rate: 300, 2400
BBS Number: (301) 498-8205
Sysop: Larry Mitchell
Help Line: (301) 776-8741

CD-ROM

⑤ *Guiness Disc of Records*
UniDisc

⑤ *Software Toolworks Game CD Pack*
Software Tookworks

⑤ *National Survey of Fishing, Hunting &*
Wildlife Recreation
CD-ROM Inc

Geography/ Culture Resources

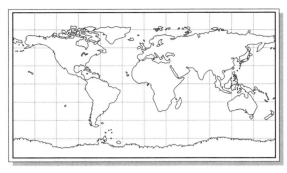

Forums & Databases
America Online (AOL)

⑨ *National Geographic Online*
Keyword: NGS
Path: Learning & Reference Department >
National Geographic Online
Offers access to feature articles from National
Geographic magazine, as well as *National
Geographic's World and Traveler* magazines.

CompuServe (CIS)
No services available.

GEnie

⑨ *Left Coast Online! RoundTable*
Keyword: B LEFT COAST or Page 1065
An information service dedicated to putting
residents and visitors to Alaska, Washington,
Oregon and California in touch with travel,
recreational, informational, and business
resources up and down the Left Coast.

⑨ *Deutschland RT*
Keyword: GERMANY or Page 725
For users interested in German culture.

⑨ *Japan RT*
Keyword: JAPAN or Page 225
For users who want to exchange information
about Japan or its culture.

⑨ *Canada RoundTable*
Keyword: CANADA or Page 1225
Enables users to learn about the Canadian
Culture, or where Canadian users can voice
their opinions on everything Canadian.

⑨ *Destination Florida RT*
Keyword: FLORIDA or Page 195
For users to post their comments about
vacationing in Central Florida.

The Well

⑨ *Aliens On the WELL (Private Conference)*
(g aliens)
For extraterrestrials, mutants, and time travelers.

⑨ *Hawaii*
(g aloha)
Discusses the island of Hawaii.

⑨ *Bay Area Tonight*
(g bat)
A short-term calendar of what's happening in
the Bay Area.

⑨ *Berkeley*
(g berk)

⑨ *Eastcoast*
(g east)
Discusses anything about the eastern half of
the United States.

⑨ *Geography*
(g geo)
Discusses the land, sea, air, and distribution of
life on the planet.

⑨ *German*
(g german)
Covers all facets of German culture.

⑨ *Gulf War*
(g gulf)
Discusses the Middle East conflicts.

⑤ *Irish/Celtic*
(g irish)
Covers the history, politics, music, dance, and art, of the Irish-American experience.

⑤ *Italian*
(g ital)

⑤ *Jewish*
(g jewish)
Offers information about being Jewish.

⑤ *Midwest*
(g midwest)
For midwesterners to discuss the happenings in their region(s) with each other and non-midwesterners.

⑤ *North Bay*
(g north)
Discusses topics of interest to users who live or like to visit the counties north of the Golden Gate.

⑤ *Pacific Northwest*
(g nw)
For users who want to talk about the Pacific Northwest.

⑤ *Oakland*
(g oak)
For users to discuss Oakland, California and its attributes.

⑤ *Pacific Rim*
(g pacrim)
Covers the culture, technology, language, economics and politics of Japan and other Pacific Rim countries.

⑤ *Peninsula*
(g pen)
Provides a place to discuss work, play, politics, transportation, and anything else related to the San Francisco Peninsula.

⑤ *Earthquake/Disaster*
(g quake)
Discusses natural disasters of all varieties from earthquakes, to locusts; droughts are major topics of discussion.

⑤ *Texas and the Southwest*
(g rodeo)
Discusses the mythic history of the southwest as the frontier, its current evolution as high tech wonderland, and as a source of cultural innovation from psychedelic rock to pomo/cyberpunk rants, and its future.

⑤ *San Francisco*
(g sanfran)
Covers all facets of the great city San Francisco.

⑤ *Southern California*
(g socal)
For discussing the city of Los Angeles and the southern part of California.

⑤ *South*
(g south)
Discusses all facets of Dixie!

⑤ *Tibet*
(g tibet)
Discusses Tibet's culture, people, traditions, religions, and political struggle.

Network Discussions Lists
Internet (Includes Bitnet & UUCPNet)

⑤ *Geographische Informationssyteme*
For the discussion and other postings about all areas of geographic information processing. Aimed at all German-speaking countries.
```
ACDGIS-L@AWIIMC12.BITNET
LISTSERV@AWIIMC12.BITNET
```
Contact: Josef Strobl
```
<STROBL@EDVZ.UNI-SALZBURG.ADA.AT>
```

Canada

⑤ *Canadian Issues Forum*
```
CANADA-L@MCGILL1.BITNET
LISTSERV@VM1.MCGILL.CA
```
Contact: Anastassia Khouri St-Pierre
```
<ED22@MUSICA.McGill.CA>
```

⑤ *Latin American and Caribbean Digest from CANADA*
```
CANALC-D@YORKVM1.BITNET
LISTSERV@YORKVM1.BITNET
```

⑤ *Canadian Association for Latin American and Caribbean list*
```
CANALC@YORKVM1.BITNET
LISTSERV@YORKVM1.BITNET
```

Geography

⑤ *CARIS Geographic Information System Users*
CARIS is a geographic information system (GIS) used for managing various kinds of spatial data, natural resources, municipalities, oceanography, charting, etc.
```
CarisUse@sun1.cogs.ns.ca
roger@sun1.cogs.ns.ca
```

Contact: Roger Mosher
  <roger@sun1.cogs.ns.ca>

⑤ *Newsletter on Chinese Community*
  CCNL@UTARLVM1.BITNET
  LISTSERV@UTARVM1.BITNET

⑤ *Central America Discussion List*
For students from Central America and users
interested in discussing issues concerning these
countries (especially those of Panama and Costa
Rica).
  CENTAM-L@UBVM.BITNET
  LISTSERV@UBVM.BITNET
Contact: Ginni Dubois
  v557nv8k@ubvms.BITNET

⑤ *Regional Development*
Discusses issues of relevance to regional
development and regional development
research in Central Europe.
  CERRO-L@AEARN.BITNET
  LISTSERV@AEARN.BITNET
Contact: Gunther Maier
  <cerro@awiwuw11.BITNET>

⑤ *Latin America Data Base*
  CH-LADB@UNMVM.BITNET
  LISTSERV@UNMVM.BITNET

⑤ *Chile Discussion List*
  CHILE-L@PURCCVM.BITNET
  LISTSERV@PURCCVM.BITNET
Contact: Antonio Mladinic
  <MLADINIC@PURCCVM.BITNET>

⑤ *China News Digest*
  CHINA-ND@KENTVM.BITNET
  LISTSERV@KENTVM.BITNET

⑤ *China News Network*
  CHINA-NN@ASUACAD.BITNET
  LISTSERV@ASUACAD.BITNET

⑤ *China-Net List*
  CHINA-NT@UGA.BITNET
  LISTSERV@UGA.BITNET

⑤ *CHINANET: Networking In China*
  CHINANET@TAMVM1.BITNET
  LISTSERV@TAMVM1.BITNET
Contact: Butch Kemper
  <X040BK@TAMVM1.BITNET>

⑤ *China Studies list*
  CHINA@PUCC.BITNET
  LISTSERV@PUCC.BITNET

⑤ *Latin America Data Base list*
  UP-LADB@UNMVM.BITNET
  LISTSERV@UNMVM.BITNET

⑤ *Events around the Berlin Wall*
Discusses events in recent German history.
  9NOV89-L@DBOTUI11.BITNET
  LISTSERV@DBOTU11.BITNET
Contact: Gerard Gschwind
  <GSCHWIND@DBOTUI11.BITNET>

⑤ *Queen's Chinese Friendship Association*
  LYH-L@QUCDN.BITNET
  LISTSERV@QUCDN.BITNET

⑤ *Slovak Issues*
  SLOVAK-L@UBVM.BITNET
  LISTSERV@UBVM.BITNET

⑤ *SM-LADB—Latin America Database list*
  SM-LADB@UNMVM.BITNET
  LISTSERV@UNMVM.BITNET

⑤ *Greek Culture*
Discusses of Greek society and culture to/from
a group of subscribers, that have NO USENET
ACCESS (people overseas, on BITNET, on
decnet, etc.).
  SOC-CULTURE-GREEK-POST@CS.WISC.EDU
  SOC-CULTURE-GREEK-REQUEST@CS.WISC.EDU
Contact: Manolis Tsangaris
  <mt@CS.WISC.EDU>

⑤ *Turkish Cultural Programs*
  TRKNWS-L@USCVM.BITNET
  LISTSERV@USCVM.BITNET

⑤ *The Tunisia Network*
  TUNISNET@PSUVM.BITNET
  LISTSERV@PSUVM.BITNET

⑤ *User Interfaces for Geographic Information
Systems*
Discusses topics related to the design and testing
of user interfaces for Geographic Information
Systems (GIS) and other geographic software.
  UIGIS-L@UBVM.BITNET
  LISTSERV@UBVM.BITNET
Contact: David M. Mark
  <GISMGR@UBVMS.BITNET>

⑤ *Geography Department Discussion List*
  UKGEG@UKCC.BITNET
  LISTSERV@UKCC.BITNET

⑤ *The Ukraine*
For the civil and thoughtful exchange and
analysis of information regarding Ukraine. Send
the command INDEX UKRAINE to the ListServ
address.
  Ukraine@INDYCMS.BITNET
  ListServ@IndyCMS.BITNET
Contact: John B Harlan
  <JBHarlan@IndyVAX.BITNET>

Regional

🕙 *African American Student Network*
```
AASNET-L@UHUPVM1.BITNET
LISTSERV@UHUPVM1.BITNET
```

🕙 *African-American Research list*
```
AFAM-L@UMCVMB.BITNET
LISTSERV@UMCVMB.BITNET
```

🕙 *African American Studies and Librarianship*
For librarians and other interested people on topics relating to the African-American experience and librarianship.
```
AFAS-L@KENTVM.BITNET
LISTSERV@KENTVM.BITNET
```
Contact: Gladys Smiley Bell
```
<gbell@kentvm.BITNET>
```

🕙 *FORUM PAN-AFRICA*
For the discussion of the interests of African peoples, and for users with an interest in the African continent and her peoples.
```
AFRICA-L@BRUFMG.BITNET
LISTSERV@BRUFMG.BITNET
```
Contact: Carlos Fernando Nogueira
```
<CTEDTC09@BRUFPB.BITNET>
```

🕙 *African-American issues in higher education.*
```
AFROAM-L@TEMPLEVM.BITNET
LISTSERV@TEMPLEVM.BITNET
```
Contact: Lee Baker
```
V1328G@<TEMPLEVM.BITNET>
```

🕙 *Baltic Republics Discussion List*
About the Baltic Republics of Lithuania, Latvia, and Estonia.
```
BALT-L@UBVM.BITNET
LISTSERV@UBVM.BITNET
```
Contact: Edis Bevan
```
<AEB_BEVAN@UK.AC.OPEN.ACS.VAX>
```

🕙 *Eastern European Business Network*
```
E-EUROPE@NCSUVM.BITNET
LISTSERV@NCSUVM.BITNET
```
Contact: James W. Reese
```
<R505040@UNIVSCVM.BITNET>
```

🕙 *People of Hellenic Descent*
```
ERMIS@VLSI.BU.EDU
listserv@vlsi.bu.edu
```

🕙 *Spain and Its People*
```
ESPANA-L@ALBNYVM1.BITNET
LISTSERV@ALBNYVM1.BITNET
```

🕙 *Yiddish Language*
```
mail.yiddish@LSUC.ON.CA
```
Contact: David Sherman
```
<dave@LSUC.ON.CA>
```

🕙 *Mardi Gras Discussion*
```
mardi_gras@mintir.fidonet.org
mardi_gras-request@mintir.fidonet.org
```
Contact: Edward J. Branley
```
<elendil@mintir.fidonet.org>
```

🕙 *Mexico—People, Places, Culture*
```
MEXICO-L@TECMTYVM.BITNET
LISTSERV@TECMTYVM.BITNET
```
Contact: Rosas Madrigal
```
koala@mtecv2.mty.itesm.mx Guillermo
```

🕙 *Muslim News Network*
```
MUSLIMS@ASUACAD.BITNET
LISTSERV@ASUACAD.BITNET
```

🕙 *Pacific Ocean and Islands*
```
PACIFIC@BRUFPB.BITNET
LISTSERV@BRUFPB.BITNET
```

🕙 *Pakistani News*
```
PAKISTAN@ASUACAD.BITNET
LISTSERV@ASUACAD.BITNET
```

🕙 *Indonesian Group—Montreal*
```
PERMIKA@MCGILL1.BITNET
LISTSERV@MCGILL1.BITNET
```

🕙 *Postmodern Culture*
```
PMC-LIST@NCSUVM.BITNET
LISTSERV@NCSUVM.BITNET
```

🕙 *Pacific Northwest Canadian Studies Conference*
```
PNWCSC@UWAVM.BITNET
LISTSERV@UWAVM.BITNET
```

🕙 *Polish Culture and Events*
```
POLAND-L@UBVM.BITNET
LISTSERV@UBVM.BITNET
```

🕙 *Turkish Issues*
```
PTT-L@LIVERPOOL.AC.UK
LISTSERV@LIVERPOOL.AC.UK
```

🕙 *News of former Soviet Union*
Provides information on the former Soviet Union and Eastern Europe. It is published Monday through Friday (except German holidays) by the RFE/RL Research Institute (a division of Radio Free Europe/Radio Liberty Inc) in Munich.
```
RFERL-L@UBVM.BITNET
LISTSERV@UBVM.BITNET
```
Contact: Dawn Mann
```
<mannd@rferl.org>
```

🕙*Russia*
```
RUSSIA@INDYCMS.BITNET
LISTSERV@INDYCMS.BITNET
```
Contact: John B Harlan
```
<IJBH200@IndyVAX.BITNET>
```

☯ *South Bend, Indiana, Notices and Events*
SBNEVENT@INDYCMS.BITNET
LISTSERV@INDYCMS.BITNET

☯ *Southeast Asian Studies List*
SEANET-L@NUSVM.BITNET
LISTSERV@NUSVM.BITNET
Contact: Paul Kratoska
 <hispaulk@nusvm.bitnet>

☯ *South East Asia*
SEASIA-L@MSU.BITNET
LISTSERV@MSU.BITNET
Contact: Elliott Parker
 <3ZLUFUR@CMUVM.BITNET>

☯ *SEELangs: Study of Slavic and Eastern Europe*
SEELANGS@CUNYVM.BITNET
LISTSERV@CUNYVM.BITNET

☯ *UPEI Institute. of Island Studies-Small Islands*
SIIN-L@UNBVM1.BITNET
LISTSERV@UNBVM1.BITNET

Geography

☯ *Geographical Issues*
GEOGRAPH@FINHUTC.BITNET
LISTSERV@FINHUTC.BITNET

☯ *Germans from Russia*
GER-RUS@NDSUVM1.BITNET
LISTSERV@NDSUVM1.BITNET GER-RUS

☯ *Geographic Information Systems Discussion List*
GIS-L@UBVM.BITNET
LISTSERV@UBVM.BITNET
Contact: David M. Mark
GEODMM@UBVMS.BITNET

☯ *Malaysian Women in U.S. and Canada*
HELWA-L@PSUVM.BITNET
LISTSERV@PSUVM.BITNET

☯ *Hindu Digest List*
HINDU-D@ARIZVM1.BITNET
LISTSERV@ARIZVM1.BITNET

☯ *Hungarian Discussion List*
HUNGARY@UCSBVM.BITNET
LISTSERV@UCSBVM.BITNET
Contact: Eric Dahlin
 <hcf2hung@ucsbuxa.BITNET>

☯ *The Indian Interest Group*
INDIA-L@UTARLVM1.BITNET
LISTSERV@UTARLVM1.BITNET
Contact: Geert K. Marien
GKMCU@CUNYVM.CUNY.EDU ()

☯ *Worldwide Irish-Interest Research Net*
IRL-NET@IRLEARN.BITNET
LISTSERV@IRLEARN.BITNET
Contact: Fionn Murtagh
FIONN@DGAES051.BITNET

☯ *IRL-POL—Current Irish Politics*
IRL-POL@IRLEARN.BITNET
LISTSERV@IRLEARN.BITNET

☯ *Latinos in the United States*
MCLR-L@MSU.BITNET
LISTSERV@MSU.BITNET

☯ *Community and Rural Economic Development International list.*
RURALDEV@KSUVM.BITNET
LISTSERV@KSUVM.BITNET

☯ *South Bend Area News*
SBNNEWS@INDYCMS.BITNET
LISTSERV@INDYCMS.BITNET

United Nations

☯ *United Nations*
UN@INDYCMS.BITNET
LISTSERV@IndyCMS.BITNE
Contact: John B Harlan
 <IJBH200@IndyVAX.BITNET>

☯ *Vietnamese Culture (BITNET)*
VIETNET@USCVM.BITNET
LISTSERV@USCVM.BITNET

Urban

☯ *Urban Planning*
URBAN-L@TREARN.BITNET
LISTSERV@TREARN.BITNET

☯ *Urban Planning Student Network*
URBANET@MSU.BITNET
LISTSERV@MSU.BITNET

☯ *Urban Self-sufficiency*
Discusses and promotes self-sufficiency in everyday life in many forms.
URBANITES@PSYCHE.MIT.EDU
strata@FENCHURCH.MIT.EDU
Contact: Stephen G. Wadlow
sgw@silver.lcs.mit.edu

Fidonet

☯ *International chat echo—Asia/North America/Europe*
ASIAN_LINK
For users interested in topics related to Asia and the Asian culture.
Moderator: Bill Oxner
1:388/8.2

Distribution: ZONE 1 BACKBONE, ZONE 2, ZONE 3, ZONE 6
Gateways: RBBS VIA 1:10/8, GT-NET VIA 6:720/616, ZONE 2 VIA 2:2405/100, ZONE 6 VIA 6:730/2 OR 6:700/300 OR 6:760/1 OR 6:751/1 SWEDEN VIA 2:203/218, NETHERLANDS VIA 2:500/1, BELGIUM VIA 2:29/777, ZONE 3 VIA 3:711/508

🌀 *Exploring Backroads*
BACKROADS
For grand touring which includes the sport touring motorcycle rider, sports cars, 4WD, RV's, and so on. Not about the vehicles except for passage conditions.
Moderator: Chuck Cole
8:973/1
Distribution: RBBS-NET
Gateways: RBBS-NET VIA 8:8/0

🌀 *Georgia Forum*
GEORGIA_FORUM
Covers life, the universe, as it relates to Georgia.
Moderator: Richard Press
1:273/201
Distribution: PRIVATE

🌀 *Greater Danbury Area Sysop Conference*
GDASYSOP
The Sysop and co-sysop echomail conference for the (extended) Greater Danbury Connecticut Area.
Moderator: Gary Snider
1:141/740
Restr: MOD-APVL
Distribution: GDA-LOCAL

🌀 *Hawaii and Pacific Island Topics*
HAWAII
A general conference that discusses things to do in Hawaii and its environs.
Moderator: PJ Estes
1:345/10
Distribution: Hawaii, California, Virginia, Panama

🌀 *Hebrew Discussions*
Moderator: Aaron Schmiedel
1:124/4104
Restr: MOD-APVL
Distribution: KESHERNET

🌀 *IOWA Echo*
IOWA_ECHO
For Iowa FidoNet BBS's and anyone else interested in maintaining contact with IOWA.
Moderator: Dan Buda
1:290/627
Distribution: REGION 14 HUBS, Iowa & Out-of-State

🌀 *Jewish Computer Users*
Moderator: Aaron Schmiedel
1:124/4104
Restr: MOD-APVL
Distribution: KESHERNET

🌀 *Jewish Discussions*
JUDAICA
Offers discussions about the Torah, about traditions, and about anything Jewish.
Moderator: Aaron Schmiedel
1:124/4104
Distribution: KESHERNET

🌀 *Jewish Education*
For teachers in the Jewish community. Includes Sunday school, yeshivot, and any Jewish learning center.
Moderator: Aaron Schmiedel
1:124/4104
Restr: MOD-APVL
Distribution: KESHERNET

🌀 *Jewish Geneaology*
For tracing your yiddische family tree.
Moderator: Aaron Schmiedel
1:124/4104
Restr: MOD-APVL
Distribution: KESHERNET

🌀 *Jewish Matchmakers!*
For finding your sweetheart. Computerized yenta!
Moderator: Aaron Schmiedel
1:124/4104
Restr: MOD-APVL
Distribution: KESHERNET

🌀 *Jews For Judaism*
For discussiing tactics used by various organizations to convert Jews.
Moderator: Ronnie Schreibe
1:120/241

🌀 *MAPPING*
For land surveyors, navigators, cartographers, geodesists, and geographers.
Moderator: Maynard Riley
1:115/678
Distribution: 1:115/678

🌀 *Modem Users of Minnesota*
MUM
For Modem users in Minnesota and users interested in MUM events, activities, and chit-chat.
Moderator: Erik Jacobson
1:282/31
Distribution: LOCAL-NET282

🖑 *New York Interests*
CALLNY
For users interested in things New York.
Moderator: Ronnie Toth
1:135/71
Distribution: BACKBONE

🖑 *Poland and Polish related topics.*
POLISH
Moderator: Henry Lukoszek
1:142/347
Distribution: BACKBONE
Gateways: 1:13/13 VIA 2:2405/100

🖑 *Where Friends Meet!*
PEN_PALS
For Canadian residents interested in keeping in touch with friends that they have made on FidoNet across Canada.
Moderator: Dean Laviolette
1:248/1
Distribution: NORTHSTAR

🖑 *Wisconsin Family Net General Chatter*
NET_WIS
For Wisconsin residents and users interested in Family Net activities in Wisconsin.
Moderator: Charles Nance
8:7480/110
Distribution: WISCONSIN

Usenet

🖑 *The state and the state of mind.*
alt.california

🖑 *British humour.*
alt.comedy.british

🖑 *What's happening to the Kurds in Iraq.*
alt.desert-thekurds

🖑 *Discussions of the Great Lakes and adjacent places.*
alt.great-lakes

🖑 *Discussion of the great little state.*
alt.rhode_island

🖑 *Eastern Europe List.*
bit.listserv.euearn-l

🖑 *The Hellenic Discussion List. (Moderated)*
bit.listserv.hellas

🖑 *Middle Europe Discussion List.*
bit.listserv.mideur-l

🖑 *Southeast Asia Discussion List.*
bit.listserv.seasia-l

🖑 *Slovak Discussion List.*
bit.listserv.slovak-l

🖑 *User Interface for Geographical Info Systems.*
bit.listserv.uigis-l

🖑 *International Intercultural Newsletter.*
bit.listserv.xcult-l

🖑 *News from Bangladesh, India, Nepal, etc. (Moderated)*
misc.news.southasia

🖑 *Discussion of the Afghan society.*
soc.culture.afghanistan

🖑 *Discussions about Africa & things African.*
soc.culture.african

🖑 *Discussions about Afro-American issues.*
soc.culture.african.american

🖑 *Technological & cultural issues, *not* politics.*
soc.culture.arabic

🖑 *Countries of the Assoc. of SE Asian Nations.*
soc.culture.asean

🖑 *Issues & discussion about Asian-Americans.*
soc.culture.asian.american

🖑 *Australian culture and society.*
soc.culture.australian

🖑 *Issues & discussion about Bangladesh.*
soc.culture.bangladesh

🖑 *Talking about the people and country of Brazil.*
soc.culture.brazil

🖑 *Issues about Britain & those of British descent.*
soc.culture.british

🖑 *Discussing Bulgarian society.*
soc.culture.bulgaria

🖑 *Discussions of Canada and its people.*
soc.culture.canada

🖑 *Life in the Caribbean.*
soc.culture.caribbean

🖑 *Irish, Scottish, Breton, Cornish, Manx & Welsh.*
soc.culture.celtic

🖑 *About China and Chinese culture.*
soc.culture.china

🖑 *Bohemian, Slovak, Moravian and Silesian life.*
soc.culture.czecho-slovak

🖑 *Discussing all aspects of all-European society.*
soc.culture.europe

🌀 *Group about the Filipino culture.*
soc.culture.filipino

🌀 *French culture, history, and related discussions.*
soc.culture.french

🌀 *Discussions about German culture and history.*
soc.culture.german

🌀 *Group about Greeks.*
soc.culture.greek

🌀 *Discussions pertaining to Hong Kong.*
soc.culture.hongkong

🌀 *Group for discussion about India & things Indian.*
soc.culture.indian

🌀 *Discussions about Iran and things Iranian/ Persian.*
soc.culture.iranian

🌀 *The Italian people and their culture.*
soc.culture.italian

🌀 *Everything Japanese, except the Japanese language.*
soc.culture.japan

🌀 *Jewish culture & religion.*
soc.culture.jewish

🌀 *Discussions about Korean & things Korean.*
soc.culture.korean

🌀 *Topics about Latin-America.*
soc.culture.latin-america

🌀 *Discussion about things Lebanese.*
soc.culture.lebanon

🌀 *The Hungarian people & their culture.*
soc.culture.magyar

🌀 *Discussion of Mexico's society.*
soc.culture.mexican

🌀 *Group for discussion about other cultures.*
soc.culture.misc

🌀 *Discussion of people and things in & from Nepal.*
soc.culture.nepal

🌀 *People from the Netherlands and Belgium.*
soc.culture.netherlands

🌀 *Discussion of topics related to New Zealand.*
soc.culture.new-zealand

🌀 *Discussion about culture up north.*
soc.culture.nordic

🌀 *Topics of discussion about Pakistan.*
soc.culture.pakistan

🌀 *Polish culture, Polish past, and Polish politics.*
soc.culture.polish

🌀 *Discussion of the people of Portugal.*
soc.culture.portuguese

🌀 *Discussion of Romanian and Moldavian people.*
soc.culture.romanian

🌀 *Topics relating to Russian or Soviet culture.*
soc.culture.soviet

🌀 *Discussion of culture on the Iberian peninsula.*
soc.culture.spain

🌀 *Things & people from Sri Lanka.*
soc.culture.sri-lanka

🌀 *Discussion about things Taiwanese.*
soc.culture.taiwan

🌀 *Tamil language, history and culture.*
soc.culture.tamil

🌀 *Thai people and their culture.*
soc.culture.thai

🌀 *Discussion about things Turkish.*
soc.culture.turkish

🌀 *The culture of the United States of America.*
soc.culture.usa

🌀 *Issues and discussions of Vietnamese culture.*
soc.culture.vietnamese

🌀 *Discussions of Yugoslavia and its people.*
soc.culture.yugoslavia

🌀 *Discussion of feminism & feminist issues. (Moderated)*
soc.feminism

Online Libraries

After Dark
No services available.

Knowledge Index
No services available.

Orbit
No services available.

NewsNet
No services available.

Bulletin Boards

PROTEUS BBS

Dedicated to the communications development with special interests in East Europe, especially Yugoslavia.
Baud Rate: 300, 1200, 2400
BBS Number: (202) 333-1484
BBS Software: MAXIMUS-CBCS
Sysop: Sinisa Mihailovic

The Dakota BBS
Bulletin Board

Dedicated to promoting the self-sufficiency and economic well-being of American Indian and rural people through the today's technology.
Baud Rate: 2400, 14.4
BBS Number: (605) 341-4552
BBS Software: RemoteAccess
Help Line: (605) 341-7293
E-Mail: anne.fallis@oldcolo.com

CD-ROM

✎ *Arctic & Antarctic*
NISC
3100 St. Paul Street
Suite 6
Baltimore, MD 21218

✎ *CIA World Factbook*
Quanta Press

✎ *Countries of the World*
Bureau of Electronic Publishing

✎ *DeLorme Streets*
DeLorme Mapping

✎ *Electronic Map Cabinet*
Highlighted Data, Inc.

✎ *GEOdisc state*
Geovision Inc.
270 Technology Pk/Atl.
Suite 1
Norcross, GA 30092

✎ *GEOVISION System*
Geovision Inc.
270 Technology Pk/Atl.
Suite 1
Norcross, GA 30092

✎ *National Register of Historic Places*
Buckmaster
P.O. Box 10
Mineral, VA 23117

✎ *Place Name Index*
Buckmaster
P.O. Box 10
Mineral, VA 23117

✎ *Supermap CountyLevel*
Chadwyck-Healey Inc.
1101 King Street
Suite 180
Alexandria, VA 22314

✎ *Supermap US Census Data*
Chadwyck-Healey, Inc.

✎ *Software Toolworks World Atlas*
Software Toolworks

✎ *Supermap USA*
Chadwyck-Healey Inc.
1101 King Street
Suite 180
Alexandria, VA 22314

✎ *US Atlas GEOdisc*
Geovision Inc.
270 Technology Pk/Atl
Suite 1
Norcross, GA 30092

✎ *US Elect*
Map Cabinet Highlighted Data
P.O. Box 17229
Washington, DC 20041

✎ *US Street ReferenceFile*
Donnelley Marketing Information
70 Seaview Avenue
Stamford, CT 06904

✎ *US Yellow Page Boundaries*
Donnelley Marketing Information
70 Seaview Avenue
Stamford, CT 06904

✎ *World Atlas*
Electromap, Inc.
P.O. Box 1153
Fayetteville, AR 72702-1153

✎ *World Factbook 1989*
Quanta Press Inc.
2550 University Avenue W.
No. 245N
St. Paul, MN 55114

Geological Resources

Forums & Databases

America Online (AOL)
No services available.

CompuServe (CIS)
No services available.

GEnie
No services available.

The Well

🕲 *Earthquake/Disaster*
(g quake)
For the discussion of natural disasters of all varieties.

Network Discussions Lists

Internet (Includes Bitnet & UUCPNet)

🕲 *Geology Discussion list.*
GEOLOGY@PTEARN.BITNET
LISTSERV@PTEARN.BITNET

🕲 *Sistemas de Informacion Geo-Referencial list.*
GEOREF@UNALCOL.BITNET
LISTSERV@UNALCOL.BITNET

🕲 *HELPNET Network Emergency Response Planning*
For users interested in the roles global computer networks might play in times of disaster, such as earthquakes and hurricanes.
HELPNET@NDSUVM1.BITNET
LISTSERV@NDSUVM1.BITNET

Contact: Marty Hoag
NU021172@NDSUVM1.BITNET

🕲 *Mineral Economics and Management Society list.*
MEMSNET@UABDPO.BITNET
LISTSERV@UABDPO.BITNET

🕲 *Ocean Drilling Program Open Discussion list.*
ODP-L@TAMVM1.BITNET
LISTSERV@TAMVM1.BITNET
Contact: Judy Duke
DUKE@TAMODP

🕲 *Oil and gas Industry list.*
For the discussion of current oil and gas industry issues, problems, events, and opportunities. Includes daily oil prices.
OIL-GAS@PAVNET.NSHOR.NCOAST.ORG
oil-gas-request@pavnet.nshore.ncoast.org

🕲 *Quake list.*
For the discussion of the ways various national and international computer networks can help during earthquakes, or how the help can be enhanced.
QUAKE-L@NDSUVM1.BITNET
LISTSERV@NDSUVM1.BITNET

🕲 *Seismological topics of general interest list.*
SEISM-L@BINGVMB.BITNET
LISTSERV@BINGVMB.BITNET
Contact: Francis Wu
BG4655@BINGVMA.BITNET

🕲 *Seismological Discussion list.*
SEISMD-L@BINGVMB.BITNET
LISTSERV@BINGVMB.BITNET

🕲 *Stat-Geo—Forum of Quantitative Methods in Geo-sciences list.*
STAT-GEO@UFRJ.BITNET
LISTSERV@UFRJ.BITNET

⚙ *Univ Consort for Geo Info & Analysis list.*
  UCGIA-L@UBVM.BITNET
  LISTSERV@UBVM.BITNET

 ⚙ *VOLCANO list.*
  VOLCANO@ASUACAD.BITNET
  LISTSERV@ASUACAD.BITNET

Fidonet

No services available.

Usenet

 ⚙ *Discussion of geophysical fluid dynamics.*
  sci.geo.fluids

 ⚙ *Discussion of solid earth sciences.*
  sci.geo.geology

Online Libraries
After Dark

 ⚙ *Current Contents*
Physical, Chemical, and Earth Sciences: A subset of Current Contents Search™ corresponding to the Current Contents: Physical, Chemical, and Earth Sciences edition.
Coverage: Most current 12 months
Updated: Weekly

 ⚙ *QUAKELINE*
Contains bibliographic information on earthquakes, earthquake engineering, natural hazard mitigation, and related topics.
Coverage: 1987 to present
Updated: Monthly

Knowledge Index

No services available.

Orbit

 ⚙ *API Energy Business News Index (APIBIZ)*
Includes 24 major news and economics publications as the primary sources for worldwide coverage of commercial, financial, marketing, and regulatory information affecting the petroleum and energy industries.
Coverage: 1975 to present
Updated: Weekly

 ⚙ *APILIT*
Covers worldwide petroleum literature starting in 1964. Available on a limited basis to non-subscribing organizations.
Coverage: 1964 to present
Updated: Monthly

 ⚙ *Electric Power Industry Abstracts*
Provides access to literature on electric power plants and related facilities. Only available on Orbit.
Coverage: 1975 to 1983

 ⚙ *Energy Bibliography*
Covers worldwide literature on energy from the Texas A&M Library collection. Features coverage of German World War II documents on synthetic fuel technology. Only available on Orbit.
Coverage: 1919 to present (some 19th century material)
Updated: Periodically

 ⚙ *ENERGYLINE*
Contains journals as well as reports, surveys, monographs, newspapers, conference proceedings, and irregular serials that are screened to provide comprehensive coverage of energy information.
Coverage: 1971 to present
Updated: Monthly

 ⚙ *GEOBASE*
Contains citations from the international literature on physical and human geography, geology, and ecology.
Coverage: 1980 to present
Updated: Monthly

 ⚙ *GeoMechanics Abstracts*
Contains bibliographic data of published literature on the mechanical performance of geological materials relevant to the extraction of raw materials for mankind from the earth and the construction of structures on or in the earth for civil engineering projects or energy generation.
Coverage: 1977 to present (some before 1977)
Updated: Bimonthly

 ⚙ *GEOREF*
Covers geo-sciences literature from 3,000 journals, including books, conference proceedings, government documents, maps, and theses, with more than 1.5 million records.
Coverage: 1785 to present
Updated: Monthly

 ⚙ *IPABASE*
Contains records on petroleum and allied literature concerning oil field exploration and development, petroleum refining and products, and economics.
Coverage: 1985 to present
Updated: Quarterly

🌐 *POWER*
Consists of catalog records for books, monographs, proceedings, journals, and other material in the collections of the technical and law libraries of the U.S. Department of Energy.
Coverage: 1950 to present
Updated: Triannually

🌐 *Remote Sensing*
Contains bibliographic references to studies, technical reports, papers, symposiums, and conference proceedings covering the instrumentation, techniques, and applications of remote sensing technology.
Coverage: 1973 to present
Updated: Monthly

🌐 *TULSA (Petroleum Abstracts)*
Contains references and abstracts to worldwide literature and patents related to oil and natural gas exploration, development, and production. On-line access is restricted to TULSA subscribers. Only available on Orbit.
Coverage: 1965 to present
Updated: Weekly

🌐 *WPIA/WPILA*
Contains records for more than 5.5 million patents covering petroleum processes, fuels, lubricants, petro-chemicals, pipelines, tankers, storage, pollution control, synthetic fuels, and other technologies. Only available on Orbit.
Coverage: 1963 to present
Updated: Weekly and monthly

NewsNet

No services available.

Bulletin Boards

Bureau of Mines Bureau-Wide (BOM-BBN) BBS

Makes BOM data available 2 to 4 weeks sooner than is now possible. The bulletins are text files that users can read when connected to BOM-BBN. Lots of information on mineral production.
Baud Rate: 300, 1200, 2400, 9600
BBS Number: (202) 501-0373
BBS Software: RBBS-PC
Help Line: (202) 501-0406

California Division of Mines and Geology (CDMG) On-line

For Geo-scientists, Geographers, and GIS Specialists. Also primarily for disseminating information of geologic interest for the state of California and for publications written by geologists with the California Division of Mines & Geology.
Availability: 24 hours/7 days
Baud Rate: 300, 1200, 2400, 9600
BBS Number: (916) 327-1208
BBS Software: WILDCAT
Sysop: Ted Smith

Computer Oriented Geological Society (COGSnet)

A professional organization that actively encourages the application of computers in the field of geology.
Availability: 24 hours/7 days
Baud Rate: 300, 1200, 2400
BBS Number: (303) 740-9493
BBS Software: OPUS-CBCS
Sysop: Tom Bresnahan

Precambrian BBS

For geological and earth sciences. Maintains a list of other geological-related bulletin boards.
Baud Rate: 300, 1200, 2400, 9600, 14.4
BBS Number: (602) 881-5836
BBS Software: WILDCAT
Help Line: (602) 323-9170

U.S. Geological Survey (USGS) BBS

CD-ROM conference and lots of geological files.
Baud Rate: 300, 1200, 2400, 9600
BBS Number: (703) 648-4168
BBS Software: PCBoard

U.S. Geological Survey (USGS) Online Info System

Contains Quick Epicenter Determinations (QED), Earthquake Lists (EQLIST), and Geomagnetic Field Values.
Baud Rate: 1200
BBS Number: (800) 358-2663
Help Line: (303) 236-1500
Comment: No registration required

CD-ROM

Earth science

♻ *Earth Science Data Directory*
OCLC
6565 Franz Road
Dublin, OH 43017

♻ *GeoIndex*
OCLC
6565 Franz Road
Dublin, OH 43017

♻ *Natural Resources Database*
NISC
3100 Paul Street, Suite 6
Baltimore, MD 21218

♻ *USGS Library*
OCLC
6565 Franz Road
Dublin, OH 43017

Geology, Geophysics, and Hydrology

♻ *CDROM Prototype*
U.S. Geological Survey
804 National Center
Reston, VA 22092

♻ *Deep Sea Drilling Project (DSDP)*
National Geophysical Data Center
325 Broadway
Dept. 731
Boulder, CO 80303

♻ *Earth Sciences Disc*
SilverPlatter Information Inc.
One Newton Executive Park
Newton Lower Falls, MA 02162

♻ *GeoRef*
SilverPlatter Information Inc.

♻ *Global Hypocenter Data Base*
U.S. Geological Survey
National Earthquake Information Center
Denver Federal Center
Box 25046 MS 967
Denver, CO 80225

♻ *GLORIA (Geological LongRange Inclined Asdisc) for Gulf of New Mexico*
National Geophysical Data Center
325 Broadway
Dept. 731
Boulder, CO 80303

♻ *NGDC-01 (Solar Terrestrial Time Series)*
National Geophysical Data Center
325 Broadway
Dept. 731
Boulder, CO 80303

♻ *NIMBUS-7 SMMR, Vol 1. (Brightness Temperature Grids)*
National Geophysical Data Center
325 Broadway
Dept. 731
Boulder, CO 80303

♻ *Publications of the U.S. Geological Survey*
American Geological Institute

♻ *Selected Water Resources Abstracts*
OCLC
6565 Franz Road
Dublin, OH 43017

Government Resources

Forums & Databases

America Online (AOL)

No services available.

CompuServe (CIS)

⑤ *Government Publications*
Keyword: GO GPO
Offers a catalog of government publications, books, and subscription services, and on-line consumer information articles from government publications.

⑤ *Health Database Plus*
Keyword: GO HLTDB
Provides information from consumer and professional health, nutrition, and fitness publications. Enables users to access the full text of articles from selected lay journals published after January 1989.

⑤ *Information USA*
Keyword: GO INFOUSA
Tells users how to use free government publications and services available, and explains the art of obtaining information from bureaucrats.

⑤ *NTIS-Government Sponsored Research*
Keyword: GO NTIS
Offers a database of references to articles from government-sponsored research, development, and engineering reports.

GEnie

No services available.

The Well

No services available.

Network Discussions Lists

Internet (Includes Bitnet & UUCPNet)

⑤ *Election Techniques*
Aimed at campaign managers, workers, and candidates at all levels of government and from all ideologies.
```
ELECT-L@PCCVM.BITNET
LISTSERV@PCCVM.BITNET
```
Contact: Brett A. Feinstein
```
<bafei@conncoll.BITNET>
```

⑤ *Republican*
For discussion of Republican and Conservative issues.
```
GOP-L@OCCVM.BITNET
LISTSERV@PCCVM.BITNET
```
Contact: Brett A. Feinstein
```
<bafei@conncoll.BITNET>
```

⑤ *United Nations*
For discussion of the United Nations.
```
UN@INDYCMS.BITNET
LISTSERV@IndyCMS.BITNE
```
Contact: John B. Harlan
```
<IJBH200@IndyVAX.BITNET>
```

Fidonet

⑤ *Civil Liberties*
```
CIVLIB
```
For discussing Civil Liberties, the Bill of Rights, and Constitution of the United States as applied to your rights.
Moderator: Bob Hirschfeld
```
1:114/74.2
```
Distribution: BACKBONE

Canadian Government Computer Systems and Vendor Chat
GOVT_CS
For discussing issues in the Canadian Federal computing industry.
Moderator: Raymond Ouellette
1:163/125
Distribution: Cross-Canada. Mainly in Ottawa-Toronto Area
Gateways: IMEX, FEDNET

 Model Government Colloquium
MODEL_GEE
For role playing.
Moderator: Rob Levin
1:3802/217
Distribution: OPEN, DIRECT, NET-3802

 World Talk Conference & United Nations News
WORLDTLK
For obtaining United Nations proceedings from General Assembly. UN press releases, global environmental news, news flashes from UNICEF, and other related UN organizations.
Moderator: James Waldron
1:2604/401
Distribution: BACKBONE (ZONE-1, ZONE-2, ZONE-3, AND ZONE-4)
Gateways: FREDMAIL RBBSNET. Internet Mailing List

Usenet

 News regarding both U.S. and international elections. (Moderated)
clari.news.election

 General Government-related stories. (Moderated)
clari.news.gov

 Government agencies, FBI, and others. (Moderated)
clari.news.gov.agency

 Budgets at all levels. (Moderated)
clari.news.gov.budget

 Government corruption, kickbacks, and more. (Moderated)
clari.news.gov.corrupt

 International government-related stories. (Moderated)
clari.news.gov.international

 Government officials and their problems. (Moderated)
clari.news.gov.officials

 State government stories of national importance. (Moderated)
clari.news.gov.state

 Tax laws, trials, and more. (Moderated)
clari.news.gov.taxes

 U.S. Federal government news. (High volume). (Moderated)
clari.news.gov.usa

 Panama and General Noriega. (Moderated)
clari.news.hot.panama

 Politicians & politics. (Moderated)
clari.news.politics

 Terrorist actions and related news around the world. (Moderated)
clari.news.terrorism

 Discussion of government document issues.
bit.listserv.govdoc-l

Online Libraries
After Dark

 GPO Monthly Catalog
Index to public documents. Includes legislative and judiciary materials, presidential publications, committee and commission reports, and documents of independent and regulatory agencies.
Coverage: July 1976 to present
Updated: Monthly

 Index to U.S. Government Periodicals
Covers nearly all fields of interest, with 185 titles from more than 100 government agencies indexed by subject and author.
Coverage: 1980 to present (partial 1979)
Updated: Monthly (about 1100 records per update)

 PAIS (Public Affairs Information Service) International
Worldwide coverage of public policy aspects of economics, business, government, law, public administration, political science, international relations, and all other social sciences.
Coverage: 1972 to present
Updated: Monthly

 Social Planning/Policy & Development Abstracts
A companion database to Sociological Abstracts (SOCA). Contains information about the

applied and social-oriented problems of sociological and social sciences literature from around the world.
Coverage: 1979 to present
Updated: Twice a year with approximately 1500 records per year

Knowledge Index

⑤ *Commerce Business Daily*
Produced by the U.S. Department of Commerce. The complete text equivalent of the print publication Commerce Business daily.
Coverage: 1982 to present
Updated: Daily

⑤ *GPO Publications Reference File*
Indexes public documents currently for sale by the Superintendent of Documents, U.S. Government Printing Office as well as forthcoming and recently out-of-print publications.
Coverage: 1971 to present
Updated: Biweekly

⑤ *NTIS*
Features government-sponsored research, development, and engineering, plus analyses prepared by federal agencies, their contractors, or grantees.
Coverage: 1964 to present
Updated: Biweekly

Orbit

No services available.

NewsNet

⑤ *Antitrust FOIA Log*
Covers legal decisions, legislative developments, and regulatory changes. Includes information on committee reports, upcoming conferences, and pertinent published articles on the latest developments in freedom of information.
Frequency: Weekly
Earliest NewsNet Issue: July 4,1986

⑤ *Congressional Activities*
Provides frequent reporting on freedom of information requests filed at the U.S. Justice Department's Anti-trust Division.
Frequency: Weekly
Retention: One year plus current year

⑤ *Federal Grants and Contracts Weekly*
Summary of upcoming Congressional events

of interest to energy industries. Includes schedule of hearings, historical items, list of bills introduced, bills reported, bills passed, laws enacted, and Congressional Record references.
Read Rate: $2.00/min.; (40cts/min.)
Frequency: Weekly
Retention: 26 weeks

⑤ *Federal/Industry Watchdog*
Provides complete records of new federal grants and contracts in research services and training. Also includes news, analysis, profiles of key agencies, and updates on new legislation, regulations, budget developments, publications, and foundations.
Frequency: Monthly
Earliest NewsNet Issue: 5/1/91

⑤ *FTC FOIA Log*
A guide to materials developed by the General Accounting Office. Each article contains a description of an original investigation, or an audit of the government, or a government contractor's activities.
Frequency: Weekly
Earliest NewsNet Issue: January 18, 1985

⑤ *The FTC Today*
Lists all of the Freedom of Information Act requests received by the U.S. Federal Trade Commission.
Frequency: Daily
Earliest NewsNet Issue: September 30, 1991

⑤ *FTC: Watch*
Provides full text of official U.S. Federal Trade Commission news releases each day as they are released.
Frequency: Biweekly
Earliest NewsNet Issue: January 8, 1982

⑤ *GAO Reports and Testimony*
Contains information and details concerning policies, programs, and personnel of the U.S. Federal Trade Commission.
Frequency: Monthly
Earliest NewsNet Issue: May 1, 1990

⑤ *Government and Regulatory (GT)*
Access Reports/Freedom of Information.
Frequency: Biweekly
Retention: Two years plus current year

⑤ *The Information Report*
Provides titles and abstracts of reports and statements of testimony issued by the U.S.

General Accounting Office. Aids readers in ordering and using cited reports and testimony.
Frequency: Monthly
Earliest NewsNet Issue: May 1, 1985

⑤ *Inside DOT & Transportation Week*
Updated on new and little-known sources of free and low-cost federal, state, local, international, professional, and trade information of interest to business executives, corporate analysts, and others.
Frequency: Weekly
Earliest NewsNet Issue: October 4, 1990

⑤ *Liability Week*
Tracks the U.S. Department of Transportation budget and how it is being spent. Covers contracts awarded by each of the DOT subsections, transportation-related debates on Capitol Hill, and international events.
Frequency: Weekly
Earliest NewsNet Issue: May 5, 1986

⑤ *NIST Update*
An authoritative report on political and legislative developments brought on by the liability insurance crisis sweeping America.
Frequency: Biweekly
Earliest NewsNet Issue: July 1, 1986

⑤ *Tactical Technology*
Covers recent activities of the United States National Bureau of Standards—the nation's physical science and engineering measurement laboratory.
Frequency: Biweekly
Earliest NewsNet Issue: October 2, 1991

⑤ *U.S. ITC Update*
Provides defense and technology executives with a comprehensive source of news, business opportunities, and timely analysis of the SO/LIC-WOD marketplace.
Frequency: Monthly
Earliest NewsNet Issue: January 1, 1991

⑤ *U.S. Newswire*
Provides news releases, full-text statements, and news advisories to the national media by-groups including U.S. government agencies, Congressional offices, national interest groups, and labor unions.
Frequency: Daily
Earliest NewsNet Issue: October 1, 1991

Bulletin Boards
Annual Wage Reporting (AWR) BBS
Provides service to users who are interested in AWR information and documentation. Offered by Social Security Administration Office of Systems Requirements Baltimore, Maryland.
Baud Rate: 300, 1200, 2400, 9600, 19.2
BBS Number: (410) 965-1133
BBS Software: TBBS
Sysop: Suzanne Ford

District of Columbia Government PMS BBS
Facilitates electronic communications among staff members and agencies of the District of Columbia Government and other users interested in local government activities and management.
Availability: 24 hours/7 days
Baud Rate: 300, 1200, 2400
BBS Software: FIDO
Sysop: Danny Weiss
Help Line: (202) 727-3377

Electronic Filing Service (EFS) BBS
Offered by the U.S. Department of Treasury Internal Revenue Service Systems for the exchange of information about electronic filing.
Baud Rate: 300, 1200, 2400, 9600
BBS Number: (202) 927-4180
BBS Software: RBBS-PC
Sysop: Harry Eisenberg
Help Line: (202) 927-3463

The Energy & Regulatory Matters BBS
Sponsored by the Michigan Public Service Commission. Provides energy, environmental, public information, software and computer, telecommunication, and PSC forums.
Availability: 24 hours/7 days
Baud Rate: 300, 2400
BBS Number: (517) 882-1421
BBS Software: The Major BBS
Help Line: (517) 334-6264

FCC Public Access Link (PAL)

Contains public notices, rule makings, and equipment approval status and other Commission activities and procedures.
Baud Rate: 1200
BBS Number: (301) 725-1072
Help Line: (301) 725-1585

The Federal Bulletin Board

From the U.S. Government Printing Office (GPO). Enables all federal agencies to give the public immediate, self-service access to government information electronically at reasonable rates. Users need to purchase a GPO deposit account to order any of the on-line publications. Minimum download charge is $2 per file up to 50k files.
Availability: 22 hours (not available 3-5 a.m.) /7 days
Baud Rate: 2400
BBS Number: (202) 512-1387
Help Line: (202) 512-1524

The Federal Whistleblower BBS

Helps the United States Congress identify waste, fraud, and abuse in the federal government.
Availability: 24 hours/7 days
Baud Rate: 300, 1200, 2400, 9600
BBS Number: (202) 225-5527
BBS Software: RBBS-PC
Sysop: Congressman Bob Wise from West Virginia.

General Services Administrations' Information Resources Services Center

Provides information on federal acquisition regulation changes (FACs), and contracts and schedules.
Baud Rate: 300, 1200, 2400, 9600
BBS Number: (703) 305-6229
BBS Software: CTUS-BBS

Information Reporting Project, IRS BBS

Provides information, services, and the option of filing your information returns electronically.
Baud Rate: 300, 1200, 2400, 9600, 14.4
BBS Number: (304) 263-2749
BBS Software: TBBS

IRS Statistics of Income Division Bulletin Board

Disseminates statistical information to the public.
Baud Rate: 300, 1200, 2400, 9600
BBS Number: (202) 874-9574
BBS Software: PCBoard
Sysop: Jim Willis and Kristine Zahm
Help Line: (202) 874-0408, (202) 874-0273

MEGAWATTS

General computer board with lots of files.
Availability: 24 hours/7 days
Baud Rate: 300, 1200, 2400, 9600
BBS Number: (202) 586-0739
BBS Software: RBBS-PC
Sysop: Bruce Birnbaum

National Technical Information Service (NTIS) BBS

Availability: 24 hours/7 days
Baud Rate: 2400, 9600
BBS Number: (703) 321-8020 or (703) 321-8970 (9600)
BBS Software: RBBS-PC
Sysop: Ken Royer
Help Line: (703) 487-4620/4007
Comment: The following other BBS are located on these systems: CALS (Computer-aided Acquisition & Logistic Support) BBS, Bob Freeman, (703) 487-4829; CTN CALS Test Network Bulletin Board, Michael Christie, (301) 227-5497; and MODIL Manufacturing Operations Development and Integration Laboratory, Arnold Johnson, (301) 975-3247

OPM Atlanta Region Bulletin Board

Provides job information for individuals seeking federal employment. Also provides information for federal personnel to improve communication between the U.S. Office of Personnel Management and other agencies.
Baud Rate: 300, 1200, 2400
BBS Number: (404) 730-2370
BBS Software: PCBoard
Help Line: (404) 331-3459

OPM Pay Per Net Bulletin Board System

Provides information to federal agencies on the federal personnel community. Contains information and programs relating to Title 5. Open to all federal agencies and general public.
Availability: 24 hours/7 days
Baud Rate: 300, 1200, 2400
BBS Number: (202) 606-2675/1876
BBS Software: PCBoard
Sysop: Denise Jenkins
Help Line: (202) 606-2092

PerManNet BBS

Serves various interest groups including: associates of the U.S. Agency for International Development; scientific researchers; writers and global networkers; users needing access to the Internet or certain message conferences; users looking for state-of-the-art PC communications software; and more.
Baud Rate: 300, 1200, 2400, 9600, 14.4
BBS Number: (202) 296-6304, or (202) 466-5353
Sysop: Mark Prado
Help Line: (202) 466-6275
Comment: Internet address: permannet@f349.n109.z1.fidonet.org; Fidonet addresses: 1:109/349 (2400 baud) 1:109/10 (9600 and 14,400 baud)

SBA Online

Covers women, international trade, veterans, general business development files, business initiatives, education and training, service corps of retired executives (score), procurement assistance, minority small business, small business innovation research, surety guarantee, small business investment, financial assistance, disaster assistance, legislation and regulations, small business development center files, and miscellaneous files. Provided by U.S. Small Business Administration Electronic Bulletin Board.
Baud Rate: 300, 1200, 2400, 9600
BBS Number: (202) 205-7265 or (800) 697-4636 (9600 bps), (800) 859-4636 (2400 bps)
Help Line: (800) 827-5722

State and Local Emergency Management Data Users Group (SALEMDUG) BBS

SALEMDUG is an association of state, local, and Federal Emergency Management Agency (FEMA). It promotes information exchange, encourages standardization throughout the emergency management community, and facilitates application of computer technology to emergency management problems.
SALEMDUG is open to anyone who is affiliated with or has an expressed interest in Emergency Management.
Availability: 24 hours/7 days
Baud Rate: 300, 1200, 2400, 9600, 14.4
BBS Number: (202) 646-2887 or (202) 646-3639
BBS Software: PCBoard
Sysop: Rod Renner (202) 646-3528, Chip Hines (202) 646-3115
Help Line: (202) 646-3115

U.S. Small Business Administration (SBA) BBS

For the sole use of the small business administration and affiliated contractors.
Baud Rate: 300, 1200, 2400, 9600
BBS Number: (202) 205-6269 or (202) 205-6272
BBS Software: RBBS-PC
Sysop: Rick Butler and Ed Watkins
Help Line: (202) 205-6244 or (202) 205-6259

CD-ROM

❦ *Federal Register Compact Disc*
Counterpoint Publishing

❦ *GAO Masterfile*
Chadwyck-Healey

❦ *Government Documents Catalog*
Auto-Graphics Inc.
3201 Temple Avenue
Pomona, CA 91768

❦ *GPO*
SilverPlatter Information Inc.

❦ *Marcive/GPO Catalog*
Marcive, Inc.
P.O. Box 47508
San Antonio, TX 78265

❦ *NTIS*
Dialog Information Services

History/ Genealogy Resources

Forums & Databases
America Online (AOL)

◔ *Baby Boomers Club*
Keyword: Baby Boomers
Path: Lifestyles & Interests Department > Baby Boomers Club
Enables users to talk about the music, historical and cultural events, and styles that have shaped their lives and world view.

CompuServe (CIS)

◔ *Genealogy Forum*
Keyword: GO ROOTS
Enables users to find their roots. Provides list of Irish genealogy societies and addresses of vital records departments in all the Canadian provinces.

GEnie

No services available.

The Well

◔ *History*
   (g hist)
For anyone interested in history. Topics include everything from Medieval heretics to World War II trivia.

Network Discussions Lists
Internet (Includes Bitnet & UUCPNet)

◔ *Association for History & Computing*
   AHC-L@DGOGWDG1.BITNET
   LISTSERV@DGOGWDG1.BITNET
Contact: Manfred Thaller
   <MTHALLE1@DGOGWDG1.BITNET>

◔ *British and Irish History*
   ALBION-L@UCSBVM.BITNET
   LISTSERV@UCSBVM.BITNET

◔ *American Studies list.*
   AMERSTDY@MIAMIU.BITNET
   LISTSERV@MIAMIU.BITNET

◔ *American West History Forum list.*
   AMWEST-H@USCVM.BITNET
   LISTSERV@USCVM.BITNET

◔ *History of the Ancient Mediterranean*
For the debate, the discussion, and the exchange of information by students and scholars of the history of the Ancient Mediterranean.
   ANCIEN-L@ULKYVM.BITNET
   LISTSERV@ULKYVM.BITNET
Contact: James A. Cocks
   <JACOCK01@ULKYVM.BITNET>

🖙 *ANSAXNET Discussion Forum*
For scholars of the culture and history of
England before 1100 C.E.
```
ANSAX-L@WVNVM.BITNET
LISTSERV@WVNVM.BITNET
```
Contact: Patrick W. Conner
```
<U47C2@WVNVM.BITNET>
```
For scholars of the culture and history of
England before 1100 C.E.

🖙 *Mailing List for Irish and UK Architectural
Librarians*
```
ARCLIB-L@IRLEARN.BITNET
LISTSERV@IRLEARN.BITNET
```
Contact: Julia Barrett
```
JBARRETT@IRLEARN.BITNET>
```

🖙 *Theatre History Discussion list.*
```
ASTR-L@UIUCVMD.BITNET
LISTSERV@UIUCVMD.BITNET
```

🖙 *ERASMUS Discussion list.*
```
bowen@vm.epas.utoronto.ca
bowen@vm.epas.utoronto.ca
```

🖙 *CELTIC-L—The Celtic Culture discussion
list.*
```
CELTIC-L@IRLEARN.BITNET
LISTSERV@IRLEARN.BITNET
```

🖙 *Cross-disciplinary analysis of ancient texts.*
For scholarly, informal, and polite discussion
of the social worlds behind and within the
texts of antiquity—including those of the
Hebrew bible, early Christianity, Rabbinic
Judaism, and all of the literature associated
with the Graeco-Roman world.
```
CONTEX-L@UOTTAWA.BITNET
LISTSERV@UOTTAWA
```
Contact: Michael Strangelove
```
<441495@ACADVM1.UOTTAWA.CA>
```

🖙 *Society of Early Americanists list.*
```
EARAM-L@KENTVM.BITNET
LISTSERV@KENTVM.BITNET
```

🖙 *Han and Tang dynasties list.*
For the discussion on the studies of Chinese
history between the Han and the Tang dynasties
(3rd through 6th centuries A.D.).
```
EMEDCH-L@USCVM.BITNET
LISTSERV@USCVM.BITNET
```

🖙 *Early Modern History Forum list.*
```
EMHIST-L@RUTVM1.BITNET
LISTSERV@RUTVM1.BITNET
```

🖙 *History of the Iberian Peninsula*
For the debate, the discussion, and the exchange
of information by students and scholars of the
history of the Iberian Peninsula from the earliest
time to the present.
```
ESPORA-L@UKANVM.BITNET
LISTSERV@UKANVM.BITNET
```
Contact: Richard Clement
```
<RCLEMENT@UKANVM.BITNET>
```

🖙 *General Ethnology and History Discussion
list.*
For the discussion on the intersection of
ethnology and history.
```
ETHNOHIS@HEARN.BITNET
LISTSERV@HEARN.BITNET
```
Contact: Fred Melssen
```
<u211610@hnykun11.urc.kun.nl>
```

🖙 *FICINO Discussion—Renaissance and
Reformation list.*
```
FICINO@UTORONTO.BITNET
LISTSERV@UTORONTO.BITNET
```

🖙 *Folklore Discussion list.*
```
FOLKLORE@TAMVM1.BITNET
LISTSERV@TAMVM1.BITNET
```

🖙 *FRANCEHS list for French history scholars.*
```
FRANCEHS@UWAVM.BITNET
LISTSERV@UWAVM.BITNET
```

🖙 *German History*
For the discussion of German History from 800
to 1992.
```
GRMNHIST@DGOGWDG1.BITNET
LISTSERV@DGOGWDG1.BITNET
```
Contact: Thomas Zielke
```
<113355@DOLUNI1.BITNET>
```

🖙 *Austrian History*
For the discussion of Austrian History since
1500.
```
HABSBURG@PURCCVM.BITNET
LISTSERV@PURCCVM.BITNET
```

🖙 *HISTORYA History Department list.*
```
HISTORYA@UWAVM.BITNET
LISTSERV@HISTORYA.BITNET
```

🖙 *HistOwnr—Discussion list.*
```
HISTOWNR@UBVM.BITNET
LISTSERV@UBVM.BITNET
```

🖙 *History and Philosophy of Science and
Science list.*
```
HPSST-L@QUCDN.BITNET
LISTSERV@QUCDN.BITNET
```

🖙 *Study of Classical India*
For academics interested in the study of Classical
India.
```
INDOLOGY@LIVERPOOL.AC.UK
LISTSERV@LIVERPOOL.AC.UK
```

Contact:Dominik Wujastyk
<D.WUJASTYK@UCL.AC.UK>

🕲 *Pop Culture & Recent History*
INMYLIFE@WKUVX1.BITNET
LISTSERV@WKUVX1.BITNET
For the discussion of Beatle era popular culture. Topics include history, politics, culture, music, literature, collectibles, comic books, comics, counter culture, drugs, Vietnam (and the war), the Cold War, and more.
Contact: Matt Gore
<goremh@WKUVX1.BITNET>

🕲 *First Century Judaism Discussion Forum*
Explores first-century Judaism. Specializes in the writings of Philo of Alexandria and Flavius Josephus.
IOUDAIOS@YORKVM1.BITNET
LISTSERV@YORKVM1.BITNET
Contact: Veronica Timm
<VERONICA@YORKVM1.BITNET>

🕲 *History at the University of Kansas list.*
KUHIST-L@UKANVM.BITNET
LISTSERV@UKANVM.BITNET

🕲 *Lifeline Genealogical Database*
For topics related to the enhancement of LifeLines Genealogical Database and Report Generator, an experimental, second-generation genealogical system.
LINES-L@NDSUVM1.BITNET
LISTSERV@NDSUVM1.BITNET
Contact: Cliff Manis
<cmanis@csoftec.csf.com>

🕲 *LORE—Folklore list.*
For users interested in Folklore.
LORE@NDSUVM1.BITNET
LISTSERV@NDSUVM1.BITNET

🕲 *Medieval History Discussion list.*
For scholars and students of the Middle Ages.
MEDIEV-L@UKANVM.BITNET
LISTSERV@UKANVM.BITNET
Contact: Jeff Gardner
<JGARDNER@UKANVM.BITNET>

🕲 *Medieval Text—Philology, Codicology list.*
MEDTEXTL@UIUCVMD.BITNET
LISTSERV@UIUCVMD.BITNET

🕲 *MELLON Fellows Discussion Forum*
For anyone holding a Mellon Fellowship or interested in Mellon-related events.
MELLON-L@YORKVM1.BITNET
LISTSERV@YORKVM1.BITNET
Contact: Robert Stainton
GL250264@YUORION

🕲 *Aztec studies in general and Nahuatl (the Aztec language)*
Focuses on Aztec studies in general and the Aztec language, Nahuatl, in particular.
NAHUAT-L@FAUVAX.BITNET
NAHUAT-REQUEST@FAUVAX.BITNET
Contact: J.F. Schwaller
(schwallr@acc.fau.edu/schwallr@fauvax.bitnet)

🕲 *North American Society for the Study of Roman list.*
NASSR-L@WVNVM.BITNET
LISTSERV@WVNVM.BITNET

🕲 *History of the Renaissance*
For the debate, the discussion, and the exchange of information by students and scholars of the history of the Renaissance.
RENAIS-L@ULKYVM.BITNET
LISTSERV@ULKYVM.BITNET
Contact: James A. Cocks
<JACOCK01@ULKYVM.BITNET>

🕲 *ROOTS-L Genealogy list.*
For the discussion of geneaological matters.
ROOTS-L@NDSUVM1.BITNET
LISTSERV@NDSUVM1.BITNET
Contact: Alf Christophersen
ROOTS-OP@NDSUVM1.BITNET

🕲 *RusHist—Russian History 1462-1917*
For the discussion of any aspect of Russian history from the reign of Ivan III (1462-1505) to the end of the Romanov dynasty by Nicholas II (1894-1917).
RusHist@USCVM.BITNET
LISTSERV@USCVM.BITNET
Contact: Valentine Smith
<cdell@vax1.umkc.edu>

🕲 *RusHist—Russian History Forum*
RUSHIST@USCVM.BITNET
LISTSERV@USCVM.BITNET

🕲 *History of Computing*
For scholars and researchers to discuss topics of interest to The Society for History of Technology (SHOT) Special Interest Group on Information, Computing and Society.
SHOTHC-L@SIVM.BITNET
LISTSERV@SIVM.BITNET

🕲 *History of Computers*
For the discussion and research of the history of computers.
SIGPAST@List.Kean.EDU
SIGPAST-Request@List.Kean.EDU

ⓢ *New Social History List.*
Emphasizes quantitative data rather than an analysis of prose sources; borrows methodologies from the social sciences, such as linguistics, demographics, and anthropology; and examines groups that have been ignored by traditional disciplines.
```
SOCHIST@USCVM.BITNET
LISTSERV@USCVM.BITNET
```
Contact: Bob Pasker
```
<bob@halfdome.sf.ca.us>
```

ⓢ *SovHist—Soviet History 1917-1991*
For the discussion of any aspect of the history of the Soviet Union from the February Revolution of 1917 to the breakup of the U.S.S.R.on 25 December, 1991.
```
SovHist@USCVM.BITNET
LISTSERV@USCVM.BITNET
```
Contact: Valentine Smith
```
<cdell@vax1.umkc.edu>
```

ⓢ *SovHist—Soviet History Forum list.*
```
SOVHIST@USCVM.BITNET
LISTSERV@USCVM.BITNET
```

ⓢ *History ANSAXNET*
```
U47C2@WVNVM.WVNET.EDU
U47C2@WVNVM.WVNET.EDU
```
Contact: C.E Patrick W. Conner
```
<U47C2@WVNVM.WVNET.EDU>
```

ⓢ *Non-Eurocentric History*
Discusses the teaching, methodology, and theory of a scientific and non-Eurocentric world history.
```
WORLD-L@UBVM.BITNET
LISTSERV@UBVM.BITNET
```
Contact: Haines Brown
```
<BROWNH@CTSTATEU.BITNET>
```

Fidonet

ⓢ *Civil War*
```
CIVIL_WAR
```
For the discussion of the Civil War's causes and effects.
Moderator: Al Thorley
```
1:387/628.1
```
Distribution: ZONE-1 BACKBONE

ⓢ *Genealogy Database*
```
GENDATA
```
For a method of circulation for one form of genealogy information. These messages consist of a predetermined format and are called Tiny Tafels.
Moderator: John Grove
```
1:18/230
```
Distribution: FIDONET ZONE 1 BACKBONE

ⓢ *National Genealogical Conference*
```
GENEALOGY
```
For the exchange of data on all aspects of genealogy. Primarily oriented toward U.S.-Canadian research and includes queries, requests for help, and product/software announcements.
Moderator: Don Wilson
```
1:109/302
```
Distribution: WORLD-WIDE

ⓢ *Genealogy and Family History International*
```
GENEALOGY.EUR
```
For the discussion of genealogy and family history anywhere in the world except within the U.S.A. (But immigration to or from the U.S.A. is acceptable.)
Moderator: Steve Hayes
```
5:7101/20
```
Distribution: ZONE-1-BACKBONE, ZONE-5-BACKBONE, ZONE-2, ZONE-3, ZONE-6
Gateways: GTNET RBBSNET

ⓢ *Genealogy Forum: "Who's Got What" (WGW)*
```
GENEALOGY:_WGW
```
For genealogy researchers who want to find out who possesses what research material.
Moderator: Jack Williams
```
1:274/30
```
Distribution: BACKBONE

ⓢ *Genealogy Software*
```
GENSOFT
```
For dealing with genealogy software, hardware, utilities. Includes instructions, reviews, announcements from suppliers, help with problems.
Moderator: Richard Pence
```
1:109/302
```
Distribution: WORLD-WIDE

ⓢ *Genealogy Sysop Echo*
```
GENSYSOP
```
For systems operators and co-systems operators of genealogy-oriented systems.
Moderator: Wayne Silsbee
```
1:105/223.1
```
Distribution: Z1 BACKBONE; Z2

ⓢ *History Topics in Spanish*
```
HISTORIA
```
For the exchange of information and opinions on historical topics from a wide perspective, not with a rigorously scientific orientation.
Moderator: Luis Garcia-Barrio
```
1:273/909
```
Distribution: ZONE-1, ZONE-2, ZONE-4
Gateways: ZONE-2 VIA 1:273/909 ZONE-4 VIA 1:367/1

◊ *International History Echo*
HISTORY
For the discussion of historical events, their impacts, causes, and interpretation.
Moderator: Dixon Kenner
1:243/5
Distribution: BACKBONE

◊ *Pioneer Journals and Diaries*
JOURNAL
For users interested in history or genealogy.
Moderator: Jim Henry
1:273/408
Distribution: ZONE 1

◊ *Medieval studies, recreation, arts, and more.*
MEDIEVAL
For the discussion of medieval things and medieval hobbies, especially those practiced by such groups as the SCA, Markland, and MSR.
Moderator: Dave Aronson
1:109/120
Distribution: Z1, PODS, GT-NET, WWIVNET, MORE; TRYING TO GO BACKBONE

◊ *South Eastern U.S. Genealogy Conference*
SE_GENEALOGY
For genealogy buffs interested in the specific areas of the South Eastern United States that were considered Confederates during the United States Civil War.
Moderator: Debbi McKay
1:271/23
Distribution: BACKBONE

◊ *Spanish Genealogy*
SPANISH.GEN
For questions and answers about genealogical research on Spanish surnames.
Moderator: John Grove
1:18/230
Distribution: ZONE ONE BACKBONE
Gateways: ALL OF SPAIN VIA 273/60, ZONE 2 AND 3 VIA 2:440/50, BRASIL VIA 18/90.

◊ *Genealogy Forum: "Who's Got What" (WGW)*
WGW
For supplying inputs and queries to the WGW data base. The WGW data base is a -DIRECTORY- of who possesses what genealogy-related research material.
Moderator: Jack Williams
1:274/30
Distribution: BACKBONE

Usenet

◊ *The Kennedy assassination.*
alt.conspiracy.jfk

◊ *The war against Iraq in Kuwait.*
alt.desert-storm

◊ *For factual information on The Gulf War.*
alt.desert-storm.facts

◊ *What's happening to the Kurds in Iraq?*
alt.desert-thekurds

◊ *Some say he did it to himself.*
alt.gorby.gone.gone.gone

◊ *"It CAN'T be that way 'cause here's the FACTS."*
alt.revisionism

◊ *Not just collateral damage.*
alt.war

◊ *Lest we forget.*
alt.war.civil.usa

◊ *18th Century Interdisciplinary discussion.*
bit.listserv.c18-l

◊ *The Hellenic discussion list. (Moderated)*
bit.listserv.hellas

◊ *History list.*
bit.listserv.history

◊ *Studying classical history, languages, art, and more.*
sci.classics

◊ *Discussions of things historical.*
soc.history

◊ *Genealogical matters.*
soc.roots

Online Libraries
After Dark
No services available.

Knowledge Index

◊ *America: History and Life (AHL)*
Abstracts and indexes over 2,000 journals in the sciences and humanities as well as monographs and dissertations that cover U.S. and Canadian history and current affairs.
Coverage: 1964 to present
Updated: three times per year

Historical Abstracts
A reference service that abstracts and indexes the world's periodical literature in history and the related social sciences and humanities. Covers the history of the world from 1450 to present, excluding the U.S. and Canada.
Coverage: 1973 to present
Updated: Quarterly

Orbit
No services available.

NewsNet
No services available.

Bulletin Boards
National Genealogical Society
NGS/CIG BBS
Contains lots of genealogical files and user information in the form of messages from around the World. Also has text files offering information and hints to assist in your research.
Baud Rate: 300, 1200, 2400, 9600
BBS Number: (703) 528-2612
BBS Software: TBBS
Sysop: Don Wilson
Help Line: (703) 525-0050

CD-ROM

Desert Storm: The War in the Persian Gulf
Warner News Media

Middle East Diary
Quanta Press

National Register of Historic Places
Buckmaster Publishing

North American Indians
Quanta Press

USA Wars: Civil War
Quanta Press

USA Wars: Korea
Quanta Press

USA Wars: Vietnam
Quanta Press

U.S. Civics
Quanta Press

U.S. History on CD-ROM
Bureau of Electronic Publishing
18 Louisburg Square
Verona, NJ 07044

U.S. Presidents
Quanta Press

Humanities Resources

Forums & Databases

America Online (AOL)
No services available.

CompuServe (CIS)
No services available.

GEnie
No services available.

The Well
No services available.

Network Discussions Lists

Internet (Includes Bitnet & UUCPNet)

🌀 *Noticias Acerca de la Cooperacion Franco-Chile*
AMFCH-L@UCHCECVM.BITNET
ISTSERV@UCHCECVM.BITNET

🌀 *Turk Amigacilar listesi.*
AMIGA-TR@TREARN.BITNET
LISTSERV@TREARN.BITNET

🌀 *American Parliamentary Debate Association*
APDA@PUCC.BITNET
LISTSERV@PUCC.BITNET

🌀 *The Brazilian Interest Continental list.*
BRAS-CON@FRORS12.BITNET
LISTSERV@FRORS12.BITNET

🌀 *Brown University Computing in the Humanities*
CHUG-L@BROWNVM.BROWN.EDU
LISTSERV@BROWNVM.BROWN.EDU
Contact: Elli Mylonas
<ELLI@BROWNVM.BROWN.EDU>

🌀 *CompCiv-L list.*
COMCIV-L@IUBVM.BITNET
LISTSERV@IUBVM.BITNET
Contact: Warren Lewis
<wwlewis@iubvm.BITNET>

🌀 *Debate list.*
DEBATE@LMUACAD.BITNET
LISTSERV@LMUACAD.BITNET

🌀 *Diversity Concerns Exchange*
For people of all backgrounds interested in the exchange of information on diversity.
DIVERS-L@PSUVM.BITNET
ISTSERV@PSUVM.BITNET
Contact: Howard Lawrence
<HRL@PSUARCH.BITNET>

🌀 *Dead Teachers Society Discussion list.*
DTS-L@IUBVM.BITNET
LISTSERV@IUBVM.BITNET

🌀 *Programme International de Formation*
ECP-PIF@FRECP12.BITNET
LISTSERV@FRECP12.BITNET

🌀 *Humanities Computing Forum*
HCFNET@UCSBVM.BITNET
LISTSERV@UCSBVM.BITNET

🌀 *Human Resource Development*
HRD-L@UMCVMB.BITNET
LISTSERV@UMCVMB.BITNET

🌀 *Human Nets Digest list.*
HUMANETS@RUTVM1.BITNET
LISTSERV@RUTVM1.BITNET

Contact: Charles McGrew
    Human-Nets@Red.Rutgers.Edu

⚲ *Humanist Discussion list.*
For discussion among computing humanists
and users who support the application of
computers to humanities scholarship.
    HUMANIST@BROWNVM.BROWN.EDU
    LISTSERV@BROWNVM.BROWN.EDU

⚲ *Hume Society Discussion list.*
    HUME@WMVM1.BITNET
    LISTSERV@WMVM1.BITNET

⚲ *Humanist Special list.*
    HUMSPC-L@BROWNVM.BROWN.EDU
    LISTSERV@BROWBVM.BITNET

⚲ *Les Arts et les nouvelles technologies.*
L-ARTECH s'adresse aux organisations (centre,
studio, association, etc.) et aux individus
s'interessant a l'art et aux nouvelles technogiles.
L-ARTECH est en premier lieu une liste de
discussions et d'echanges. De plus, L-ARTECH
donne acces a deux annuaires: le premier re
groupe les organisations, et le deuxieme, les
individus.
    L-ARTECH@UQAM.BITNET
    LISTSERV@UQAM.BITNET

⚲ *Mass Communications and New*
    Technologies list.
    MASSCOMM@RPICICGE.BITNET
    COMSERVE@RPIECS.

⚲ *Multicriteria Discussion list.*
    MCRIT-L@HEARN.BITNET
    LISTSERV@HEARN.BITNET
Contact: MCRIT@HROEUR1

⚲ *Nota Bene list.*
News and information exchange for Nota Bene
users.
    NOTABENE@TAUNIVM.BITNET
    LISTSERV@TAUNIVM.BITNET
Contact: Itamar Even-Zohar
    B10@TAUNIVM.BITNET

⚲ *Communication in Organizations*
    ORGCOMM@RPICICGE.BITNET
    COMSERVE@RPIECS.BITNET

⚲ *Project on Ethnic Relations*
    PER$L@PLEARN.BITNET
    LISTSERV@PLEARN.BITNET

⚲ *Lista De Poetas Latinoamericanos*
    POESIA@UNALCOL.BITNET
    LISTSERV@UNALCOL.BITNET

⚲ *Hebrew University Center for Rationality list.*
    RATION-L@TAUNIVM.BITNET
    LISTSERV@TAUNIVM.BITNET

⚲ *Rhetoric, Social Movements, Persuasion list.*
    RHETORIC@RPICICGE.BITNET
    COMSERVE@RPIECS.BITNET

⚲ *Risk Management list.*
For communications related to risk man-
agement and insurance.
    RISK@UTXVM.CC.UTEXAS.EDU
    LISTSERV@UTXVM.CC.UTEXAS.EDU
Contact: James R. Garven
    <Garven@UTXVM.CC.UTEXAS.EDU>

⚲ *Second European Conference on Social*
    Networks list.
    SOCNETW2@FRORS12.BITNET
    LISTSERV@FRORS12.BITNET

⚲ *Social Work Discussion list.*
    SOCWORK@UMAB.BITNET
    LISTSERV@UMAB.BITNET

⚲ *Tamil Studies list.*
    TAMIL-L@DHDURZ1.BITNET
    LISTSERV@DHDURZ1.BITNET

⚲ *WHIM—Humor Studies list.*
    WHIM@TAMVM1.BITNET
    LISTSERV@TAMVM1.BITNET

Fidonet

⚲ *International Humanities Echo*
    HUMANITIES
For interdisciplinary discussions within the
humanities.
Moderator: George Mosley
    1:3641/1.911
Distribution: AD HOC

Usenet

No services available.

Online Libraries
After Dark

⚲ *Arts & Humanities Search®*
A citation index to the arts and humanities.
Coverage: 1980 to present
Updated: Weekly

❆ *Current Contents: Arts & Humanities.*
A subset of Current Contents Search™ corresponding to the *Current Contents: Arts & Humanities* print edition.
Coverage: Most recent 12 months
Updated: Weekly

❆ *Wilson Humanities Index*
Provides indexing of over 350 English-language periodicals in the humanities.
Coverage: 1984 to present
Updated: Monthly

Knowledge Index
No services available.

Orbit
No services available.

NewsNet
No services available.

Bulletin Boards

Black Data Processing Associates (BDPA)—Bay Area Chapter BBS
Sustains a network of minority data-processing professionals, sharing information, providing education, and performing community services. Maintains a list of minority bulletin boards across the country.
Availability: 24 hours/ 7 days
Baud Rate: 2400,19.2
BBS Number: (707) 552-3314
BBS Software: WILDCAT!
Sysop: Jerry Kirkpatrick
Help Line: (707) 552-1982

The SF NET
A network of computers with conferences found throughout 19 San Francisco coffee houses. Interactive games, matchmaking, chess, and Fidonet/Usenet conferences.
Availability: 24 hours/ 7 days
Baud Rate: 2400
BBS Number: (415) 824-7603

CD-ROM

❆ *Humanities Index*
H.W. Wilson

Language/ Linguistics Resources

Buon Giorno

Bon Jour

Jó Napot

Buenos Dias

Guten Tag

Forums & Databases

America Online (AOL)

No services available.

CompuServe (CIS)

Foreign Language Forum
Keyword: GO FLEFO
Provides a service to both general and specific interests in foreign languages and foreign language learning.

GEnie

No services available.

The Well

Spanish
(g spanish)
Offers discussion of anything in Spanish or anything about the Spanish language.

Words
(g words)
For all lovers of words to discuss the peculiarities, oddities, beauties, and inanities of language.

Network Discussions Lists

Internet (Includes Bitnet & UUCPNet)

Linguist-Abstracts list.
ABSTRACT@TAMVM1.BITNET
LISTSERV@TAMVM1.BITNET

American Dialect Society list.
ADS-L@UGA.BITNET
LISTSERV@UGA.BITNET

American Sign Language list.
ASLING-L@YALEVM.BITNET
LISTSERV@YALEVM.BITNET

Computer-Assisted Language Learning—Courseware list.
CALLCD@SIUCVMB.BITNET
LISTSERV@SIUCVMB.BITNET

Department of English Discussion
For faculty in English Departments in Canada who are using mainframes for teaching and research, and who may be using microcomputers as well.
ENGLISH@UTARLVM1.BITNET
LISTSERV@UTARLVM1.BITNET
Contact: Marshall Gilliland
GILLILAN@SASK.BITNET

Experimental list.
For the teaching and the study of language.
ERIC-L@IUBVM.BITNET
LISTSERV@IUBVM.BITNET

Esperanto list.
A list on the Esperanto Language.
ESPER-L@TREARN.BITNET
LISTSERV@TREARN.BITNET
Contact: Turgut Kalfaoglu
<TURGUT@TREARN.BITNET>

Esperanto Language
For people interested in the neutral international language Esperanto.
ESPERANTO@LLL-CRG-LLNL.GOV
ESPERANTO-REQUEST@LLL-CRG-LLNL.GOV
Contact: Mike Urban
<ESPERANTO-REQUEST@LLL-CRG-LLNL.GOV>

⟲ *Ethnomethodology list.*
Ethnomethodology and conversation analysis list.

```
ETHNO@RPICICGE.BITNET
COMSERVE@RPIECS.BITNET
```

⟲ *foNETiks Phonetic Science*
Offers information to researchers and students interested in speech production and speech perception, speech disorders, automatic speech recognition, and speech synthesis.

```
FONETIKS <R34334@UQAM.BITNET>
ERIC KELLER <R34334@UQAM.BITNET>
```
Contact: Eric Keller
```
<r34334@UQAM.BITNET>
```

⟲ *GAELIC Language Bulletin Board*
Facilitates the exchange of news, views, and information in Irish and Scottish Gaelic.

```
GAELIC-L@IRLEARN.BITNET
LISTSERV@IRLEARN.BITNET
```
Contact: K.P.Donnelly
```
@EDINBURGH.AC.UK
```

⟲ *Older Germanic Languages (to 1500) list.*
```
GERLINGL@UIUCVMD.BITNET
LISTSERV@UIUCVMD.BITNET
```

⟲ *The Hellenic Discussion list.*
A means of communication for Greeks of BitNet. The language preferably used is Greek (with Latin characters, "Vlachofragika").

```
HELLAS@AUVM.BITNET
LISTSERV@AUVM.BITNET
```
Contact: Alexandros Couloumbis
```
ALEX@AUVM.BITNET
```

⟲ *Japanese Teachers and Instructional Technology*
For Japanese teachers and media professionals to exchange and discuss ideas and information.

```
JTIT-L@PSUVM.BITNET
LISTSERV@PSUVM.BITNET
```
Contact: Hideo Tomita
```
<tomita@Vax001.Kenyon.Edu>
```

⟲ *Discussione Centri Linguistici Italiani list.*
```
LANGIT@IVEUNCC.BITNET
LISTSERV@IVEUNCC.BITNET
```

⟲ *Langues Enseignement du Francais par Ordinate.*
Cette liste est dediee a l'enseignement des langues secondes par ordinateur, ainsi qu'aux systemes-experts et a l'analyse linguistique par ordinateur. Le volet INTERCULTUREL traite desrapports et des transferts culturels.

```
LANGUES@UQUEBEC.BITNET
LISTSERV@UQUEBEC.BITNET
```

⟲ *Interpreting (and) Translating*
For all aspects of translating and interpreting natural languages including computer aids for translating and interpreting.

```
LANTRA-L@FINHUTC.BITNET
LISTSERV@FINHUTC.BITNET
```
Contact: Helge Niska
```
Helge.Niska@qz.se
```

⟲ *Linguistics and Related Fields*
For issues concerning the academic discipline of linguistics and related fields.

```
LINGUIST@TAMVM1.BITNET
LISTSERV@LINGUIST.BITNET
```

⟲ *Literature and Related Fields*
Offers the exchange of ideas about literature and related topics, like linguistics, semantics, and philology.

```
LITERA-L@TECMTYVM.BITNET
LISTSERV@TECMTYVM.BITNET
```

⟲ *Language, Learning, and Technology*
A distribution point for information on language learning and technology with an international perspective.

```
LLTI@DARTCMS1.BITNET
LISTSERV@DARTCMS1.BITNET
```

⟲ *Langage Naturel list.*
```
LN@FRMOP11.BITNET
LISTSERV@FRMOP11.BITNET
```

⟲ *Yiddish language*
Offers a discussion of the Yiddish language, literature, and culture. Some of the discussion is in translated Yiddish.

```
mail.yiddish@LSUC.ON.CA
David Sherman <dave@LSUC.ON.CA>
```
Contact: David Sherman
```
<dave@LSUC.ON.CA>
```

⟲ *Academically Oriented Yiddish Digest*
For everything that touches on the Yiddish language and literature, such as linguistics, literary criticism, history, and news.

```
MENDELE@TRINCC.BITNET
NMILLER@TRINCC.BITNET
```
Contact: Norman (Noyekh) Miller
```
<nmiller@trincc.BITNET>
```

⟲ *Language and Education in Lingual Setting list.*
```
MULTI-L@BARILVM.BITNET
LISTSERV@BARILVM.BITNET
```

⟲ *Nihongo*
Offers discussion of the Japanese language, including spoken and written forms.

```
NIHONGO@MITVMA.BITNET
LISTSERV@MITVMA.BITNET
```

Contact: Steve Strassmann
    `<straz@MEDIA-LAB.MEDIA.MIT.EDU>`

🖲 *Natural Language*
Offers a discussion of any topic related to natural language and knowledge representation.
    `NL-KR@CS.RPI.EDU`
    `NL-KR-REQUEST@CS.RPI.EDU`
Contact: Christopher Welty
    `weltyc@cs.rpi.edu`

🖲 *Oxford English Dictionary Discussion list.*
    `OED-L@LIVERPOOL.AC.UK`
    `LISTSERV@LIVERPOOL.AC.UK`

🖲 *Rhetoric, Language, Professional Writing*
Offers discussion of current issues or "topoi" in the fields of rhetoric and composition, professional writing, and language research.
    `PURTOPOI@PURCCVM.BITNET`
    `LISTSERV@PURCCVM.BITNET`
Contact: Tharon Howard
    `ucc@mace.cc.purdue.edu`

🖲 *Russian Language Issues (Preferably in Russian)*
For topics that include (but are not limited to) Russian language, linguistics, grammar, translations, literature. Geared toward students of Russian.
    `RUSSIAN@ASUACAD.BITNET`
    `LISTSERV@ASUACAD.BITNET`
Contact: Andrew Wollert
    `<ISPAJW@ASUACAD.BITNET>`

🖲 *Semiotics Discussion*
Offers discussion of semiotics, verbal and non-verbal communication, language behavior, visual issues, and linguistics.
    `SEMIOS-L@ULKYVM.BITNET`
    `LISTSERV@ULKYVM.BITNET`
Contact: Steven Skaggs
    `<S0SKAG01@ULKYVM.BITNET>`

🖲 *Second Language Acquisition Research and Teaching (SLART)*
For those involved in or interested in second language acquisition research and teaching SLART.
    `SLART-L@PSUVM.BITNET`
    `LISTSERV@PSUVM.BITNET`
Contact: Joyce Neu
    `JN0@PSUVM.BITNET`

🖲 *Sign Language Linguistics list.*
    `SLLING-L@YALEVM.BITNET`
    `LISTSERV@YALEVM.BITNET`

🖲 *Telugu Language and Culture list.*

    `TELUGU@NDSUVM1.BITNET`
    `LISTSERV@NDSUVM1.BITNET`

🖲 *Teachers of English to Students list.*
    `TESL-L@CUNYVM.BITNET`
    `LISTSERV@CUNYVM.BITNET   TESL-L:`

🖲 *Fluency First and Whole Language list.*
    `TESLFF-L@CUNYVM.BITNET`
    `LISTSERV@CUNYVM.BITNET`

🖲 *Intensive English Program list.*
    `TESLIE-L@CUNYVM.BITNET`
    `LISTSERV@CUNYVM.BITNET`

🖲 *Welsh Language Bulletin Board list.*
    `WELSH-L@IRLEARN.BITNET`
    `LISTSERV@IRLEARN.BITNET`

🖲 *English Language Discussion Group*
Offers discussion of the English language.
    `WORDS-L@UGA.BITNET`
    `LISTSERV@UGA.BITNET`
Contact: Natalie Maynor
    `<nm1@ra.msstate.edu>`

Fidonet

🖲 *American Sign Language*
    `ASL`
Offers discussion of American Sign Language and of the Deaf.
Moderator: James Womack
    `94:94/98`
Distribution: ADANET INTERNATIONAL DISABILITY NETWORK

🖲 *Disabilities Support Echo in Spanish*
    `DESHABILITADO`
Offers discussion of disability in Spanish.
Moderator: ADAnet
    `94:94/1`
Distribution: ADANET INTERNATIONAL DISABILITY NETWORK
Gateways: ADANET (94:94/1)

🖲 *FRANCAIS*
    `FRANCAIS`
Offers discussions in French. This conference is echoed in the United States and Canada and is based in Quebec, Canada.
Moderator: Alain Lachapelle
    `1:167/90.13`
Distribution: BACKBONE

🖲 *Disabilities Support Echo in French*
    `FRANCO_HANDICAP`
Offers discussion of disability in French.
Moderator: Daniel Coulombe
    `94:2050/1`

Distribution: ADANET INTERNATIONAL DISABILITY NETWORK
Gateways: ADANET (94:94/1)

🕲 *Latino's Spanish International Conference*
LATINO
For the Spanish language for all Latin Americans and others interested in speaking Spanish.
Moderator: Juan Davila
1:367/1
Distribution: BACKBONE

🕲 *International Portuguese Language Echo*
PORTUGUES
For all countries that use the Portuguese language. Contains general common interest topics in Portuguese.
Moderator: Leslie Scofield
1:18/90
Distribution: ZONE-1, ZONE-2, ZONE-4, ZONE-6, IDS
Gateways: 1:18/90 VIA 4:802/1 1:18/90 VIA 2:362/2 1:18/90 VIA 1:102/631 2:362/2 VIA 6:701/1

General Quotes and Puns
QUOTES_2
Enables users to share their favorite quotes and puns with others.
Moderator: Chris Nunn
1:382/98
Distribution: BACKBONE

🕲 *Wayward Witticisms, Stray Puns, Other Linguistic Outcasts.*
WITS_END
Offers wit and humor that comes from and is a tribute to the richness of the human language.
Moderator: Alan Gilbertson
1:3603/230
Distribution: ECHONET BACKBONE (ZONE 50)

🕲 *Words, Words, Words*
WORDS_WORDS
Offers a discussion on the meanings, origins, and uses of the spoken and written word employed in our communication with each other.
Moderator: Sue Oakes
1:226/50
Distribution: BACKBONE

Usenet

🕲 *For and about people who can't spell*
alt.flame.spelling

🕲 *English grammar, word usages, and related topics*
alt.usage.english

🕲 *Rhetoric, social movements, persuasion*
bit.listserv.rhetoric

🕲 *English Language Discussion Group*
bit.listserv.words-l

🕲 *Studying classical history, languages, art, and more*
sci.classics

🕲 *Natural languages, communication, and more*
sci.lang

🕲 *The Japanese language, both spoken and written*
sci.lang.japan

Online Libraries
After Dark

🕲 *Linguistics and Language Behavior Abstracts*
Offers worldwide coverage of the literature in language behavior, linguistics, and related topics.
Coverage: 1973 to present
Updated: Quarterly

Knowledge Index

🕲 *Linguistics and Language Behavior Abstracts*
Provides current selective access to the world's literature on linguistics and language behavior.
Coverage: 1969 to present
Updated: Monthly

🕲 *MLA Bibliography*
Provides the first on-line access to comprehensive bibliographies of humanistic studies produced annually by the Modern Language Association.
Coverage: 1963 to present
Updated: Annually

Orbit
No services available.

NewsNet
No services available.

Bulletin Boards
No services available.

CD-ROM

🕲 *Languages of the World*
NTC Publishing

Law/Justice Resources

Forums & Databases

America Online (AOL)

No services available.

CompuServe (CIS)

🌎 *Legal Forum*
Keyword: GO LAWSIG
For attorneys, corrections officers, paralegals, court reporters, or lay persons interested in law.

🌎 *Legal Research Center*
Keyword: GO LEGALRC
Provides access to seven databases.

🌎 *The Electronic Frontier Foundation Forum*
Users can share facts and opinions about issues concerning computer-based communication.

GEnie

🌎 *A Law Enforcement RoundTable*

Keyword: ALERT or Page 255
Run by the San Jose Police Officers' Association, the forum is for people in law enforcement and allied occupations.

🌎 *Law RoundTable*
Keyword: LAW or Page 570
For learning about the law, law practice, and the American legal system. Contact Robert Kohn (BOB.KOHN).

The Well

🌎 *Firearms, Military, Police & True Crime*
(g firearms)
Discusses topics like police (pro and con), true crime books, military technology and affairs, firearms (pro and con), self-defense, sword fighting, and knives.

🌎 *First Amendment*
(g first)
An electronic way to chronicle and discuss attempts to stifle free expression.

🌎 *Legal*
(g legal)
For discussing everyday legal problems that affect us all. Attorney postings are conversations, not deeply researched advice.

🌎 *Scams, Swindles, Cons, and Hoaxes*
(g scam)
Discusses schemes, scams, hoaxes, and con artists, and loss of money due to a savings and loan stock purchase.

Network Discussions Lists

Internet (Includes Bitnet & UUCPNet)

🌎 *ADA Law*
ADA-LAW@NDSUVM1.BITNET
LISTSERV@NDSUVM1.BITNET

🌎 *Artificial Intelligence and Law*
Discusses topics related to artificial intelligence and law.
AIL-L@austin.onu.edu
listserv@austin.onu.edu
Contact: David R. Warner Jr.
<WARNER@AUSTIN.ONU.EDU>

🌀 *AJCU Law Librarians/Interlibrary Loan Contact list.*
AJCUILL@GUVM.BITNET
LISTSERV@GUVM.BITNET

🌀 *ALA Washington Office Update list.*
ALA-WO@UICVM.BITNET
LISTSERV@UICVM.BITNET

🌀 *ALA Filelist.*
ALA@UICVM.BITNET
LISTSERV@UICVM.BITNET

🌀 *ALA Council list.*
ALACOUN@UICVM.BITNET
LISTSERV@UICVM.BITNET

🌀 *ALA Membership Committee list.*
ALAMEMB@UICVM.BITNET
LISTSERV@UICVM.BITNET

🌀 *ALA Treasurer-COPES Chair-ALA Financial Staff list.*
ALATREAS@UICVM.BITNET
LISTSERV@UICVM.BITNET

🌀 *Canadian Law Libraries Discussion list.*
CALL-L@UNBVM1.BITNET
LISTSERV@UNBVM1.BITNET

🌀 *Criminal Justice Discussion list.*
CJUST-L@IUBVM.BITNET
LISTSERV@IUBVM.BITNET
<FLOOD@IUBVM>

🌀 *Computers and Legal Education*
Discussions from the 4th Annual Computers and the Law Teaching Process Conference.
COMLAW-L@UALTAVM.BITNET
LISTSERV@UALTAVM.BITNET
Contact: John Boeske
<JBOESKE@UALTAVM.BITNET>

🌀 *Computer Privacy*
A list gatewayed into the moderated USENET newsgroup comp.society.privacy for discussion on how technology impacts privacy.
comp-privacy@pica.army.mil
comp-privacy-request@pica.army.mil
Contact: Dennis G. Rears
<drears@pilot.njin.net>

🌀 *The Law and Policy of Computer Networks list.*
CYBERLAW@WMVM1.BITNET
LISTSERV@WMVM1.BITNET

🌀 *Law and Education list.*
EDLAW@UKCC.BITNET
LISTSERV@UKCC.BITNE

🌀 *Law and Education*
For users who teach and practice law.
EdLaw@UKCC.BITNET
LISTSERV@UKCC.BITNET
Contact: Virginia Davis-Nordin
<NORDIN@ukcc.uky.edu>

🌀 *Exchange of Information Regarding the Issues of Fathers' Rights*
Discusses divorce issues, custody disputes, and visitation and child-support arrangements.
FREE-L@INDYCMS.BITNET
LISTSERV@INDYCMS.BITNET
Contact: Dale Marmaduke
<ITOG400@INDYCMS.IUPUI.EDU>

🌀 *Fathers' Rights and Equality Exchange list.*
FREE-L@INDYCMS.BITNET
LISTSERV@INDYCMS.BITNET

🌀 *History of the Law*
For debate, discussion, and exchange of information by students and scholars of the history of the law (Feudal, Common, Canon).
HISLAW-L@ULKYVM.BITNET
LISTSERV@ULKYVM.BITNET
Contact: James A. Cock
<JACOCK01@ULKYVM.BITNET>

🌀 *Computers and the law*
For anyone interested in computers and the law.
INFO-LAW@BRL.MIL
INFO-LAW-REQUEST@BRL.MIL
Contact: Mike Muuss
<INFO-LAW-REQUEST@BRL.MIL>

🌀 *Foreign and International Law Librarians*
For librarians and others interested in exchanging information on foreign, comparative, and international legal materials and issues.
INT-LAW@UMINN1.BITNET
LISTSERV@UMINN1.BITNET
Contact: Lyonette Louis-Jacques
<L-LOUI@UMINN1.BITNET>

🌀 *Law School Financial Aid Discussion list.*
LAWAID@RUTVM1.BITNET
LISTSERV@RUTVM1.BITNET

🌀 *Law School Discussion list.*
Discusses topics of concern that affect all law students.
LAWSCH-L@AUVM.BITNET
LISTSERV@AUVM.BITNET
Contact: Ed Kania
<EKANIA@AUVM.BITNET>

Villanova Law Review Symposium list.
```
LREVSYMP@VILLVM.BITNET
LISTSERV@VILLVM.BITNET
```

National Crime Survey Discussion
Discusses the design and use of the National Crime Survey—a large and continuous survey of housing units in the U.S. to produce national estimates of criminal victimization.
```
NCS-L@UMDD.BITNET
LISTSERV@UMDD.BITNET
```
Contact: Brian Wiersema
```
BRIANW@UMDD.BITNET
```

Security
For discussion of the field of security.
```
SECURITY@AIM.RUTGERS.EDU
SECURITY-REQUEST@AIM.RUTGERS.EDU
```
Contact: *Hobbit*
```
<Hobbit@AIM.RUTGERS.EDU>
```

Security mailing list.
For discussion of the field of security.
```
SECURITY@FINHUTC.BITNET
LISTSERV@FINHUTC.BITNET
```
Contact: *Hobbit*
```
<AWalker@RUTGERS.BITNET>
```

United Nations Criminal Justice Information list.
```
UNCJIN-L@ALBNYVM1.BITNET
LISTSERV@ALBNYVM1.BITNET
```

Fidonet

Human Rights Issues, News, and Concerns
```
AI_HUM_R
```
Discusses human rights issues, news, and concerns.
Moderator: Randy Edwards
```
1:128/105
```
Distribution: INTERNATIONAL

Amnesty International
```
AMNESTY_INT.CAN
```
For members of the public interested in the work of Amnesty International, a worldwide human rights organization.
Moderator: Mike Blackstock
```
1:163/508.1
```
Distribution: ZONE-1

Ask a Cop
```
ASKACOP
```
Enables users to ask street line cops questions.
Moderator: Randy White
```
1:124/6106
```
Distribution: BACKBONE

Ask a Cop
```
ASKACOP2
```
Enables users to question police officers, federal agents, and other law enforcement officials across the USA and Canada.
Moderator: Nolan Shapiro
```
1:3620/14
```
Distribution: BACKBONE

Civil Liberties
```
CIVLIB
```
Gives information about civil liberties, the Bill of Rights, and the Constitution of the United States as applied to individual rights.
Moderator: Bob Hirschfeld
```
1:114/74.2
```
Distribution: BACKBONE

Conference on Police Dogs
```
K9COPS
```
For the exchange of information and ideas for users interested in the breeding, raising, training, and application of police dogs.
Moderator: Bob Eden 1:153/900
Distribution: INTERNATIONAL

Legal Issues Conference
```
LAW
```
For exchanging new cases, decisions, procedures, and technology to advance the judicial systems and legal profession.
Moderator: Bill McMahon
```
8:965/10.69
```
Distribution: BACKBONE FIDONET RBBSNET

"Law and Disorder" Discussion Area
```
LAW_DISORDER
```
Discusses laws and the disorder that results from the enforcement (or lack thereof) of these laws.
Moderator: Alan Hess
```
1:261/1000
```
Distribution: BACKBONE

Piracy and Computer Crime Prevention Forum
```
NOPIRACY
```
Discusses the various types of computer crimes and how to prevent them.
Moderator: Dan McCarriar
```
1:261/1056.6
```
Distribution: BACKBONE

Police Pin/Patch Collectors Echo
```
PIN_PATCH
```
For officers interested in collecting police or law enforcement patches, pins, caps, and more.
Moderator: Dave Johnson
```
1:260/204
```

Distribution: 1:260/204 1:340/48 2:252/150 3:713/611
No. of Nodes: 25
Volume: five per day

↺ *Citizen's Rights*
  PN-RIGHTS
Discussion of United States Citizens' rights.
Moderator: Paul Hancock
  1:114/143
Distribution: ZONE-30

↺ *Law Enforcement Officers Nat'l Echo*
  POLICE
Discussion for sworn law enforcement officers.
Moderator: Dave Johnson
  1:260/204
Restr: MOD-APVL MEMBER
Distribution: 1:260/204 1:340/48 2:252/150 3:713/611

↺ *RTKBA*
  RTKBA
Discusses the political aspects of firearms, firearms ownership, and second amendment rights.
Moderator: Bob Kohl
  1:102/861
Distribution: BACKBONE, 10/8, 19/3 NET-102, NET-103, NET-105, NET-109, NET-129, NET-135, NET-137, NET-147, NET-151, NET-300, NET-372

Usenet

↺ *Academic freedom issues related to computers. (Moderated)*
  alt.comp.acad-freedom.news

↺ *Academic freedom issues related to computers.*
  alt.comp.acad-freedom.talk

↺ *Be paranoid—they're out to get you.*
  alt.conspiracy

↺ *The Kennedy assassination*
  alt.conspiracy.jfk

↺ *"...EXCEPT THAT Congress shall limit...."*
  alt.freedom.of.information.act

↺ *Philosophies where individual rights are paramount.*
  alt.individualism

↺ *Worse than banana slug fleas*
  alt.lawyers.sue.sue.sue

↺ *Four of a kind beat a king*
  alt.rodney.king

↺ *Pointers to good stuff in {alt,misc}.security. (Moderated)*
  alt.security.index

↺ *Individual rights*
  alt.society.civil-liberties

↺ *To balance out all the false crime on the net*
  alt.true.crime

↺ *Discussion of ethics in computing*
  bit.listserv.ethics-l

↺ *Law School Discussion list.*
  bit.listserv.lawsch-l

↺ *Lawsuits and business-related legal matters. (Moderated)*
  clari.biz.courts

↺ *Government agencies, FBI, and more. (Moderated)*
  clari.news.gov.agency

↺ *Tax laws, trials, and more. (Moderated)*
  clari.news.gov.taxes

↺ *Freedom, Racism, Civil Rights Issues. (Moderated)*
  clari.news.issues.civil_rights

↺ *Family, child abuse, and more. (Moderated)*
  clari.news.issues.family

↺ *General group for law-related issues. (Moderated)*
  clari.news.law

↺ *Civil trials & litigation. (Moderated)*
  clari.news.law.civil

↺ *Major crimes. (Moderated)*
  clari.news.law.crime

↺ *Sex crimes and trials. (Moderated)*
  clari.news.law.crime.sex

↺ *Trials for criminal actions. (Moderated)*
  clari.news.law.crime.trial

↺ *Violent crime & criminals. (Moderated)*
  clari.news.law.crime.violent

↺ *Drug-related crimes & drug stories. (Moderated)*
  clari.news.law.drugs

↺ *Investigation of crimes. (Moderated)*
  clari.news.law.investigation

↺ *Police & law enforcement. (Moderated)*
  clari.news.law.police

↺ *Prisons, prisoners & escapes. (Moderated)*
  clari.news.law.prison

Lawyers, judges, and more. (Moderated)
`clari.news.law.profession`

U.S. Supreme Court rulings & news. (Moderated)
`clari.news.law.supreme`

Sexual issues, sex-related political stories. (Moderated)
`clari.news.sex`

Terrorist actions & related news around the world. (Moderated)
`clari.news.terrorism`

Legalities and the ethics of law
`misc.legal`

Discussing the legal climate of the computing world
`misc.legal.computing`

Tax laws and advice
`misc.taxes`

Online Libraries
After Dark

Legal Resource Index™
Includes more than 960 law revisions, bar association journals, and legal newspapers covering all English-language secondary legal literature.
Coverage: January 1980 to present
Updated: Monthly (over 3000 records per update)

Public Affairs Information Service (PAIS) International
Offers worldwide coverage of the public policy aspects of all social sciences.
Coverage: 1972 to present
Updated: Monthly

Wilson Index to Legal Periodicals
Indexes articles from 476 legal periodicals published in the United States, Canada, Great Britain, Ireland, Australia, and New Zealand.
Coverage: 1983 to present
Updated: Monthly

Knowledge Index

Bureau of National Affairs (BNA) Daily News
Produced by BNA, it offers daily news publications on developments from the White House, Congress, federal and state agencies, the courts, international, and private organizations.
Coverage: 1990 to present
Updated: Daily

Legal Resource Index™
Provides a complete index of over 750 key law journals, six law newspapers, and legal monographs. Also includes relevant law articles from Magazine Index™, National Newspaper Index™, and Trade And Industry Index™.
Coverage: 1980 to present
Updated: Monthly

Orbit

Legal Status
Records thousands of actions that can affect the legal status of a patented document after it has been published and after the patent has been granted. Also includes an Intellectual Property Organization.
Coverage: 1959 to present
Updated: Weekly

LitAlert
Includes more than 20,000 notices of filing and subsequent actions for patent and trademark infringement suits filed in the U.S. District Courts. Only available on ORBIT.
Coverage: 1970 to present
Updated: Weekly

NewsNet
No services available.

Bulletin Boards
Court Information Transmitted Electronically (C.I.T.E.) Bulletin Board

Enables users to obtain up-to-date information on cases in the U.S. Court of Appeals for the Sixth Circuit. Includes docket information on individual cases, full text of newly filed slip opinions, and other legal items.
Baud Rate: 300, 1200, 2400
BBS Number: (202) 684-2842
Help Line: (202) 633-6393
Comments: Logon with CITE and NEWUSER for password.

Judge Advocate General's Information Network (JAGNET) BBS

Provided by the Naval-Marine Corps Appellate Review to facilitate communication within the legal community.
Availability: 24 hrs/7 days
Baud Rate: 300, 1200, 2400
BBS Number: (703) 325-0748
BBS Software: PCBoard
Sysop: Ron Stokes
Help Line: (703) 325-2924

Legal Ease BBS

For legal issues and living trust information. Contains a legal BBS list and searchable databases such as the Washington Digital Law Library System.
Availability: 24 hrs/7 days
Baud Rate: 16.8
BBS Number: (509) 326-3238
BBS Software: PCBoard
Sysop: Bill Sorcinelli
Help Line: (509) 325-0432

National Criminal Justice Reference (NCJRS) Electronic Bulletin Board

A public bulletin board established by the National Institute of Justice to share current information from various participating Office of Justice Programs agencies. Includes current news and announcements.
Baud Rate: 300, 1200, 2400, 9600
BBS Number: (301) 738-8895
BBS Software: MMB TEAMate
Comments: Logon as "ncjrs"

PD-BBS

An experimental BBS provided by Arlington County, Virginia Police Department and Emergency Communications Center. Specializes in information for law enforcement officers, fire fighters and emergency medical services personnel.
Baud Rate: 300, 1200, 2400, 9600
BBS Number: (703) 358-3949
BBS Software: TCOMM

7th Circuit Court of Appeals Bulletin Board

Contains court dockets, cases, and more, provided by the United States Court of Appeals.
Baud Rate: 300, 1200, 2400
BBS Number: (312) 435-5560
BBS Software: PCBoard
Help Line: (312) 435-5528

YE OLDE BAILEY

Provides information and discussions on your legal rights. Maintains a list of legal BBSs from around the country.
Availability: 24 hours/7 days
Baud Rate: 300,38.4
BBS Number: (713) 520-1569
BBS Software: PCBoard
Sysop: Reginald Hirsch

CD-ROM

❧ *Drugs & Crime CDROM*
Abt Books

❧ *Federal Decisions*
ROM Publishers, Inc.
1033 "O" Street, Mezzanine Level
Lincoln, NE 68508

❧ *Federal Supplemental*
ROM Publishers, Inc.

❧ *Index Legal Periodicals*
H.W. Wilson Co.
950 University Avenue
Bronx, NY 10452

❧ *Justis CDROM*
Context Limited

❧ *Law Cataloging Collection*
OCLC

❧ *PAIS on CD-ROM*
Public Affairs Info Service
11 West 40th Street
New York, NY 10008

Library
Science
Resources

Forums & Databases
America Online (AOL)
No services available.

CompuServe (CIS)
No services available.

GEnie
No services available.

The Well

↳ *Apple Library User's Group*
(g alug)
Over 19,000 members worldwide. All types of libraries and librarians are represented.

↳ *Books*
(g books)
A place to talk about books—books you've read, books you haven't, books you've never heard of, books you're bound to want to read after hearing about them.

↳ *Computer Books*
(g cbook)
Discusses all facets of the computer book business.

↳ *Factsheet Five*
(g f5)
An electronic extension of the traditional paper magazine of the same name. The most comprehensive review of the fanzine press—those thousands of publications out there with a circulation under 5,000.

↳ *Indexing*
(g indexing)
Discussions for users interested in the process of indexing and the retrieval of information through indexing structures.

↳ *Periodical/Newsletter*
(g per)
A place for publishers of newsletters and other small periodicals to share resources, informational and otherwise.

Network Discussions Lists
Internet (Includes Bitnet & UUCPNet)

↳ *Association of College and Research Libraries list.*
ACRL@UICVM.BITNET
LISTSERV@UICVM.BITNET

↳ *Geac Advance Library System list.*
Discusses the Geac Advance Library System, used for cataloging, circulation, book acquisitions, and journal control.
ADVANC-L@IDBSU.BITNET
LISTSERV@IDBSU.BITNET
Contact: Dan Lester
<ALILESTE@IDBSU.BITNET>

↳ *African-American Studies and Librarianship Discussion list.*
Discussions for librarians and interested users relating to African-American experience and librarianship.
AFAS-L@KENTVM.BITNET
LISTSERV@KENTVM.BITNET
Contact: Gladys Smiley Bell
<gbell@kentvm.BITNET>

🔄 *Discussione Associazione Italiana Biblioteche list.*
AIB-CUR@IVEUNCC.BITNET
LISTSERV@IVEUNCC.BITNET

🔄 *Academic Librarian's Forum*
Explores news and views on developments affecting academic librarians.
ALF-L@YORKVM1.BITNET
LISTSERV@YORKVM1.BITNET
Contact: Tiit Kodar
<TKODAR@VM2.YORKU.CA>

🔄 *Indexing and Annotated Lists-of-Things Discussion list.*
ANN-LOTS@NDSUVM1.BITNET
LISTSERV@NDSUVM1.BITNET

🔄 *Archives & Archivists list.*
Discusses archives; for users involved or interested in archival theory and practice.
ARCHIVES@INDYCMS.BITNET
LISTSERV@INDYCMS.BITNET
Contact: Donna B Harlan
<Harlan@IUBACS.BITNET>

🔄 *Irish and UK Architectural Librarians Mailing list.*
ARCLIB-L@IRLEARN.BITNET
LISTSERV@IRLEARN.BITNET
Contact: Julia Barrett
JBARRETT@IRLEARN.BITNET>

🔄 *RLG Ariel Document Transmission System list.*
Discusses the usage of the Ariel document transmission system for the Internet.
ARIE-L@IDBSU.BITNET
LISTSERV@IDBSU.BITNET
Contact: Dan Lester
<ALILESTE@IDBSU.BITNET>

🔄 *Library Science Conference list.*
ARIZSLS@ARIZVM1.BITNET
LISTSERV@ARIZVM1.BITNET

🔄 *Arts Libraries Discussion list.*
ARLIS-L@UKCC.BITNET
LISTSERV@UKCC.BITNET
Contact: Mary Molinaro
<MOLINARO@UKCC.BITNET>

🔄 *Library Cataloging and Authorities Discussion list.*
AUTOCAT@UVMVM.BITNET
LISTSERV@UVMVM.BITNET

🔄 *Boston Area Business Librarians Discussion list.*
BABL-L@MITVMA.BITNET
LISTSERV@MITVMA.BITNET

🔄 *Bibliographic Instruction Discussion Group.*
Discusses ways of assisting library users exploit the resources available through the library of the 1990s.
BI-L@BINGVMB.BITNET
LISTSERV@BINGVMB.BITNET
Contact: Martin Raish
<MRAISH@BINGVMA.BITNET>

🔄 *Research Library User Services list.*
BIBLIST@SEARN.BITNET
LISTSERV@SEARN.BITNET

🔄 *Software for Personal Bibliographic Database Management list.*
Discusses how to choose a program, comparisons of programs, downloading from library catalogs, and other databases.
BIBSOFT@INDYCMS.BITNET
LISTSERV@INDYCMS.BITNET
Contact: Sue Stigleman
<stigle@cs.unca.edu>

🔄 *Conference of Black Librarians list.*
BLACKLIB@GUVM.BITNET
LISTSERV@GUVM.BITNET

🔄 *ACRL Canadian Studies Librarians' Discussion list.*
CANST-LI@UVMVM.BITNET
LISTSERV@UVMVM.BITNET

🔄 *CARL User's Information list.*
CARL-L@UHCCVM.BITNET
LISTSERV@UHCCVM.BITNET

🔄 *Circplus—Library Circulation list.*
Deals with issues related to circulation control in libraries, including circulation, shelving, reserve room or reserve desk operations, stacks maintenance, and so on.
CIRCPLUS@IDBSU.BITNET
LISTSERV@IDBSU.BITNET
Contact: Dan Lester
<ALILESTE@IDBSU.BITNET>

🔄 *Community of Industrial Relations Librarians*
CIRLNET@RUTVM1.BITNET
LISTSERV@RUTVM1.BITNET

🔄 *CLA Collections Development Interest Group*
COLDEV-L@UNBVM1.BITNET
LISTSERV@UNBVM1.BITNET

🔄 *Library Collection Development*
Discussions primarily for library collection-development officers, bibliographers, and selectors, plus others involved with library

collection development, including interested publishers and vendors.
```
COLLDV-L@USCVM.BITNET
LISTSERV@USCVM.BITNET
```
Contact: Lynn Sipe
```
<LSIPE@USCVM.BITNET>
```

🍾 *South Asian Libraries Discussion list.*
```
CONSALD@UTXVM.BITNET
LISTSERV@UTXVM.BITNET
```

🍾 *Library Cooperative Cataloging list.*
A clearinghouse of information to aid in the formation of cooperative cataloging arrangements among libraries.
```
COOPCAT@NERVM.BITNET
LISTSERV@NERVM.BITNET
```
Contact: Carol Walton
```
<carwalt@nervm.BITNET>
```

🍾 *Dance Librarians Discussion Group list.*
```
DLDG-L@IUBVM.BITNET
LISTSERV@IUBVM.BITNET
```

🍾 *ASEE Engineering Libraries Division Network list.*
```
ELDNET-L@UIUCVMD.BITNET
LISTSERV@UIUCVMD.BITNET
```

🍾 *Open Library/Information Science Research Forum*
Devoted to research in library and information science.
```
ELEASAI@ARIZVM1.BITNET
LISTSERV@ARIZVM1.BITNET
```
Contact: Gretchen Whitney
```
<GWHITNEY@ARIZVMS.BITNET>
```

🍾 *Greek Library Automation System list.*
```
ELLASBIB@GREARN.BITNET
LISTSERV@GREARN.BITNET
```

🍾 *Southeast Document Librarians list.*
```
FLADOCS@NERVM.BITNET
LISTSERV@NERVM.BITNET
```

🍾 *Florida Librarians Preservation/Education Discussion list.*
```
FLIPPER@NERVM.BITNET
LISTSERV@NERVM.BITNET
```

🍾 *Federal Depository Libraries Information/ Discussion list.*
Issues discussed include the electronic dissemination policies of the Government Printing Office, the 1990 census, access to federal documents (Freedom of Information Act), automation of document collections in libraries, and more.
```
GOVDOC-L@PSUVM.BITNET
LISTSERV@PSUVM.BITNET
```

🍾 *UTK Graduate School of Library and Information Science list.*
```
GSLIS-L@UTKVM1.BITNET
LISTSERV@UTKVM1.BITNET
```

🍾 *HARLIC Libraries Discussion Group list*
```
HARLIC-L@RICELIBR.BITNET
LISTSERV@RICELIBR.BITNET
```

🍾 *Israeli Information Retrieval Specialists list.*
```
IIRS@TAUNIVM.BITNET
LISTSERV@TAUNIVM.BITNET
```

🍾 *Interlibrary Loan Discussion Group list.*
```
ILL-L@UVMVM.BITNET
LISTSERV@UVMVM.BITNET
```

🍾 *Indiana NOTIS Sites and Users list.*
```
IN-NOTIS@IRISHVMA.BITNET
LISTSERV@IRISHVMA.BITNET
```

🍾 *Indexers Discussion Group*
Promotes good indexing practices by providing a forum for aspiring and professional indexers to share information and ideas.
```
INDEX-L@BINGVMB.BITNET
LISTSERV@BINGVMB.BITNET
```
Contact: Charlotte Skuster
```
<skuster@bingvmb.BITNET>
```

🍾 *Information and Referral list.*
Discussions for users involved or interested in information and referral services.
```
INFO+REF@INDYCMS.BITNET
LISTSERV@INDYCMS.BITNET
```
Contact: John B Harlan
```
<IJBH200@IndyVAX.BITNET>
```

🍾 *III Online Public Access Catalog Discussion list.*
Discusses Innovative Interfaces' Online Public Access Catalog and related subjects.
```
INNOPAC@MAINE.BITNET
LISTSERV@MAINE.BITNET
```
Contact: Marilyn Lutz
```
LUTZ@MAINE.BITNET
```

🍾 *Research Support for Indiana University Librarians list.*
```
IULRES-L@IUBVM.BITNET
LISTSERV@IUBVM.BITNET
```

🍾 *Open Library/Information Science Education Forum*
Discusses teaching and educational concerns in library and information science.
```
JESSE@ARIZVM1.BITNET
LISTSERV@ARIZVM1.BITNET
```
Contact: Gretchen Whitney
```
<GWHITNEY@ARIZVMS.BITNET>
```

⑤ *Librarian Systems and Databases Discussion list.*
KATALIST@HUEARN.BITNET
LISTSERV@HUEARN.BITNET

⑤ *KU Library Humanities Bibliographers list.*
KULHUM-L@UKANVM.BITNET
LISTSERV@UKANVM.BITNET

⑤ *Turkish Libraries Discussion list.*
KUTUP-L@TRMETU.BITNET
LISTSERV@TRMETU.BITNET

⑤ *Latin Americanist Librarians' Announcements list.*
LALA-L@UGA.BITNET
LISTSERV@UGA.BITNET

⑤ *Library Administration Issues Discussion list.*
Discusses issues of library administration and management.
LIBADMIN@UMAB.BITNET
LISTSERV@UMAB
Contact: Pamela Bluh
pbluh@umab.BITNET

⑤ *Southern California Library list.*
Lists library-related events occurring in Southern California.
LIBEVENT@USCVM.BITNET
LISTSERV@uscvm.BITNET
Contact: Karen Howell
<khowell@vm.usc.edu>

⑤ *Exhibits and Academic Libraries Discussion list.*
LIBEX-L@MAINE.BITNET
LISTSERV@MAINE.BITNET

⑤ *LIBINFO—Harvard Library Information Discussion list.*
LIBINFO@HARVARDA.BITNET
LISTSERV@HARVARDA.BITNET

⑤ *The Library Master Bibliographic Database list.*
For users of the Library Master bibliographic and textual database management system.
LIBMASTR@UOTTAWA.BITNET
LISTSERV@UOTTAWA.BITNET
Contact: Michael Strangelove
<441495@Uottawa.BITNET>

⑤ *Libraries and Networks in North Carolina list.*
LIBNET-L@NCSUVM.BITNET
LISTSERV@NCSUVM.BITNET

⑤ *Library Personnel Issues list.*
LIBPER-L@KSUVM.BITNET
LISTSERV@KSUVM.BITNET

⑤ *University Library Planning Discussion list.*
LIBPLN-L@QUCDN.BITNET
LISTSERV@QUCDN.BITNET

⑤ *Libraries & Librarians list.*
General news and information of interest to libraries, their employees, and users.
LIBRARY@INDYCMS.BITNET
LISTSERV@INDYCMS.BITNET
Contact: Donna B Harlan
<Harlan@IUBACS.BITNET>

⑤ *Discussion of Library Reference Issues list.*
Discusses the changing environment of library reference services and activities.
LIBREF-L@KENTVM.BITNET
LISTSERV@KENTVM.BITNET
Contact: Diane Kovacs
<dkovacs@kentvm.BITNET>

⑤ *Library and Information Science Research list.*
Discusses library and information science research; supports the development of our knowledge base.
LIBRES@KENTVM.BITNET
LISTSERV@KENTVM.BITNET
Contact: Diane Kovacs
<dkovacs@kentvm.BITNET>

⑤ *LIBSUP-L UW Cataloging list.*
LIBSUP-L@UWAVM.BITNET
LISTSERV@UWAVM.BITNET

⑤ *EARCH—Library Discussion list.*
LISR-ALL@NMSUVM1.BITNET
LISTSERV@NMSUVM1.BITNET ACRL RES

⑤ *Acrl Research—Bibliographic Control list.*
LISRBC1L@NMSUVM1.BITNET
LISTSERV@NMSUVM1.BITNET

⑤ *Each—Collection Management list.*
LISRCM-L@NMSUVM1.BITNET
LISTSERV@NMSUVM1.BITNET ACRL RES

⑤ *Acrl Research—Expert Systems list.*
LISRES-L@NMSUVM1.BITNET
LISTSERV@NMSUVM.BITNET

⑤ *Acrl Research—Library Effectiveness list.*
LISRLE-L@NMSUVM1.BITNET
LISTSERV@NMSUVM1.BITNET

⑤ *Acrl Research—Scholarly Communication list.*
LISRSC-L@NMSUVM1.BITNET
LISTSERV@NMSUVM1.BITNET

⑤ *Library Media Network list.*
Serves the school library media community worldwide.
LM_NET@SUVM.BITNET
LISTSERV@SUVM.BITNET

Contact: Peter Milbury
    <PMILBUR@ATL.CALSTATE.EDU>

⟲ *Journal of Academic Media Librarianship
    list.*
An electronic publication whose scope encompasses all aspects of academic media librarianship.
    MCJRNL@UBVM.BITNET
    LISTSERV@UBVM.BITNET
Contact: Lori Widzinski
    <HSLLJW@ubvm.bitnet>

⟲ *Medical Libraries Discussion list.*
Discussions for librarians in the health sciences.
    MEDLIB-L@UBVM.BITNET
    LISTSERV@UBVM.BITNET
Contact: Nancy Start
    <HSLSTART@UBVM.BITNET>

⟲ *MIT Industrial Relations Library list.*
    MITIRLIB@MITVMA.BITNET
    LISTSERV@MITVMA.BITNET

⟲ *Music Library Association list.*
For announcements of deadlines for NOTES and the MLA newsletter, news items, general inquiries about MLA activities, and more.
    MLA-L@IUBVM.BITNET
    LISTSERV@IUBVM.BITNET
Contact: A. Ralph Papakhian
    <PAPAKHI@IUBVM.BITNET>

⟲ *Association of Government Archivists list.*
    NAGARA-L@UMDD.BITNET
    LISTSERV@UMDD.BITNET

⟲ *Rare Book and Special Collections Cataloging
    Discussion list.*
    NOTRBCAT@INDYCMS.BITNET
    LISTSERV@INDYCMS.BITNET

⟲ *Music Library Association (New York/
    Ontario) list.*
Discusses topics related to the New York State/
Ontario chapter of the MLA.
    NYSO-L@UBVM.BITNET
    LISTSERV@UBVM.BITNET
Contact: Rick McRae
    <mmlrick@UBVM.BITNET>

⟲ *Online Computer Library list.*
For press releases and other official communications from Online Computer Library Center, Inc. (OCLC).
    OCLC-NEWS@OCLC.ORG
    LISTSERV@OCLC.ORG
Contact: Marifay Makssour
    <marifay_makssour@oclc.org>

⟲ *Off-Campus Library Services list.*
    OFFCAMP@WAYNEST1.BITNET
    LISTSERV@WAYNEST1.BITNET

⟲ *Online Research Services list.*
For information or questions concerning the on-line world .
    online@uunet.ca
    online-request@uunet.ca
Contact: Jim Carroll
    <jcarroll@jacc.uucp>

⟲ *Personal Bibliographic Software Discussion
    list.*
For users interested in the bibliographic textbase software program PRO-CITE and its companion BIBLIO-LINK, published by Personal Bibliographic Software.
    PRO-CITE@IUBVM.BITNET
    LISTSERV@IUBVM.BITNET
Contact: Mark Day
    <DAYM@IUBACS.BITNET>

⟲ *RLG Archives, Manuscripts, and Special
    Collections list.*
    RLGAMSC@RUTVM1.BITNET
    LISTSERV@RUTVM1.BITNET

⟲ *RLG Art and Architecture list.*
    RLGART-L@YALEVM.BITNET
    LISTSERV@YALEVM.BITNET

⟲ *RLGLAW-L RLG Law Library list.*
    RLGLAW-L@UMINN1.BITNET
    LISTSERV@UMINN1.BITNET

⟲ *RLG Library Systems Officer Forum list.*
    RLGLOC-L@BINGVMB.BITNET
    LISTSERV@BINGVMB.BITNET

⟲ *RLG Preservation list.*
    RLGPRE-L@YALEVM.BITNET
    LISTSERV@YALEVM.BITNET

⟲ *RLG Public Service and Collection
    Development list.*
    RLGPSCD@BROWNVM.BROWN.EDU
    LISTSERV@BROWNVM.BROWN.EDU

⟲ *RLG Technical Services list.*
    RLGTECH@RUTVM1.BITNET
    LISTSERV@RUTVM1.BITNET

⟲ *Serials in Libraries User Discussion list.*
    SERIALST@UVMVM.BITNET
    LISTSERV@UVMVM.BITNET

⟲ *Special Resource Committee on Medical
    School Libraries in Canada list (closed).*
    SRCMSL-L@MCMVM1.BITNET
    LISTSERV@MCMVM1.BITNET

⟲ *SUNY Library Association list.*
    SUNYLA-L@BINGVMB.BITNET
    LISTSERV@BINGVMB.BITNET

- *Technical Standards for Library Automation list.*
  ```
  TESLA@NERVM.BITNET
  LISTSERV@NERVM.BITNET
  ```

- *UNICORN Library Catalog System list.*
  ```
  UNICRN-L@PSUORVM.BITNET
  LISTSERV@PSUORVM.BITNET
  ```

- *USMARC Advisory Group Forum*
For members of the USMARC Advisory Group and anyone interested in discussing the implementation, maintenance, changes, and development of USMARC formats.
  ```
  USMARC-L@MAINE.BITNET
  LISTSERV@MAINE.BITNET
  ```
Contact: William E. Moen
  ```
  wmoe@seq1.loc.gov
  ```

- *Virtual International Faculty in Library and Information Science list.*
  ```
  VIFLIS@ARIZVM1.BITNET
  LISTSERV@ARIZVM1.BITNET
  ```

- *Library of the Future list.*
  ```
  VIRTUAL@INDYCMS.BITNET
  LISTSERV@INDYCMS.BITNET
  ```

- *Scholarly Electronic Journals list.*
Discusses electronic publishing issues, especially those related to scholarly electronic journals. Covers SGML, PostScript, and other electronic journal formats, as well as software and hardware considerations.
  ```
  VPIEJ-L@VTVM1.BITNET
  LISTSERV@VTVM1.BITNET
  ```
Contact: James Powell
  ```
  <JPOWELL@VTVM1.BITNET>
  ```

- *Health Sciences Library Discussion list.*
  ```
  WHSCL-L@EMUVM1.BITNET
  LISTSERV@EMUVM1.BITNET
  ```

Fidonet

- *Information Power!*
  ```
  LIBRARY
  ```
For librarians exploring technological access to information. Gated to Usenet as the newsgroup k12.library.
Moderator: Janet Murray
  ```
  1:105/23
  ```
Distribution: NATIONAL BACKBONE

Usenet

- *Geac Advance Integrated Library System users.*
  ```
  bit.listserv.advanc-l
  ```

- *Business libraries list.*
  ```
  bit.listserv.buslib-l
  ```

- *Circulation reserve and related library issues.*
  ```
  bit.listserv.circplus
  ```

- *Discussion of government document issues.*
  ```
  bit.listserv.govdoc-l
  ```

- *Library reference issues. Moderated.*
  ```
  bit.listserv.libref-l
  ```

- *Library and information science research issues.*
  ```
  bit.listserv.libres
  ```

- *Discussing all aspects of libraries.*
  ```
  soc.libraries.talk
  ```

Online Libraries
After Dark

- *Wilson Library Literature*
Shows the latest trends in rapidly evolving fields by indexing English and foreign-language library periodicals, selected state journals, monographs, conference proceedings, pamphlets, and library school theses.
Coverage: 1983 to present
Updated: Monthly

Knowledge Index
No services available.

Orbit

- *National Union Catalog Codes*
Contains the names, complete addresses, and National Union Catalog codes for libraries cited in the Chemical Abstracts Service Source Index (CASSI) database. All data is searchable. Coverage includes approximately 400 libraries in 28 countries.
Coverage: Current
Updated: Periodically

- *Scientific and Technical Books & Serials in Print*
Provides a comprehensive subject selection of books and serials in scientific and technical fields. All aspects of physical and biological sciences and their applications are included, as well as engineering and technology. Includes over 160,000 book titles and more than 40,000 serial titles.
Coverage: Current
Updated: Monthly

SciSearch

Provides a multidisciplinary index to the international journal literature of science and technology. With approximately 10 million records, it corresponds to the printed *Science Citation Index* and contains additional records from the *Current Contents* series of publications.
Coverage: 1974 to present
Updated: Weekly

NewsNet

No services available.

Bulletin Boards

ALIX—Automated Library Information eXchange

For exchange of information on innovative library and information center automation programs, solutions to library and information center automation problems, and microcomputer experience and techniques. Federal library jobs, federal agency library information, conferences, and library administration are covered.
Baud Rate: 300, 1200, 2400, 9600
BBS Number: (202) 707-4888
BBS Software: TBBS
Help Line: (202) 707-4848

The Friends Forum

Friends of the library, Montgomery County, Maryland. Offered as a public service to facilitate interchange of information and ideas related to public libraries.
Availability: 24 hours/ 7 days
Baud Rate: 300, 1200, 2400, 9600, 14.4
BBS Number: (301) 217-3913
BBS Software: RBBS-PC
Help Line: (301) 217-3810

CD-ROM

ABI/INFORM (most recent 5 years)
UMI
300 North Zeeb Road
Ann Arbor, MI 48106

Academic Index
Information Access Co.
362 Lakeside Drive
Foster City, CA 94404

Applied Science and Technical Index
H.W. Wilson Co.
950 University Avenue
Bronx, NY 10452

Books In Print Plus
Bowker Electronic Publishing
245 West 17th Street
New York, NY 10011

Books Out of Print Plus
Bowker Electronic Publishing
245 West 17th Street
New York, NY 10011

Dissertation Abstracts
UMI
300 North Zeeb Road
Ann Arbor, MI 48106

Education Index
H.W. Wilson Co.
950 University Avenue
Bronx, NY 10452

General Science Index
H.W. Wilson Co.
950 University Avenue
Bronx, NY 10452

Government Documents Catalog Service
Auto-Graphics, Inc.
3201 Temple Avenue
Pamona, CA 91768

GPO Monthly Catalog
SilverPlatter Information Inc.
One Newton Executive Park
Newton Lower Falls, MA 02162

Periodic Abstracts
UMI
300 North Zeeb Road
Ann Arbor, MI 48106

Resource/One Ondisc
UMI
300 North Zeeb Road
Ann Arbor, MI 48106

Sci-Tech Reference +
Bowker Electronic Publishing
245 West 17th Street
New York, NY 10011

Literature Resources

Forums & Databases
America Online (AOL)

✑ *Book Bestsellers*
Keyword: Books
Path: Entertainment Department > Book Bestsellers
Bestseller lists are compiled by Publishers Weekly and are supplied by Cineman Syndicate, Inc. Categories include fiction, non-fiction, paperback trade, and mass market paperbacks. Users can post their own reviews or respond to reviews posted by other members.

CompuServe (CIS)

✑ *Literary Forum*
    GO LITFORUM
A gathering place for professional writers, literature readers, journalists, humorists and users with an interest in any related field.

GEnie
No services available.

The Well
No services available.

Network Discussions Lists
Internet (Includes Bitnet & UUCPNet)

✑ *American Literature Discussion List*
Discusses topics and issues on American Literature among a world-wide community interested in the subject.
    AMLIT-L@UMCVMB.BITNET
    LISTSERV@UMCVMB.BITNET
Contact: Michael O'Conner
    <ENGMO@UMCVMB.BITNET>

✑ *Discussion of Isaac Asimov's works.*
    ASIMOV-L@UTDALLAS.BITNET
    LISTSERV@UTDALLAS.BITNET

✑ *Readers of Jane Austen*
Discusses Jane Austen's novels and her contemporaries, such as Fanny Burney, Maria Edgeworth and Maria Wollstonecraft.
    AUSTEN-L@MCGILL1.BITNET
    CCMW@MUSICA.MCGILL.CA

✑ *Quebec Literature Studies*
    AXE-LIST@MCGILL1.BITNET
    LISTSERV@MCGILL1.BITNET

✑ *Discusses all Arthurian fields of interest.*
    camelot@castle.ed.ac.uk
    camelot-request@castle.ed.ac.uk

✑ *Medieval English Literature*
    CHAUCER@SIUCVMB.BITNET
    LISTSERV@SIUCVMB.BITNET
Contact: Jeff Taylor
    <GR4302@SIUCVMB.BITNET>

✑ *Chaucer Scholars*
Discusses the works of Geoffrey Chaucer and medieval English literature and culture in the period 1100-1500.
    chaucer@unlinfo.unl.edu
    listserv@unlinfo.unl.edu
Contact: Thomas Bestul
    <tbestul@crcvms.unl.edu>

꙳ *Chicano literature discussion list.*
CHICLE@UNMVM.BITNET
LISTSERV@UNMVM.BITNET

꙳ *Classics and Latin discussion group list.*
CLASSICS@UWAVM.BITNET
LISTSERV@UWAVM.BITNET

꙳ *Fans of Katherine Kurtz' novels set in the Deryni universe*
DERYNI-L@mintir.new-orleans.la.us
MAIL-SERVER@mintir.new-orleans.la.us
Contact: Edward J. Branley
<elendil@mintir.new-orleans.la.us>

꙳ *DOROTHYL is a discussion list for lovers of the mystery genre*
DOROTHYL@KENTVM.BITNET
LISTSERV@KENTVM.BITNET
Contact: Harriet Vane
<Harriet@e-math.ams.com>

꙳ *Albert Einstein Papers Project and Discussion*
EPP-L@BUACCA.BITNET
LISTSERV@BUACCA.BITNET
Contact: Adam Bryant, Coordinator
adb@bu-it.bu.edu

꙳ *Faulkner Journal Editor List*
FJ-ROSA@AKRONVM.BITNET
LISTSERV@AKRONVM.BITNET

꙳ *Finnegans Wake (by James Joyce) Discussion List*
FWAKE-L@IRLEARN.BITNET
LISTSERV@IRLEARN.BITNET
Contact: Michael O'Kelly
MOKELLY@IRLEARN.BITNET

꙳ *Finnegans Wake—Textual Notes*
FWAKEN-L@IRLEARN.BITNET
LISTSERV@IRLEARN.BITNET

꙳ *List for the discussion of Buckminster Fuller*
GEODESIC@UBVM.BITNET
LISTSERV@UBVM.BITNET
Contact: Patrick G. Salsbury
<V291NHTP@UBVMSC.CC.BUFFALO.EDU>

꙳ *The Works of Hermann Hesse*
HESSE-L@UCSBVM.BITNET
LISTSERV@UCSBVM.BITNET
Contact: Gunther Gottschalk
<hcf2hess@ucsbvm.bitnet>

꙳ *Society for Literature and Science*
LITSCI-L@UIUCVMD.BITNET
LISTSERV@UIUCVMD.BITNET

꙳ *John Milton List*
MILTON-L@URVAX.BITNET
MILTON-REQUEST@URVAX.BITNET
Contact: Kevin J.T. Creamer
<CREAMER@URVAX.BITNET>

꙳ *Irish British Literature*
For scholars, teachers, and students of Modern British and Irish literature (1895-1955) and those who share their interests.
MODBRITS@KENTVM.BITNET
LISTSERV@KENTVM.BITNET

꙳ *Mystery Science Theater 3000*
For fans of the television show "Mystery Science Theater 3000" that is shown on the Comedy Channel (available on various cable networks in North America).
MST3K@gynko.circ.upenn.edu
MST3K-Request@gynko.circ.upenn.edu
Contact: Rich Kulawiec
<rsk@gynko.circ.upenn.edu>

꙳ *Thomas Pynchon*
Discusses the works of Thomas Pynchon, a notoriously publicity-shy, contemporary American novelist.
PYNCHON@SFU.BITNET
JODY GILBERT <USERDOG1@SFU.BITNET>
Contact: Jody Gilbert
<USERDOG1@SFU.BITNET>

꙳ *Discusses topics related to the books by Ceanne DeRohan.*
Right_Use_of_Will@kether.webo.dg.com
Will-Request@kether.webo.dg.com

꙳ *Romance Readers Anonymous*
RRA-L@KENTVM.BITNET
LISTSERV@KENTVM.BITNET
Contact: Jayne A. Krentz
<lhaas@kentvm.BITNET>

꙳ *SUNY/Stony Brook Literary Underground*
SBRHYM-L@SBCCVM.BITNET
LISTSERV@SBCCVM.BITNET
Contact: Kristofer Munn
KMUNN@SBCCVM.BITNET

꙳ *Citations for Serial Literature list*
SERCITES@MITVMA.BITNET
LISTSERV@MITVMA.BITNET

꙳ *Science Fiction-Lovers List*
SFLOVERS@RUTVM1.BITNET
LISTSERV@RUTVM1.BITNET
Contact: Saul Jaffe
<sf-lovers-request@rutgers.edu>

꙳ *Shakespeare Electronic Conference*
SHAKSPER@UTORONTO.BITNET
LISTSERV@UTORONTO.BITNET
Contact: Ken Steele
<KSTEELE@vm.epas.utoronto.ca>

⑤ *History of the printed word*
SHARP-L@IUBVM.BITNET
LISTSERV@IUBVM.BITNET
Contact: Patrick Leary
<pleary@IUBACS.BITNET>

⑤ *Superguy*
A multi-author world of superheroes.
SUPERGUY@UCF1VM.BITNET
LISTSERV@UCF1VM.BITNET
Contact: Tad Simmons
<SIMMONS@UCF1VM.BITNET>

⑤ *For readers of J.R.R.Tolkien.*
TOLKIEN@JHUVM.BITNET
LISTSERV@JHUVM.BITNET

⑤ *Mark Twain Forum*
For users having a scholarly interest in the life and writings of Mark Twain. The archives of TWAIN-L files are stored in the TWAIN-L FILELIST.
TWAIN-L@YORKVM1.BITNET
LISTSERV@YORKVM1.BITNET
Contact: Taylor Roberts
<TROBERTS@YORKVM1.BITNET>

⑤ *The Urantia Book*
Discusses "The Urantia Book" to gain integration of knowledge and consolidation of worldviews toward an improved life for all on Earth.
URANTIAL@UAFSYSB.BITNET
LISTSERV@UAFSYSB.BITNET

⑤ *Writers Lists Works*
WORKS-L@NDSUVM1.BITNET
LISTSERV@NDSUVM1.BITNET

⑤ *Mytacist Manufacture*
For bizarre/disturbing/offensive short stories and ramblings, not humor.
WEIRD-L@BROWNVM.BROWN.EDU
LISTSERV@BROWNVM.BROWN.EDU
Contact: Jeremy Bornstein
(jeremy@brownvm.BITNET)

Fidonet

⑤ *Douglas Adams Fan Club*
ADAMS
For fans of Hitchhiker's guide to the galaxy-triology and Meaning of Life and all other books by Douglas Adams, humour being one of the main issues.
Moderator: Andreas Birgerson
2:200/407
Distribution: WORLD

⑤ *Comics Echo*
COMICS
For the discussion of comic books and all sorts of related topics such as adaptations in other media, newspaper comic strips, comics related RPGs and the like.
Moderator: Dave Thomer
1:161/42
Distribution: BACKBONE

⑤ *Comics For Sale*
CMX4SALE
To buy, sell, and trade comics and comic character toys.
Moderator: Walter Tietjen
1:151/114

⑤ *Mystery books and stories*
MYSTERY
Discusses literary works of mystery, espionage, and related genres.
Moderator: David Dyer-Bennet
1:282/341
Distribution: BACKBONE, ZONE 1

⑤ *Reviews of almost anything.*
REVIEWS
For reviews of just about anything, including movies, tv programs, restaurants, books, software.
Moderator: Kurt Reisler
1:109/101

⑤ *Science Fiction and Fantasy Literature*
SF
Discusses literary works of science fiction and fantasy, science fiction fandom and conventions, and writing and publishing.
Moderator: David Dyer-Bennet
1:282/341
Distribution: BACKBONE, ***E-1, ZONE-2, ZONE-3, ALTERNET
Gateways: ALTERNET VIA 1:141/488, ZONE-3 VIA 1:1/3

⑤ *Science Fiction Literature*
SF-LIT
Discusses science fiction in its written (and published) form.
Moderator: Carlos Benitz
1:125/17

⑤ *Star Trek Books/Tech Manuals*
STBOOKS
For topics including various *Star Trek* Novels, *Star Trek* Technical Manuals and Comic Books.
Moderator: Nathan Moschkin
1:109/427

↻ Stephen King Discussion—International
S_KING
Moderator: Tina Lymburner
1:110/15
Distribution: BACKBONE, INTERNATIONAL
Gateways: RBBS-NET, CHATEAUNET,
PCBUSINESS NET

Usenet

*↻ Author of "The Meaning of Life", & other
fine works.*
alt.fan.douglas-adams

↻ Anne McCaffery's s-f oeuvre.
alt.fan.pern

↻ For fans of Terry Pratchett, s-f humor writer.
alt.fan.pratchett

↻ A novelist of quaint and affecting tales.
alt.fan.tom-robbins

↻ The horror genre.
alt.horror

↻ Discussion of non-Western comics.
alt.manga

↻ Discussion of Government Document Issues.
bit.listserv.govdoc-l

↻ GUTNBERG Discussion List.
bit.listserv.gutnberg

↻ Discussions about Literature.
bit.listserv.literary

↻ Erotic fiction and verse. (Moderated)
rec.arts.erotica

↻ Discussions about interactive fiction.
rec.arts.int-fiction

*↻ Reviews of science fiction/fantasy/horror
works. (Moderated)*
rec.arts.sf.reviews

Online Libraries
After Dark

↻ Wisconsin Reader's Guide
Indexes more than 60,000 articles per year on
a wide range of newsworthy topics, from
scientific breakthroughs to international
politics, to theater news.
Coverage: 1983 to present
Updated: Monthly

↻ Wilson Readers' Guide Abstracts
Combines Readers Guide indexing with high
quality informative abstracts to create a unique
information service.
Coverage: 1983 to present
Updated: Monthly

Knowledge Index

↻ MLA Bibliography
Provides the first online access to the dis-
tinguished and comprehensive bibliography
of humanistic studies produced annually by
the Modern Language Association.
Coverage: 1963 to present
Updated: Annual

Orbit

No services available.

NewsNet

No services available.

Bulletin Boards
Book Stacks Unlimited, Inc.

An on-line bookstore and readers' conference
system accessible by modem from anywhere in
the world. Enables users to search for books by
author or title, or just browse the shelves by
subject.
Availability: 24 hrs/7 days
Baud Rate: 300-2400
BBS Number: (216) 861-0469

BOOK BBS

Provides free information to consumers about
non-fiction technical books, primarily
computer books. They specialize in books and
related materials about computers, business,
travel & language and are experts on personal
computer books.
Availability: 24 hrs/ 7 days
Baud Rate: 2400
BBS Number: (215) 657-6130 or
(215) 657-4783
BBS Software: TBBS
Sysop: Ken Taylor, Business & Computer
Bookstore
Help Line: mail-order/phone orders: call
(800) 233-0233 or (215) 657-8300.

CD-ROM

❧ *CD Theses*
Chadwyck-Healey

❧ *Columbia Granger's World of Poetry*
Columbia University Press

❧ *Electronic Home Library*
World Library, Inc.

❧ *Essay and General Literature Index*
H.W. Wilson

❧ *Library of the Future Series*
World Library, Inc.

❧ *MLA International Bibliography*
H.W. Wilson

❧ *Shakespeare on Disk*
CMC Research

❧ *Sherlock Holmes on Disk*
CMC Research

Mathematics Resources

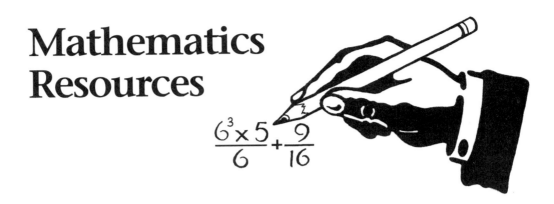

$$\frac{6^3 \times 5}{6} + \frac{9}{16}$$

Forums & Databases
America Online (AOL)
No services available.

CompuServe (CIS)

🕈 *Science/Math Education Forum*
GO SCIENCE
Serves science educators, students and others in science and science education. Includes a large software library for downloading into class and home computers. Makes available practice problems for science and math college boards.

GEnie
No services available.

The Well
No services available.

Network Discussions Lists
Internet (Includes Bitnet & UUCPNet)

🕈 *Algebraic Geometry list.*
ALG-GEOL@JPNYITP.BITNET
LISTSERV@JPNYITP.BITNET

🕈 *Forum de Computacao Algebrica list.*
ALGCOMP@BRLNCC.BITNET
LISTSERV@BRLNCC.BITNET

🕈 *North Carolina Science and Mathematics Alliance list.*
ALLIANCE@NCSUVM.BITNET
LISTSERV@NCSUVM.BITNET

🕈 *COM-ALG—Commutative Algebra list.*
Discussions for professionals in commutative algebra.
COM-ALG@NDSUVM1.BITNET
LISTSERV@NDSUVM1.BITNET
Contact: Joseph Brennan
<NU160025@NDSUVM1.BITNET>

🕈 *Forum on Cryptology and Related Mathematics*
CRYPTO-L@JPNTOHOK.BITNET
LISTSERV@JPNTOHOK.BITNET
Contact: Hiroki Shizuya
SHIZUYA@JPNTOHOK.BITNET

🕈 *Chinese Statistical Archive list.*
CSA-DATA@UICVM.BITNET
LISTSERV@UICVM.BITNET

🕈 *Statistics Education Discussion list.*
Discussions of techniques and philosophies of teaching statistics.
EDSTAT-L@NCSUVM.BITNET
LISTSERV@NCSUVM.cc.ncsu.edu
Contact: Tim Arnold
<arnold@stat.ncsu.edu

🕈 *Educacion Matematica en Chile list.*
EDUMATE@USACHVM1.BITNET
LISTSERV@USACHVM1.BITNET

🕈 *EGRET Epidemiological Software Discussion list.*
For discussions relative to the EGRET software package.
EGRET-L@DARTCMS1.BITNET
LISTSERV@DARTCMS1.BITNET
Contact: Stephen P. Baker
<SBAKER@UMASSMED.UMMED.EDU>

🕈 *European Women in Mathematics (EWM) list.*
EWM@ICNUCEVM.BITNET
LISTSERV@ICNUCEVM.BITNET

Contact: Laura Tedeschini Lalli
LAURATED@IRMUNISA

✪ *Grafos-l Aspectos matematicos e computacionai list.*
GRAFOS-L@UFRJ.BITNET
LISTSERV@UFRJ.BITNET

✪ *GRAPHNET—Graph Theory Discussion list.*
Discussions of graph theory for mathematicians.
GRAPHNET@NDSUVM1.BITNET
LISTSERV@NDSUVM1.BITNET
Contact: GRAPHNET@VM1.NoDak.EDU

✪ *HP Calculator Discussion list.*
For discussions of the HP-28S and HP-28C calculators.
HP-28@NDSUVM1.BITNET
LISTSERV@NDSUVM1.BITNET

✪ *International Linear Algebra list.*
Operated by the International Linear Algebra Society. Encourages activities in linear algebra.
ILAS-NET@TECHNION.BITNET
LISTSERV@TECHNION.BITNET
Contact: Danny Hershkowitz
<mar23aa@technion.BITNET>

✪ *Teachers International Study Program in Statistics list.*
ISPS@BLEKUL11.BITNET
LISTSERV@BLEKU11.BITNET

✪ *Journal of Computers in Mathematics and Science list.*
JCMST-L@PURCCVM.BITNET
LISTSERV@PURCCVM.BITNET

✪ *Symbolic Math list.*
Discussions of symbolic math algorithms, applications, and problems relating to the various symbolic math languages. It is primarily the USENET newsgroup sci.math.symbolic.
<leff%smu.uucp@UUNET.UU.NET>
leff%smu.uucp@UUNET.UU.NET
Contact: Laurence Leff
<leff%smu.uucp@UUNET.UU.NET>

✪ *Mathematica list.*
For discussions concerning the Mathematica product.
mathgroup@yoda.ncsa.uiuc.edu
mathgroup-request@yoda.ncsa.uiuc.edu
Contact: Timothy Buck
<timbuck@vtvm1.cc.vt.edu>

✪ *Number Theory list.*
For discussions of the Number Theory Net.
NMBRTHRY@NDSUVM1.BITNET
LISTSERV@NDSUVM1.BITNET
Contact: Victor Miller
<TheoryNet-Request@IBM.COM>

✪ *Casio Calculators and Microcomputers list.*
Discussions relative to Casio calculators and microcomputers (models PB and FX).
PB-FX@PUCING.BITNET
LISTSERV@PUCING.BITNET
Contact: Italo@pucing.BITNET

✪ *P-STAT Stats and Programming Discussion list.*
For information on the P-STAT data management and statistics package: codes, macros, applications, user news, and so on.
PSTAT-L@IRLEARN.BITNET
LISTSERV@IRLEARN.BITNET
Contact: Peter Flynn
CBTS8001@IRUCCVAX.BITNET

✪ *Q Methodology Network list.*
Discussions of all aspects of Q methodology as developed by the late William Stephenson (1902-1989).
Q-METHOD@KENTVM.BITNET
LISTSERV@KENTVM.BITNET
Contact: Steven R. Brown
<SBrown@KENTVM.BITNET>

✪ *Quantitative Methods: Theory and Design list.*
QNTEVA-L@PSUVM.BITNET
LISTSERV@PSUVM.BITNET

✪ *Qualitative Research for the Human Sciences list.*
QUALRS-L@UGA.BITNET
LISTSERV@UGA.BITNET

✪ *Qualitative Research in Education list.*
QUALRSED@UNMVM.BITNET
LISTSERV@UNMVM.BITNET

✪ *Symbolic and Algebraic Manipulation list.*
SAME@FRULM11.BITNET
LISTSERV@FRULM11.BITNET

✪ *Arkansas Science and Math Education list.*
SCIMAT-L@UAFSYSB.BITNET
LISTSERV@UAFSYSB.BITNET

✪ *Sociedad Matematica de Chile list.*
SOMACHI@PUCING.BITNET
LISTSERV@PUCING.BITNET

✪ *Forum of Quantitative Methods in Geosciences list.*
STAT-GEO@UFRJ.BITNET
LISTSERV@UFRJ.BITNET

✪ *Sander Wasser Statistical Consulting list.*
For discussions dealing with statistical consulting at university computing centers.
STAT-L@MCGILL1.BITNET
CCMW@MCGILLA.BITNET

Contact: Michael Walsh
<CCMW@MCGILLA.BITNET>

- *Mathematics Teaching list.*
  SUSIG@MIAMIU.BITNET
  LISTSERV@MIAMU.BITNET

- *Turkish Mathematicians Discussion list.*
  TURKMATH@TRMETU.BITNET
  LISTSERV@TRMETU.BITNET

- *UIC Mathematics list.*
  UICMATH@UICVM.BITNET
  LISTSERV@UICVM.BITNET

- *UIC Mathematics Majors list.*
  UICMATHS@UICVM.BITNET
  LISTSERV@UICVM.BITNET

- *Vital Statistics at Albnydh2 list.*
  VSTAT-L@ALBNYDH2.BITNET
  LISTSERV@ALBNYDH2.BITNET

Fidonet

No services available.

Usenet

- *Statistics education discussion list.*
  bit.listserv.edstat-l

- *Social science data list.*
  bit.listserv.sos-data

- *Scientific image processing and analysis.*
  sci.image.processing

- *Logic—math, philosophy & computational aspects.*
  sci.logic

- *Mathematical discussions and pursuits.*
  sci.math

- *Discussion of current mathematical research. Moderated.*
  sci.math.research

- *Statistics discussion.*
  sci.math.stat

- *Symbolic algebra discussion.*
  sci.math.symbolic

Online Libraries

After Dark

- *Current Contents: Engineering, Technology & Applied Sciences*

A subset of Current Contents Search™ corresponding to the Current Contents: Engineering, Technology & Applied Sciences print edition.
Coverage: Most current 12 months
Updated: Weekly

- *MathSci®*

Covers world mathematical research literature. Approximately 1,600 journals are scanned for inclusion, including 400 core mathematics journals which are indexed cover-to-cover. Most mathematical reviews are in English.
Coverage: 1973 to present
Updated: Monthly

Knowledge Index

- *MathSci®*

Covers world mathematical research literature. Approximately 1,600 journals are scanned for inclusion, including 400 core mathematics journals which are indexed cover-to-cover. Most mathematical reviews are in English.
Coverage: 1973 to present
Updated: Monthly

Orbit

No services available.

NewsNet

No services available.

Bulletin Boards

Pi Square BBS

Dedicated to resources on technical topics in science, engineering and math
Availability: 24 hours/ 7 days
Baud Rate: 2400
BBS Number: (301) 725-9080
BBS Software: Searchlight
Sysop: A. Hermida

CD-ROM

- *MathSci*

SilverPlatter Information Inc.
One Newton Executive Park
Newton Lower Falls, MA 02162

Meteorology Resources

Forums & Databases

America Online (AOL)

No services available.

CompuServe (CIS)

🖐 *EMI Non-graphic Map*
GO AERORAD
Maps showing radar precipitation with numerical indicators of precipitation intensity. Weather data updated every hour with National Weather Service information

🖐 *NWS Aviation Weather*
GO AWX
Provides instant weather information for pilots using the NOAA "A" weather wire. Includes hourly reports, updated continuously, including terminal forecasts, area forecasts, radar summaries, and more.

🖐 *Weather Maps*
GO MAPS
Accesses display of 16-color or black-and-white maps of North America, Europe, and the Pacific. Offers satellite maps, current conditions, and forecast maps; additional maps available for the United States.

🖐 *UK Weather*
GO UKWEATHER
Short-term weather reports and maps for cities in England, Scotland, Wales, and Northern Ireland. Also available are reports and maps for sites in continental Europe, North America and the Pacific rim.

🖐 *Weather Reports*
GO WEA
Short-term and extended forecasts, severe weather alerts, daily climatological reports, and more for U.S. locations.

🖐 *Weather*
GO WEATHER
Makes available, for the U.S,, a wide variety of National Weather Service reports and Accu-Weather maps; for locations outside the U.S., Accu-Weather maps and current condition / three-day forecast reports.

GEnie

🖐 *Space and Science Information Center*
Keyword: SCIENCE CENTER or Page 461
Daily weather maps provided in GIF format. The database is searchable by keyword.

The Well

No services available.

Network Discussions Lists
Internet (Includes Bitnet & UUCPNet)

🖐 *Climatologists list.*
CLIMLIST@OHSTVMA.BITNET
LISTSERV@OHSTVMA.BITNET

🖐 *The Energy and Climate Information Exchange*
A project of EcoNet, ECIX aims to educate the environmental community and general public

about options to reduce the use of fossil fuels and their effects on climate.

```
ecixfiles@igc.org
ecixfiles@igc.org
```

Contact: Lelani Arris

```
<larris@igc.org>
```

✸ *HELPNET Network Emergency Response Planning*

For those interested in the roles global computer networks play in times of disasters. Send LISTSERV the commands INDEX HELPNET and INFO DATABASE for more information.

```
HELPNET@NDSUVM1.BITNET
LISTSERV@NDSUVM1.BITNET
```

Contact: Marty Hoag

```
NU021172@NDSUVM1.BITNET
```

✸ *Weather list.*

For discussions of weather-related phenomena.

```
WX-TALK@UIUCVMD.BITNET
LISTSERV@UIUCVMD
```

Fidonet

No services available.

Usenet

✸ *Major problems, accidents, and natural disasters. (Moderated)*

```
clari.news.disaster
```

✸ *Weather and temperature reports. (Moderated)*

```
clari.news.weather
```

✸ *Discussions of meteorology and related topics.*

```
sci.geo.meteorology
```

Online Libraries

After Dark

No services available.

Knowledge Index

No services available.

Orbit

No services available.

NewsNet

No services available.

Bulletin Boards
National Oceanographic and Atmospheric Administration (NOAA) BBS

Provided by the Space Environment Laboratory (SEL) of NOAA, monitors solar activity in collaboration with the U.S. Air Force. Provides advisories and forecasts; covers geomagnetic, ionospheric, atmospheric, and space environment effects.

Baud Rate: 300, 1200, 2400
BBS Number: (301) 770-0069

CD-ROM

✸ *Climatedata-Cen/East*
US WEST Optic

✸ *Climatedata NCDC 15 minute*
EarthInfo, Inc.
90 Madison Street, Suite 200
Denver, CO 80206

✸ *Climatedata-Precipitation*
US WEST.Optic

✸ *Climatedata-WestStat*
US WEST Optic

✸ *Gale Experiment Daty*
University of Washington
Department of Atmospheric Sciences
Seattle, WA 98195

✸ *Hydrodata*
EarthInfo, Inc.
90 Madison Street, Suite 200
Denver, CO 80206

✸ *Hydrodata II Climate*
EarthInfo, Inc.
90 Madison Street, Suite 200
Denver, CO 80206

✸ *Meteorological Grid*
University of Washington
Department of Atmospheric Sciences
Seattle, WA 98195

✸ *National Meterological Center*
University of Washington

🌐 *NCDC Hourly Precipitation*
EarthInfo, Inc.
90 Madison Street, Suite 200
Denver, CO 80206

🌐 *North American Observational Data*
University of Washington

🌐 *World WeatherDisc*
National Climatic Data Center

Military/ Weapons/ Peace Resources

Forums & Databases
America Online (AOL)

✎ *Military & Vets Club*
Keyword: Military
Path: Lifestyles & Interests Department >
Military & Vets Club
Offers discussion on military issues. Message
boards host discussion on everything from
veteran's benefits to military humor.

CompuServe (CIS)

✎ *Military and Veterans Forum*
Keyword: GO MILITARY
Offers discussion of military topics and includes
a section for veterans to inquire about benefits
and data library files on the MIA/POW issue,
military hardware, Atomic Vets, veterans
organizations, and member writings.

GEnie

✎ *Air Force Small Business RoundTable*
Keyword: AFSB3 or Page 1035
Offers information to small businesses about
doing business with the Air Force and the
Department of Defense.

✎ *Military RoundTable*
Keyword: MILITARY or Page 155
Offers discussion of military subjects by
members of the military, civilians working in
the defense industry, or other civilians.

The Well

✎ *Firearms, Military, Police & True Crime*
(g firearms)
Offers discussion on various subjects, including
police (pro and con), true crime books, military
technology and affairs, firearms (pro and con),
self-defense, sword fighting, knives, and more
.

✎ *Gulf War*
(g gulf)
Offers discussion on the Middle East crisis.

✎ *Veterans*
(g veterans)
Offers discussion of issues for veterans of all
wars.

Network Discussions Lists
Internet (Includes Bitnet & UUCPNet)

✎ *Activists for Peace, Empowerment, Human
Rights*
ACTIV-L@UMCVMB.BITNET
LISTSERV@UMCVMB.BITNET
Contact: Rich Winkel
<MATHRICH@UMCVMB.BITNET>

✎ *Amnesty International list.*
A monthly distribution of Amnesty Inter-
national's urgent action newsletters. Contains
stories on political prisoners.
AMNESTY@JHUVM.BITNET
LISTSERV@JHUVM.BITNET
Contact: Jeffrey James Carpenter
<jjc@UNIX.CIS.PITT.EDU>

⑨ *Arms and Disarmament*
Offers comments and questions on policy issues related to peace, war, national security, weapons, the arms race, and more.
```
ARMS-D@XX.LCS.MIT.EDU
ARMS-D-REQUEST@XX.LCS.MIT.EDU
```

⑨ *Arms Mailing list.*
```
ARMS-L@BUACCA.BITNET
LISTSERV@BUACCA.BITNET
```
Contact: Rob Gross
```
<GROSS@BCVMS.BITNET>
```

⑨ *Disarmament Discussion Monthly Digest*
A digest of selected mail discussions processed through DISARM-L. Also includes more substantial contributions written specially for the DISARM-D digest.
```
DISARM-D@ALBNYVM1.BITNET
LISTSERV@ALBNYVM1.BITNET
```
Contact: Donald F. Parsons
```
DFP10@ALBNYVM1.BITNET
```

⑨ *Disarmament Discussion list.*
Offers discussions and monthly digests of military and political strategy, technology, sociology, and popular peace activism involved in accelerating disarmament of military weapons.
```
DISARM-L@ALBNYVM1.BITNET
LISTSERV@ALBNYVM1.BITNET
```
Contact: Donald F. Parsons
```
DFP10@ALBNYVM1.BITNET
```

⑨ *Firearms Discussion list.*
```
FIREARMS@UTARLVM1.BITNET
LISTSERV@UTARLVM1.BITNET
```
Contact: Gordon Keegan
```
C145GMK@UTARLG
```

⑨ *Gun Control*
Offers announcements and discussion on coordination of firearms legislation, and about Second Amendment rights.
```
firearms-politics@TUT.CIS.OHIO-STATE.EDU
firearms-politics-request@TUT.CIS.OHIO-
STATE.EDU
```

⑨ *Guns and firearms used by sportsmen.*
Offers discussion for sportsmen on issues of concern such as hunting, firearms safety, the law, reloading tips, maintenance suggestions, target shooting, and more.
```
firearms@TUT.CIS.OHIO-STATE.EDU
firearms-request@TUT.CIS.OHIO-STATE.EDU
```

⑨ *News and Information Related to Firearms list.*
```
GUN-NEWS@PCCVM.BITNET
LISTSERV@PCCVM.BITNET
```

⑨ *Human rights*
Offers discussion on human rights.
```
HR-L@VMS.CIS.PITT.EDU
HR-L-REQUEST@VMS.CIS.PITT.EDU
```
Contact: Jeff Carpenter
```
<HR-L-REQUEST@VMS.CIS.PITT.EDU>
```

⑨ *Military technology*
Offers discussion of military technology and related matters.
```
military@ATT.ATT.COM
military-request@ATT.ATT.COM
```
Contact: Bill Thacker
```
<military@ATT.ATT.COM>
```

⑨ *Peace Corps Volunteers*
Offers discussion for current, returned, and potential volunteers on the "Peace Corps experience" and related subjects.
```
PCORPS-L@CMUVM.BITNET
LISTSERV@CMUVM.BITNET
```
Contact: Elliott Parker
```
<3ZLUFUR@CMUVM.BITNET>
```

⑨ *Peace studies list.*
```
PEACE@INDYCMS.BITNET
LISTSERV@INDYCMS.BITNET
```

⑨ *Supply Assistance Team (SAT)*
For the Mainz Army Depot and its SAT concerns.
```
sat@mainz-emh2.army.mil
sat-request@mainz-emh2.army.mil
```

⑨ *Vietnam War*
Offers communication among scholars, teachers, veterans, and anyone who is interested in the Vietnam War.
```
VWAR-L@UBVM.BITNET
LISTSERV@UBVM.BITNET
```
Contact: Lydia Fish
```
<FISHLM@SNYBUFVA.BITNET>
```

⑨ *World War II Discussion list.*
Offers discussion on World War II issues such as history, strategy, technology, personalities, political issues, general information, and trivia.
```
WWII-L@UBVM.BITNET
LISTSERV@UBVM.BITNET
```
Contact: Larry W. Jewell
```
<jewell@mace.cc.purdue.edu>
```

Fidonet

⑨ *Beyond War*
```
BEYOND_WAR
```
Offers a discussion of alternatives to war for resolving conflicts.
Moderator: Ken Peck
```
1:388/21
```
Distribution: BACKBONE

‍ *Civil War*
CIVIL_WAR
Offers discussion on the Civil War, its causes, and effects.
Moderator: Al Thorley
1:387/628.1
Distribution: ZONE-1 BACKBONE

‍ *Firearms*
FIREARMS
Offers discussion for shooters—from novice to expert—on topics ranging from hunting to self-defense.
Moderator: Bob Kohl
1:102/861
Distribution: BACKBONE, 10/8, 19/3 NET-102, NET-103, NET-105, NET-109, NET-129, NET-135, NET-137, NET-147, NET-151, NET-300, NET-372

‍ *In Country*
IN_COUNTRY
For veterans who have received a campaign ribbon denoting service combat.
Moderator: Lefty Frizzell
1:106/449
Distribution: NATIONAL BACKBONE
Gateways: ALTERNET VIA 106/449, ALAMONET VIA 36:1836/2000

‍ *Maritime Conference*
MARITIME
Offers discussion of topics on ships—military and commercial—and related topics.
Moderator: J.M. Peeler
1:3631/60
Distribution: NET 1:3631

‍ *Military Issues of All Kinds*
MILITARY_PEOPLE
Offers discussion on active duty, retirement, veterans, and disabled veterans. Open to all nations.
Moderator: Joan Renne
1:285/662
Distribution: INTERNATIONAL

‍ *RTKBA*
RTKBA
Offers discussion on the political aspects of firearms, firearms ownership, and Second Amendment rights.
Moderator: Bob Kohl
1:102/861
Distribution: BACKBONE, 10/8, 19/3 NET-102, NET-103, NET-105, NET-109, NET-129, NET-135, NET-137, NET-147, NET-151, NET-300, NET-372

‍ *USS Liberty (AGTR-5) Incident of June 8, 1967*
USS_LIBERTY
Offers discussion of the Israeli attack on the USS Liberty on June 8, 1967, and all related issues.
Moderator: Joe Meadors
1:160/230
Distribution: BACKBONE

‍ *Vietnam Vets*
VIETNAM_VETS
Offers discussion of international Vietnam veterans' issues.
Moderator: Joseph Peck
1:321/203
Distribution: BACKBONE, VETNET, ALTERNET, METROLINK, WORLDNET, AKANET, ETC.
Gateways: 1:8003/0 19:2/1 66:4400/203 11:555/0

Usenet

‍ *The war against Iraq in Kuwait.*
alt.desert-storm

‍ *For factual information on The Gulf War.*
alt.desert-storm.facts

‍ *What's happening to the Kurds in Iraq.*
alt.desert-thekurds

‍ *Not just collateral damage.*
alt.war

‍ *Lest we forget...*
alt.war.civil.usa

‍ *Disarmament Discussion list.*
bit.listserv.disarm-l

‍ *Clashes around the world. (Moderated)*
clari.news.fighting

‍ *The Gulf Crisis*
clari.news.hot.iraq

‍ *Panama and General Noriega. (Moderated)*
clari.news.hot.panama

‍ *Conflict between groups around the world. (Moderated)*
clari.news.issues.conflict

‍ *Military equipment, people & issues. (Moderated)*
clari.news.military

‍ *Defense industry issues. (Moderated)*
clari.tw.defense

🖙 *Discussion about science & the military.
(Moderated)*
`sci.military`

🖙 *Social issues relating to military veterans.*
`soc.veterans`

Online Libraries
After Dark
No services available.

Knowledge Index
No services available.

Orbit
No services available.

NewsNet

🖙 *Defense (DE)*
Offers an intimate look at current requests for proposals (RFPs), contract awards, subcontracting and "teaming" opportunities, and significant developments in defense programs and technology.
Earliest NewsNet Issue: 9/1/86-10/8/90

🖙 *Defense/Aerospace Business Digest*
Covers every area of Defense Department activity that is important to business, including news from the Pentagon and Capitol Hill.
Frequency: Archive file only; not currently updated
Earliest NewsNet Issue: 8/1/83-6/26/91

🖙 *Defense & Aerospace Electronics*
Monitors opportunities available for command, control, communications, intelligence contracts, and research in the defense industry.
Frequency: Biweekly
Earliest NewsNet Issue: 3/23/87

🖙 *Defense Daily*
Provides extensive coverage of all major U.S. and international defense and space programs—from concept to implementation.
Frequency: Daily
Earliest NewsNet Issue: 8/13/86

🖙 *Defense Marketing International*
Covers the world of international defense. Reports on international marketing opportunities, defense and aerospace marketing

trends, and defense budgeting by individual nations.
Frequency: Biweekly
Earliest NewsNet Issue: 6/12/89

🖙 *Defense R&D Update*
Helps companies identify and track the emerging research and development programs in aeronautics and electronic systems.
Issues Available: 9/1/83 to 10/1/87

🖙 *Defense Technology Business*
Explores new trends and developments within the defense and space industries and how companies are using advanced technology to remain competitive as defense spending drops.
Frequency: Biweekly
Earliest NewsNet Issue: 12/5/89

🖙 *Defense Week*
Covers defense policy, military budget news, weapons research and development, acquisition issues, space-based defense, and the international defense marketplace.
Frequency: Weekly
Earliest NewsNet Issue: 4/10/89

🖙 *The Evans & Novak Defense Letter*
Provides expert political analysis of the global defense situation. Reports on decisions at the Pentagon and on Capitol Hill and on the political and fiscal aspects of defense policy.
Frequency: Biweekly
Earliest NewsNet Issue: 3/12/91

🖙 *For Your Eyes Only*
A comprehensive summary of military affairs, including battlefield reports, arms sales, weapons tests, space programs, SDI, tactics, technology, espionage, and terrorism.
Frequency: Biweekly
Earliest NewsNet Issue: 10/26/87

🖙 *GPS Report*
Provides in-depth news and analysis on military and commercial applications of the global positioning system.
Frequency: Biweekly
Earliest NewsNet Issue: 11/1/91

🖙 *Military & Commercial Fiber Business*
Focuses on the development and use of fiber optic cables in defense projects and federal government agency programs, and commercial businesses that supply fiber for government programs.
Frequency: Biweekly
Earliest NewsNet Issue: 8/8/86

✎ Military Robotics
Discusses government and defense applications of robotics, including remotely piloted aircraft, unmanned submarines, teleoperated and autonomous combat vehicles and weapons, and more.
Frequency: Biweekly
Earliest NewsNet Issue: 11/15/87

✎ Military Robotics Sourcebook 1991-92
An abstract of unmanned vehicles and systems for the U.S. military and government market.
Frequency: Annually

✎ Military Space
A comprehensive source for the latest developments in space-based programs, policy, and technology.
Frequency: Biweekly
Earliest NewsNet Issue: 9/1/86

✎ Navy News & Undersea Technology
Reports on contracts, congressional debates, emerging technology, and Department of Defense funding that enables companies to gain an edge in the competition for contracts.
Frequency: Weekly
Earliest NewsNet Issue: 8/28/89

✎ PAC-Rim Defense Marketing
Provides news of business opportunities in the rapidly expanding Pacific Rim defense marketplace.
Earliest NewsNet Issue: 7/23/90 to 6/10/91

✎ Periscope—Daily Defense News Capsules
Abstracts compiled from hundreds of news sources from around the world.
Frequency: Daily
Earliest NewsNet Issue: 4/2/90

✎ SDI Intelligence Report
A comprehensive report on Strategic Defense Initiative (SDI) contract solicitations and awards, technological developments, and appropriations.
Frequency: Biweekly
Earliest NewsNet Issue: 1/7/86

✎ SDI Monitor
Offers quick, accurate, and comprehensive review of contract and research opportunities in the Strategic Defense Initiative (SDI).
Frequency: Biweekly
Earliest NewsNet Issue: 9/8/86

✎ Soviet Aerospace & Technology
Reports on new Soviet programs and weapons systems, space launches, technology, treaty violations, and much more.
Frequency: Biweekly
Earliest NewsNet Issue: 10/6/86

✎ Strategic Defense
Reports on developments in Strategic Defense Initiative (SDI) applications, including surveillance, acquisitions, military weapons in space, and much more.
Issues Available: 4/23/87 to 10/6/89

Bulletin Boards
ADA Technical Support Bulletin Board System
Contains technical support for the ADA programming language. Operated by the Naval Computer and Telecommunications Area Master Telecommunications Command.
Availability: 24 hours
Baud Rate: 300, 1200, 2400, 9600,16.8
BBS Number: (804) 444-7841
Sysop: Dave Parker
Help Line: (804) 444-4680

Bumpers Access
Provides communication between the Chief of Naval Personnel and the U.S. Naval fleet.
Baud Rate: 300, 1200, 2400, 9600
BBS Number: (703) 614-8059
Help Line: (703) 624-8083

Defense Communications Agency Acquisition Bulletin Board System (DCAABBS)
Provides information from Defense Commercial Communications Office Communications Center (DECCO) to the telecommunications industry
Availability: 24 hours/7 days
Baud Rate: 300, 1200, 2400, 9600
BBS Number: (618) 256-8200
BBS Software: WILDCAT
Sysop: Mitch Cooley
Help Line: (618) 256-9380

Defense Technology Security Administration Export License Status Advisor (DTSA-ELISA1) BBS

For export license applicants and other export information.
Baud Rate: 300, 1200, 2400
BBS Number: (703) 697-6109
BBS Software: RBBS-PC
Sysop: Ron Ramos
Help Line: (703) 693-1098, Fax (703) 693-5305

DODIGNET

Provides job vacancy announcement information for the Office of the Inspector General, Department of Defense. Offers users information on the latest job opportunities.
Baud Rate: 300, 1200, 2400, 9600
BBS Software: RBBS-PC
Sysop: Karen Lewi or Amy Jacobs

Judge Advocate General's Information Network (JAGNET) BBS

Enables Naval Legal Service Command center and Staff Judge Advocate offices to pass along questions, suggestions, and other information about their experiences with Judge Advocate General's Management Information System (JAGMIS).
Availability: 24 hours
Baud Rate: 300, 1200, 2400
BBS Number: (703) 325-0748
BBS Software: PCBoard
Sysop: Ron Stokes
Help Line: (703) 325-2924

MetroNet BBS

For employees of Morale, Welfare, and Recreation (MWR) of the U.S. Army Military District of Washington (MDW). Provides users access to a local and wide area electronic message system.
Availability: 24 hours
Baud Rate: 300, 1200, 2400
BBS Number: (202) 475-2517
BBS Software: PCBoard
Help Line: (202) 475-2513, FAX: 475-2751

Naval Computer and Telecommunications Station (NCTS) BBS

Operated by the NCTS, Washington, D. C. to provide marketing information and a forum for technical support for its clients.
Baud Rate: 300, 1200, 2400, 9600
BBS Number: (202) 475-7885
BBS Software: PCBoard
Sysop: James Svendsen and Allen Ford
Help Line: (202) 475-7685

NAVCOMTELSTA WASHINGTON (N9121) Bulletin Board

Contains lots of information on Milnet, DOD software, contracts, and conferences.
Baud Rate: 300, 1200, 2400
BBS Number: (301) 238-2131
BBS Software: RBBS-PC
Sysop: Art Lyndon
Help Line: (301) 238-2181

Navy Alcohol and Drug Abuse Prevention and Control (NADAP) BBS

Offers discussion on drug and alcohol abuse issues and is operated by the Alcohol Abuse Prevention and Control Division of the Naval Military Personnel Command.
Availability: 24 hours/7 days
Baud Rate: 300, 1200, 2400, 9600
BBS Number: (703) 693-3831
BBS Software: WILDCAT
Sysop: NADAP

Online Automated System (OASYS)

For active military personnel, civil service employees, and civilians who are calling on official government business.
Baud Rate: 300, 1200, 2400, 9600, 38,400 bps
BBS Number: (804) 445-1121
Sysop: Bill Hay
Help Line: (804) 444-8487

PPCUG/RDAMIS BBS

A large general purpose board with many conferences on science and technology, military, DOD, and general computers.
Baud Rate: 300, 1200, 2400 9600-14400
BBS Number: (703) 614-4114
BBS Software: WILDCAT
Sysop: John Forbes

CD-ROM

⌕ *Aerospace*
Dialog Information Services

⌕ *Aircraft Encyclopedia*
Quanta Press

⌕ *Officers Bookcase*
Quanta Press

⌕ *USA Wars: Civil War*
Quanta Press

⌕ *USA Wars: Korea*
Quanta Press

⌕ *USA Wars: Vietnam*
Quanta Press

Music/Dance Resources

Forums & Databases
America Online (AOL)

✪ *Bose Express Music*
Path: Travel & Shopping Department > Bose Express Music
Enables user to order the Bose Express Music Catalog and then place on-line orders for records, tapes, and CDs.

✪ *Grateful Dead Forum*
Keyword: Grateful Dead
Path: Entertainment > Grateful Dead Forum
Message board provides a medium for exchange of Dead trivia and concert memories. In the forum software library, you can download graphic files of Jerry, Jerry with the guys, the Skull and Roses image, Bob Weir's guitar, and more.

✪ *Music and Sound Forum*
Path: Computing & Software Department > Music & Sound
Keywords: Mac music, PC music
File libraries contain sound clips and utilities under such categories as Amiga Music, Digitized Sounds, Programs and Utilities, Tandy Music, Movie Themes and Clips, MIDI/Music Technology, and Commercial Demos. The Mac forum features a special interest group for music programmers.

✪ *RockLink*
Keyword: RockLink
Path: Entertainment Department > RockLink
Supplies rock music industry news and gossip,

as well as message board exchange on various rock music genres. Regular on-line conferences feature performers and writers from all over America. Concert dates, reviews, and charts are updated regularly.

CompuServe (CIS)

✪ *RockNet*
GO ROCK
Provides current news and information on the world of rock. It contains The RockNet Forum (GO ROCKNET), rock news, a list of top albums and tapes, and articles.

✪ *RockNet (Rock Music) Forum*
GO ROCKNET
This forum has many members within the record industry; users may learn news items before they appear in newspapers.

GEnie

✪ *MIDI RoundTable*
Keyword: MIDI or Page 430
Deals with MIDI—computer-based music systems. Supports all computers.

✪ *The Music RoundTable*
Keyword: MUSIC or Page 135
Information about the latest music releases on LP, cassette, CD, and video. Trade music news, information, and opinions, and keep up with the latest concerts. Download and read the Online Digital Music Review (ODMR), containing reviews of new releases on CD in all musical categories.

The Well

ॐ *Audio*
(g aud)
For neophytes and techies, music and video lovers and equipment mavens.

ॐ *Band (Private Conference)*
(g band)
A private forum for semi-pro (and professional) musicians to talk the business.

ॐ *Beatles*
(g beat)
Discussions for all Beatlemaniacs.

ॐ *Audio-Image (CDs)*
(g cd)
Reviews of digital audio software and discussions of compact disc technology and sound recordings.

ॐ *Deadlit*
(g deadlit)
Coordinates scholarly discussions of the Grateful Dead.

ॐ *Deadplan (Private Conference)*
(g deadplan)
Used from time to time to discuss sensitive Grateful Dead-related matters out of view of the general public.

ॐ *Digital Domain*
(g dig)
Discusses digital technical matters, digital equipment reviews, digital purveyors of information, and digital tape recording.

ॐ *Grateful Dead Feedback*
(g feedback)
Posts comments and requests to various organizations and publications of interest to Deadheads.

ॐ *Grateful Dead*
(g gd)
For announcements, general discussions, and lots of playful topics on the Dead.

ॐ *Grateful Dead Hour*
(g gdh)
Enables Deadheads to conspire to get the program on the air in new cities and collect comments on the show itself.

ॐ *Grateful Dead Rumors (Private conference)*
(g grapevine)
Fans discuss rumors of the Dead, upcoming shows, new tune breakouts, who's leaving the band this week, and the like.

ॐ *Jazz*
(g jazz)
Discussions of the many different styles, sounds, and musical visions of jazz.

ॐ *MIDI*
(g midi)
Discusses issues pertaining to making music with the aid of electronics or computers.

ॐ *Music*
(g music)
For general discussions of music.

ॐ *Onstage!*
(g onstage)
For musicians, dancers, actors, or other performers.

ॐ *Grateful Dead Audio*
(g tapes)
For tape collectors to arrange trades, ask technical questions, and the like.

ॐ *Grateful Dead Tickets*
(g tix)
Information on new shows, ticket trades, and more.

ॐ *Grateful Dead Tours and Trips*
(g tours)
Fans talk about tours and shows before they happen, post set lists and reviews as tours occur, and compare notes.

Network Discussions Lists Internet (Includes Bitnet & UUCPNet)

ॐ *4AD Recording Artists list.*
A repository for 4AD information, as well as a forum for discussing 4AD artists/groups.
4AD-L@JHUVM.BITNET
LISTSERV@JHUVM.BITNET
Contact: Jim Jones
L64A0110@JHUVM.BITNET

ॐ *Music and Recordings of the Pre-LP Era list.*
For collectors and lovers of all kinds of music of this era, such as early jazz and blues, big bands, show music, vaudeville, classical, and so on, as well as spoken word and other historical recordings.
78-L@CORNELL.EDU
LISTSERV@CORNELL.EDU
Contact: Doug Elliot
<de3@cornellc.cit.cornell.edu>

❧ *Association for Chinese Music Research Network list.*
ACMR-L@UHCCVM.BITNET
LISTSERV@UHCCVM.BITNET

❧ *Severed Heads Music.*
Discusses the music of the Severed Heads and of bands on the Ralph label.
adolph-a-carrot@ANDREW.CMU.EDU
adolph-a-carrot-request@andrew.cmu.edu
Contact: Yary Richard Phillip Hluchan
<yh0a+@ANDREW.CMU.EDU>

❧ *Alice Cooper Fans list.*
Discussions among fans of Alice Cooper.
ALICEFAN@WKUVX1.BITNET
LISTSERV@WKUVX1.BITNET
Contact: Hunter Goatley
<goathunter@WKUVX1.BITNET>

❧ *Music discussion list.*
Talk about all forms of music.
ALLMUSIC@AUVM.BITNET
LISTSERV@AUVM.BITNET
Contact: Mike Karolchik
U6183@<WVNVM.BITNET>

❧ *ALLMUSIC Digest list.*
AMUSIC-D@AUVM.BITNET
LISTSERV@AUVM.BITNET

❧ *The Art of Noise discussion list.*
Discussions about the music group The Art of Noise.
aon@POLYSLO.CALPOLY.EDU
aon-request@POLYSLO.CALPOLY.EDU
Contact: Cliff Tuel
<ctuel@POLYSLO.CALPOLY.EDU>

❧ *Allan Holdsworth Discussion Digest*
Offers discussions and information on the works of guitarist Allan Holdsworth.
ATAVACHRON@MOREKYPR.MOREHEAD-ST.EDU
PRESTON@MOREKYPR.MOREHEAD-ST.ED
Contact: Jeff Preston
<preston@morekypr.MOREHEAD-ST.EDU>

❧ *Audio discussion list.*
AUDIO-L@VMTECMEX.BITNET
LISTSERV@VMTECMEX.BITNET

❧ *Ballroom and Swing Dancing discussion list.*
ballroom@athena.mit.edu
ballroom-request@athena.mit.edu

❧ *Bluegrass Music discussion list.*
Discussion of issues related to the International Bluegrass Music Association (IBMA) and bluegrass music in general.
BGRASS-L@UKCC.BITNET
LISTSERV@UKCC.BITNET
Contact: Frank Godbey
<UKA016@UKCC.BITNET>

❧ *Performing Musicians*
Discussions intended mainly for musicians performing in small brass ensembles, but with other interested parties welcome.
BRASS@geomag.gly.fsu.EDU
BRASS-REQUEST@geomag.gly.fsu.EDU
Contact: Ted Zateslo
<zateslo@geomag.glyFSU.EDU>

❧ *Bruce Springsteen list.*
For fans of the music of Bruce Springsteen.
BSTREETS@VIRGINIA.BITNET
Backstreets-Request@VIRGINIA.EDU
Contact: Marc Rouleau
<mer6g@VIRGINIA.EDU>

❧ *Debbie Gibson list.*
For Debbie Gibson fans.
BtL@bullwinkle.ucdavis.edu
ez000018@bullwinkle.ucdavis.edu

❧ *Classical Music list.*
Discusses classical music of all kinds and periods.
CLASSM-L@BROWNVM.BROWN.EDU
LISTSERV@BROWNVM.BROWN.EDU
Contact: Catherine "Pumpkin" Yang
<CYANG@BROWNVM.BROWN.EDU>

❧ *Folkdance and Traditional Dance list.*
DANCE-L@HEARN.BITNET
LISTSERV@HEARN.BITNET

❧ *Grateful Dead Music list.*
A digest for fans of Grateful Dead music. Bidirectionally gatewayed with the USENET newsgroup rec.music.gdead.
DEAD-FLAMES@VIRGINIA.EDU
Dead-Flames-Request@VIRGINIA.EDU
Contact: Marc Rouleau
<mer6g@VIRGINIA.EDU>

❧ *DJ-L - Campus Radio Disk Jockeys*
For discussions of interest to campus radio station disk jockeys.
DJ-L@NDSUVM1.BITNET
LISTSERV@NDSUVM1.BITNET
Contact: Andrew Tabar
ARTABAR@MTUS5.BITNET

❧ *Pink Floyd list.*
eclipse@reef.cis.ufl.edu
eclipse-request@reef.cis.ufl.edu

❧ *Electronic Music discussion list.*
EMUSIC-L@AUVM.BITNET
LISTSERV@AUVM.BITNET
Contact: Joe McMahon
XRJDM@VPFVM.BITNET

❧ *EthnoFORUM—Global Ethnomusicology list.*
ETHMUS-L@UMDD.BITNET
LISTSERV@UMDD.BITNET

⑤ *Folk Music list.*
Discusses music of the recent wave of American singer/songwriters like Shawn Colvin, Mary Chapin Carpenter, David Wilcox, Nanci Griffith, Darden Smith, Maura O'Connell, Don Henry, and others.

```
Folk_Music@nysernet.org
sub_folk@nysernet.org
```
Contact: Alan Rowoth
```
<alanr@nysernet.org>
```

⑤ *GEAC Music Users list.*
```
GEACMUS@RUTVM1.BITNET
LISTSERV@RUTVM1.BITNET
```

⑤ *Grunge Rock discussion list.*
Discusses any and all topics related to the form of music known as grunge rock, not just Seattle or Sub Pop.
```
GRUNGE-L@UBVM.BITNET
LISTSERV@UBVM.BITNET
```
Contact: Jon Hilgreen
```
hilgreen@acsu.buffalo.edu
```

⑤ *Harmonica Playing list.*
For discussion of all forms and styles of harmonica playing and theory.
```
HARP-L@WKUVX1.BITNET
LISTSERV@WKUVX1.BITNET
```
Contact: Chris Pierce
```
<pierccm@WKUVX1.BITNET>
```

⑤ *Mike Oldfield list.*
For devotees of Mike Oldfield and his music.
```
hart@vtcc1.cc.vt.edu
hart@vtcc1.cc.vt.edu
```

⑤ *IMUG-L—Innopac Music Users Group list.*
```
IMUG-L@OHSTVMA.BITNET
LISTSERV@OHSTVMA.BITNET
```

⑤ *Compact Disc list.*
For the exchange of subjective comments about the CD audio medium and related hardware.
```
INFOCD@CISCO.NOSC.MIL
CDREQUEST@CISCO.NOSC.MIL
```
Contact: Michael Pawka
```
<MIKE@CISCO.NOSC.MIL>
```

⑤ *Unmoderated Music of Jamie Notarthomas list.*
For discussions of Jamie Notarthomas, an up-and-coming acoustic guitarist/singer/songwriter.
```
JAMIE-L@CORNELL.BITNET
LISTSERV@CORNELL.BITNET
```
Contact: Jeffrey Anbinder
```
<bory@cornella.cit.cornell.edu>
```

⑤ *Jane's Addiction list.*
Discusses anything relating to the musical group Jane's Addiction.
```
janes-addiction@ms.uky.edu
janes-addiction-request@ms.uky.edu
```
Contact: Joel Abbott
```
<abbott@ms.uky.edu>
```

⑤ *Jazz Lovers' list.*
```
JAZZ-L@TEMPLEVM.BITNET
LISTSERV@TEMPLEVM.BITNET
```

⑤ *Sinead O'Connor list.*
For discussion of the music and recordings of Sinead O'Connor, and related matters such as lyrics and tour information.
```
jump-in-the-river@PRESTO.IG.COM
jump-in-the-river-request@PRESTO.IG.COM
```
Contact: Michael C. Berch
```
<mcb@PRESTO.IG.COM>
```

⑤ *KISS Fan discussion list.*
```
KISSARMY@WKUVX1.BITNET
LISTSERV@WKUVX1.BITNET
```
Contact: Hunter Goatley
```
<goathunter@WKUVX1.BITNET>
```

⑤ *Clarinet Player's Network*
News, information, research, and items of interest, plus other information concerning clarinet players, teachers, students, and enthusiasts.
```
KLARINET@VCCSCENT.BITNET
LISTSERV@VCCSCENT.BITNET
```
Contact: Jim Fay
```
<NVFAYXJ@VCCSCENT.BITNET>
```

⑤ *Latin American Music discussion list.*
```
LATAMMUS@ASUACAD.BITNET
LISTSERV@ASUACAD.BITNET
```

⑤ *Kate Bush list.*
For discussion of Kate Bush's music (and any other artistic music or anything else for that matter).
```
Love-Hounds@EDDIE.MIT.EDU
Love-Hounds-Request@EDDIE.MIT.EDU
```
Contact: Doug Alan
```
<nessus@EDDIE.MIT.EDU>
```

⑤ *U2 list.*
```
METZ@JHUVMS.BITNET
metz@jhuvms.hcf.jhu.edu
```

⑤ *MUSIC/SP discussion list.*
```
MUG@MARIST.BITNET
LISTSERV@MARIST.BITNET
```
Contact: A. Harry Williams
```
HARRY@MARIST.BITNET
```

⑤ *Music Education list.*
```
MUSIC-ED@UMINN1.BITNET
LISTSERV@UMINN1.BITNET
```

⑤ *MUSIC/SP User discussion list.*
```
MUSIC-L@MARIST.BITNET
LISTSERV@MARIST.BITNET
```

⑤ *Computers in Music Research list.*
Brings together musicologists, music analysts, computer scientists, and others working on applications of computers in music research.
```
music-
research%prg.oxford.ac.uk@NSS.CS.UCL.AC.UK
music-research-request@prg.oxford.ac.uk
```

⑤ *Music-Research Redistribution list.*
```
MUSIC@FINHUTC.BITNET
LISTSERV@FINHUTC.BITNET
```

⑤ *NACO Music Project list.*
```
NMP-L@IUBVM.BITNET
LISTSERV@IUBVM.BITNET
```

⑤ *Opera Lovers list.*
```
OPERA-L@BRFAPESP.BITNET
MAILSERV@BRFAPESP.BITNET
```

⑤ *Music discussion list.*
```
RMUSIC-L@GITVM1.BITNET
LISTSERV@GITVM1.BITNET
```

⑤ *Sun Ra list.*
For discussion of Sun Ra's music, albums, videos, poetry, and philosophy.
```
SATURN@HEARN.BITNET
LISTSERV@HEARN.BITNET
```
Contact: Tom Buck
```
<TBuck@KNOX.BITNET>
```

⑤ *Brothers of Phi Mu Alpha Sinfonia (Professional Fraternity in Music).*
```
SINFONIA@ASUACAD.BITNET
LISTSERV@ASUACAD.BITNET
```

⑤ *Siouxsie and The Banshees list.*
Discussion of Siouxsie and The Banshees and its offshoots.
```
Siouxsie@tjhsst.vak12ed.edu
Siouxsie-request@tjhsst.vak12ed.edu
```

⑤ *Roy Harper list.*
```
stormcock@cs.qmw.ac.uk
stormcock-request@cs.qmw.ac.uk
```

⑤ *Redistribution of rec.music.synth list.*
```
SYNTH-L@AUVM.BITNET
LISTSERV@AUVM.BITNET
```

⑤ *Tangerine Dream Discussion list.*
Discusses the music of electronic group Tangerine Dream and related artists.
```
tadream@vacs.uwp.wisc.edu
tadream-request@vacs.uwp.wisc.edu
```

⑤ *Tuba Players Mailing list.*
```
TUBA-L@VTVM2.BITNET
LISTSERV@VTVM2.BITNET
```

⑤ *Rolling Stones discussion list.*
```
UNDERCOVER@SNOWHITE.CIS.UOGUELPH.CA
undercover-request@snowhite.cis.uoguelph.ca
```
Contact: Steve Portigal
```
<stevep@snowhite.cis.uoguelph.ca>
```

⑤ *Update-Electronic-Music-News list.*
For "underground" music—independent and major label artists and companies. Contains record reviews, interviews, perspectives, and a host of other topics.
```
UPNEWS@MARIST.BITNET
LISTSERV@MARIST.BITNET
```
Contact: Christopher DeRobertis
```
<UICD@MARIST.BITNET>
```

⑤ *Urusei Yatsura list.*
For Urusei Yatsura fans.
```
URUSEI-YATSURA@PANDA.COM
URUSEI-YATSURA-REQUEST@PANDA.COM
```
Contact: Mark Crispin
```
<MRC@PANDA.COM>
```

⑤ *Early Music list.*
For anything about early music (medieval, renaissance and the like), including comments/ questions about new records, books, performances, song texts and translations, and encoding early music scores in electronic form.
```
VW5EARN@AWIWUW11.BITNET
VW5EARN@AWIWUW11.BITNET
```
Contact: Gerhard Gonter
```
<GONTER@AWIWUW11.BITNET>
```

Fidonet

⑤ *Amiga Music/Sound Topics*
```
AMIGA_MUSIC
```
For Commodore Amiga owners using their computers for music, composing, sampling, and so on.
Moderator: Nathan Barber
```
1:366/3
```
Distribution: BACKBONE

⑤ *Grateful Dead Topics*
```
DEADHEAD
```
For fans of the Grateful Dead. Features concert reviews, schedules, rumor control, and chit-chat.
Moderator: Kay Akagi
```
1:105/642
```
Distribution: BACKBONE

꙳ *Guitar Topics*
GUITAR

For guitar players, builders, and techs. Includes playing styles and techniques, building and modifying guitars and guitar-related devices, accessories, amplifiers, more.
Moderator: Tom Rieger
1:260/242
Distribution: ZONE-1 BACKBONE

꙳ *Central Indiana Musician's Conference*
IMUSICIAN

Devoted to the music industry in central Indiana.
Moderator: Richard Holler
1:231/290
Distribution: NET-231

꙳ *Jazz*
JAZZ

Discussions pertaining to jazz, including jazz styles, artists, recording labels, and other related subjects.
Moderator: James Downie
1:153/733.2
Distribution: INDEPENDENT FEED ARRANGEMENTS

꙳ *K12net Performing Arts Education Conference*
K12_MUSIC_ED

For discussions relating to elementary and secondary performing arts education. Not available singly; see K12.SYSOP for details.
Moderator: Jack Crawford
1:260/620

꙳ *Kate Bush Appreciation*
KATEBUSH

For devotees of Kate Bush, a musician quite popular in Europe.
Moderator: Richard Bollar
1:133/110
Distribution: ZONE 1, CHATEAUNET

꙳ *MIDI Software Programmer Conference*
MIDI-PROGRAMMING
Moderator: Rick Ashworth
1:108/90.96
Distribution: INTERNATIONAL

꙳ *Music*
MUSIC

For anything related to music.
Moderator: David Bloomberg
1:233/12
Distribution: BACKBONE, INTERNATIONAL

꙳ *Music Composition Conference*
MUSIC_COMP_101

For composers/arrangers/theorists.
Moderator: Rick Ashworth
1:108/90
Distribution: INTERNATIONAL

꙳ *Musician's Classified Conference*
MUSICIAN'S_SERVICES

A musician's for sale/help wanted area.
Moderator: Rick Ashworth
1:108/90.96
Distribution: INTERNATIONAL

꙳ *Music-Syn*
MUSICSYN

For synthesizer-related topics.
Moderator: Richard Holler
1:231/290
Distribution: BACKBONE

꙳ *Discussions on any kind of music.*
SHARPS&FLATS
Moderator: Tina Braun
50:5011/1
Distribution: ECHONET BACKBONE (ZONE 50)

꙳ *Saint Elvis Echo*
ST_ELVIS

For fans of Elvis.
Moderator: Alan Jennings
1:3800/6

꙳ *Studio and Live Music Performance Conference*
STUDIO_101

For performing musicians, studio and live.
Moderator: Rick Ashworth
1:108/90.96
Distribution: INTERNATIONAL

꙳ *Frank Zappa Forum*
ZAPPA

Discusses the life and works of Frank Zappa.
Moderator: Tom Rieger
1:260/242
Distribution: PRIVATE VIA 1:260/242

Usenet

꙳ *For bass guitarists, not fish.*
alt.bass

꙳ *Marching bands and the like.*
alt.colorguard

꙳ *Drum and bugle corps discussion.*
alt.drumcorps

- Ethnic, exotic, electronic, elaborate, etc. music.
  alt.emusic

- Is that a Sears poncho?
  alt.fan.frank-zappa

- Classical music composer.
  alt.fan.shostakovich

- Guitar enthusiasts.
  alt.guitar

- For groups having 2 or less Platinum-selling albums.
  alt.music.alternative

- Gaelic set to spacey music.
  alt.music.enya

- For Rushheads.
  alt.music.rush

- Don't stand so close.
  alt.music.the.police

- For fans of rap music.
  alt.rap

- Fans of the Grateful Dead and rap.
  alt.rap-gdead

- Techno-culture: music, dancing, drugs, dancing...
  alt.rave

- Counterpart to alt.sex and alt.drugs.
  alt.rock-n-roll

- For the headbangers on the net.
  alt.rock-n-roll.metal

- Non-sissyboy metal bands.
  alt.rock-n-roll.metal.heavy

- Discussions on all forms of music.
  bit.listserv.allmusic

- Electronic music discussions.
  bit.listserv.emusic-l

- Reviews and issues concerning music and musicians. Moderated.
  clari.news.music

- Any aspects of dance not covered in another newsgroup.
  rec.arts.dance

- Folk dances, dancers, and dancing.
  rec.folk-dancing

- Music with afro-latin influences.
  rec.music.afro-latin

- Postings about the Fab Four and their music.
  rec.music.beatles

- Discussion of jazz, blues, and related types of music.
  rec.music.bluenote

- CDs—availability and other discussions.
  rec.music.cd

- Christian music, contemporary and traditional.
  rec.music.christian

- Discussion about classical music.
  rec.music.classical

- Country and western music, performers, performances, and so on.
  rec.music.country.western

- Discussion of comedy and novelty music.
  rec.music.dementia

- Discussion of Bob's works and music.
  rec.music.dylan

- Discussion of pre-classical European music.
  rec.music.early

- Folks discussing folk music.
  rec.music.folk

- Funk, rap, hip-hop, house, soul, r&b and related.
  rec.music.funky

- Discussion of Kate Bush and other alternative music. Moderated.
  rec.music.gaffa

- A group for (Grateful) Dead-heads.
  rec.music.gdead

- Hindustani and Carnatic Indian classical music.
  rec.music.indian.classical

- Discussing Indian music in general.
  rec.music.indian.misc

- Discussion of all industrial music styles.
  rec.music.industrial

- News and announcements on musical topics. Moderated.
  rec.music.info

- For performers and their discussions.
  rec.music.makers

- Records, tapes, and CDs: wanted, for sale, and so on.
  rec.music.marketplace

- *Music lovers' group.*
  rec.music.misc

- *New Age music discussions.*
  rec.music.newage

- *Discussing the musical group Phish.*
  rec.music.phish

- *Reviews of music of all genres and mediums. Moderated.*
  rec.music.reviews

- *Synthesizers and computer music.*
  rec.music.synth

- *Discussion of music videos and music video software.*
  rec.music.video

Online Libraries
After Dark
No services available.

Knowledge Index
No services available.

Orbit
No services available.

NewsNet
No services available.

Bulletin Boards
Washington MIDI Users' Group BBS
Dedicated to users of equipment employing the MIDI (Musical Instrument Digital Interface) protocol, electronic musicians, and people into sound and recording technology. Exchange questions, answers, information, tips, tricks, experiences, and public-domain voice patches and programs with other people in the MIDI community.
Baud Rate: 300, 1200, 2400
BBS Number: (703) 532-7860
BBS Software: PCBoard
Sysop: Mike Rivers

CD-ROM

- *Music Cataloging Collection*
OCLC

News/Current Events Resources

Forums & Databases

America Online (AOL)

News Search
Keyword: News search
Path: News & Finance Department > Search News Stories
Enables users to easily search for the day's top news stories by typing in key words or phrases that describe topics of interest to them.

USA Today
Keyword: USA Today
Path: News & Finance Department > USA Today
Covers the day's top stories from the familiar USA Today categories of news, money, sports, and life.

Mike Keefe Editorial Cartoons
Keyword: Keefe
Path: News & Finance Department > Mike Keefe Editorial Cartoons
Offers downloadable editorial cartoons from award-winning Denver Post cartoonist Mike Keefe. New cartoons are posted on America Online 3 times a week.

Newsbytes
Keyword: Newsbytes
Path: News & Finance Department > Newsbytes
Newsbytes News Network is the largest independent computer industry news service in the world, published continuously since May 1983. Newsbytes is available on other online services; no surcharges or citation fees are charged on America Online.

Express Yourself
Keyword: Express Yourself
Path: News & Finance Department > Express Yourself
Enables members to debate the top news, social, and political issues on this very active message board.

The New Republic
Keyword: New Republic
Path: News & Finance Department > New Republic
The nation's oldest magazine of political opinion, public policy, and the arts. Founded in 1914, the New Republic is prepared for the future of publishing with its online version on America Online.

CompuServe (CIS)

AIDS News Clips
`GO AIDSNEWS`
Enables members to review the latest full text news reports about AIDS including international news and reports and the most recent AIDS research results.

Apple News Clips
`GO APPLENEWS`
Enables members to review the latest full-text articles and reports about Apple Corporation and Apple products from AP, UPI, Reuters and other news wires.

AP Online
`GO APO`
Gives the latest news from Associated Press.

⑤ *Associated Press Sports Wire*
   GO APSPORTS
Gives the latest scores, news, and league leaders in football, baseball, basketball, soccer, hockey, tennis, and golf as well as information on college sports, Olympic competitions, and other sports.

⑤ *The Business Wire*
   GO TBW
Offers press releases, news articles and other information from the world of business. Updated continuously throughout the day.

⑤ *Executive News Service*
   GO ENS
Enables members to keep informed of news affecting their business and personal interests with the Executive News Service.

⑤ *Issues Forum*
   GO ISSUESFORUM
For the free exchange of ideas about current issues and names in the news.

⑤ *NewsGrid*
   GO NEWSGRID
A comprehensive news service compiled from several global news wire services.

⑤ *Newspaper Library*
   GO NEWSLIB
Offers full-text articles from more than 50 newspapers from across the United States (classified ads not included). There is a two-day delay in making today's articles available.

⑤ *Outdoors News Clips*
   GO OUTNEWS
Enables members to review the latest full-text news reports on issues concerning the environment and outdoors activities including hunting and fishing. News items are extracted from major news sources such as AP and UPI.

⑤ *UK News Clips*
   GO UKNEWS
Offers full-text stories on the United Kingdom from the Reuters World news wire. Stories are held within this clipping file for 24 hours.

⑤ *UK Newspaper Library*
   GO UKPAPERS
Contains articles from the leading United Kingdom newspapers.

⑤ *Journal Graphics Transcripts*
   GO TRANSCRIPTS
Enables members to order printed television broadcast transcripts through Journal Graphics Transcripts.

GEnie

⑤ *Newsbytes News Network*
Keyword: NEWSBYTES or Page 316
The largest independent computer industry news service in the world, published continuously since May, 1983. It publishes daily significant microcomputer and consumer technology news.

⑤ *Reuter Newswires*
Keyword: REUTERS or Page 344
Provides round-the-clock news coverage from around the world, including breaking news stories, features, and domestic and international market analysis.

⑤ *GEnie QuikNews*
Keyword: QUIKNEWS or Page 341
For a flat monthly fee, QuikNews enables users to select up to ten (10) fulltext search terms (additional search terms can be defined for an additional charge), then performs full text searches of all incoming stories from Reuters World Service, Reuters Business Report and Newsbytes using the search terms from your profile. QuikNews continually scans the wires for new stories which match your customized profile of search terms and standing stories. As soon as a story is received, it is sent to your GE Mail address.

⑤ *Public Forum * NonProfit Connection*
Keyword: NPC or Page 545
Provides a place to discuss news, current events and societal issues that affect society.

⑤ *Public Opinion Online Database*
Keyword: POLL or Page 1120
Covers a wide spectrum of public interest from politics, government, public institutions, international affairs, business, social issues and attitudes to consumer issues and preferences.

The Well

⑤ *Current Events*
   (g current)
Enables users to discuss current events of interest: political, social, economic, and technical.

⑤ *Gulf War*
   (g gulf)
Discusses the Middle Eastern problems.

Network Discussions Lists
Internet (Includes Bitnet & UUCPNet)

🕙 *Algeria News List*
ALGNEWS@GWUVM.BITNET
LISTSERV@GWUVM.BITNET

🕙 *Blind News Digest list*
BLINDNWS@NDSUVM1.BITNET
LISTSERV@NDSUVM1.BITNET

🕙 *CAROLINA—E-mail news weekly list.*
CAR-ENG@CSEARN.BITNET
LISTSERV@CSEARN.BITNET

🕙 *Journalism*
Communication between working journalists (any media), journalism educators, and news librarians and researchers. The topic is focussed on the use of computers in journalism, not general journalism.
CARR-L@ULKYVM.BITNET
LISTSERV@ULKYVM.BITNET
Contact: Elliott Parker
<3ZLUFUR@CMUVM.CSV.CMICH.EDU>

🕙 *Coalition of Essential Schools News*
CESNEWS@BROWNVM.BITNET
LISTSERV@BROWNVM.BITNET

🕙 *Center for Electronic Texts in the Humanities*
CETH@PUCC.BITNET
LISTSERV@PUCC.BITN

🕙 *CND Chinese Magazine Network list.*
CCMAN-L CCMAN-L@UGA.BITNET
LISTSERV@UGA.BITNET

🕙 *China News Digest*
CHINA-ND@KENTVM.BITNET
LISTSERV@KENTVM.BITNET

🕙 *Distribution List of the News list.*
CIUW-L@PLEARN.BITNET
LISTSERV@PLEARN.BITNET

🕙 *China News (Canada)*
CNC-L@UVVM.BITNET
LISTSERV@UVVM.BITNET

🕙 *CND-OSU China News Service for Eastern USA*
CND-OSU@OHSTVMA.BITNET
LISTSERV@OHSTVMA.BITNET

🕙 *China News Digest at Penn State*
CNDPSU-L@PSUVM.BITNET
LISTSERV@PSUVM.BITNET

🕙 *China News Digest (Global Service)*
CNDUB-L@UBVM.BITNET
LISTSERV@UBVM.BITNET

🕙 *DevelopNet News distribution list.*
DNN-L@AUVM.BITNET
LISTSERV@AUVM.BITNET

🕙 *News of India*
INDIANWS@PCCVM.BITNET
LISTSERV@PCCVM.BITNET

🕙 *Magazine Publishing*
MAGAZINE@RPIECS.BITNET
LISTSERV@RPIECS.BITNET

🕙 *Media Journal Distribution*
MCJRNL@UBVM.BITNET
LISTSERV@UBVM.BITNET

🕙 *Media in Education*
MEDIA-L@BINGVMB.BITNET
LISTSERV@BINGVMB.BITNET
Contact: Jeff Donahue
JDONAHUE@BINGVAXC

🕙 *Navy News Service*
Contains official news and information about fleet operations and exercises, personnel policies, budget actions, and more.
NAVNEWS@nctamslant.navy.mil
navnews@nctamslant.navy.mil
Contact: CDR Tim Taylor
USN <navnews@nctamslant.navy.mil>

🕙 *ComServe News Service*
NEWSLINE@RPICICGE.BITNET
COMSERVE@RPIECS.BITNET

🕙 *Network-News*
NNEWS@NDSUVM1.BITNET
LISTSERV@NDSUVM1.BITNET
Contact: Dana Noonan
<noonan@msus1.msus.edu>
For library and information resources on the Internet. It updates the information found in *A Guide to Internet/Bitnet*.

🕙 *Progressive/Alternative Publications and Media*
PROG-PUBS@fuggles.acc.virginia.edu
PROG-PUBS-request@fuggles.acc.virginia.edu

🕙 *Polish News*
(przemek@ndcvx.cc.nd.edu)
(przemek@ndcvx.cc.nd.edu)

Fidonet

🕭 *Bible News*
BIBLE_NEWS
For news of interest to Bible believing Christians.
READ ONLY.
Moderator: Bob Hoffman
8:70/0
Distribution: 1:11/50 8:8/7001
Gateways: FIDONET 8:8/7001<>1:11/50

🕭 *FidoNet News Chat Conference*
NEWSCHAT
For users and sysops to read the Fidonet News
online comment and chat about what's
happening in Fidonet. No article submissions
are accepted. Topics limited to 2 weeks.
Moderator: Michele Stewart
1:369/21
Distribution: BACKBONE

🕭 *Gays/Lesbians News Echo*
GAYNEWS
For current gay/lesbian news.
Moderator: Robert Bayron
1:107/810
Distribution: ZONE-1 ZONE-3 BACKBONE
FIDONET

🕭 *Human Rights Issues, News, and Concerns*
AI_HUM_R
For human rights issues, news, and concerns.
Moderator: Randy Edwards
1:128/105
Distribution: INTERNATIONAL

🕭 *Jewish News*
For news clips from various sources dealing
with all aspects of Judaism and Israel.
Moderator: Aaron Schmiedel
1:124/4104
Distribution: KESHERNET

🕭 *K12net News Conference*
K12_NEWS
A READ-ONLY conference that provides news
pertinent to K12net and education.
Moderator: Jack Crawford
1:260/620

🕭 *National Federation of the Blind news/
discussion*
NFB-TALK
For news and discussion of topics of specific
interest to members of the National Federation
of the Blind.
Moderator: David Andrews
1:261/1125

Distribution: ZONE-1 1:261/1125
Gateways: ADANET VIA 1:3602/24

🕭 *News of the US and World*
ANEWS
For current events and interesting news items
from today's news.
Moderator: Joe Delassus
1:100/355
Distribution: INTERNATIONAL

🕭 *Odyssey Newsclipping and Announcement
Echo*
CLIPPINGS
For posting of news clippings of fringe science
events. Echo restricted to Odyssey BBS Networks
only.
Moderator: Jerry Woody
1:3607/20
Restr: MEMBER
Distribution: FIDONET ECHOMAIL, ODYSSEY
BACKBONE

🕭 *Media Review*
For metaphysical books, movies, music, and
magazines.
Moderator: Jeanne Garner
1:267/128
Restr: MOD-APVL
Distribution: PRIVATELY DISTRIBUTED

🕭 *Progressive News & Views*
P_NEWS
For progressive discussions and news, and
poetry if it is related to the human condition.
Moderator: Hank Roth
1:151/101
Distribution: ZONE-1

Usenet

🕭 *News from Bangladesh, India, Nepal, etc.
(Moderated)*
misc.news.southasia

🕭 *ClariNet UPI general news wiregroups.*
clari.news

🕭 *Temporary groups for hot news stories.*
clari.news.hot

🕭 *ClariNet UPI business news wiregroups.*
clari.biz

🕭 *ClariNet UPI sports wiregroups.*
clari.sports

🕭 *ClariNet UPI technology related news
wiregroups.*
clari.tw

- *ClariNet broadcast style news about Canada.*
  `clari.canada`
- *Feature columns and products.*
  `clari.feature`
- *Columns of humorist Dave Barry. (Moderated)*
  `clari.feature.dave_barry`
- *Chicago Opinion Columnist Mike Royko. (Moderated)*
  `clari.feature.mike_royko`
- *Judith Martin's Humorous Etiquette Advice. (Moderated)*
  `clari.feature.miss_manners`
- *Richard Lederer's "Looking at Language". (Moderated)*
  `clari.feature.lederer`
- *Sex Q & A and Advice from Kinsey Institute. (Moderated)*
  `clari.feature.kinsey`
- *Regular newscast for Canadians. (Moderated)*
  `clari.canada.newscast`
- *Regular updates of Canadian News in Brief. (Moderated)*
  `clari.canada.briefs`
- *News briefs for Ontario and Toronto. (Moderated)*
  `clari.canada.briefs.ont`
- *News briefs for Alberta, the Prairies & B.C. (Moderated)*
  `clari.canada.briefs.west`
- *Short items on Canadian News stories. (Moderated)*
  `clari.canada.general`
- *Canadian Business Summaries. (Moderated)*
  `clari.canada.biz`
- *Daily almanac—quotes, 'this date in history' etc. (Moderated)*
  `clari.news.almanac`
- *Stage, drama & other fine arts. (Moderated)*
  `clari.news.arts`
- *Aviation industry and mishaps. (Moderated)*
  `clari.news.aviation`
- *Books & publishing. (Moderated)*
  `clari.news.books`
- *Regular news summaries. (Moderated)*
  `clari.news.briefs`
- *Major breaking stories of the week. (Moderated)*
  `clari.news.bulletin`
- *News related to Canada. (Moderated)*
  `clari.news.canada`
- *Summary of top radio news stories. (Moderated)*
  `clari.news.cast`
- *Stories related to children and parenting. (Moderated)*
  `clari.news.children`
- *Consumer news, car reviews etc. (Moderated)*
  `clari.news.consumer`
- *Demonstrations around the world. (Moderated)*
  `clari.news.demonstration`
- *Major problems, accidents & natural disasters. (Moderated)*
  `clari.news.disaster`
- *General economic news. (Moderated)*
  `clari.news.economy`
- *News regarding both US and international elections. (Moderated)*
  `clari.news.election`
- *Entertainment industry news & features. (Moderated)*
  `clari.news.entertain`
- *News related to Europe. (Moderated)*
  `clari.news.europe`
- *Unclassified feature stories. (Moderated)*
  `clari.news.features`
- *Clashes around the world. (Moderated)*
  `clari.news.fighting`
- *Ultra-important once-a-year news flashes. (Moderated)*
  `clari.news.flash`
- *Stories of success and survival. (Moderated)*
  `clari.news.goodnews`
- *General Government related stories. (Moderated)*
  `clari.news.gov`
- *Government agencies, FBI etc. (Moderated)*
  `clari.news.gov.agency`
- *Budgets at all levels. (Moderated)*
  `clari.news.gov.budget`

🕥 *Government corruption, kickbacks etc. (Moderated)*
`clari.news.gov.corrupt`

🕥 *International government-related stories. (Moderated)*
`clari.news.gov.international`

🕥 *Government officials & their problems. (Moderated)*
`clari.news.gov.officials`

🕥 *State government stories of national importance. (Moderated)*
`clari.news.gov.state`

🕥 *Tax laws, trials, etc. (Moderated)*
`clari.news.gov.taxes`

🕥 *US Federal government news. (High volume) (Moderated)*
`clari.news.gov.usa`

🕥 *News of interest to black people. (Moderated)*
`clari.news.group.blacks`

🕥 *Homosexuality & Gay Rights. (Moderated)*
`clari.news.group.gays`

🕥 *Jews & Jewish interests. (Moderated)*
`clari.news.group.jews`

🕥 *Women's issues and abortion. (Moderated)*
`clari.news.group.women`

🕥 *Top news headlines—one sentence per story. (Moderated)*
`clari.news.headlines`

🕥 *News from Eastern Europe. (Moderated)*
`clari.news.hot.east_europe`

🕥 *Human interest stories. (Moderated)*
`clari.news.interest`

🕥 *Animals in the news. (Moderated)*
`clari.news.interest.animals`

🕥 *Human interest stories & history in the making. (Moderated)*
`clari.news.interest.history`

🕥 *Famous people in the news. (Moderated)*
`clari.news.interest.people`

🕥 *Unusual or funny news stories. (Moderated)*
`clari.news.interest.quirks`

🕥 *Stories on major issues not covered in their own group. (Moderated)*
`clari.news.issues`

🕥 *Freedom, Racism, Civil Rights Issues. (Moderated)*
`clari.news.issues.civil_rights`

🕥 *Conflict between groups around the world. (Moderated)*
`clari.news.issues.conflict`

🕥 *Family, Child abuse, etc. (Moderated)*
`clari.news.issues.family`

🕥 *Unions, strikes. (Moderated)*
`clari.news.labor`

🕥 *Civil trials & litigation. (Moderated)*
`clari.news.law.civil`

🕥 *Major crimes. (Moderated)*
`clari.news.law.crime`

🕥 *Trials for criminal actions. (Moderated)*
`clari.news.law.crime.trial`

🕥 *Violent crime & criminals. (Moderated)*
`clari.news.law.crime.violent`

🕥 *Drug related crimes & drug stories. (Moderated)*
`clari.news.law.drugs`

🕥 *Investigation of crimes. (Moderated)*
`clari.news.law.investigation`

🕥 *Police & law enforcement. (Moderated)*
`clari.news.law.police`

🕥 *Prisons, prisoners & escapes. (Moderated)*
`clari.news.law.prison`

🕥 *U.S. Supreme court rulings & news. (Moderated)*
`clari.news.law.supreme`

🕥 *Military equipment, people & issues. (Moderated)*
`clari.news.military`

🕥 *Politicians & Political Personalities. (Moderated)*
`clari.news.politics.people`

🕥 *Terrorist actions & related news around the world. (Moderated)*
`clari.news.terrorism`

🕥 *Weather and temperature reports. (Moderated)*
`clari.news.weather`

🕥 *Good news.*
`alt.good.news`

Online Libraries

After Dark

❧ *Magazine Index*™
Bibliographic information for articles published in general interest magazines covering business, current affairs, consumer information, education, performing arts, science and travel.
Coverage: 1959 to present
Updated: Monthly, over 70,000 records per update

❧ *National Newspaper Index*™
Articles from The New York Times, The Wall Street Journal, and The Christian Science Monitor are indexed, as well as national and international news items from The Washington Post, and The Los Angeles Times.
Coverage: 1979 to present
Updated: Monthly with over 12,000 records per update

❧ *NEWSEARCH*™
A bibliographic file containing the daily updates of five databases: Magazine Index, National Newspaper Index, Legal Resource Index, Management Contents and Computer Database.
Coverage: 2 to 6 weeks
Updated: Daily

Knowledge Index

❧ *Current Digest Of The Soviet Press.*
Contains translations and abstracts from Soviet newspapers and magazines. The Current Digest of the Soviet Press covers the general press and all areas except the hard sciences.
Coverage: January 1982 to the present
Updated: Weekly

❧ *Facts On File*®.
A weekly record of contemporary history compiled from worldwide news sources. Facts On File® corresponds to the printed *Facts on File World News Digest.*
Coverage: 1982 to the present
Updated: Weekly

❧ *National Newspaper Index*
Provides front-to-back indexing of The Christian Science Monitor, The New York Times, and The Wall Street Journal.
Coverage: 1979 to present (1982 to present for the Los Angeles Times, and The Washington Post.)
Updated: Monthly

❧ *Newsearch*
A daily index of more than 2000 news stories, articles, and book reviews from over 1700 important newspapers, magazines, and periodicals.
Coverage: Current month only
Updated: Daily

❧ *UPI News.*
Contains the full text of news stories carried on the United Press International wire. File 261 is the current file with daily updates; up to six months of information is available within 48 hours of the present date. File 260 contains the backfile, providing information from April 1983 to five months prior to the current date.
Coverage: April 1983 to the present (see below)
Updated: Daily (File 261); Monthly (File 260)

Orbit

No services available.

NewsNet

❧ *Agence France-Presse International News Wire*
AGENCE FRANCE-PRESSE (AF)
Frequency: Continuous wire feed with 15 minute delay; ten week retention of articles.
Provides continuous reporting on international news, consisting of about 60 percent general news, 20 percent sports, and 20 percent economic and business news.

❧ *ASSOCIATED PRESS (AP)*
Publisher: Associated Press
Read Rate: $1.20/min.
Frequency: Continuous wire feed with immediate updating; ten week retention of articles.
World's largest supplier of general interest news to the media, provides two real-time newswire feeds to NewsNet. Full-text searching of all articles is available within one hour of release.

⑤ *AP DataStream Business News Wire—
APOlW*
Cross-referenced: Fl, GB, Wlres, Bwires
Continuous reporting on business and financial news.

⑤ *AP DataStream Washington News Wire—
AP03W*
Cross-referenced: GT, PO, Wkes
Continuous reporting on political news from the U.S. capital.

⑤ *AP DataStream International News Wire—
AP04W*
Cross-referenced: IT, PO, Wires, l~ires
Continuous reporting on international news, including the United Nations.

⑤ *Business Wire*
Frequency: Continuous wire feed with immediate updating; ten-week retention of articles.
Delivers timely, full-text press releases and announcements prepared and transmitted to Business Wire by over 10,000 U.S. companies.NewsNet monitors Business Wire on a 24-hour basis. Full-text searching of all articles is available within one hour of release.

⑤ *Catholic News Service*
Frequency: Daily
Earliest NewsNet Issue: 1/4/88
Compiled daily from the previous day's Catholic News Service newswire.

⑤ *Catholic Trends*
Frequency: Biweekly
Earliest NewsNet Issue: 4/2/88

⑤ *News and analyses of Catholic activities.*
Origins: Catholic Documentary Service
Frequency: Weekly
Earliest NewsNet Issue: 3/31/88

⑤ *Commerce Business Daily (CB)*
Six separate services comprising the full text of the printed edition of Commerce Business Daily, published each business day by the U.S. Department of Commerce.
Electronic Provider: Mercury Computer Services Inc.
Frequency: Daily
Earliest NewsNet Issue: 4 week retention

Commerce Business Daily

⑤ *CBD: Procurements—Services—CBOlT*
Online equivalent of the Services section of U.S. Government Procurements listings from the printed edition of Commerce Business Daily.

⑤ *CBD: Procurements—Supplies—CB02T*
Online equivalent of the Supplies section of U.S. Government Procurements listings from the printed edition of Commerce Business Daily.

⑤ *CBD: Contract Awards—Services—CB03T*
Online equivalent of the services section of the Contract Award listings from the printed edition of Commerce Business Daily.

⑤ *CBD: Contract Awards—Supplies—CB04T*
Online equivalent of the services section of the Contract Award listings from the printed edition of Commerce Business Daily.

⑤ *CBD: Special Notices—CBOS*
Online equivalent of the special notices section of the printed edition of Commerce Business Daily. Includes special notices of government actions affecting commerce and standards.

⑤ *CBD: Foreign Government Standards—CB06*
Online equivalent of the Foreign Government Standards section of the printed edition of Commerce Business Daily. Lists notices of proposed changes in foreign standards and certification systems that could affect U.S. exports.

Federal News Service (FN)

Frequency: Continuous wire feed with immediate updating; ten-week retention of all articles; selected items are permanently archived. Federal News Service provides verbatim transcripts of all major press briefings, speeches, Congressional hearings, and conferences involving leading U.S. government policymakers at home and abroad.

⑤ *Federal News Service Transcripts—FNOlW*
Continuous delivery of transcripts originating from Washington and major U.S. television new programs.

⑤ *Federal News Service Washington Daybook—
FN02W*
Provides daily and weekly schedules of U.S. government events and key private-sector events in the Washington area.

⑤ *Federal News Service Kremlin Transcripts—FN03W*
Verbatim transcripts, in English, of speeches and press conferences by key government officials in the USSR.

⑤ *Federal News Service Transcript Archive—FN04*
Archived transcripts of substantive proceedings and speeches originally filed in Federal News Service Transcripts and Federal News Service Kremlin Transcripts.

REUTER NEWS (RN)

Frequency: Continuous wire feed; ten-week retention of articles.
Provides around-the-clock coverage of breaking news in concise and authoritative reports.

⑤ *Reuter News Reports—RN0lW*
Twenty-four-hour coverage from around the globe assembled by experienced editors who put international news into perspective. (This service is also known as the LBY or "Library" service.)

⑤ *Reuter Business Report—RN02W*
Edited in New York for the North American market, this service draws upon the worldwide Reuter network of real-time financial news and information. It also includes analysis and interviews with business leaders.

⑤ *Reuter Transcript Report—RN03W*
Verbatim transcripts of important news events from Washington, including presentations and speeches by all major U.S. policymakers. Reuters services are not available via NewsNet to users outside North America.

United Press International (UP)

Frequency: Continuous wire feed with immediate updating; ten week retention of articles NewsNet monitors five national and international newswires from United Press International on a 24 hour basis.

⑤ *UPI Business & Financial Wire—UP0lW*
Continuous reporting on business and financial news.

⑤ *UPI Domestic News Wire—UP02W*
Continuous reporting on all domestic news other than financial, political, and sports.

⑤ *UPI Political Wire—UP03W*
Continuous reporting on political news.

⑤ *UPI International Wire—UP04W*
Continuous reporting on international news.

⑤ *UPI Sports Wire—UP0SW*
Continuous reporting on sports news.

XINHUA NEWS (XN)

⑤ *Xinhua English Language News Service*
Frequency: Continuous wire feed with immediate updating; ten-week retention of articles.
Originates in Beijing, People's Republic of China, and provides 24 hour coverage of important political, economic, social, and sporting events in the PRC and from more than 80 international bureaus.

Bulletin Boards
COMMUNITY NEWS SERVICE
A BBS that has lots of general news.
Availability: 24 hrs/ 7 days
Baud Rate: 2400
BBS Number: (719) 520-5000

CD-ROM

⑤ *News Digest 1980-87*
Facts On File, 460 Park Avenue South, New York, NY 10016

⑤ *Info Trac II*
Information Access Co.
362 Lakeside Drive
Foster City, CA 94404

⑤ *Atlanta Constitution 1985+*
UMI
300 N. Zeeb Road
Ann Arbor, MI 48106

⑤ *Chicago Tribune 1985+*
UMI
300 N. Zeeb Road
Ann Arbor, MI 48106

⑤ *Christian Science Monitor 1985 +*
UMI
300 N. Zeeb Road
Ann Arbor, MI 48106

٩ *Daily Oklahoman*
DataTimes
11400 Quail Springs Pkwy #450
Oklahoma City, OK 73134

٩ *NY Times 1987+*
UMI
300 N. Zeeb Road
Ann Arbor, MI 48106

٩ *Pravda (trans 86-87)*
Alde Publishing
7840 Computer Avenue
Minneapolis , MN 55435

٩ *Wall St. Journal Abstracts 1985+*
UMI
300 N. Zeeb Road
Ann Arbor, MI 48106

٩ *Washington Post 1989+*
UMI
300 N. Zeeb Road
Ann Arbor, MI 48106

٩ *Newspaper Abstracts OnDisc (contains most
of the above)*
UMI
300 N. Zeeb Road
Ann Arbor, MI 48106

٩ *Congress Stack*
Highlighted Data, Inc.

٩ *Consumers Reports on CDROM*
National Information Services Corp.

٩ *Consumers Reference Disc*
National Information Services Corp.

٩ *Desert Storm-The War in the Persian Gulf*
Warner New Media

٩ *Drugs & Crime CDROM*
Abt Books, Inc.

٩ *Electronic Blue Book*
DISC

٩ *Middle East Diary*
Quanta Press

٩ *Boston Globe*
Dialog Information Services.

٩ *Detroit Free Press*
Dialog Information Services.

٩ *Front Page News*
Buckmaster Publishing

٩ *Los Angeles Times*
Dialog Information Services

٩ *Magazine Article Summaries*
EBSCO Publishing

٩ *Miami Herald*
Dialog Information Services

٩ *Newsday & New York Newsday*
Dialog Information Services.

٩ *Online Hotline News*
Information Intelligence Inc.

٩ *Phildelphia Inquirer*
Dialog Information Services

٩ *San Francisco Chronicle*
Dialog Information Services

٩ *San Jose Mercury News*
 Dialog Information Services

٩ *Time Magazine Compact Almanac*
Compact Publishing, Inc.

٩ *News Scan*
Newsreel Access Systems
885 3rd Avenue, 28th Flr.
New York, NY 10022

Philosophy Resources

Forums & Databases
America Online (AOL)

⟲ *Ethics and Religion Forum*
Explores religious and ethical issues facing society. Multiple boards facilitate discussion; library contains religious software.

CompuServe (CIS)
No services available.

GEnie

⟲ *Religion and Philosophy RoundTable*
Keyword: RELIGION or Page 390
Exchange of news, information, and opinions pertaining to all aspects of world religion, philosophy, and ethics.

The Well
No services available.

Network Discussions Lists
Internet (Includes Bitnet & UUCPNet)

⟲ *Ayn Rand Philosophy Discussion list.*
    AYN-RAND@UA1VM.BITNET
    LISTSERV@UA1VM.BITNET

⟲ *New Ways of Thinking list.*
Discussions of various views presented by Robert Anton Wilson, Timothy Leary, John Lilly, Antero Alli, Christopher Hyatt, and others.
    FNORD-L@UBVM.BITNET
    LISTSERV@UBVM.BITNET

Contact: Patrick G. Salsbury
    <salsbury@acsu.buffalo.edu>

⟲ *Noble Savage Philosophers Mailing list.*
For undergraduate/graduate discussion of various philosophical topics.
    NSP-L@RPICICGE.BITNET
    COMSERVE@RPIECS.BITNET
Contact: Barry B. Floyd
    USERF98F@RPITSMTS.BITNET

⟲ *Philosophy of Communication list.*
    PHILCOMM@RPICICGE.BITNET
    COMSERVE@RPIECS.BITNET

⟲ *Philosophy Discussion list.*
For philosophers (waged or unwaged) in the United Kingdom to discuss matters of mutual concern, and to encourage others to converse via computer mail.
    PHILOS-L%liverpool.ac.uk@NSFNET-RELAY.AC.UK
    LISTSERV%LIVERPOOL.AC.UK@NSFNET-RELAY.AC.UK
Contact: S. Clark
    <AP01@LIVERPOOL.AC.UK>

⟲ *Students and Teachers Discussing Philosophy list.*
    PHILOSED@SUVM.BITNET
    LISTSERV@SUVM.BITNET

⟲ *Philosophy Discussion Forum*
Allows posting of files of interest to academic philosophy: works in progress, conference advertisements, newsletters, journals, associations, job postings, and more.
    PHILOSOP@YORKVM1.BITNET
    LISTSERV@YORKVM1.BITNET
Contact: Nollaig MacKenzie
    <GL250011@YUORION.BITNET>

⟡ *Philosophy, Religion, and Society Debate list.*
PHILRELSOC@HAMPVMS.BITNET
PHILRELSOC@HAMPVMS.BITNET

⟡ *Social Organization of Knowledge Discussion.*
SOCORG-K@UTORONTO.BITNET
LISTSERV@UTORONTO.BITNET
Contact: Dr. Alison Griffith
aigel@uno.BITNET

⟡ *Society for Women in Philosophy Information list.*
SWIP-L@CFRVM.BITNET
LISTSERV@CFRVM.BITNET

Fidonet

⟡ *Awakenings Forum*
For the New consciousness (techniques, and discussions). Topics include meditation, chakra, body of light, visualization, global consciousness, and more.
Moderator: Jeanne Garner
1:267/128
Restr: MOD-APVL
Distribution: Privately distributed

⟡ *Non-violence & Vegetarianism Forum*
AHIMSA
Discussions of the Buddhist principle and practice of Ahimsa, or non-injury to sentient beings, whether by word, thought, or act; discussions of vegetarianism as an ethical choice.
Moderator: Barry Kapke
1:125/33

Distribution: *DHARMANET*
Gateways: DHARMANET VIA 1:125/33

⟡ *Buddhist Philosophy and Practice Forum*
DHARMA
For Buddhist theory, philosophy, and practice. All schools welcome.
Moderator: Barry Kapke
1:125/33
Distribution: FIDONET, DHARMANET
Gateways: DHARMANET VIA 1:125/33

⟡ *Holistic Thought and Lifestyle Forum*
HOLISTIC
Discussions of the interconnectedness of body, mind, spirit, and planet.
Moderator: Barry Kapke
1:125/33
Distribution: FIDONET, ADANET, DHARMA-NET
Gateways: ADANET VIA 1:3602/24, DHARMANET VIA 1:125/33

⟡ *Krishna Consciousness Movement, Vedic Philosophy Forum.*
KRISHNA
Discussions about issues relating to Krishna philosophy.
Moderator: Vaishnava dasa
1:115/800
Restr: MOD-APVL
Distribution: BACKBONE

⟡ *Objectivist Forum.*
OBJECTIV
Discussions of topics relating to the philosophy of objectivism or its founder, Ayn Rand.
Moderator: Joe Dehn
1:104/418

⟡ *Philosophy Forum*
PHIL
Discussions of philosophical topics such as epistemology, metaphysics, ethics, and so on.
Moderator: Aaron Boyden
1:282/50

⟡ *Disability and the Philosophy of Disability Forum*
PHILO
Discussions of philosophical issues bearing on disability.
Moderator: George Tracy
94:7040/1

Distribution: *ADANET INTERNATIONAL DISABILITY NETWORK*
Gateways: ADANET 94:94/1

⟡ *Dharma Events & Community Listings.*
SANGHA
A national calendar for the Buddhist community. Timely listings of classes, retreats, dharma events, sitting groups, visiting teachers, and so on.
Moderator: Barry Kapke
1:125/33
Distribution: DHARMANET
Gateways: DHARMANET 1:125/33

Usenet

⟡ *Philosophies where individual rights are paramount.*
alt.individualism

⟡ *Discussion of intellectual property rights.*
misc.int-property

⟡ *Technical philosophy: math, science, logic, and so on.*
sci.philosophy.tech

⑤ *Philosophical musings on all topics.*
`talk.philosophy.misc`

Online Libraries
After Dark
No services available.

Knowledge Index

⑤ *Philosopher's Index*
Provides indexing and abstracts from books and over 270 journals of philosophy and related fields. Covers aesthetics, epistemology, ethics, logic, and metaphysics; also a rich source of material on the philosophy of various disciplines.
Coverage: 1940 to present
Updated: Quarterly

Orbit
No services available.

NewsNet
No services available.

Bulletin Boards
Modern Technology BBS
Devoted to philospohy and the home of a weekly cable TV philosophy show. Seeks to "act as a socratic philosophical agent in the emerging videopolis being created by the technology of signal."
Baud Rate: 300, 1200, 2400
BBS Number: (703) 920-7564
BBS Software: WILDCAT!
Help Line: (703) 920-1973

CD-ROM

⑤ *KANT CD.*
Incom GmbH

⑤ *Philosopher's Index*
Dialog Information Services

Photography Resources

Forums & Databases
America Online (AOL)

↺ *Kodak Photography Forum*
Path: Lifestyles & Interests > Kodak Photography Forum
Keyword: photography
Sponsored by the Eastman Kodak Company. Provides information exchange, as well as message boards and a for sale board.

CompuServe (CIS)

↺ *Photography Forum*
GO PHOTOFORUM
Discussions of photography equipment, film types, camera techniques, and money-making ideas for professionals.

GEnie

↺ *Photo & Video RT*
Keyword: PHOTO or Page 660
Covers video, cinema, and many areas of graphic arts, offering a photo gallery using digitized photos viewable on any computer.

↺ *PhotoSource International*
Keyword: PSI or Page 355
Gives photographers a direct avenue to photo sales by listing specific needs of buyers in the publishing and promotion industries.

The Well

↺ *Photography*
(g pho)
Discussion and information forum for photographers at all levels.

Network Discussions Lists
Internet (Includes Bitnet & UUCPNet)

↺ *3-D Photography*
3D@BFMNY0.UU.NET
3D-REQUEST@BFMNY0.UU.NET
Contact: Tom Neff
<tneff%bfmny0@UUNET.UU.NET>

↺ *Photography Phorum*
Discussions of photography, including aesthetics, equipment, and technique.
PHOTO-L@BUACCA.BITNET
LISTSERV@BUACCA.BITNET
Contact: Mark Hayes
CCMLH@BUACCA.BITNET

↺ *Pinhole Camera*
Discussions of pinhole photography.
pinhole@mintir.fidonet.org
pinhole-request@mintir.fidonet.org
Contact: Richard R. Vallon, Jr.
<rvallon@mintir.fidonet.org>

Fidonet
No services available.

Usenet

↺ *Hobbyists interested in photography.*
rec.photo

Online Libraries
After Dark
No services available.

Knowledge Index
No services available.

Orbit
No services available.

NewsNet

 PhotoBulletin
Weekly market service linking photo buyers with members of the photosupplier community, listing photo needs of major markets.
Frequency: Weekly
Earliest NewsNet issue: Issues retained for 17 weeks

 The Photoletter
Pairs picture buyers with photographers. Issues contain 20-30 photo requests from editors with descriptions, prices, deadlines, and contact information.
Frequency: Monthly
Earliest NewsNet issue: Issues retained for 17 weeks

 PhotoMarket
Pairs photo buyers at mid-range publishing houses, magazines, ad agencies, and so on, with photographers' collections.
Frequency: Biweekly
Earliest NewsNet issue: Issues retained for 17 weeks

Bulletin Boards
SKYLAND

For nature photographers, writers, and nature lovers. Files include the Smokies, environment, flora and fauna, geography, new age, and the outdoors.
Availability: 24 hours/ 7 days
Baud Rate: 300, 1200, 2400
BBS Number: (704) 254-7800
BBS Software: PCBoard
Parameters: 8-0-1
Sysop: Michael Havelin

CD-ROM

 Comstock Desktop Photography
Comstock Desktop Publishing

Physics Resources

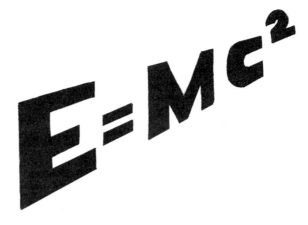

Forums & Databases
America Online (AOL)
No services available.

CompuServe (CIS)
No services available.

GEnie
No services available.

The Well
No services available.

Network Discussions Lists
Internet (Includes Bitnet & UUCPNet)

↻ *L3 Alpha Physics Block Analysis Diagram Group list.*
ALPHA-L@LEPICS.BITNET
LISTSERV@LEPICS.BITNET
Contact: Richard Mount
<MOUNT@LEPICS.BITNET>

↻ *Astrophysics list.*
ASTRO-PL@JPNYITP.BITNET
LISTSERV@JPNYITP.BITNET

↻ *Unified Physics list.*
Discussions of topics related to Comprehensive Unified Physics Learning Environment (CUPLE) software for PCs.
CUPLE-L@UBVM.BITNET
LISTSERV@UBVM.BITNET
Contact: Jack Wilson
<Jack_Wilson@mts.rpi.edu>

↻ *Redistribution list of* sci.physics.fusion.
FUSION@NDSUVM1.BITNET
LISTSERV@NDSUVM1.BITNET

↻ *Nuclear Fusion Discussion list.*
fusion@ZORCH.SF-BAY.ORG
LISTSERV@NDSUVM1.BITNET
Contact: Scott Hazen Mueller
<scott@ZORCH.SF-BAY.ORG>

↻ *Preprint server for General Relativity list.*
GR-QC-L@JPNYITP.BITNET
LISTSERV@JPNYITP.BITNET

↻ *Preprint Server for Particle Phenomenology list.*
HEP-PH-L@JPNYITP.BITNET
LISTSERV@JPNYITP.BITNET

↻ *Preprint Server for String/Conformal/Field Theory list.*
HEP-TH-L@JPNYITP.BITNET
LISTSERV@JPNYITP.BITNET

↻ *Preprint Server for Nuclear Theory list*
NUCL-THL@JPNYITP.BITNET
LISTSERV@JPNYITP.BITNET

↻ *Israeli Optics and Lasers list.*
Information exchange for the Israeli research community involved in optics, electro-optics, and lasers.
OPTICS-L@TAUNIVM.BITNET
LISTSERV@TAUNIVM.BITNET

↻ *Optics list.*
Facilitates the interchange of ideas, discussions, and meeting announcements in the field of optics.
OPTICS@TOE.TOWSON.EDU
MAILSERV@TOE.TOWSON.EDU

↪ *Electro- and Photo-Nuclear Reaction Discussion list.*
```
PHOTREAC@JPNTOHOK.BITNET
LISTSERV@JPNTOHOK.BITNET
```

↪ *Forum for Physics Teachers.*
For teachers of college and university physics courses.
```
PHYS-L@UWF.BITNET
LISTSERV@UWF.BITNET
```
Contact: Dick Smith
```
RSMITH@UWF.BITNET
```

↪ *Physics Student Discussion list.*
```
PHYS-STU@UWF.BITNET
LISTSERV@UWF.BITNET
```

↪ *High School Physics Resource Sharing list.*
```
PHYSHARE@PSUVM.BITNET
LISTSERV@PSUVM.BITNET
```

↪ *Israeli Physics list.*
Announcements of upcoming weekly colloquia and seminars in physics at all Israeli universities, except the Technion.
```
PHYSIC-L@TAUNIVM.BITNET
LISTSERV@TAUNIVM.BITNET
```

↪ *Physics Discussion list.*
```
PHYSICS@EB0UB011.BITNET
LISTSERV@EB0UB011.BITNET
```

↪ *Physics Discussion list.*
Discussions of topics in physics, with some reasonable speculation allowed.
```
PHYSICS@UNIX.SRI.COM
PHYSICS-REQUEST@UNIX.SRI.COM
```
Contact: Andrew Knutsen
```
<knutsen@UNIX.SRI.COM>
```

↪ *Physics Jobs Discussion list.*
```
PHYSJOB@WAYNEST1.BITNET
LISTSERV@WAYNEST1.BITNET
```

↪ *Polymer Physics Discussion list.*
```
POLYMERP@HEARN.BITNET
LISTSERV@HEARN.BITNET
```
Contact: Jan Scheutjens
```
SCHEUTJE@HWALHW50.BITNET
```

↪ *Superconducting Supercollider list.*
Informs the high-energy physics community of events and activites related to the Superconducting Supercollider.
```
SSCNEWS@UTARLVM1.BITNET
LISTSERV@UTARLVM1.BITNET
```

↪ *Superconductivity list.*
Covers current events and advances in superconductivity.
```
SUP-COND@TAUNIVM.BITNET
LISTSERV@TAUNIVM.BITNET
```
Contact: Jo van Zwaren
```
JO@ILNCRD.BITNET
```

↪ *Workshop Physics list.*
```
WKSPHYS@IDBSU.BITNET
LISTSERV@IDBSU.BITNET
```

Fidonet

↪ *Health Physics Society Conference*
```
HPS
```
Discussions of topics relating to industrial hygiene and radiation safety. Linked to Internet via the *hps@ux1* mailing list.
Moderator: Hector Mandel
```
1:233/15
```

Restr: MOD-APVL
Distribution: 1:233/13

↪ *(Out On) The Perimeter*
```
PERIMETR
```
For those "between the cutting edge and the lunatic fringe." Discussion of physics, metaphysics, paraphysics, "fringe science," and the paranormal.
Moderator: Jonny Vee
```
1:215/606
```
Distribution: ZONE-1

↪ *Physics Discussion list*
```
PHYSICS
```
Moderator: Morton Sternheim
```
1:321/109
```
Distribution: BACKBONE

Usenet

↪ *Sound advice.*
```
alt.sci.physics.acoustics
```

↪ *Scientific theories you won't find in journals.*
```
alt.sci.physics.new-theories
```

↪ *Issues of physics in medical testing/care.*
```
sci.med.physics
```

↪ *Discussion relating to the science of optics.*
```
sci.optics
```

↪ *Physical laws, properties, and so on.*
```
sci.physics
```

↪ *Info on fusion, especially "cold" fusion.*
```
sci.physics.fusion
```

Online Libraries

After Dark

No services available.

Knowledge Index

No services available.

Orbit

No services available.

NewsNet

No services available.

Bulletin Boards

Spacemet Central/Physics Forum BBS

Primarily for teachers in Massachusetts; operated by the University of Massachusetts. Makes available space, physics, astronomy, and educational text and program files and an on-line database. A user manual available for downloading.
Availability: 24 hours/ 7 days
Baud Rates: 3/12/2400
Parameters: 8-N-1
BBS Number: (413) 545-1959; (413) 545-4453; Boston line (617) 265-8972
BBS Software: Maximus-CBCS
Sysop: Helen Sternheim
Help Line: (413) 545-3697 or (413) 545-2548

CD-ROM

꙳ *Mass Spectral Data*
John Wiley & Sons, Inc.
605 Third Avenue
New York, NY 10158

꙳ *Plus_37*
Philips Electronic Instruments
85 McKee Drive
Mahwah, NJ 07430

꙳ *Resors*
PCI Inc.
80 Bloor Street 0WX, Suite 1100
Toronto, Ontario M5S 2V1 Canada

Planning/ Transportation/ Travel Resources

Forums & Databases

America Online (AOL)

No services available.

CompuServe (CIS)

⌕ *ABC Worldwide Hotel Guide*
  GO ABC

Provides a current comprehensive listing of over 68,000 hotel properties worldwide, giving location, local and toll-free telephone numbers, credit cards accepted, rates and facilities. Updated every three months.

⌕ *Adventures in Travel*
  GO AIT

Contains travel articles covering all aspects of travel, written by travel writer Lee Foster and other professional travel writers. New articles appear every two weeks. Updated twice a month.

⌕ *Air Information/Reservations*
  GO FLIGHTS

Contains EAASY SABRE, the Official Airline Guide Electronic Edition Travel Service, WORLDSPAN Travelshopper and WORLDSPAN Travelshopper (CIM). Each offers complete schedule and fare information for all commercial flights throughout the world. When using any of these products, you will be asked for your departure and destination cities and your date of travel. All systems offer reservations and ticketing options as well as other travel information.

⌕ *Florida Forum*
  GO FLORIDA

Allows anyone with an interest in Florida to share information about the sunshine state. Members can talk with residents to find out the best places to stay, eat, or visit if you're planning a vacation. Access the Disneymania section for topics about DisneyWorld.

⌕ *Hotel Information*
  GO HOTELS

Contains menu options for finding information on accommodations in the U.S. and around the world.

⌕ *OAG Electronic Edition Travel Service*
  GO OAG

Provides travel news, frequent flyer/lodger information, hotel information, ski reports and country and traveler's information, plus the schedules and availability for all commercial flights operating throughout the world. *The World Travel Guide* contains travel information about more than 300 countries; *Zapodel's Adventure Atlas* describes 5,000 adventure tours; *Frequent*, a monthly newsletter for frequent flyers, includes information about frequent flyer programs and contests. Make reservations on-line. Updated continually.

⌕ *EAASY SABRE*
  GO SABRE

Provides flight schedules for almost all commercial airlines, information on more than 45 million airfares and access to more than 27,000 hotels and 52 car rental agencies. Use EAASY SABRE to find the fastest route to a destination, check weather reports and take advantage of the lowest airfares with the Bargain Finder feature. Book flights, rent cars and reserve condo vacations, cruises and hotels. Save up to 25% on vacation travel and up to 65% on short-notice travel. Updated continually.

⑤ EAASY SABRE (CIM)
GO SABRECIM

EAASY SABRE has been CIMplified. Use the CompuServe Information Manager (CIM) to access EAASY SABRE and access flights, fares, hotel and car rental information and reservations. With CIM, you can easily scroll through pages of flights and fares.

⑤ Department of State Advisories
GO STATE

Maintains a continuously updated information service for Americans traveling abroad. Advisories and warnings cover conditions such as warfare, political unrest, hotel/motel shortages, currency regulations and other information of interest to the American traveler. Updated constantly.

⑤ Travel Forum
GO TRAVSIG

Exchange travel stories, ideas, and travel information with other forum members. Talk with others who have already been to your destination to find the best (or worst) restaurants and hotels. Members can learn about the customs in foreign countries and other important information.

⑤ VISA Advisors
GO VISA

A passport and visa expediting firm located in Washington D.C. Charges a service fee per document and hand carries member documents to the embassies or consulates involved. VISA and passport requirements updated monthly.

⑤ West Coast Travel
GO WESTCOAST

This travel guide by Lee Foster promotes the many pleasures of the western United States. For each area, Lee describes the flavor, how to get there, history, the main attractions, nearby trips and where to get more information. Questions may be left for Lee, which he answers in future columns. Updated weekly.

⑤ WORLDSPAN Travelshopper (CIM)
GO WORLDCIM

CompuServe and WORLDSPAN Travelshopper provide this new interface to the WORLDSPAN Reservation System for members who use CompuServe Information Manager (CIM). WORLDSPAN Travelshopper (CIM) allows you to navigate easily through flights, fares, fare restrictions and flight details.

⑤ WORLDSPAN Travelshopper
GO WORLDSPAN

Gives direct access to the WORLDSPAN reservation system (formerly PARS). Members can look up flight availability and fares for any airline in the world. Travelshopper also provides the lowest fares available with Travelshopper's Low Fare Finder. Members can book hotel rooms and rental cars, and can make reservations online. Additional services and travel information are also provided.

⑤ Zagat Restaurant Survey
GO ZAGAT

Features thousands of reviews based on annual surveys of restaurant patrons. Search for old and new restaurants in more than 20 cities and regions across the U.S. by name, location, type of cuisine, or price.

GEnie

⑤ Adventure Atlas
Keyword: ATLAS or Page 775
Helps users find trips that match personal criteria. Choose a trip category and respond to queries; the atlas will list a number of trips that match the criteria. From there, users can select individual trips and display the details of each.

⑤ American Airlines EAASY SABRE
Keyword: SABRE or Page 760
Enables users to retrieve flight, hotel, and weather information. Set up an account on the EAASY SABRE system, book flights, and make hotel reservations on-line.

⑤ Destination Florida RoundTable
Keyword: FLORIDA or Page 195
Users post their comments about vacationing in Central Florida. The library area is stocked with related data files.

⑤ Official Airline Guides
Keyword: OAG or Page 761
Contains several travel related databases. Enables users to view schedules for over 600 airlines updated weekly, millions of fares updated daily, and over 37,500 hotels in North America, Europe, and the Pacific. Also provides the unique ability to compare the lowest available airfares before you book on-line.

⑤ Traveler's Information RoundTable
Keyword: TIS or Page 560
For users who want to learn about new travel locations and great travel bargains. The library

is full of information such as Tourist Authority addresses, toll-free numbers for car rental agencies and cruise lines.

The Well

CoHousing
(g coho)
Discusses cohousing, a type of living community first developed in Denmark, increasingly common throughout Northern Europe, and just starting to appear in the United States.

WELL Adopt-A-Highway
(g highway)
Concerns the WELL's initial and ongoing efforts to adopt a stretch of California highway.

Transportation
(g transport)
Discusses all aspects of transportation.

Travel
(g travel)
For discussions among travellers.

Network Discussions Lists

Internet (Includes Bitnet & UUCPNet)

Land Information Access Discussion Forum list.
ACCESS-L@UNBVM1.BITNET
LISTSERV@UNBVM1.BITNET

Railroad Transportation list.
Discusses urban transportation issues with emphasis on rail transportation.
GKMCU@CUNYVM.CUNY.EDU
GKMCU@CUNYVM.CUNY.EDU
Contact: Geert K. Marien
<GKMCU@CUNYVM.CUNY.EDU>

HHI Research Findings list.
For discussion of matters of general interest to real estate researchers and students.
HHI-RES@UTARLVM1.BITNET
LISTSERV@UTARLVM1.BITNET
Contact: Hans Isakson
B581HRI@UTARLVM1.BITNET

Hospitality Exchanges list.
For hospitality exchange discussions.
HOSPEX-L@PLEARN.BITNET
LISTSERV@PLEARN.BITNET
Contact: Wojtek Sylwestrzak
<wojsyl@appli.mimuw.edu.pl>

Railfans and Railroaders list.
Discusses anything about railroads, real and model.
RAILROAD@CUNYVM.BITNET
LISTSERV@CUNYVM.BITNET
Contact: Geert K. Marien
<GKMQC@CUNYVM.CUNY.EDU>

Rural Development list.
For users interested in rural development.
RURALAM@MSU.BITNET
LISTSERV@MSU.BITNET
Contact: Shawn Lock
<22331MOM@MSU.BITNET>

Community and Rural Economic Development International list.
RURALDEV@KSUVM.BITNET
LISTSERV@KSUVM.BITNET

Urban Public Transportation Discussion list.
TRANSIT@GITVM1.BITNET
LISTSERV@GITVM1.BITNET

Transportation and Traffic Engineering Discussion list.
TRANSP-L@ASUACAD.BITNET
LISTSERV@ASUACAD.BITNET

U.S. State Department Travel Advisories list.
Distributes US State Department Travel Advisories.
travel-advisories@stolaf.edu
travel-advisories-request@stolaf.edu
Contact: Craig D. Rice
<cdr@stolaf.edu>

Tourism Discussions
TRAVEL-L@TREARN.BITNET
LISTSERV@TREARN.BITNET
Contact: Esra Delen
ESRA@TREARN

Urban Planning list.
URBAN-L@TREARN.BITNET
LISTSERV@TREARN.BITNET

Urban Planning Student Network list.
URBANET@MSU.BITNET
LISTSERV@MSU.BITNET

Urban Self-Sufficiency list.
Discusses and promote self-sufficiency in everyday life.
URBANITES@PSYCHE.MIT.EDU
strata@FENCHURCH.MIT.EDU
Contact: Stephen G. Wadlow
sgw@silver.lcs.mit.edu

Fidonet

🕉 *Railfans, Train Watching, Prototype Railroads*
RAILFANS
Discusses what is happening, railroad-wise, across the country.
Moderator: Charlie Baden
1:207/117.1
Distribution: BACKBONE, FIDONET, RBBS-NET
Gateways: RBBS-NET VIA 1:10/8

Usenet

🕉 *Flaming the German rail system.*
alt.deutsche.bundesbahn.kotz.kotz.kotz

Online Libraries
After Dark

🕉 *HUD User Online*
Abstracts of reports on housing and urban development produced by HUD's Office of Policy Development and Research.
Coverage: 1967 to present
Updated: Quarterly

🕉 *PAIS (Public Affairs Information Service) International*
Worldwide coverage of the public policy aspects of economics, business, government, law, public administration, political science, international relations, legislation, demography, and other social sciences.
Coverage: 1972 to present
Updated: Monthly

🕉 *Social Planning/Policy & Development Abstracts*
A companion database to Sociological Abstracts (SOCA), containing information about applied and social problems-oriented aspects of social sciences literature from around the world.
Coverage: 1979 to present
Updated: Semiannually

Knowledge Index

🕉 *OAG Electonic Edition Travel Service*
Provides current travel-related infomration.
Coverage: Current
Updated: Weekly for schedules, daily for fares

Orbit
No services available.

NewsNet
No services available.

Bulletin Boards
No services available.

CD-ROM

🕉 *AmericanProfile*
Donnelley Marketing Information
70 Seaview Avenue
Stamford, CT 06904

🕉 *Cluster+ Workstation*
Donnelley Marketing Information
70 Seaview Avenue
Stamford, CT 06904

🕉 *Connecticut Real Estate Transfer Database 87-89*
Abt Books

🕉 *Conquest/Canada*
Donnelley Marketing Information
70 Seaview Avenue
Stamford, CT 06904

🕉 *Consumer Lifestyles*
Donnelley Marketing Information
70 Seaview Avenue
Stamford, CT 06904

🕉 *County & City Databook.*
Bureau of the Census

🕉 *County & City Statistics*
Slater Hall Information Products

🕉 *County Business Patterns 86&87*
Bureau of the Census

🕉 *Demographics Intelligence*
Strategic Intelligence System
404 Park Avenue South, Suite 1301
New York, NY 10016

🕉 *Economic Census 1987*
Bureau of the Census

🕉 *GraphicProfile*
Donnelley Marketing Information
70 Seaview Avenue
Stamford, CT 06904

✎ *Income By Age*
Donnelley Marketing Information
70 Seaview Avenue
Stamford, CT 06904

✎ *Market Potential*
Donnelley Marketing Information
70 Seaview Avenue
Stamford, CT 06904

✎ *Massachusetts and Connecticut Real Estate Transfer Database*
Abt Books

✎ *Population Statistics*
Slater Hall Information Products

✎ *Supermap US Census Data*
Chadwyck-Healey, Inc.

✎ *TargetScan*
Donnelley Marketing Information
70 Seaview Avenue
Stamford, CT 06904

✎ *Voter Lists*
Aristotle Industries

Politics
Resources

Forums & Databases
America Online (AOL)

✪ *Express Yourself*
Keyword: Express Yourself
Path: News & Finance Department > Express Yourself
Offers debate of the top news, social, and political issues. Virtually every subject under the sun is open to discussion.

✪ *The New Republic*
Keyword: New Republic
Path: News & Finance Department > New Republic
Offers articles from the latest edition of the magazine. Enables users to discuss the ideas and issues raised in the magazine with New Republic editors and other America Online members.

CompuServe (CIS)

✪ *CONGRESSgrams*
Keyword: GO CONGRESS
Enables users to express opinions or views to members of the United States Congress or to the President or Vice President of the United States. Members also can use the Congressional database to look up information about any Congressman.

GEnie
No services available.

The Well

✪ *Gulf War*
(g gulf)
Offers discussion of Middle East events.

✪ *Liberty*
(g liberty)
Offers discussion on alternatives to "politics-as-usual."

✪ *Politics*
(g pol)
Offers exchange of ideas.

Network Discussions Lists
Internet (Includes Bitnet & UUCPNet)

✪ *George Bush's Presidential Campaign*
Offers discussion on George Bush's 1992 campaign for President.
BUSH@MARIST.BITNET
LISTSERV@MARIST.BITNET
Contact: Martha McConaghy
<URMM@VM.MARIST.EDU>

✪ *Bill Clinton's Presidential Campaign*
Offers discussion of Bill Clinton's 1992 campaign for President.
CLINTON@MARIST.BITNET
LISTSERV@MARIST.BITNET
Contact: Lee Sakkas
<URLS@MARISTC.BITNET>

GOP List
Offers a discussion of all things Republican and Conservative.

```
GOP-L@PCCVM.BITNET
LISTSERV@PCCVM.BITNET
```

Discussion of Current Irish Politics
Offers a discussion of current Irish Politics, which includes the Republic of Ireland (26 counties) since 1922.

```
IRL-POL@IRLEARN.BITNET
LISTSERV@IRLEARN.BITNET
```
Contact: James P McBride
```
<bridec92@irlearn.ucd.ie>
```

Missouri Political Issues
Offers a discussion on Missouri political issues.

```
MOPOLY-L@UMCVMB.BITNET
LISTSERV@UMCVMB.BITNET
```
Contact: Len Rugen
```
<C4322LR@UMVMA.BITNET>
```

Peace Corps Volunteers
Enables current, returned, and potential volunteers to discuss the "Peace Corps experience" and related subjects.

```
PCORPS-L@CMUVM.BITNET
LISTSERV@CMUVM.BITNET
```
Contact: Elliott Parker
```
<3ZLUFUR@CMUVM.BITNET>
```

H. Ross Perot's Presidential Campaign
Offers a discussion of H. Ross Perot's 1992 campaign for President.

```
PEROT@MARIST.BITNET
LISTSERV@MARIST.BITNET
```
Contact: Charlie Murphy
```
<URMC@MARISTC.BITNET>
```

Forum for the Discussion of Politics
Offers a discussion of politics, hosted by the University of Central Florida.

```
POLITICS@UCF1VM.BITNET
LISTSERV@UCF1VM.BITNET
```

Politics in the American States list.
```
STATEPOL@UMAB.BITNET
LISTSERV@UMAB.BITNET
```

United Nations
Offers a discussion of the United Nations.

```
UN@INDYCMS.BITNET
LISTSERV@IndyCMS.BITNE
```
Contact: John B Harlan
```
<IJBH200@IndyVAX.BITNET>
```

Fidonet

Alpha-Omega—Open Forum
```
ALPHA
```
Offers a discussion of all viewpoints on all subjects, including science, politics, religion, the paranormal, history, and more.
Moderator: EA Richards
```
1:154/414
```
Distribution: BACKBONE

Animal Rights Conference
```
ANIMAL_RIGHTS
```
Offers a discussion of the pros and cons of various animal rights issues.
Moderator: Mike Adams
```
1:19/10
```
Distribution: BACKBONE

Canadian Politics Conference
```
CANPOL
```
Offers a discussion of political affairs pertaining to Canada.
Moderator: Dixon Kenner
```
1:243/5
```
Restr: SYSOP MOD-APVL
Distribution: BACKBONE

Concord Coalition
```
CONCORD
```
For The Concord Coalition, a non-profit, bi-partisan organization dedicated to educating the people about America's ever increasing debt.
Moderator: Brenda Donovan
```
1:202/701
```
Distribution: ZONE1

Libertarian Politics—Theory and Practice
```
LIBERTY
```
Offers news and discussion relating to the Libertarian movement, including both political philosophy and activism.
Moderator: Joe Dehn
```
1:104/418
```

Perot & Political Change
```
PEROT
```
Offers a discussion of changes in the American political system caused largely by Ross Perot and his volunteers, as well as other groups.
Moderator: Dave Stoddard
```
1:260/246
```
Distribution: BACKBONE

Exchange of Radical Ideas
```
PN-RADICAL
```
Offers a discussion of U.S. politics and of radical ideas.
Moderator: Dan Sjolseth
```
30:201/101
```
Distribution: ZONE-30

⤳ *Technology and Politics*
PN-TECH
Offers a discussion of U.S. politics, the effects of technology on politics, and vice versa.
Moderator: Bryan Hanes
30:301/108
Distribution: ZONE-30

⤳ *Scandals of Political Office*
PN-SCANDAL
Offers a discussion of U.S. politics and of scandals in politics.
Moderator: Eric Kimmet
30:30/1
Distribution: ZONE-30

⤳ *USPolNet Sysops' Discussion area*
PN-SYSOP
Offers a discussion of U.S. politics and systems operations.
Moderator: Paul Hancock
30:30/0
Restr: SYSOP
Distribution: ZONE-30

⤳ *Politics*
POLITICS
Offers open debate for general political discussion.
Moderator: Ed Cleary
1:157/200.19
Distribution: BACKBONE

⤳ *Survnet Politics*
SURV_POLITICS
Offers a discussion of political topics and how they may affect survivalists.
Moderator: Dave Skinner
1:105/711
Distribution: SURVNET

Usenet

⤳ *The Kennedy assassination.*
alt.conspiracy.jfk

⤳ *The war against Iraq in Kuwait.*
alt.desert-stormms

⤳ *For factual information on The Gulf War.*
alt.desert-storm.facts

⤳ *What's happening to the Kurds in Iraq.*
alt.desert-thekurds

⤳ *For discussion of the U.S. Vice President.*
alt.fan.dan-quayle

⤳ *Some say he did it to himself.*
alt.gorby.gone.gone.gone

⤳ *Politics and a real Queen, too.*
alt.politics.british

⤳ *Discussing Slick Willie and Co.*
alt.politics.clinton

⤳ *A Neil Bush fan club.*
alt.politics.correct

⤳ *Everyone who votes for Quayle gets a free lollipop.*
alt.politics.elections

⤳ *As the name implies*
alt.politics.homosexuality

⤳ *Discussion of the non-candidate.*
alt.politics.perot

⤳ *"It CAN'T be that way 'cause here's the FACTS."*
alt.revisionism

⤳ *Independantistes, unite!*
alt.society.sovereign

⤳ *Disarmament Discussion list.*
bit.listserv.disarm-l

⤳ *Forum for the Discussion of Politics*
bit.listserv.politics

⤳ *Demonstrations around the world. (Moderated)*
clari.news.demonstration

⤳ *The Gulf Crisis.*
clari.news.hot.iraq

⤳ *Politicians & politics. (Moderated)*
clari.news.politics

⤳ *Politicians & Political Personalities. (Moderated)*
clari.news.politics.people

⤳ *Current interest: drug testing, terrorism, and more*
misc.headlines

⤳ *Political problems, systems, solutions. (Moderated)*
soc.politics

⤳ *Arms discussion digest. (Moderated)*
soc.politics.arms-d

⤳ *Human rights & activism (for example, Amnesty International).*
soc.rights.human

⤳ *All sorts of discussions and arguments on abortion.*
talk.abortion

- ꔄ *The unusual, bizarre, curious, and often stupid.*
  `talk.bizarre`

- ꔄ *Discussing the state of the environment & what to do.*
  `talk.environment`

- ꔄ *Evolution versus creationism (sometimes hot!).*
  `talk.origins`

- ꔄ *Discussion of political issues related to China.*
  `talk.politics.china`

- ꔄ *The politics of drug issues.*
  `talk.politics.drugs`

- ꔄ *The politics of firearm ownership and use and misuse.*
  `talk.politics.guns`

- ꔄ *Discussion and debate over Middle Eastern events.*
  `talk.politics.mideast`

- ꔄ *Political discussions and ravings of all kinds.*
  `talk.politics.misc`

- ꔄ *Discussion of Soviet politics, domestic and foreign.*
  `talk.politics.soviet`

- ꔄ *Non-technical issues affecting space exploration.*
  `talk.politics.space`

- ꔄ *Theory of politics and political systems.*
  `talk.politics.theory`

Online Libraries

After Dark
No services available.

Knowledge Index
No services available.

Orbit
No services available.

NewsNet

ꔄ *The Hotline*
Provides timely information and insights into the American political scene. Compiled from contacts in government, business, and academia.
Frequency: Daily
Retention: One year plus current year

ꔄ *Japan Policy and Politics*
Reports on policy-making decisions, new political appointees, and various political parties within Japan.
Frequency: Weekly
Earliest NewsNet Issue: 5/29/89

ꔄ *National Minority Politics*
Provides the latest information on political trends, issues, and elections that impact minority groups.
Frequency: Monthly
Earliest NewsNet Issue: 9/1/91

ꔄ *PACs & Lobbies*
Includes the latest available lobby and foreign agent registrations from Congress and the Department of Justice as well as the newest political action committees (PACs) at the Federal Election Commission.
Frequency: Biweekly
Earliest NewsNet Issue: 6/2/82

ꔄ *POLITICS (PO)*
Covers news on the major players in the Far East, including South Korea, China, Taiwan, Thailand, the Philippines, Hong Kong, Singapore, and Malaysia.
Frequency: Weekly
Earliest NewsNet Issue: 5/29/89

ꔄ *PR Newswire*
Full text of press releases prepared by corporations, public-relations agencies, labor unions, civic and cultural organizations, political parties, and government agencies.
Frequency: Continuous wire feed with immediate updating; ten-week retention of articles.

Bulletin Boards

The Capitol Hill Hub: For Public Policy Issues
Offers the exchange of ideas and information on public policy issues and contains the text for the Declaration of Independence, Additional Amendments, the Constitution of the U.S., the Bill of Rights, and Jefferson on Religious Freedom.
Baud Rate: 300, 1200, 2400, 9600
BBS Number: (703) 709-6436

The Free American BBS

Enables users to write on political matters.
Baud Rate: 300, 1200, 2400, 9600
BBS Number: (703) 768-3733
BBS Software: WILDCAT!
Sysop: Jean Blevins

Imad-ad-Dean BBS

Offers discussion for the Libertarian Party and for Islam.
BBS Number: (301) 656-4714
Baud Rate: 300, 1200, 2400, 9600, 14.4
Sysop: Dean Ahmad

John Birch BBS

Offers information on the John Birch Society.
Baud Rate: 300, 1200, 2400, 9600
BBS Number: (703) 754-0899
Sysop: Mason Gardner

Superdemocracy Foundation BBS

Offers debate and the exchange of ideas in conjunction with the concepts of Superdemocracy.
Availability: 24 hrs/7 days
Baud Rate: 2400
BBS Number: (305) 370-9376
BBS Software: The Major BBS
Help Line: (305) 370-7850

CD-ROM

✺ *CIA World Factbook*
Quanta Press

✺ *Congress Stack*
Highlighted Data, Inc.

✺ *Seals of the UG Government*
Quanta Press

Political Science Resources

Forums & Databases

America Online (AOL)

🖐 *Library of Congress Online*
Path: Learning & Reference Department >
Library of Congress Online
The Library of Congress is working with America
Online to bring some of their most important
exhibits on-line.

🖐 *The New Republic*
Keyword: New Republic
Path: News & Finance Department > New
Republic
Members can refer to articles from the latest
edition of the magazine. Offers a searchable
database of past issues that enables users to
search full-text articles by keywords and phrases.
Users can submit Letters to the Editor on-line.

CompuServe (CIS)
No services available.

GEnie
No services available.

The Well
No services available.

Network Discussions Lists
Internet (Includes Bitnet & UUCPNet)

🖐 *POLCAN Canadian Political Science
Discussion*
For Canadian political scientists to access papers,
exchange news, and look up the electronic
mail addresses of other political scientists.
```
POLCAN@YORKVM1.BITNET
LISTSERV@YORKVM1.BITNET
```

🖐 *Political Communication list.*
For discussion on issues of interest to professional political scientists.
```
POLCOMM@RPICICGE.BITNET
COMSERVE@RPIECS.BITNET
```

🖐 *Political Science Digest*
A spinoff from the HUMAN-NETS discussion
list.
```
POLI-SCI@RUTVM1.BITNET
LISTSERV@RUTVM1.BITNET
Poli-Sci-Request@Aramis.Rutgers.Edu
```

🖐 *POLITICA—Discussoes sobre a Politica
Nacion list.*
```
POLITICA@UFRJ.BITNET
LISTSERV@UFRJ.BITNET
```

🖐 *Political Science Research and Teaching list.*
```
PSRT-L@UMCVMB.BITNET
LISTSERV@UMCVMB.BITNET
```
Contact: Bill Ball
```
<C476721@UMCVMB.BITNET>
```

Fidonet
No services available.

Usenet

No services available.

Online Libraries

After Dark

No services available.

Knowledge Index

No services available.

Orbit

No services available.

NewsNet

No services available.

Bulletin Boards

Superdemocracy Foundation BBS

A Florida-based, not-for-profit corporation used as a forum for people interested in Superdemocracy.

BBS Number: (305) 370-9376
Baud Rate: 2400
Availability: 24 hrs/ 7 days
Help Line: (305) 370-7850
BBS Software: The Major BBS

THE CAPITOL HILL HUB: For Public Policy Issues

For exchange of ideas and information on topical public policy issues. Contains text of Declaration of Independence, additional Amendments, Constitution of the U.S., George Mason's Bill of Rights, Bill of Rights, and Jefferson on Religious Freedom.

BBS Number: (703) 709-6436
Baud Rate: 300, 1200, 2400, 9600

CD-ROM

- *CIA World Factbook*
  Quanta Press
- *Congress Stack*
  Highlighted Data, Inc.
- *Seals of the UG Government*
  Quanta Press

Potpourri Resources

Forums & Databases
America Online (AOL)

⑤ *AutoVantage*
Keyword: Autoadvantage
Path: Travel & Shopping Department > AutoVantage
Provides on-line information about bargains on cars and car parts, new car summaries, used car information, and locations of service centers for your car.

⑤ *Horoscopes*
Keyword: Horoscopes
Path: Entertainment Department > Horoscopes
Offers a posting of new horoscopes every day of the week.

⑤ *LaPub*
Keyword: LaPub
Path: Entertainment > LaPub
A unique on-line bar that enables users to experience the bar scene.

⑤ *Classifieds*
Keyword: Classified
Path: Travel & Shopping Department > Classified
Offers an on-line classifieds ad listing service for no extra charge.

⑤ *Comp-U-Store OnLine*
Keyword: Compustore
Path: Travel & Shopping > Comp-U-Store OnLine
Offers a database of over 250,000 brand name products from manufacturers.

⑤ *Cooking Club*
Keyword: Cooking
Path: Lifestyles & Interests Department > Cooking Club
Features recipe exchange and some interesting cookbook reviews and preparation techniques.

⑤ *EAASY SABRE Travel Service*
Keyword: EAASY SABRE
Path: Travel & Shopping Department > EAASY SABRE
Provides a gateway to the computers of American Airline's EAASY SABRE Travel Service, that enables users to book reservations on over 350 airlines, view flight schedules, reserve hotel rooms, and rent cars.

⑤ *Flower Shop*
Keyword: Flowers
Path: Travel & Shopping Department > The Flower Shop
Enables users to send a limited selection of roses, orchids, and simple arrangements to anyone within the continental United States.

⑤ *Gay and Lesbian Community Forum*
Keyword: GLCF
Path: Lifestyles & Interests Department > Gay and Lesbian Community Forum
Offers on-line center for the gay community to interact and socialize.

⑤ *Genealogy Club*
Keyword: Genealogy
Path: Lifestyles & Interests Department > Genealogy Club
Offers beginner and advanced classes in genealogy, and hosts semiweekly on-line conferences for America Online members interested in getting involved in genealogy.

⑤ *The Independent Traveler*
Path: Travel & Shopping Department > The Independent Traveler
Offers the exchange of information on travel ranging from weekend getaways and romantic hideaways to international travel in both traditional and exotic locations.

⑤ *Online Cartoons*
Keyword: Cartoons
Path: Entertainment Department > Online Cartoons
Offers access to the newest form of cartoon entertainment—regular ongoing cartoon features not found anywhere else.

⑤ *Pennywise Office Products*
Keyword: Pennywise
Path: Travel & Shopping Department > Pennywise Office Products
Enables users to purchase brand-name office supplies at discount prices.

⑤ *People Connection*
Keyword: People Connection
Path: People Connection
Schedules and hosts a number of rooms every night, including TeenChat, RecoveryLink, Romance Connection, Over 35, POWs, Parents, and many more.

⑤ *Wine and Dine Online*
Keyword: Wine
Path: Lifestyles & Interests Department > Wine & Dine Online
Offers restaurant, winery and merchant guides, wine ratings, a beer and brewing message board, a travel guide, and plenty of resources for people who love good food and spirits.

CompuServe (CIS)

⑤ *Phone*File*
Keyword: GO PHONEFILE
Contains the names, addresses and phone numbers of more than 75 million U.S. households.

GEnie

⑤ *GEnie Banner Maker*
Keyword: BANNER or Page 839
Enables users to display a text banner anywhere.

⑤ *TeleJoke RT*
Keyword: JOKE or Page 230
Posts daily jokes.

The Well
No services available.

Network Discussions Lists
Internet (Includes Bitnet & UUCPNet)

⑤ *Miscellaneous non-computer requests*
Offers information, requests, problems, or searches NOT related to computers.
    MISC@TREARN.BITNET
    LISTSERV@TREARN.BITNET
Contact: Esra Delen
    <ESRA@TREARN.BITNET>

Fidonet

⑤ *EmergNet Operation & Mission Discussion*
    CRASH
Offers discussion on EmergNet Operation, an organization of emergency services related Computer BBS systems.
Moderator: Gary Reardon
    1:321/131
Distribution: NORTH AMERICA, BACKBONE
Gateways: EMERGNET VIA 1:2610/14, GTNET VIA 1:116/36

⑤ *Disaster Info/Relief/Recovery*
    DISASTERS
Offers worldwide disaster information, notices, and relief efforts, including messages to and about people in the disaster area.
Moderator: Marianne Cowley
    1:377/3
Distribution: ZONE 1 BACKBONE, ZONE 3 BACKBONE
Gateways: 3:632/387 VIA 1:374/14

⑤ *Emergency and Public Safety Communications*
    ECOMNET
For all individuals who are interested in Emergency and Public Safety Communications systems.
Moderator: Steve Collins
    1:260/236
Distribution: NATIONAL

⑤ *Emergency Medical Services*
    EMS
Offers discussion of topics related to Emergency Medical Services.
Moderator: Gary Reardon
    1:321/131

Distribution: NORTH AMERICA, BACKBONE
Gateways: EMERGNET VIA 1:2610/14, GTNET VIA 1:116/36

🕙 *Fire and Emergency Medical Related Topics*
FIRENET

Offers discussion on dealing with fire, EMS, SCBA, hazardous materials, and other related topics.
Moderator: Chuck Sanders
1:128/16
Distribution: BACKBONE, RACENET
Gateways: USENET VIA 343/94, BITNET VIA 343/94 a

Usenet

🕙 *Forum for paramedics & other first responders.*
misc.emerg-services

🕙 *Devoted to issues concerning rural living.*
misc.rural

Online Libraries
After Dark
No services available.

Knowledge Index
No services available.

Orbit
No services available.

NewsNet

🕙 *Futurehome Technology News*
Devoted exclusively to the latest news and analysis of new residential information and entertainment media, along with the business opportunities they create.
Frequency: Biweekly
Earliest NewsNet Issue: 9/10/90

Bulletin Boards
Volunteers in Technical Assistance (VitaNet)

Provides private and public messages and files, distributed conferencing, special access to the Disaster Information Center, a private VITA overseas network, and network access to the

Internet and Fidonet.
Baud Rate: 300, 1200, 2400
BBS Number: (703) 527-1086
Sysop: Gary Garriott
Help Line: (703) 276-1800

CD-ROM

🕙 *Grants Database*
Dialog Information Services

🕙 *World Almanac*
Discovery Systems

Preservation Resources

Forums & Databases
America Online (AOL)
No services available.

CompuServe (CIS)
No services available.

GEnie
No services available.

The Well
No services available.

Network Discussions Lists
Internet (Includes Bitnet & UUCPNet)

✎ *Museum discussion list.*
Discussions among museum professionals and others concerning museum-related issues.
```
MUSEUM-L@UNMVM.BITNET
LISTSERV@UNMVM.BITNET
```
Contact: John Chadwick
```
<chadwick@unmb.BITNET>
```

Fidonet
No services available.

Usenet

✎ *Discussions concerning antiques and vintage items.*
```
rec.antiques
```

Online Libraries
After Dark
No services available.

Knowledge Index
No services available.

Orbit
No services available.

NewsNet
No services available.

Bulletin Boards
National Genealogical Society BBS
Supports genealogical researchers using computers to enhance their work. Offers support files for genealogy database programs and unique stand-alone utility files.
Baud Rate: 300, 1200, 2400, 9600
BBS Number: (703) 528-2612
BBS Software: TBBS
Sysop: Don Wilson
Help Line: (703) 525-0050

CD-ROM

✎ *National Register of Historic Places*
Buckmaster Publishing

Psychology/ Psychiatry Resources

Forums & Databases
America Online (AOL)

⑤ *disABILITIES Club*
Keyword: Disabilities
Path: Lifestyles & Interests Department > disABILITIES Club
Focuses on a number of special interests concerning the disabled. Also offers insurance information.

CompuServe (CIS)

⑤ *PsycINFO—Psychological Abstracts*

Keyword: GO PSYCINFO
Provides abstracts of articles from international literature in psychology and behavioral sciences.

GEnie
No services available.

The Well

⑤ *Dreamland*
(g dreams)
To record, discuss, and interpret users' dreams. Includes latest dream research and books available on the subject.

⑤ *Mind*
(g mind)
For discussions on the mind—human and otherwise—in the broadest possible sense.

⑤ *Psychology*
(g psy)
For discussions on all aspects of the field.

⑤ *Psychotherapy*
(g therapy)
For psychotherapists, psychotherapy patients, and other interested parties.

⑤ *True Confessions*
(g tru)
Dedicated to personal stories.

Network Discussions Lists
Internet (Includes Bitnet & UUCPNet)

⑤ *A Research Psychology Network*
APASD-L@VTVM2.BITNET
LISTSERV@VTVM2.BITNET
Contact: Cheri Fullerton
<APASDCF@GWUVM.BITNET>

⑤ *APA Science Leaders Network*
APASLN@GWUVM.BITNET
LISTSERV@GWUVM.BITNET

⑤ *APA Scientific Grassroots Network*
APASPAN@GWUVM.BITNET
LISTSERV@GWUVM.BITNET
Contact: Stephanie Holaday
<APASDSDH@GWUVM.BITNET>

⑤ *Advancement of Paradigmatic Behaviorism*
APB-L@LAVALVM1.BITNET
LISTSERV@LAVALVM1.BITNET

⑤ *Adancement du Behaviorisme Paradigmatique list.*
APB-UL-L@LAVALVM1.BITNET
LISTSERV@LAVALVM1.BITNET

☙ *American Psychological Society Student Caucus*
```
APSSCNET@MCGILL1.BITNET
LISTSERV@MCGILL1.BITNET
```

☙ *Research in Auditory Perception List*
```
AUDITORY@MCGILL1.BITNET
LISTSERV@MCGILL1.BITNET
```

☙ *Behavioral and Emotional Disorders in Children*
```
BEHAVIOR@ASUACAD.BITNET
LISTSERV@ASUACAD.BITNET
```
Contact: Samuel A. DiGangi
```
<ATSAD@ASUACAD.BITNET>
```

☙ *Mind-Brain Discussion Group list.*
```
BRAIN-L@MCGILL1.BITNET
LISTSERV@MCGILL1.BITNET
```

☙ *Behavioral Research in Transplantation list.*
```
BRIT-L@KSUVM.BITNET
LISTSERV@KSUVM.BITNET
```

☙ *Historical Conflict Simulation list.*
For discussion of historical conflict simulation games, particularly games published in Strategy and Tactics and Command magazines. Also includes boxed games from The Avalon Hill Game Company, Victory Games, and Game Designers Workshop.
```
CONSIM-L@UALTAVM.BITNET
LISTSERV@UALTAVM.BITNET
```

☙ *Forum on Environment and Human Behavior*
For discussion on topics concerning the relationship between people and their physical environments.
```
ENVBEH-L@POLYGRAF.BITNET
LISTSERV@POLYGRAF.BITNET
```
Contact: Richard Wener
```
RWENER@POLYVM.BITNET
```

☙ *Interamerican Psychologists List*
El proposito de IAPSY es facilitar y fomentar la comunicacion y la colaboracion entre los psicologos de todas las Americas y el Caribe, y ayudar en el trabajo de la Sociedad Interamericana de Psicologia. Los idiomas de la lista son espanol, frances, ingles, y portuges (los idiomas de la SIP).
```
IAPSY-L@ALBNYVM1.BITNET
LISTSERV@ALBNYVM1.BITNET
```
Contact: (Bernardo Ferdman)
```
bmf13@ALBNYVM1.BITNET
```

☙ *Industrial Psychology*
For discussions dedicated to Industrial/organizational psychology and organizational behavior (IOOB).
```
IOOB-L@UGA.BITNET
LISTSERV@UGA.BITNET
```
Contact: John L. Cofer
```
<COFER@UTKVX.BITNET>
```

☙ *Industrial Psychology Forum*
```
IOOBF-L@UGA.BITNET
LISTSERV@UGA.BITNET
```

☙ *Society for Mathematical Psychology List.*
```
MPSYCH-L@BROWNVM.BROWN.EDU
LISTSERV@BROWNVM.BROWN.EDU
```

☙ *Parapsychology Discussion Forum*
For discussing experiences, questions, ideas, or research on psi—for example, ESP, out-of-body experiences, dream experiments, and altered states of consciousness.
```
PSI-L@RPIECS.BITNET
LISTSERV@RPIECS.BITNET
```
Contact: Lusi Ngai
```
<LUKQC@CUNYVM.BITNET>
```

☙ *Psychology Newsletter*
For news items of interest to organizational researchers. Can be used to disseminate information related to professional organizations and journals, job announcements, openings in professional positions, abstracts or preprints, and more.
```
PSYC@PUCC.BITNET
LISTSERV@PUCC.BITNET
```
Contact: Alison Davis-Blake
```
<mtbx612@utxvm.BITNET>
```

☙ *Psychology Graduate Student Forum*
For graduate students to communicate efficiently with each other.
```
PSYCGRAD@UOTTAWA.BITNET
LISTSERV@UOTTAWA.BITNET
```
Contact: Matthew Simpson
```
<054340@UOTTAWA.BITNET>
```

☙ *Graduate Students in Psychology list.*
```
PSYCH-L@UOTTAWA.BITNET
LISTSERV@UOTTAWA.BITNET
```

☙ *PSYCGRAD Digest Redistribution list*
```
PSYGRD-D@UOTTAWA.BITNET
LISTSERV@UOTTAWA.BITNET
```

☙ *Psychology Statistics discussion list.*
```
PSYSTS-L@MIZZOU1.BITNET
LISTSERV@MIZZOU1.BITNET
```

⑤ Teaching in the Psychological Sciences
For discussion of all aspects of teaching in PSYCHOLOGY.

```
TIPS@FRE.FSU.UMD,EDU
LISTSERV@FRE.FSU.UMD.EDU
```

Contact: Bill Southerly

```
<TIPSOWNER@FRE.FSU.UMD.EDU>
```

Fidonet

⑤ Mental Health

```
MENTAL_HEALTH
```

For individuals suffering from depression, phobias, schizophrenia and other mental health impairments.
Moderator: Butch Walker

```
1:157/2
```

Distribution: BACKBONE

⑤ Public Psychology

```
PUBLIC_PSYCH
```

For discussion of Psychology by the general public.
Moderator: Bob Johnstone

```
42:1001/24
```

Distribution: BACKBONE AND GROUPMAIL

⑤ Mental Power & Stress Management

```
STRESS_MGMT
```

A HOW-TO conference by Sciences of the Mind.
Moderator: Bob Johnstone

```
42:1001/24
```

Distribution: BACKBONE AND GROUPMAIL

Usenet

⑤ Anxiety in the Modern World.

```
alt.angst
```

⑤ Tightening the Screws of Your Existence.

```
alt.angst.xibo.sex
```

⑤ Be Paranoid—They're out To Get You.

```
alt.conspiracy
```

⑤ What Do They Mean?

```
alt.dreams
```

⑤ For Discussion about Supernatural Arts.

```
alt.magick
```

⑤ Contemplation of States Beyond the Teeth.

```
alt.meditation.transcendental
```

⑤ Geek Seeks Dweeb. Object: Low-level Interfacing.

```
alt.personals
```

⑤ Techno-culture: Music, Dancing, Drugs, Dancing...

```
alt.rave
```

⑤ Dealing With Emotional Situations & Experiences.

```
alt.support
```

⑤ Industrial Psychology.

```
bit.listserv.ioob-l
```

⑤ Psychology Grad Student Discussions.

```
bit.listserv.psycgrad
```

⑤ Exercise and Sports Psychology.

```
bit.listserv.sportpsy
```

⑤ Topics Related to Psychology.

```
sci.psychology
```

⑤ PSYCOLOGY: Referred Psychology Journal and Newsletter (Moderated)

```
sci.psychology.digest
```

Online Libraries
After Dark

⑤ PsycINFO®
Offers worldwide literature in psychology and related topics such as psychiatry, sociology, anthropology, education, linguistics, and pharmacology.
Coverage: 1967 to date
Updated: Approx. 3200 citations added monthly

Knowledge Index

⑤ Mental Health Abstracts
Cites worldwide infomration relating to the general topic of mental health. Includes information from 1200 journals from 41 different coutries.
Coverage: 1969 to present
Updated: Monthly

⑤ PsycINFO ®
Formerly Psychological Abstracts. Covers world's literature in psychology and related disciplines in the behavioral sciences.
Coverage: 1967 to present
Updated: Monthly

Orbit

No services available.

NewsNet

No services available.

Bulletin Boards

CD-ROM

❊ *Excerpta Medica CD-Psychiatry*
SilverPlatter Information Inc.
One Newton Executive Park
Newton Lower Falls, MA 02162

❊ *PsycLIT*
SilverPlatter Information Inc.

❊ *Psyndex*
SilverPlatter Information Inc.

Publications Resources

Forums & Databases
America Online (AOL)

✤ *Home-Office Computing Magazine*
Path: News & Finance Department > Home-Office Computing
Link Resources' National Work-at-Home Survey estimates that 4.2 million people started up home businesses last year. Most of them rely on their trusty computers to be organized and productive in running their business. Does not include the full-text of the monthly magazine, but does have some useful resources.

✤ *PC Novice/PC Today Magazines*
Path: News & Finance Department > PC Novice/ PC Today Magazines
Designed specifically for users who are getting started with personal computers. Monthly articles explain the "basics." New articles are added to America Online each month.

✤ *Compton's Encyclopedia*
Keyword: Encyclopedia
Path: Learning & Reference Department > Compton's Encyclopedia
Published by Britannica Software, Inc., features 8,784,000 words; 5,200 full length articles; 26,023 capsule articles; and 63,503 index entries.

✤ *National Geographic Online*
Keyword: NGS
Path: Learning & Reference Department > National Geographic Online
Users have access to feature articles from National Geographic magazine, as well as National Geographic's World and Traveler magazines.

✤ *The New Republic*
Keyword: New Republic
Path: News & Finance Department > New Republic
The nation's oldest magazine of political opinion, public policy, and the arts. Founded in 1914, the New Republic is prepared for the future of publishing with its online version on America Online.

✤ *Macworld Online*
Keyword: Macworld
Path: Computing & Software Department > Macworld Online
The online version of the popular magazine for Macintosh users. Users can read the most recent reviews and product news, search past issues of the magazine for articles of interest, discuss current issues with other Mac users, and even communicate with the editors of Macworld magazine.

CompuServe (CIS)

✤ *Book Review Digest*
  GO BOOKREVIEW
Provides references to over 26,000 fiction and nonfiction English language books. The digest maintains a full citation and abstract for each book included and is updated twice weekly.

✤ *Books in Print*
  GO BOOKS
Enables members to find books distributed in the U.S. for single- or multiple-copy purchase, books currently in print, books to be published in the next six months, and books that went out of print or out of stock in the last two years.

꘠ *Magazine Database Plus*
  GO MAGDB
Enables members to find full-text magazine articles in more than 90 publications.

GEnie

꘠ *Comics RoundTable*
Keyword: COMICS or Page 1320
Specializes in comic books, their creators and their publishers, comic strips, collecting comics, fan humor and fiction, animated toons in full length films and television shows.

꘠ *DTP RoundTable*
Keyword: DTP or Page 590
For the desktop publishing and electronic pre-press profession.

꘠ *GEnie BookShelf*
Keyword: BOOKSHELF or Page 1250
Contains records for more than 1 Million books in print, reviews for more than 40 thousand and listings for more than 50,000 publishing organizations. BookShelf accesses the *Books In Print* database.

꘠ *Rainbo Electronic Reviews*
Keyword: RAINBO or Page 325
Rainbo Electronic Reviews covers popular books, books for children, cookbooks, and computer books.

The Well

꘠ *Books*
  (g books)
For talking about books.

꘠ *Comics*
  (g comics)
This area is to have four-color fun in a two-color medium. Share your views on the past, present, and future of our favorite funnybooks.

꘠ *Computer Books*
  (g cbook)
About writing computer books and learning the business.

꘠ *Factsheet Five*
  (g f5)
An electronic extension of the traditional paper magazine of the same name. The magazine is a comprehensive review of the fanzine press.

꘠ *Microtimes*
  (g microx)
A place to communicate with the staff and writers of MicroTimes magazine, that is published and distributed in the Bay Area and Los Angeles/Orange County.

꘠ *Mondo 2000*
  (g mondo)
Covers the leading edge in hyperculture.

꘠ *Netweaver*
  (g netweaver)
The online monthly newsletter of the Electronic Networking Association (ENA).

꘠ *Options*
  (g options)
An experiment in the interrelationship of print and electronic media. Options is a magazine by and for the progressives in Marin.

꘠ *Periodical/Newsletter*
  (g per)
For publishers of newsletters and other small periodicals to share resources, informational and otherwise.

꘠ *Whole Earth*
  (g we)
For readers of and contributors to the Whole Earth Review, an eclectic, forward-looking quarterly that helped create the WELL.

꘠ *Zine*
  (g zine)
An ongoing anthology of The Well.

Network Discussions Lists
Internet (Includes Bitnet & UUCPNet)

꘠ *CONTENTS-Alert by Elsevier Science Publishers*
  C-ALERTL@JPNYITP.BITNET
  LISTSERV@JPNTITP.BITNET

꘠ *Board of Advisors for CONTENTS Projects*
  C-BOARD@UOTTAWA.BITNET
  LISTSERV@UOTTAWA.BITNET

꘠ *Canadian Association of Electronic Journal Publishers*
  CAEJ-L@UOTTAWA.BITNET
  LISTSERV@UOTTAWA.BITNET

⤷ *Chinese Magazine at Penn State*
CMPSU-L@PSUVM.BITNET
LISTSERV@PSUVM.BITNET

⤷ *Electronic Hebrew User*
E-HUG@DARTCMS1.BITNET
LISTSERV@DARTCMS1.BITNET
Contact: Ari Davidow
ari!wlll@apple.com
This is electronic-only, and mandated, like the original, to cover all things relating to use of Hebrew, Yiddish, Judesmo, and Arabic on computers.

⤷ *Rare Books Discussion*
EXLIBRIS@RUTVM1.BITNET
LISTSERV@RUTVM1.BITNET

⤷ *Material Management Department Newsletter.*
MMDNEWS@UCSFVM.BITNET
LISTSERV@UCSFVM.BITNET

⤷ *A Culturel Studies Journal on The Americas*
SOUTH@TCSVM.BITNET
LISTSERV@TCSVM.BITNET

⤷ *Technical Report Redistribution*
TRLIST@UXA.ECN.BGU.EDU
trlist-request@uxa.ecn.bgu.edu

Fidonet

⤷ *MS-DOS to CBM-DOS porting + CBM Publications*
PCWRITE
For discussions concerning the porting of programs from MS-DOS to CS-DOS, various Commodore Publications with particular emphasis on C64 ALIVE!, other growing Jack Vanderwhite productions, and rare bovine diseases.
Moderator: Jack Vanderwhite
1:203/999
Distribution: BACKBONE

⤷ *Electronic Publishing*
E_PUB
Discusses the writing, distribution, and reading of publications entirely by computer.
Moderator: Kief Morris
1:3603/210
Distribution: NET 3603, 377, 363

⤷ *TOONS, cartoon/animation echo.*
TOONS
Discusses cartoons, animation, anime, comics, computer animation, and related topics.
Moderator: Jan Maaskant
1:387/255
Distribution: BACKBONE

Usenet

⤷ *Books & publishing. (Moderated)*
clari.news.books

⤷ *Discussion of books about technical topics.*
misc.books.technical

⤷ *Books of all genres, and the publishing industry.*
rec.arts.books

⤷ *Discussion of written science fiction and fantasy.*
rec.arts.sf.written

⤷ *New Star Trek shows, movies and books.*
rec.arts.startrek.current

⤷ *Magazine summaries, tables of contents, and so on.*
rec.mag

Online Libraries
After Dark

⤷ *Books in Print*
References to scholarly, popular, adult, juvenile, reprint and all other types of books covering all subjects, published or exclusively distributed in the United States and available to the general public for purchase.
Coverage: All books in print
Updated: Monthly

⤷ *Magazine Index*™
Bibliographic information for articles published in general interest magazines covering business, current affairs, consumer information, education, performing arts, science, and travel.
Coverage: 1959 to present
Updated: Monthly, over 70,000 records per update

⤷ *National Newspaper Index*™
Indexes articles from the New York Times, The Wall Street Journal, and The Christian Science Monitor, as well as national and international news items from The Washington Post and The Los Angeles Times.
Coverage: 1979 to present
Updated: Monthly with over 12000 records per update

⤷ *NEWSEARCH*™
A bibliographic file containing the daily updates of five databases: Magazine Index, National

Newspaper Index, Legal Resource Index, Management Contents and Computer Database.
Coverage: 2 to 6 weeks
Updated: Daily

٭ *UMI Article Clearinghouse*
Records for more than 11,000 periodicals and conference proceedings covering computer science, engineering, life sciences, medicine, business, education, humanities, and social sciences.
Coverage: 1978 to date
Updated: Monthly

Knowledge Index

٭ *Books in Print*
The major source of information on books currently in print in the United States. The database provides a record of forthcoming books, books in print, and books out of print. Scientific, technical, medical, scholarly, and popular works, as well as children's books, are included in the file.
Coverage: Currently in-print books
Updated: Monthly

٭ *Canadian Business and Current Affairs (CBCA)*
Provides indexing to more than 100,000 articles per year appearing in more than 500 Canadian business periodicals and 10 newspapers. From 1986 forward, event- and activity-related corporate filings deposited with the Ontario Securities Commission (OSC) are also included. CBCA is available from Dialog for searching both online and in compact-disc format.
Coverage: July 1980 to the present
Updated: Monthly

٭ *Consumer Reports*
Consumer Reports contains the complete text of the 11 regular monthly issues of the print, *Consumer Reports*, and the 12 monthly issues each of the *Consumer Reports Travel Letter*, and the *Consumer Reports Heath Letter*.
Coverage: 1982 to present; *Consumer Reports Health Letter*, September 1989 to present.
Updated: Monthly

٭ *Dissertation Abstracts Online*
A definitive guide to virtually every American dissertation accepted at an accredited institution since 1861. In addition, Masters Abstracts from Spring 1988 to the present are included.

Coverage: 1861 to present
Updated: Monthly

٭ *GPO Publications Reference File*
Indexes public documents currently for sale by the Superintendent of Documents, U.S. Government Printing Office, as well as forthcoming and recently out-of-print publications.
Coverage: 1971 to present
Updated: Biweekly

٭ *Magazine Index*
Covers more than 435 popular magazines, providing extensive coverage of current affairs, the performing arts, business, sports, recreation and travel, consumer product evaluations, science and technology, leisure-time activities, and other areas.
Coverage: 1959 to March 1970, 1973 to present
Updated: Weekly

٭ *Marquis Who's Who*
Contains detailed biographies on over 77,000 individuals. Top professionals in business, sports, government, the arts, entertainment, science, and technology are included.
Coverage: Current
Updated: Quarterly

Orbit

No services available.

NewsNet

٭ *BP Report*
Frequency: Weekly
Earliest NewsNet Issue: 1/7/91
Monitors trends and developments in book publishing worldwide. Regularly reports on trade, professional, specialty, and academic publishing.

٭ *The Business Publisher*
Frequency: Biweekly
Earliest NewsNet Issue: 12/15/90
Covers the trade magazine and business and professional publishing industries. Reports on start-ups, mergers, acquisitions, trade advertising, personnel changes, and association news.

٭ *The Cole Papers*
Frequency: Monthly
Earliest NewsNet Issue: 10/1/91
Examines professional publishing technology, including suppliers and their products, users

and their problems, as well as how newspaper and magazine publishers operate. Includes evaluating methods and techniques.

Editors Only
Frequency: Monthly
Earliest NewsNet Issue: 10/26/83
Offers advice for editors for successful editing, writing, and management. Includes editorial survey results, a freelance directory, and other reference tools.

Educational Marketer
Frequency: Biweekly
Earliest NewsNet Issue: 1/7/91
Monitors, analyzes, and reports on trends and developments in educational publishing worldwide, including trends and developments, industry events, and enrollment trends.

Electronic Services Update
Frequency: Monthly
Earliest NewsNet Issue: 5/1/88
A monthly newsletter for executives concerned with a broad range of interactive communications, information processing, and entertainment services—the electronic services industry.

Friday Memo
Frequency: Biweekly
Earliest NewsNet Issue: 1/8/82
Covers the national public policy positions of the information industry in the U.S., product and technology reports, and new research and publications.

IDP Report
Frequency: Weekly
Earliest NewsNet Issue: 1/11/91
Monitors trends and developments in information services, including new storage and distribution media, databases, electronic publishing, value-added fax, online, and voice services.

Inside Market Data
Frequency: Biweekly
Earliest NewsNet Issue: 1/1/88
Focuses on the business of real-time financial information. Covers digital data feeds, quote terminals, brokerage branch systems, and product marketing strategies of major information providers.

MIN Media Industry Newsletter
Frequency: Weekly
Earliest NewsNet Issue: 10/7/91
Provides information for publishers and presidents in the competitive media industry. Reports on frontpage news of interest to the industry, circulation figures, and advertising revenues.

Morgan Report on Directory Publishing
Frequency: Monthly
Earliest NewsNet Issue: 8/20/86
Provides a comprehensive international overview of directory publishing, buying guide and yellow page markets. Articles cover new products, acquisitions, vendor profiles, editorial and circulation workshops, and more.

Multimedia Publisher
Frequency: Monthly
Earliest NewsNet Issue: 5/1/90
Provides news and information on the multimedia publishing industry and explores the trends, latest developments, and marketing strategies of the vendors and publishers of information and entertainment products.

NewsNet Action Letter
Frequency: Monthly
Includes features on use of NewsNet commands, newservices, and major software enhancements, plus search tips, customer questions and answers, and interest-category spotlights.

NewsNet's Online Bulletin
Frequency: As News Develops—Four Week Retention
Includes up-to-the-minute coverage on new services, software enhancements, price changes, and service changes.

Bulletin Boards

Book Stacks Unlimited, Inc.

An on-line Bookstore and Readers' Conference System accessible by modem from anywhere in the world and has 600,000 titles. Users can search for books by author or title, or browse the 'shelves' by subject.
Availability: 24 hrs/7 days
Baud Rate: 300-2400
BBS Number: (216) 861-0469

BOOK BBS

Provides free information to consumers about non-fiction technical books, primarily computer books. Specializes in books and related materials about computers, business, travel, and language and are experts on personal computer books.
Availability: 24 hrs/ 7 days
Baud Rate: 2400
BBS Number: (215) 657-6130
or (215) 657-4783
BBS Software: TBBS
Sysop: Ken Taylor, Business & Computer Bookstore
Help Line: mail-order/phone orders: call (800) 233-0233 or (215) 657-8300.

The Federal Bulletin Board

Enables all Federal agencies to provide the public immediate, self service access to government information in electronic form at reasonable rates. Users need to purchase a GPO deposit account to order any of the online publications. There is an online users guide. Minimum download charge is $2 per file up to 50k size files.
Availability: 22 hrs (not available 3-5AM)/ 7 days
Baud Rate: 2400
BBS Number: (202) 512-1387
Help Line: (202) 512-1524

CD-ROM

✒ *Bookshelf- Microsoft*
Microsoft Corp.

✒ *Books in Print*
R.R. Bowker Electronic Publishing

✒ *CD Wordlibrary*
CD Wordlibrary Inc.

✒ *Consumer Reports*
National Information Services Corp.

✒ *Consumer Reference Disc*
National Information Services Corp.

✒ *Cumulitive Books Index*
H.W. Wilson

✒ *Directory of Library and Information Professionals*
American Library Association

✒ *Electronic Blue Book*
DISC

✒ *Electronic Encyclopedia*
Grolier Electronic Publishing

✒ *Gale Global Access Associations*
SilverPlatter

✒ *Guiness Disc of Records*
UniDisc

✒ *Serials Directory*
EBSCO Publishing

✒ *SciTech Reference*
R.R. Bowker Electronic Publishing

✒ *World Amanac*
Discovery Systems

Public Health Resources

Forums & Databases
America Online (AOL)

⑨ *Emergency Response Club*
Keyword: Emergency Response
Path: Lifestyles & Interests Department >
Emergency Response Club
Covers everything from CPR and stress to
hazardous spills and field intubation, in this
club especially for those in the emergency
response professions.

⑨ *disABILITIES Club*
Keyword: Disabilities
Path: Lifestyles & Interests Department >
disABILITIES Club
Focuses on a number of special interests
concerning the disabled, with special areas for
learning disabilities, blindness, deafness, and
physical disabilities, and insurance information.

CompuServe (CIS)

⑨ *AIDS Information*
GO AIDS
Lists products that contain information
pertaining to AIDS, the Acquired Immune
Deficiency Syndrome.

⑨ *CCML AIDS Articles*
GO AIDSNEWS
Enables users to find full text AIDS-related
articles.

⑨ *AIDS News Clips*
GO AIDSNEWS
Enables members to review the latest full text
news reports about AIDS including
international news and reports and the most
recent AIDS research results.

⑨ *Cancer Forum*
GO CANCER
Provides information about cancer and support
for people with cancer, their friends, and
relatives. Support is provided by forum members
and the Cancer Hotline in Kansas City. No
medical opinions or diagnoses are given.

⑨ *Diabetes Forum*
GO DIABETES
For users interested in diabetes, hypoglycemia
or related genetic autoimmune conditions.

⑨ *Disabilities Forum*
GO DISABILITIES
A communication facility and support group
for anyone interested in disabilities to exchange
information.

⑨ *Health and Fitness Forum*
GO GOODHEALTH
Provides the member with general health-
related information and support groups.

⑨ *Health/Fitness*
GO HEALTH
Contains options for information on health-
related matters including sports medicine,
sexuality, mental health and general health
topics.

⑨ *Health Database Plus*
GO HLTDB
Provides information from consumer and
professional health, nutrition, and fitness
publications.

HealthNet
GO HNT

A comprehensive online medical reference source containing a reference library and section about sports medicine. The Sports Medicine section contains information on nutrition, exercise, and injuries incurred from some specific sports.

Handicapped Users' Database
GO HUD

Provides articles and topics of interest both for and about the handicapped.

Human Sexuality Databank and Forums
GO HUMAN

Questions and problems are answered in an informative manner. Enables members to share their feelings, experiences and relationships with others in a warm, supportive environment.

IBM Special Needs Forum
GO IBMSPECIAL

Addresses all aspects of special education—from education of the handicapped to bilingual and vocational education, from K-12 to adult literacy programs.

Sports Medicine
GO INFOUSA

Provides information on basic exercise, physiology, exercise testing, training, nutrition and the general risks versus benefits of exercise.

IQuest Medical InfoCenter
GO IQMEDICINE

Enables users to find information such as medical practice, research, pharmaceutical news and allied health studies.

AMIA Medical Forum
GO MEDSIG

Represents all segments of the professional medical community; use this forum to exchange ideas and information on medically related topics.

NORD Services/Rare Disease Database
GO NORD

Provides members with current and accurate information on rare disorders and diseases.

Physicians Data Query
GO PDQ

Comprises four databases published by the National Cancer Institute. One database contains material written for the lay person covering more than 80 cancer types, treatment alternatives, stage expectations, and general prognoses. Another is written for health care providers, making current information on most major cancers available. A directory database contains organizational and physician listings, with names, addresses, and other information provided for cancer centers, programs and specialists. A protocol database contains the treatment and medications used for different cancers.

PaperChase
GO PCH

Enables users to have access to MEDLINE, the National Library of medicine's database of references to biomedical literature.

Safetynet
GO SAFETYNET

The gathering place for law enforcement officials, firefighters and emergency medical professionals.

GEnie

disABILITIES RT
Keyword: ABLE or Page 970

Discusses issues relating to various types of disABILITIES, sharing information, and meeting others with similar experiences and needs.

Consumer Medicine
Keyword: MEDICINE or Page 1258

Enables users to quickly locate information in the world's largest collection of medical research. More than 3 million articles have been summarized on all aspects of human medicine.

Medical RoundTable
Keyword: MEDICAL or Page 745

For medical professionals, and other associated professions such as nursing, pharmacy, optometry, podiatry, dentistry and others, as well as for anyone interested in medicine and health.

The Well

AIDS
(g aids)

Discusses matters related to AIDS.

Drugs
(g drugs)

Discusses drugs.

⤶ *Aging*
(g gray)

⤶ *Health*
(g heal)
Discusses health and healing.

⤶ *Holistics*
(g holistic)
Enables users to explore, inquire, discuss, and relate personal stories, and anecdotal evidence of all that may fall into the category of alternative healing.

⤶ *Optical*
(g optical)
Available to anyone involved in the optical field.

⤶ *Recovery (Private Conference)*
(g recovery)
A private conference for people actively involved in 12-step programs, including Alcoholics Anonymous, AlAnon and Overeaters Anonymous. E-mail dhawk or jrc for entry.

Network Discussions Lists
Internet (Includes Bitnet & UUCPNet)

⤶ *Mature discussion of addiction related topics.*
ADDICT-L@KENTVM.BITNET
LISTSERV@KENTVM.BITNET
Contact: David Delmonico
<Ddelmoni@kentvm.kent.edu>

⤶ *American Health Line News Service*
AHL@GWUVM.BITNET
LISTSERV@GWUVM.BITNET

⤶ *Artificial Intelligence & Medicine*
For computer scientists and engineers with interest in biomedical and clinical research, and for physicians with interest in medical informatics.
AI-MEDICINE@VUSE.VANDERBILT.EDU
ai-medicine-request@vuse.vanderbilt.edu
Contact: Serdar Uckun, MD
<serdar@vuse.vanderbilt.edu>

⤶ *AIDs Statistics*
For the distribution of AIDS statistics from various agencies. The prime information being distributed will be the Center for Disease Control's monthly AIDS Surveillance Report.
AIDS-STAT@WUBIOS.WUSTL.EDU
AIDS-STAT-REQUEST@WUBIOS.WUSTL.EDU

Contact: David Dodell
<ddodell@stjhmc.fidonet.org>

⤶ *Sci.Med.AIDS Newsgroup*
AIDS@RUTVM1.BITNET
LISTSERV@EB0UB011.BITNET

⤶ *AIDS/HIV News*
Discusses any issue relating to AIDS/ARC. AIDS Treatment News reports on experimental and alternative treatments, especially those available now.
AIDSNEWS@RUTVM1.BITNET
LISTSERV@RUTVM1.BITNET
Contact: Michael Smith
<MSMITH@UMAECS.BITNET>

⤶ *Alchol & Drug Studies*
ALCOHOL@LMUACAD.BITNET
LISTSERV@LMUACAD.BITNET
Contact: Phillip Charles Oliff
<FXX1@LMUACAD.BITNET>

⤶ *Dental AMALGAM and MERCURY Poisoning*
Provides information about "silver" dental fillings and some special aspects of chronic mercury poisoning. For more information send the following command to LISTSERV@ds0rus1i.BITNET via MAIL or message: INDex AMALGAM
AMALGAM@DS0RUS1I.BITNET
LISTSERV@DS0RUS1I.BITNET
Contact: Siegfried Schmitt
<UJ21@DKAUNI2.BITNET>

⤶ *American Medical Informatics Association Education List*
AMIED-L@MCGILL1.BITNET
LISTSERV@MCGILL1.BITNET

⤶ *Anesthesiology*
Discusses topics related to anesthesiology and collection of any information related to anesthesiology.
ANEST-L@UBVM.BITNET
LISTSERV@UBVM.BITNET
Contact: Andrew M. Sopchak
<sopchaka@snysyrv1>

⤶ *Developmentally Disabled and Autism*
For people who are developmentally disabled, their teachers, and users interested in this area.
AUTISM@SJUVM.BITNET
LISTSERV@SJUVM.BITNET
Contact: Bob Zenhausern
<drz@sjuvm.bitnet>

⤶ *BACKS-L: Research on lower back pain and disability list.*

BACKS-L@UVMVM.BITNET
LISTSERV@UVMVM.BITNET

❧ *Bureau of Health Resources Development list*
BHRD-L@ALBNYDH2.BITNET
LISTSERV@ALBNYDH2.BITNET

❧ *Blind Computer Users*
Discusses computer use by the blind and visually impaired. Topics relating to use of VM/CMS and PCs are of particular interest, but discussion of other systems is also welcome.
BLIND-L@UAFSYSB.BITNET
LISTSERV@UAFSYSB.BITNET

❧ *Computing and Health*
Shares information, experiences, concerns, and advice about computers and health.
C+HEALTH@IUBVM.BITNET
LISTSERV@IUBVM.BITNET
Contact: Kimberly Updegrove
<kimu@dairp.upenn.edu>

❧ *History of Medicine Collections Forum*
A discussion for the members of the Association of Librarians in the History of the Health Sciences, and other individuals interested in medical history collections.
CADUCEUS@UTMBEACH.BITNET
CADUCEUS@UTMBEACH.BITNET

❧ *WVNET CANCER discussion list.*
A public list for the discussion of cancer related topics.
CANCER-L@WVNVM.BITNET
LISTSERV@WVNVM.BITNET
Contact: Susan Rodman
<U0AC3@WVNVM.BITNET>

❧ *Chronic Fatigue Syndrome Discussion CFIDS/ME*
For users with chronic fatigue syndrome, a broad discussion of CFS-related topics.
CFS-L@NIHLIST.BITNET
LISTSERV@NIHLIST.BITNET
Contact: Roger Burns
<BFU@NIHCU.BITNET>

❧ *Chronic Fatigue Syndrome Newsletter CFIDS/ME*
Disseminates information about current medical research on CFS.
CFS-NEWS@NIHLIST.BITNET
ISTSERV@NIHLIST.BITNET
Contact: Roger Burns
<BFU@NIHCU.BITNET>

❧ *Canadian Medical Student Societies*
CMEDSSOC@UTORONTO.BITNET
LISTSERV@UTORONTO.BITNET

❧ *School of Medicine Conference List*
CONFLIST@UCSFVM.BITNET
LISTSERV@UCSFVM.BITNET

❧ *Croatian Medical List*
Informs an international community on current events in Croatia, particularly in the sphere of medicine.
CROMED-L@AEARN.BITNET
LISTSERV@AEARN.BITNET

❧ *The Oral Microbiology/Immunology Interest Group*
D-ORAL-L@NIHLIST.BITNET
LISTSERV@NIHLIST.BITNET
Contact: Dr. John Spitznagel
<jks@giskard.uthscsa.edu>

❧ *Deaf List*
DEAF-L@SIUCVMB.BITNET
LISTSERV@SIUCVMB.BITNET

❧ *Cosine Project—Dental Research Unit, UCC List*
DENTAL-L@IRLEARN.BITNET
LISTSERV@IRLEARN.BITNET

❧ *Dentistry related articles and reports.*
DENTALMA@UCF1VM.BITNET
LISTSERV@UCF1VM.BITNET
Contact: Karl-Johan Soderholm
<SODERHOL@UFFSC.BITNET>

❧ *International Research Project on Diabetes*
DIABETES@IRLEARN.BITNET
LISTSERV@IRLEARN.BITNET
Contact: Jill Foster
<JILL.FOSTER@NEWCASTLE.AC.UK>

❧ *Open Discussion forum for diabetic patient concerns.*
To aid diabetic people in the exchange of views, problems, anxieties, and other aspects of their condition.
DIABETIC@PCCVM.BITNET
LISTSERV@PCCVM.BITNET
Contact: R N Hathhorn
<sysmaint@PCCVM.BITNET>

❧ *Support and Discussion of Weight Loss*
DIET@UBVM.BITNET
LISTSERV@UBVM.BITNET
Contact: Roger Campbell
<CAMPBELL@UBVM.BITNET>

❧ *Drug Abuse Education Information and Research*
DRUGABUS@UMAB.BITNET
LISTSERV@UMAB.BITNET
Contact: Trent Tschirgi
ttschirg@umab.BITNET

🍥 *Drug Abatement Research*
```
DRUGHIED@TAMVM1.BITNET
LISTSERV@TAMVM1.BITNET
```

🍥 *Cultural Food History/International Recipe Exchange*
```
EAT-L@VTVM2.BITNET
LISTSERV@VTVM2.BITNET
```

🍥 *Environmental Health System List*
```
EHS-L@ALBNYDH2.BITNET
LISTSERV@ALBNYDH2.BITNET
```

🍥 *Collegiate Emergency Medical Services*
```
EMERG-L@MARIST.BITNET
LISTSERV@MARIST.BITNET
```

🍥 *Electromagnetics in Medicine, Science & Communication*
```
EMFLDS-L@UBVM.BITNET
LISTSERV@UBVM.BITNET
```
Contact: David Rodman
```
OOPDAVID@UBVMS.BITNET
```

🍥 *EMS Issues for NYS Providers*
```
EMSNY-L@ALBNYDH2.BITNET
LISTSERV@ALBNYDH2.BITNET
```

🍥 *Family Practice and Clinical Medicine*
```
FAMILY-L@UMCVMB.BITNET
LISTSERV@UMCVMB.BITNET
```

🍥 *Family Science Network*
For researchers and scholars whose work focusses on family science, marriage and family therapy, family sociology, and the behavioral science aspects of family medicine.
```
FAMLYSCI@UKCC.BITNET
LISTSERV@UKCC.BITNET
```
Contact: Greg Brock
```
GWBROCK@UKCC.BITNET
```

🍥 *Food and Agriculture Organization*
```
FAO-BULL@IRMFAO01.BITNET
LISTSERV@IRMFAO01.BITNET
```

🍥 *Food and Agriculture Organization— Computer List*
```
FAO-DOC@IRMFAO01.BITNET
LISTSERV@IRMFAO01.BITNET
```

🍥 *The Food and Agriculture Organization INFO List*
```
FAO-INFO@IRMFAO01.BITNET
LISTSERV@IRMFAO01.BITNET
```

🍥 *Food and Agriculture Organization Open Discussion*
```
FAOLIST@IRMFAO01.BITNET
LISTSERV@IRMFAO01.BITNET
```

🍥 *Health Care Financial list*
```
FINAN-HC@WUVMD.BITNET
LISTSERV@WUVMD.BITNET
```

🍥 *Wellness, Exercise, Diet*
```
FIT-L@ETSUADMN.BITNET
LISTSERV@ETSUADMN.BITNET
```
Contact: Chris Jones
```
<JONES@ETSUADMN.BITNET>
```

🍥 *Fitness and the IUPUI Campus*
```
FITNESS@INDYCMS.BITNET
LISTSERV@INDYCMS.BITNET
```

🍥 *The Academic Study of Food*
For the study of food and its accompaniments, from a variety of disciplines, such as marketing, communications, hospitality, consumer affairs, hotel and catering management.
```
FOODWINE@CMUVM.BITNET
LISTSERV@CMUVM.BITNET
```
Contact: Musa Knickerbocker
```
<32HYFEV@CMUVM>
```

🍥 *Discussion List for Food and Wine*
```
FOODWINE@CMUVM.BITNET
LISTSERV@CMUVM.BITNET
```

🍥 *Forensic Medicine and Sciences Interest Group*
```
FORENS-L@FAUVAX.BITNET
MAILSERV@FAUVAX.BITNET
```
Contact: M. Yasar Iscan
```
<Iscan@FAUVAX.BITNET>
```

🍥 *Federal Service Doctoral Nurses List.*
```
FSDNURSE@UNCVM1.BITNET
LISTSERV@UNCVM1.BITNET
```

🍥 *Clinical Human Genetic*
Discusses clinical human genetics.
```
GENETICS@INDYCMS.BITNET
LISTSERV@INDYCMS.BITNET
```
Contact: Luis Fernando Escobar MD
```
<IZED100@INDYVAX.BITNET>
```

🍥 *Geriatric Health Care Discussion Group*
For users interested in geriatric health care.
```
GERINET@UBVM.BITNET
LISTSERV@UBVM.BITNET
```
Contact: Robert S. Stall, M.D.
```
DRSTALL@UBVMS.BITNET
```
Contact: Vegetarian Discussion List
```
GRANOLA@GITVM1.BITNET
LISTSERV@GITVM1.BITNET   GRANOLA:
```
Contact: Carole Mah
```
ST701852@BROWNVM.BROWN.EDU
```

🍥 *International Discussion on Health Research*
```
HEALTH-L@IRLEARN.BITNET
LISTSERV@IRLEARN.BITNET
```

Contact: Jill Foster
    JILL.FOSTER@NEWCASTLE.AC.UK

↳ *Communication in health/medical context list.*
    HEALTHCO@RPICICGE.BITNET
    COMSERVE@RPIECS.BITNET

↳ *Holistic Information*
For information and discussion on holistic concepts and methods of living which provide a natural way of dealing with the challenges of life.
    HOLISTIC@SIUCVMB.BITNET
    LISTSERV@SIUCVMB.BITNET
Contact: Curt Wilson
    <ST9996@SIUCVMB.BITNET>

↳ *Hospital computer network discussion group.*
Provides consultation, a monthly digest, and a data base of hospital networks.
    HSPNET-D@ALBNYDH2.BITNET
    LISTSERV@ALBNYDH2.BITNET
Contact: Donald F. Parsons MD
    DFP10@ALBNYVM1

↳ *HyperBaric Medicine*
For issues, questions, comments, ideas, and procedures on virtually anything dealing with medicine in relation to diving and HyperBaric Medicine.
    HYPBAR-L@TECHNION.BITNET
    LISTSERV@TECHNION.BITNET

↳ *Inflammatory Bowel Diseases*
    IBDlist%mvac23@udel.edu
    ibdlist-request%mvac23@udel.edu

↳ *Diseases involving the immune system.*
For people with immune-system breakdowns (and their symptoms) such as Chronic Fatigue Syndrome, Lupus, Candida, Hypoglycemia, Multiple Allergies, Learning Disabilities, etc, and their SO's, and medical caretakers.
    immune@weber.ucsd.edu
    immune-request@weber.ucsd.edu
Contact: Cyndi Norman
    <cnorman@ucsd.edu>

↳ *Medical Decision Making List*
    SMDM-L@DARTCMS1.BITNET
    LISTSERV@DARTCMS1.BITNET

↳ *Smoking Addiction*
For people recovering from addiction to cigarettes.
    SMOKE-FREE@RA.MSSTATE.EDU
    LISTSERV@RA.MSSTATE.EDU
Contact: Natalie Maynor
    <maynor@ra.msstate.edu>

↳ *Shared Medical Systems (SMS) National User Group (SNUG)*
For communication concerning technical, operational, and business issues involved in the use of the SMS Inc. products.
    SMS-SNUG@UNVCM1.BITNET
    LISTSERV@UNVCM1.BITNET
Contact: Lyman A. Ripperton III
    <Lyman@unchmvs.unch.unc.edu>

↳ *SUNYA/DOH/AMC School of Public Health*
    SPHALB-L@ALBNYDH2.BITNET
    LISTSERV@ALBNYDH2.BITNET

↳ *Exercise and Sports Psychology list*
    SPORTPSY@TEMPLEVM.BITNET
    LISTSERV@TEMPLEVM.BITNET
Contact: Michael Sachs
    V5289E@TEMPLEVM.BITNET

↳ *UVic Health Info Science Bulletins*
    UVHINF-L@UVVM.BITNET
    LISTSERV@UVVM.BITNET

↳ *Medical Administration network and application list*
    WHSCAB-L@EMUVM1.BITNET
    LISTSERV@EMUVM1.BITNET

↳ *Endometriosis*
Covers all aspects of endometriosis, with emphasis on coping with the disease and its treatment.
    WITSENDO@DARTCMS1
    LISTSERV@DARTCMS1

↳ *Medical Journal Discussion Club list*
    JMEDCLUB@BROWNVM.BITNET
    LISTSERV@BROWNVM.BITNET

↳ *Lactic Acid Bacteria Forum*
For the discussion and information exchange on all aspects related to the BIOLOGY and USES of lactic acid bacteria.
    LACTACID@SEARN.BITNET
    LISTSERV@SEARN.BITNET

↳ *Laser Medicine*
A BITNET newsletter on lasers in medicine.
    LASMED-L@TAUNIVM.BITNET
    LISTSERV@TAUNIVM.BITNET
Contact: Dr. M. Wolff

↳ *Veterinary Laboratories*
Offers the discussion between veterinary diagnostic laboratories and members of the AAVLD.
    LD-L@UCDCVDLS.BITNET
    LISTSERV@UCDCVDLS.BITNET
Contact: Jim Case DVM,Ph.D
    <JCASE@UCDCVDLS.BITNET>

⑤ *Medcons (Medical consulting and case descriptions)*
Enables medical consulting for physicians and investigators on a voluntary basis.
    MEDCONS@FINHUTC.BITNET
    LISTSERV@FINHUTC.BITNET

⑤ *Medical Student Organization/Policy Forum list*
    MEDFORUM@ARIZVM1.BITNET
    LISTSERV@ARIZVM1.BITNET

⑤ *Medical Imaging Discussion List*
    MEDIMAGE@POLYGRAF.BITNET
    LISTSERV@POLYGRAF.BITNET
Contact: Michael Smith
    MNSMITH@UMAECS.BITNET

⑤ *Medical Informatics*
    MEDINF-L@DEARN.BITNET
    LISTSERV@DEARN.BITNET
Contact: Prof. Dr. Claus O. Koehler
    DOK205@DHDDKFZ1

⑤ *Medical Computer Networks*
For users interested in the roles global computer networks might play in clinical, research, and administrative areas of medicine.
    MEDNETS@NDSUVM1.BITNET
    LISTSERV@NDSUVM1.BITNET

⑤ *MEDNEWS—Health Info-Com Network Newsletter*
For the distribution of the Health Info-Com Network medical newsletter. It is distributed weekly and contains the latest MMWR from the Center for Disease Control, weekly AIDS Statistics, FDA bulletins, medical news from the United Nations, and other medical news items.
    MEDNEWS@ASUACAD.BITNET
    LISTSERV@ASUACAD.BITNET

⑤ *EFOMP Medical Physics Information Services*
    MEDPHY-L@AWIIMC12.BITNET
    LISTSERV@AWIIMC12.BITNET

⑤ *Marine Biology of the Adriatic Sea*
    MEDSEA-L@AEARN.BITNET
    LISTSERV@AEARN.BITNET

⑤ *Medical Students Discussion*
    MEDSTU-L@UNMVM.BITNET
    LISTSERV@UNMVM.BITNET
Contact: Art St. George
    <STGEORGE@UNMB.BITNET>

⑤ *Managed Health Care*
    MHCARE-L@MIZZOU1.BITNET
    LISTSERV@MIZZOU1.BITNET

⑤ *Nursing Informatics List*
    NRSING-L@UMSSMDVM.BITNET
    LISTSERV@UMSSMDVM.BITNET

⑤ *Nursing School Project*
    NURSE-L@EMUVM1.BITNET
    LISTSERV@EMUVM1.BITNET

⑤ *Nursing Centers List*
    NURCENS@UNCVM1.BITNET
    LISTSERV@UNCVM1.BITNET

⑤ *Nutritional Epidemiology*
    NUTEPI@DB0TUI11.BITNET
    LISTSERV@DB0TUI11.BITNET

⑤ *Pharmacy Mail Exchange*
    Pharmex@leicester-poly.ac.uk
    Pharmex-request@leicester-poly.ac.uk
Contact: Paul Hodgkinson
    <phh@leicp.ac.uk>

⑤ *Prenatal Outcomes List*
    PRENAT-L@ALBNYDH2.BITNET
    LISTSERV@ALBNYDH2.BITNET

⑤ *RHCFRP-L Residential Health Care Facilities*
    RHCFRP-L@ALBNYDH2.BITNET
    LISTSERV@ALBNYDH2.BITNET

⑤ *Risks*
For safety people interested in the various environmental, health and safety issues and problems on college and university campuses.
    SAFETY@UVMVM.BITNET
    LISTSERV@UVMVM.BITNET

⑤ *Student Health Services*
    SHS@UTKVM1.BITNET
    LISTSERV@UTKVM1.BIT

Fidonet

⑤ *12 Steps Discussion*
    12_STEPS
Discusses participants' experience, strength, and hope in taking the 12 steps suggested as a program of recovery in various Anonymous self-help groups.
Moderator: Howie Ducat
    1:278/3
Distribution: BACKBONE
Gateways: RBBSNET

⑤ *Abled Athletes*
    ABLED_ATHLETE
For the impaired individual that still participates in athletics, or athletic competition.
Moderator: Butch Walker

1:157/2
Distribution: BACKBONE

🔖 *Abortion Issues*
   ABORTION
A general debate and information conference regarding current abortion issues, and legislation.
Moderator: Kevin Watkins
   1:389/6
Distribution: BACKBONE, NETWORK
Gateways: FMLYNET VIA 11/50, FMLYNET VIA 389/6, AGAPNET VIA 389/6

🔖 *Adult Children of Alcoholics*
   SIP_ACA
For people who have been raised in an alcoholic or otherwise dysfunctional family.
Moderator: Joe Jared
   1:125/1212
Distribution: BACKBONE

🔖 *AIDS-HIV Discussion Echo*
   AIDS-HIV
Moderator: Howie Ducat
   1:278/0
Distribution: BACKBONE

🔖 *AIDS/ARC*
   AIDS/ARC
For the discussion of AIDS/ARC/HIV related topics for all audiences.
Moderator: Mary Elizabeth
   1:103/927
Distribution: BACKBONE

🔖 *Alcoholism & Recovery*
   SIP_AA
Enables users practicing the 12-step recovery program to share the experience, strength, and hope.

🔖 *Alcoholics Anonymous*
Moderator: Gary Clark
   1:134/28
Distribution: BACKBONE

🔖 *Alzheimers*
   ALZHEIMERS
An electronic support group for the discussion of Alzheimers, Dementias, and other forms of senility.
Moderator: Butch Walker
   1:157/2
Distribution: 157/3

🔖 *American Red Cross Volunteers Information Exchange*
   REDCROSS

For volunteers to discuss nation and world wide ideas, opinions, and exchange information.
Moderator: Kevin Watkins
   1:389/6
Distribution: NEW

🔖 *Amputee Support*
   AMPUTEE
Provides support, comfort, and the exchange of information between amputees.
Moderator: Butch Walker
   1:157/2.1
Distribution: BACKBONE

🔖 *Ask a Nurse*
   ASK_A_NURSE
Interacts with registered nurses for answers to specific health care issues or trends.
Moderator: Sheila Curtis
   1:2260/160
Distribution: FIDONET REGION 11 BACKBONE

🔖 *Assistive Devices for Sale (Used and New)*
   ASSIST_4SALE
Provides a list of devices for sale that can assist a disabled person.
Moderator: Rick Catania
   94:2190/2
Distribution: ADANET INTERNATIONAL DISABILITY NETWORK
Gateways: FIDONET VIA 1:3602/24

🔖 *Attention Deficit Hyperactivity Disorders*
   ADHD
Provides discussions about children with learning disabilities caused by attention deficits or hyperactivity.
Moderator: Butch Walker
   1:157/2
Distribution: BACKBONE

🔖 *Biomedical and Clinical Engineering Topics*
   BIOMED
For employees of hospitals, clinics, and biomedical service organizations that work on medical equipment, or for biomedical equipment technicians or clinical engineers, or for all others to learn what BMET/CBET/CEs are and what they do.
Moderator: Ray Brown
   1:135/70
Distribution: BACKBONE

🔖 *Blindness-related topics and discussions.*
   BLINDTLK
For the blind and visually impaired persons, our friends and relatives and anyone else who is interested.

Moderator: David Andrews
1:261/1125
Distribution: ZONE-1 1:261/1125
Gateways: ADANET VIA 1:3602/24

↺ *Bodywork & Massage Therapy Forum*
BODYWORK
Moderator: Barry Kapke
1:125/33
Distribution: FIDONET BACKBONE, ADANET,
DHARMANET
Gateways: ADANET VIA 1:3602/24,
DHARMANET VIA 1:125/33

↺ *Brain Injuries*
THI_CVA
Moderator: Butch Walker
1:157/2
Distribution: BACKBONE

↺ *California ABLED News Conference*
CA-ABLED
Provides news about legislation and other issues
concerning the disabled community in the
state of California.
Moderator: Guy Thomas
1:161/40
Distribution: FIDONET-ONLY REGION-10

↺ *Cancer Survivors*
CARCINOMA
Moderator: Butch Walker
1:157/2.1
Distribution: BACKBONE

↺ *Cancer/Leukemia/blood & immune system/*
coping with adversity.
SURVIVOR
Moderator: Dallas Hinton
1:153/715
Distribution: BACKBONE

↺ *Carpal Tunnel Syndrome*
CTS
Moderator: ADAnet
94:94/1
Distribution: ADANET INTERNATIONAL
DISABILITY NETWORK

↺ *Care Giver*
CARE_GIVER
Enables users who care for physically disabled
people to share information, offer help, and
provide ideas, support, and comfort.
Moderator: Butch Walker
1:157/2.1
Distribution: BACKBONE

↺ *Cerebral Palsy*
CPALSY

Moderator: Cliff Jones
2:254/71
Distribution: BACKBONE

↺ *Chronic Fatigue Syndrome*
CFS
For anyone with CFS, involved in treating it, or
just interested in the disease.
Moderator: Preston Richardson
1:279/14
Distribution: FIDONET BACKBONE, ADANET

↺ *Chronic Pain Discussion Area*
CHRONIC_PAIN
Discusses ailments causing chronic pain,
treatments for pain, coping methods, and so
on.
Moderator: Alan Hess
1:261/1000
Distribution: BACKBONE, GATED TO ADANET

↺ *Conference for the Deaf and Hard of Hearing*
SILENTTALK
Discusses all forms of hearing impairment,
sharing information on assistive devices, the
ADA, TDD/TT's, various communication
modes, organizations, and anything of general
interest to the deaf and hard of hearing.
Moderator: Ann Stalnaker
1:124/2120
Distribution: BACKBONE

↺ *Cross-Disability Awareness*
CROSS
For Cross-Disability Awareness—general
disability awareness originating within
ADAnet ™.
Moderator: ADAnet
94:94/1
Distribution: ADANET INTERNATIONAL
DISABILITY NETWORK

↺ *Diabetes discussions and support.*
DIABETES
For messages to/from diabetics relating to the
control of the disease.
Moderator: John Hargrove
1:382/68
Restr: SYSOP
Distribution: BACKBONE

↺ *Diets and Dieting*
DIETS
For anything having to do with dieting,
including the discussion of exercise.
Moderator: Brian Cooney
1:261/1081
Distribution: ECHONET BACKBONE (ZONE
50)

🕭 *Disabilities Support Echo in French*
FRANCO_HANDICAP
Moderator: Daniel Coulombe
94:2050/1
Distribution: ADANET INTERNATIONAL
DISABILITY NETWORK
Gateways: ADANET (94:94/1)

🕭 *Disabilities Support Echo in Spanish*
DESHABILITADO
Moderator: ADAnet
94:94/1
Distribution: ADANET INTERNATIONAL
DISABILITY NETWORK
Gateways: ADANET (94:94/1)

🕭 *Mobility Impairment*
MOBILITY
Moderator: Bill Freeman
94:2050/1
Distribution: ADANET INTERNATIONAL
DISABILITY NETWORK
Gateways: ADANET (94:94/1)

🕭 *Muscular Dystrophy*
MUSCULAR_DYST
Moderator: Bill Freeman
94:2050/1
Distribution: ADANET INTERNATIONAL
DISABILITY NETWORK
Gateways: ADANET (94:94/1)

🕭 *Lung and Respiratory Diseases Discussion*
RESPIRATORY
Moderator: Randall Dickerson
94:2050/3
Distribution: ADANET INTERNATIONAL
DISABILITY NETWORK
Gateways: ADANET (94:94/1)

🕭 *Disability and Adaptive Technology*
ADAPTIVE
Moderator: Bill Baughn
94:2050/1
Distribution: ADANET INTERNATIONAL
DISABILITY NETWORK
Gateways: ADANET (94:94/1)

🕭 *Disability and Advocacy Issues*
ADVOCACY
Moderator: ADAnet
94:94/1
Distribution: ADANET INTERNATIONAL
DISABILITY NETWORK
Gateways: ADANET (94:94/1)

🕭 *Disability and Aging Issues*
GOLDEN_YEARS
Moderator: ADAnet
94:94/1

Distribution: ADANET INTERNATIONAL
DISABILITY NETWORK
Gateways: ADANET (94:94/1)

🕭 *Disability and Allergy Issues*
ALLERGIES
Moderator: ADAnet
94:94/1
Distribution: ADANET INTERNATIONAL
DISABILITY NETWORK
Gateways: ADANET (94:94/1)

🕭 *Disability and Architectural Barriers*
BARRIERS
Moderator: ADAnet
94:94/1
Distribution: ADANET INTERNATIONAL
DISABILITY NETWORK
Gateways: ADANET (94:94/1)

🕭 *Disability and Arthritis Management*
ARTHRITIS
Moderator: ADAnet
94:94/1
Distribution: ADANET INTERNATIONAL
DISABILITY NETWORK
Gateways: ADANET (94:94/1)

🕭 *Disability and Burn Management*
BURN
Moderator: ADAnet
94:94/1
Distribution: ADANET INTERNATIONAL
DISABILITY NETWORK
Gateways: ADANET (94:94/1)

🕭 *Disability and Dialysis Management*
DIALYSIS
Moderator: ADAnet
94:94/1
Distribution: ADANET INTERNATIONAL
DISABILITY NETWORK
Gateways: ADANET (94:94/1)

🕭 *Disability and Distance Education Issues*
EDUTEL
Moderator: ADAnet
94:94/1
Distribution: ADANET INTERNATIONAL
DISABILITY NETWORK
Gateways: ADANET (94:94/1)

🕭 *Disability and Employment*
ADAJOBS
Moderator: Waddell Robey
94:2050/1
Distribution: ADANET INTERNATIONAL
DISABILITY NETWORK
Gateways: ADANET (94:94/1)

⑤ *Disability and Independent Living*
INDEP
Moderator: George Tracy
94:7040/1
Distribution: ADANET INTERNATIONAL DISABILITY NETWORK
Gateways: ADANET (94:94/1)

⑤ *Disability and Job Accommodation Issues*
ACCOMMODATION
Moderator: ADAnet
94:94/1
Distribution: ADANET INTERNATIONAL DISABILITY NETWORK
Gateways: ADANET (94:94/1)

⑤ *Disability and Medication Discussion*
MEDICATION
Moderator: ADAnet
94:94/1
Distribution: ADANET INTERNATIONAL DISABILITY NETWORK
Gateways: ADANET (94:94/1)

⑤ *Disability and Medicine*
MEDICAL
Moderator: Jesse Massengill
94:2050/1
Distribution: ADANET INTERNATIONAL DISABILITY NETWORK
Gateways: ADANET (94:94/1)

⑤ *Disability and Occupational Injury*
OCC_INJURY
Moderator: ADAnet
94:94/1
Distribution: ADANET INTERNATIONAL DISABILITY NETWORK
Gateways: ADANET (94:94/1)

⑤ *Disability and Online Learning Opportunities*
LEARNING
Moderator: Bill Freeman
94:2050/1
Distribution: ADANET INTERNATIONAL DISABILITY NETWORK
Gateways: ADANET (94:94/1)

⑤ *Disability and Outdoors Recreation*
ADA_OUTDOORS
Moderator: ADAnet
94:94/1
Distribution: ADANET INTERNATIONAL DISABILITY NETWORK

⑤ *Disability and Political Empowerment*
ADARIGHTS
Moderator: John Desantis
94:2050/1

Distribution: ADANET INTERNATIONAL DISABILITY NETWORK
Gateways: ADANET (94:94/1)

⑤ *Disability and Retardation*
RETARDATION
Discusses how retardation affects children and adults.
Moderator: Bob Moylan
94:8040/1
Distribution: ADANET INTERNATIONAL DISABILITY NETWORK
Gateways: ADANET (94:94/1)

⑤ *Disability and Sexuality*
ADA_SEXUALITY
Moderator: Linda Cummings
94:2051/2
Distribution: ADANET INTERNATIONAL DISABILITY NETWORK

⑤ *Disability and the Family Discussions*
ADA_FAMILY
Discusses how disability issues affect the family.
Moderator: Waddell Robey
94:2050/1
Distribution: ADANET INTERNATIONAL DISABILITY NETWORK

⑤ *Disability and Vocational Rehabilitation*
ADA_OCCUPATION
Moderator: ADAnet
94:94/1
Distribution: ADANET INTERNATIONAL DISABILITY NETWORK

⑤ *Disability Beginner's Conference*
README.ADA
Enables network beginners to ask questions about disability.
Moderator: ADAnet
94:94/1
Distribution: ADANET INTERNATIONAL DISABILITY NETWORK
Gateways: ADANET (94:94/1)

⑤ *Disability Issues Which Affect Children*
ADACHILD
Discusses how disability issues affect children. Includes the effects of a disabled parent on a child and child-related disabilities. Enables adults to discuss how they feel as parents of a disabled child.
Moderator: Bonnie Snyder
94:4020/8
Distribution: ADANET INTERNATIONAL DISABILITY NETWORK
Gateways: ADANET (94:94/1)

❧ *Disability Law Topics*
  HANDILAW
Discusses the development, implementation, and underlying philosophy of disability law.
Moderator: Bill Freeman
  94:2050/1
Distribution: ADANET INTERNATIONAL DISABILITY NETWORK
Gateways: ADANET (94:94/1)

❧ *Disability Sysop Forum within ADAnet*
  ADASYSOP
Moderator: ADAnet
  94:94/1
Restr: SYSOP
Distribution: ADANET INTERNATIONAL DISABILITY NETWORK
Gateways: ADANET (94:94/1)

❧ *Disabled persons share experiences.*
  SAFE_SPACE
For people with physical or emotional disabilities.
Moderator: Phil Scovell
  1:104/810
Distribution: ECHONET BACKBONE (ZONE 50)

❧ *Disabled Users Information Exchange*
  ABLED
For information, help, and support Echo for the Handicapped.
Moderator: Stu Turk
  1:129/26
Distribution: BACKBONE

❧ *Dwarfism and Disability Conference*
  DWARFISM
Moderator: Rob Jacobsen
  94:2060/1
Distribution: ADANET INTERNATIONAL DISABILITY NETWORK (ZONE 94) AND INTERNET
Gateways: INTERNET VIA 94:121/10 (AKA 1:351/233) ADANET.MED.DWARFISM

❧ *Electronic Media Venture Marijuana Information*
  NORML
Moderator: David Rains
  1:133/602
Distribution: REQUEST

❧ *Emergency Medical Services*
  EMS
Moderator: Gary Reardon
  1:321/131
Distribution: NORTH AMERICA, BACKBONE

Gateways: EMERGNET VIA 1:2610/14, GTNET VIA 1:116/36

❧ *EmergNet Operation & Mission Discussion*
  CRASH
Moderator: Gary Reardon
  1:321/131
Distribution: NORTH AMERICA, BACKBONE
Gateways: EMERGNET VIA 1:2610/14, GTNET VIA 1:116/36

❧ *Fire and emergency medical related topics.*
  FIRENET
Moderator: Chuck Sanders
  1:128/16
Distribution: BACKBONE, RACENET
Gateways: USENET VIA 343/94, BITNET VIA 343/94

❧ *General health questions discussed.*
  ASK_THE_DOCTOR
Moderator: Ed Lawyer
  1:261/1056
Distribution: ECHONET BACKBONE (ZONE 50)

❧ *Health Physics Society Conference*
  HPS
Moderator: Hector Mandel
  1:233/15
Restr: MOD-APVL
Distribution: 1:233/13
Gateways: INTERNET VIA 1:233/13

❧ *Independent Living Conference*
  ILC
Discusses personal care attendants, adaptive technology, Independent Living Center issues, and other topics of interest to disabled people who want to live independently.
Moderator: Guy Thomas
  1:161/40
Distribution: FIDONET-ONLY

❧ *International Post-Polio Survivors Forum*
  POST_POLIO
Moderator: Tom McKeever
  1:374/22
Distribution: ADANET, BRAZIL_VIA_18/90, BACKBONE
Gateways: BRAZIL VIA 18/90

❧ *JADA Discussion and Article Submission*
  DIGEST
Moderator: Linda Cummings
  94:2051/2
Distribution: ADANET INTERNATIONAL DISABILITY NETWORK
Gateways: ADANET (94:94/1)

⌕ *Medical Discussion Conference*
GRAND_ROUNDS
Moderator: David Dodell
1:114/15
Distribution: BACKBONE

⌕ *Multiple Personality Disorder*
M_P_D
Moderator: Jack Zeller
1:369/34
Distribution: BACKBONE, ADANET

⌕ *Multiple Sclerosis Support Group*
MULT-SCLEROSIS
Moderator: Butch Walker
1:157/2.1
Distribution: BACKBONE

⌕ *Weight Training, Nutrition, and Fitness*
PA-CENTRAL
Moderator: Jim Kennedy
1:270/116
Distribution: LOCAL-NATIONAL

⌕ *Muscle and Fitness Echo*
MUSCLE
Moderator: Jim Kennedy
1:270/116
Distribution: FIDONET-ONLY

⌕ *Muscular Dystrophy Conference*
MDYSTROPHY
Moderator: Guy Thomas
1:161/40
Distribution: FIDONET-ONLY

⌕ *Narcotics Anonymous Echo*
SIP_NA
Moderator: Bob R.
1:154/40
Distribution: BACKBONE RECOVERYNET

⌕ *National Federation of the Blind news/
discussion.*
NFB-TALK
Moderator: David Andrews
1:261/1125
Distribution: ZONE-1 1:261/1125
Gateways: ADANET VIA 1:3602/24

⌕ *Natural Healing*
NHEAL
Moderator: Jeanne Garner
1:267/128
Distribution: PRIVATELY DISTRIBUTED

⌕ *NurseNet International*
NURSES_NETWORK
For nurses and users interested in nursing and
health care, and its impact upon nursing.

Moderator: Jim Rankin
1:10/475
Distribution: BACKBONE

⌕ *Nutrition and Diet*
NUTRITION
Moderator: Lawrence London
1:151/502
Distribution: BACKBONE

⌕ *OASIS for Compulsive Overeaters*
OASIS
Moderator: Phillip Z.
1:125/32
Distribution: BACKBONE

⌕ *Optometry/Eyecare Topics*
OPTOMETRY
Moderator: Walt Mayo
1:3627/101

⌕ *Radiology (X-Ray, Ultrasound, Nuclear Med.
& Rad Therapy)*
MED_RAYS
Moderator: Daniel Hagan
1:381/61
Distribution: BACKBONE
Gateways: ZONE 2 ZONE 3 VIA 396/1

⌕ *Rare Diseases*
RARE_CONDITION
Enables users to find other people with the
same condition.
Moderator: Butch Walker
1:157/2
Distribution: BACKBONE

⌕ *Recovery (International 12-Step Oriented)*
RECOVERY
Moderator: Rich Ward
1:102/402
Distribution: n/a

⌕ *Sex Addicts Anonymous*
SIP_SAA
Moderator: Bill E.
1:102/749
Distribution: BACKBONE

⌕ *Singleness in Purpose—Multiple Personality
Disorder*
SIP_MPD
Moderator: Chris E.
1:153/740
Distribution: BACKBONE

⌕ *Spinal Cord Injury Topics*
SPINAL_INJURY
Moderator: Alan Hess
1:261/1000
Distribution: BACKBONE, GATED TO ADANET

꠵ *Sysops interested in disability advances.*
HANDY.SYSOP

Enables Sysops to discuss various disability related accessibility issues related to BBS and non-BBS questions.
Moderator: Les Barr
1:147/41
Restr: SYSOP
Distribution: FIDO BACKBONE
Gateways: ADANET

꠵ *Traditional Asian Medicine & Bodywork*
TCM
Moderator: Barry Kapke
1:125/33
Distribution: FIDONET, ADANET, DHARMANET
Gateways: ADANET VIA 1:3602/24, DHARMANET VIA 1:125/33

꠵ *Vibrational Healing*
VHEAL

Discusses the various approaches to health that focus on the "subtle" body. Balneology (therapeutic baths), flower essences, aromatherapy, radionics, homeopathy, uropathy, dowsing, magnets, crystals, and so on.
Moderator: Barry Kapke
1:125/33
Distribution: FIDONET, ADANET, DHARMANET
Gateways: ADANET VIA 1:3602/24, DHARMANET VIA 1:125/33

꠵ *Visual Disabilities Echo*
BLINKTALK

Discusses topics of special interest to blind and partially sighted individuals.
Moderator: William Wilson
1:129/89
Distribution: BACKBONE 129/89

Usenet

꠵ *Anxiety in the modern world.*
alt.angst

꠵ *Recreational pharmaceuticals and related flames.*
alt.drugs

꠵ *Many things are addictive besides pills.*
alt.drugs.usenet

꠵ *You WILL read this group and ENJOY it!*
alt.mindcontrol

꠵ *For people in recovery programs (AA, ACA, GA).*
alt.recovery

꠵ *Is that last name, first?*
alt.suicide.finals

꠵ *Talk of why suicides increase at holidays.*
alt.suicide.holiday

꠵ *Dealing with emotional situations & experiences.*
alt.support

꠵ *Seeking enlightenment through weight loss.*
alt.support.diet

꠵ *Autism and Developmental Disability List*
bit.listserv.autism

꠵ *Computer and Health Discussion List*
bit.listserv.c+health

꠵ *Deaf List*
bit.listserv.deaf-l

꠵ *Medical Libraries Discussion List*
bit.listserv.medlib-l

꠵ *MEDNEWS—Health Info-Com Network Newsletter.*
bit.listserv.mednews

꠵ *Disease, medicine, health care, sick celebs. (Moderated)*
clari.tw.health

꠵ *AIDS stories, research, political issues. (Moderated)*
clari.tw.health.aids

꠵ *Items of interest for/about the handicapped. (Moderated)*
misc.handicap

꠵ *Current interest: drug testing, terrorism, etc.*
misc.headlines

꠵ *Medicine and its related products.*
sci.med

꠵ *Environmental news, hazardous waste, forests. (Moderated)*
regulations.clari.tw.environment

꠵ *AIDS: treatment, pathology/biology of HIV, prevention. (Moderated)*
sci.med.aids

꠵ *Issues of physics in medical testing/care.*
sci.med.physics

꠵ *The politics of drug issues.*
talk.politics.drugs

Online Libraries
After Dark

✪ *ABLEDATA*
Contains detailed information on rehabilitation products and technical aids for people with disabilities, from personal care to vocational and transportation aids.
Coverage: current
Updated: Monthly

✪ *AgeLine*
A bibliographic database with abstracts on middle age and ageing. Includes research and consumer-orented materials.
Coverage: 1978 to present
Updated: Bimonthly

✪ *AIDS Abstracts from the Bureau of Hygiene and Tropical Diseases*
Abstracts of papers on all viruses in the HIV/HTLV family and AIDS-related retroviruses and associated infections covering clinical aspects, treatment, etiology, pathology, serology, immunology, virology, epidemiology and more.
Coverage: 1983 to present
Updated: Monthly with about 120 documents added per update.

✪ *Alcohol and Alcohol Problems Science Database*
Contains bibliographic records with abstracts and alcohol-related scientific references from US and foreign sources. Covers all apsects of alcoholism research.
Coverage: 1972 to present
Updated: Monthly

✪ *Alcohol Information for Clinicians and Educators*
Offers a collection of information about alcohol, alcoholism, and other drugs in the Project Cork Resource Center.
Coverage: 1978 to present
Updated: Quarterly

✪ *Birth Defects Encyclopedia Online*
A comprehensive, systematic, knowledge base of the biomedical sciences as they relate to human anomalies of clinical relevance, with emphasis on the applications of that knowldege to patient care.
Coverage: Current
Updated: Quarterly

✪ *CAB: Human Nutrition*
A subset of CABA containing all documents from the Nutrition Abstracts and Reviews Series A.
Coverage: 1973 to present
Updated: Monthly

✪ *CANCERLIT*
Bibliographic documents about published, cancer-related materials.
Coverage: 1980 to present
Updated: Monthly

✪ *Combined Health Information Database*
Offers citations and programmatic materials intended for health professionals, health educators, patients and the general public relating to AIDS, information and education programs, Alzheimer's disease, arthritis, blood resource information, cardiovascular diseases, diabetes, and other health topics.
Coverage: 1973 to present
Updated: Quarterly

✪ *Computer Retrieval of Information on Scientific Projects*
Contains major scientific information on the research projects supported by the US Public Health Service.
Coverage: 1986 to present
Updated: Monthy

✪ *Consumer Drug Information*
Full-text information on uses, undesired effects, precautions, dosages, and methods of drug administration and storage.
Coverage: Current material
Updated: Reloaded annually, with updates as needed

✪ *Current Contents Search*
Offers two databases, a table of contents, and a bibliography to correspond with the seven Current Contents Print editions: clinical medicine; life sciences; physical, chemical, and earth sciences; engineering, technology, and applied sciences; agriculture, biology, and environmental science; and arts, humanities, and social and behavioral sciences.
Coverage: Most current 12 months
Updated: Weekly

✪ *Current Contents: Clinical Medicine*
A subset of Current Contents Search™ corresponding to the Current Contents: Clinical Medicine print edition.
Coverage: Most current 12 months
Updated: Weekly

Disclosure/Health
A subset of Disclosure Database containing annual and quarterly financial and management information on companies publicly traded in the U.S. which deal with health care, pharmaceuticals and/or medical equipment.
Coverage: Current
Updated: Weekly

Drug Information Fulltext
Full text of Handbook on Injectable Drugs and American Hospital Formulary Service Drug Information, providing detailed information on virtually every drug entity available in the United States.
Coverage: Current material
Updated: Three times a year, plus annual reload

DRUGINFO and Alcohol Use and Abuse
This database is for social workers, therapists, social scientists, and educators.
Coverage: 1968 to present
Updated: Quarterly

Health and Psychosocial Instruments
Contains information on national and international instruments for researchers, practitioners, educators, and others in health-related fields.
Coverage: 1985 to present
Updated: Quarterly

HEalth Periodicals Database
Provides consumer summaries and full text on health, medicine, fitness, and nutrition.
Coverage: 1976 to present
Updated: Weekly

Health Planning and Administration
Index and abstracts of national and international publications in health care planning, organization, financing, management, manpower, and related subjects.
Coverage: Primarily 1974 to date, with some earlier documents
Updated: Monthly with 2500-3000 citations

International Pharmaceutical Abstracts
Worldwide literature from pharmaceutical, medical, and related journals covering drug therapy, toxicity, and pharmacy practice.
Coverage: 1970 to present
Updated: Monthly

Iowan Drug Information Service
Contains indexed records and articles on human drug therapy.

Coverage: 1966 to present:
Updated: Monthly

Medical and Psychological Previews
Provides current literature of clinical medicine and psychology .
Coverage: Current three months
Updated: Weekly with about 1000 documents (4-5000 older docs purges monthly)

MediConf
Provides information on worldwide medical and pharmaceutical conferences and exhibitions. Lists more than 4000 future events in all fields of medicine and health care from allergies to veterinary medicine up to the year 2000.
Coverage: Sept 1991 to 2000
Updated: Monthly

MEDLINE and Backfiles
Covers all aspects of biomedicine, including the allied health fields, and how they relate to medicine and health care on national and international levels.
Coverage: 1966 to present
Updated: Monthly

National Epilepsy Library Database
Coverage: 1982 to present
Updated: Quarterly

Nursing & Allied Health
Covers English-language journals and books in nursing and 13 allied health fields, including health education, rehabilitation, emergency services and health science librarianship.
Coverage: 1983 to date
Updated: Every two months, with about 3500 documents

NTIS (National Technical Information Service)
Covers U.S. and foreign government-sponsored research reports and studies in the physical sciences, technology, engineering, biological sciences, medicine and health sciences, agriculture, and social sciences.
Coverage: 1970 to present
Updated: Monthly

REHABDATA
Covers research and literature relevant to the rehabilitation of persons with physical or mental disabilities.
Coverage: 1956 to present
Updated: Monthly

Knowledge Index

◈ AIDSLINE
Contains records representing the scientific literature concerning AIDS (Acquired Immunodeficiency Syndrome). References cover the clinical and research aspects of the disease, epidemiology, and health policy issues.
Coverage: 1980 to the present
Updated: Monthly

◈ CANCERLIT®
Contains abstracts that appeared in Carcinogenesis Abstracts from 1963 to 1969 and in Cancer Therapy Abstracts from 1967 to 1979. Covers all aspects of cancer from research to the different diseases.
Coverage: 1963 to the present
Updated: Monthly

◈ Consumer Drug Information Fulltext
Contains in-depth descriptions of more than 260 drug entities, which make up over 80% of all prescription drugs, and a number of important non-prescription drugs. Offers information from descriptions of drugs and how they work, to storing the drugs.
Coverage: Current edition
Updated: Quarterly (with annual reloads)

◈ Drug Information Fulltext
Drug Information Fulltext corresponds to two print publications: The American Hospital Formulary Service, which contains information on 1,000 drugs available commercially in the United States, and The Handbook on Injectable Drugs, which covers commercially available and investigational drugs in use in the U.S.
Coverage: Current
Updated: Quarterly

◈ Embase
Provides abstracts and citations of articles from biomedical journals from around the world.
Coverage: 1974 to present
Updated: Weekly

◈ Health Planning and Administration®
Contains references to nonclinical literature on all aspects of health care planning and facilities, health insurance, and the aspects of financial management, personnel administration, manpower planning, and licensure and accreditation that apply to the delivery of health care.
Coverage: 1975 to the present
Updated: Monthly

◈ International Pharmaceutical Abstracts
Provides information on all phases of the development and use of drugs and on professional pharmaceutical practice.
Coverage: 1970 to the present
Updated: Monthly

◈ Life Sciences Collection
Contains abstracts of information in the fields of animal behavior, biochemistry, ecology, endocrinology, entomology, genetics, immunology, microbiology, oncology, neuroscience, toxicology, virology and related fields.
Coverage: 1978 to present
Updated: Monthly

◈ MEDLINE
Covers virtually every subject in the field of biomedicine, indexing articles from over 3000 journals published in the United States and 70 other countries. MEDLINE is the equivalent of three printed indexes: *Index Medicus, Index to Dental Literature,* and *International Nursing Index.*
Coverage: 1966 to present
Updated: Twice a month

◈ Mental Health Abstracts
Cites worldwide information relating to the general topic of mental health.
Coverage: 1969 to present
Updated: Monthly

◈ Pharmaceutical News Index
Contains international information on pharmaceuticals cosmetics, medical devices, and health related industries.
Coverage: Dec 1975 to present
Updated: monthly

◈ Smoking and Health
Contains bibliographic citations and abstracts to journal articles, reports, and other literature that discusses the effects of smoking on health.
Coverage: 1960 to the present (some older material)
Updated: Every two months

◈ The Merck Index Online
Discusses a single chemical entity or a small group of very closely related compounds. Records contain molecular formulas and weights, systematic chemical names (including CAS names), generic and trivial names, trademarks and their owners, company codes, CAS Registry Numbers, physical and toxicity data, therapeutic and commercial uses, and

bibliographic citations to the chemical, biomedical, and patent literature.
Coverage: Late 19th Century to the present
Updated: Semiannual reloads

Orbit

↻ *Aqualine*
Covers the world's literature on water and wastewater technology and environmental protection. Only available on Orbit.
Coverage: 1960 to present
Updated: Biweekly

↻ *Chemical Safety NewsBase*
Covers a wide range of information on the health and safety affects of hazardous chemicals encountered by employees in industry and laboratories.
Coverage: 1981 to present
Updated: Monthly

↻ *CISDOC*
Provides international coverage of all topics related to general safety and health conditions at work.
Coverage: 1972 to present
Updated: Bimonthly

↻ *Drug Patents International*
Provides evaluated product patent coverage for more than 800 pharmaceutical compounds, either marketed or in active R&D.
Coverage: Current
Updated: Monthly

↻ *ENVIROLINE*
Provides records with abstracts on air environment, environmental health, land environment, resource management, and water environment.
Coverage: 1971 to present
Updated: Monthly

↻ *Food Science and Technology Abstracts*
Covers the literature on food science and technology. FSTA includes articles on the basic food sciences, food safety, engineering, packaging, food products and food processes.
Coverage: 1969 to present
Updated: Monthly

↻ *Health and Safety Executive*
Contains bibliographic references from journals, books, pamphlets, government publications, and conference proceedings. Covers occupational health and safety aspects.
Coverage: 1977 to present
Updated: Monthly

↻ *National Institute for Occupational Safety and Health Technical Information Center (NIOSHTIC)*
Contains records covering all aspects of occupational safety and health from the National Institute for Occupational Safety and Health.
Coverage: 19th century to present
Updated: Quarterly

↻ *PESTDOC*
Covers worldwide literature on pesticides, herbicides, and plant protection designed specifically for the information requirements of analysis, biochemistry, chemistry, toxicology, insecticides, herbicides, fungicides, molluscicides, and rodenticides. Access is limited to PESTDOC subscribers.
Coverage: 1964 to present
Updated: Quarterly

↻ *Pharmaceutical News Index (PNI)*
Contains cover-to-cover indexing to 23 major industry newsletters.
Coverage: 1974 to present
Updated: Weekly

↻ *RINGDOC*
Covers worldwide pharmaceutical literature, specifically designed to meet the information needs of pharmaceutical manufacturers. Access is restricted to RINGDOC subscribers.
Coverage: 1964 to present
Updated: Monthly

↻ *Safety Science Abstracts*
Covers the interdisciplinary science of safety—identifying, evaluating, and eliminating or controlling hazards.
Coverage: 1981 to present
Updated: Monthly

↻ *Standard Drug File*
A companion to the RINGDOC Unified Database (UDB) file, SDF is a listing of approximately 7,500 known drugs and other commonly occurring compounds, including the full name and a standard registry name, pharmacological classification of standard activities, if any, chemical substructure terms, chemical ring codes, and other codes. Available to all RINGDOC subscribers.
Coverage: Current
Updated: Periodically

WasteInfo

Contains bibliographic references on all aspects of non-radioactive waste management with extensive coverage in the areas of waste disposal and treatment, waste recycling, environmental hazards of wastes, waste management policy, guidelines, legislation, regulations, economics, and more. Available only on ORBIT.
Coverage: 1973 to present
Updated: Monthly

NewsNet

Health and Hospitals (HH)

AIDS Weekly
Frequency: Weekly
Earliest NewsNet Issue: 11/7/88
AIDS epidemic. AIDS news and research findings from all countries are featured each week. Included are reviews of published articles about AIDS, and a calendar of relevant meetings.

Cancer Weekly
Frequency: Weekly
Earliest NewsNet Issue: 12/19/88
Contains extensive medical and therapy cancer news, research, as well as reviews of major periodicals and a calendar of relevant meetings from around the world.

Health Business
Frequency: Weekly
Provides late-breaking business, financial, legal, and regulatory news.

Health Care Competition Week
Frequency: Weekly
Earliest NewsNet Issue: 1/4/88
Contains concise, timely reports, and provides critical coverage of the business of health care.

Health Grants and Contracts Weekly
Frequency: Weekly
Earliest NewsNet Issue: 2/22/88
Provides timely and comprehensive record of health-related federal grants and contracts.

Health Legislation and Regulation
Frequency: Weekly
Earliest NewsNet Issue: 11/20/91
Provides briefs of late-breaking House and Senate bills and agency proposals, and offers an insider's perspective on lobbying initiatives and more.

Health Manager's Update
Frequency: Biweekly
Earliest NewsNet Issue: 11/6/91
Provides briefings on business, legislative, and regulatory developments affecting health-care costs, Medicare/Medicaid, and managed care.

Health News Daily
Frequency: Daily
Earliest NewsNet Issue: 6/21/88
Provides information on health business coverage, and reports on corporate financial performance and results, mergers and acquisitions, new ventures and products, and advancements in technology and science.

Health Week
Frequency: Biweekly
Earliest NewsNet Issue: 10/22/90
Covers business news of the health industry and offers solutions to vital management issues and concerns faced by senior business executives and clinical/ technical managers who work for major healthcare provider organizations.

Long Term Care Management
Frequency: Biweekly
Earliest NewsNet Issue: 11/21/91
Provides information and guidance that can help long-term care facilities survive and prosper.

Managed Care Law Outlook
Frequency: Monthly
Earliest NewsNet Issue: 2/7/89
A monthly legal briefing on HMOs, PPOs, and benefit options. Covers court cases, decisions, and legal and legislative trends involving managed care systems.

Managed Care Outlook
Frequency: Biweekly
Earliest NewsNet Issue: 1/8/88
An executive insider business briefing on all aspects of managed care—health maintenance organizations (HMOs), preferred provider organizations (PPOs), triple-option plans, utilization review, information systems, and contracting.

Medical Research Funding News
Frequency: Biweekly
Earliest NewsNet Issue: 11/13/91
Provides information on funding from the government and the private sector, including how to prepare for and respond to NIH policy

developments affecting budgets, funding priorities, application requirements, and more.

⑤ *Medical Utilization Review*
Frequency: Biweekly
Earliest NewsNet Issue: 11/14/91
Offers late-breaking developments affecting cost containment, data disclosure, private standards, PROs, and Medicare/Medicaid.

⑤ *Medicine & Health*
Frequency: Weekly
Earliest NewsNet Issue: 11/1/91
Monitors the legislators, regulators, and industry leaders who shape health policy.

⑤ *Washington Health Record*
Frequency: Weekly
Earliest NewsNet Issue: 11/11/91
Delivers a quick-reference compilation of new regulations and late-breaking legislative activity. Provides updates on final and proposed rules, notices, and agency meetings and hearings from the Federal Register, House and Senate bills, and more.

Medicine (ME)

⑤ *The Physician & Sportsmedicine*
Frequency: Monthly
Earliest NewsNet Issue: 10/1/91
Reports on medical principles involved in training and conditioning of sports participants, including nutrition, exercise methods, and evaluation of physical fitness.

⑤ *Postgraduate Medicine*
Frequency: Monthly
Earliest NewsNet Issue: 9/15/91
Offers original clinical articles stressing the diagnosis and treatment of problems encountered in general medical practice, such as coronary disease, strokes, AIDS, diabetes, hypertension, and asthma.

⑤ *Transplant News*
Frequency: Biweekly
Earliest NewsNet Issue: 10/25/91
Up-to-date reports on the latest developments in organ and tissue procurement, and transplantation. Provides concise briefings on the industry's legal, financial, and policy concerns from Washington and around the U.S..

Bulletin Boards
DCRT Personal Computing Branch Bulletin Board (PCBull)
Access to this service is mainly for NIH (National Institute of Health) employees.
Baud Rate: 300, 1200, 2400, 9600
BBS Number: (301) 480-8400
BBS Software: RBBS-PC
Help Line: 496-2282

OASH BBS
National AIDS Program Office
Baud Rate: 300, 1200, 2400, 9600
BBS Number: (202) 245-1423
BBS Software: RBBS-PC
Sysop: TED FOOR

NADAP BBS
Navy Alcohol and Drug Abuse Prevention and Control (NADAP) "NADAP is operated for the use by the personnel of the Drug and Alcohol Abuse Prevention and Control Division of the Naval Military Personnel Command. It serves as an E-mail point, and a forum to discuss problems and issues for addicted people. "
Availability: 24 hrs/7 days
Baud Rate: 300, 1200, 2400, 9600
BBS Number: (703) 693-3831
BBS Software: WILDCAT
Sysop: NADAP

TEDDY BEAR HOLLOW
Adult Children Educational Foundation: Recovery Educational Foundation
Dedicated to the alcohol and drug recovery community, and contains materials available from recovery books and tapes, resources for the recovery community, professional treatment providers, information & resources for the professional, and other topics of interest to the recovery community
Baud Rate: 300, 1200, 2400
BBS Number: (703) 821-2925
BBS Software: RBBS-PC
Sysop: Ray Walsh
Help Line: (703) 356-6064

TEDI-NET BBS

Operated by Telecommunications Exchange for the Deaf, Inc., a non-profit organization that provides services to the speech- and hearing-impaired. Primary service is the relay of telephone calls between the hearing and hearing- or speech impaired.
Baud Rate: 300, 1200, 2400
BBS Number: (703) 242-8117
BBS Software: Searchlight
Sysop: Esther Schaeffer, Bill Smith, and Randy Mays
Help Line: (703) 759-2993

Bureau of Health Professions

Dedicated to the nation's health care, it monitors and guides the development of health resources by providing leadership to improve the education, training, distribution, utilization, supply and quality of the Nation's health personnel.
Baud Rate: 300, 1200, 2400, 9600
BBS Number: (301) 443-5913
BBS Software: WILDCAT!
Sysop: Larry DiGiulio

HEX: The Handicapped Educational Exchange

The world's first tdd-compatible bbs, serving the disabled since 1979, it serves as a clearinghouse for information about the use of technology to aid the disabled, and as a way for handicapped people and their friends to ask questions and exchange information.
Baud Rate: 300, 1200, 2400
BBS Number: (301) 593-7357 or 593-7033 (TTY or 300bps)
BBS Software: TODAY/PC
Help Line: (301) 763-4640

Centers for Disease Control Laboratory Performance Information Exchange System (LPIES)

LPIES is an electronic communications system that was designed to assist laboratory personnel in maintaining an awareness of the latest developments in human retroviral laboratory testing technology.

Baud Rate: 300, 1200, 2400, 9600
BBS Number: (800) 522-6388
Help Line: (800) 322-4383

FDA/CDRH (Center for Devices dn Radiological Health)

Contains draft FDA guidance documents from the FDA division of mechanics and material science as it relates to the use of scientific equipment that use radioactive substances.
Baud Rate: 300, 1200, 2400
BBS Name/Sponsor: FDA/CDRH Guidelines
BBS Number: (301) 443-7496
BBS Software: RBBS-PC
Parameters: 8-N-1
Sysop: Ed Mueller
Help Line: (301) 443-7003

St. Joseph's Hospital BBS

This board is medical oriented, but has FDA news and releases, latest AIDS information, employment opportunities, and medical news, and Center for Disease Control reports.
Availability: 24 hours/7 days
Baud Rate: 330, 1200, 2400, 9600
BBS Name/Sponsor: St. Joseph's Hospital BBS
BBS NUMBER: (602) 235-9653
BBS Software: OPUS-CBCS
Parameters: 8-0-1
Sysop: David Dodell
Comments: Started in 1982

Black Bag BBS

Carries many science and public health echos like the Science National, National Physics, and Radiology Echo. It is a member of the Fidonet so you can send email to the Internet and Bitnet.
Availability: 24 hours/7day
Baud Rate: 300, 1200, 2400
BBS Name/Sponsor: Black Bag BBS
BBS Number: (302) 731-1998
Parameters: 8-0-1
Sysop: Ed Del Grosso M.D
BBS Software: OPUS-CBCS

Occupational Safety and Health BBS

For organizations and individuals with occupational health and safety concerns to

exchange information and ideas, get technical assistance with occupational health problems, and gain access to a variety of information resources.
Availability: 24 hrs/7 days
Baud Rate: 2400
BBS Number: (212) 385-2034
BBS Software: PCBoard
Sysop: Michael McCann
Help Line: (212) 227-6220

Vitality Directory

Contains health care conferences; Natural Health Care: Providers, Services and Products; News articles on various subjects relating to people's health; Calendar of Events for the country; a Speakers Bureau; Environmental Groups listing: Private and Government; Local and National Resources for Men, Woman, and Families; National Products & Services for over 60 categories; Personal Ad section: Men & Women looking for a mate; Catalogs, book reviews, and more
Availability: 24 hrs/7 days
Baud Rate: 14.4
BBS Number: (619) 634-1912
Help Line: (619) 634-1846
BBS Software: WILDCAT!

CD-ROM

Drugs & Pharmaceuticals

✎ *Drug Information Compact Cambridge*
7200 Wisconsin Avenue
Bethesda, MD 20814

Health

✎ *Health All-Primary CD Resources*
1123 Broadway, #902
New York, NY 10010

✎ *Health Index Information Access Co.*
362 Lakeside Drive
Foster City, CA 94404

✎ *Hospital Facilities*
Donnelley Marketing Information
70 Seaview Avenue
Stamford, CT 06904

✎ *OHS MSD*
TMS Inc.
110 West Third Street
Stillwater, OK 74076.

✎ *OSH-ROM*
SilverPlatter Information Inc.
One Newton Executive Park
Newton Lower Falls, MA 02162.

Health Safety

✎ *CCINFOdisc*
CCOHS
250 Main St., E.
Hamilton, ON L8N 1H6 Canada.
Medicine/Medical Research

✎ *10 Yearbooks on disc 1988 (Text only)*
CMC ReSearch, Inc.
7150 SW Hampton, Suite C-120
Portland, OR 97223

✎ *12 Yearbooks on disc 1989 (Text only)*
CMC ReSearch, Inc.
7150 SW Hampton, Suite C-120
Portland, OR 97223

✎ *AIDS Information*
CD Resources
1123 Broadway, #902
New York, NY 10010

✎ *American Family Physician*
CMC ReSearch, Inc.
7150 SW Hampton, Suite C-120
Portland, OR 97223

✎ *American Journal Diseases of Children (AJDC)*
CMC ReSearch, Inc.
7150 SW Hampton, Suite C-120
Portland, OR 97223 .

✎ *Archives of Dermatology*
CMC ReSearch, Inc.
7150 SW Hampton, Suite C-120
Portland, OR 97223

✎ *Archives of General Psychiatry*
CMC ReSearch, Inc.
7150 SW Hampton, Suite C-120
Portland, OR 97223

✎ *Archives of Internal Medicine*
CMC ReSearch, Inc.
7150 SW Hampton, Suite C-120
Portland, OR 97223
Portland, OR 97223

✎ *Archives of Neurology*
CMC ReSearch, Inc.
7150 SW Hampton, Suite C-120
Portland, OR 97223

꙰ *Archives of Ophthalmology*
CMC ReSearch, Inc.
7150 SW Hampton, Suite C-120,
Portland, OR 97223

꙰ *Archives of Otolaryngology/Head and Neck Surgery*
CMC ReSearch, Inc.
7150 SW Hampton, Suite C-120

꙰ *Archives of Pathology/Lab Med*
CMC ReSearch, Inc.
7150 SW Hampton, Suite C-120
Portland, OR 97223

꙰ *Archives of Surgery*
CMC ReSearch, Inc.
7150 SW Hampton, Suite C-120
Portland, OR 97223

꙰ *BiblioMED*
Digital Diagnostics, Inc.
601 University Avenue, Suite 255
Sacramento, CA 95825

꙰ *Cancer-CD*
SilverPlatter Information Inc.
One Newton Executive Park
Newton Lower Falls, MA 02162

꙰ *Cancer 1988*
CMC ReSearch, Inc.
7150 SW Hampton, Suite C-120
Portland, OR 97223

꙰ *Cancer 1989*
CMC ReSearch, Inc.
7150 SW Hampton, Suite C-120
Portland, OR 97223

꙰ *Cancerlit (Macintosh only)*
Aries Systems Corp.
1 Dundee Park
Andover, MA 01810

꙰ *CD-Gene*
Bureau of Electronic Publishing
18 Louisburg Square
Verona, NJ 07044

꙰ *ClinMED-CD*
SilverPlatter Information Inc.
One Newton Executive Park
Newton Lower Falls, MA 02162

꙰ *Compact Med Base*
Online Research Systems
2901 Broadway, Suite 154
New York, NY 10025

꙰ *Comprehensive MEDLINE*
EBSCO Electronic Information
P.O. Box 325
Topsfield, MA 01983

꙰ *CONSULT*
Compact Cambridge
7200 Wisconsin Avenue
Bethesda, MD 20814
Cost: $375.00

꙰ *Core MEDLIN*
EBSCO Electronic Information
P.O. Box 325
Topsfield, MA 01983

꙰ *Critical Care Medicine*
85-89 CMC ReSearch, Inc.
7150 SW Hampton, Suite C-120
Portland, OR 97223

꙰ *Dictionary of Medicine & Biology*
John Wiley & Sons, Inc.
605 Third Avenue
New York, NY 10158

꙰ *DRG Forecasting Model*
Donnelley Marketing Information
70 Seaview Avenue
Stamford, CT 06904

꙰ *DRUGDEX*
Micromedex Inc.
660 Bannock Street, 3rd Flr.
Denver, CO 80204

꙰ *EMBASE*
SilverPlatter Information Inc.
One Newton Executive Park
Newton Lower Falls, MA 02162.

꙰ *EMBASE-Excerpta Medica*
Elsevier Science Public
52 Vanderbilt Avenue
New York, NY 10017

꙰ *EMERGINDEX*
Micromedex Inc.
660 Bannock Street, 3rd Flr.
Denver, CO 80204

꙰ *Gastroenterology*
SilverPlatter Information Inc.
One Newton Executive Park
Newton Lower Falls, MA 02162

꙰ *IDENTIDEX*
Micromedex Inc.

660 Bannock Street, 3rd Flr.
Denver, CO 80204

✒ *Immunology and AIDS*
SilverPlatter Information Inc.
One Newton Executive Park
Newton Lower Falls, MA 02162.

✒ *Journal of American Medical Association*
(Update every 6 months)
CMC ReSearch, Inc.
7150 SW Hampton, Suite C-120
Portland, OR 97223

✒ *Journal of Trauma*
CMC ReSearch, Inc.
7150 SW Hampton, Suite C-120
Portland, OR 97223

✒ *MEDLINE*
Compact Cambridge
7200 Wisconsin Avenue
Bethesda, MD 20814

✒ *MEDLINE (1984-88)*
Dialog Information Service
3460 Hillview Avenue
Palo Alto, CA 94304

✒ *MEDLINE (1987-88)*
Dialog Information Service
3460 Hillview Avenue
Palo Alto, CA 94304

✒ *MEDLINE (unabridged)*
Faxon Co.
15 Southwest Park
Westwood, MA 02090

✒ *MEDLINE (current year)*
SilverPlatter Information Inc.
One Newton Executive Park
Newton Lower Falls, MA 02162.

✒ *MEDLINE (current yr+1)*
SilverPlatter Information Inc.

✒ *MEDLINE (current yr+2)*
SilverPlatter Information Inc.

✒ *MEDLINE (current yr+3)*
SilverPlatter Information Inc.

✒ *MEDLINE (current yr+4)*
SilverPlatter Information Inc.

✒ *MEDLINE Knowledge Finder (Macintosh only)*

Aries Systems Corp.
1 Dundee Park
Andover, MA 01810

✒ *Neurosciences*
SilverPlatter Information Inc.
Nurse Library

✒ *(The) Ellis Enterprises Inc.*
225 NW Thirteenth Street
Oklahoma City, OK 73103

✒ *Nursing Indisc*
Knowledge Access International
2685 Marine Way, Suite 1305
Mountain View, CA 94043

✒ *Nursing&Allied Health*
CINAHL
1509 Wilson Terrace
Glendale, CA 91209-0871

✒ *Obstetrics & Gynecology 85-89*
CMC ReSearch, Inc.
7150 SW Hampton, Suite C-120
Portland, OR 97223

✒ *Oncodisc*
J.B. Lippincott Co.
East Washington Square
Philadelphia, PA 19105

✒ *Oxford Text*
Medicine Bureau of Electronic Publishing
18 Louisburg Square
Verona , NJ 07044

✒ *Pathline Biomedical Macintosh only*
Aries Systems Corp.
1 Dundee Park
Andover, MA 01810

✒ *PDR Direct Access*
EBSCO Electronic Information
P.O. Box 325
Topsfield, MA 01983

✒ *Pediatric Infectious Disease Journal 84-89*
CMC ReSearch, Inc.
7150 SW Hampton, Suite C-120
Portland, OR 97223

✒ *Pediatrics 1983-89*
CMC ReSearch, Inc.
7150 SW Hampton, Suite C-120
Portland, OR 97223

✤ *Pediatrics in Review/Redbook*
CMC ReSearch, Inc.
7150 SW Hampton, Suite C-120
Portland, OR 97223

✤ *Medicine Physician Specialty*
Donnelley Marketing Information
70 Seaview Avenue
Stamford, CT 06904

✤ *Physicians' Desk Reference*
Medical Economics Co., Inc.
680 Kinderkamac Road
Oradell, NJ 07649

✤ *POISONDEX*
Micromedex Inc.
660 Bannock Street
3rd Flr., Denver, CO 80204

✤ *Psychiatry*
SilverPlatter Information Inc.
One Newton Executive Park
Newton Lower Falls, MA 02162.

✤ *Renal Tumors of Children*
CMC ReSearch, Inc.
7150 SW Hampton, Suite C-120
Portland, OR 97223

✤ *Specialty Series (Macintosh only)*
Aries Systems Corp.
1 Dundee Park
Andover, MA 01810

Nutrition

✤ *Food/Analyst*
Hopkins Technology
421 Hazel Lane
Hopkins, MN 55343

✤ *Food/Analyst Plus*
Hopkins Technology
421 Hazel Lane
Hopkins, MN 55343

Religion Resources

Forums & Databases

America Online (AOL)

Ethics and Religion Forum
Keyword: Ethics
Path: Lifestyles & Interests Department > Ethics and Religion Forum
Dedicated to the exploration of ethical and religious issues that face today's society. Members of all beliefs can participate in message board and live online discussion.

CompuServe (CIS)

New Age Forum
GO NEWAGE
Discusses "new age" topics such as psychic arts and sciences; yoga and meditation; Eastern and occult religions and beliefs; natural foods/ healing; and environmental issues.

Religion Forum
GO RELIGION
For users to share discussions, opinions and information, as well as ask questions on topics that relate to religion.

GEnie

Religion & Philosophy RoundTable
Keyword: RELIGION or Page 390
Enables users to exchange news, information, and opinions pertaining to all aspects of world religions, philosophies, and ethics.

The Well

Christianity
(g cross)
Dicusses all facets of Christianity

Jewish
(g jewish)
Covers everything about being Jewish.

Spirituality
(g spi)
Enables users to arrive at a common spiritual consensus in spite of a difference in backgrounds.

Buddhist
(g wonder)

Network Discussions Lists

Internet (Includes Bitnet & UUCPNet)

Computerized Analysis of Biblical Texts
AIBI-L@UOTTAWA.BITNET
LISTSERV@UOTTAWA.BITNET The Comp

History of American Catholicism
AMERCATH@UKCC.BITNET
LISTSERV@UKCC.BITNET
Contact: Anne Kearney
<JCCANNEK@UKCC.BITNET>

Episcopal Mailing List
ANGLICAN@AUVM.BITNET
LISTSERV@AUVM.BITNET

American Theological Library Discussion list
ATLANTIS@HARVARDA.BITNET
LISTSERV@HARVARDA.BITNET

Theology
For issues and questions of concern to observant Jews.
BALTUVA@MCGILL1.BITNET
LISTSERV@MCGILL1.BITNET
Contact: Claire Austin
<CZCA@MUSICA.MCGILL.CA>

❧ *Personal Ideologies Discussion List*
BELIEF-L@BROWNVM.BROWN.EDU
LISTSERV@BROWNVM.BROWN.EDU
Contact: David B. O'Donnell
<EL407006@brownvm.BITNET>

❧ *Muslim Students Association*
For the Muslim Students Association; operates in English and Indonesian.
boulalem@eleceng.ee.queensu.caBoualem
Sekhri<boulalem@eleceng.ee.queensu.ca>

❧ *Buddhism Discussion Group*
BUDDHA-L@ULKYVM.BITNET
LISTSERV@ULKYVM.BITNET
Contact: James A. Cocks
<JACOCK01@ULKYVM.BITNET>

❧ *Indian and Buddhist Studies List*
BUDDHIST@JPNTOHOK.BITNET
LISTSERV@JPNTOHOK.BITNET

❧ *Catholic Evangelism*
Covers Catholic evangelism, church revitalization, and preservation of Catholic teachings, traditions, and values.
Catholic-action@cvpnet.chi.il.us
Catholic-action-request@cvpnet.chi.il.us
Contact: Catholic Evangelism
<rfreeman@vpnet.chi.il.us>

❧ *Free Catholic Mailing List*
CATHOLIC@AUVM.BITNET
LISTSERV@AUVM.BITNET

❧ *Practical Christian Life*
CHRISTIA@FINHUTC.BITNET
LISTSERV@FINHUTC.BITNET
Contact: Bill Sklar Mailing
<EL407007@BROWNVM.BROWN.EDU>

❧ *Religious Studies Publications*
An electronic journal that disseminates table of contents, abstracts, reviews, and ordering information on new and recent print and electronic publications of relevance to religious studies.
CONTENTS@UOTTAWA.BITNET
LISTSERV@UOTTAWA.BITNET
Contact: Michael Strangelove
<441495@Uottawa.BITNET>

❧ *Christian Thought and Literature in Late Antiquity*
Discussions of the thought and literature of Christianity during the period 100 to 500 a.d.
ELENCHUS@UOTTAWA.BITNET
LISTSERV@UOTTAWA.BITNET
Contact: Gregory Bloomquist
<GBLOOMQ @UOTTAWA.BITNET>

❧ *Eastern Orthodox Christianity*
EOCHR-L@QUCDN.BITNET
LISTSERV@QUCDN.BITNET

❧ *Eastern Orthodox Christian Discussion Group*
The discussion and exchange of ideas by members, and people interested, of the various Eastern and Oriental Orthodox churches around the world.
EOCHR@QueensU.CA
Dragic.Vukomanovic@QueensU.CA
Contact: Dragic V.Vukomanovic
<Dragic.Vukomanovic@QueensU.CA>

❧ *Feminist Theology*
A discussion and resource list concerning women & religion and feminist theology.
FEMREL-L@UMCVMB.BITNET
LISTSERV@UMCVMB.BITNET
Contact: Cathy Quick
<c497487@UMCVMB.BITNET>

❧ *Global Christianity*
GLOBLX-L@QUCDN.BITNET
LISTSERV@QUCDN.BITNET

❧ *Hebrew-L Jewish and Near East list*
HEBREW-L@UMINN1.BITNET
LISTSERV@UMINN1.BITNET

❧ *History of Evangelical Christianity*
HISTEC-L@UKANVM.BITNET
LISTSERV@UKANVM.BITNET
Contact: Daniel H. Bays
<BAYS@UKANVM.BITNET>

❧ *History of Islam*
For the discussion, debate, and the exchange of information by students and scholars of the history of Islam.
ISLAM-L@ULKYVM.BITNET
LISTSERV@ULKYVM.BITNET
Contact: James A. Cocks
<JACOCK01@ULKYVM.BITNET>

❧ *Intervarsity Christian Fellowship Discussion*
For a discussion related to InterVarsity Christian Fellowship, a multi-denominational Christian group.
IVCF-L@UBVM.BITNET
LISTSERV@UBVM.BITNET
Contact: Mark E. Keating
V067PXNR@UBVMS.BITNET

❧ *The Ibycus Scholarly Computer discussion list.*
For scholarly computing and word processing primarily in Classics and in Biblical Studies. It is integrated with CD-ROMs to search and

display texts in Greek, Hebrew, Coptic, and languages using the Roman alphabet.

```
IBYCUS-L@USCVM.BITNET
LISTSERV@USCVM.BITNET
```

Contact: Sterling G. Bjorndahl

```
BJORNDAS@CLARGRAD.BITNET
```

❧ *Discussion on Judaism and Databases*

```
JU-DA@BARILVM.BITNET
LISTSERV@BARILVM.BITNET
```

❧ *Judaic Studies Newsletter*

For information, work-in-progress, electronic applications, and, especially, new approaches, that relate to Judaic studies.

```
JUDAICA@TAUNIVM.BITNET
LISTSERV@TAUNIVM.BITNET
```

Contact: Yechiel Greenbaum

```
WWRMK@HUJIVM1.BITNET
```

❧ *The Krishna Consciousness Club*

```
KRSNANET@ARIZVM1.BITNET
LISTSERV@ARIZVM1.BITNET
```

❧ *Christian Liturgy*

```
LITURGY@MAILBASE.AC.UK
MAILBASE@MAILBASE.AC.UK
```

Contact: Michael Fraser

```
<m.a.fraser@durham.ac.uk>
```

❧ *Christian Discussion*

```
mailjc@GRIAN.CPS.ALTADENA.CA.US
mailjc-request@GRIAN.CPS.ALTADENA.CA.US
```

Contact: Liz Allen-Mitchell

```
<liz@GRIAN.CPS.ALTADENA.CA.US>
```

❧ *Religion and the Ministry*

A discussion of the concerns and experiences of people who are planning a career in religious ministry, or for those considering such a move.

```
MINISTRY-L@GACVAX1.BITNET
MAILSERV@GACVAX1
```

Contact: Charles Piehl

```
<UNDERHILL@GACVAX1.BITNET>
```

❧ *Muslim News Network*

```
MUSLIMS@ASUACAD.BITNET
LISTSERV@ASUACAD.BITNET
```

❧ *National List for Jewish Students*

```
NHILLEL@GWUVM.BITNET
LISTSERV@GWUVM.BITNET
```

❧ *New Testament Greek Studies Conference*

```
NT-GREEK@VIRGINIA.EDU
NT-GREEK-REQUEST@VIRGINIA.EDU
```

Contact: David John Marotta

```
<djm5g@virginia.edu>
```

❧ *Orthodox Christianity*

For the exchange of information regarding Orthodox Christianity worldwide, especially its impact upon and resurgence within Russia and her neighbors.

```
ORTHODOX@INDYCMS.BITNET
LISTSERV@INDYCMS.BITNET
```

Contact: John B Harlan

```
<IJBH200@IndyVAX.BITNET>
```

❧ *Pagan Religion and Philosophy*

```
PAGAN@DRYCAS.CLUB.CC.CMU.EDU
PAGAN-REQUEST@DRYCAS.CLUB.CC.CMU.EDU
```

Contact: Stacey Greenstein

```
<UTHER@DRYCAS.CLUB.CC.CMU.EDU>
```

❧ *Philosophy*

A philosophy, religion, and society magazine for intense debate.

```
PHILRELSOC@HAMPVMS.BITNET
PHILRELSOC@HAMPVMS.BITNET
```

❧ *Progressive Jewish Activism List*

```
PJAL@UTXVM.BITNET
LISTSERV@UTXVM.BITNET
```

Contact: Steve Carr

```
<RTFC507@UTXVM>
```

❧ *Progressive Jewish Mailing List*

```
PJML@UTXVM.BITNET
LISTSERV@UTXVM.BITNET
```

Contact: Steve Carr

```
<RTFC507@UTXVM.BITNET>
```

For sharing information on Jewish concerns.

❧ *Quakerism/the Religious Society of Friends*

```
QUAKER-L@UIUCVMD.BITNET
LISTSERV@UIUCVMD.BITNET
```

Contact: Bruce Dienes

```
<bdienes@psych.uiuc.edu>
```

❧ *RELIGCOM— A discussion forum list*

```
RELIGCOM@UKCC.BITNET
LISTSERV@ULCC.BITNET
```

❧ *Religious Studies Publications*

A list for users who want to receive the full text of all reviews and book notes published by the *Religious Studies Publications Journal.*

```
REVIEW-L@UOTTAWA.BITNET
LISTSERV@UOTTAWA.BITNET
```

Contact: Michael Strangelove

```
<441495@Uottawa.BITNET>
```

❧ *Seventh-Day Adventists*

```
SDA-L@LLUVM.BITNET
LISTSERV@LLUVM.BITNET
```

❧ *United Society of Believers*

For users interested in the history, culture, artifacts, and beliefs of the Shakers (The United Society of Believers).

```
SHAKER@UKCC.BITNET
LISTSERV@UKCC.BITNET
```

🕉 *Scientific Study of Religion*
SSREL-L@UTKVM1.BITNET
LISTSERV@UTKVM1.BITNET

🕉 *Discussion of Religion*
THEOLOGY <U16481@UICVM.BITNET>
CHARLEY EARP <U16481@UICVM.BITNET>

🕉 *Unitarian Universalists*
A global meeting place for Unitarian Universalists and anyone following their beliefs.
UUs-L@UBVM.CC.BUFFALO.EDU
LISTSERV@ubvm.cc.buffalo.edu
Contact: Steve Traugott
<uus-lman@TerraLuna.SpaceCoast.Org>

Fidonet

🕉 *Abortion discussion from the Christian perspective.*
KILLBABY
Moderator: Steve Winter
98:98/1
Gateways: PRIME NETWORK

🕉 *A-Theism Education and Enlightenment Echo*
A_THEIST
For free thought and with the understanding that the Constitutional separation of state and church is not only desirable but absolutely mandated by the U.S. Constitution and works toward that end with education and source information.
Moderator: Christopher Baker
1:374/14
Distribution: LOCAL, ZONE1 BACKBONE, ZONE3, ZONE2, ZONE6
Gateways: 3:800/857 2:241/6001 6:600/403

🕉 *Baha'i Faith*
BAHAI
Moderator: Pam Cammack
1:352/19
Distribution: PRIVATE, REQUESTING BACKBONE ACCESS

🕉 *Bible News*
BIBLE_NEWS
A read-only forum for information for bible believing Christians.
Moderator: Bob Hoffman
8:70/0
Distribution: 1:11/50 8:8/7001
Gateways: FIDONET 8:8/7001<>1:11/50

🕉 *Bnai Noachim*
For followers of the Noahide Covenant.
Moderator: Aaron Schmiedel
1:124/4104

Restr: MOD-APVL
Distribution: KESHERNET

🕉 *Buddhist Philosophy & Practice*
DHARMA
Moderator: Barry Kapke
1:125/33
Distribution: FIDONET, DHARMANET
Gateways: DHARMANET VIA 1:125/33

🕉 *CHASSIDUS*
For the "PIOUS ONES." learning about the ways, customs, and laws of the Chassidim.
Moderator: Aaron Schmiedel
1:124/4104
Restr: MOD-APVL
Distribution: KESHERNET

🕉 *Christian Action Line*
C_ACTLINE
Lists legislative and corporate attacks on traditional family values.
Moderator: Ruth Grove
1:387/507
Distribution: FAMILYNET BACKBONE, OR PICKUP FROM MODERATOR

🕉 *Dharma Events & Community Listings*
SANGHA
A national "calendar" for the Buddhist community.
Moderator: Barry Kapke
1:125/33
Distribution: DHARMANET
Gateways: DHARMANET VIA 1:125/33

🕉 *Divining*
For Tarot, Runes, I Ching, Scrying, and other means of divination
Moderator: Jeanne Garner
1:267/128
Restr: MOD-APVL
Distribution: PRIVATELY DISTRIBUTED

🕉 *Engaged Buddhism*
PEACEWORK
Discusses ethics, social responsibility and engaged Buddhism.
Moderator: Barry Kapke
1:125/33
Distribution: DHARMANET
Gateways: DHARMANET VIA 1:125/33

🕉 *FidoNet International Open Bible Conference*
OPEN_BIBLE
For users seeking biblical truth, and truth about the Bible.
Moderator: Mike Wallace
1:100/519
Distribution: BACKBONE

InterFaith Religious Exchange Echo
INTERFAITH
For members of all religions and denominations to meet and discuss and promote their views in a non-confrontational atmosphere.
Moderator: Jason Steck
1:104/424
Restr: MOD-APVL
Distribution: LDSNET, PODS, METRONET, PRIVATE

International Bible Conference
BIBLE
For strictly Bible oriented conversations, primarily for Fundamental Bible believers.
Moderator: Bob Hoffman
8:70/0
Distribution: 1:13/13 8:8/7001
Gateways: FIDONET 8:8/7001<>1:11/50 8:70/0<>1:11/50

KESHERnet—International Jewish Echos
K_TORAH
Moderator: Aaron Schmiedel
1:124/4104
Restr: MOD-APVL
Distribution: KESHERNET

Missionary Newsletter Conference
MISSIONS
For missionary letters from the mission fields. Read only!
Moderator: Bob Hoffman
8:70/0
Distribution: 1:11/50 8:8/7001
Gateways: FIDONET 8:8/7001<>1:11/50 8:70/0<>1:11/50

Mormon Echo
MORMON
Discusses the Church of Jesus Christ of Latter-Day Saints—its theology, traditions, history, and people.
Moderator: Malin Jacobs
1:104/438
Distribution: LDSNET
Gateways: FIDONET VIA 1:104/424

Osho/Sannyas
OSHO
For the discussion of texts, experiences, issues related to Osho (aka Bhagwan Shree Rajneesh) and the sannyas experience.
Moderator: Premananda
1:125/1066
Distribution: FIDONET, DHARMANET
Gateways: DHARMANET VIA 1:125/33

PARish COMputing: Computers in the Church
PARCOM
For authors and users of Church Management, Bible, and Christian Education/Games software share tricks and tips on automating elements of the Church's work.
Moderator: Lou Pascazi
1:129/75
Distribution: NON-BACKBONE
Gateways: GT:001/060 VIA 1:106/960 NETWORK:70/0 VIA 1:11/50

Prayer Now!
PRAYER_NOW
Operates in the light of what Jesus states in Matthew 18:20, "For where two or three are gathered together in my name, there am I in the midst of them."
Moderator: Greg Kudasz
1:379/26
Restr: MOD-APVL
Distribution: 379/26 OR MODERATOR APPROVED LINK

Religion Debate Echo
HOLYSMOKE
For the discussion and argument of religions, religious tenets, and practices with a jaundiced eye.
Moderator: Frederick Leff
1:152/20
Distribution: ZONE1 BACKBONE, ZONE3, ZONE2, ZONE6
Gateways: 3:800/857 2:241/6001 6:600/403

Religion
RELIGION
For users who want to discuss religion without flaming those who hold opposing views.
Moderator: Ed Lawyer
1:261/1056
Distribution: ECHONET BACKBONE (ZONE 50)

Shepherd's Chapel Bible Conference
S_CHAPEL
This forum is on Bible study.
Moderator: William Le Var
1:102/481
Distribution: NET-102, SCBN, CLINK
Gateways: CLINK VIA 911:5150/22, SCBN VIA 777:777/0

Swedenborgian Ideas
SWEDENBORG
For discussing the spiritual and philosophical ideas of the New Christianity as envisioned by

Emanuel Swedenborg (1688-1772).
Moderator: Lee Woofenden
   1:3401/101
Distribution: ZONE 1 FROM 1:3401/101.0

ꕷ *Talmudic Studies*
For Shi'urim (classes) in Talmud, ON-LINE!
Some real talmid chochim here!
Moderator: Aaron Schmiedel
   1:124/4104
Restr: MOD-APVL
Distribution: KESHERNET

ꕷ *Tibetan Buddhism & Culture*
   TIBET_NEWS
Moderator: Barry Kapke
   1:125/33
Distribution: DHARMANET
Gateways: DHARMANET VIA 1:125/33

ꕷ *Torah Portion*
Comments on the weekly Torah portion.
Moderator: Aaron Schmiedel
   1:124/4104
Restr: MOD-APVL
Distribution: KESHERNET

ꕷ *Universal Life Church Chat*
   ULC_CHAT
A contact-point for users interested in learning
more about the ULC.
Moderator: Alan Jennings
   1:3800/6
Restr: MEMBER
Distribution: 1:3800/6,COMPUCHURCH

ꕷ *Universal Life Church Ministers*
   ULC_MINISTERS
Moderator: Alan Jennings
   1:3800/6
Restr: MEMBER
Distribution: 1:3800/6,COMPUCHURCH

ꕷ *Wholly Bible Related Discussions*
   HOLY_BIBLE
Explores the Christian Holy Bible (serious Bible
study only).
Moderator: Steve Winter
   98:98/1
Distribution: BACKBONE
Gateways: PRIME NETWORK

Usenet

ꕷ *Godless Heathens*
   alt.atheism

ꕷ *Focused Godless heathens. (Moderated)*
   alt.atheism.moderated

ꕷ *Contemplation of states beyond the teeth.*
   alt.meditation.transcendental

ꕷ *Messianic traditions.*
   alt.messianic

ꕷ *Discussions about paganism and religion.*
   alt.pagan

ꕷ *Phenomena which are not scientifically
explicable.*
   alt.paranormal

ꕷ *Flaming the merits of the Sigler-Lear
ADM3A.*
   alt.religion.adm3a

ꕷ *Grokking the Church of All Worlds from
Heinlein's book.*
   alt.religion.all-worlds

ꕷ *He's Fred, Jim*
   alt.religion.kibology

ꕷ *He's dead, Jim*
   alt.religion.scientology

ꕷ *Not such a bad dude once you get to know
him.*
   alt.satanism

ꕷ *Practical Christian Life*
   bit.listserv.christia

ꕷ *Religion, religious leaders, televangelists.
(Moderated)*
   clari.news.religion

ꕷ *Discussion of the Baha'i Faith. (Moderated)*
   soc.religion.bahai

ꕷ *Christianity and related topics. (Moderated)*
   soc.religion.christian

ꕷ *Discussions of Eastern religions. (Moderated)*
   soc.religion.eastern

ꕷ *Discussions of the Islamic faith. (Moderated)*
   soc.religion.islam

ꕷ *Religious, Ethical, and Moral Implications*
   talk.religion.misc

ꕷ *Esoteric and Minority Religions &
Philosophies*
   talk.religion.newage

Online Libraries
After Dark

⑨ *Religion Index*
Contains current and retrospective scholary material on religion, theology, and scriptural and ministerial studies.
Coverage: 1949 to 1959; 1975 to current
Updated: Monthly

Knowledge Index

⑨ *Bible (King James Version)*
Contains the complete text of the modern Thomas Nelson revision of the 1769 editon of the King James version of the Holy Bible.
Updates: closed

⑨ *Religion Index*
Provides indexing and abstracts to article for over 200 journals, and indexing for over 300 multiple author works.

Orbit
No services available.

NewsNet

Social Sciences

⑨ *ChurchNews International*
Frequency: Daily
Earliest NewsNet Issue: 11/3/82
Monitors religion worldwide, including news, advance alerts, backgrounders, features, personalities, and resources covering all major churches.

⑨ *Lutheran News Service*
Frequency: Weekly
Earliest NewsNet Issue: 1/10/86
News of the Lutheran Church in America and the American Lutheran Church.

⑨ *RNS Daily News Reports*
Frequency: Daily
Earliest NewsNet Issue: 8/20/84
Provides comprehensive coverage of significant religious developments in the U.S. and abroad, and of the interaction of religion and society. Impartial and inter-religious.

⑨ *United Methodist Information*
Frequency: Weekly
Earliest NewsNet Issue: 5/18/83
A news and human-interest service of particular significance to people and organizations related to the United Methodist Church.

Bulletin Boards
Mended Vessels
Contains a major religious segment.
Baud Rate: 300, 1200, 2400, 9600
BBS Number: (301) 705-6907
BBS Software: TriBBS
Sysop: Tom Watson.

Readers! of the Lost Ark!
Promoted as a religious board.
Baud Rate: 300, 1200, 2400
BBS Number: (301) 871 1809
BBS Software: Major BBS

CD-ROM

⑨ *The Bible Library*
Ellis Enterprises

⑨ *FABS Reference Bible*
FABS International Inc

⑨ *Master Search Bible*
TriStar Publishing

⑨ *Multi-Bible CDROM*
Innotech, Inc

⑨ *Religion Indexes*
American Theological Library Associates

Science Resources

Forums & Databases

America Online (AOL)

No services available.

CompuServe (CIS)

⟲ *Science/Math Education Forum*
  GO SCIENCE
For science educators, students, and others with interests in science and science education. Includes a large data library of downloadable software and practice problems for science and math college boards.

GEnie

⟲ *Space and Science Information Center*
Keyword: SCIENCE CENTER or Page 461
Supports space exploration, astronomy issues, and all avenues of science.

The Well

⟲ *Science*
  (g science)
A general conference on things scientific.

Network Discussions Lists

Internet (Includes Bitnet & UUCPNet)

⟲ *AIR-L—Institutional Researchers/University list.*
  AIR-L@UNMVM.BITNET
  LISTSERV@UNMVM.BITNET
Contact: Tom K. Field
  <TFIELD@UNMB.BITNET>

⟲ *North Carolina Science and Mathematics Alliance list.*
  ALLIANCE@NCSUVM.BITNET
  LISTSERV@NCSUVM.BITNET

⟲ *L3 Alpha Physics Block Analysis Diagram Group list.*
  ALPHA-L@LEPICS.BITNET
  LISTSERV@LEPICS.BITNET
Contact: Richard Mount
  <MOUNT@LEPICS.BITNET>

⟲ *Annealing list.*
For discussion of simulated annealing techniques and analysis, as well as related issues.
  ANNEAL@CS.UCLA.EDU
  ANNEAL-REQUEST@CS.UCLA.EDU
Contact: Daniel R. Greening
  <dgreen@CS.UCLA.EDU>

⟲ *APRX-NET—Approximation Theory Network list.*
  APRX-NET@TECHNION.BITNET
  LISTSERV@TECHNION.BITNET

⟲ *Aquaculture discussion list.*
Individuals interested in the science, technology and business of rearing aquatic species.
  AQUA-L@UOGUELPH.BITNET
  LISTSERV@UOGUELPH.BITNET
Contact: Ted White
  <ZOOWHITE@UOGUELPH.BITNET>

⟲ *Pollution and Groundwater Recharge list.*
For dicussions on aquifers.
  AQUIFER@IBACSATA.BITNET
  LISTSERV@IBACSATA.BITNET
Contact: S. Troisi
  <1026TRO@ICSUNIV.BITNET>

⟲ *Alliance for Teaching of Science list.*
  ASCD-SCI@PSUVM.BITNET
  LISTSERV@PSUVM.BITNET

♻ *Approximation Theory Network*
AT-NET@TECHNION.BITNET
LISTSERV@TECHNION.BITNET

♻ *Electromagnetic Transients Program*
ATP-EMTP@NDSUVM1.BITNET
LISTSERV@NDSUVM1.BITNET

♻ *Biomedical Ethics*
For discussion of medicine and medical technology.
BIOMED-L@NDSUVM1.BITNET
LISTSERV@NDSUVM1.BITNET
Contact: Bill Sklar
<86730@LAWRENCE.BITNET>
LISTSERV@FRMOP11.BITNET

♻ *Secondary Biology Teacher Enhancement*
BIOPI-L@KSUVM.BITNET
LISTSERV@KSUVM.BITNET

♻ *Bureau International des Poids et Mesures*
BIPM-L@FRORS12.BITNET
LISTSERV@FRORS12.BITNET

♻ *BrainWave Systems Corporation Product User List*
BIXANET@JHUVM.BITNET
LISTSERV@JHUVM.BITNET

♻ *Bureau of Public Water Supply Protect*
BPWSP-L@ALBNYDH2.BITNET
LISTSERV@ALBNYDH2.BITNET

♻ *Research and Advanced Study: Canada and Italy*
For the research communities in Canada and Italy.
CACI-L@UALTAVM.BITNET
LISTSERV@UALTAVM.BITNET

♻ *Canadian Coordinating Committee for Research*
CCCRN@NRCVM01.BITNET
LISTSERV@NRCVM01.BITNET

♻ *CHAOPSYC: Society for Chaos*
CHAOPSYC@UVMVM.BITNET
LISTSERV@UVMVM.BITNET

♻ *Correspondants Scientifiques du GS Chimie Moleculaire*
CHIMIECH@FRMOP11.EITNET
LISTSERV@FRMOP11.BITNET
Contact: Jean-Marie Teuler
<UCIR044@FRORS31.BITNET>

♻ *Correspondants Techniques du GS Chimie Moleculaire*
CHIMIECT@FRMOP11.BITNET
LISTSERV@FRMOP11.BITNET

♻ *Groupement Scientifique Chimie Moleculaire*
CHIMIEGS@FRMOP11.BITNET
LISTSERV@FRMOP11.BITNET

♻ *Climatologists list.*
CLIMLIST@OHSTVMA.BITNET
LISTSERV@OHSTVMA.BITNET

♻ *Coastal GIS Distribution list.*
COASTGIS@IRLEARN.BITNET
LISTSERV@IRLEARN.BITNET

♻ *Computers in Canadian Medical Education*
COCAMED@UTORONTO.BITNET
LISTSERV@UTORONTO.BITNET

♻ *Cognitive Science Center*
For faculty and students in a variety of disciplines, including psychology, philosophy, linguistics, computer science, music and others interested in the study of cognition.
COGSCI-L@MCGILL1.BITNET
LISTSERV@MCGILL1.BITNET
Contact: Michael Friendly
<FRIENDLY@YORKVM1.BITNET>

♻ *Comparative Medicine*
COMPMED@WUVMD.BITNET
LISTSERV@WUVMD.BITNET

♻ *Consultation and Discussion of Research and Policy list.*
CONSLT-L@IUBVM.BITNET
LISTSERV@IUBVM.BITNET

♻ *CORRIM-L Committee On Renewable Resources*
CORRIM-L@UWAVM.BITNET
LISTSERV@UWAVM.BITNET

♻ *The Color and Vision Network list.*
For users in vision research and in color research who utilize E-mail communication.
CVNET@YORKVM1.BITNET
CVNET@YORKVM1.BITNET
Contact: Peter K. Kaiser
<pkaiser@YORKVM1.BITNET>

♻ *The Cyanobacterial Toxins discussion list.*
Information about cyanobacterial toxins, toxic cyanobacteria (blue-green algae) and related topics.
CYAN-TOX@GREARN.BITNET
LISTSERV@GREARN.BITNET
Contact: Jussi Meriluoto
JMERILUOTO@FINABO

♻ *Cybernetics and Systems List*
Users interested in the interdisciplinary fields of systems science and cybernetics, and related fields.

CYBSYS-L@BINGVMB.BITNET
LISTSERV@BINGVMB.BITNET

↻ *Turkish Scientists' Discussion Group list.*
DOST@TREARN.BITNET
LISTSERV@TREARN.BITNET

↻ *Computers in Biotechnology, Research and Education*
EBCBBUL@HDETUD1.BITNET
LISTSERV@HDETUD1.BITNET
Contact: Arie Braat
RCSTBRA@HDETUD1.BITNET

↻ *Catalogue of Biotechnological Software*
Information about public domain and commercially available software for use in biotechnological research and teaching.
EBCBCAT@HDETUD1.BITNET
LISTSERV@HDETUD1.BITNET
Contact: Arie Braat
RCSTBRA@HDETUD1.BITNET

↻ *The Energy and Climate Information Exchange*
A project of EcoNet, aimed at educating the environmental community and the general public on the potential of energy efficiency and renewable energy to reduce the use of fossil fuels and their contribution to climate change.
ecixfiles@igc.org
ecixfiles@igc.org
Contact: Lelani Arris
<larris@igc.org>

↻ *Ecole d'ete de mecanique de l'Ecole Centrale*
ECP-MECH@FRECP12.BITNET
LISTSERV@FRECP12.BITNET

↻ *EHS-L Environmental Health System list.*
EHS-L@ALBNYDH2.BITNET
LISTSERV@ALBNYDH2.BITNET

↻ *Grupo de discussao na area de eletromagnetism list.*
ELTMAG-L@BRUFMG.BITNET
LISTSERV@BRUFMG.BITNET

↻ *Grupo de discussao na area de eletronica list.*
ELTPOT-L@BRUFMG.BITNET
LISTSERV@BRUFMG.BITNET

↻ *Electromagnetics in Medicine, Science and Communication list.*
For users interested in electromagnetic fields.
EMFLDS-L@UBVM.BITNET
LISTSERV@UBVM.BITNET
Contact: David Rodman
OOPDAVID@UBVMS.BITNET

↻ *Energy list.*
A BITNET newsletter on energy research in Israel.
ENERGY-L@TAUNIVM.BITNET
LISTSERV@TAUNIVM.BITNET
Contact: Joseph van Zwaren de Zwarenstein
<JO@ILNCRD.BITNET>

↻ *EU-SOAR European SOAR research communications list.*
EU-SOAR@HEARN.BITNET
LISTSERV@HEARN.BITNET

↻ *EV Electric Vehicle Discussion*
Discusses the current state of the art and future direction of electric vehicles.
EV@SJSUVM1.SJSU.EDU
LISTSERV@sjsuvm1.sjsu.edu
Contact: Clyde R. Visser
<cvisser@ucrmath.ucr.edu

↻ *Eye Movement Network*
For investigators representing a range of research interests in eye movements.
EYEMOV-L@SPCVXA.BITNET
EYEMOV-R@SPCVXA.BITNET
Contact: Dennis Carmody
<carmody_d@spcvxa.spc.edu>

↻ *Research in Fetal and Perinatal Development list.*
FET-NET@HEARN.BITNET
LISTSERV@HEARN.BITNET

↻ *Feminism in Science and Technology list.*
For discussion of feminism and science and technology.
FIST@hamp.hampshire.edu
FIST-request@hamp.hampshire.edu
Contact: Michelle Murrain
<mmurrain@hamp.hampshire.edu>

↻ *Preprint server for Functional Analysis list.*
FUNCT-AL@JPNYITP.BITNET
LISTSERV@JPNYITP.BITNET

↻ *HC-L HEALTHCOM/VM Discussion list.*
HC-L@ALBNYDH2.BITNET
LISTSERV@ALBNYDH2.BITNET

↻ *Hadron Calorimeter Database forum.*
HCDB-L@LEPICS.BITNET
LISTSERV@LEPICS.BITNET
Contact: Geoffrey B. Mills
GEOFFREY@LEPICS.BITNET

↻ *High Resolution Infrared Spectroscopy list.*
HIRIS-L@IVEUNCC.BITNET
LISTSERV@IVEUNCC.BITNET

๑ *History of Philosophy of Science list.*
For the exchange of information, ideas, queries, job notices, course syllabi, conference announcements, and other news of interest to scholars in this area.
```
HOPOS-L@UKCC.BITNET
LISTSERV@UKCC.BITNET
```
Contact: Don Howard
```
<einphil@ukcc.uky.edu>
```

๑ *History and Philosophy of Science and Science list.*
```
HPSST-L@QUCDN.BITNET
LISTSERV@QUCDN.BITNET
```

๑ *International Arctic Project Planning list.*
```
IAP-PLAN@NDSUVM1.BITNET
LISTSERV@NDSUVM1.BITNET
```

๑ *International Arctic Project Student Projects list.*
```
IAPCIRC@NDSUVM1.BITNET
LISTSERV@NDSUVM1.BITNET
```

๑ *International Arctic Project Expeditions list.*
```
IAPEXPED@NDSUVM1.BITNET
LISTSERV@NDSIVM1.BITNET
```

๑ *International Arctic Project Wildlife list.*
```
IAPWILD@NDSUVM1.BITNET
LISTSERV@NDSUVM1.BITNET
```

๑ *22nd International Cosmic Ray Conference*
```
ICRC-L@IRLEARN.BITNET
LISTSERV@IRLEARN.BITNET
```

๑ *International Chemometrics Society*
```
ICS-L@UMDD.BITNET
LISTSERV@UMDD.BITNET
```

๑ *Interfacial Phenomena Interest list.*
```
IFPHEN-L@WSUVM1.BITNET
LISTSERV@WSUVM1.BITNET
```

๑ *International Medical Informatics Association Board list.*
```
IMIA-L@UMAB.BITNET
LISTSERV@UMAB.BITNET
```

๑ *INFO-GCG: GCG Genetics Software Discussion list.*
Topics in computer-aided molecular biology and of particular interest to users and managers of the Genetics Computer Group software from the University of Wisconsin.
```
INFO-GCG@UTORONTO.BITNET
LISTSERV@UTORONTO.BITNET
```
Contact: John Cargill
```
<CARGILL@UTOROCI.BITNET>
```

๑ *Intuition in Decisionmaking list.*

To discuss, conduct, and promote inter-disciplinary research on the use of intuition in decisionmaking.
```
INTUDM-L@UTEPA.BITNET
LISTSERV@UTEPA.BITNET
```
Contact: Weton H. Agor
```
<HY00@UTEP.BITNET>
```

๑ *Dendrochronology Forum/International Tree Ring Databank list.*
```
ITRDBFOR@ASUACAD.BITNET
LISTSERV@ASUACAD.BITNET
```
Contact: Tom Nash
```
ATTHN@ASUACAD.BITNET
```

๑ *Society for Literature and Science— Philosophy list.*
```
LITSCI-L@UIUCVMD.BITNET
LISTSERV@UIUCVMD.BITNET
```

๑ *Maps and Air Photo Systems Forum list.*
```
MAPS-L@UGA.BITNET
LISTSERV@UGA.BITNET
```

๑ *Marine Studies/Shipboard Education Discussion list.*
```
MARINE-L@UOGUELPH.BITNET
LISTSERV@UOGUELPH.BITNET
```

๑ *Forum on Materials Design by Computer list.*
```
MAT-DSGN@JPNTOHOK.BITNET
LISTSERV@JPNTOHOK.BITNET
```

๑ *Forum on Materials Database System list.*
```
MATDB-L@JPNIMRTU.BITNET
LISTSERV@JPNIMRTU.BITNET
```

๑ *Material list.*
Provides information on the subject in Israel and to distribute it quickly through the computer network.
```
MATERI-L@TAUNIVM.BITNET
LISTSERV@TAUNIVM.BITNET
```
Contact: M. Wolff
```
WOLFF@ILNCRD.BITNET
```

๑ *Materials Synthesis list.*
```
MATLS-L@PSUVM.BITNET
LISTSERV@PSUVM.BITNET
```

๑ *Metallibrary list.*
```
METALIB@JPNTOHOK.BITNET
LISTSERV@JPNTOHOK.BITNET
```

๑ *Methodologie quantitative, sciences sociales list.*
```
METHO@UQUEBEC.BITNET
LISTSERV@UQUEBEC.BITNET
```
Contact: Simon Langlois
```
LANGLOIS@LAVALVM1.BITNET
```

⅏ *BIOSCI Methods-and-Reagents Bulletin Board list.*
METHODS@IRLEARN.BITNET
LISTSERV@IRLEARN.BITNET

⅏ *Modal Analysis list.*
MODAL@VTVM1.BITNET
LISTSERV@VTVM1.BITNET

⅏ *Mossbauer Spectroscopy, Software & Forum list.*
MOSSBA@USACHVM1.BITNET
LISTSERV@USACHVM1.BITNET

⅏ *Nutrient Cycling Issues—Worldwide at Yale University list.*
NCIW-L@YALEVM.BITNET
LISTSERV@YALEVM.BITNET

⅏ *Science Education Reform list.*
NCPRSE-L@ECUVM1.BITNET
LISTSERV@CUVM1.BITNET

⅏ *Nonlinear Dynamics Research Group list.*
Discussion of applications of nonlinear dynamics to science, engineering, and economics.
NDRG-L@WVNVM.BITNET
LISTSERV@WVNVM.BITNET
Contact: Charles Jaffe
U0D96@WVNVM.BITNET

⅏ *NEUCHILE: Chilean Neurosciences Discussion list.*
NEUCHILE@CUNYVM.BITNET
LISTSERV@CUNYVM.BITNET

⅏ *Neural Networks list.*
Deals with all aspects of neural networks (and any type of network or neuromorphic system).
NEURON@HPLABS.HP.COM
neuron-request@HPLABS.HP.COM
Contact: Peter Marvit
<marvit@HPLABS.HP.COM>

⅏ *Neuroscience Information Forum list.*
NEURO1-L@UICVM.BITNET
LISTSERV@UICVM.BITNET

⅏ *Methods in Modern Neuroscience list.*
NEUS582@UICVM.BITNET
LISTSERV@UICVM.BITNET

⅏ *NO-L-ARG : Nitric Oxide/L-Arginine discussion list.*
NO-L-ARG@UKACRL.BITNET
LISTSERV@UKACRL.BITNET

⅏ *Nonmem and the Use of Population Pharacokinet list.*
NONMEM-L@UBVM.BITNET
LISTSERV@UBVM.BITNET

⅏ *Bitnet Redistribution of NSF STIS Documents list.*
NSFDOC-L@JHUVM.BITNET
LISTSERV@JHUVM.BITNET

⅏ *Organization for Tropical Studies at Yale University list.*
OTS-L@YALEVM.BITNET
LISTSERV@YALEVM.BITNET
Contact: Phil Sollins
SOLLINS@YALEVM.BITNET

⅏ *Oxygen Free Radical Biology and Medicine Discussion list.*
OXYGEN-L@UMCVMB.BITNET
LISTSERV@UMCVMB.BITNET

⅏ *POLAR-L Discussion list.*
POLAR-L@UOGUELPH.BITNET
LISTSERV@UOGUELPH.BITNET

⅏ *Qualitative Research for the Human Sciences list.*
QUALRS-L@UGA.BITNET
LISTSERV@UGA.BITNET

⅏ *Regional Science Information Exchange list.*
REGSCI-L@WVNVM.BITNET
LISTSERV@WVNVM.BITNET

⅏ *Group 1—Special Relativity list.*
RELATIV1@UWF.BITNET
LISTSERV@UWF.BITNET

⅏ *Group 2—Special Relativity list.*
RELATIV2@UWF.BITNET
LISTSERV@UWF.BITNET

⅏ *Campus Environmental, Health, and Safety Issues list.*
SAFETY@UVMVM.BITNET
LISTSERV@UVMVM.BITNET

⅏ *Science Awareness and Promotion list.*
For exchanging innovative ideas about making science more appealing to students.
SAIS-L@UNB.CA
LISTSERV@UNB.ca
Contact: Keith W. Wilson
<SAIS@UNB.ca>

⅏ *Fraud in Science list.*
For discussion of fraud in science.
SCIFRAUD@ALBNYVM1.BITNET
LISTSERV@ALBNYVM1.BITNET
Contact: Al Higgins
ACH13@ALBNYVMS.BITNET

⅏ *Arkansas Science and Math Education list.*
SCIMAT-L@UAFSYSB.BITNET
LISTSERV@UAFSYSB.BITNET

ᕗ *Societe canadienne de science economique list.*
SCSE@UQUEBEC.BITNET
LISTSERV@UQUEBEC.BITNET

ᕗ *Spectroscopic Happenings on Actinides and Rare list.*
SHARE-L@FRORS12.BITNET
LISTSERV@FRORS12.BITNET

ᕗ *Small Ruminant Discussion list.*
SM-RUM@ICNUCEVM.BITNET
LISTSERV@ICNUCEVM.BITNET
Contact: Alessio Valentini
TUSCIAZO@ICNUCEVM.BITNET

ᕗ *Discussion of Carpal Tunnel Syndrome, Tendonitis list.*
SOREHAND@UCSFVM.BITNET
LISTSERV@UCSFVM.BITNET

ᕗ *Southern Regional Science Association list.*
SRSA-L@WVNVM.BITNET
LISTSERV@WVNVM.BITNET

ᕗ *System Science discussion list.*
SYSCI-L@UOTTAWA.BITNET
LISTSERV@UOTTAWA.BITNET

ᕗ *Textile Discussion list.*
Discussion and development of textiles and clothing related studies.
TEXTILES@TREARN.BITNET
LISTSERV@TREARN.BITNET
Contact: Haluk Demirbag
<TEX5HAD@CMS1.LEEDS.AC.UK>

ᕗ *Journal des theoriciens des particules list.*
THEO-L@FRCPN11.BITNET
LISTSERV@FRCPN11.BITNET

ᕗ *TheoryNet list.*
For theoretical computer science.
THEORYNT@DEARN.BITNET
LISTSERV@DEARN.BITNET
Contact: Victor Miller
<TheoryNet-Request@IBM.COM>

ᕗ *Thermal Physiology*
For accelerating exchanges of information between scientists working in the field of thermal physiology.
THPHYSIO@FRMOP11.BITNET
LISTSERV@FRMOP11.BITNET
Contact: Michel Jorda
JORDA@FRSUN12.BITNET

ᕗ *Technical Report Redistribution list.*
TRLIST@UXA.ECN.BGU.EDU
trlist-request@uxa.ecn.bgu.edu

ᕗ *Tunisian Scientific Society Scientific Activity list.*
TSSACT-L@UTKVM1.BITNET
LISTSERV@UTKVM1.BITNET

ᕗ *Tunisian Scientific Society News list.*
TSSNEWS@PSUVM.BITNET
LISTSERV@PSUVM.BITNET

ᕗ *Turkish Science and Technology Policy Discussion list.*
TURKSCI@TRITU.BITNET
LISTSERV@TRITU.BITNET

ᕗ *Teaching Science in Elementary Schools list.*
T321-L@MIZZOU1.BITNET
LISTSERV@MIZZOU1.BITNET

ᕗ *University Communications Research Committee list.*
UCRC-L@VTVM1.BITNET
LISTSERV@VTVM1.BITNET

ᕗ *Discussion for University of Science and Technology list.*
USTC85-L@RICEVM1.BITNET
LISTSERV@RIVEVM1.BITNET

ᕗ *Expert Systems and Vision list.*
Discussion for artificial intelligence vision researchers.
VISION-LIST@ADS.COM
Vision-List-Request@ADS.COM
Contact: Tod Levitt
<levitt@ADS.COM>

ᕗ *APT and HRPT Features of TIROS-N and GOES Satellites list.*
weifax@IDA.ORG
wefax-request@IDA.ORG TIROS-N
Contact: Dr. Eric Roskos
<roskos@IDA.ORG>

ᕗ *Models of Welds*
A special interest group for computer modelling welds, run from CASCADE (Centre for Advanced Studies in Computer Aided Design and Engineering) at Carleton University.
WELDCOMP%cascade@alfred.ccs.carleton.ca
WELDCOMP-REQ%cascade@alfred.ccs.carleton.ca
Contact: Warren Hik
<hik%cascade@alfred.ccs.carleton.edu

ᕗ *Women In Science and Engineering net.*
Women in science, mathematics or engineering and students interested in those disciplines .
WISENET@UICVM.BITNET
LISTSERV@UICVM.BITNET
Contact: Dr. Alice Dan
<U16715@UICVM.BITNET>

◈ *Ciencia & Tecnologia (Science & Technology) list.*
XXI@UCHCECVM.BITNET
LISTSERV@UCHCEVM.BITNET

Fidonet

◈ *Science and Technology Conference*
SCI&TECH
For discussions about science and technology.
Moderator: Hector Mandel
1:233/15
Restr: MOD-APVL
Distribution: BACKBONE

◈ *National Science Echo*
SCIENCE
A general-interest science forum.
Moderator: Jeff Otto
1:154/32
Distribution: BACKBONE

◈ *National General Technical Discussion Conference*
TECH
For discussion of all technical subjects, including but not limited to computers and software, electronics, automotive technology, and all general tech and science subjects.
Moderator: Jim Gifford
1:203/289
Distribution: INTERNATIONAL

Usenet

◈ *Technology and use of the boomerang.*
alt.boomerang

◈ *Discussion of telecommunications technology.*
alt.dcom.telecom

◈ *The folklore of science, not the science of folklore.*
alt.folklore.science

◈ *Discussions on the Astronomical Image Processing System.*
alt.sci.astro.aips

◈ *Sound advice.*
alt.sci.physics.acoustics

◈ *Scientific theories you won't find in journals.*
alt.sci.physics.new-theories

◈ *EDTECH—Educational Technology. Moderated.*
bit.listserv.edtech

◈ *INFO-GCG: GCG Genetics Software Discussion.*
bit.listserv.info-gcg

◈ *Qualitative research of the human sciences.*
bit.listserv.qualrs-l

◈ *ClariNet UPI technology-related news wiregroups.*
clari.tw

◈ *Electronics makers and sellers. Moderated.*
clari.tw.electronics

◈ *General technical industry stories. Moderated.*
clari.tw.misc

◈ *Nuclear power & waste. Moderated.*
clari.tw.nuclear

◈ *General science stories. Moderated.*
clari.tw.science

◈ *Phones, satellites, media and general telecommunictaions. Moderated.*
clari.tw.telecom

◈ *The science of aeronautics and related technology.*
sci.aeronautics

◈ *All aspects of studying humankind.*
sci.anthropology

◈ *Scientifically-oriented postings about aquaria.*
sci.aquaria

◈ *Studying antiquities of the world.*
sci.archaeology

◈ *Biology and related sciences.*
sci.bio

◈ *Chemistry and related sciences.*
sci.chem

◈ *Studying classical history, languages, art, and more.*
sci.classics

◈ *Perception, memory, judgement, and reasoning.*
sci.cognitive

◈ *The use of computers as tools in scientific research.*
sci.comp-aided

◈ *Theory and practice of biostasis, suspended animation.*
sci.cryonics

- *Methods of data encryption and decryption.*
  sci.crypt
- *The science of economics.*
  sci.econ
- *The science of education.*
  sci.edu
- *Circuits, theory, electrons, and discussions.*
  sci.electronics
- *Discussions about energy, science, and technology.*
  sci.energy
- *Technical discussions about engineering tasks.*
  sci.engr
- *Discussing the field of biomedical engineering.*
  sci.engr.biomed
- *All aspects of chemical engineering.*
  sci.engr.chem
- *Topics related to civil engineering.*
  sci.engr.civil
- *The field of mechanical engineering.*
  sci.engr.mech
- *Discussions about the environment and ecology.*
  sci.environment
- *Discussion of geophysical fluid dynamics.*
  sci.geo.fluids
- *Discussion of solid earth sciences.*
  sci.geo.geology
- *Discussion of meteorology and related topics.*
  sci.geo.meteorology
- *Scientific image processing and analysis.*
  sci.image.processing
- *Natural languages, communication, and so on.*
  sci.lang
- *The Japanese language, both spoken and written.*
  sci.lang.japan
- *Logic—math, philosophy, and computational aspects.*
  sci.logic
- *All aspects of materials engineering.*
  sci.materials
- *Mathematical discussions and pursuits.*
  sci.math
- *Discussion of current mathematical research. (Moderated.)*
  sci.math.research
- *Statistics discussion.*
  sci.math.stat
- *Symbolic algebra discussion.*
  sci.math.symbolic
- *Medicine and its related products and regulations.*
  sci.med
- *AIDS: treatment, pathology/biology of HIV, prevention. (Moderated.)*
  sci.med.aids
- *Issues of physics in medical testing and care.*
  sci.med.physics
- *Discussion about science and the military. (Moderated.)*
  sci.military
- *Short-lived discussions on subjects in the sciences.*
  sci.misc
- *Self-reproducing molecular-scale machines. (Moderated.)*
  sci.nanotech
- *Discussion relating to the science of optics.*
  sci.optics
- *Technical philosophy: math, science, logic, and so on.*
  sci.philosophy.tech
- *Physical laws, properties, more.*
  sci.physics
- *Info on fusion, especially cold fusion.*
  sci.physics.fusion
- *Topics related to psychology.*
  sci.psychology
- *Refereed Psychology Journal and Newsletter. Moderated.*
  sci.psychology.digest
- *Research methods, funding, ethics, and whatever.*
  sci.research
- *Issues relevant to careers in scientific research.*
  sci.research.careers

⑤ *Skeptics discussing pseudo-science.*
`sci.skeptic`

⑤ *Space, space programs, space related research, and so on.*
`sci.space`

⑤ *Announcements of space-related news items. (Moderated)*
`sci.space.news`

⑤ *The space shuttle and the STS program.*
`sci.space.shuttle`

⑤ *The theory and application of systems science.*
`sci.systems`

⑤ *Modelling the universe. (Moderated)*
`sci.virtual-worlds`

Online Libraries
After Dark

⑤ *Cambridge Scientific Abstracts Engineering*
Brings together information from CSA abstracting services.
Coverage: 1981 to present
Updated: Monthly

⑤ *Current Contents: Engineering, Technology and Applied Sciences*
A subset of Current Contents Search™ corresponding to the *Current Contents: Engineering, Technology & Applied Sciences* print edition.
Coverage: Current 12 months
Updated: Weekly

⑤ *Current Contents: Physical, Chemical and Earth Sciences*
Corresponds to *Current Contents: Physical, Chemical, and Earth Sciences®* print edition. The database is a 12-month rolling file updated every week.
Coverage: Current 12 months
Updated: Weekly

⑤ *Current Contents Search™*
A multidisciplinary database corresponding to the seven *Current Contents®* print editions: Clinical Medicine; Life Sciences; Physical, Chemical Earth Sciences; Engineering, Technology, and Applied Sciences; Agriculture, Biology, and Environmental Sciences; Arts and Humanities, and Social and Behavioral Sciences.
Coverage: Current 3 months
Updated: Weekly

⑤ *Encyclopedia of Polymer Science and Engineering*
The full text on-line version of *Wiley's Encyclopedia of Polymer Science and Engineering* (2nd edition). Contains the complete text of all articles plus an abstract of each, index terms, cited and general reference, tables, and other cititation information.
Coverage: 1984
Updated: Concurrent with the publication of each new volume

⑤ *INSPEC and Backfile*
Access to international literature, journal articles, conferences, reports, dissertations, and books covering physics, electronics, computers, electrical engineering and information technology.
Coverage: 1969 to present
Updated: Monthly

⑤ *National Technical Information Service (NTIS)*
A bibliographic database covering U.S. and foreign government-sponsored research reports and studies in the physical sciences, technology, engineering, biological sciences, medicine and health sciences, agriculture and social sciences.
Coverage: 1970 to present
Updated: Monthly

⑤ *Wilson Applied Science and Technology Index*
Contains articles, product evaluations, and book reviews on over 390 leading English-language periodicals published in the U.S. and elsewhere.
Coverage: 1983 to present
Updated: Monthly

⑤ *Wilson General Science Index*
A guide to current information in 111 English-language periodicals in the physical, life, and health sciences, designed for students and non-specialists.
Coverage: 1984 to present
Updated: Monthly

Knowledge Index

⑤ *Food Science and Technology Abstracts*
Provides access to research and new developments in food science/technology and allied disciplines. Includes Vitis, a subfile on viticulture and enology. Indexes over 1200 journals from over 50 countries, patents from 20 countries, and books in any language.

Coverage: 1969 to present
Updated: Monthly

❧ *Japan Technology*
Contains English-language abstracts of articles from the leading Japanese business, technical, and scientific journals.
Coverage: 1985 to present
Updated: Monthly

Orbit

❧ *American Men and Women of Science*
Contains an active register of U.S. and Canadian scientists in the physical and biological sciences, as well as public health scientists, engineers, mathematicians, statisticians and computer scientists. A total of 160 major disciplines and 800 subdisciplines are classified. Biographical citations for 125,000 scientists include what the individual has accomplished, current affiliations and contact information.
Coverage: Current
Updated: Every three years

❧ *Ceramic Abstracts*
Covers scientific, engineering, and commercial literature pertaining to ceramics and related materials, including processing and manufacturing aspects. More than 130,000 records are included.
Coverage: 1976 to present
Updated: Bimonthly

❧ *Directory of American Research & Technology*
Contains the research and development capabilities of approximately 12,000 industrial organizations in the U.S. Also includes non-profit and privately financed firms doing research, development, engineering, consulting or behavioral research for industry.
Coverage: Current
Updated: Annually

❧ *Imaging Abstracts*
Contains more than 75,000 abstracts and references to the international literature on all aspects of imaging.
Coverage: 1977 to present
Updated: Monthly

❧ *ISTP Search*
Covers proceedings literature published internationally in journal issues, journal supplements, serials and monographs. This multidisciplinary file, with more than a million records, includes the following major areas: agriculture; applied sciences; biology; chemical sciences; clinical medicine; engineering; environmental sciences; life sciences; mathematics; physical sciences; technology, and more.
Coverage: 1982 to present
Updated: Monthly

❧ *Japan Technology*
Covers the science, technology, and business of Japan by providing more than 170,000 English abstracts of Japanese journal articles and special reports. Emphasis is on chemistry, computers, electronics, materials science, and manufacturing. Sources include over 500 journals published in Japan. Produced in the U.S.
Coverage: 1985 to present
Updated: Monthly

❧ *Materials Business File*
Covers all commercial aspects of iron and steel, non-ferrous metals and non-metallic materials, including ceramics, polymers, composites, and plastics. Articles are abstracted from over 2,000 worldwide technical and trade journals in more than 50,000 records.
Coverage: 1985 to present
Updated: Monthly

❧ *METADEX*
Provides more than 830,000 records from the international literature on metals and alloys. Sources include journal articles, conference papers, technical reports and books. Cross-references to translations are also covered.
Coverage: 1966 to present
Updated: Monthly

❧ *Metals Data File*
Provides designation and specification numbers, composition, forms, applications, manufacturers, element concentrations, mechanical and physical properties for ferrous and non-ferrous metals and alloys. Contains more than 45,000 records.
Coverage: 1983 to present
Updated: Monthly

❧ *National Union Catalog Codes*
Contains the names, complete addresses, and National Union Catalog codes for libraries cited in the Chemical Abstracts Service Source Index (CASSI) database. Serves as a companion to the CASSI file for identification of library codes

and listings of library addresses. Coverage includes approximately 400 libraries in 28 countries.
Coverage: Current
Updated: Periodically

National Technical Information Service (NTIS)
Covers completed U.S. government-sponsored research from hundreds of federal government agencies, their contractors and grantees. Includes technical reports, reprints, computer software and datafiles, subscriptions and bibliographies. The database announces U.S. government-owned inventions (patents and patent applications) available for licensing by the public. Contains more than 1.5 million records.
Coverage: 1964 to present
Updated: Biweekly

RAPRA Abstracts
The world's primary database on technical and commercial aspects of the rubber, plastics, and polymer composites industries. Covers the world's polymer literature including journals, conference proceedings, books, specifications, reports and trade literature. Contains over 375,000 records.
Coverage: 1972 to present
Updated: Biweekly

Safety Science Abstracts
Covers the broad interdisciplinary science of safety—identifying, evaluating and eliminating or controlling hazards; Contains 61,000 records.
Coverage: 1981 to present
Updated: Monthly

Scientific and Technical Books and Serials in Print
Provides a comprehensive subject selection of books and serials in scientific and technical fields. All aspects of physical and biological sciences and their applications are included as well as engineering and what can generally be called technology. Over 160,000 book titles and more than 40,000 titles of serials are included.
Coverage: Current
Updated: Monthly

SciSearch
Provides a multidisciplinary index to the international journal literature of science and technology. With approximately 10 million records, it corresponds to the printed *Science Citation Index* and contains additional records from the Current Contents series of publications. Indexes all significant items from approximately 4,400 scientific and technical journals and permits searching by cited references.
Coverage: 1974 to present
Updated: Weekly

World Ceramics Abstracts
Provides coverage of the world's literature on all aspects of ceramics. Contains more than 53,000 records.
Coverage: 1978 to present
Updated: Biweekly

NewsNet

Battery & EV Technology
Frequency: Monthly
Earliest NewsNet Issue: 9/1/89
Covers technical and economic developments in primary and secondary batteries and all forms of portable electric ground transportation.

Flame Retardancy News
Frequency: Monthly
Earliest NewsNet Issue: 6/1/91
Reports on the new developments and trends in flame-retardancy technologies, products, and processes. Provides news and analysis on worldwide R&D, corporate activities, and product comparisons.

Futuretech
Frequency: Monthly
Earliest NewsNet Issue: 1/1/88
Provides briefings on focused, strategic technologies that have been judged capable of making an impact on industry. Includes forecasts of marketable products and services resulting from the uncovered technology.

Innovator's Digest
Frequency: Biweekly
Earliest NewsNet Issue: 8/2/83
Reviews selected reports and documentation dealing with innovative multidisciplinary activities worldwide.

Inside R&D
Frequency: Weekly
Earliest NewsNet Issue: 1/4/89
Provides detailed reports on current research

and development around the world, concentrating on the trends and breakthroughs that affect business.

๑ *Japan Science Scan*
Frequency: Weekly
Provides news on physics, chemistry, pharmaceuticals, and environmental issues, including events which affect earth warming and deforestation and awards given to noted scientists and professional researchers.

๑ *New Technology Week*
Frequency: Weekly
Earliest NewsNet Issue: 1/30/89
Provides inside information and analysis on new developments in a wide range of important technologies.

๑ *Tech Transfer Report*
Frequency: Monthly
Earliest NewsNet Issue: 10/1/91
Reports on business opportunities at federal labs under the U.S. Departments of Energy, Defense and Commerce. Covers tech transfer laws, licensing arrangements, and cooperative R&D agreements.

๑ *Technology Access Report*
Frequency: Monthly
Earliest NewsNet Issue: 8/1/91
Helps companies locate, acquire, develop, and deploy technology from universities, research hospitals, and federal laboratories.

Bulletin Boards
Amateur Scientist BBS

For users interested in science, especially students and other amateurs but including professionals who like to discuss their own and other fields with nonspecialists. Includes *Journal of Student Research*, devoted to research papers by high school students, tutorial articles, and essays of interest to young scientists. Maintains a library of programs useful in amateur scientific work.
Availability: 24 hours/ 7 days
Baud Rate: 300, 1200, 2400
BBS Number: (503) 843-4214
BBS Software: Wildcat
Sysop: Gerry Roe

Building and Fire Research BBS

Devoted to fire research.
Baud Rate: 300, 1200, 2400, 9600
BBS Number: (301) 921-6302
BBS Software: TCOMMnet
Sysops: Scot Deal and Charley Arnold
Help Line: (301) 975-6891

FDA Guidance BBS

Operated by the FDA Division of Mechanics and Materials Science; contains drafts of FDA guidance documents.
Baud Rate: 300, 1200, 2400, 9600
BBS Number: (301) 443-7496
BBS Software: RBBS-PC
Sysop: Edward Mueller
Help Line: (301) 443-7003

National Geographic Kids Network

For teachers and schools that want to teach students how to use on-line communications and learn science and environmental issues. Students conduct experiments and research on an issue, and organize their findings with teammates across the world. A professional scientist on the network works with the students. Requires Apple II computers.

National Science Foundation (NSF) BBS

Operated by the NSF Division of Science Resources Studies.
Baud Rate: 300, 1200, 2400, 9600
BBS Number: (202) 634-1764
Help Line: (202) 634-4250

Science Line BBS

Sponsored by the National Science Teachers Association (NSTA). Provides a wealth of information and files for science teachers in astronomy, communications, earth science, medicine, psychology, general science, science for the handicapped, and more.
Availability: 24 hours/ 7 days
Baud Rate: 2400
BBS Number: (202) 328-5853, (202) 265-4496
BBS Software: RBBS-PC
Sysop: Alex Mondale
Help Line: (202) 328-5800 x57

Science Resources Studies BBS

Operated by the National Science Foundation, Division of Science Resources Studies. Provides bulletins and information regarding grants in the sciences.
Baud Rate: 300, 1200, 2400
BBS Number: (202) 634-4250
BBS Software: RBBS-PC
Help Line: (202) 634-4250

The Scientist's and Musician's BBS

Dedicated to finding the best scientific, engineering, medicine, C/C++, freeware, and shareware available throughout the world.
Baud Rate: 300, 1200, 2400, 9600
BBS Number: (216) 639-9508
BBS Software: PCBoard

Skyland BBS

Designed for nature photographers, writers, and nature lovers. Provides lists of wildlife and natural science bulletin boards.
Availability: 24 hours/ 7 days
Baud Rate: 300, 1200, 2400
BBS Number: (704) 254-7800
BBS Software: PCBoard
Parameters: 8-0-1
Sysop: Michael Havelin

STIS BBS

Replaces the SRS BBS; contains a great deal of information on NSF programs, grants, and bulletins.
Baud Rate: 300, 1200, 2400
BBS Number: (202) 357-0359 and 0360
BBS Software: SunOS
Help Line: (202) 357-7555
Comments: Logon with PUBLIC, select VT100 or VT100nkp terminal type.

CD-ROM

↻ *Apple Science CD*
Apple Computer Inc.
20525 Mariani Avenue
Cupertino, CA 95014

↻ *Earth Science Database*
OCLC
6565 Franz Road
Dublin, OH 43017

↻ *General Science Index*
H.W. Wilson

↻ *NTIS*
SilverPlatter Information Inc.
One Newton Executive Park
Newton Lower Falls, MA 02162

↻ *Science Helper K-8*
PC-SIG, Inc.

↻ *Science/Science Citation Index*
Institute For Scientific Information
3501 Market Street
Philadelphia, PA 19104

↻ *SciTech Reference Plus/Europe.*
R.R. Bowker Electronic Publishing

↻ *Selected Water Resources*
OCLC
6565 Franz Road
Dublin, OH 43017

↻ *Time Table of Science (Macintosh only)*
Xiphias
13464 Washington Boulevard
Marina Del Rey, CA 90292

Science Fiction Resources

Forums & Databases
America Online (AOL)

⑨ *Science Fiction & Fantasy Club*
Keyword: Science fiction
Path: Lifestyles & Interests Department >
Science Fiction & Fantasy Club
Contains categories for horror and mystery,
comics, Star Wars, Star Trek (Next Generation
and original show), Television, and Fantasy.

CompuServe (CIS)

⑨ *Sci-Fi and Fantasy Forum*
Keyword: GO SCIFI
Offers discussion for science fiction lovers.
Also provides conferences with famous authors,
producers, and publishers.

GEnie

⑨ *Science Fiction and Fantasy RT*
Keyword: SFRT or Page 470
Covers science fiction, fantasy, and horror
as well as comic books, science fiction
conventions, music and the visual arts as they
relate to science fiction and fantasy.

The Well

⑨ *Science Fiction and Fantasy*
  (g sf)
Features science authors, books, stories, and
more. A conference about the future and the
past.

Network Discussions Lists
Internet (Includes Bitnet & UUCPNet)

⑨ *Asimov list.*
Offers discussion of Isaac Asimov's works.
  ASIMOV-L@UTDALLAS.BITNET
  LISTSERV@UTDALLAS.BITNET

⑨ *Highly Imaginative Technologies*
Offers discussion on any technology that could
be implemented in the future.
  HIT@UFRJ.BITNET
  LISTSERV@UFRJ.BITNET
Contact: Geraldo Xexeo
  GXEXEO@CERNVM.BITNET

⑨ *Horror*
  HORROR@PACEVM.BITNET
  LISTSERV@PACEVM.BITNET
Contact: Cliff Brenner
  VMAN@PACEVM.BITNET

⑨ *Science Fiction Journal*
For Quanta, the moderated, electronically
distributed journal of Science Fiction and
Fantasy.
  Quanta@ANDREW.CMU.EDU
  quanta+request-ascii@ANDREW.CMU.EDU
Contact: Pierette Maniago
  <pierette+@ANDREW.CMU.EDU>

⑨ *Science Fiction Lovers list.*
Offers many topics related to the theme of
science fiction or fantasy.
  SFLOVERS@RUTVM1.BITNET
  LISTSERV@RUTVM1.BITNET
Contact: Saul Jaffe
  <sf-lovers-request@rutgers.edu>

⑤ *Star Trek Fan Club (Digests) list.*
```
STREK-D@PCCVM.BITNET
LISTSERV@PCCVM.BITNET
```

⑤ *Star Trek Fan Club list.*
Offers discussion of the different aspects of Star Trek.
```
STREK-L@PCCVM.BITNET
LISTSERV@PCCVM.BITNET
```
Contact: R N Hathhorn
```
<SYSMAINT@PCCVM.BITNET>
```

⑤ *Starfleet forum*
```
STRFLEET@PCCVM.BITNET
LISTSERV@PCCVM.BITNET
```
Contact: Brian Hartsfield
```
<BH@ENG.AUBURN.EDU>
```

⑤ *TRAVELLER Role Playing Game*
Offers discussion of the TRAVELLER series Science Fiction Role Playing Game, published by Game Designers' Workshop.
```
TRAVELLER@DADLA.WR.TEK.COM
traveller-request@DADLA.WR.TEK.COM
```
Contact: James T Perkins
```
<jamesp@DADLA.WR.TEK.COM>
```

⑤ *Vampires*
Offers vampire lore, fact, and fiction.
```
VAMPYRES@GUVM.BITNET
LISTSERV@GUVM.BITNET
```

⑤ *War of the Worlds*
Offers discussion of Paramount's syndicated science fiction TV series "War of the Worlds."
```
war-worlds@PANARTHEA.EBAY.SUN.COM
war-worlds-request@PANARTHEA.EBAY.SUN.COM
```
Contact: Steven Grimm
```
<sgrimm@SUN.COM>
```

Fidonet

⑤ *Douglas Adams FanClub*
```
ADAMS
```
For fans of Douglas Adams and his books.
Moderator: Andreas Birgerson
```
2:200/407
```
Distribution: WORLD

⑤ *Discussions germane to TREK movies & TV shows*
```
ALL_TREK
```
Offers discussion of any facet of the TREK phenomena.
Moderator: Mike Gurski
```
1:261/1062
```
Distribution: ECHONET BACKBONE (ZONE 50)

⑤ *Odyssey UFO Echo*
```
BAMA
```

Offers discussion of UFOs and related topics.
Moderator: Jerry Woody
```
1:3607/20
```
Distribution: FIDONET BACKBONE, ODYSSEY NET BACKBONE

⑤ *Odyssey Newsclipping and Announcement Echo*
```
CLIPPINGS
```
Enables users to post news clippings of fringe science events.
Moderator: Jerry Woody
```
1:3607/20
```
Restr: MEMBER
Distribution: FIDONET ECHOMAIL, ODYSSEY BACKBONE

⑤ *Deals with all science fiction topics.*
```
FANTA-SCI
```
For the serious and fun-loving addicts of science fiction.
Moderator: Mike Gurski
```
1:261/1062
```
Distribution: ECHONET BACKBONE (ZONE 50)

⑤ *Science Fiction Fannish Folksongs*
```
FILK
```
Devoted to fannish folksongs, or "filksongs," a long-established science fiction fannish tradition.
Moderator: Kay Shapero
```
1:102/524
```
Distribution: BACKBONE

⑤ *Anthropomorphics (funny human-like animals).*
```
FURRY
```
Offers discussion of science fiction and folk tales related to "funny animals."
Moderator: Nicolai Shapero
```
1:102/524
```
Restr: MOD-APVL

⑤ *Anthropomorphics, the technical side.*
```
FUR_TECH
```
Features the technical side of Anthropomorphics. Includes costuming tricks and design, relevant biological science discussions, and computer animation tricks, traps, and techniques.
Moderator: Nicolai Shapero
```
1:102/524
```
Restr: MOD-APVL

⑤ *Multiversal Party Line Storyboard*
```
INTERCEPTED
```
An on-line version of the magazine INTERCEPTED.

Moderator: Kay Shapero
1:102/524
Restr: MOD-APVL

✪ *Klingon Legion of Assault Warriors*
KLAW
A Star Trek role-playing fan club with emphasis on the Klingons.
Moderator: Bob Ferguson
1:273/935
Distribution: ZONE-1

✪ *Odyssey Monsters Echo*
MONSTERS
Offers discussion of cryptozoology, mythical, or real monsters.
Moderator: Jerry Woody
1:3607/20
Restr: MOD-APVL
Distribution: FIDONET ECHOMAIL, ODYSSEY BACKBONE

✪ *OTHER SUNS Science Fiction Role Playing Game (SFRPG)*
OTHER_SUNS
Offers discussion of rules revisions, new races, historical background, and second edition rules revisions. Devoted to the SFRPG OTHER SUNS, published by Fantasy Games Unlimited.
Moderator: Nicolai Shapero
1:102/524
Restr: MOD-APVL

✪ *Conversations about "The Unknown"*
PARA_REALM
Offers discussion of the occult and the unknown.
Moderator: Cathy Emerson
1:369/66
Distribution: ECHONET BACKBONE (ZONE 50)

✪ *(Out On) The Perimeter*
PERIMETR
Offers discussion of physics, metaphysics and paraphysics, "fringe science," and the paranormal.
Moderator: Jonny Vee
1:215/606
Distribution: ZONE-1

✪ *Science Fiction and Fantasy Literature*
SF
Offers discussion of literary works of science fiction and fantasy, science fiction fans and conventions, and writing and publishing.
Moderator: David Dyer-Bennet
1:282/341

Distribution: BACKBONE, ***E-1, ZONE-2, ZONE-3, ALTERNET
Gateways: ALTERNET VIA 1:141/488, ZONE-3 VIA 1:1/3

✪ *SF Convention Running*
SFCON
Features discussion among people running science fiction and fantasy conventions.
Moderator: David Dyer-Bennet
1:282/341
Restr: MOD-APVL
Distribution: 1:282/341

✪ *Science Fiction and Fandom*
SFFAN
Offers discussion of anything that is related to science fiction or science fiction fandom.
Moderator: Nicolai Shapero
1:102/524
Distribution: BACKBONE

✪ *Science Fiction Literature*
SF-LIT
Offers discussion of written and published science fiction.
Moderator: Carlos Benitz
1:125/17

✪ *Skeptical Inquiry Echo*
SKEPTIC
Offers discussion of skeptical and critical examination of paranormal claims such as psychic powers, UFOs, astrology, Bigfoot, biorhythms, and crystals.
Moderator: Jackson Harding
3:800/857
Distribution: LOCAL, ZONE1 BACKBONE, ZONE2, ZONE3, ZONE6
Gateways: 1:374/14 2:241/6001 6:600/403

✪ *Odyssey UFO Reporting Echo*
SKYWATCH
Enables users to report UFO sightings from UFOBASE and Official Odyssey sighting forms.
Moderator: Jerry Woody
1:3607/20
Restr: MEMBER
Distribution: FIDONET ECHOMAIL

✪ *Star Trek Role-Playing Game Echo*
STARTREK
For individuals who wish to participate in Role-Playing Games (RPGS) based on the popular Star Trek, Star Trek Movies, and the TNG theme.
Moderator: Mike Shepherd
1:151/2395
Distribution: BACKBONE

☙ *Star Wars Echo*
STARWARS

Features *Star Wars* memorabilia ranging from the three movies, to the multitude of books and comics.

Moderator: Skip Shayotovich
1:161/42

Distribution: BACKBONE

☙ *Star Trek Books and Technical Manuals*
STBOOKS

Offers discussion of topics such as *Star Trek* Novels, *Star Trek* Technical Manuals and Comic Books, NO SPOILERS, or Television Shows.

Moderator: Nathan Moschkin
1:109/427

☙ *Star Trek: Deep Space Nine*
STDSN

Offers discussion on the new televison series, *Star Trek: Deep Space Nine.*

Moderator: Ray Brown
1:135/70

Distribution: BACKBONE

Gateways: METRONET VIA 1:104/43

☙ *Star Trek: The Next Generation*
STTNG

Offers discussion on *Star Trek: The Next Generation* only.

Moderator: Joe Siegler
1:273/928

Distribution: BACKBONE

☙ *Star Trek*
TREK

Offers discussion on all aspects of the *Star Trek* phenomenon, including the original series, the movies, and *The Next Generation.*

Moderator: Marshall Presnell
1:203/1701

Distribution: BACKBONE GROUPMAIL

☙ *Star Trek Technical Discussions*
TREKTECH

Offers discussion of the technology of *Star Trek* in the films, movies, episodes, animation, novels, games, and fan publications.

Moderator: Brandon Campbell
1:3818/1701

Distribution: ZONE-1

☙ *UFO Topics*
UFO

Features general UFO information and related topics.

Moderator: Don Allen
1:363/81.1

Distribution: BACKBONE

☙ *Odyssey Paranormal and Unknown Events Echo*
UNKNOWN

Offers discussion of paranormal events such as ghosts, ESP, and psychics.

Moderator: Jerry Woody
1:3607/20

Restr: MEMBER

Distribution: FIDONET ECHOMAIL

☙ *The International Doctor, Who, and British Science Fiction-TV Conference*
WHO

Offers conversations between *Doctor Who* enthusiasts and related British SF-TV shows.

Moderator: *Romana
1:362/708

Restr: MOD-APVL

Distribution: BACK-BONE

Gateways: ZONE 2 VIA 1:362/708

☙ *Science Fiction, Fantasy, Filk, Fen, Faire, Pagan, Anarchy, Anachrony*
WUNDERMENT

For users who wonder at the world.

Moderator: Rob Levin
1:3802/217

Distribution: BACKBONE

Usenet

☙ *Space Aliens on Earth. !Abduction! Gov't Coverup!*
alt.alien.visitors

☙ *Deteriorata meets the Space Orphans.*
alt.destroy.the.earth

☙ *We just can't get enough of him.*
alt.ensign.wesley.die.die.die

☙ *Tales from the Dark Side*
alt.evil

☙ *Anne McCaffery's s-f oeuvre.*
alt.fan.pern

☙ *For fans of Terry Pratchett, s-f humor writer.*
alt.fan.pratchett

☙ *Announcements of conventions (SciFi and others).*
alt.fandom.cons

☙ *Picard, you are not yourself lately.*
alt.french.captain.borg.borg.borg

☙ *Entries for the actual Hitchhiker's Guide to the Galaxy.*
alt.galactic-guide

- *More Stardrek.*
  `alt.lwaxana-troi.die.die.die`

- *More Stardrek.*
  `alt.sexy.bald.captains`

- *Stories and parodies related to Star Trek.*
  `alt.startrek.creative`

- *Major announcements of the SF world. (Moderated)*
  `rec.arts.sf.announce`

- *Discussions of SF fan activities.*
  `rec.arts.sf.fandom`

- *Personal for sale notices of SF materials.*
  `rec.arts.sf.marketplace`

- *Science fiction lovers' newsgroup.*
  `rec.arts.sf.misc`

- *Discussing SF motion pictures.*
  `rec.arts.sf.movies`

- *Reviews of science fiction, fantasy, and horror works. (Moderated)*
  `rec.arts.sf.reviews`

- *Real and speculative aspects of SF science.*
  `rec.arts.sf.science`

- *Discussion of the Star Wars universe.*
  `rec.arts.sf.starwars`

- *Discussing general television SF.*
  `rec.arts.sf.tv`

- *Discussion of written science fiction and fantasy.*
  `rec.arts.sf.written`

- *New Star Trek shows, movies, and books.*
  `rec.arts.startrek.current`

- *Star Trek conventions and memorabilia.*
  `rec.arts.startrek.fandom`

- *Information about the universe of Star Trek. (Moderated)*
  `rec.arts.startrek.info`

- *General discussions of Star Trek.*
  `rec.arts.startrek.misc`

- *Star Trek's depiction of future technologies.*
  `rec.arts.startrek.tech`

Online Libraries

After Dark
No services available.

Knowledge Index
No services available.

Orbit
No services available.

NewsNet
No services available.

Bulletin Boards

DOPPLER BASE BBS
Offers a wide variety of files with emphasis on computing, education, space exploration, science fiction, and games.
Availability: 24 hours/7 days
Baud Rate: 1200-14.4
BBS Number: (410) 922-1352
BBS Software: REMOTE ACCESS
Sysop: Dan Myers

CD-ROM
No services available.

Security Resources

Forums & Databases
America Online (AOL)
No services available.

CompuServe (CIS)
No services available.

GEnie
No services available.

The Well
No services available.

Network Discussions Lists
Internet (Includes Bitnet & UUCPNet)

⑤ *Computer Privacy list.*
Discussions of how technology impacts upon privacy. Gatewayed into the moderated USENET newsgroup `comp.society.privacy`.
```
comp-privacy@pica.army.mil
comp-privacy-request@pica.army.mil
```
Contact: Dennis G. Rears
```
<drears@pilot.njin.net>
```

⑤ *Disaster Plans and Recovery Resources list.*
```
DISASTER@UTXVM.BITNET
LISTSERV@UTXVM.BITNET
```

⑤ *Network Emergency Response Planning list.*
Discusses the roles global computer networks play in times of disaster. Archives are kept; send

LISTSERV the commands INDEX HELPNET and INFO DATABASE for more information (note that the commands are sent to `LISTSERV@NDSUVM1`).
```
HELPNET@NDSUVM1.BITNET
LISTSERV@NDSUVM1.BITNET HELPNET
```
Contact: Marty Hoag
```
NU021172@NDSUVM1.BITNET
```

⑤ *Security list.*
General discussions of the field of security (electronic, physical, or computer-related).
```
SECURITY@AIM.RUTGERS.EDU
SECURITY-REQUEST@AIM.RUTGERS.EDU
```

⑤ *Security Mailing list.*
General discussions in the field of security.
```
SECURITY@FINHUTC.BITNET
LISTSERV@FINHUTC.BITNET
```
Contact: A. Walker
```
<AWalker@RUTGERS.BITNET>
```

Fidonet
No services available.

Usenet

⑤ *Pointers to good stuff in security. (Moderated)*
```
alt.security.index
```

Online Libraries
After Dark
No services available.

Knowledge Index

No services available.

Orbit

No services available.

NewsNet

No services available.

Bulletin Boards
AIS Security Branch
Computer Security OnLine
Information System

Information on computer security issues. Devoted to the management of the information systems security program for the U.S. Department of the Treasury, Bureau of Public Debt.
Baud Rate: 300, 1200, 2400
BBS Number: (304) 420-6083
BBS Software: RemoteAccess

National Computer Systems
Laboratory Computer
Security BBS

Maintained by the Computer Systems Laboratory, National Institute of Standards and Technology. Encourages information exchange regarding methods of data and systems protection.
Availability: 24 hours/ 7 days
Baud Rate: 300, 1200, 2400, 9600
BBS Number: (301) 948-5717 (2400 bps), or 5140 (9600 bps, 2 nodes)
BBS Software: RBBS-PC
Sysop: Marianne Swanson
Help Line: (301) 975-3359, John Wack
Internet: Telnet to cs-bbs.ncsl.nist.gov (129.6.54.30); download files available via anonymous ftp from csrc.ncsl.nist.gov (129.6.54.11)

CD-ROM

↻ *CIA World Fact Book*
Quanta Press

Social Issues

Forums & Databases
America Online (AOL)

🕤 *disABILITIES Club*
Keyword: Disabilities
Path: Lifestyles & Interests Department > disABILITIES Club
Focuses on special interests concerning the disabled, with areas for learning disabilities, blindness, deafness, and physical disabilities, and insurance information. Message board discussion includes information and experience sharing among disabled members and their families.

🕤 *Express Yourself*
Keyword: Express Yourself
Path: News & Finance Department > Express Yourself
Enables users to debate the top news, social, and political issues. Virtually any subject is fair game.

CompuServe (CIS)

No services available.

GEnie

🕤 *Astrology RoundTable*
Keyword: ASTROLOGY or Page 1180
Meets the needs of the astrological community and provides services to all.

🕤 *Astro News and Events*
Keyword: ASTRO or Page 1165
Provides daily guides for all signs from *American Astrology* magazine, a schedule of astrological conferences, lectures, and seminars, and astrological organizations.

🕤 *Family RoundTable*
Keyword: FAMILY or Page 1235
For families interested in interpersonal relationships and individual personal development. Supplies areas for every member of the family, from young children to working couples to single parents to empty nesters.

The Well

🕤 *Computers, Freedom, and Privacy*
(g cfp)
Distributes information about the face-to-face First Conference on Computers, Freedom, and Privacy, held on March 25-28, 1991. Includes general information, edited highlights and full transcripts of the program and sessions.

🕤 *Cohousing*
(g coho)
Discusses cohousing, a type of living community first developed in Denmark, becoming increasingly common in Northern Europe, and just starting to appear in the United States.

🕤 *Consumers*
(g cons)
Discussions for consumers concerning which goods and services they have had good and bad experiences with.

🕤 *Computer Professionals for Social Responsibility*
(g cpsr)
Discusses issues related to computers and society.

🕤 *Disability*
(g disability)
Enables the disabled community to connect, discuss, and conjecture; also a place for the

non-disabled to do the same about disability issues.

☙ *Electronic Frontier Foundation*
   (g eff)
Covers a wide range of subjects, including computing and civil liberties, new metaphors for digital media, the clash of property interests, and the right to communicate freely.

☙ *Eros*
   (g eros)
Discusses the physical, spiritual, and psychological aspects of human sexuality.

☙ *First Amendment*
   (g first)
An electronic forum to chronicle and discuss attempts to stifle free expression.

☙ *Futures*
   (g future)
Discusses general trends, uncertainties, critical issues, and alternative scenarios.

☙ *Gay Private (Private Conference)*
   (g gaypriv)
Discusses matters of concern to gay men, lesbian women, and bisexuals. Membership is open to all people regardless of their sexual orientation.

☙ *Generation X*
   (g genx)
If you look at a chart of U.S. birthrates from 1940 or so to the present, you'll notice something interesting around 1960. The birth rate began to decline, bottoming out around 1967, then jumped up and leveled off. Why did this anomaly produce a generation that was hypnotized by the Brady Bunch, armageddon, and the excesses of its predecessors?

☙ *Homeowners*
   (g home)
A forum where homeowners can share knowledge and grow together.

☙ *Men on the Well (Private Conference)*
   (g mow)
Encourages candid and sensitive exchange among gendermates.

☙ *Peace*
   (g peace)
Discusses peace issues.

☙ *Sexuality*
   (g sex)
Discusses sexuality and relationships .

☙ *Singles*
   (g sin)
Post personal ads, discuss problems, encounters, and philosophies of the single life, and talk about topics such as opening lines, where to meet members of the opposite sex, and what to do when you have.

☙ *Statements*
   (g statements)
Create a topic or three of your very own: an announcement, a pronouncement, a mission statement, a self-portrait, a creative exploration, a page out of your high school yearbook, scribblings in your slam book—a topic about you.

☙ *Unity*
   (g unity)
Discuss and organize around issues affecting minority peoples. A supportive atmosphere minimizes hostility and prejudice.

☙ *Women on the Well (Private Conference)*
   (g wow)
A private conference for women only.

☙ *Workers Conference*
   (g workers)
Discussions on socialism, utopian and scientific.

Network Discussions Lists Internet (Includes Bitnet & UUCPNet)

☙ *The 12-Step list.*
   12step@trwrb.dsd.trw.com
   12step-request@trwrb.dsd.trw.com
Contact: Maurice Suhre
   <Suhre@trwrb.dsd.trw.com>

☙ *21st Century Discussion list.*
   21ST-C-L@BRUFPB.BITNET
   LISTSERV@BRUFPB.BITNET

☙ *Act Up Hotline list.*
   act-up@world.std.com
   act-up-request@world.std.com

☙ *College Activism/Information list.*
Acts as an information repository for data on college activism, events and items of importance. College students can discuss events and their implications.
   ACTNOW-L@BROWNVM.BROWN.EDU
   LISTSERV@BROWNVM.BROWN.EDU

❧ *Amnesty International list.*
Distributes Amnesty International's urgent action newsletters, approximately one a month. These are single-page summaries of a prisoner's situation, what he or she was arrested for, who to write to, and so on.
```
AMNESTY@JHUVM.BITNET
LISTSERV@JHUVM.BITNET
```
Contact: Jeffrey James Carpenter
```
<jjc@UNIX.CIS.PITT.EDU>
```

❧ *Animal Rights discussion list.*
```
ANIMAL-RIGHTS@CS.ODU.EDU
Animal-Rights-Request@XANTH.CS.ODU.EDU
```
Contact: Chip Roberson
```
<csrobe@CS.WM.EDU>
```

❧ *Bisexual Activists' discussion list.*
```
BIACT-L@BROWNVM.BITNET
LISTSERV@BROWNVM.BITNET
```

❧ *Bisexual Women's discussion list.*
```
BIFEM-D@BROWNVM.BROWN.EDU
LISTSERV@BROWNVM.BROWN.EDU
```
Contact: Elaine Brennan and Tina Mancuso
```
<el406014@brownvm.brown.edu>
```

❧ *Bisexuality discussion list.*
```
BISEXU-D@BROWNVM.BROWN.EDU
LISTSERV@BROWNVM.BROWN.EDU
```

❧ *Coalition of Lesbian and Gay Student Groups list.*
```
CLGSG-L@RICEVM1.BITNET
LISTSERV@RICEVM1.BITNET
```

❧ *Lesbian/Gay/Bisexual Commission of the Democratic Socialists of America list.*
Discussions for users interested in the connections between sexual identity and the democratic socialist movement in the U.S. and other nations.
```
DSA-LGB@midway.uchicago.edu
DSA-LGB-request@midway.uchicago.edu
```

❧ *ALA Feminist Task Force discussion list.*
```
FEMINIST@MITVMA.BITNET
LISTSERV@MITVMA.BITNET
```

❧ *Stony Brook Feminist Philosophy Mailing list.*
```
FEMSEM@SBCCVM.BITNET
LISTSERV@SBCCVM.BITNET
```

❧ *Fathers' Rights discussion list.*
Discusses issues of divorce, custody, and visitation/child-support arrangements. Sponsored by the Fathers' Rights and Equality Exchange (FREE).
```
FREE-L@INDYCMS.BITNET
LISTSERV@INDYCMS.BITNET
```
Contact: Dale Marmaduke
```
<ITOG400@INDYCMS.IUPUI.EDU>
```

❧ *Lesbian and Gay Concerns list.*
For lesbian and gay concerns on college campuses including, but not limited to, outreach programs, political action, AIDS education, dealing with school administrations, social programs, and just finding out what other support and social groups are doing.
```
GayNet@ATHENA.MIT.EDU
gaynet-request@ATHENA.MIT.EDU
```
Contact: Mark Rosenstein
```
<mar@MIT.EDU>
```

❧ *International Committee for Electronic Communication on AIDS list.*
Foster international coordination of electronic activities on AIDS.
```
ICECA@RUTVM1.BITNET
LISTSERV@RUTVM1.BITNET
```
Contact: Michael Smith
```
MNSMITH@UMAECS.BITNET
```

❧ *Men's Issues discussion list*
Discusses men's issues; open to everyone.
```
MAIL-MEN@usl.com
mail-men-request@ATTUNIX.ATT.COM
```
Contact: Marcel-Franck Simon
```
<mingus@usl.COM>
```

❧ *Mardi Gras discussion list.*
```
MARDI-GRAS@mintir.new-orleans.la.us
MAIL-SERVER@mintir.new-orleans.la.us
```
Contact: Edward J. Branley
```
<elendil@mintir.new-orleans.la.us>
```

❧ *Freemasonry list.*
For discussion of Freemasonry, its affiliated bodies, and other (non-university) fraternities.
```
MASONIC <PTREI@ASGARD.BBN.COM
<PTREI@ASGARD.BBN.COM>
```
Contact: Peter Trei
```
<PTREI@ASGARD.BBN.COM>
```

❧ *Medievalist Feminists discussion list.*
```
MEDFEM-L@INDYCMS.BITNET
LISTSERV@INDYCMS.BITNET
```

❧ *Senior Citizen Health and Quality of Life list.*
Discusses all issues relating to the health and lives of senior citizens.
```
SENIOR@INDYCMS.BITNET
LISTSERV@INDYCMS.BITNET
```
Contact: John B Harlan
```
<IJBH200@IndyVAX.BITNET>
```

❧ *Paranormal discussion list.*
Discussions for philosophers, psychologists, natural and biological scientists, and writers, to take a scientifically informed look at claims of the paranormal.
```
SKEPTIC@YORKVM1.BITNET
LISTSERV@YORKVM1.BITNET SKEPTIC
```

Contact: Norman R. Gall
```
gall@yunexus
```

⑨ *Sexual Assault Activist list.*
Connects anti-rape campus activists from all
over the country.
```
STOPRAPE@BROWNVM.BROWN.EDU
LISTSERV@BROWNVM.BROWN.EDU
```
Contact: M. Moore Robinson
```
<ST102199@BROWNVM.BROWN.EDU>
```

⑨ *WIML-L (Women's Issues) list.*
```
WIML-L@IUBVM.BITNET
LISTSERV@IUBVM.BITNET
```

⑨ *Women's Studies list.*
Discusses women's studies issues, especially
those concerned with research, teaching, and
program administration. Publicizes relevant
conferences, job announcements, calls for
papers, publications, and the like.
```
WMST-L@UMDD.BITNET
LISTSERV@UMDD.BITNET
```
Contact: Joan Korenman
```
<KORENMAN@UMBC.BITNET>
```

⑨ *Children's Rights list.*
Discusses the rights of children and adolescents.
```
Y-RIGHTS@SJUVM.BITNET
LISTSERV@SJUVM.BITNET
```
Contact: Kenneth Udut
```
<KUDUT@hamp.hampshire.edu>
```

⑨ *Youth Net list.*
```
YOUTHNET@INDYCMS.BITNET
LISTSERV@INDYCMS.BITNET
```

Fidonet

⑨ *Abortion Issues*
```
ABORTION
```
A general debate and information conference
regarding current abortion issues, legislation,
and so on.
Moderator: Kevin Watkins
```
1:389/6
```
Distribution: BACKBONE, NETWORK
Gateways: FMLYNET VIA 11/50, FMLYNET
VIA 389/6, AGAPNET VIA 389/6

⑨ *Adoption Information Exchange*
```
ADOPTION
```
A general conference for those persons looking
to adopt, and for general discussion of state
adoption policies, and so on.
Moderator: Kevin Watkins
```
1:389/6
```
Distribution: ZONE 1, NETWORK

⑨ *Human Rights Issues, News, and Concerns*
```
AI_HUM_R
```
Discusses human rights issues, news, and
concerns. Contains general human rights
information and news, along with Amnesty
International Urgent Action notices of human
rights abuses, conversation about human rights,
and more.
Moderator: Randy Edwards
```
1:128/105
```
Distribution: INTERNATIONAL

⑨ *Amnesty International*
```
AMNESTY_INT.CAN
```
For users interested in the work of Amnesty
International, a worldwide human rights
organization.
Moderator: Mike Blackstock
```
1:163/508.1
```
Distribution: ZONE-1

⑨ *Consumer Self-Defense and Scam Alert*
```
ANTI_SCAM
```
Discusses consumer self-defense and remedies
against scams, con-games, unethical business
practices, and unresponsive bureauracies.
Moderator: Jack Feka
```
1:153/615
```
Distribution: NET-153, LOCAL-VANCOUVER

⑨ *Family Violence*
```
BATTERED
```
Covers the topic of battered and abused spouses
and children, family violence, and
dysfunctional families.
Moderator: Butch Walker
```
1:157/2
```
Distribution: BACKBONE

⑨ *Naturist Lifestyle and Discussion*
```
BAYNUDE
```
For discussion of issues and choices related to
a clothing-optional lifestyle.
Moderator: Barry Kapke
```
1:125/33
```
Distribution: REGIONAL (NORTHERN
CALIFORNIA)

⑨ *Birthparents' Discussion Area*
```
BIRTHPARENTS
```
For users with biologically-parented children
subsequently surrendered for adoption.
Moderator: Donna
```
1:114/113.11
```

⑨ *Free-form Free-speech Echo*
```
CHAOS_LANDING
```
Topics range from silly to sublime, from serious
to surreal.

Moderator: Dale Springfield
1:124/5114
Distribution: BACKBONE

🔊 *Child Abuse Information and Recovery*
CHILD_ABUSE
For people who were abused as children either sexually, physically, or emotionally, to share their recovery, and for anyone interested in stopping the cycle of abuse. Recovering perpetrators of sexual abuse are welcome to share.
Moderator: Chris E.
1:153/740
Distribution: BACKBONE

🔊 *Civil Liberties*
CIVLIB
Discusses civil liberties; the Bill of Rights and Constitution of the United States. Discussion of Supreme Court cases, interpretation, freedom of speech, freedom of religion and government influence on religion, search and seizure, abortion, privacy, death penalty, more.
Moderator: Bob Hirschfeld
1:114/74.2
Distribution: BACKBONE

🔊 *Consumer Advocate*
C_ADVOCAT
Discusses consumer issues, legislation, boycotts, economic issues, anything "for the consumer."
Moderator: Al Thorley
1:387/628
Distribution: ZONE-1 BACKBONE

🔊 *Cohousing discussion, networking, and meetings*
COHOUSING
For cohousers, cohousing groups, and interested individuals.
Moderator: Wilma Keppel
1:283/657
Distribution: LOCAL-IOWA CITY, LOCAL-OMAHA

🔊 *Consumer Report*
CONSUMER_REPORT
Discussioms regarding products and services, pro/con.
Moderator: Doug Wittich
1:261/1082
Distribution: ZONE-1 BACKBONE

🔊 *Survnet Current Events*
CURRENT_EVENTS
Public announcements for SURVNET systems.
Moderator: Dave Skinner
1:105/711
Distribution: SURVNET

🔊 *Dads*
DADS
Regarding father-child relationships, parenting skills, role models, nurturing, dealing with problems of divorce/custody/visitation, recreation, communication, discipline, more.
Moderator: Bob Hirschfeld
1:114/74.2
Distribution: BACKBONE

🔊 *Teenage chatter*
ECHO_TEEN
Discusses topics concerning teenagers.
Moderator: Mike Gurski
1:261/1062
Distribution: ECHONET BACKBONE (ZONE 50)

🔊 *Feminism and Gender Issues*
FEMINISM
Moderator: Donna.
1:114/113.11

🔊 *People Looking for Other People/Missing Persons*
FINDERS
A place to post messages looking for out-of-touch friends, missing persons—a national and global people-finders echo.
Moderator: Sir James
1:215/53

🔊 *The Flirt's Nook*
FLIRTS_NOOK
For compulsive flirts.
Moderator: Josh Burke
1:138/174

🔊 *Light-hearted humor.*
FRIVOLOUS_FOLLIES
For light-hearted, good-natured humor—silliness, not vulgarity.
Moderator: Ed Lawyer
1:261/1056
Distribution: ECHONET BACKBONE (ZONE 50)

🔊 *Funny Stories and Jokes*
FUNNY
A place for funny jokes and stories.
Moderator: Sean Dorsey
1:115/911
Distribution: BACKBONE
Gateways: ZONE 6 VIA 1:10/8

🔊 *Gay Fandom Discussions*
GAY_FANDOM
Discusses fandom with emphasis on gay/lesbian/bisexual issues. Not limited to one genre; discussions so far have included science

fiction, fantasy, animation, and comics.
Moderator: Rick Giguere
1:101/165
Distribution: VIA 1:101/165

✎ *Gaylink*
GAYLINK
Discusses the positive aspects of homosexual lifestyles.
Moderator: Sid Balcom
1:109/343
Distribution: BACKBONE
Gateways: ZONE 2 VIA 109/343

✎ *Gays/Lesbians News Echo.*
GAYNEWS
For current gay/lesbian news.
Moderator: Robert Bayron
1:107/810
Distribution: ZONE-1 ZONE-3 BACKBONE FIDONET

✎ *Gender Dysphoria Information and Support Echo*
GENDER
Discusses issues related to gender roles, such as transsexualism, transvestism, cross-dressing, and so on.
Moderator: Heather James
1:109/443
Distribution: BACKBONE

✎ *Gaylactic Network Echo*
GNE
An unofficial conference for users interested in the Gaylactic Network, a science-fiction organization for gays, lesbians, and bisexuals.
Moderator: Joe Leonard
1:267/202
Distribution: VIA 1:101/165

✎ *Humor*
HUMOR
For all humorous experiences.
Moderator: Bob Johnstone
42:1001/24
Distribution: BACKBONE OVER 750 BBS' AND GROUPMAIL

✎ *Issues Concerning Gays and Lesbians*
ICGAL
Discusses real-world issues facing homosexuals.
Moderator: Robert Bayron
1:107/800
Distribution: ZONE-1 ZONE-2 ZONE-3 BACKBONE FIDONET

✎ *Indian_Affairs*
INDIAN_AFFAIRS

Covers Native American issues.
Moderator: Dolores Jensen
1:327/999
Distribution: NATIONAL BACKBONE ZONE 1

✎ *International Cooking*
INTERCOOK
A multilingual conference related to culinary interests.
Moderator: Perry Lowell
1:322/359.1
Distribution: BACKBONE
Gateways: 2:310/11 VIA 1:260/340, 3:690/625 VIA 1:260/340

✎ *Pre-teen Conversations*
KID_POWER
Provides users under 13 a place of their own for posting messages for their national friends.
Moderator: Bonnie Lind
1:369/18
Distribution: ECHONET BACKBONE (ZONE 50)

✎ *Abortion discussion from the Christian perspective.*
KILLBABY
Discusses abortion.
Moderator: Steve Winter
98:98/1
Gateways: PRIME NETWORK

✎ *LAUGH*
LAUGH
A G-rated joke conference—family-rated jokes only.
Moderator: Don Morgan
8:7001/2
Distribution: 1:11/50 8:8/7001
Gateways: FIDONET 8:8/7001<>1:11/50

✎ *Lovers and Other Strangers*
LOVELINE
Looking for that love of your life? For G-rated chatter and flirting between the sexes.
Moderator: Burt Juda
1:107/1
Distribution: 107/1 107/10 107/3 107/323 107/519 107/5001 107/3000
Gateways: GROUPMAIL VIA 1:107/3

✎ *Men's Issues*
MENS_ISSUES
An issues-oriented conference with a focus on men's issues, including general sexual-politics issues, divorce, custody/support, men and spirituality, men in recovery, the men's movement, more.

Moderator: Mike Arst
1:343/8.9

ⓢ *New York Metro Area Gay/Lesbian Conference*
METROGAY
For gay and lesbian people to air views on all subjects.
Moderator: Michael Stewart
1:278/6969
Restr: MOD-APVL
Distribution: NY-METRO-AREA-ONLY

ⓢ *National Missing Persons Echo*
MISSING
For locating living friends, relatives, and acquaintances you have lost track of over the years.
Moderator: Russell Coombs
1:2612/107
Distribution: BACKBONE BACKBONE
Gateways: GTPOWER RHIME RELAY_NET

ⓢ *National Missing Children Echo*
MISSING_CHILD
For help locating missing children.
Moderator: Marv Cotton
1:387/622
Distribution: BACKBONE
Gateways: GT-NET FAMILY_NET USENET GTPOWER RIME RBBS_NET

ⓢ *Naturist echo*
NATURIST
For the serious naturist, the wannabe, and even the simply curious. Topics include skinny dipping, clothing-optional beaches, organized clubs, where to go, why participate, how to get more information for your area, family involvement, current official attitudes, and much more.
Moderator: Wayne Silsbee
1:105/223.1
Distribution: PRIVATE/ZONE 1

ⓢ *Parenting humans*
PARENTING
Share technical support, experiences and opinions related to the topic of parenting humans. Inclined towards the Christian perspective.
Moderator: Steve Winter
98:98/1
Gateways: PRIME NETWORK

ⓢ *Parents Echo*
PARENTS
For parents, expectant parents, and wannabees.
Moderator: Donna Ransdell

1:202/1311.100
Distribution: BACKBONE
Gateways: INTO FAMILYNET VIA 1:115/887

ⓢ *Please stop the cycle of child abuse*
PLEASE
For users abused as children either sexually, physically, or emotionally, to share their recovery, and for anyone interested in stopping the cycle of abuse.
Moderator: Chris E.
1:153/740
Distribution: BACKBONE

ⓢ *Problem Children*
PROBLEM_CHILD
Discusses juvenile delinquency, chronic underachievement, substance abuse or anti-social behavior; for the discussion of any child with problems.
Moderator: Butch Walker
1:157/2
Distribution: BACKBONE

ⓢ *American Red Cross Volunteers Information Exchange*
REDCROSS
A general conference for volunteers to discuss ideas, opinions, and exchange information.
Moderator: Kevin Watkins
1:389/6
Distribution: NEW

ⓢ *Reproductive Rights (Choice) Issues*
REPRO_RIGHTS
A support group and clearinghouse for information that affects our most personal family decisions.
Moderator: Donna
1:114/113.11

ⓢ *Mens Rights and Gender Equality*
RIGHTS
Discusses issues relating to gender equality from the male perspective.
Moderator: Ken Vandergriff
1:362/901
Distribution: BACKBONE OR DIRECT FEED
Gateways: NONE Rule File: n/a

ⓢ *Are ritual abuse survivor stories to be believed?*
RITUAL_ABUSE
Discusses evaluating the veracity of satanic ritual abuse survivor stories. Believers and skeptics welcome.
Moderator: Gary Moore
1:161/210

⑤ *International Scouting Conference*
SCOUTING

Meet and discuss matters with scouts from around the world. A general conference for members of the Boy Scouts, Girl Scouts, and all scouting organizations throughout the world.
Moderator: Dave Tracewell
   1:208/302
Distribution: BACKBONE, ZONE 1, ZONE 2, ZONE 3
Gateways: RBBS

⑤ *Support for Abused People*
SILENT_CRY

For users who have or are suffering from abuse of any kind. Handles allowed.
Moderator: Cindy Barnes
   94:2051/1
Distribution: ADANET INTERNATIONAL DISABILITY NETWORK

⑤ *Survivors of Incest and Childhood Sexual Abuse*
SIP_INCEST

For users recovering from incest and childhood sexual abuse.
Moderator: Mark Smith
   1:125/32.3
Distribution: BACKBONE

⑤ *Sex Addicts Anonymous*
SIP_SAA

For users recovering from addiction to sex.
Moderator: Bill E.
   1:102/749
Distribution: BACKBONE

⑤ *Survnet Soapbox*
SOAP_BOX

For ranting and raving, as long as participants remain civil. All topics except abortion are allowed.
Moderator: Dave Skinner
   1:105/711
Distribution: SURVNET

⑤ *Satanic Ritual Abuse*
SRA

For victims of satanic ritual abuse.
Moderator: Meghan Langley
   1:273/207

⑤ *Survnet Politics*
SURV_POLITICS

For discussion of political topics and how they may affect survivalists.
Moderator: Dave Skinner
   1:105/711
Distribution: SURVNET

⑤ *Survnet General Discussions*
SURVIVAL_ORIENTED

For the exchange of survival-oriented information such as tips and techniques for wilderness survival, questions regarding survival topics, product opinions, and so on.
Moderator: Dave Skinner
   1:105/711
Distribution: SURVNET

⑤ *Survivalist*
SURVIVALIST

For users interested in survival tactics, practices, plans, and anything associated with the same.
Moderator: Dave Paxton
   1:369/3

⑤ *International Teenagers' Echo*
TEEN

A forum by teenagers for teenagers; for general chat, discussion of controversial issues related to teens, and any other teen-related problem or situation.
Moderator: Jimmy Kitchens
   1:124/3106
Distribution: BACKBONE, RBBS-NET
Gateways: 1:10/8

⑤ *Relationships*
TOGETHER

Discusses relationships of all types, not just romantic.
Moderator: Sonya Whitaker-Quandt
   1:369/3
Distribution: NET-369, NET 260, NET 3609, NET 3638, NET 130

⑤ *Tott Echo*
TOTT

Discusses issues and problems facing teens today.
Moderator: Faye Johnson
   1:205/80
Restr: MOD-APVL
Distribution: BACKBONE

⑤ *TOTT Sysop Echo [See Elist]*
TOTT_SYSOP

For sysops who wish to carry the TOTT echo, an administrative area intended to allow sysops to discuss ideas, explore options, and brainstorm about problems posted on the TOTT echo.
Moderator: Faye Johnson
   1:205/80
Restr: MOD-APVL
Distribution: BACKBONE

⑤ *Victims of False Accusations of Abuse*
VFALSAC

Discusses of the tragedy of false accusations of child physical abuse, child sexual abuse, spouse abuse, and other domestic accusations, often in the context of ongoing litigative disputes over child custody.
Moderator: Bob Hirschfeld
1:114/74.2
Distribution: BACKBONE

🕭 *Gay/Lesbian/Transexual/Subculture Spirituality*
VOICES
Discusses spirituality in daily life with emphasis on the issues of interest to gays, lesbians, and transsexuals.
Moderator: Jeanne Re Montandon
1:3800/17

🕭 *Welfare Conference*
WELFARE
Discusses social service programs such as food stamps, aid to families with dependent children, medicaid, day care, and any other relevant program.
Moderator: Mike Adams
1:19/10
Distribution: BACKBONE, ADANET

🕭 *Men and Women's Social Issues*
WO/MEN
For men and women to come together and talk about mutual issues: friendship, dating, marriage, parenting, more.
Moderator: Donna
1:114/113.11

🕭 *Young Adult Forum*
YOUNG_ADULT
Discussions for the young at heart, to talk about problems and feelings of youth and growing up.
Moderator: Kevin McNeil
1:128/45
Distribution: ZONE-1

🕭 *Zoophilia ("Bestiality") discussion*
ZOOPHILE
Discusses social, legal, and personal issues among zoophiles and interested parties.
Moderator: Dr. Doolittle
1:286/66

Usenet

🕭 *Activities for activists.*
alt.activism

🕭 *A place to discuss issues in alt.activism.*
alt.activism.d

🕭 *Twinkle, twinkle, little planet.*
alt.astrology

🕭 *Discussion about restricting speech/press.*
alt.censorship

🕭 *Raising children in a split family.*
alt.child-support

🕭 *Academic freedom issues related to computers. Moderated.*
alt.comp.acad-freedom.news

🕭 *Academic freedom issues related to computers.*
alt.comp.acad-freedom.talk

🕭 *Be paranoid—they're out to get you.*
alt.conspiracy

🕭 *Rights of fathers trying to win custody in court.*
alt.dads-rights

🕭 *Quotas, affirmative action, bigotry, persecution.*
alt.discrimination

🕭 *Divination techniques (for example, I Ching, Tarot, runes).*
alt.divination

🕭 *Recreational pharmaceuticals and related flames.*
alt.drugs

🕭 *Many things are addictive besides pills.*
alt.drugs.usenet

🕭 *Learning experiences for the disabled.*
alt.education.disabled

🕭 *Other topics for fans of various kinds.*
alt.fandom.misc

🕭 *The ancient secrets revealed.*
alt.fax.bondage

🕭 *Most folks like it.*
alt.food

🕭 *"...EXCEPT THAT Congress shall limit...".*
alt.freedom.of.information.act

🕭 *The gothic movement: things mournful and dark.*
alt.gothic

🕭 *Recipes & cooking info. Moderated.*
alt.gourmand

🕭 *Philosophies where individual rights are paramount.*
alt.individualism

🆂 *Locating missing children.*
alt.missing-kids

🆂 *Issues for and about native Americans.*
alt.native

🆂 *Parent-teenager relationships.*
alt.parents-teens

🆂 *Are you tied up this evening?*
alt.personals.bondage

🆂 *Dweeb seeks Geek. Object: low-level interfacing.*
alt.personals.misc

🆂 *As the name implies.*
alt.politics.homosexuality

🆂 *For those who maintain multiple love relationships.*
alt.polyamory

🆂 *Privacy issues in cyberspace.*
alt.privacy

🆂 *Better living through chemistry.*
alt.psychoactives

🆂 *For people in recovery programs (e.g., AA, ACA, GA).*
alt.recovery

🆂 *Four of a kind beat a king.*
alt.rodney.king

🆂 *Discussion about the romantic side of love.*
alt.romance

🆂 *Talk about no sex.*
alt.romance.chat

🆂 *Self-improvement in less than 14 characters.*
alt.self-improve

🆂 *Postings of a prurient nature.*
alt.sex

🆂 *Postings of a very prurient nature.*
alt.sex.aluminum.baseball.bat

🆂 *Happiness is a warm puppy.*
alt.sex.bestiality

🆂 *Tie me, whip me, make me read the net!*
alt.sex.bondage

🆂 *Extracting yourself from a quagma.*
alt.sex.bondage.particle.physics

🆂 *For those who fall asleep BEFORE.*
alt.sex.boredom

🆂 *Where Carasso's SO is himself.*
alt.sex.carasso

🆂 *I can't talk, my mouth is full.*
alt.sex.carasso.snuggles

🆂 *As the name implies.*
alt.sex.homosexual

🆂 *Where one's SO is oneself.*
alt.sex.masturbation

🆂 *Jesse Helms would not subscribe to this group.*
alt.sex.motss

🆂 *Discussing the ins and outs of certain movies.*
alt.sex.movies

🆂 *For those who've had enough of sex, or else want to.*
alt.sex.NOT

🆂 *Yesssss....*
alt.sex.sonja

🆂 *For those who need it NOW.*
alt.sex.stories

🆂 *Requests for erotica, either literary or in the flesh.*
alt.sex.wanted

🆂 *Questions for only true sex wizards.*
alt.sex.wizards

🆂 *Helping others deal with traumatic experiences.*
alt.sexual.abuse.recovery

🆂 *The skinhead culture/anti-culture.*
alt.skinheads

🆂 *The Activist Times Digest. Moderated.*
alt.society.ati

🆂 *Individual rights.*
alt.society.civil-liberties

🆂 *Is that last name, first?*
alt.suicide.finals

🆂 *Talk of why suicides increase at holidays.*
alt.suicide.holiday

🆂 *Seeking enlightenment through weight loss.*
alt.support.diet

🆂 *GayNet Discussion list. Moderated.*
bit.listserv.gaynet

🆂 *Handicap list. Moderated.*
bit.listserv.l-hcap

🆂 *Stories related to children and parenting. Moderated.*
clari.news.children

❅ *News of interest to black people. (Moderated)*
clari.news.group.blacks

❅ *Homosexuality and Gay Rights. (Moderated)*
clari.news.group.gays

❅ *Jews and Jewish interests. (Moderated)*
clari.news.group.jews

❅ *Women's issues and abortion. (Moderated)*
clari.news.group.women

❅ *Freedom, Racism, Civil Rights Issues. (Moderated)*
clari.news.issues.civil_rights

❅ *Family, child abuse, and related issues. (Moderated)*
clari.news.issues.family

❅ *Fashion, leisure, and so on. (Moderated)*
clari.news.lifestyle

❅ *Sexual issues, sex-related political stories. (Moderated)*
clari.news.sex

❅ *Terrorist actions and related news around the world. (Moderated)*
clari.news.terrorism

❅ *Nuclear power & waste. (Moderated)*
clari.tw.nuclear

❅ *Information for progressive activists. (Moderated)*
misc.activism.progressive

❅ *Consumer interests, product reviews, and so on.*
misc.consumers

❅ *Discussion about owning and maintaining a house.*
misc.consumers.house

❅ *Physical fitness, exercise, and so on.*
misc.fitness

❅ *Items of interest for/about the handicapped. (Moderated)*
misc.handicap

❅ *Current interest: drug testing, terrorism, and so on.*
misc.headlines

❅ *Children, their behavior and activities.*
misc.kids

❅ *Discussions of bisexuality.*
soc.bi

❅ *Discussions for couples (cf. soc.singles).*
soc.couples

❅ *Discussion of feminism and feminist issues. (Moderated)*
soc.feminism

❅ *Issues related to men, their problems, and relationships.*
soc.men

❅ *Socially-oriented topics not in other groups.*
soc.misc

❅ *Issues pertaining to homosexuality.*
soc.motss

❅ *Announcements, requests, and so on about people on the net.*
soc.net-people

❅ *In search of netfriendships.*
soc.penpals

❅ *Newsgroup for single people, their activities, and so on.*
soc.singles

❅ *Social issues relating to military veterans.*
soc.veterans

❅ *Issues related to women, their problems and relationships.*
soc.women

❅ *All sorts of discussions and arguments on abortion.*
talk.abortion

❅ *The politics of drug issues.*
talk.politics.drugs

❅ *Discussions on stopping rape; not to be crossposted.*
talk.rape

Online Libraries
After Dark

❅ *Family Resources Database*
Responds to the needs of educators, researchers, counselors, public officials, the media, professional therapists, social services personnel, and others interested in marriage and family literature.
Coverage: 1970 to present
Updated: Bimonthly

❅ *Social Work Abstracts*
Contains abstracts of articles published in more than 400 social work journals and journals in related fields.

Coverage: July 1977 to present
Updated: Quarterly

Knowledge Index

No services available.

Orbit

No services available.

NewsNet

No services available.

Bulletin Boards

GLIB BBS

Discusses gay and lesbian issues.
Baud Rate: 300, 1200, 2400, 9600
BBS Number: (703) 578-4542
BBS Software: TBBS
Help Line: (703) 379-4568

Mars Station BBS

Helps survivors of sexual abuse recover from their ordeals. Run and operated by a rape survivor; offers a special message group just for survivors; offers many files on the issues of sexual abuse; contains nationwide treatment facility listings.
Baud Rate: 300, 1200, 2400
BBS Number: (301) 294-5182
BBS Software: WILDCAT!
Help Line: (301) 294-5321

Women's World BBS

A large network of conferences of interest to women. Most conferences are women-only.
Baud Rate: 300, 1200, 2400, 9600
BBS Number: (301) 431-0647
BBS Software: PCBoard

CD-ROM

✎ *AIDSLINE*
SilverPlatter

✎ *Consumer Reports*
National Information Services Corporation

✎ *Consumers Reference Disc*
National Information Services Corporation

✎ *Drugs and Crime CDROM*
Abt Books

✎ *Excerpta Medica, Immunology and AIDS*
SilverPlatter Information, Inc.

✎ *Health and Medical Care Directory*
Innotech, Inc.

✎ *Physician's Desk Reference*
Medical Economics Data

✎ *Voter's Lists on CD*
Aristotle Industries

Sociology Resources

Forums & Databases
America Online (AOL)
No services available.

CompuServe (CIS)
No services available.

GEnie
No services available.

The Well
No services available.

Network Discussions Lists
Internet (Includes Bitnet & UUCPNet)

⑨ *Association of Black Sociologists*
    ABSLST-L@CMUVM.BITNET
    LISTSERV@CMUVM.BITNET

⑨ *Association canadienne des sociologues et des list.*
    ACSALF@UQUEBEC.BITNET
    LISTSERV@UQUEBEC.BITNET

⑨ *Discussion Group for the Game Diplomacy*
For the game Diplomacy as played via electronic mail.
    DIPL-L@MITVMA.BITNET
    LISTSERV@MITVMA.BITNET
Contact: Eric Klien
    <portal!cup.portal.com!Eric_S_Klien@SUN.COM>

⑨ *National Social Sciences and Humanities*
    NA-L@UOTTAWA.BITNET
    LISTSERV@UOTTAWA.BITNET

⑨ *Social Science Data list.*
    SOS-DATA@UNCVM1.BITNET
    LISTSERV@UNCVM1.BITNET

Fidonet

⑨ *Computer Users in the Social Sciences*
    CUSS
For students, professionals, and interested individuals who want to discuss issues involving computers in the social sciences.
Moderator: Bill Allbritten
    1:11/301
Distribution: BACKBONE, 1:11/301

Usenet
No services available.

Online Libraries
After Dark

⑨ *Current Contents*
Social Behavioral Sciences: A subset of Current Contents Search™ corresponding to the Current Contents: Social Behavioral Sciences print edition.
Coverage: Most current 12 months
Updated: Weekly

꙳ *International Review of Publications in Sociology*
Enhanced bibliographic citations of book reviews that appear in the journals abstracted by Sociological Abstracts. Plus detailed abstracts of books in sociology and related topics.
Coverage: 1980 to present
Updated: Five times a year (1300 records per update)

꙳ *Social Planning/Policy & Development Abstracts*
A companion database to Sociological Abstracts (SOCA). Contains information about the applied and social problems-oriented aspects of sociological and social sciences literature from around the world.
Coverage: 1979 to present
Updated: Twice a year with about 1500 records per year

꙳ *Social SciSearch®*
A citation index to research in the social and behavioral sciences or related interdisciplinary areas.
Coverage: 1972 to present
Updated: Monthly

꙳ *Sociological Abstracts*
Worldwide coverage of journal articles, books, association papers, conference reports, and other publications in sociology and related topics.
Coverage: 1963 to present
Updated: five times a year

꙳ *Sociological Abstracts, Social Planning/Policy & Development Abstracts, International Review of Publications in Sociology: Merged.*
A concatenation of these three sociology databases.
Coverage: 1963 to present
Updated: Five times a year

꙳ *Wilson's Social Science Index*
Contains article and book reviews in over 350 key English language periodicals on the social sciences.
Coverage: 1983 to present
Updated: Monthly

Knowledge Index

꙳ *Ageline*
Focuses exclusively on aspects of middle age and aging from a social-psychological perspective, examining such issues as economics, family, demographic trends, health care, and political action.

꙳ *PAIS International*
A bibliographic index to the public policy literature of business, economics, finance, law, international relations, government, political science, and other social sciences.
Coverage: 1972 to present (PAIS Foreign Language Index); 1976 to present (PAIS Bulletin)
Updated: Monthly

꙳ *Sociological Abstracts*
Covers the world's literature in sociology and related topics in the social and behavioral sciences.
Coverage: 1963 to present
Updated: Five times a year

Orbit
No services available.

NewsNet
No services available.

Bulletin Boards
No services available.

CD-ROM

꙳ *Cross Cultural*
SilverPlatter Information Inc.
One Newton Executive Park
Newton Lower Falls, MA 02162

꙳ *PAIS International*
SilverPlatter Information, Inc.

꙳ *Sociofile*
SilverPlatter Information, Inc.

꙳ *Social Sciences Index*
H.W. Wilson

Sports/ Recreation Resources

Forums & Databases
America Online (AOL)

✪ *BikeNet*
Keyword: Bikenet
Path: Lifestyles & Interests Department > BikeNet
Dedicated to the art, sport, and science of bicycling. Hosts weekly live conferences online and includes message boards, a classifieds area, and information about trails.

✪ *Scuba Forum*
Keyword: Scuba
Path: Lifestyles & Interests Department > Scuba Forum
Offers the exchange of information on general diving, dive instruction, dive medicine, wreck, cavern and cave diving, and still and video photography.

✪ *The Independent Traveler*
Path: Travel & Shopping Department > The Independent Traveler
Offers exchange of information about travel ranging from weekend getaways and romantic hideaways to international travel in both traditional and exotic locations.

✪ *TraveLink*
Keyword: TraveLink
Path: Travel & Shopping Department > TraveLink
Offers listings of upcoming festivals and events throughout the United States.

CompuServe (CIS)

✪ *Associated Press Sports Wire*
Keyword: GO APSPORTS
Provides the latest scores, news, and league leaders in football, baseball, basketball, soccer, hockey, tennis, and golf as well as information on other sports.

✪ *Scuba Forum*
Keyword: GO DIVING
Offers a wide range of information from seeking scuba instruction to pursuing a career in diving.

✪ *Sports Forum*
Keyword: GO FANS
Offers a discussion on NFL football, major league baseball, NHL hockey, and NBA basketball.

✪ *Sports Medicine*
Keyword: GO INFOUSA
Provides information on basic exercise physiology, exercise testing, training, nutrition, and the general risks versus benefits of exercise.

✪ *NCAA Collegiate Sports Network*
Keyword: GO NCAA
Updates members on their favorite college football, basketball, and baseball and softball, Division I, II, and III teams.

✪ *Outdoor Forum*
Keyword: GO OUTDOOR
Enables outdoor lovers to share information. Topics include camping, climbing, backpacking, fishing, hunting, cycling, sailing, and winter sports.

Outdoor ForumOutdoors News Clips
Keyword: `GO OUTNEWS`
Reviews the latest full-text news reports on issues concerning the environment and outdoor activities like hunting and fishing.

Motor Sports Forum
Keyword: `GO RACING`
Provides driver biographies, track information, sanctioning organization addresses and contact information, schedules, and other information of interest to motor sports fans.

Sailing Forum
Keyword: `GO SAILING`
Offers discussion and education about all aspects of sailing.

UK Sports Clips
Keyword: `GO UKSPORTS`
Contains full-text sports stories from the Reuters World news wire, including cricket, football (soccer), snooker (billiards), athletics (track and field), and rugby.

GEnie

Motorcycling RoundTable
Keyword: `MOTO` or Page 1155
For motorcycling enthusiasts.

Sports RT
Keyword: `SPORTS` or Page 215
Follows and discusses all types of sports.

The Well

The Bicycling Channel
`(g bike)`
Offers 24-hour interactive bicycle talk, information, and resources.

Motoring
`(g car)`
For all car-related things.

Flying
`(g flying)`
Offers information on anything that flies and other related topics.

Motorcycling
`(g ride)`
Enables cyclists to meet, swap information on products, bikes, and good rides.

Sports and the Outdoors
`(g spo)`
Offers sports talk for cyclists, hikers, swimmers, and other active individuals.

Boating
`(g wet)`
Offers discussion of water sports.

Network Discussions Lists

Internet (Includes Bitnet & UUCPNet)

The List for Classic and Sports Cars
`AUTOS-L@TRITU.BITNET`
`LISTSERV@TRITU.BITNET`

Bicycles
Offers bicycle-related topics.
`bicycles@BBN.COM`
`bicycles-request@BBN.COM`
Contact: Craig MacFarlane
<cmacfarl@SOCRATES.BBN.COM>

College Bowl Teams and Officials list.
`C-BOWL@RICEVM1.BITNET`
`LISTSERV@RICEVM1.BITNET`

Cars
Offers discussion about cars.
`CARS-L@SAUPM00.BITNET`
`LISTSERV@SAUPM00.BITNET`
`Gandal@GGRCRVAX1.BITNET`

Cleveland Sports Mailing list.
Offers discussion of Cleveland sports teams.
`cle-list@tribe.b15.ingr.com`
`aj755@Cleveland.Freenet.Edu`
Contact: Ron Graham
<ecaxron@ariel.lerc.nasa.gov>

Cricket Magazine
Features the score sheets of first-class matches and itineraries of the tours.
`CRICKET@VM1.NODAK.EDU`
`LISTSERV@NDSUVM1.BITNET`
Contact: K. Sankara Rao
<ksrao@power.eee.ndsu.nodak.edu>

Running
Offers discussion for people who like to talk about running.
`DRS@UTXVM.CC.UTEXAS.EDU`
`LISTSERV@UTXVM.CC.UTEXAS.EDU`

> *Fishing*
> FLYFISH@UMAB.BITNET
> LISTSERV@UMAB.BITNET
Contact: Tom Williams
> tw@umab.BITNET

> *Golfers list.*
Offers a discussion on golf and all topics related to golf.
> Golf-L@UBVM.BITNET
> LISTSERV@ubvm.BITNET
Contact: Chris Tanski
> <captanski33@snycorva.BITNET>

> *Hang Gliding*
> hang-gliding@virginia.edu
> hang-gliding-request@virginia.edu
Contact: Galen Hekhuis
> <gjh@virginia.edu

> *College Hockey discussion list.*
Offers a discussion of collegiate ice hockey, including scores, team information, and schedules.
> HOCKEY-L@MAINE.BITNET
> LISTSERV@MAINE.BITNET
Contact: Wayne T. Smith
> WTS@MAINE.BITNET

> *Honda Digest*
Offers a discussion about Honda automobiles.
> HONDA-L@BROWNVM.BITNET
> LISTSERV@BROWNVM.BITNET
Contact: Marshall Vale
> <mjv@brownvm.BITNET>

> *Lacrosse Information list.*
Offers any discussion about lacrosse .
> LACROS-L@VILLVM.BITNET
> LISTSERV@VILLVM.BITNET
Contact: Alec Plotkin
> 18542228@VUVAXCOM.BITNET

> *Martial arts*
> martial-arts@DRAGON.CSO.UIUC.EDU
> martial-arts-request@DRAGON.CSO.UIUC.EDU
Contact: Steven Miller
> <smiller@DRAGON.CSO.UIUC.EDU>

> *Missouri Caving Discussion list.*
> MOCAVES@UMSLVMA.BITNET
> LISTSERV@UMSLVMA.BITNET

> *Motorcycle design*
For the theory and practice of motorcycle chassis design and construction.
> moto.chassis@OCE.ORST.EDU
> moto.chassis-request@OCE.ORST.EDU
Contact: Paul O'Neill
> <pvo@OCE.ORST.EDU>

> *Mountaineering Discussion list.*
Offers a discussion and communication among mountaineers.
> MOUNT-L@TRMETU.BITNET
> LISTSERV@TRMETU.BITNET
Contact: Metin Turan

> *Outdoor Discussion Group list.*
> OUTDOR-L@ULKYVM.BITNET
> LISTSERV@ULKYVM.BITNET

> *Paintball discussion list.*
> PAINTBOL@TCSVM.BITNET
> LISTSERV@TCSVM.BITNET

> *Play-by-Play Sportscasters*
> PBP-L@ETSUADMN.BITNET
> LISTSERV@ETSUADMN.BITNET
Contact: John Hendry
> <HENDRY@ETSUADMN.BITNET>

> *Runners*
Offers a discussion for runners and joggers.
> RUNNERS@VMTECSLP.BITNET
> LISTSERV@VMTECSLP.BITNET

> *SBN Sport*
For South Bend area sports.
> SBNSPORT@INDYCMS.BITNET
> LISTSERV@INDYCMS.BITNET

> *Scuba Digest Redistribution*
A digest version of the Usenet rec.scuba list.
> SCUBA-D@BROWNVM.BROWN.EDU
> LISTSERV@BROWNVM.BROWN.EDU
Contact: Catherine Yang
> <cyang@brownvm.brown.edu>

> *Scuba diving discussion list.*
Offers a discussion on all aspects of scuba diving.
> SCUBA-L@BROWNVM.BROWN.EDU.BITNET
> LISTSERV@BROWNVM.BROWN.EDU.BITNET

> *Figure Skating Fans list.*
> SKATING@UMAB.BITNET
> LISTSERV@UMAB.BITNET

> *Ski Vermont—Area Snow Reports list.*
> SKIVT-L@UVMVM.BITNET
> LISTSERV@UVMVM.BITNET

> *Soccer Boosters list.*
> SOCCER-L@UKCC.BITNET
> LISTSERV@UKCC.BITNET

> *Sport Management list.*
> SPORTMGT@UNBVM1.BITNET
> LISTSERV@UNBVM1.BITNET

> *Use of computers in sport list.*
> SPORTPC@UNBVM1.BITNET
> LISTSERV@UNBVM1.BITNET

⟲ *Exercise and Sports Psychology*
      SPORTPSY@TEMPLEVM.BITNET
      LISTSERV@TEMPLEVM.BITNET
Contact: Michael Sachs
      V5289E@TEMPLEVM.BITNET

⟲ *BITNET Baseball League and Discussion*
A rotisserie league for baseball fans.
      STATLG-L@SBCCVM.BITNET
      LISTSERV@SBCCVM.BITNET
Contact: Kristofer Munn
      KMUNN@SBCCVM

⟲ *Swimmer's list.*
Offers a discussion on all phases of swimming.
      SWIM-L@UAFSYSB.BITNET
      LISTSERV@UAFSYSB.BITNET
Contact: L.C. Jones
      <LJ27524@UAFSYSB.BITNET>

⟲ *Rice Fencing Club list.*
      TOUCHE@RICEVM1.EITNET
      LISTSERV@RICEVM1.BITNET

⟲ *Princeton Ultimate Frisbee list.*
      ULTIMATE@PUCC.BITNET
      LISTSERV@PUCC.BITNET

⟲ *Corvette Discussion—Service Info, Shows list.*
      VETTE-L@EMUVM1.BITNET
      LISTSERV@EMUVM1.BITNET

⟲ *White water Recreation*
Offers a discussion on white water kayaking, rafting, and canoeing.
      whitewater@IUVAX.CS.INDIANA.EDU
      whitewater-request@IUVAX.CS.INDIANA.EDU
Contact: Charles Daffinger
      <cdaf@IUVAX.CS.INDIANA.EDU>

⟲ *Woodworking Discussions Weekly Digest list.*
      WOODWEEK@IPFWVM.BITNET
      LISTSERV@IPFWVM.BITNET

⟲ *Woodworking*
Offers a discussion of the tools, methods, and techniques used in working with wood.
      WOODWORK@IPFWVM.BITNET
      LISTSERV@IPFWVM.BITNET
Contact: Larry Rondot
      <RONDOT@IPFWVM.BITNET>

⟲ *Yachting, Sailing, and amateur Boat Building*
Enables people interested in yachting, sailing, design, and boat building to communicate, share ideas and exchange information.
      YACHT-L@GREARN.BITNET
      LISTSERV@GREARN.BITNET
Contact: Kostas Antonopoulos

Fidonet

⟲ *Bicycling and human powered vehicles*
      BIKENET
Offers a discussion of bicycle riding, racing, touring, commuting, technology, repairs, and any form of human-powered vehicle.
Moderator: Howard Gerber
      1:106/88
Distribution: BACKBONE

⟲ *Boating*
      BOATING
Offers a discussion of boating topics and items of interest to boaters.
Moderator: Geno DellaMattia
      1:106/141
Distribution: BACKBONE

⟲ *Spelunker's Forum*
      CAVERS
Offers a discussion about caving. This echo is linked to the Cavers-Request@m2c.org internet mailing list.
Moderator: Hector Mandel
      1:233/15
Restr: MOD-APVL
Distribution: 1:233/15
Gateways: INTERNET VIA 1:233/13

⟲ *All-Sports Echo*
      EN_SPORTS
Offers a discussion of anything directly related to regulation sports, armchair participants, and Monday Morning Quarterbacks.
Moderator: Sonya Whitaker-Quandt
      1:369/3
Distribution: ECHONET BACKBONE (ZONE 50)

⟲ *Fishing discussions of all kinds*
      FISHING
Offers a discussion of fishing of all types.
Moderator: John Parker
      1:383/10

⟲ *Hanglider's Forum*
      HANGLIDE
Offers a discussion about hanggliding.
Moderator: Hector Mandel
      1:233/15
Restr: MOD-APVL
Distribution: 1:233/15
Gateways: INTERNET VIA 1:233/13

⟲ *North American Hockey Echo*
      HOCKEY
Offers discussion of all aspects of ice hockey in North America and the world.

Moderator: Tim Eichman
 1:2607/107
Restr: MOD-APVL
Distribution: ZONE-1 BACKBONE

🖑 *Las Vegas Gambler and Information*
 LV_GAMBLER
Enables experienced gamblers from Las Vegas to discuss winning systems and hints.
Moderator: Nick Hard
 1:209/777
Distribution: BACKBONE

🖑 *Major League Baseball*
 ML-BASEBALL
Offers a discussion on all topics that directly concern Major League Baseball.
Moderator: Kent Ogle
 1:286/777
Distribution: BACKBONE

🖑 *Inter-National MOTORCYCLE Conference*
 MOTORCYCLE
Offers a discussion of motorcycles, riding, accessories, repairs, and tips about anything associated with motorcycle riding.
Moderator: Bob Johnstone
 42:1001/24
Distribution: BACKBONE AND GROUPMAIL

🖑 *Muscle and Fitness Echo*
 MUSCLE
Offers a discussion of weight training, nutrition, and fitness issues.
Moderator: Jim Kennedy
 1:270/116

🖑 *National Football League*
 NFL
Offers a discussion of professional football only.
Moderator: Kent Ogle
 1:286/777
Distribution: REGIONAL ONLY.

🖑 *RVs and camping.*
 RV_CAMP
Offers a discussion of RVs, trailers, or other camping vehicles.
Moderator: Barbara O'Keefe
 1:135/54
Distribution: ECHONET BACKBONE (ZONE 50)

🖑 *Sailing*
 SAILING
Offers a discussion of sailing topics and of items of interest to sailors.
Moderator: Geno DellaMattia
 1:153/764
Distribution: BACKBONE

🖑 *Self Contained Underwater Breathing Apparatus*
 SCUBA
Offers a discussion for divers, from novice to professional.
Moderator: Tom Haycraft
 1:124/2107.2
Distribution: FIDONET BACKBONE

🖑 *Skydiving, Parachuting, and Paragliding*
 SKYDIVE
Offers a discussion of skydiving, parachuting, and paragliding.
Moderator: Hector Mandel
 1:233/15
Restr: MOD-APVL
Distribution: BACKBONE

🖑 *Wilderness Experience*
 WILDRNSS
Provides fundamentals of wilderness travel, including mountaineering, backpacking, camping, hiking, and various modes of human- or animal-powered transportation in the wilderness.
Moderator: Kim Erdman
 1:135/19
Distribution: BACKBONE
Distribution: FIDONET-ONLY

Usenet

🖑 *Robin Hood had the right idea.*
 alt.archery

🖑 *Fishing as a hobby and sport.*
 alt.fishing

🖑 *High-horsepower sleds in the powder.*
 alt.snowmobiles

🖑 *In the gutter again.*
 alt.sport.bowling

🖑 *Like alt.suicide with rubber bands.*
 alt.sport.bungee

🖑 *Look what you've done to the wall!*
 alt.sport.darts

🖑 *Indoor splatball with infrared lasers.*
 alt.sport.lasertag

🖑 *Riding the ocean waves.*
 alt.surfing

🖑 *Scuba diving Discussion list.*
 bit.listserv.scuba-l

🖑 *Exercise and Sports Psychology.*
 bit.listserv.sportpsy

- *ClariNet UPI sports wiregroups.*
  `clari.sports`
- *Baseball scores, stories, games, stats. (Moderated)*
  `clari.sports.baseball`
- *Basketball coverage. (Moderated)*
  `clari.sports.basketball`
- *Sports feature stories. (Moderated)*
  `clari.sports.features`
- *Pro football coverage. (Moderated)*
  `clari.sports.football`
- *NHL coverage. (Moderated)*
  `clari.sports.hockey`
- *Other sports, plus general sports news. (Moderated)*
  `clari.sports.misc`
- *Racing, Motor Sports. (Moderated)*
  `clari.sports.motor`
- *Tennis news & scores. (Moderated)*
  `clari.sports.tennis`
- *Top sports news. (Moderated)*
  `clari.sports.top`
- *Activities in the Great Outdoors.*
  `rec.backcountry`
- *Climbing techniques, competition announcements, and so on.*
  `rec.climbing`
- *Running for enjoyment, sport, exercise, and so on.*
  `rec.running`
- *Discussion about baseball.*
  `rec.sport.baseball`
- *Baseball on the collegiate level.*
  `rec.sport.baseball.college`
- *Rotisserie (fantasy) baseball play.*
  `rec.sport.baseball.fantasy`
- *Hoops on the collegiate level.*
  `rec.sport.basketball.college`
- *Discussion about basketball.*
  `rec.sport.basketball.misc`
- *Talk of professional basketball.*
  `rec.sport.basketball.pro`
- *Discussion about the sport of cricket.*
  `rec.sport.cricket`
- *Scores from cricket matches around the globe. (Moderated)*
  `rec.sport.cricket.scores`
- *Discussion of flying disc-based sports.*
  `rec.sport.disc`
- *Discussion of Australian (Rules) Football.*
  `rec.sport.football.australian`
- *U.S.-style college football.*
  `rec.sport.football.college`
- *Discussion about American-style football.*
  `rec.sport.football.misc`
- *U.S.-style professional football.*
  `rec.sport.football.pro`
- *Discussion about all aspects of golfing.*
  `rec.sport.golf`
- *Discussion about ice hockey.*
  `rec.sport.hockey`
- *Discussion of the sport of field hockey.*
  `rec.sport.hockey.field`
- *Spectator sports.*
  `rec.sport.misc`
- *All aspects of the Olympic Games.*
  `rec.sport.olympics`
- *Discussing all aspects of the survival game paintball.*
  `rec.sport.paintball`
- *Discussion about professional wrestling.*
  `rec.sport.pro-wrestling`
- *Discussion about the game of rugby.*
  `rec.sport.rugby`
- *Discussion about soccer (Association Football).*
  `rec.sport.soccer`
- *Training for and competing in swimming events.*
  `rec.sport.swimming`
- *Things related to the sport of tennis.*
  `rec.sport.tennis`
- *Discussing all aspects of multi-event sports.*
  `rec.sport.triathlon`
- *Discussion about volleyball.*
  `rec.sport.volleyball`

Online Libraries
After Dark

⑤ *Sport and Fitness Thesaurus*
Contains all terminology used in the index of
the SPORT database.
Coverage: Current edition
Updated: Semiannually

⑤ *Sport Database*
Contains bibliographic records covering the
world's practical and research literature for all
sport and fitness disciplines.
Coverage: 1949 to present
Updated: Monthly

Knowledge Index
No services available.

Orbit
No services available.

NewsNet
No services available.

Bulletin Boards
Match Up League (MUL) BBS
Devoted to sports.
Availability: Closed Monday through
Wednesday, 8:30 a.m. to 4:30 p.m.
Baud Rate: 1200, 2400, 9600
BBS Number: (703) 920-0548

National Association for Cave Diving BBS
Dedicated to cave diving.
Availability: 24 hours/7 days
Baud Rate: 300, 2400
BBS Number: (912) 246-3280
Sysop: SYSOP

Track Stats BBS
Reserved solely for the topic of horse racing.
Baud Rate: 300, 1200, 2400
BBS Number: (703) 938-4705
BBS Software: QuickBBS
Sysop: Tom Warakomski

CD-ROM

⑤ *Guiness Disc of Records*
UniDisc

⑤ *National Survey of Fishing, Hunting, &
Wildlife Recreation*
CD-ROM, Inc.

⑤ *Sport Discuss*
SilverPlatter Information Inc.

⑤ *Sporting News Baseball Guide/Baseball
Register*
Quanta Press

TV/Radio/ Film/Theater Resources

Forums & Databases
America Online (AOL)

❧ *Baby Boomers Club*
Keyword: Baby Boomers
Path: Lifestyles & Interests Department > Baby Boomers Club
Enables Boomers to talk about the music, historical and cultural events, and styles that have shaped their lives and worldview. Old television shows, the Vietnam War, and music are popular conversation topics.

❧ *Video Database*
Keyword: Movies
Path: Entertainment Department > Movies Reviews & News > Video Database
A searchable database of video reviews. Type in a word or words that describe what you are looking for—for example: "action" and "police." A list of movies will appear, and you can select any of these to read a review of it.

CompuServe (CIS)

❧ *Broadcast Professionals Area*
GO BPF
Contains several sections of interest to television and radio broadcast professionals in fields such as engineering, production, programming, promotion, and land mobile service.

❧ *Broadcast Professional Forum*
GO BPFORUM

Covers the major publications, manufacturers and trade associations, conventions, organizations, and seminars related to the fields of broadcast and audio engineering, production and land mobile communications. Also includes the latest FCC news as it relates to the broadcast and communications professions.

❧ *Roger Ebert's Reviews and Features*
GO EBERT
Reviews of the most recent box-office hits and flops. The well-known critic also provides the moviegoer with celebrity interviews, a Movie Lover's Source List, a list of the top ten movies of all time, and advice on attending film festivals. A feedback section is available to communicate directly with Ebert.

❧ *HamNet (Ham Radio) Forum*
GO HAMNET
Enables users to converse with other users interested in amateur radio and shortwave listening.

❧ *Hollywood Hotline*
GO HOLLYWOOD
A news and information service of noteworthy events in motion pictures, television programs, and music recordings. Includes a trivia quiz, entertainment features, and an entertainment encyclopedia. Offers members reviews of the most recently released movies in the theater.

❧ *Magill's Survey of Cinema*
GO MAGILL
Provides a database of in-depth articles covering films released since 1902. Files contain the film

title, information about its release date, country of release, cast, credits, MPAA rating, running time, and production studio. Plots and significant influences are summarized and discussed.

✪ *Showbiz Forum*
GO SHOWBIZ

Enables users to share information and opinions with others about their favorite movies, plays, celebrities, and television shows.

✪ *Soap Opera Summaries*
GO SOAPS

Provides daily summaries of soap plots, news of what is happening in real life to your favorite stars, cast lists, where to write to soap stars, and fan club news.

✪ *Journal Graphics Transcripts*
GO TRANSCRIPTS

Order printed television broadcast transcripts; transcripts are available for selected shows.

GEnie

✪ *CINEMAN Entertainment Information*
Keyword: CINEMAN or Page 330
1. Movies (930201)

2. Reviews (930201)

3. Box Office Report (930202)

4. Coming Attractions (930201)

5. Home Video Update (930201)

6. Academy Awards

✪ *Hollywood Hotline(tm)*
Keyword: HOTLINE or Page 350
The lowdown on the top 50 current movies. Each capsule movie review is 500 to 600 words long and covers the film's major credits, a summary of the storyline, and reviewer comments.

✪ *Radio and Electronics RoundTable*
Keyword: RADIO or Page 345
For users interested in electronics and radio hobbies, including amateur radio, shortwave and scanner listening, CB, audio and video, experimentation, and technology advances.

✪ *Show Biz RoundTable*
Keyword: SHOWBIZ or Page 185
Information on movies, television, the stage, home entertainment technology, and more.

✪ *Soap Opera Summaries*
Keyword: SOAPS or Page 280
Available by 5:00 PM EST, Monday through Friday, with prime-time summaries updated the morning after they air during the regular season. On weekends, "The Soap Report" provides plot information, guest star listings, and special events.

The Well

✪ *Filmmaking*
(g film)
For amateurs and pros alike. Discuss what goes on behind the camera.

✪ *Onstage!*
(g onstage)
Provides information on lighting, sound, stage, and makeup.

✪ *Packet Radio*
(g packet)
Covers the technology of packet radio, as well as related questions such as how to design packet networks, building ham gear for use with computers, and so on.

✪ *Producers (Private Conference)*
(g pro)
The on-line meeting place for Producing Members, the Association of Independents in Radio (AIR).

✪ *Radio*
(g radio)
A gathering place for radio workers and listeners.

✪ *Theater*
(g theater)
Discusses live theater, from Sophocles and Shakespeare to Shaffer and Shaw.

✪ *Television*
(g tv)
Discusses specific programs, technology, the politics of television and television technology, the nature of the medium, and more.

Network Discussions Lists

Internet (Includes Bitnet & UUCPNet)

Cable TV list.
For users interested in cable television programming, technology, regulation, and so on.
CATV@quack.sac.ca.us
catv-request@quack.sac.ca.us
Contact: Nick Sayer
<mrapple@quack.sac.ca.us>

Cinema Discussion list.
Discusses all forms of cinema.
CINEMA-L@AUVM.BITNET
LISTSERV@AUVM.BITNET
Contact: Mike Karolchik
<U6183@WVNVM.BITNET>

Hispanic Classic Theater list.
COMEDIA@ARIZVM1.BITNET
LISTSERV@ARIZVM1.BITNET

Discovery Communications On-Line Listings
For advanced listings and curriculum material for educational programming on The Discovery Channel and The Learning Channel.
DISC-L@SENDIT.NODAK.EDU
listserv@sendit.nodak.edu
Contact: Gleason Sackmann
<sackman@sendit.NoDak.edu>

Campus Radio Disk Jockeys list.
Discussions of interest to campus radio station disk jockeys.
DJ-L@NDSUVM1.BITNET
LISTSERV@NDSUVM1.BITNET
Contact: Andrew Tabar
ARTABAR@MTUS5.BITNET

Filmmaking and Reviews list.
For different points of view about cinema: film as an art, entertainment, business, or communications medium. Serves as a source for help of amateur filmmakers on any format.
FILM-L@VMTECMEX.BITNET
LISTSERV@VMTECMEX.BITNET
Contact: Alejandro Kurczyn
499229@VMTECMEX.BITNET

Parker Lewis list.
Discusses the television series *Parker Lewis Can't Lose.*
flamingo@ddsw1.mcs.com
flamingo-request@ddsw1.mcs.com
Contact: David W. Tamkin
flamingo-request@ddsw1.mcs.com

College and University-Based Amateur Radio Clubs list.
HAM-UNIV@UIUCVMD.BITNET
LISTSERV@UIUCVMD.BITNET

Licensing Matters in Ham Radio Discussion list.
A splinter group from the USENET newsgroup rec.ham-radio and the digest INFO-HAMS@WSMR-SIMTEL20.ARMY.MIL; separates the high traffic of the licensing discussions.
HAMLICEN@VMD.CSO.UIUC.EDU
PHILIP HOWARD <PHIL@UIUCVMD.BITNET>
Contact: Philip Howard
<PHIL@UIUCVMD.BITNET>

Home Satellite Technology list.
HOMESAT@NDSUVM1.BITNET
LISTSERV@NDSUVM1.BITNET

Info-Hams Redistribution list.
For amateur radio (not CB) operators. Gatewayed to/from Usenet's rec.ham-radio.
INFO-HAMS@WSMR-SIMTEL20.ARMY.MIL
INFO-HAMS-REQUEST@WSMR-SIMTEL20.ARMY.MIL
Contact: Keith Petersen
<W8SDZ@WSMR-SIMTEL20.ARMY.MIL>

TCP/IP AMPR Ham Radio AX25 list.
listserv@mtsu.edu
Packet High Speed Switch
Contact: Mark
<nobody@msen.com>

NBS-AEP: National Broadcasting Society list.
NBS-AEP@CUNYVM.BITNET
LISTSERV@CUNYVM.BITNET

Packet Radio discussion list.
Enables users to exchange ideas about packet radio and discuss projects they are working on. Gatewayed to/from Usenet's rec.ham-radio.packet.
PACKET-RADIO@WSMR-SIMTEL20.ARMY.MIL
PACKET-RADIO-REQUEST@WSMR-SIMTEL20.ARMY.MIL
Contact: Keith Petersen
<W8SDZ@WSMR-SIMTEL20.ARMY.MIL>

Medieval Performing Arts list.
PERFORM@IUBVM.BITNET
LISTSERV@IUBVM.BITNET

Packet Radio Internet Extension list.
PRIE-L@UCSFVM.BITNET
LISTSERV@UCSFVM.BITNET

Public Radio discussion group list.
PUBRADIO@IDBSU.BITNET
LISTSERV@IDBSU.BITNET

↺ *REED-L: Records of Early English Drama Discussion list.*
REED-L@UTORONTO.BITNET
LISTSERV@UTORONTO.BITNET
Contact: Dr. Abigail Young
reed@utorepas.BITNET

↺ *Satellite TV Discussion list.*
SATTV-L@VMTECMEX.BITNET
LISTSERV@VMTECMEX.BITNET

↺ *Film and TV Studies Discussion list.*
For users who study, teach, theorize about, or research film and television—mostly in an academic setting, but not necessarily so.
SCREEN-L@UA1VM.BITNET
LISTSERV@UA1VM.BITNET
Contact: Jeremy Butler
<JBUTLER@UA1VM>

↺ *Stagecraft list.*
Discusses stage work, including (but not limited to) special effects, sound effects, sound reinforcement, stage management, set design and building, lighting design, company management, hall management, hall design, and show production.
Stagecraft@jaguar.CS.UTAH.EDU
stagecraft-request@JAGUAR.CS.UTAH.EDU
Contact: Brad Davis
<b-davis%CAI@CS.UTAH.EDU>

↺ *Short Wave Listener's list.*
SWL-L@CUVMA.BITNET
LISTSERV@CUVMA.BITNET

↺ *Short Wave Listening in Turkey list.*
SWL-TR@TRITU.BITNET
LISTSERV@TRITU.BITNET

↺ *Theater Discussion list.*
For all people who are or want to be involved with theater as a hobby (or maybe more).
THEATRE@GREARN.BITNET
LISTSERV@GREARN.BITNET
Contact: Theodore J. Soldatos
SYSTU003@GRCRUN11.BITNET

↺ *TV Discussion list.*
For all kinds of TV program discussions.
TV-L@TREARN.BITNET
LISTSERV@TREARN.BITNET
Contact: Esra
ESRA@TREARN

↺ *VHF Radio list.*
For discussion of VHF radio propagation, equipment, and activity related to amateur radio.
vhf@w6yx.Stanford.EDU
vhf-request@w6yx.Stanford.EDU

Contact: Paul Flaherty
N9FZX <paulf@stanford.edu>

↺ *War of the Worlds Discussion list.*
For discussion of Paramount's syndicated science fiction TV series "War of the Worlds."
war-worlds@PANARTHEA.EBAY.SUN.COM
war-worlds-request@PANARTHEA.EBAY.SUN.COM
Contact: Steven Grimm
<sgrimm@SUN.COM>

↺ *WVU Video Technology Coordinating Council list.*
WVUVTC-L@WVNVM.BITNET
LISTSERV@WVNVM.BITNET

Fidonet

↺ *Discussions of Trek movies and TV shows.*
ALL_TREK
Discusses any facet of the Trek phenomena.
Moderator: Mike Gurski
1:261/1062
Distribution: ECHONET BACKBONE (ZONE 50)

↺ *Amateur Radio Conference*
AMATEUR_RADIO
Discusses amateur radio and related topics.
Moderator: Glen Johnson
1:2605/269
Distribution: SECONDARY BACKBONE

↺ *General Broadcasting Discussions*
BROADCAST
A general chatter conference for radio, TV, and broadcast engineering topics.
Moderator: John Anderson
1:128/59

↺ *Cable Television Echo*
CABLE-TV
For current pro-consumer information about the cable television industry.
Moderator: Frank Kennedy
1:124/4115.225
Distribution: NET-260 NET-124

↺ *Dementia Discussion Echo*
DEMENTIA
This forum is for discussion about Dementia in general.
Moderator: Steven Blodgett
1:203/19
Distribution: LOCAL-SACRAMETRO, 1:108/250, 1:134/67, 1:202/1005, 1:207/117

꙳ *Radio and Data Telecommunications Regulation*
FCC
Discusses any form of telecommunications regulation.
Moderator: Alan Boritz
1:2604/102
Distribution: 1:2604/102, BACKBONE

꙳ *Film and Movie Review*
FILM
Deals with all facets of filmed entertainment, including movies, videos, and television.
Moderator: Mat Hough
1:379/1
Distribution: BACKBONE

꙳ *Amateur Radio Interest*
HAM
For licensed amateur radio operators and users interested in becoming ham operators.
Moderator: Lee Laird
1:124/7009
Distribution: BACKBONE

꙳ *Amateur (Ham) Radio Swap n' Shop*
HAM4SALE
For exchange of messages by ham radio operators concerning the swapping, buying, and selling of personal electronic equipment.
Moderator: W8GRT
1:234/1
Restr: MOD-APVL
Distribution: ECHOMAIL AND GROUPMAIL FROM THE MODERATOR

꙳ *Amateur Radio File Announcements and File Requests*
HAM_REQ
Announces new files and bulletins hatched in HDN. May also be used to locate amateur radio, shortwave, and scanner radio-related files.
Moderator: Lee Laird
1:124/7009
Distribution: BACKBONE

꙳ *Amateur (Ham) Radio Technology Conference*
HAM_TECH
For the exchange of messages by ham radio operators on the technical aspects of amateur radio, DXing, antennas, modifications, towers, shack designs, amateur radio software, and technical discussion.
Moderator: Wayne Sarosi
1:374/73.2
Distribution: FIDONET BACKBONE VIA ECHOMAIL

꙳ *Radio Ham Band Intruder Monitoring and Tracking*
INTRUDER
For the exchange of information on the discovery, identification, and elimination of non-ham operation in the ham bands.
Moderator: W8GRT
1:234/1
Restr: MOD-APVL
Distribution: ECHOMAIL AND GROUPMAIL FROM THE MODERATOR
Gateways: BY MODERATOR BETWEEN FIDONET & HAMLINK ZONE 73

꙳ *Rush Limbaugh/EIB Topics*
LIMBAUGH
A general chatter conference for fans of Rush Limbaugh's radio and TV shows.
Moderator: Douglas Luurs
1:228/52
Distribution: LOCAL-228NET / BACKBONE

꙳ *Monty Python Conference*
MONTE
Devoted to fans of the British comedy group Monty Python.
Moderator: Bill Fisch
1:264/174
Distribution: NET 264
Gateways: RBBS NET VIA 1:10/8

꙳ *Movies and TV Discussions*
MOVIES_&_TV
Users chat about movies and TV shows.
Moderator: Ed Lawyer
1:261/1056
Distribution: ECHONET BACKBONE (ZONE 50)

꙳ *Amateur Radio Packet Echo*
PACKET
Designed to discuss packet and other digital amateur radio communications.
Moderator: Jim Beeler
1:130/22
Distribution: BACKBONE

꙳ *All aspects of telecommunications.*
PHONE_LINE
Discusses phone lines and phone companies, phones (regular, cellular, cordless, and pay), amateur and commercial broadcasting and CATV, fiber optics and lasers, microwave, satellites, modems, fax machines, even two tin cans with string tied between them.
Moderator: Alan Gilbertson
1:3603/230
Distribution: ECHONET BACKBONE (ZONE 50)

⮑ *RTTY, SITOR, FAX, CW Over Radio*
RTTY

For the monitoring of and the use/applications of various digital communications and FAX signals sent via radio.
Moderator: Nolan Lee
1:390/5
Distribution: ZONE 1 AND 2, AND THE ZONE 3 BACKBONE

⮑ *Scanner and Frequency Discussion*
SCANRADIO

For scanner receiver users (police, fire, amateur, and others) and the sharing of information regarding active frequencies in use, type of equipment used, and the like.
Moderator: Ken Storm
1:267/108
Distribution: BACKBONE—ALL ZONES
Gateways: FAMILYNET VIA 1:115/887

⮑ *Star Wars Echo*
STARWARS

Discusses all materials concerning the world of *Star Wars,* ranging from the movies to the multitude of books and comics and the infinite number of games and action figures.
Moderator: Skip Shayotovich
1:161/42
Distribution: BACKBONE

⮑ *Star Trek: Deep Space Nine*
STDSN

A forum for the new televison series, *Star Trek: Deep Space Nine.*
Moderator: Ray Brown
1:135/70
Distribution: BACKBONE
Gateways: METRONET VIA 1:104/43

⮑ *Howard Stern Discussion Area*
STERN-SHOW

Discussions pertaining to Howard Stern, the morning DJ broadcasting out of New York.
Moderator: Joe Siegler
1:273/928
Distribution: PRIVATE VIA 1:273/928

⮑ *Star Trek: The Next Generation*
STTNG

Discussions on *Star Trek: The Next Generation* only.
Moderator: Joe Siegler
1:273/928
Distribution: BACKBONE

⮑ *Star Trek*
TREK

Discusses all aspects of the *Star Trek* phenomenon, including the original series, movies, and *The Next Generation,* as well as collectibles, comic books, and more.
Moderator: Marshall Presnell
1:203/1701
Distribution: BACKBONE GROUPMAIL

⮑ *Star Trek Technical Discussions*
TREKTECH

Discusses the technology of *Star Trek* in the films, movies, episodes, animation, novels, games, and fan publications.
Moderator: Brandon Campbell
1:3818/1701
Distribution: ZONE-1

⮑ *Television Forum*
TV

Discusses tv shows and programming.
Moderator: Rod Bowman
1:10/8
Distribution: BACKBONE (RBBS-NET.NA AND FIDONET.NA)

⮑ *Satellite Television Echo*
TVRO

Discusses all aspects of the satellite tv industry.
Moderator: Frank Kennedy
1:124/4115.225
Distribution: BACKBONE

⮑ *Video Making! Video Toaster and Home/ Semi-Pro Video*
VIDEO

A forum for discussing desktop videomaking. camcorders, VCRs, and other videomaking equipment.
Moderator: Ron Kramer
1:228/13
Distribution: BACKBONE

⮑ *The International Dr. Who and British Science Fiction TV Conference*
WHO

For conversations between *Doctor Who* enthusiasts and related British science fiction tv shows.
Moderator: Romana
1:362/708
Restr: MOD-APVL
Distribution: BACK-BONE
Gateways: ZONE 2 VIA 1:362/708

Usenet

🕭 *German TV cartoon characters.*
`alt.aeffle.und.pferdle`

🕭 *Fans of the abrasive radio and TV personality.*
`alt.fan.howard-stern`

🕭 *Bart Simpson's favorite TV cartoon.*
`alt.fan.itchy-n-scratchy`

🕭 *Electronic fan club for those wacky Brits.*
`alt.fan.monty-python`

🕭 *Mystery Science Theater 3000 TV show.*
`alt.fan.mst3k`

🕭 *Breathtaking adventure stories.*
`alt.fan.suicide-squid`

🕭 *For the college radio show "T n A".*
`alt.fan.tna`

🕭 *Picard, you are not yourself lately.*
`alt.french.captain.borg.borg.borg`

🕭 *More Stardrek.*
`alt.lwaxana-troi.die.die.die`

🕭 *Hide the gear, here come the magic station wagons.*
`alt.radio.pirate`

🕭 *Discussion of scanning radio receivers.*
`alt.radio.scanner`

🕭 *Fans of the conservative activist radio announcer.*
`alt.rush-limbaugh`

🕭 *More Stardrek.*
`alt.sexy.bald.captains`

🕭 *Fans of the new "The Antagonists" TV show.*
`alt.tv.antagonists`

🕭 *The bigger they are...*
`alt.tv.dinosaurs`

🕭 *For the folks out in la-law land.*
`alt.tv.la-law`

🕭 *"The Prisoner" television series from years ago.*
`alt.tv.prisoner`

🕭 *Some change from Lassie, eh?*
`alt.tv.ren-n-stimpy`

🕭 *Don't have a cow, man!*
`alt.tv.simpsons`

🕭 *Discussion about the "Tiny Toon Adventures" show.*
`alt.tv.tiny-toon`

🕭 *Discussion about the popular (and unusual) TV show.*
`alt.tv.twin-peaks`

🕭 *Movies with a cult following (for example, "The Rocky Horror Picture Show").*
`alt.cult-movies`

🕭 *Technical theater issues.*
`alt.stagecraft`

🕭 *Filmmaking and reviews.*
`bit.listserv.film-l`

🕭 *Discussions on all forms of cinema.*
`bit.listserv.cinema-l`

🕭 *Stage, drama, and other fine arts. (Moderated)*
`clari.news.arts`

🕭 *Entertainment industry news and features. Moderated.*
`clari.news.entertain`

🕭 *Reviews, news, and stories on movie stars. Moderated.*
`clari.news.movies`

🕭 *TV schedules, news, reviews, and stars. Moderated.*
`clari.news.tv`

🕭 *Discussion of the art of cinema. (Moderated)*
`rec.arts.cinema`

🕭 *Discussion about Dr. Who.*
`rec.arts.drwho`

🕭 *Discussions of movies and moviemaking.*
`rec.arts.movies`

🕭 *Reviews of movies. Moderated.*
`rec.arts.movies.reviews`

🕭 *Discussing science fiction motion pictures.*
`rec.arts.sf.movies`

🕭 *Discussing general television science fiction.*
`rec.arts.sf.tv`

🕭 *New Star Trek shows, movies and books.*
`rec.arts.startrek.current`

🕭 *Discussion of all aspects of stage work and theatre.*
`rec.arts.theatre`

🕭 *The boob tube, its history, and past and current shows.*
`rec.arts.tv`

🔊 Postings about soap operas.
rec.arts.tv.soaps

🔊 Discussions of telly shows from the UK.
rec.arts.tv.uk

🔊 "A Prairie Home Companion" radio show discussion.
rec.arts.wobegon

🔊 Amateur radio practices, contests, events, rules, and so on.
rec.radio.amateur.misc

🔊 Discussion about packet radio setups.
rec.radio.amateur.packet

🔊 Radio use and regulation policy.
rec.radio.amateur.policy

🔊 Local area broadcast radio. Moderated.
rec.radio.broadcasting

🔊 Citizen-band radio.
rec.radio.cb

🔊 Topics relating to noncommercial radio.
rec.radio.noncomm

🔊 Shortwave radio enthusiasts.
rec.radio.shortwave

🔊 Offers to trade and swap radio equipment.
rec.radio.swap

🔊 Video and video components.
rec.video

🔊 Technical and regulatory issues of cable television.
rec.video.cable-tv

🔊 Making professional quality video productions.
rec.video.production

🔊 Prerecorded video releases on laserdisc and videotape.
rec.video.releases

🔊 Getting shows via satellite.
rec.video.satellite

Online Libraries
After Dark
No services available.

Knowledge Index

🔊 *Magill's Survey of Cinema*
Contains complete text articles on over 1,800 notable films.
Coverage: 1902 to present
Updated: Monthly

Orbit
No services available.

NewsNet

🔊 *Data Broadcasting Report*
Frequency: Monthly
Earliest NewsNet Issue: 1/1/88
Provides exclusive information on point-to-multipoint digital communications. Regular coverage includes FM sidebands, vertical blanking intervals (VBI), small-dish satellites, real-time data services, messaging systems, and distributed database applications.

🔊 *HDTV Newsletter*
Frequency: Monthly
Earliest NewsNet Issue: 6/30/88
Provides complete coverage of fast-breaking events regarding high-definition television. Coverage includes standard issues, new applications, and political considerations.

🔊 *HDTV Report*
Frequency: Biweekly
Earliest NewsNet Issue: 4/15/91
Reports on all-digital television, including displays, transmission, production, recording, programming, computers, and competing media.

🔊 *Public Broadcasting Report*
Frequency: Biweekly
Earliest NewsNet Issue: sn/82
Specializes in reporting on public TV and radio, focusing on key events at PBS, NPR, and CPB. Also includes information on programming, regulatory actions, and fundraising.

🔊 *Television Digest*
Frequency: Weekly
Earliest NewsNet Issue: 3/15/82
Covers broadcasting, cable, and allied fields since 1945, focusing on key events at the FCC and Congress. Provides exclusive coverage of technical, financial, and marketing developments.

🕙 *Videonews International*
Frequency: Monthly
Earliest NewsNet Issue: 7/1/89
Covers new media throughout the world, including home video, broadcasting, cable TV satellites, theatrical exhibition, and new technologies such as HDTV, reports on promotion, distribution, mergers, acquisitions, and more.

🕙 *Video Technology News*
Frequency: Biweekly
Earliest NewsNet Issue: 9/26/88
Devoted exclusively to emerging media and the business opportunities they create. Delivers the latest news and analysis of video technology business opportunities in such areas as broadcast, cable, computer video, consumer electronics, fiber, new media, satellites, telecommunications, education, and training.

🕙 *Video Week*
Frequency: Weekly
Earliest NewsNet Issue: 4/12/82
Covers the business of program sales and distribution for videocassette, disc, pay TV, and allied new electronic media.

Bulletin Boards

Broadcaster's Information System BBS

Sponsored by T.Z. Sawyer Technical Consultants. A board for the broadcasting industry.
Baud Rate: 300, 1200, 2400
BBS Number: (301) 654-6462
Help Line: (301) 913-9287
Comment: Operates in English (default), French, Dutch, Spanish, Portuguese, and Slavic.

FCC Public Access Link (PAL) BBS

Contains public notices, rulemakings, and equipment approval status and other FCC activities and procedures.
Baud Rate: 1200
BBS Number: (301) 725-1072
Help Line: (301) 725-1585

The Frequency Forum BBS

Dedicated exclusively to the radio listening hobby, with a primary focus on monitoring public safety radio communications.

Baud Rate: 300, 1200, 2400
BBS Number: (703) 207-9622
BBS Software: RBBS-PC
Sysop: Jack Anderson

Janus BBS

A place for ham radio operators and scanner buffs to talk and exchange information.
Availability: 24 hours/ 7 days
Baud Rate: 300, 1200, 2400, 9600, 14.4
BBS Number: (703) 869-3843
BBS Software: TriBBS
Sysop: Sean McClanahan

Movies-By-Modem

An on-line video store accessible by modem. Users must be 18 or older to use this board. Search for videos and laserdiscs by title or subject and place orders to be shipped directly to your home or office.
Availability: 24 hours/ 7 days
Baud Rate: 2400
BBS Number: (216) 694-5736
Help Line: (216) 861-0467

The Movie BBS

Makes available movie and video reviews, star and movie profiles, *Star Trek* and science fiction, and over 7,000 graphic files and on-line games.
Availability: 24 hours/ 7 days
Baud Rate: 1200, 2400, 9600
BBS Number: (718) 939-5462
BBS Software: PCBoard
Sysop: Clarke H. Ulmer Jr.

VideoPro BBS

Provides support to professionals in the video and audio production, and post-production fields.
Baud Rate: 300, 1200, 2400, 9600, 14.4
BBS Number: (703) 455-1873
BBS Software: PCBoard
Sysop: Tom Hackett

CD-ROM

🕙 *A/V Online*
SilverPlatter Information Inc.

🕙 *Electronic Encyclopedia*
Grolier Electronic Publishing

🕙 *Variety's Video Directory Plus/Europe*
R.R. Bowker Electronic Publishing

Technology Resources

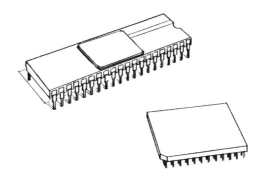

Forums & Databases
America Online (AOL)

🖙 *Newsbytes*
Keyword: Newsbytes
Path: News & Finance Department > Newsbytes
Complete computer industry news. New issues appear daily. Current and back issues are searchable; download an entire issue to your hard drive by clicking on a few icons, and refer to it later off-line.

CompuServe (CIS)
No services available.

GEnie
No services available.

The Well
No services available.

Network Discussions Lists
Internet (Includes Bitnet & UUCPNet)

🖙 *Information Technology and Africa list.*
For sharing and exchanging information on the field of information technology in Africa.
```
AFRICANA@WMVM1.BITNET
LISTSERV@WMVM1.BITNET
```
Contact: Paa-Bekoe Welbeck
```
<PBWELB@WMVM1.BITNET>
```

🖙 *Cellular Telephone list.*
Discusses cellular telephones and technology.
```
CELLULAR@yngbld.gwinnett.com
Mail-Server@yngbld.gwinnett.com
```
Contact: Gregory S. Youngblood
```
<zeta@yngbld.gwinnett.com>
```

🖙 *The Cracow Institute of Technology Discussion list.*
```
CIT$W@PLEARN.BITNET
LISTSERV@PLEARN.BITNET
```

🖙 *Volunteers in Technical Assistance list.*
Discusses technology transfer in international development.
```
DEVEL-L@AUVM.BITNET
LISTSERV@AUVM.BITNET
```
Contact: R. R. Ronkin
```
<VITA@GMUVAX.BITNET>
```

🖙 *Educational Technology list.*
```
EDTECH@OHSTVMA.BITNET
LISTSERV@OHSTVMA.BITNET
```

🖙 *European Training and Technology list.*
```
EEC-L@AUVM.BITNET
LISTSERV@AUVM.BITNET
```

🖙 *Educational Uses of Information Technology list.*
```
EUITLIST@BITNIC.BITNET
LISTSERV@BITNIC.BITNET
```

🖙 *Image Processing And Applications*
For image processing and related issues, focusing on video compression for multimedia applications, image processing applications, object isolation, linear predictive systems, motion detection, and motion video compression.
```
IMAGE-L@TREARN.BITNET
LISTSERV@TREARN.BITNET
```
Contact: Yusuf Ozturk
```
<BILYOZ@TREARN.BITNET>
```

ↄ *Future of Technology list.*
Analyzes current and likely events in technology as they will affect computing and related areas.
```
INFO-FUTURES@ENCORE.COM
INFO-FUTURES-REQUEST@ENCORE.COM
```
Contact: Barry Shein
```
<bzs@ENCORE.COM>
```

ↄ *Journal of Technology Education list.*
```
JTE-L@VTVM1.BITNET
LISTSERV@VTVM1.BITNET
```
Contact: Mark Sanders
```
<MSANDERS@VTVM1.BITNET>
```

ↄ *Technical Report lists.*
The redistribution list of technical reports from universities and R&D labs.
```
TECHNICAL REPORTS REDISTRIBUTION
E1AR0002@SMUVM1.BITNET
```

ↄ *Issues In Technology Licensing list.*
```
TECHNO-L@MITVMA.BITNET
LISTSERV@MITVMA.BITNET
```

ↄ *Technology Transfer discussion list.*
```
technology-transfer-list@sei.cmu.edu
technology-transfer-list-
request@sei.cmu.edu
```

ↄ *NIST Technology Transfer list.*
Discusses the technology transfer products, programs, resources and services of the Technology Services unit of the National Institute of Standards and Technology (NIST).
```
TECHSERV@NIST.GOV
TECHSERV-REQUEST@NIST.GOV
```
Contact: John Makulowich
```
<johnjohn@micf.nist.gov>
```

ↄ *Enhanced Telephone discussion list.*
Deals with telecom privacy issues.
```
telecom-priv@pica.army.mil
telecom-priv-request@pica.army.mil
```
Contact: Dennis Rears
```
<drears@pica.army.mil>
```

ↄ *Telecommunications discussion list.*
Discusses telecommunictions technology: the telephone system, modems, and other technical aspects of telecommunications systems.
```
TELECOM@EECS.NWU.EDU
TELECOM-REQUEST@EECS.NWU.EDU
```
Contact: Patrick Townson
```
<PTOWNSON@EECS.NWU.EDU>
```

ↄ *Technoculture discussion list.*
```
TNC@GITVM1.BITNET
LISTSERV@GITVM1.BITNET
```

Fidonet

ↄ *Disability and Adaptive Technology*
ADAPTIVE
Discusses disability and adaptive technology.
Moderator: Bill Baughn
94:2050/1
Distribution: ADANET INTERNATIONAL DISABILITY NETWORK
Gateways: ADANET (94:94/1)

ↄ *Amateur (Ham) Radio Technology Conference*
HAM_TECH
For the exchange of messages by ham radio operators.
Moderator: Wayne Sarosi
1:374/73.2
Distribution: FIDONET BACKBONE VIA ECHOMAIL

ↄ *K12net Technology and Vocational Education Conference*
K12_TECH_ED
For curriculum-oriented discussion broadly relating to educating elementary and secondary-school students about robotics, engineering, industrial and manufacturing technologies, drafting, CAD/CAM, and all forms of skilled trades.
Moderator: Jack Crawford
1:260/620

ↄ *Main Distribution Frame (MDF)— Telecommunications Topics*
MDF
Discusses telecommunications technology, issues, and ideas. Aimed primarily at telecom professionals.
Moderator: William Degnan
1:382/39
Distribution: BACKBONE

ↄ *Technology and Politics*
PN-TECH
Discusses the effects of technology on politics, and vice versa.
Moderator: Bryan Hanes
30:301/108
Distribution: ZONE-30

ↄ *Postal Opinion Forum*
POST_OP
Debate on divisive issues in the mailing community. Covers topics such as the wisdom and validity of the postal monopoly, the

positions and bargaining tactics of different postal labor unions, and whether to encourage or discourage alternative delivery.
Moderator: Charles Lasitter
  1:3641/277
Distribution: PRIVATE

⑤ *National Pyrotechnic Echo*
  PYRO
Seeks the advancement of the art and technique of safe and legal pyrotechnics.
Moderator: Mark Buda
  1:132/777
Distribution: BACKBONE

⑤ *Robotix and related discussions*
  ROBOTIX
A general chatter conference for users interested in all aspects of robots and automation.
Moderator: Dave Funk
  1:106/1555
Distribution: BACKBONE

⑤ *Technology-Related Assistance Act of 1988*
  TECH_ACT
The gathering place for Tech Act States citizens to share information regarding this federal project.
Moderator: ADAnet
  94:94/1
Distribution: ADANET INTERNATIONAL DISABILITY NETWORK

Usenet

⑤ *Discussions about energy, science, and technology.*
  sci.energy

Online Libraries
After Dark
No services available.

Knowledge Index
No services available.

Orbit

⑤ *CorpTech*
Provides company information on over 35,000 U.S. manufacturers and developers of high-tech products. Technologies covered include computer hardware and software, environmental, photonics, robotics, artificial intelligence, biotechnology, advanced materials, and other high-tech products. Search by any combination of 20+ criteria.
Coverage: Current
Updated: Quarterly

⑤ *Directory of American Research and Technology*
Contains information on the research and development capabilities of approximately 12,000 industrial organizations in the United States.
Coverage: Current
Updated: Annually

⑤ *Food Science and Technology Abstracts*
Covers the literature on food science and technology; includes articles on the basic food sciences, food safety, engineering, packaging, food products and food processes Contains approximately 380,000 records.
Coverage: 1969 to present
Updated: Monthly

⑤ *INSPEC*
Provides worldwide coverage of the literature in physics, electrical and electronics engineering, computers and control, and information technology. Contains more than 4 million records.
Coverage: 1969 to present
Updated: Biweekly

⑤ *Japan Technology*
Covers the science, technology, and business of Japan. Emphasis is on chemistry, computers, electronics, materials science, and manufacturing.
Coverage: 1985 to present
Updated: Monthly

⑤ *Scientific and Technical Books and Serials in Print*
Provides a comprehensive subject selection of books and serials in scientific and technical fields. All aspects of physical and biological sciences and their applications are included, as well as engineering and technology. Over 160,000 book titles and more than 40,000 titles of serials.
Coverage: Current
Updated: Monthly

Supertech
Combines the following high-tech files from Bowker Electronic Publishing: Artificial Intelligence, CAD/CAM, and Robotics. Covers a wide variety of areas within the subject scope of the three files; contains more than 40,000 records.
Coverage: 1973 to present
Updated: Monthly

Who's Who on Technology
Contains biographic details and career histories (including publications and patents) of over 37,000 leaders of American technology.
Coverage: Current
Updated: Biennially

NewsNet

411 Newsletter
Frequency: Biweekly
Earliest NewsNet Issue: 1/2/89
The telecom manager's information source. Offers practical, proven tips that help telecommunications managers run efficient, low-cost telecommunications networks.

Advanced Wireless Communications
Frequency: Biweekly
Earliest NewsNet Issue: 11/7/91
Concentrates on the business of personal communications, digital cellular, digital radio, miniature paging, in-flight phones, local loop alternatives, low-orbit satellites, spectrum allocation, and other advanced technologies.

AIN Report
Frequency: Biweekly
Earliest NewsNet Issue: 6/10/91
Follows the step-by-step development and deployment of advanced intelligent networks, providing insight into RBOC marketing and management strategies, and comprehensive coverage of vendor offerings and emerging AIN applications.

AT&T's Products and Services
Frequency: Annual
Alphabetically lists and explains AT&T's products and services. Includes long distance services, computers, net- work transmissions, local area networks, electronic components, as well as customer premises equipment such as PBXs, key systems, and phones.

Audiotex Update
Frequency: Monthly
Earliest NewsNet Issue: 8/1/89
Provides the latest news and information about the audiotex industry, including voice processing information, products, services, companies, marketing strategies, and research and development.

Broadband Networking News
Frequency: Monthly
Earliest NewsNet Issue: 11/1/91
Contains incisive news and analysis on high-speed data transfer strategies, in-depth case studies, comparison charts on the latest broadband products and services, and ideas to help boost data transfer efficiencies and cut costs.

Common Carrier Week
Frequency: Weekly
Earliest NewsNet Issue: 4/16/84
Comprehensive news coverage of all aspects of the telecommunications industry, including legal and regulatory decisions; local, long distance and international carriers; and business and consumer communications equipment.

Communications Daily
Frequency: Daily
Earliest NewsNet Issue: 1/4/82
Executive news service covering the world of electronic communications, including broadcasting, cable, telephone and data communications, satellites, and more.

Communications Week
Frequency: Weekly
Earliest NewsNet Issue: 9/24/90
Covers late-breaking news in computer networking, private networking, and public networking. Provides timely business analysis and in-depth features on specific market segments in addition to product and technology news.

Cellular Sales and Marketing
Frequency: Monthly
Earliest NewsNet Issue: 2/1/87
Reports, analyzes and evaluates how cellular systems, agents, dealers, resellers, manufacturers, and others in the cellular industry are advertising, promoting, and marketing their products and services. Includes information on how to sell more cellular phones, peripherals, and services.

Comline Japan Daily: Telecommunications
Frequency: Daily
Earliest NewsNet Issue: 1/5/90
Covers developments in new communications equipment, including transceivers, microwave equipment, telephones, facsimiles, paging systems, optical transmission devices, and interfaces.

Communications Week International
Frequency: Biweekly
Earliest NewsNet Issue: 10/15/90
Includes worldwide coverage of the convergence of computers and communications, regulatory and public policy issues, national policies, international standards deliberations, emerging worldwide networks, management strategies, and more.

Data Channels
Frequency: Biweekly
Earliest NewsNet Issue: 1/11/82
Covers the full spectrum of data communications: local and wide area networking, bypass technologies, videotex, regulatory, legislative and business trends.

Data Communications
Frequency: Monthly
Earliest NewsNet Issue: 10/1/91
Written for users of computer communications systems, local- and wide-area networks, and voice/data information systems. Subjects include software, hardware, transmission media, automation, processing, and electronic mail.

DBS News
Frequency: Monthly
Earliest NewsNet Issue: 7/1/90
Provides in-depth coverage of the direct broadcast satellite industry. Covers areas such as technology, regulation and DBS activity in the former U.S.S.R. and Europe.

Eastern European and Soviet Telecom Report
Frequency: Monthly
Earliest NewsNet Issue: 12/1/90
Focuses on the telecom, information processing, and broadcasting sectors of Central and Eastern Europe. Issues cover political, regulatory, and business developments that influence telecom development.

Edge: On and About AT&T
Frequency: Weekly
Earliest NewsNet Issue: 11/10/86
A consulting firm's view of AT&T in the computer and telecom industry. Published to provide information on current product and organization changes within AT&T and external developments affecting AT&T.

EDI News
Frequency: Biweekly
Earliest NewsNet Issue: 9/1/87
Devoted solely to the electronic data interchange arena. Documents strategies of industry network providers, hardware and software suppliers, and end users.

Electronic Messaging News
Frequency: Biweekly
Earliest NewsNet Issue: 8/8/89
Reports on the strategic use of electronic messaging technology (primarily electronic mail) to cut costs and improve inter- and intra-corporate communications. Offers non-technical, executive reporting on strategies and applications.

En Route Technology
Frequency: Biweekly
Earliest NewsNet Issue: 10/2/91
Covers the broad spectrum of innovative mobile information technologies deployed to link a mobile workforce with computing networks. Focuses on challenges involved in the commercial integration of these systems.

Enhanced Services Outlook
Frequency: Monthly
Earliest NewsNet Issue: 1/1/88
Covers Bell Operating Companies' development of transmission services for the enhanced services industry, marketing of information services, and development of new technologies. Includes developments affecting enhanced-service providers, BOCs and trade groups, as well as key Washington action.

Exchange
Frequency: Weekly
Earliest NewsNet Issue: 1/17/92
Coverage of Australian and New Zealand telecommunications. Focuses on regulatory developments, government policy, new technologies, carrier and value-added services, as well as pertinent overseas developments.

Executive Briefing on State Telecom Laws
Frequency: Annual
Contains executive summaries of the 80 state telecommunications laws enacted in 1988. Entries are listed by state and category of regulation. Each entry contains the bill or chapter number of the law and an effective date.

✑ FCC Daily Digest
Frequency: Daily
Earliest NewsNet Issue: 11/20/85
The official daily summary of public notices, texts, agendas, and other Federal Communications Commission business.

✑ FCC Week
Frequency: Weekly
Earliest NewsNet Issue: 11/25/85
In-depth reports on key federal regulatory developments involving all segments of the telecommunication industry, including interexchange carriers, cable TV systems, cellular service, large telephone companies, international carriers, and radio and TV broadcasting.

✑ Fiber Optics News
Frequency: Weekly
Earliest NewsNet Issue: 1/8/82
Provides coverage of fiber-optic and laser markets and technologies. Reports on what both corporations and government are doing to accelerate the growth of these industries.

✑ Imaging News
Frequency: Biweekly
Earliest NewsNet Issue: 10/9/91
Covers the latest revolution in high-speed office communications, providing in-depth reports on rapidly emerging technologies including video conferencing, desktop image-transmission, high resolution graphics, and document scanning.

✑ Independent Telco News
Earliest NewsNet Issue: 6/21/90
Delivers news and analysis on the independent telco field. Covers new services, technological breakthroughs, landmark regulatory decisions and rulings, and more.

✑ Industrial Communications
Frequency: Weekly
Earliest NewsNet Issue: 8/16/85
Comprehensive source of weekly news in the land mobile radio industry, including cellular mobile telephone, business radio, special mobilized radio services, public safety, frequency coordination areas. Extensive FCC regulation coverage.

✑ Global Telecom Report
Frequency: Monthly
Analyzes news and identifies strategic opportunities in the international telecommunications marketplace. Explains international regulatory and public policy issues, and provides companies with valuable, actionable information.

✑ Information and Interactive Services Report
Frequency: Monthly
Earliest NewsNet Issue: 7/15/84
Exclusive reports and analyses of new products, marketing, regulation, hardware and software, technical developments, and financial data in the electronic publishing business. Covers charts, statistics, and corporate profiles of leading videotex and teletext organizations.

✑ Information Week
Frequency: Weekly
Earliest NewsNet Issue: 10/22/90
Covers the information services marketplace from a broad perspective. Includes news, features, and tips for IS management.

✑ Inside the Independents
Frequency: Annual
Covers the independent telephone companies of Centel, Contel, GTE, Southern New England Telephone, and United Telecom. Includes financial results, organizational charts, and names and addresses of key people.

✑ Inside the RHCs
Frequency: Annual
Covers the seven Bell regional holding companies, their 22 operating companies, and more than 100 subsidiaries. Tracks new business ventures, and examines their regulatory status and financial health.

✑ Intelligent Network News
Frequency: Monthly
Earliest NewsNet Issue: 2/1/89
The exclusive report on signaling system 7, integrated services digital networks, and advanced network service. Coverage includes wide-area Centrex, calling card validation, 800 service, standards, virtual networks, fiber optics, alternate operator services, customer premises equipment, and much more.

✑ ISDN News
Frequency: Biweekly
Earliest NewsNet Issue: 8/3/88
Provides actionable information on the integrated services digital networks marketplace. Includes in-depth case studies on ISDN implementation, product and service offerings, trends, marketing strategies, and standards.

Japan Telecommunications Scan
Frequency: Weekly
Earliest NewsNet Issue: 7/1/84
Discusses the Nippon Telegraph and Telephone Public Corporation of Japan. Examines NTT's telecommunications role in Japan, including the latest technological developments and marketing in the telecommunications and electronics fields.

Local Area Networking Sourcebook
Frequency: Annual
This directory provides information on local area networks (LANs), including profiles of LAN manufacturers and network specifications; listings of manufacturers that provide bridges, cables, gateways, interfaces, and other LAN hardware; descriptions of software providers; suppliers of business and technical services; and descriptions of LAN standards and standards groups.

Long-Distance Letter
Frequency: Monthly
Earliest NewsNet Issue: 1/1/85
Provides in-depth analysis of all key developments in the rapidly changing long-distance telephone marketplace.

Microcell Report
Frequency: Monthly
Earliest NewsNet Issue: 1/1/90
Provides authoritative coverage of the personal communications market, including portable telephones, PCNs, telepoints, and wireless PBX activity in the U.S. and abroad. Reports on manufacturers, operators, technologies, and government activity.

Mobile Data Report
Frequency: Monthly
Earliest NewsNet Issue: 3/15/89
Analyzes the rapidly expanding market for portable data communications. Reports on dedicated UHF and VHF networks, cellular telephones, specialized mobile radios, alphanumeric radio pagers, land mobile satellites, aeronautical radios, and FM radio subcarriers. Applications covered include remote database access, vehicle dispatching, location and navigation, electronic mail, news reports, and medical/industrial telemetry.

Mobile Phone News
Frequency: Biweekly
Earliest NewsNet Issue: 1/11/84
Covers mobile communications with an emphasis on cellular radio and new venture radio industries. Includes regulation, new company news, services and technologies, corporate developments, and marketing.

Mobile Satellite News
Frequency: Monthly
Earliest NewsNet Issue: 10/1/89
Covers the news and trends from all three areas of the mobile satellite industry—land-based, aeronautical, and maritime. Focuses on the mobile satellite marketplace and related business information.

Mobile Satellite Reports
Frequency: Biweekly
Earliest NewsNet Issue: 9/1/89
Devoted entirely to news of aeronautical, maritime, and mobile satellites, and radio determination services. Covers the FCC, NASA, and Congress, earth station and equipment manufacturers, major conferences and seminars, and more.

New Era: Japan
Frequency: Biweekly
Earliest NewsNet Issue: 5/1/86
Keeps on top of in-field R&D, equipment and systems applications, and other noteworthy developments in the database, VAN and network fields. Procurement needs by Japanese firms are explained.

Online Product News
Frequency: Monthly
Earliest NewsNet Issue: 2/15/84
Covers news and reports on videotex/teletext products and services, including on-line databases and telecommunications hardware and software. Emphasis is on videotex as it relates to personal computers. Also covered are electronic mail, E-COM, and noncommercial bulletin boards.

Outlook on AT&T
Earliest NewsNet Issues: 8/1/86-7/1/88 available
A source of analysis and interpretation on every aspect of AT&T and its activities. Covers AT&T's marketing stance, advertising plans, finances, joint ventures, strategic planning, and more.

PCN News
Frequency: Monthly
Earliest NewsNet Issue: 10/1/90
Covers the microcell industry, new product and service offerings from vendors, regulatory issues, U.S. and European business opportunities, and initiatives such as CT-2, CT-3, and DECT.

Report on AT&T
Frequency: Weekly
Earliest NewsNet Issue: 11/11/85
Covers AT&T only. Includes exclusive coverage of AT&T's new PBXs, key systems, computers and network products. Covers AT&T's long-distance arm, international marketing, and joint ventures.

Residential Communications Marketplace
Frequency: Monthly
Earliest NewsNet Issue: 8/1/89
Provides ratings and statistics on mass-market videotex services. Features analysis and profiles of major on-line services, including RBOC gateways, national system operators, and local bulletin boards.

The Satellite Directory
Frequency: Annual
Lists equipment manufacturers and distributors: satellite operators, transmission services, uplinks/downlinks, consultants, engineering and technical services, and other satellite industry suppliers worldwide.

Satellite News
Frequency: Weekly
Earliest NewsNet Issue: 1/4/82
Covers the commercial satellite industry, including spacecraft, terrestrial systems, service companies, regulation, finance, and general business.

The Spectrum Report
Frequency: Biweekly
Earliest NewsNet Issue: 1/1/91
Dedicated to the global frequency allocation battle and to offering the facts, analysis, and breadth of perspective needed to protect your interests. Includes coverage of regulatory actions, WARC '92, new technologies, and international coverage.

State Telephone Regulation Report
Frequency: Biweekly
Provides a clear, concise look at rate cases filed by large telcos and long distance carriers, telcos' tariffs for new services, bills in state legislatures, and court rulings.

TDS Telecom Calendar
Frequency: 3-5 times weekly
Earliest NewsNet Issue: Current edition only
A listing of events of interest to the telecommunications industry. Includes seminars, conferences, congressional hearings, FCC meetings, and trade shows.

Telecom Outlook
Frequency: Monthly
Earliest NewsNet Issue: 7/1/89
Provides in-depth news and analysis on the telecommunications industry, including national and international marketing trends, distribution channels, new product and service announcements, and interviews with industry executives.

Telecom Today
Frequency: Monthly
Earliest NewsNet Issue: 4/1/91
Provides key information on the U.S. and international telecommunications industry, including trends in technology, new equipment and services.

Telecommunications Alert
Frequency: Daily
Earliest NewsNet Issue: 6/1/87
Highlights the news of the voice and data communications industry. Each issue contains over 150 stories, short takes, and listings, with reference material from a broad range of telecom publications. Includes calendar, index, and bimonthly Canadian supplement.

Telecommunications Reports
Frequency: Weekly
Earliest NewsNet Issue: 8/5/85
Weekly news service covering the telecommunications, voice, record, and data service fields. Offers in-depth articles covering the latest trends and developments in these fields, with particular emphasis on regulatory affairs and telephone issues.

Telecommunications Week
Frequency: Weekly
Earliest NewsNet Issue: 1/5/87
Contains a weekly digest of important developments in the telecommunications industry, including legal cases, mergers, acquisitions, federal regulations, and analysis of trends.

Telephone Industry Directory
Frequency: Annual
This directory lists equipment manufacturers and distributors: telephone companies,

common carriers, consultants, engineering and technical services, and other telecommunications industry suppliers.

 ✑ *Telephone News*
Frequency: Biweekly
Earliest NewsNet Issue: 1/11/82
A comprehensive source on the telephone industry, covering marketing, new products and services, regulation, and more. Written for industry executives.

 ✑ *Telephone Week*
Frequency: Weekly
Earliest NewsNet Issue: 11/25/85
Focuses on the activities of the Bell Operating Companies (BOC). News from the nation's biggest telcos includes new network services, BOC construction plans, cellular offerings, CPE marketing, rate restructuring, new digital services, and centrex enhancements.

 ✑ *Tele-Service News*
Frequency: Monthly
Earliest NewsNet Issue: 2/1/90
Covers the services, products, and research and development making news in the telephone industry. Reports on RBOC, long distance carriers, and other industry vendors.

 ✑ *TRWirelessNews*
Frequency: Biweekly
Earliest NewsNet Issue: 11/21/91
Covers all major developments in the cellular, personal communications, land mobile, messaging, and other spectrum-based services. Focuses on public policy and technology, and covers FCC and state regulatory activities.

 ✑ *Viewtext*
Frequency: Monthly
Earliest NewsNet Issue: 5/1/82
Reports on interactive telecommunications covering videotex and teletext worldwide. Also includes coverage of on-line databases and optical-disc storage technology.

 ✑ *Voice Technology News*
Frequency: Biweekly
Earliest NewsNet Issue: 7/18/89
Covers the voice processing industry, including voice mail, voice recognition, and voice synthesis. Provides the facts and analysis needed by industry executives and users, including business news, new products, and company strategies.

 ✑ *Washington Telecommunications Directory*
Frequency: Annual
Provides a comprehensive list of key telecom contacts in Washington, D.C. Includes names, phone numbers and addresses of key people at the FCC and Commerce, Defense, Justice, and State Departments, ITC, Congress, embassies, associations and U.S. trade representatives.

 ✑ *Worldwide Telecom*
Frequency: Monthly
Earliest NewsNet Issue: 11/1/89
Covers international telecommunications products, services, and contracts, with emphasis on U.S. telecommunications companies doing business in foreign markets.

Bulletin Boards
Aerospace Technology BBS
Home to the International Emergency Network. One of the most extensive series of BBS listings, covering astronomy, CAP, USCATCOM, aviation, military, and 9600 baud BBSs.
Availability: 24 hours/ 7 days
Baud Rates: HST 14.4K
BBS Number: (707) 437-5389
BBS Software: Opus 1.03b
Parameters: 8-0-1
Sysop: Guy Hokanson

NSSDC'S On-Line Data and Information Service (NODIS) BBS
An intensive space science and earth science system.
Baud Rate: 300, 1200, 2400
BBS Number: (301) 286-9000, (301) 2860-9500
Sysop: Angelia Bland
Help Line: (301) 513-1687
Comment: Type NSSDC after connect (or when asked for a number) then for user enter NSSDC or NODIS.

CD-ROM

 ✑ *Composite: Index for CRC Handbooks*
CRC Press

 ✑ *INIS*
SilverPlatter Information Inc.

Writing/ Journalism Resources

Forums & Databases

America Online (AOL)

No services available.

CompuServe (CIS)

Marquis Who's Who
Keyword: GO BIOGRAPHY
Provides information on key North American professionals obtained directly from the individual.

Journalism Forum
Keyword: GO JFORUM
Offers journalists a variety of services and specialized data libraries, including radio, TV, print and photo/video journalists.

Media Services
Keyword: GO MEDIA
Contains services for people in media, including broadcasting, marketing, and engineering.

Media Newsletters
Keyword: GO MEDIANEWS
Offers full-text articles from several leading newsletters covering the broadcasting and publishing industries.

GEnie

Romance Writers Exchange RoundTable
Keyword: ROMANCE or Page 1330
Devoted to the discussion about women's fiction and romance, and all of its sub-genres. Readers and writers of women's fiction are welcome to participate.

Writers' Ink RoundTable
Keyword: WRITERS or Page 440
An electronic association of novelists, journalists, technical writers, dramatists, poets, screenwriters, humorists, and others who discuss getting published.

The Well

Archives
(g archives)
Enables users to record memories of specific events.

Computers, Freedom, and Privacy
(g cfp)
Offers information about the face-to-face First Conference on Computers, Freedom & Privacy, held March 25-28, 1991.

Computer Journalism
(g cpj)
Discusses issues of special interest to computer journalists as well as general issues of interest to all computer users.

Electronic Frontier Foundation
(g eff)
Discusses computing and civil liberties, new metaphors for digital media, the clash of property interests and the right to communicate freely, EFF activities, and more.

First Amendment
(g first)
Offers the discussion of the many attempts to stifle free expression.

Media
(g media)
Offers the discussion on all aspects of media and propaganda. Emphasizes print and electronic journalism, and its legal and ethical problems.

❧ *Options*
   (g options)
An experiment on the interrelationship of print and electronic media.

❧ *Writers*
   (g wri)
Enables users to get answers to questions on submissions, query letters, grants and awards, and writers colonies.

❧ *WELL Writer's Workshop (Private Conference)*
   (g www)
An on-line writing workshop where members post their writing and other members post constructive criticism.

Network Discussions Lists
Internet (Includes Bitnet & UUCPNet)

❧ *The Academically, Artistically, and Athletically Able*
A journal for the study and advancement of the academically, artistically, and athletically able.
   ABILITY@ASUACAD.BITNET
   LISTSERV@ASUACAD.BITNET
Contact: A. DiGangi
   <SAMUEL@ASUACAD.BITNET>

❧ *Journal—Discussion & Submission*
   ABLE-L@ASUACAD.BITNET
   LISTSERV@ASUACAD.BITNET ABILITY
Contact: Sanford J. Cohn
   <ATSJC@ASUACAD.BITNET>

❧ *Campus Computing Newsletter Editors*
A forum for Campus Computing Newsletter Editors to exchange ideas, problems, and experiences in editing, producing, and disseminating printed and electronic newsletters.
   CCNEWS@BITNIC.BITNET
   LISTSERV@BITNIC.BITNET
Contact: Wendy Rickard

❧ *Comic Writers Workshop list.*
   COMICW-L@UNLVM.BITNET
   LISTSERV@UNLVM.BITNET
   <RICKARD@BITNIC.BITNET>

❧ *Creative Writing Pedagogy for Teachers and Students*
Offers a discussion on how and why creative writing is being taught at colleges and universities.
   CREWRT-L@UMCVMB.BITNET
   LISTSERV@UMCVMB.BITNET

Contact: Eric Crump
   <LCERIC@UMCVMB.BITNET>

❧ *Computers and Writing list.*
   CW-L@TTUVM1.BITNET
   LISTSERV@TTUVM1.BITNET

❧ *Fiction writers group*
Offers a support group for professional fiction writers.
   fiction-writers%studguppy@LANL.GOV
   writers-request%studguppy@LANL.GOV
Contact: Doug Roberts
   <roberts%studguppy@LANL.GOV>

❧ *Journalism/Mass Comm Document Database list.*
   JDOCS-DB@TEMPLEVM.BITNET
   LISTSERV@TEMPLEVM.BITNET

❧ *Discussion List for Journalism Education*
Offers discussion of topics of interest to journalists and journalism educators.
   JOURNET@QUCDN.BITNET
   LISTSERV@QUCDN.BITNET
Contact: George Frajkor
   FRAJKOR@CARLETON.BITNET

❧ *Dargon Project Writers Forum*
Only for writers involved in the Dargon Project.
   L@NCSUVM.BITNET
   LISTSERV@NCSUVM.BITNET

❧ *Megabyte University (Computers & Writing)*
   MBU-L@TTUVM1.BITNET
   LISTSERV@TTUVM1.BITNET

❧ *Athene Is a Free Network "Magazine"*
Devoted to amateur fiction written by the members of the on-line community.
   MCCABE@MTUS5.BITNET
   MCCABE@MTUS5.BITNET
Contact: Jim McCabe
   <MCCABE@MTUS5.BITNET>

❧ *Rhetoric, Language, Professional Writing*
Offers a discussion of current issues in rhetoric and composition, professional writing, and language research.
   PURTOPOI@PURCCVM.BITNET
   LISTSERV@PURCCVM.BITNET
Contact: Tharon Howard
   ucc@mace.cc.purdue.edu

❧ *Screen Writing Discussion list.*
Offers a discussion on the joy and challenge of screen writing for film and TV.
   SCRNWRIT@TAMVM1.BITNET
   LISTSERV@TAMVM1.BITNET
Contact: Jack Stanley

🔗 *German Students Press Discussion list.*
Fosters the communication among the German students press.

```
S-PRESS@DCZTU1.BITNET
PTWURZEL@DCZTU1.BITNET
```

Contact: Red Wurzelmaennchen

```
<PTWURZEL@DCZTU1.BITNET>
<JRS4284@PANAM.BITNET>
```

🔗 *Writers Lists Works*

```
WORKS-L@NDSUVM1.BITNET
LISTSERV@NDSUVM1.BITNET
```

🔗 *Brown University Women Writer's Project*
For the Women Writer's Project at Brown University.

```
WWP-L@BROWNVM.BROWN.EDU
LISTSERV@BROWNVM.BROWN.EDU
```

Contact: Allen Renear

```
ALLEN@BROWNVM.BROWN.EDU
```

Fidonet

🔗 *The Business of Writing*
```
PROWRITE
```
A forum for the business of writing.
Moderator: Roger Franz
1:100/520

🔗 *For Those Interested in Writing*
```
WRITERS
```
For published and unpublished authors and others just curious about writing.
Moderator: Alan Gilbertson
```
1:3603/230
```
Distribution: ECHONET BACKBONE (ZONE 50)

🔗 *Writing*
```
WRITING
```
Offers the discussion of all aspects of the art, craft, and business of writing, both fiction and non-fiction.
Moderator: Don Freidkin
```
1:280/9.3
```
Distribution: BACKBONE

Usenet

🔗 *Electronic fan club for humorist Dave Barry.*
```
alt.fan.dave_barry
```

🔗 *Entertaining, utter drek.*
```
alt.national.enquirer
```

🔗 *Don't believe the hype.*
```
alt.news-media
```

🔗 *Postings of original writings, fictional and otherwise.*
```
alt.prose
```

🔗 *Discussions about postings in alt.prose.*
```
alt.prose.d
```

🔗 *Paperback fiction, newsprint production, orange juice.*
```
alt.pulp
```

🔗 *Megabyte University—Computers and Writing.*
```
bit.listserv.mbu-l
```

🔗 *Discussion of writing in all of its forms.*
```
misc.writing
```

🔗 *For the posting of poems.*
```
rec.arts.poems
```

Online Libraries
After Dark
No services available.

Knowledge Index
No services available.

Orbit
No services available.

NewsNet
No services available.

Bulletin Boards
Society for Technical Communication (STC) BBS
Offers members access to the STC mailing list available, job leads, calendar of events, research request for proposals, member services, internships, and more.
Availability: 24 hours/7 days
Baud Rate: 300, 1200, 2400, 9600, 19.2
BBS Number: (703) 522-3299
BBS Software: WILDCAT
Sysop: Peter Herbst
Help Line: (703) 522-4114

CD-ROM

🔗 *Findit Webster*
Innotech, Inc.

🔗 *Oxford English Dictionary on CDROM*
Oxford University Press

Zoology
Resources

Forums & Databases
America Online (AOL)

✎ *Pet Care Forum*
Keyword: Pet care
Path: Lifestyles & Interests Department > Pet Care Forum
Provides discussion of dogs & cats, horses & farm animals, reptiles & marine life, wild & exotic animals, and birds. Weekly live conferences are scheduled on a variety of topics, mostly of interest to household pet owners.

CompuServe (CIS)

✎ *Pets/Animal Forum*
Keyword: GO PETS
Deals with all kinds of animals.

GEnie

✎ *Maggie Mae's PET-NET & Co. RT*
Keyword: PET or Page 295
A support center for all those who enjoy animals.

The Well

No services available.

Network Discussions Lists
Internet (Includes Bitnet & UUCPNet)

✎ *American Association of Vet Lab Diagnosticians list.*
AAVLD-L@UCDCVDLS.BITNET
LISTSERV@UCDCVDLS.BITNET

✎ *Animal Rights*
Offers a discussion of animal rights.
ANIMAL-RIGHTS@CS.ODU.EDU
Animal-Rights-Request@XANTH.CS.ODU.EDU
Contact: Chip Roberson
<csrobe@CS.WM.EDU>

✎ *Aquaculture Discussion list.*
Offers a discussion of science, technology, and business of rearing aquatic species.
AQUA-L@UOGUELPH.BITNET
LISTSERV@UOGUELPH.BITNET
Contact: Ted White
<ZOOWHITE@UOGUELPH.BITNET>

✎ *Discussion of Bee Biology*
Offers a discussion of research and information on the biology of bees, including honey bees and other bees.
BEE-L@ALBNYVM1.BITNET
LISTSERV@ALBNYVM1.BITNET
Contact: Mary Jo Orzech
<MJO@BROCK1P.BITNET>

✎ *Beef Specialists list.*
BEEF-L@WSUVM1.BITNET
LISTSERV@WSUVM1.BITNET

✎ *National Birding Hotline Cooperative Expands Again*
Offers bird banders a chance to discuss their trade.
BIRDBAND@ARIZVM1.BITNET
LISTSERV@ARIZVM1.BITNET
Contact: Charles B. Williamson
<CHUCKW@ARIZEVAX.BITNET>

✎ *National Birding Hotline Cooperative Expands Again*
Offers transcripts of current eastern U.S. hotlines only.
BIRDEAST@ARIZVM1.BITNET
LISTSERV@ARIZVM1.BITNET

Contact: Charles B. Williamson
<CHUCKW@ARIZEVAX.BITNET>

✯ *NBHC Birding Trip Reports*
BIRDTRIP@ARIZVM1.BITNET
LISTSERV@ARIZVM1.BITNET

✯ *National Birding Hotline Cooperative Expands Again*
Offers transcripts of current western U.S. hotlines only.
BIRDWEST@ARIZVM1.BITNET
LISTSERV@ARIZVM1.BITNET
Contact: Charles B. Williamson
<CHUCKW@ARIZEVAX.BITNET>

✯ *Brine Shrimp Discussion list.*
BRINE-L@UGA.BITNET
LISTSERV@UGA.BITNET

✯ *Camel Research*
For the field of Camel research and study. It is launched by the Camel Research Center at King Faisal University, Saudi Arabia.
CAMEL-L@SAKFU00.BITNET
LISTSERV@SAKFU00.BITNET
Contact: Mustafa Ghazal
<Devmtg12@Sakfu00.Bitnet>

✯ *Dog Fanciers*
CANINE-L@PSUVM.BITNET
LISTSERV@PSUVM.BITNET
Contact: W. K. Gorman
<34AEJ7D@CMUVM>

✯ *Ethology*
Offers a discussion of animal behavior and behavioral ecology.
ETHOLOGY@FINHUTC.BITNET
LISTSERV@FINHUTC.BITNET
Contact: Jarmo Saarikko
SAARIKKO@FINUHB.BITNET

✯ *Equestrian Digest*
A redistribution of articles from the USENET rec.equestrian newsgroup for people without USENET access.
EQUINE-D@PSUVM.BITNET
LISTSERV@PSUVM.BITNET
Contact: W. K. Gorman
<34AEJ7D@CMUVM.BITNET>

✯ *Discussion Forum for Horse Fanciers*
Offers a discussion of all phases of horse ownership, management, use, and related concerns for all horse breeds, including hot and cold blood.
EQUINE-L@PSUVM.BITNET
LISTSERV@PSUVM.BITNET
Contact: W. K. Gorman
<34AEJ7D@CMUVM.BITNET>

✯ *A list for Cat Fanciers.*
FELINE-L@PSUVM.BITNET
FELINE-L@PSUVM.BITNET

✯ *A list for frogs.*
FROGTALK@BITNIC.BITNET
LISTSERV@BITNIC.BITNET

✯ *Horse enthusiasts*
A bi-directional gateway of the "rec.equestrian" newsgroup for users who do not have USENET access.
HORSE@BBN.COM
HORSE-REQUEST@BBN.COM
Contact: Ken Rossen
<kenr@BBN.COM>

✯ *Model Horses*
For model horses of all makes (for showing, remaking, collecting, and more).
model-horse@xzact.com
model-horse-request@xzact.com
Contact: Darci L. Chapman
<dlc@gasco.uucp>

✯ *Domestic Animal Care and Education list*
PETS-L@VMTECMEX.BITNET
LISTSERV@VMTECMEX.BITNET
Contact: Alejandro Kurczyn
499229@VMTECMEX.BITNET

✯ *Pferde Diskussions liste.*
Offers horse discussion in German.
PFERDE@DLRVM.BITNET
LISTSERV@DLRVM.BITNET
Contact: Heike Mueller

✯ *South Bend Area Birds list.*
Offers news and discussion of birds living in and flying through the South Bend community.
SBNBIRDS@INDYCMS.BITNET
LISTSERV@INDYCMS.BITNET

✯ *Veterinary Medicine Computer Assisted Instruction list.*
VETCAI-L@KSUVM.BITNET
LISTSERV@KSUVM.BITNET

✯ *Veterinary Immunology Discussion Group list.*
VETIMM-L@UCDCVDLS.BITNET
LISTSERV@UCDCDLS.BITNET

✯ *Veterinary Medicine*
Offers discussion on Informatics, with a special reference to the field of Veterinary Medicine.
VETINFO@UCDCVDLS.BITNET
LISTSERV@UCDCVDLS.BITNET
Contact: Jim Case DVM, Ph.D
<JCASE@UCDCVDLS.BITNET>

⤷ *Veterinary Medicine Library Issues and Information list.*
VETLIB-L@VTVM2.BITNET
LISTSERV@VTVM2.BITNET

⤷ *Veterinary Microbiology Discussion Group list.*
VETMICRO@UCDCVDLS.BITNET
LISTSERV@UCDCDLS.BITNET

⤷ *Veterinary Mycoplasma Discussion Group list.*
VETMYCOP@UCDCVDLS.BITNET
LISTSERV@UCDCDLS.BITNET
<RZ4P@DLRVMGO.BITNET>

Fidonet

⤷ *Animal Rights Conference*
ANIMAL_RIGHTS
Discusses the pros and cons of various animal rights issues.
Moderator: Mike Adams
1:19/10
Distribution: BACKBONE

⤷ *ANIMED*
ANIMED
Offers a discussion of animal sickness and cures.
Moderator: Bob Kohl
1:102/861

⤷ *Fishkeeping, fresh, and marine tanks*
AQUARIUM
Offers a discussion of all aspects of keeping fish, in either salt or marine tanks.
Moderator: Vern Faulkner
1:340/44
Distribution: BACKBONE

⤷ *Parrots and Other Cage Birds Echo*
AVICULTURE
Offers a discussion on the raising and caring of birds, especially wild birds in captivity.
Moderator: Tom Hendricks
1:261/662
Distribution: BACKBONE

⤷ *Reptile, Amphibian and Exotic Pets Discussion Area*
CHAMELEON
Offers a discussion of reptiles, amphibians, and exotic pets.
Moderator: Stephen Kunc
1:163/227
Distribution: BACKBONE

⤷ *Dog Lovers' Discussions*
DOGHOUSE
Enables users to share favorite canine stories. Also offers discussion of health care, news, and general socializing about dogs.
Moderator: Missy Cauldwell
1:231/370
Distribution: BACKBONE

⤷ *Equus*
EQUUS
Offers discussion of horses and horsemanship, all breeds and all styles of riding.
Moderator: Bob Kohl
1:102/861
Distribution: BACKBONE, NET-13 NET-102, NET-103, NET-124, NET-170, NET-202, NET-203, NET-265, NET-322, NET-388, NET-396,

⤷ *Exotic Birds Echo*
EXOTIC_BIRDS
Offers a discussion of all aspects of the avian world, from keeping birds as pets, to bird watching, to the natural histories of wild bird species.
Moderator: Dee Lamzaki
1:125/102
Distribution: BACKBONE
Gateways: RBBS-NET

⤷ *FERRET FORUM*
FERRET_FORUM
Offers information about ferrets. Also provides information, articles, and bulletins provided by members of the Ferret News Network and the International Ferret News Service (IFNS).
Moderator: Roger McMillian
1:115/622
Distribution: BACKBONE

⤷ *Anthropomorphics, the Current Magazines*
FUR_MAG
Devoted to anthropomorphic fans (YARF!, FURVERSION, FURTHERANCE, FURN-OGRAPHY, and more).
Moderator: Nicolai Shapero
1:102/524

⤷ *Cat Conference*
KATTY_KORNER
Offers anecdotes and tips on care and feeding of cats.
Moderator: Debbi Brown
1:388/33
Distribution: BACKBONE

⑤ *For animal lovers*
PET_TALK
Offers discussion of all animals.
Moderator: Jeff Emerson
1:369/66
Distribution: ECHONET BACKBONE (ZONE 50)

⑤ *Parrots/Hookbill Conference*
PARROTS
Offers discussion of jungle/equatorial birds, such as Amazons, Macaws, Conures, African Greys, as well as the ones from Australia.
Moderator: Doris Marsh
1:125/20
Distribution: BACKBONE

⑤ *Save Our Sealife Committee Echo for Florida*
S.O.S.
Dedicated to a grassroots petition campaign to amend the Constitution of Florida to prohibit the use of gill nets and other entangling nets.
Moderator: Christopher Baker
1:374/14
Distribution: LOCAL, FLORIDA

Usenet

⑤ *Ethology list.*
bit.listserv.ethology

⑤ *Animals in the news. (Moderated)*
clari.news.interest.animals

⑤ *Hobbyists interested in bird watching.*
rec.birds

⑤ *Pets, pet care, and household animals in general.*
rec.pets

⑤ *The culture and care of indoor birds.*
rec.pets.birds

⑤ *Discussion about domestic cats.*
rec.pets.cats

⑤ *Any and all subjects relating to dogs as pets.*
rec.pets.dogs

⑤ *Reptiles, amphibians, and other exotic vivarium pets.*
rec.pets.herp

⑤ *The use and abuse of animals.*
talk.politics.animals

Online Libraries
After Dark

⑤ *CAB: Veterinary and Medical*
Contains all documents from nine veterinary publications.
Coverage: 1972 to present
Updated: Monthly

Knowledge Index
No services available.

Orbit

⑤ *VETDOC*
Covers worldwide journal literature on veterinary applications of drugs, hormones, vaccines, growth promotants, and more, for use in domestic and farm animals.
Coverage: 1968 to present
Updated: Quarterly

NewsNet
No services available.

Bulletin Boards
AmNet On-Line New York City
Promotes positive human-animal relationships and concern for the environment upon which sentient beings depend.
Baud Rate: 300, 1200, 2400
BBS Number: (212) 724-6826 or (303) 223-1297 for Ft. Collins, Co.
BBS Software: TBBS
Sysop: John Frederick

The Animal Bytes BBS
Devoted to animal rights.
Baud Rate: 300, 1200, 2400
BBS Number: (301) 891-2646
Sysop: Paul Nahay

Osprey's Nest
Offers a discussion and the exchange of information on birdwatching and bird feeding in the Washington Metropolitan area.

Availability: 24 hours/7 days
Baud Rate: 300,1200,2400
BBS Number: (301) 989-9036
BBS Software: ROBBS
Parameters: 8-0-1
Sysop: Fran and Norm Saunders

CD-ROM

❧ *About Cows*
Quanta Press

❧ *Aquatic Sciences & Fisheries Abstracts*
Cambridge Scientific Abstracts

❧ *Wildlife & Fish Worldwide*
National Information Services Corp.

FREE TRIAL SUBSCRIPTION

The Modem User's Resource

CONNECT brings the telecomputing community up-to-date and timely news, reviews and information about the products and services available for *all* computer and modem users.

Each bi-monthly issue includes columns covering:
- America Online
- BIX
- CompuServe
- Delphi
- GEnie
- Internet
- BBS Networks
- IBM and Macintosh products
- Palmtops
- and *The Inside Line* by Michael Banks!

FREE 3-issue Trial Subscription!

Just fill out and return this form to receive three issues of **CONNECT** absolutely *free.* There's no further obligation, but we're sure you'll find **CONNECT** well worth the normal $18/yr subscription rate and that you'll sign up once your trial subscription expires!

NOTE: This offer is only good for subscriptions mailed to U.S. addresses.

☐ Please sign me up for your *free* trial subscription!

Name: _____

Company: _____

Address: _____

City: _____ State: _____ Zip: _____

Phone: _____

Where can we reach you online?

_____

_____

Return this form to *CONNECT* Free Offer, 3487 Braeburn Circle, Ann Arbor, MI 48108-2619 or Fax to (313) 973–0411.